THE UNITED STATES AND THE TWENTIETH CENTURY

THE UNITED STATES AND THE TWENTIETH CENTURY

GEORGE H. MAYER
WALTER O. FORSTER
PURDUE UNIVERSITY

HOUGHTON MIFFLIN COMPANY · BOSTON
The Riverside Press Cambridge

The Riverside Press
CAMBRIDGE · MASSACHUSETTS
PRINTED IN THE U.S.A.

PREFACE

THIS BOOK is the direct outgrowth of more than a decade of classroom experience with twentieth-century American History courses on the part of both authors. They soon learned that the field is much richer in texts that feature narrative than in those that explain its meaning. Such offerings do not, as a rule, forego "interpretation." It is achieved by selection and indirection rather than by a systematic presentation of the "facts" within a meaningful framework. Yet just the latter is the urgent need of the student. A structure for correlation and evaluation of the information he is to acquire is implicit in every textbook, whether stated or not. It is better that the student be brought face to face with this fact than that he be subjected to unstated assumption, insinuation, or the pretense that interpretation is not taking place.

Therefore, in this text the writers have chosen frankly to confront the student with an analytical framework, even at the risk that it may coincide neither with the one he eventually selects, nor with the one preferred by his instructor. In fact, in order to enhance the range of choices some suggestions for additional readings are included. Any other group of equally stimulating selections that teachers might wish to substitute from the voluminous literature in the field will serve as well, since the sole purpose is to expand and illuminate the forum of competing ideas.

In domestic affairs the impression is commonly conveyed that since 1900 America has preserved an ideological consistency in dealing with the manifold problems which threatened a pre-existing pattern of beliefs and institutions. Either explicitly or implicitly, the accepted solutions to these problems have been represented as procedural changes rather than as substantive departures from original principles. Such an impression is strengthened by the use of words like "democratic" and "liberal" to describe changing beliefs or political programs. In the process, basic changes in the content of democracy are explained away as mere additions of "new dimensions" to democracy.

This volume recognizes the dynamism of American society in its efforts to adjust to a shifting environment without feeling any compulsion to blur the fundamental nature of the transformation that has resulted. Americans at the beginning of the century are pictured as believing that they can preserve nineteenth-century ideals despite the challenge of a new technology. By the time of the New Deal, the majority of the American people have shifted to the view that they must alter the old ideals to make them conform to their present environment and immediate purposes. If the term "democracy" is to be used of the United States in the 1950's, this cannot properly be done without making it clear that the term has quite a different content than it did in 1900. The student must have some clue to the great difference between trends which are merely extensions of familiar developments and those that constitute a basic departure from the past.

As the foregoing implies, this book is more than a political history, and involves a more extensive treatment of matters religious, cultural, and social than is traditional. Emphasis has been placed on intellectual development in the last two generations and on the interplay between ideas and institutions. In doing this, a special effort has been made to show the place of literature in the main current of history.

More than ordinary attention has also been given to the emergence of the United States as a great power in a world-wide system of international politics. It is, of course, possible to *say* that the United States is a "world power," deeply involved in "world affairs," and yet to treat these subjects from a strictly American point of view. When this is done, inadequate attention is accorded the fact that these "affairs" are conducted within an existing framework of concepts, practices, and institutions. Usually "the system" is recognized, if at all, only to condemn it. Thus American "history" is adjusted to American preferences for ignoring the historic fact that the United States is a product and a part of the international community which has developed over the last few centuries. Misunderstanding of the motives of American policy and the means it must use to be effective is virtually assured. It becomes easy to cater to the notion that the function of American foreign affairs is to create an international order rather than to cope with an existing one. The tension between this version of *Weltpolitik* and the realities of United States operations remains unresolved — unless it can be called a solution to denounce the actions of rival states abroad or of the rival party at home.

The present approach to American foreign affairs is a different one. Of course, the facts of the historical setting it describes have long been acknowledged in writing the history of other countries; and the principles of international politics which it sets forth have long been known to other disciplines. What is distinctive in this textbook is that these matters have been brought to bear upon the American record. Foreign relations are examined with this broader view as a point of departure, rather than as a final perspective attained only in the melancholy of mid-century sophistication. Accordingly the authors have felt no need to pretend that America has no special interests, or that national interest acquires a special virtue when it is American. Instead they have been at pains to show that the United States has interests like any other state, pursuing some deliberately and others instinctively. Admitting to national interests suggested modifying the traditional treatment of foreign policy according to administrations. A regional approach has been substituted at many points, on the assumption that situations are at least as important in determining the policy followed as the question of which party is in power in the United States.

At the same time the authors have felt no obligation to refrain from evaluating developments that reflect unfavorably on America or minimizing the consequences of those that cannot be concealed. The word "defeat" has hitherto seldom been employed in telling the American story except in the narrow context of presidential elections, domestic party warfare, Senate votes on treaties, and propaganda efforts attending the launching of earth satellites. Yet the United States has failed in building a durable peace or even in maintaining her favorable position after the twentieth century's two world wars: she possessed the decisive physical power to win them but lacked the incisive intellectual resources to cope with their consequences. This fact seems to the authors to demand a systematic and searching examination of the most basic presuppositions of Americans about foreign affairs which motivated their policy. They feel themselves bound to point out, at whatever cost in disillusionment to their readers, that pleas for "international cooperation" or even "peace" designed to protect the American *status quo* will lack widespread appeal. Indeed, they do not stop short of the conclusion that the pursuit of an "internationalism" which seeks to impose American ideological preferences on the world is merely a more virulent and implausible form of nationalism than the older and more exclusive variety.

Optimism has its uses. But if the historian intends to draw lessons from the last fifty-odd years of American history for the future guidance of the United States, he needs more than a blind faith that everything will come out all right in the end because his country has a "destiny." He needs to be critical — even severely critical — where the facts cry for such an evaluation. Those who cannot bear such judgments about American conduct from time to time will probably prefer to put down this book now rather than later. For the present volume proceeds on the premise that the function of history is not to defend America but to explain her, and that the end aim of a useful evaluation is better served by analytical than by evangelical efforts. Feeling the need for such a history text, we have tried to write it.

GEORGE H. MAYER
WALTER O. FORSTER

Purdue University

CONTENTS

THE UNITED STATES AND THE TWENTIETH CENTURY

CHAPTER ONE

THE TURN OF THE CENTURY: AMERICA FACES THE FUTURE

TRANSITIONAL PAINS AT THE END OF THE NINETEENTH CENTURY

"The tents have been struck and the great caravan of humanity is once again on the march." In these words the Boer statesman, Jan Christiaan Smuts, asserted his belief that the twentieth century would be an era of unparalleled human progress. He spoke in the idealistic afterglow of World War I. A similar optimism had been expressed at the turn of the new century by self-confident Americans who not only proclaimed their faith in the high destiny of the human race but regarded the United States as the custodian and architect of future progress.

The attitude of Americans in 1900 was hardly modest, though their achievements somewhat justified their pride and sense of mission. In a hundred years they had tamed half a continent, converted a wilderness into a mineral and agricultural empire, linked east to west by an intricate transportation network, and set up democratic institutions in the new areas. They had built an industrial system on a greater scale than Great Britain and had won a war to preserve their national unity. And at the very end of the century they had stated their accomplishments in a language the world could understand: they had created an overseas empire at the expense of a crumbling Spain.

All these successes promised still more success in the new century, and true to her expectation the United States continued to grow economically and to emerge as a major world power. But the generation which had seen such fabulous material growth and well-being had witnessed a different development in spiritual and intellectual affairs. A revolution in technology in the last quarter of the nineteenth century created vast wealth and demanded armies of humble laborers, with the result that the old idea of America as a land of equal opportunity became harder and harder to believe in. At the same time radical developments in science and scientific thought, notably the widespread effect of the theory of evolution, cast doubt upon the old American view of a world ruled by a Deity who stood outside of nature and operated through rational principles. The result was a period of stress and crisis during which the time-honored beliefs on which American government and society had been founded were called into question. Much of the domestic history of twentieth-century United States can therefore be written in terms of the conflicts and shifting alignments in allegiance between these older and newer views. Most Americans reacted in one of three ways. Some wanted to bend the new forces to fit the framework of the old ideological and institutional structure. Others wanted to change ideals and institutions to conform to the changing balance of material forces. But the majority wanted the best of both worlds: to preserve the comforting ideology they had grown up with and at the same time to retain the material riches and the ideas which were forcing it to change. In 1900 most Americans were optimistic about containing new forces within the traditional pattern of values. By mid-century they were modifying their values to accommodate new social and economic forces. To see just why these conflicts existed and in what way they created a kind of spiritual crisis, we must briefly sketch the preconceptions and intellectual trends involved.

Toward the end of the last century the newer forces of science and technology came into conflict with an older system of thought compounded of seventeenth-century and eighteenth-century beliefs which Americans had adjusted to suit their convenience. From the rationalistic philosophy of the Enlightenment they had drawn the view that the universe was organized in terms of natural law and that the precepts of law applicable to human society could be discovered by the intellect. As interpreted by the Constitution makers, natural law required government to preserve the life, liberty, and property of the individual. Natural law drew a protective circle around man, safeguarding him from both a privileged aristocracy and a tyrannical government. He was free to worship, speak, and accumulate property without interference. He was granted equality of opportunity and was expected to compete with his neighbors in wresting a livelihood from nature. The proponents of this philosophy felt that the prosperity of the individual and the progress of society would automatically follow if such rights were guaranteed. Confident that they had discovered eternally valid principles for a properly functioning society, the Founding Fathers anchored them in the Constitution of 1787. They also tried to guard against the vagaries of future generations by making amendment of the Constitution extremely difficult.

The credo of the Enlightenment was grafted onto an older body of religious thought brought to the New World in the seventeenth century by settlers preoccupied with the salvation of their souls. Usually referred to as Puritanism, this brand of Protestantism based its view of human destiny on John Calvin's interpretation of the Bible. Whereas the philosophers of the En-

From the depths. (William Balfour Ker, 1906.)

lightenment assumed that human beings were basically good and capable of perfection if guided by the dictates of natural law, Calvin emphasized the biblical idea that all men are tainted by the original sin of Adam. Both he and the American Puritans considered predisposition to sin a fixed quality of human nature and asserted that only God could save mankind from hell. Further analysis of the Scriptures convinced the Puritans that God arbitrarily elected some men for salvation and others for damnation. In their view, human conduct had no effect on God's decision. Nevertheless, they believed that conduct provided evidence of election or damnation: the elect were sober, honest, energetic, thrifty and hard-working. If these qualities brought prosperity, the Puritans regarded it as a sign of God's favor rather than of human greed. Conversely, they expected the damned to be extravagant, addicted to pleasure, and poor. The Puritans did not, of course, let sinners behave as they pleased, but supervised their conduct so that they would not affront God.

This austere code relaxed in the eighteenth century. Except on the frontier, where revivalist preachers continued to make hell seem a very real menace to sinners, congregations paid lip service to the doctrines of original sin and election and increasingly stressed the benevolence of God. Religious philosophies like Perfectionism, Unitarianism, and Emersonian Transcendentalism, with their higher view of human nature, aided this trend. By the middle of the nineteenth century, the unofficial Protestantism of the worshippers had become a sort of religious version of the Enlightenment.

The unplanned convergence of Puritanism and the Enlightenment led to a mixed rather than a systematic world view. It drew optimism, individualism, and a belief in progress from the Enlightenment — and aggressiveness, thrift, and the sanctification of wealth, from Puritanism. Both sources assumed that the values for which they stood could be deduced rationally either from the law of nature or from scriptural revelation, and that these values were eternal and unchanging. Such a patchwork could hold together only as long as: (1) the economic environment favored individualism; (2) science supported the concept of a static, rational universe; (3) nobody challenged the Enlightenment's interpretation of Scripture. For better or for worse, these three props disappeared shortly after the Civil War.

SIGNIFICANCE OF THE INDUSTRIAL REVOLUTION

Many forces created pressure for institutional change, but perhaps the most important was the Industrial Revolution. The effect of this new technological system is best introduced with a word about the system of production which developed along with it.

The crucial source of all later industrial development was the discovery of a reliable method for generating power on a large scale, thus providing for rapid transportation and mass production. Until the eighteenth century, wind, water, charcoal, animals, and human beings had furnished the requisite energy with only modest results, but about 1750 the use of coke assured an unprecedented supply of heat and energy. This revolution in technique took place first in England and spread gradually to the western half of Europe and to America. But it was impossible to reap the full benefits of factories driven by mechanical power until scientific research developed machines capable of using this energy efficiently, metal alloys tough enough to stand up under sustained operation, and a transportation system which could assemble fuel, raw materials, and labor cheaply at a central point.

To describe these developments in a few phrases may give the impression that they were swiftly and simply completed. Actually it took over a century to move from a transportation system where rickety coal cars were pulled slowly over wooden tracks by women and mules to one where durable all-purpose freight cars were pulled rapidly over steel rails by huge steam locomotives. Other developments occurred at the same slow rate. In the United States, an industrial system capable of large-scale operation did not materialize until the network of railroads was completed and the production of steel integrated in the early 1880's. Even then, few could have predicted the spectacular strides in technology that were to make the United States the leading industrial power of the world.

These developments foreshadowed painful adjustments for a nation which was 90 per cent agricultural and which treasured initiative, independence, and self-reliance. The farmers first weakened their rugged individualism by demanding government-subsidized railroads. For they soon learned that the railroads controlled the avenues to market, and that the manufacturers of farm equipment held the key to cheap, efficient agricultural production. When corporations of both types created monopolies to charge what the traffic would bear, the farmers invoked action by the government to regulate their "oppressors" and formed agricultural organizations as weapons of their own to smash the industrial giants. Paradoxically, either method of retaliation could be applied only at the expense of the very individualism which farmers were trying to preserve.

Industrialization threatened to eliminate individual initiative at another crucial point by changing traditional methods of urban production. Three-quarters of a century earlier, Thomas Jefferson had predicted that the growth of cities would endanger the values of a democratic society. Now the new technology gave substance to his fears in two ways. First, it created in the cities an environment where group cooperation was essential to health, sanitation, and safety. This led in turn to devaluation of the initiative and aggressiveness traditionally cherished on the frontier. Defiance of authority abated as the citizen was relentlessly integrated into community life, and the sheer complexity of his new existence gradually wore down his resistance to government supervision and direction. Second, new technology gave the death blow to equality of opportunity by producing monopolies and hardening class lines. Business combination developed because the high initial investment in factory equipment, plus fixed costs of production, meant that the industrial corporation had to make a profit in order to survive. Competition led to price wars, which in turn resulted in bankruptcy. This sequence was repeated so often in the 1870's that in the ensuing decade competing firms stampeded into mergers. By the end of the century the basic industries were so far integrated that competition was seldom practiced though often praised. Furthermore, the new corporative structure, like the iceberg, concealed its lethal bulk beneath the surface; that is, important policies were not always formulated by the active officers of a corporation but by a compact group of industrialists and bankers who came to exercise almost absolute power over the whole economy.

Beyond the immediate problems of shrinking opportunity for small businessmen and high prices for consumers, monopoly raised the larger question whether free enterprise could be restored. A negative answer came from Henry Demarest Lloyd who in his penetrating analysis of trusts, *Wealth Against Commonwealth* (1894), had written that competition was a transitional phase of economic development rather than a way of life, a process that never reached equilibrium but ended in the victory of the most skillful or the most ruthless monopolists. Lloyd went on to assert that government was the sole agency capable of disciplining the industrial giants for the benefit of the people. To the great majority of Americans, however, the alternatives that Lloyd's conclusion seemed to suggest were equally distasteful. Inveterate believers in competition, they were no more willing to accept monopoly supervised by government than monopoly supervised by private stockholders.

Lloyd had expressed concern for the American workman, whose tradition of independence also was threatened by the industrial revolution. Before the appearance of the large factory, the employer and the laborer had frequently worked side by side in the mill or shop. Under the new productive system, this personal relationship threatened to disappear entirely as the employer-entrepreneur was replaced by a remote group of stockholders who hired a manager chiefly for his ability to create profits. At the same time new industrial machinery, easy to operate, destroyed the premium which the old system had placed upon skilled labor. And so the craftsman was exposed to competition from the hordes of unskilled hands who made up the bulk of the new immigration.

The independent position of the American workman was further undermined in the 1890's by the disappearance of the frontier, which had always helped to keep labor relatively scarce and wages relatively high. Even if flight to the unsettled West had not been practical for most of the individual workmen stranded in the large cities by unemployment, the theoretical opportunity to escape had made the frontier a psychologically valuable symbol of opportunity. The invariable support given by organized labor to subsidies for improving the remaining public lands attested to the perennial strength of the symbol. But by the end of the century the frontier was gone, and this avenue to independence vanished.

The cumulative effect of these developments was to impair the dignity of manual workers and diminish their chance to rise in the economic scale. As technology leveled them, they lost their bargaining power. The right of the individual to make free contracts regarding wages, hours, and working conditions disappeared in practice, and the clichés about "equality of opportunity" took on a hollow ring. John Mitchell, president of the United Mine Workers, said after the coal strike of 1901 that the members of his organization were reconciled to their fixed class status and henceforward would try to improve their lot within that class rather than aspire to move up the social scale. His prediction was premature, but it gave an indication of working-class disillusionment at that time.

If the Industrial Revolution put in jeopardy the credo of individualism and equal opportunity, it also threatened cultural uniformity by stimulating immigration. Before 1890 most of the migrants had come from northwestern Europe where beliefs, customs, and institutions resembled those already prevailing in America. Even so, similarity of background had failed to protect the Irish and the Germans against the resentment of the native-born. Social tensions were further aggravated by the influx of southern Europeans, especially after 1900 when they began to arrive at the rate of a million a year. The immigrants from the Latin and Balkan states brought with them a low standard of living, meager experience in self-government, and Catholicism. Devout Protestants were disturbed by the religious affiliations of the immigrants; organized labor was alarmed by their willingness to work for low wages; and strong nationalists were repelled by their clannishness, illiteracy, and high birth rate. Some nativist groups wanted to exclude them, while others wanted to speed the process of assimilation and coerce the laggards. But public opinion did not crystallize behind the move to restrict immigration until after World War I.

The friction between the predominantly Anglo-Saxon groups and the new immigrants served to divert attention from the serious split within the Anglo-Saxon majority itself. The cultural and social unity, shaken by the sectional conflicts leading up to the Civil War, had not been restored by the victory of the North. Reconstruction left the South with a permanent bitterness which expressed itself in the emergence of a distinctively regional outlook. The persistence of social and cultural schism in the twentieth century was to weaken the national will to resist the forces which challenged traditional institutions.

THE IMPACT OF SCIENTIFIC THOUGHT

Less immediately shattering than the revolution in industrial technology, but more unsettling in the long run, was the intellectual revolution of the 1880's and 1890's, sparked by the impact of science on philosophic thought. Usually theories that emerge from the laboratory are applied in a limited field. As such, they seldom provide decisive support or opposition for a particular system of philosophy. The scientific theories of the mid-nineteenth century seemed, however, to have very broad application. Geology, physics, and biology alike pointed to the conclusion that the universe and everything in it was in a process of constant, unrepetitive change. The pioneer work of the British geologist, Sir Charles Lyell, in analyzing rock strata, glaciation, and river valleys revealed that the hills were not eternal, as poets loved to say, but subject to a variety of changes. Experiments in physics indicated that the conversion of matter into radiation was irreversible and that no new matter could be created. As formulated by Lord Kelvin in the second law of thermodynamics, this steady process of change pointed to the ultimate dissolution of the universe. But the most spectacular assertion about the plastic, provisional character of nature was made by a British biologist, Charles Darwin. In the famous *Origin of Species* (1859), he argued that all life including man had evolved from more primitive forms. He thought that the chief factor in this evolution was the struggle of organisms over an inadequate food supply and that this led to the survival of the fittest species. He recognized that each species usually breeds true to type, and he explained organic mutuation or change as the accumulation of slight variations which eventually produce new species.

In aggregate, these new scientific ideas cast doubt on the older Newtonian view of the universe as a machine incapable of motion or change except in a repetitive pattern governed by mathematical law. Since American ideals and institutions had often been defended as projections of Newtonian law in the social order, their status was indirectly challenged by the new world view. Thereafter, reformers would not be so easily discouraged by the assertion that national institutions reflected unchanging, eternal laws of the universe and hence were exempted from all tinkering. They drew the sweeping inference that society partook of the same plasticity as the universe at large and that institutional values should change as rapidly as the environment.

Analogies pointing to this view were provided in most spectacular form by Darwinian biology. Enthusiastic evolutionists quickly moved from the specific hypothesis that some species develop new properties for survival in a particular environment, to the broad statement that no form of life has fixed properties or functions in terms of eternal law. It was thence a short step to the corollary that what exists at any given moment is relative to time and place, or — to put it another way — that the environment determines all standards and values.

The expansion of Darwinian evolution into a world view forced interpreters to take positions on many philosophical questions which biology left unanswered. Their speculations divided evolutionary thought into at least three schools. One group accepted the Darwinian view that the human being was as much the slave of blind evolutionary processes as the lower animals and could not guide his own destiny. However, it put so much faith in the survival of the fittest that it believed progress would occur even if men made no conscious effort to promote it. An eminent Yale sociologist, William Graham Sumner, translated this outlook into a laissez-faire social and economic program. Opposing all government legislation or subsidies for depressed groups as the coddling of the weak or unfit, Sumner proclaimed that a policy of nonintervention would lead to the rapid progress of society. He conceded misery and suffering would be the lot of the unfit, but regarded their distress as a necessary incident of the evolutionary process. The theory of Sumner, and of his British mentor, Herbert Spencer, brought great comfort to American captains of industry, who used it to justify the creation of monopolies and the destruction of labor unions. In fact, at the end of the nineteenth century it became the watchword of dominant economic interests desirous of stifling demand for reform.

The second group, chiefly writers, accepted the same unflattering view of man as a participant in the jungle warfare of the species but refused to regard his emergence at the top of the evolutionary heap as a guarantee for progress or an indication of cosmic design. Usually referred to as the Naturalists, these authors used the novel as a vehicle for their melancholy belief that creation is purposeless, the moral code meaningless, and man a two-legged animal motivated by the primitive drives of sex and hunger. Stephen Crane, a popular author of the nineties, echoed the mood of the Naturalists when he said the world was like a ship which God had made and then abandoned.

The third group shared the position that change is the dominant principle of the universe. It accepted Darwinian evolution among the lower organisms but regarded man as exempt from the primitive struggle for survival. Despite a wide variety of views within the group, all thought the human being was capable of guiding evolutionary processes and curbing the waste in nature. Some, like Henry George, argued that human intelligence, though a product of evolution, could harness nature for the welfare of society. Others, like Lester Ward, called for careful statistical studies as a basis for orderly, systematic planning. Many people who agreed with Ward that man ought to remake the environment along rational lines refused to accept his corollary that a constructive central government was the only agency which could undertake the task. Though he made little impression on contemporary opinion, his outlook was to be adopted a generation later by the New Deal.

Pragmatists, who made a point of declaring their independence of all philosophical systems, including Darwinism, were partly indebted to evolutionary theory for their belief in the provisional character of the universe. The shifting content in Pragmatist thought, caused by the quarrels of its chief spokesmen, makes generalizations about the philosophy hazardous. But, like the third group of Darwinians, the Pragmatists believed that the human will was free to direct the operations of nature. They proposed that man select or reject programs solely on the criterion of workability, experimenting freely in the process. A leading Pragmatist, John Dewey, favored almost the same kind of practical program as Lester Ward. Dewey placed special emphasis on education as a tool which would enable men to control social processes and share common goals.

Darwinism was not welcomed in all quarters otherwise sympathetic to the concept of evolution. Idealists, for instance, found change at the very core of reality. Strongly indebted to the German philosopher Hegel, they insisted that the grand design of evolutionary development was imposed upon nature by mental or spiritual absolutes. Matter, whether animate or inanimate, mirrored the transcendent reality — the metaphysical stuff to which it aspired. The accuracy of this reflection depended on the stage of development. Conflict and change might characterize the process through which the actual evolved toward the ideal, but the motive power was provided by the ideal or absolute itself. In short, the world view of the Idealists reversed the terms in the Darwinian equation which ascribed to natural selection all mental or spiritual phenomena.

The Idealists dominated the philosophy departments of American universities, and their chief spokesman, Josiah Royce, was much admired for his demonstration of the existence of God and spiritual absolutes without recourse to Christian revelation. In *The Religious Aspect of Philosophy* (1885) and *The World and the Individual* (1900–1901), he denied the Darwinian thesis that ideas about God, the self, and the universe originated in the brutal warfare of nature. But the popularity of Idealism ebbed steadily at the close of the century. The explanation of change offered by the Darwinians seemed to tally more closely with the facts of experience than did the abstract propositions of the Idealists.

Yet the challenge of Darwinism to the Idealists was not nearly so direct as its challenge to religion — especially Christianity. Evolutionary theory proclaimed that man was distinguishable from the rest of organic nature only by the high degree of his development, which he had attained through conflict with other species and by progressive adaptation to his physical environment. This hypothesis whittled all absolute ethical standards down to provisional rules of behavior associated with a particular environment and stage of development. Thus evolution courted collision at some point with most major religious faiths or moral systems. It specifically contradicted biblical assertions that man was a unique creature with a mind and soul, created in the image of a perfect Deity, but fallen from his high estate through original sin and therefore in need of a Saviour. If Christianity admitted the validity of these contradictions, it would be repudiating the revelation that distinguished it from other religions. Unless it held to the view that regeneration was the absolute and unconditional gift of God bestowed in the process of saving sinful man, there would be no need for a Christ in Christianity.

Theists, like John Fiske, who did not regard Christ as a Saviour in any case, greeted evolution rapturously, seeing it as the guarantee of unlimited progress in the universe and unlimited improvement in the moral constitution of man. Some went beyond Theism to Naturalism, arguing that life emerged from non-life and that all psychic phenomena were the product of the same blind evolutionary forces that shaped physical developments. They were to rest assured that they had grasped the basic law of the universe until the catastrophes of world wars and depressions shook their faith in inevitability of progress.

Distinguished Protestants, like Henry Ward Beecher and James McCosh, capitulated to the Darwinians in the 1880's by conceding the primacy of science and accepting evolutionary development as a scientific fact. They sought to gloss over the superfluity of Christ in a cosmic order where man rose without divine aid, by insisting that God was sponsering evolution as the vehicle of His Providence. Most Protestants who followed them sought to escape the troubling implications of the new theory by consoling themselves with the idea that the human soul was a unique creation of God, and hence exempted from the evolutionary principles governing the body.

The theologians and philosophers who made their peace with Darwinism in the closing years of the nineteenth century did not speak for the average man. The latter had only an inaccurate second-hand acquaintance with evolutionary theory and required some years to digest its implications. Ultimately, he saw that science and evolution challenged the supra-natural elements of Christian theology. Then, deprived of most of the ablest leadership in the Protestant denominations, he fought back furiously but often blindly in the Fundamentalist movement of the twenties. At the turn of the century, however, most people still lived in the Age of Confidence. Unconscious of their inconsistency, they hailed the promise of progress underwritten by the new theories and continued to cherish the familiar landmarks of the older theology. Yet the Age of Confidence was drawing to a close. The twin revolutions in industrial technology and thought had already taken some of the gaiety out of the Gay Nineties. Both were to gather momentum and shake American society to its foundations in the new century.

SUGGESTED READINGS

1. Commager, H. S., *The American Mind.*
2. Curti, Merle, *The Growth of American Thought.*
3. Gabriel, R. H., *The Course of American Democratic Thought.*
4. Hofstadter, R., *Social Darwinism in American Thought.*
5. Riley, W., *American Thought from Puritanism to Pragmatism.*

CHAPTER TWO

THE FOUNDATIONS OF AMERICAN FOREIGN POLICY

AMERICA ACHIEVES HEMISPHERIC PREDOMINANCE

The turn of the century was a transition period for America in foreign as well as in domestic affairs, because at that time she made her debut as a world power. The victory of the Union forces in the Civil War had resulted in the creation of a state strong enough to hold its own against any single great power in Europe. Forty more years of uninterrupted growth conferred so much additional strength that other states could no longer ignore the United States in the formulation of foreign policy anywhere in the world.

Evidence of increasing might accumulated in the decades when most citizens of the American Republic were focusing their attention on domestic questions like Reconstruction, the protective tariff, and agricultural depression. For one thing, rapid mastery of industrial techniques speeded the westward movement in the 1870's and 1880's, and this in turn enlarged the geographical base of power. Moreover, as continental expansion drew to a successful close, the architects of foreign policy began projecting this power into even more distant areas. Alaska was purchased in 1867; Midway and a few dozen small Pacific islands were occupied by the Navy in the same year. Eleven years later Samoa yielded naval rights in the harbor of Pago Pago, free admission of American goods, and a voice in the foreign relations of that faraway Polynesian island. During the 1870's, the government also negotiated canal treaties with Nicaragua and Colombia, secured transit rights across Nicaragua, and cooperated enthusiastically with the European powers in expanding commerce with China and Japan. Other ambitious schemes for the purchase of the Danish West Indies, the annexation of Santo Domingo, and the opening of Korea to American trade had to be dropped for a variety of reasons, but the fact that responsible officials seriously considered such projects indicates the widening of the American horizon.

Another post-Civil War manifestation of expanding power was the energetic enforcement of the Monroe Doctrine. This policy had been formulated in 1823 to serve notice on European states that the United States would tolerate neither intervention in the Western Hemisphere nor extension of colonization by outside powers. On that occasion American pretensions had been much greater than American strength; the large degree of compliance during the next four decades was due to the fact that Great Britain supported the Doctrine for reasons of her own. Only after the victory of the Northern armies in 1865 was the United States strong enough to function alone as a hemispheric policeman. During the Civil War Napoleon III had provided America with an occasion for demonstrating her intentions and strength: he had installed an Austrian Hapsburg, Maximilian, on the throne of Mexico, supporting him with French bayonets. Before demobilizing the military machine that had beaten the Confederacy, Secretary of State Seward invited Napoleon III to withdraw the French troops. The latter hastened to comply. Maximilian stayed on, but was captured and executed (1867) by Mexican revolutionaries under the leadership of Juarez. Thereafter neither an outside nor a resident power dared dispute American predominance in the Western Hemisphere.

AMERICA AS A WORLD POWER

The growth of the United States continued at such a rapid rate during the last decades of the nineteenth century that she seemed destined to become the world's most powerful state. On the eve of the Spanish-American War, her assets were unmatched in most respects and adequate in the rest to support all but extravagant objectives. Her territory, situated in the most temperate zone of the North American land mass, consisted of 2,974,159 square miles and was exceeded in size only by Russia, China, Canada, and Brazil. These four countries, however, contained far more unproductive land in proportion to their size. Geographical position also provided America with a strategic advantage unmatched by any power in history — an extensive frontage on the two most important ocean areas in the world, the North Atlantic and the North Pacific. The empire that lay between these oceans was knit together with a superb rail and inland-waterways system. It already supported a larger and younger population than most of the states of Europe, while a falling death rate and a rising volume of immigration assured a rapid increase in the decades after 1900. The diverse ethnic backgrounds of the people did not prevent them from engaging in an energetic exploitation of the rich and varied natural endowments of their country. Traditional Yankee ingenuity provided the inspiration for the development of a mass-production system that converted natural resources into finished products at a minimum cost. By the end of the nineteenth century, Americans were exporting everything from wheat to

A sudden awakening. (W. A. Rogers, Harper's Weekly, *1901.)*

machinery, often at prices which enabled them to undersell competitors. Still expanding at a prodigious rate in the 1890's, the industrial economy threatened to grow even faster than the population in the century ahead. In aggregate the United States became as nearly self-sufficient as large, modern states can be.

Besides the resources within her boundaries, the United States could command those of the entire Western Hemisphere also. As the sole resident great power in North and South America, she was in a position to organize the Hemisphere both as a bastion for defense and as a nucleus for the outward projection of strength. Her neighbors, it is true, did not contribute very much to her total power despite their considerable land mass. Latin America was disappointingly weak. The states south of the Rio Grande habitually cultivated petty rivalries and were often convulsed by internal strife. Most of them were sparsely settled, technologically retarded, and saddled with inefficient governments. The people lived in a social and intellectual atmosphere closer to that of feudal Spain than modern Europe or America. Their cultural pattern, sharply different from the Anglo-Saxon tradition, reinforced their aversion to change. Thus they were prevented from developing assets that could be used effectively in international politics, while their chronic fear of imperialism from the north impaired their will to mobilize for hemispheric solidarity.

Canada, on the other hand, had more of the endowments necessary for developing a powerful state under modern conditions. She held a larger portion of the continent than the United States, was blessed with abundant mineral resources, and had been settled by hardy pioneer stock. Offsetting these advantages were a cold climate which limited the agricultural growing season, a scarcity of capital for industrial production, and a small, dispersed population. Moreover, as a part of the British Empire, Canada had European connections from the consequences of which the United States might have to defend her.

The weakness of hemispheric neighbors was to be a problem only in the event of all-out war; at the turn of the century it assured the American hegemony of both continents through the domination of one of them. The combination of position and assets gave Americans a unique status. No state had hitherto arisen under quite the same political-geographical circumstances or operated from such a powerful base.

The strength of the United States was not recognized by the major European states until the very end of the nineteenth century. During the period of her rapid post-Civil War growth, they had been preoccupied with the problems on their own continent and with the race for colonies in Asia and Africa. What was needed to call attention to the impending shift in the center of power was some test of American strength. This occurred in 1898 with the outbreak of the Spanish-American War. It did not matter that Spain was a third-rate power or that the United States was to defeat her with ridiculous ease. The war suddenly made Europe aware of a new world giant who seemed to have materialized out of thin air. Especially disconcerting was the fact that this colossus began to operate in the arena of international politics with a bland disregard of traditional procedures.

All states succumb in varying degrees to the temptation to regard the motives of their international behavior as purer and more disinterested than those of their neighbors. Most of them, however, without apology or embarrassment, frankly pursue a large number of policies aimed at their own advancement. The United States, in contrast, has been exceptional in her capacity for self-deception regarding her own motives. Rarely has she admitted that she possessed interests. She justifies her conduct by appealing to ideals which her spokesmen assume to be self-evident and universally valid. Protestations of virtue have not, however, led to the extinction of concrete interests, but have encouraged a subconscious rather than an explicit pursuit of those interests. The refusal to spell out specific goals or devise systematic policies to implement them did not become serious as long as the United States remained weak and expanded only into the western part of the continent. But when she appeared on the world stage, her attitude produced recurring troubles for herself and others. Ultimately, it led her to commit her power in two wars on a basis which deprived her of some important fruits of military victory. To understand the frequent frustrations and disappointments that were to beset her foreign policy in the twentieth century, the reader must take two factors into account: (1) the pre-existent international community of which she was a part and (2) the developments that caused her to deny the implications of her membership in this society.

THE WESTERN STATE SYSTEM

The international community from which the United States in the mid-nineteenth century thought she had seceded is commonly known as the "Western State System." It owes its name to the fact that the basic unit is the state and that its current form emerged in Europe in the seventeenth century. There were, however, earlier variants of the structure because the problems that led to its creation have always existed. Over the centuries, the Western State System came to have an unwritten constitution with a definite set of principles underlying its rules and methods of operation. An elementary knowledge of its aims and techniques is indispensable for evaluating twentieth-century American foreign policy.

The durability of the system has depended on a commonplace fact: the persistent inability of successive generations of humanity to live either under one political organization or under none at all. Habitually men have identified the bulk of their interests and efforts to protect themselves with a smaller unit than mankind and have usually called it the state. The latter institution possesses many characteristics, but its indispensable ones are territory, people, and an ability to protect both against any threat from an external authority. In modern times the discharge of this function was facilitated by a marriage of convenience between the nation and the state. After the French Revolution, the nation became an especially important historical force. It was a group based on some combination of social, cultural, linguistic, and ethnic traits which sought to protect its common values. The nation needed statehood to achieve this protection, while the state needed a loyal and unified body of subjects to exist. The result was the nation-state. Historical circumstances assured a variable pattern of unification. Sometimes the national group tried to become a state by achieving its independent existence from a larger group organized on a non-national basis. Such an effort frequently involved the nation in wars of rebellion. Alternately, the state attempted to turn its subjects into a nation through indoctrination, suppression, or extermination. Whatever the process, the nation-state was a reality in much of Europe and also in America by 1900.

This historical development increased the odds against the triumph of either the anarchists or the "One Worlders" in the first half of the twentieth century. The pretensions of the state to supreme power when linked with the egocentrism of the nation as a social group gave each of the units in the combination fresh incentive to maintain its sovereignty against all comers. Therefore, Americans would have to cope with two conditions which had given birth to the Western State System and similar versions of the international community — the simultaneous existence of more states than one, and the refusal of any single state to accept a superior authority. The assertion of sovereignty by the modern state took on a familiar double aspect: supremacy over the area and people under its control, and assertion of equality with other states. Since the Treaty of Westphalia in 1648, the possession of sovereignty had automatically qualified a state for membership in the system. Thereafter political units became *de facto* members whenever they gave a pragmatic demonstration of sovereign power. Europe and its colonial empires in the Americas quickly blossomed into the largest multistate system yet known, with the state replacing other institutions as the supreme authority in human affairs. Moreover, the system continued to expand in the eighteenth and nineteenth centuries until at the end of the two-hundred-year period it encircled the globe.

Whether she understood it or not, America was a sovereign state and hence a member of the system. Only three broad methods of dealing with other states were open to her; she could attempt (1) to conquer them, (2) to achieve isolation from them, or (3) to get along with them. History offered little encouragement to would-be conquerors; no power has ever succeeded in completely eliminating its rivals. History also frowned on isolation. Occasionally a state has managed to make a policy of aloofness succeed for brief periods, but the combination of circumstances that blesses such enterprises usually turns out to be temporary. The only workable alternative over the centuries has been to seek stable relations with other states. Though none of the stabilizing devices evolved by the Western State System is a permanent guarantee against friction between powers, these devices do minimize the chances of disturbing the equilibrium.

Her ideology made it unthinkable for America to embark deliberately on a policy of world conquest. Isolation, however, had worked well enough in the mid-nineteenth century to encourage the conviction that she was not a part of the system and hence was not bound to its stabilizing devices. The persistence of this attitude, after aloofness became impossible, prevented the United States from exercising the leadership to which her strength entitled her. She denied herself the benefits of her position in the system.

The devices which the United States was to ignore had evolved in response to the determination of each state to perpetuate itself. Since survival depends upon the possession of power, which is never distributed evenly or in unchanging amounts, the chief stabilizing device aims at the control of power. It is usually called the "balance of power," and it expresses itself in the effort of states belonging to a particular group to maintain an equilibrium among themselves. Usually they have more to lose than to gain by disruption of the balance. Under normal circumstances, therefore, they try to meet changes in the relative strength of individual powers by peaceful adjustments aimed at the establishment of a new equilibrium. If, however, they cannot reconstitute the balance by orderly methods, they often resort to war. They will invariably do so if disruption of the equilibrium jeopardizes their independent existence. Occasionally, a state sets out to destroy the balance by trying to dominate all of the members; whenever this happens, the latter promptly coalesce in sufficient numbers to discourage the enterprise or to defeat it in a trial of arms. More rarely, circumstance enables a state to avoid commitments temporarily at no cost to itself or the equilibrium. America enjoyed such an opportunity briefly in the mid-nineteenth century and was thus encouraged in her illusion that participation in the balance would never be mandatory.

Until the end of the century, balances tended to be primarily regional. Thereafter they became interlocking, with world powers affecting more than one balance simultaneously. A unique stabilizing opportunity is conferred by the system on any great power which belongs to one or more balances but can avoid joining any major regional alliance without endangering its position. Only a few states have had such an opportunity because to qualify they must possess important interests in a regional balance but more freedom of action than the resident powers. A state so situated may, without war, block efforts to disrupt the regional balance by deliberately placing its weight in the scale against a potential aggressor and thus diminishing his prospect of success. The architect of such a policy is known as "the holder of the balance," and his action, if successful, may result in a prolonged period of equilibrium. As we shall see, the role of "holder of the balance" on two continents devolved on the United States in the opening decade of the twentieth century.

If the control of power is achieved by the balancing device, the desire of states for contact with each other opens the way for utilization of two other techniques. The first is the practice of diplomacy. This solves the dilemma of states which insist at one and the same time on separation and on contact. Conventionally, it is carried on by each state through the medium of a foreign office at home and embassies in the capitals of other countries, thus providing the contact necessary for friendly intercourse and the adjustment of disputes. The second technique is international law, a codification of the rudimentary rules of the state system evolved over a period of three and a half centuries. This code offers a provisional answer to the paradox arising out of the fact that states insist on legal equality and legal rights but deny the existence of a superior authority. Because it is the product of contradictory impulses and lacks a central enforcement agency, the coverage of international law depends on the attitude of individual states. At any given time no more of it will be honored than states are willing to enforce. This limitation does not destroy its effectiveness but emphasizes the danger of blind reliance on it.

The cornerstone of the international community is the unswerving determination of each state to safeguard its existence as a sovereign entity. This compulsion, rather than universally cherished principles of conduct, has provided the impulse for the development of the balance of power, diplomacy, and international law. Born of expediency, these stabilizing devices have worked imperfectly and provoked repeated criticism, but they could not be dispensed with as long as states clung to their sovereignty. Nevertheless, the United States remained jealous of her sovereignty while unilaterally repudiating some of the principles on which it depended. This action deprived her of certain advantages of the system without providing compensating benefits. It also caused her to misunderstand the motives of other states who shaped their foreign policies as before, unpersuaded by the American performance. Only her tremendous strength prevented the consequences of her disregard for her obligations under the state system from being more serious in the early twentieth century.

THE ORIGINS OF AMERICAN ATTITUDES

Why did the United States enter the twentieth century unwilling to acknowledge her membership in the international community? She had not always believed that she lived in a world of her own. Indeed, three generations of leaders, starting with those who achieved independence from Great Britain, showed a lively recognition of the Western State System, operated within its framework, and consciously used its procedures to strengthen the position of the fledgling republic. The fact that they repeatedly expressed the desire to escape involvement in international politics is misleading in one crucial sense: they seldom permitted their desire to withdraw from the affairs of Europe to become the basis for any assumption that withdrawal was possible. They avoided confusing hopes with facts. This attitude distinguished them from isolationists at the end of the century who equated their wishes with reality and allowed such wishes to become the basis for their policies.

A brief glance at the power situation in 1787 and the response of American policy makers to it confirms their reputation for realism. Despite the feat of the United States in achieving independence, the North American continent was clearly an area of contention in the balance of world power. The new republic was clearly the weakest of the four contestants for regional supremacy (i.e., Great Britain, the United States, France, and Spain). Only by virtue of her physical proximity to the disputed territory west of the Appalachians was she able to compete with any prospect of success. Whatever the policy may be called, until the middle of the nineteenth century it aimed at the enhancement of her power position by appropriating the assets of her neighbors. Successively, the British were eliminated from the forts on the Great Lakes, the French from Louisiana, and the Spanish from Florida. Revolutions were encouraged in South America to exclude the great powers from the Western Hemisphere.

As soon as the United States had rooted out the powers barring her westward expansion, she began to exploit her new position. Texas was acquired by infiltration and annexation; New Mexico, Arizona, and California, by conquest; and Oregon by shouting and colonizing. America did not reap this impressive harvest by repudiating the conventional aims of states or ignoring the balance of power. She single-mindedly pursued her security, unity, and prosperity. In fact, she took advantage of the periodic preoccupation of the colonizing powers with European politics to improve her position at their expense. By mid-century, she had laid the basis for dominating both North America and the Hemisphere.

Even during the pre-Civil War era, when foreign policy was often very realistic, Americans had begun to deceive themselves about the motives for their behavior. Although highly critical of other states for engaging in territorial expansion and carving out spheres of influence, they slipped into the same policies on idealistic grounds. "Manifest Destiny" was invoked to justify the conquest of the Southwest, and the Monroe Doctrine to justify the conversion of the entire Hemisphere into a sphere of influence. Americans imagined that Indian tribes and Mexicans wanted Anglo-Saxon institutions and that Hemisphere republics would welcome their protection. They thought of themselves as the bearers of a unique and morally superior way of life based on democratic principles and devotion to peace. It never occurred to them that the other peoples of the Hemisphere saw the Monroe Doctrine as a bid for Yankee dominance rather than as an unselfish offer of protection from European powers. They considered it to be a hemispheric Declaration of Independence from the power politics, alliances, and wars of Europe.

America's conception of her mission stimulated the assumption that the republics of the Western Hemisphere constituted a separate world devoid of obligations to the Western State System. It gave rise to three myths: (1) that the oceans provided a barrier against attack; (2) that trade was a right guaranteed under most circumstances by international law; (3) that the United States could enjoy permanent peace by minding her own business. Each of these comforting conclusions was based on the temporary existence of conditions underwritten by England rather than the United States. The maintenance of the ocean barrier and freedom of the seas depended on the British Navy, while the century of peace from 1815 to 1914 depended on London's ability to act as holder of the balance of power. With John Bull on the verge of abdicating all three roles in 1900, America faced some painful readjustments.

Before reality intruded on nineteenth-century myth, the United States had devised regional policies for dealing with the Western Hemisphere, Europe, and Asia. In the New World where she had achieved one-power domination, her objective was to maintain her position by excluding intruders. If the Monroe Doctrine did not provide sufficient justification for intervention south of the Rio Grande, she was prepared to redefine it and to develop corollaries that would cover all contingencies. Interests and ideals converged in a determination to preserve American hegemony. Under the proposed arrangement, the United States would supervise the political and commercial relations of Europe with the Western Hemisphere. On the other hand, she expected to trade in Europe without supervision. In return, she repeatedly promised not to interfere in the affairs of the European continent or to make entangling alliances. This renunciation cost little, since neither strategic nor economic objectives warranted American intervention in Europe. The balance of power was so stable that no single state nor group of states could shut America out of Continental trade. The only inconvenience was a rising tariff wall. This uncomplicated arrangement, which Washington regarded as self-sustaining, came to an end from 1900 to 1914 when the great powers went to war and promptly interfered with American trade.

In the Western Pacific and Asia where her commercial interests were not nearly so great at the end of the century as in Europe, the United States would have liked to pursue a similar policy. Lured by the prospects of the large undeveloped markets of Asia, she hoped to trade on equal terms with other states established in the area but to remain aloof from power commitments. This expectation was also to be shattered before the first decade of the twentieth century had ended.

THE EXPANSION OF THE WESTERN STATE SYSTEM

The most important factor in the destruction of international stability at the end of the nineteenth century was the expansion of the Western State System. Originally a regional system aimed at the preservation of an Atlantic balance, it bid fair to become world-wide in the thirty years after the Civil War. Several developments interacted to produce this trend. One was the emergence of four new great powers: Germany and Italy in Europe; and the United States and Japan outside the Continent. A second was the accumulated changes in transportation and communication which enabled the recently industrialized states to project their power successfully thousands of miles overseas. The revolution in production provided the great powers with a third incentive to expand. They needed to open up new areas which would serve as markets for surplus industrial goods, furnish raw materials, and offer attractive prospects to the investor. Seldom content with the opportunity to trade in Asia and Africa on a basis of equality with other states, the great powers carved out spheres of influence. Sometimes they annexed areas outright, but frequently they contented themselves with establishing protectorates.

Where economic considerations were not enough to stimulate overseas expansion, nationalism often provided a fourth and decisive motive. Properly indoctrinated citizens demanded that their state have "a place in the sun" and a power position comparable to that of their rivals. Closely akin to the nationalistic appeal was the enchantment of "the civilizing mission." Whether the state wished to export the Christian religion, its cultural tradition, or Western methods of sanitation, it relied on the nationalistic sense of superiority to command the support of self-proclaimed humanitarians. The assumption of "the white man's burden" — as Kipling called it — popularized what would otherwise have been a distasteful business to many citizens of expanding states.

A detailed box-score of the expansion of the Western State System lies beyond the boundaries of twentieth-century American history. For our purposes, it suffices to say that in the final three decades of the nineteenth century the European great powers opened up and subdued the hitherto dark continent of Africa, and carved out numerous spheres of influence in the Far East. This expansionist movement involved traditional colonizing states like Great Britain, newly created great powers like Germany, and miniature kingdoms like Belgium.

The same forces which caused colonization overseas by the European states motivated similar drives by the United States and Japan. As early as the 1870's and 1880's American policy makers were hatching schemes for expansion beyond the limits of the continent. President Andrew Johnson spoke for the expansionists of that era in his annual message to Congress on December 9, 1868, when he announced that the administration favored "the acquisition and incorporation into the Federal Union of the several adjacent continental and insular communities as speedily as it can be done peacefully, lawfully, and without any violation of national justice, faith, or honor." Until the late 1890's, annexationist sentiment was greater in the State Department than in the country at large. Popular hostility blocked the ratification of a treaty annexing Hawaii until 1898, although a coup d'état had given the United States virtual control of the island chain in 1891.

THE WAR WITH SPAIN

The excuse for the great expansionist drive at the end of the century was a dispute with Spain over her Caribbean colony, Cuba. A curious air of unreality hung over the ensuing war because America, true to her tradition of ideological self-deception, thought she was entering the war to free Cuba rather than to build an overseas empire. If, as is sometimes said, Great Britain accumulated her global possessions in a fit of absent-mindedness, America created her empire in a fit of anti-imperialism.

The United States had considered the acquisition of Cuba since the 1820's. Three pre-Civil War Presidents had unsuccessfully tried to purchase the "Pearl of the Antilles" from Spain. Congress had rejected by a narrow margin a resolution to intervene in behalf of Cuban rebels in 1870. On these, and on other occasions, America had always stopped short of decisive action for a variety of reasons, most of which boiled down to the fact that annexation did not justify the risks of war. After 1870 American interests, partly in the form of investments in sugar plantations, increased rapidly. Simultaneously Cuban revolutionaries, who sought to oust the Spanish, stepped up their activity. Disorder broke out periodically and the insurrectionists seldom showed a sense of discrimination in the destruction of property. American interests suffered almost as much as Spanish interests. A large-scale insurrection broke out in 1895, and by this time the American stake in Cuba was large enough to build up formidable pressure for intervention. A clumsy and ill-advised Spanish effort to put down the revolt by detaining rebels in overcrowded concentration camps was magnified by the yellow press in the United States. Lurid accounts of Spanish cruelty whipped up humanitarian sentiment, and the newspapers also exploited nationalistic impulses by demanding war, especially after the mysterious explosion of the American battleship, the *Maine,* in Havana Harbor on February 15, 1898. Eventually the agitation flowered in the passage of a war resolution by Congress (April 19–20, 1898), despite Spain's repeated efforts to effect a compromise. Although American action was a wholly normal climax to several generations of annexationist agitation, the United States insisted on misunderstanding her own motives. The Teller Amendment to the war resolution concluded its fourth point by stating that

> The United States hereby disclaims any disposition or intention to exercise sovereignty, jurisdiction, or control over said Island except for the pacification thereof and asserts its determination when that is accomplished, to leave the government and control of the Island to its people.

Within four months Spain had collapsed so completely that she accepted an agreement ending hostilities on August 12, 1898. By this time, the Spanish fleet in Philippine waters had been annihilated; Admiral George Dewey, commander of America's Far Eastern Squadron, had gained control of Manila Bay; and American troops were in process of capturing the city. Spanish ineptness had helped a small American army to occupy Cuba. In the same theater, the Spanish Caribbean fleet had been destroyed outside the harbor of Santiago. Puerto Rico had also been occupied after only token resistance.

It was doubtful whether the United States needed to engage in such far-flung military operations to liberate Cuba from a third-rate power. It was beyond dispute that she had tacitly modified her professed war aims during treaty negotiations. After ineffectual objection, Spain agreed to terms in which she gave up sovereignty over Cuba and ceded the Philippines, Puerto

Rico, and Guam outright to the United States. Signed on December 10, 1898, and presented to the Senate for ratification thereafter, the proposed treaty formally invited the United States to enter the scramble of the great powers for overseas colonies. If the Senate obliged, it would commit America to expansion in areas where collisions with other states were likely to be frequent and where the traditional precepts of United States foreign policy were certain to be unworkable. In any event America could no longer be insulated from the consequences of a century of uninterrupted growth which conferred on her membership in the select club of world powers. Sooner or later isolation would have to be abandoned. The history of our twentieth-century foreign policy properly begins with a discussion of the American reaction to victory in the Spanish-American War.

SUGGESTED READINGS

1. Bailey, T. A., *A Diplomatic History of the American People.* (General reference.)
2. Bemis, S. F., *A Diplomatic History of the United States.*
3. Kennan, George, *American Diplomacy, 1900–1950.* (General reference.)
4. Lippmann, Walter, *United States Foreign Policy: Shield of the Republic.*
5. Wight, Martin, *Power Politics.*

CHAPTER THREE

AMERICAN OVERSEAS EXPANSION

THE PRESSURES FOR ANNEXATION

Parker Moon, in describing how the great powers adopted a policy of colonialism, once observed: "On the eve of conversion individual sinners often possess a dual personality." The United States certainly had to wrestle with this psychological anxiety during the "great debate" over the treaty which concluded the war with Spain. Having launched what Secretary of State John Hay called "a splendid little war" for the liberation of Cuba, America wound up four months later committed to building an overseas empire.

The reversal of position protruded most clearly in the decision of the administration to annex the Philippines. It is not easy to isolate all the motives that caused President McKinley to move from a prewar declaration that "forceable annexation . . . cannot be thought of" to a postwar assertion that "there was nothing to do but to take them all." One of the pressures was the tireless activity of a group of expansionists strategically placed in the administration. Before he went a-soldiering in Cuba, Theodore Roosevelt as Assistant Secretary of the Navy had done everything he could to precipitate the war. After the termination of the conflict he took an even more outspoken stand for an annexationist policy. His successor on the Naval Board, Admiral Mahan, was author of a famous book, *The Influence of Sea Power on History,* and a long-time exponent of the view that a strong navy would assure national greatness. The Admiral's vision of "naval power" did not exhaust itself in demands for a strategically located string of coaling stations; he wanted "all that tends to make a people great upon the sea or by sea." This goal clearly involved substantial overseas possessions. Senatorial spokesmen for the Mahan viewpoint included Henry Cabot Lodge of Massachusetts, a close friend both of the Admiral and of

Theodore Roosevelt, as well as Cushman K. Davis of Minnesota, chairman of the Foreign Relations Committee.

A second group that applied pressure on McKinley was the commercial interests. Americans had long displayed enthusiasm for the so-called "China trade" and had taken the initiative in opening up Japan in 1853. Popular reluctance to project United States power into the Atlantic had never acted as a brake on expansionist enterprises in the Pacific. Indeed, after the Civil War there developed a policy of picking up Pacific island bases as rapidly as possible. Business groups favorable to this policy regarded the annexation of the Philippines as the next logical step, and hoped that the newly occupied island chain would provide a suitable springboard for a dive into the China market. Simultaneously, events in the Far East placed the interests of commerce in a more patriotic context. During 1897 and 1898, the European great powers extracted railroad concessions, commercial privileges, and leases on harbors from the collapsing Manchu empire of China. Russia, Great Britain, Germany, France, and Japan carved out spheres of influence so rapidly that the complete disintegration of China and the curtailment of American commercial opportunities seemed probable. These developments provided fresh ammunition to proponents of Philippine annexation. They organized an American Asiatic Association to lobby for the protection of Far Eastern trade.

Many Christian denominations also favored a colonial policy to convert and civilize the heathen peoples of the Pacific. The assumption of American superiority implicit in their attitude was even more baldly stated by the political theorists and anthropologists responsive to Darwinism. Whether the alleged superiority of Anglo-Saxon institutions or of the Nordic race provided the point of departure for their assertions, these groups hailed any extension of American dominion as a blessing to the world. Jingoes echoed this judgment and applied it specifically to the Philippine situation. They felt that any withdrawal from what she already possessed would humiliate America and make her seem ridiculous in the eyes of the world.

A fourth type of persuasion to which McKinley responded was a "grass-roots" demand for expansion. George F. Kennan has come closest to assessing the attitude of the man in the street:

> . . . when one notes the variety of arguments put up by the expansionists for the territorial acquisitions of 1898, one has the impression that none of them was the real one — that at the bottom of it all lay something deeper, something less easy to express, probably the fact that the American people of that day, or at least many of their more influential spokesmen, simply liked the smell of empire and felt an urge to range themselves among the colonial powers of the time, to see our flag flying on distant tropical isles, to feel the thrill of foreign adventure and authority, to bask in the sunshine of recognition as one of the great imperial powers of the world.

The sentiment described by Kennan was an instinctive manifestation of the popular desire for an expansionist policy bold enough to keep the

McKinley: *"Oh, well! I've got him anyhow!"* (Kladderadatsch, *Berlin, 1899.*)

United States abreast of other growing powers. If Americans had admitted their membership in the Western State System, they would have recognized their thrust for empire as an effort to maintain their position in the race for power by expanding as rapidly as rival states. Unwilling to think in such terms, they stumbled into the policy without being prepared for the consequences. McKinley labored under the same limitations as the rank and file. Whether he responded to the multiple pressures summarized above or acted on the guidance of God — as he told a group of Methodist clergymen — he insisted that Spain cede the Philippines, Guam, and Puerto Rico.

It was easier to bully Spain than the United States Senate. McKinley presented the treaty for ratification on January 4, 1899, and the result was a long debate. Senator Orville H. Platt of Connecticut argued for annexation by trying to establish a connection between Plymouth Rock and Manila Bay. He claimed that destiny had decreed American possession of both. Kindred views were expressed by a colleague from Indiana, Albert J. Beveridge, who demanded that the United States assume the white man's burden:

> The Philippines are ours forever . . . we will not repudiate our duty in the archipelago . . . we will not renounce our part in the mission of our race, trustee, under God, of the civilization of the world. And we will move forward to our work, not howling out regrets like slaves whipped to their burdens . . .

To senatorial apostles of expansion, the opportunity to annex the Philippines looked like the first step in the fulfillment of John Fiske's Darwinian prophecy that "the day is at hand when four-fifths of the human race will trace its pedigree to English forefathers."

OPPOSITION TO EXPANSION

A determined and vocal opposition emerged in 1899 as it had done on earlier occasions when the United States threatened to spill over its boundaries. The philosopher William James argued that if America annexed the Philippines she would "puke her ancient soul." Annexation was denounced as a policy unworthy of a nation whose history was tied to the cause of independence. However, the anti-imperialists suffered from a fatal handicap. They could not afford to argue against all expansion as such without committing political suicide, because the most cherished pages of American history recorded the physical growth of the country. Hence they had to confine their objections to the particular phase of expansion undertaken in 1898, proclaim it different from earlier westward movements, and condemn the deviation as evil. These considerations compelled them to assert that the current version of expansion was morally wrong because it involved the United States overseas, whereas previous physical growth had carried her only into contiguous areas. The argument implied that the actual process of subduing peoples overseas was more reprehensible than the same activity in adjacent territory. Opposition orators conscripted an old term, "imperialism," for duty in this particular enterprise and used it to sum up everything evil and derogatory about expansion. In fact, they made "imperialism" seem so odious that citizens never subsequently applied the term to American policy except when they wished to discredit it.

Notwithstanding the efforts of the anti-annexationists, their definition of imperialism failed to sustain the distinction they sought to make. Earlier generations had expanded into fresh territory whenever they wanted it and had the strength to take it. Moreover, there was little to choose morally between methods of uprooting and exterminating the Indians and of subduing rebel populations overseas. Continguity was a side issue. The Stars and Stripes fluttered over Alaska, Hawaii, and several Pacific islands while Senators lamented the obvious but irrelevant fact that the Philippines were overseas.

The logic of the debaters who called themselves anti-imperialists did not improve when they employed other arguments. Warnings that ratification of the treaty would involve the United States in the Caribbean and Pacific overlooked the fact that America had held a place in both for several decades and was currently trying to improve her position. Strategic interests had not been created by possessions. The former had developed first and made possessions desirable. The objection that the coveted territories were not likely to become states of the Union swayed few people. The parallel argument that peoples overseas ought not to be annexed because they were unsuitable material for citizenship also ignored a traditional attitude. Americans had never been deterred from overrunning Indian country by the probability that Indians would not qualify as citizens. They simply conquered the aborigines and conferred on them a status other than full citizenship. Neither the political nor the cultural problem of assimilating people with a non-Anglo-Saxon background had dampened American enthusiasm for expansion in the past. Whatever the theoretical merit of the views expressed by the foes of annexation, they assumed a standard of behavior which was contradicted by the facts of American history. The program of 1899 simply did not inaugurate a revolution in foreign policy. If it led to unprecedented results, this development was due to the fact that for the first time in over seventy-five years expansion brought collision with the great powers. The aquatic character of the new expansion did not distinguish it in any fundamental way from the westward movement over the North American continental land mass.

The groups that supported McKinley ignored the facts as stubbornly as his foes. They managed to convince themselves that the United States could annex an island chain seven thousand miles beyond the California coast and remain as unencumbered as before. They also thought that by doing what others were doing we could enhance our position proportionately. Neither belief was grounded in logic or actuality, as later developments showed. The oratory set a pattern that was to be duplicated many times in the twentieth century — a pattern that featured impassioned disagreements about unreal alternatives.

AMERICAN COMMITMENT

In the end, it made no difference whether the arguments of either side were valid. The fact that Americans had committed themselves to empire building outweighed criticism of the administration's inconsistencies and errors. Even so, the treaty with Spain was ratified on February 6, 1899, by only one vote more than the necessary two-thirds majority. This narrow victory was due to William Jennings Bryan, the staunch foe of imperialism, who persuaded several Democratic senators to support the treaty. He adopted this unusual strategy because he thought the Republicans could be defeated on the issue of expansion in the election of 1900.

Bryan's political judgment proved to be wrong. His hope for a renewal of the "great debate" never materialized. Because the Democrats again chose him as their presidential candidate, they lost the initiative. The country feared the Great Commoner more for his agrarian radicalism than it cherished him for his anti-imperialism. The Republicans, of course, were delighted by the opportunity to exploit domestic issues. Identified with continuing tensions in Cuba and desultory civil war in the Philippines, they avoided discussions of foreign policy and denounced Bryan as a threat to prosperity. The Democrats could not afford to advocate the withdrawal of American troops under attack in faraway areas, and so they also soft-pedaled the issue of colonialism.

The Republican presidential ticket of 1900 resembled the two-faced god Janus. Top billing went to the incumbent McKinley, who was associated with rising farm prices and the full dinner pail. Second place went to Theodore Roosevelt, the hero of San Juan Hill and proponent of colonial expansion. Thus the party could flash the spotlight on McKinley and exploit gratitude for prosperity, or on the Rough Rider and stimulate patriotic pride. Since the people were presented with no clear-cut choice on foreign policy, they voted solidly for prosperity. McKinley carried two more states than he did in 1896. He received 7,219,530 popular votes and 292 electoral votes as opposed to 6,358,071 and 155 for Bryan.

All this did not settle the question whether the United States had become an imperialist power in 1898–99. The answer turns largely on how the term is defined. A blanket formula that covers any extension of national influence is not very useful. Less vague definitions create other problems. If imperialism is limited to cases covering the extinction of sovereignty, it does not apply to great-power expansion in most of Africa, which until recently has lacked recognized sovereign governments. Alternately, if the term is applied to so-called civilized peoples who expand into backward areas, it perpetuates the absurdity that imperialistic enterprises are a matter of direction. Under such a definition Russia would be "imperialist" when it subdues the nomads of Central Asia, but not "imperialist" when it conquers a Balkan state in Europe.

Perhaps the best definition relates the term to the power position of expanding states in the Western State System. In this context, states are regarded as imperialistic when their expansion aims at the modification of the existing balance of power in their own favor, on either a regional or a global basis. States fall outside the terms of the definition when their expansion aims at the preservation of their relative position in the existing balance. The establishment of this distinction does not remove all difficulties; human judgment is still required to appraise the course of any given state. Moreover, the definition does not concern itself with the mechanics of expansion or the reaction of the conquered. The service it does perform is to apply to national policy the distinction between revisionist and *status quo* powers that is to be observed in the sphere of international relations.

The application of this definition to successive stages of American history involves an inversion. It points to the conclusion that the real period of American imperialism occurred in the first half of the nineteenth century when the United States sought hemispheric domination. The overseas expansion of 1898, which contemporaries denounced as imperialism, falls outside that category. America's aims were limited to keeping her position relative to other growing powers. Outside the Western Hemisphere she did not seek domination but the more modest goal of keeping abreast of others. Within the Hemisphere domination had already been established, and further extensions of American influence were designed to implement it. The distinction between these two types of expansion does not, however, depend on acceptance of the foregoing definition of imperialism. Whether Americans realized it or not, they had entered the race for overseas colonies to maintain their status in a configuration of dynamic, expanding powers.

A CUBAN PROTECTORATE

After the victory celebrations Americans had to settle down to the task of organizing their island empire. Besides acquiring Puerto Rico, Guam, and the Philippines from Spain, they had managed to annex Hawaii in 1898 and also faced a decision regarding Cuba. Ostensibly liberated, the "Pearl of the Antilles" was still occupied by American forces when the Spanish treaty cleared the Senate.

Neither the McKinley administration nor rank-and-file citizens possessed any clear theories about the organization and management of a colonial empire, for nobody had thought much about the legal status of America's new subjects. The treaty with Spain committed the United States to maintain freedom of religion in Puerto Rico, Guam, and the Philippine Islands. Otherwise Congress remained free to establish or withhold civil rights among the island peoples on any basis it chose. The pattern that subsequently crystallized varied from possession to possession. In each case it was affected by local circumstances and by the motives which had led the United States to intervene. The arrangements for Guam were the least complicated: it remained under the control of the Navy Department. Elsewhere trial and error proved to be the order of the day.

The arrangements for Cuba departed furthest from what America had led the world to expect at the outset of the war. Through the Teller Amendment, she had made a unilateral promise not to annex the island and had embodied a similar renunciation in her prewar ultimatum to Spain. The

Treaty of Paris cleared the way for the implementation of this war aim by forcing Spain to give up her sovereignty over Cuba. The logical outcome of such a chain of events and policy declarations would normally have been full independence. It soon became apparent, however, that the United States intended to "pacify" the island for a while.

Friction immediately developed between the Cuban revolutionaries and their deliverers over what the pledge of independence actually meant. Washington's view was bound to prevail because the United States could continue physical occupation until the Cubans acceded to its wishes. First peeks behind the curtain of the Teller Amendment did not reassure island patriots. In his annual message to Congress on December 5, 1899, McKinley stated his conception of legislative intentions. He asserted that the United States was responsible "for the future good government of Cuba" and went on to conclude that the island would have to be "bound to the United States by ties of singular intimacy and strength." This pronouncement was followed by modest gestures in the direction of self-government. On instructions from Washington the military governor, General Leonard Wood, held municipal elections in June 1900, and shortly thereafter issued an order for the election of delegates to a constitutional convention. Unfortunately the order stipulated that the constituent body would have to agree with the United States "upon the relations between the American government and the government of Cuba." This statement was not the prelude to the establishment of independence but to the establishment of a protectorate. To make sure that the delegates did not misunderstand the wishes of Washington, the call for the convention instructed them to incorporate the statement of government relationships in the Cuban constitution.

As it turned out, the delegates had partaken of one too many ideological "Cuba libres" to behave properly and began to act as though "Cuba" was already "libre." Their convention, which sat from November 1900 to February 1901, produced a constitution modeled on the American one. The Cuban founding fathers, however, neglected to draw up a statement of any special American-Cuban relations. And this was just as well, for Secretary of War Elihu Root did it for them. General Wood undertook to explain their duty to the Cuban delegates. When the latter continued to demur, the McKinley administration forced the terms through Congress as part of the Army Appropriation Act of March 1901. Known as the "Platt Amendment," this quasi ultimatum made the termination of military occupation dependent on Cuban acceptance of American wishes. The Amendment was to govern relations with Cuba until the 1930's and in part beyond that point. Its terms established a condition which Americans would have denounced as a protectorate if put into effect by any other state. First of all, Cuba was supposed to ratify all acts of the military government. Second, she was expected to promise that no foreign power would be granted "control over any portion of said island" but that the United States would be granted as many bases for naval or coaling stations as it desired. The

Cubans were assured that the latter provision sought to "maintain the independence of Cuba." Finally, the new republic was asked to agree to the principle that the United States could take a hand in its internal affairs.

For a time the Cuban delegates persisted in acting as though they possessed a free choice. The convention rejected the Platt Amendment by a vote of 24 to 2. This decision was followed by the personal intervention of Elihu Root, who explained that, because of the Monroe Doctrine, European nations would not interfere with American plans. Once the Secretary of War had made it clear that no force of opinion, law, or international morality would prevent the United States from keeping Cuba in a satellite status, the convention reversed itself by a narrow margin and ratified the constitution with the attached Platt Amendment. The terms of the Platt Amendment were affirmed by a formal treaty the next year to guard against unilateral Cuban repudiation through a constitutional amendment.

The compliance of the delegates paved the way for the election of President Tomás Estrada Palma on May 20, 1902, and the installation of a Cuban government in Havana. The same day the military government of General Wood, which had begun on December 13, 1899, was terminated. During his administration the General had grappled energetically with disorder, disease, and illiteracy; but the Cubans gave every indication that they would have cheerfully exchanged these gains for genuine independence.

In later practice the application of the Platt Amendment was erratic because the tastes and interpretations of successive administrations varied. It led to only one extended occupation by American troops. This occurred in 1905 when some Cubans challenged the results of the election that returned President Palma to office. Palma preferred the presence of American warships to the loss of his job and got them after several requests had been ignored in the interest of political effects elsewhere in Latin America. The ensuing occupation lasted from 1906 to early 1909, most of this time under the governorship of Charles E. Magoon. None of the subsequent interventions were so prolonged or open, but they occurred repeatedly, the most dramatic being the landing of Marines by an apprehensive Woodrow Wilson on the eve of World War I.

Often action was prompted by America's desire for stability in the Western Hemisphere. Cuba's dependence on sugar production exposed her to political and economic unrest more frequently than some of her neighbors. Hence, when sudden drops in sugar prices encouraged agitators, American investors grew nervous and clamored for help from Washington. The United States was also tempted to intervene because of a nervous preoccupation with hemispheric security — a problem we shall treat in detail in Chapter Eight. Naturally the Cubans criticized the United States for intervening. Many Americans shared their view and had less reason for restraint in expressing it. In the 1920's the complaint was replaced by charges that the United States maintained an irresponsible laissez-faire attitude toward Cuban problems. The steady drumfire of criticism suggests that a protectorate is a national headache.

The establishment of an unofficial protectorate in Cuba enabled the United States to escape some knotty problems over the legal status of the islanders that arose in the Philippines, Puerto Rico, Guam, and Hawaii, which were under direct control. The United States retained all the advantages of Cuban dependency without assuming the disadvantages of responsibility except when she deliberately chose to do so. She also avoided the opprobrium attached to the more frank arrangements between European states and their dependencies.

America would have had every reason to congratulate herself for the situation in Cuba but for the discrepancy between her promise and her performance. The failure to fulfill the pledge of independence was actually due more to inexperience in international politics than to deliberate bad faith. At the outset of the war, she looked no further than victory, failing to see that the elimination of Spain from the Hemisphere would involve her more deeply in the struggle for power and raise questions of naval strategy, trade, and the status of "liberated" areas. When she finally became aware of the relation of Cuba to these problems, she had already promised the islanders independence. Rather than throw away the benefits of victory, she established a closer relationship with Cuba than originally contemplated. The ensuing embarrassment emphasized the need for America to behave like a great power and anticipate the consequences of her actions.

HAWAII

The Spanish-American War also gave the United States an opportunity to annex the tiny chain of the Sandwich or Hawaiian islands. Ever since the revolution of 1891, expansionist groups had promoted the project. For four years, however, President Cleveland blocked annexation, and after his retirement from office in 1897, Senate Democrats successfully continued his hostile tactics. They hamstrung a treaty in March 1898, and also a substitute joint resolution submitted by administration forces to evade the necessity for a two-thirds Senate majority. The Pacific phase of the Spanish-American War highlighted the importance of the islands as a base for naval operations. After Dewey's victory on May 1 had cut the ground from under Senate obstruction, a new joint resolution cleared the House on June 15 and the Senate on July 6. As it turned out, the margin in the upper house was 42 to 21, which meant that a treaty would also have been ratified. Except for the Japanese minority, the Sandwich Islanders welcomed their new status. They had lived under virtual American control for nearly a decade and had offered every assistance, including a treaty of alliance, after the outbreak of the war.

The formal transfer of sovereignty, which took place on August 12, 1898, confronted the United States with new problems and helped to create new attitudes on colonial policy. Hitherto, American citizens had taken pride in insisting that their country did not maintain any of its possessions or peoples in a subordinate status. The Alaskan purchase had been an innovation because it added territory to the American domain without any intention of granting the new possession statehood. Hawaiian annexation pointed toward a further breach of principle inasmuch as the joint resolution promised the islanders neither citizenship nor incorporation as a state. It merely made the flat statement that Hawaii was "part of the territory of the United States" and left future Congresses to specify what that meant. However, senators who debated the joint resolution anticipated some of the troubles that would harass a country faced with a variety of present and prospective additions. Notable performances were given by Senator Platt of Connecticut and Senator Hoar of Massachusetts. Foreshadowing later Supreme Court decisions, Platt argued that the right to acquire territory was an inherent attribute of sovereignty notwithstanding the lack of detailed constitutional provisions on the subject. The United States had qualified itself for such a role when it became a sovereign state. Platt also contended that the right to govern implied the right to create whatever government seemed appropriate for the area and population. Boiled down to essentials, his doctrine constituted an assertion of America's right to be a colonial power and to make any governmental arrangements it chose in new possessions. Official acceptance of this viewpoint raised a question of classification. Neither Hawaii nor the other acquisitions qualified as "territories" in the traditional sense. Tradition forbade the employment of the word "colony" to described any relationship involving the United States after the Revolutionary War. So the new acquisitions came to be called either possessions or dependencies.

Senator Hoar also foresaw the future when he predicted that Hawaii would eventually become an "equal part of a self-governing republic." The politics of the island were sufficiently advanced to make the prospect of statehood possible, but geographical position and ethnic composition presented such novelties as to make most Americans hesitate. Eight islands large enough to be of some consequence, lying a little over two thousand miles from San Francisco, composed the bulk of the new territory. At the time of acquisition, the population totaled about 154,000. The Japanese were the largest racial group, almost 40 per cent. Native and mixed Hawaiians, Caucasians, and Chinese came next. Hawaii was the largest of the islands, which in all constituted more than six thousand square miles. Oahu was the most densely populated and most important, being the site of the chief city, Honolulu.

The Hawaiians already had a republican, constitutional government. The joint resolution of annexation permitted the existing political institutions to go on functioning so long as Congress did not provide otherwise. For almost two years Congress did not so provide. Then on April 30, 1900, it passed the Organic Act for Hawaii. Under this Act the constitutional and statutory law of the United States were extended to cover the territory. Those who were Hawaiian citizens on August 12, 1898, received recognition as American citizens. Hawaii was permitted to have its own bicameral legislature, with some restrictions on its powers. Sums in appropriations bills were to be regarded as having been reappropriated if the legislature adjourned without taking necessary action. The President was empowered to appoint the governor, but choice was limited to citizens of the territory. The Organic Act confirmed the previous right of Hawaiians to have a delegate representative in the House of Representatives at Washington. A court system was set up at two levels, one for Territorial law and one for United States Federal law. Local government was left to the Hawaiian legislature and to Hawaiian functionaries.

PUERTO RICO

Puerto Rico presented a somewhat different problem from either Cuba or Hawaii. General Miles had overcome feeble resistance and occupied the island in July 1898, before the fighting ended elsewhere. In the spirit of the times he proclaimed that Americans came to protect lives and property and to bring "the guarantees and blessings of the liberal institutions of our government." The military took over on October 18, 1898, when the Spanish authorities departed. This form of government continued until May 1900, when civilian government under the authority of the Foraker Act replaced it. Conditions confronting American military governors in Puerto Rico were in some respects more tolerable than in Cuba. There had been revolution but not the protracted wars that had torn Cuba for decades. Also it was a more manageable area, being a rectangular island of about 100 by 35 miles, with a population of just a little under a million. The military government established a distinguished record during its twenty-one months of life, especially under Brigadier General George W. Davis. Of course the Army could be depended upon to provide order and curb lawlessness among the native population, but in addition it revised the judicial system and even introduced such Anglo-Saxon novelties as *habeas corpus*. Qualifications for the franchise were established and municipal elections were held, so that the local government could be placed in native hands. The Army introduced tax reforms, as well as large-scale and unprecedented measures of sanitation and preventive medicine. For example, 750,000 persons were vaccinated during the first six months of military occupation. In fact, the civilian government was to build largely upon the very solid groundwork which had already been laid by its military predecessor.

Notwithstanding his enlightened approach to the problems of colonial government, General Davis was averse to giving the islanders any large measure of self-government at this time. He even felt it unwise to permit them to elect the lower house of their own legislative body, basing his stand on the conviction that they were not yet capable of making a democratic government work. There were many opinions and some statistics to vindicate his position: for instance, the contemporary estimate that 85 per cent could neither read nor write. Nevertheless Congress ignored his advice when it passed the Foraker Act of April 12, 1900, which was to serve as framework for Puerto Rican government during the coming decades.

This Act allowed the election of a lower house by the Puerto Ricans but qualified its authority effectively by providing for an executive council with the powers of an upper house and a governor with an absolute veto. Both council and governor were appointed by the President of the United States, but five of the eleven members of the council had to be Puerto Ricans. American responsibilities were divided among the respective bureaus of the United States government until 1909, when they were concentrated in the Bureau of Insular Affairs of the War Department. The Foraker Act and companion legislation established safeguards for fiscal and economic policies, placing restrictions upon the amount that both the national and the local government might borrow and limiting to five hundred acres the amount of land that could be controlled by any newly chartered agricultural corporation. The court system was mixed, with supreme court justices appointed by the President and the Senate of the United States, while the lower courts were controlled by the native government. Puerto Rico was given a "resident commissioner" in Washington and provisions were made for elections by popular vote every two years. In the course of time the commissioner received a seat in the House of Representatives, like the delegates of territories, although Puerto Rico did not technically qualify for territorial status.

Understandably, many Puerto Ricans felt that their political condition had retrogressed. Formerly they had been a Spanish colony enjoying Spanish citizenship and representation in the Spanish Cortes. Now, thanks to American squeamishness about the names to be used for possessions, they were something less than a colony. They had no legislative representative and their citizenship was declared by the Foraker Act to be "Puerto Rican," except for those who retained their allegiance to Spain. Puerto Rican "citizenship" entitled the islanders to the protection of the United States but did not constitute them citizens of that country or given them the rights of its citizens. The anomalies of this situation were largely corrected by a later organic act of March 2, 1917, the Jones Act. Under the terms of this legislation and with the liberal policies pursued already before its passage by the Wilson administration, Puerto Ricans gained control of the upper house of their legislature. They also received United States citizenship and were presented with a bill of rights that included most of the traditional Anglo-Saxon and a few distinctively American liberties. While Puerto Rico did not formally qualify under Supreme Court interpretations as an "incorporated territory" like Hawaii and Alaska, its status closely approximated that of the more favored "dependencies." As in the rest of the American colonial holdings, a very high degree of self-government had been achieved.

THE PHILIPPINES

The buoyant resolve of Americans not to relinquish the Philippines before they had taken the islands was one thing. To take them was quite another. Resolutions were possible in Washington, effective action only in the seven thousand islands of a mountainous archipelago that had a total area (114,830 square miles) larger than all but four of the states in the Union. The task was complicated by Filipino ideals of independence. Repeated revolts against Spanish rule had provided evidence that many of the Filipinos looked forward to freedom rather than to American domination, no matter how benevolent and well-intentioned the latter might be.

When Spanish power in the Philippines collapsed, United States forces in the Far East were in command of Manila Bay, and they continued to hold it because the Germans refrained from intervening with their superior naval power. Meanwhile, on land Americans were trying to take the city of Manila. The long-range prospects were favorable. The immediate problem was how to get control of at least a dozen or so of the largest islands which dominated the group. To establish some remote connection between military facts in the Orient and popular idealism back home, Admiral Dewey invited a young Filipino rebel leader, Emilio Aguinaldo, to return from exile in Hong Kong. The Admiral also provided Aguinaldo's supporters with arms to help oust the Spanish. No doubt military requirements justified the employment of such agents. Furthermore, both Dewey and Consul E. Spencer Pratt, at Singapore, denied categorically having made any promises regarding the Philippines' political status. Yet it was curiously risky to invite the champion of Philippine independence to help establish American rule. By the time American troops entered Manila, Aguinaldo's followers were in possession of most of the islands, including portions of the island of Luzon not occupied by Americans. They had proclaimed a Filipino Republic, established a government at Malolos, north of Manila, and begun bidding for recognition by the great powers.

The crux of the matter was the changing attitude of the United States toward the question of annexing this prize of war. American historians are still trying to determine, assess, and explain rationally the full range of motivation for the spectacular shift in national psychology of which the Philippine story is only a part, although an important one. What wonder that the Filipinos were confused! This much does seem fairly clear: in spite of vociferous protests at home and in the Philippines, American opinion and policy were swinging over to the position that the Philippine rescue could not be complete until the United States held full control. As this view crystallized, it committed America to the reduction of resistance from any source, Spanish or native. Aguinaldo and his forces plainly adopted the premise that the fight for freedom had come to a successful conclusion when the Spaniards were driven out and that it could be rekindled only by any effort of the Americans to move in.

It was a costly misunderstanding. Who fired the first shot is a matter of dispute, but two days before the Senate of the United States concluded its debate over the treaty with Spain, fighting began in the islands between native patriots and American liberators.

The Philippine imbroglio — which approval of the treaty converted into an "insurrection" — was no "splendid little war." Insurgents were quickly driven from the important towns and cities, but they carried on the war from the hills and in the open country. The bloody business dragged on for several years. The native forces eventually ran short of supplies and relied increasingly on the bolo, a long knife, while the American conquistadores ran short of patience and relied increasingly on rubber hoses. It took upwards of sixty thousand troops to hold the position. The civilizing mission was off to a bad start.

Finally the Americans, by devices somewhat less than sporting, captured Aguinaldo on March 23, 1901. Although he soon took the oath of allegiance to the United States and called upon his followers to capitulate, large numbers of guerrillas refused to do so. By July 4, 1901, a civilian replaced a military man as head of the Philippine government. On October 1 a premature claim was made that the "Philippine insurrection" was at an end. Still the fighting went on, and Moro tribesmen did not fully accept American rule for over a decade.

In the debate on Philippine policy Senator Platt had denied that the United States was obligated to grant the Philippines statehood or to confer citizenship on the Filipinos, or that the people or products of the Philippines needed to be admitted to the United States without the consent of Congress. To clarify its intentions, the Senate adopted a resolution, eight days after approving the treaty, stating that it was not the intention of the American government to incorporate the Filipinos into the body of United States citizens or to "permanently annex said islands as an integral part of the territory of the United States." Instead, the American purpose was to prepare the Philippines for self-government and eventually to dispose of them in America's and the Philippines' best interests. Although this resolution passed by a vote of only 26 to 22, it proved to be a remarkably accurate reflection of what was ultimately to happen. The Philippines may have been without experience in self-government, but the United States Congress was soon to demonstrate a comparable inexperience in the government of colonial possessions.

Even before Congress had argued to a decision, President McKinley had taken action under his war powers. A commission headed by President Schurman of Cornell University arrived in the islands shortly after the outbreak of the fighting with Aguinaldo's forces. Under the circumstances at the time of its report (November 1899), the commission did not recommend Philippine independence, which would have required American withdrawal. It did, however, take a stand in favor of a fairly advanced form of self-government and territorial status for the islands.

But with the "insurrection" still in full swing, this course seemed too generous. In fact, the problem was actually not one of turning the government over from American to Filipino hands, but of turning it over from American military to American civilian authority. Accordingly the President on April 7, 1900, instructed a second commission, headed by William Howard Taft, to effect this change. On September 1, 1900, in accordance with instructions, the civilian authorities took over legislative power from the military, and less than a year later (July 4, 1901) full executive powers as well. Mr. Taft, as a result of these developments, became the first American civilian governor of the Philippines. The judicial functions were organized by the commission itself.

For a little over two years after the ratification of the treaty of cession, the President continued to deal with the islands under his own powers. About the time that Aguinaldo's independence movement collapsed, Congress, through the Spooner Amendment to an army appropriations act of March 2, 1901, conferred blanket authority on the President. This stopgap arrangement carried over for several months, until Congress in July 1902 passed an Organic Act for the Philippines. The new legislation, which was the first of its type for the islands, approved virtually everything connected with the establishment of Philippine government up to this point. It also set the pattern for Philippine development until the end of World War I. It was a remarkable blueprint for the future of a commonwealth, and at this early stage accurately forecast the political development of the Philippines. As the commission's instructions tolerantly expressed the policy, it was an effort to weld oriental "customs," "habits," and "even their prejudices" to principles of government distilled from the Anglo-Saxon tradition and filtered through American experience.

The American pattern of tripartite division of governmental functions was transplanted to the Philippines. The civil governor, called a "Governor General" from the days of Luke E. Wright in 1905, became the chief executive. Four departments, headed by American commissioners and usefully influenced by three Filipino advisers, rounded out this branch. These same departmental commissioners and their Filipino guides doubled for some time as a legislature. As soon as the process of pacification permitted, the first reliable census was taken; it showed in 1903 a total population of 7,635,426. It also afforded a basis for electing members to a legislative body which in 1907 became the lower house of a bicameral legislature in which the commissioners, acting in legislative capacity, continued to function by now constituting the upper chamber. Two resident commissioners were elected biennially to represent the territory in Washington. A judicial system was established consisting of three levels of courts. In cases involving United States constitutional or statutory law, or for amounts over $25,000, appeal could be taken from the Philippine Supreme Court to the Supreme Court of the United States.

A sympathetic and liberal United States policy during the Roosevelt and Taft administrations took the Philippines far along the road to self-government. More and more offices went to Filipinos. By 1913 the natives held at least 50 per cent or more of all important offices except the governorship and the membership of the Council, which by this time had been enlarged to include five Americans and four Filipinos. The lower house, or Assembly, had always been predominantly Filipino and now was completely so. Over two-thirds of the classified civil service and over 90 per cent of the teachers were Filipino.

But Americans soon learned the bitter lesson that a nationalistic people is never grateful for, but ever resentful of, foreign rule, no matter how benevolent the interloper may regard himself. The Assembly soon achieved consensus on the issue of independence. Its division consisted only of a radically nationalist (Nationalist) and a moderately nationalist (Progressive) grouping. The former demanded immediate independence, and the latter were willing to settle for gradually increasing self-government looking to independence in the near future. The legislative struggle usual in the system of separated powers was intensified here by the obvious and bitter divisions along lines of Filipino patriotism and American sovereignty. By 1911 the elective lower house and the appointive upper house of the legislature were hopelessly deadlocked on the general appropriations bill. The government could function only because of the provision of the Organic Act which had made available the sums of the previous year's appropriation if a new legislative body failed to pass the necessary measure. Hence the appropriations of 1910 were used for each of the succeeding three years.

Only the general restraint and benevolence of American administrators up to this point had made the development of such vigorous self-assertion by the Filipinos possible. Yet a way had to be found for breaking the impasse. At this juncture the Democrats won the election of 1912, and on March 4, 1913, Woodrow Wilson came into office. The change in parties did not encourage a judicious evaluation of the very real progress that had been made in the Philippines. The Democrats had continued to advocate independence for the Philippines ever since 1900, and the platform of 1912 also included this well-worn plank. Wilson took full advantage of it. His new Governor General, Francis B. Harrison, conveyed the message to Filipino patriots that it was his "hope to move towards that end [ultimate independence] as rapidly as the safety and permanent interests of the Islands will permit." It was, of course, as difficult to disagree with such a pronouncement as it was to distinguish it from the settled policy already operating. If the Democrats in their role as opposition had felt that the Republicans had not moved fast enough, they soon learned that, as the responsible government, "safety and permanent interest" did not argue for immediate independence. But because a new party was in power, Washington made a compromise on more graceful terms than the Republicans might have found possible. The Filipinos were given a "majority in the appointive Commission and thus in the upper as well as the lower house of the legislature a majority representation." This was no doubt a proper step in the direction of Filipino self-government; the only impropriety would be to represent it as a departure from preceding policy rather than the logical culmination of it.

Under the pressures of war and the need for general administrative organization of territorial governments, the Jones Act was passed in 1916. Its effect upon the Philippines will be treated in another connection.

Thesc political developments were merely the framework within which a much more far-reaching and satisfying transformation was taking place in the Philippines. After all, the function of an alien people honestly trying to train a dependency in self-government is, like the function of a parent, an attempt to become superfluous. But while this end was in some measure being achieved, the social, economic, and educational changes were to be permanent American contributions to the life of the islands.

It is easy to criticize any colonial administration. Praise comes much harder. But by contrast with almost all other colonial administrations, that of the United States in the Philippines is hard to judge unfavorably and easy to view proudly. Probably nothing so pleased the Filipinos as American land policies. The natives were encouraged to own their land, and regulations made it easy for them to acquire up to about forty acres. Corporate holdings were limited by law to about 2,500 acres, and the law was reasonably well enforced. The United States finally purchased for $7,000,000 the 400,000 acres held by the religious orders, which had continued to demand payment even after the United States took over the land and separated state and church. This gigantic real estate deal was consummated after lengthy negotiations between Mr. Taft, the American representative, and the Vatican. Whatever the merits of the claims to such "friars lands," as they were called, and the advisability of our method of securing them, the outcome was good. The land found its way on easy terms into the hands of those who already were working it as tenants.

The United States handsomely redeemed the promise to educate the natives: a system of public schools was set up, ranging from the omnipresent primary school, through the high school system of the several provinces, and finally to the University of the Philippines established in Manila. In about two decades the number of children going to school rose from a few thousand to a million. Disease was attacked through improved sanitation and the application of medical science. Such formidable scourges as cholera and leprosy were all but eliminated. Conservation measures protected and developed forest and mineral resources. A new government bureau improved methods of agriculture. Police protection was provided by a well-trained native force. A civil service system was launched. The United States established civil rights and promoted a judiciary system that would protect them. Freedom of religion was introduced, and zealous American Protestants began some of the mission work promised a decade earlier.

Best of all, these improvements were paid for by the Filipinos themselves while their tax rate remained low and their indebtedness negligible. Such a happy development reflected the unprecedented prosperity which came to the islands as a result of the tremendous American-protected market opened up to them. The net result was that while the Philippines might be growing away from their protector politically — thanks to his own tutelage — they were being welded to America economically.

THE LEGAL STATUS OF THE NEW POSSESSIONS

One problem in retaining the spoils of the Spanish War was the question, what kind of possessions were they? Of all the arguments raised by the antiexpansionists during the debate on the Treaty of Paris, perhaps the most thoughtful one was that the United States could not constitutionally acquire territory not intended for statehood. Foes of annexation also contended that some of the territory which the United States then contemplated acquiring was — in the estimation of the critics, at least — unsuited for statehood. Naturally such dialectics did not serve as an effective bar to expansion in the emotionally charged atmosphere of the Senate in 1898 and 1899. But just as naturally, overriding such objections did not remove the dilemma which they seemed to pose. Congress and the Executive dealt with the new possessions as the expediency of the moment seemed to dictate. But it was only a question of time until the legal test would be made, and then some answers would have to be given on a less casual basis.

Whether or not the fundamental question had already been removed by the purchase of Alaska, the annexation of Spanish territory forced an answer to numerous queries of detail. What did the status of the new possessions imply? Were the people living in such areas citizens of the United States? Did the provisions of the Constitution apply to them? Did they possess the rights of Americans? In the popular summation of the problem, "did the Constitution follow the flag"? Out of the extensive canvassing of these problems in public discussion and learned dissertations came a series of doctrines and decisions handed down by the Supreme Court. Not even the Court was sure how it had arrived at some of them. It could only justify them one by one as it went along.

In May 1901, the Court handed down a decision in the case of *Downes* v. *Bidwell*. The substance of the case is less important than the implied question which had to be answered before a ruling could be reached: Was Puerto Rico a part of the United States? The Court said no. On the same day it ruled in the case of *De Lima* v. *Bidwell* that Puerto Rico was not a foreign country. Both decisions were rendered by a 5 to 4 vote. Eight judges were agreed that these two rulings were incompatible. But the mental flexibility of Justice Henry B. Brown, who constituted the majority of one in both cases, was equal to the task of reconciling these views. In these and subsequent cases the varying opinions of the Court began to develop a pattern. All territory acquired by the United States was annexed to it; but thereafter the territory might be classified "incorporated" or "unincorporated." Incorporated territories, like states, were subject to all provisions of the Constitution, except those obviously intended to apply only to states. Incorporation came only by direct congressional action. Unincorporated territories became so simply by the fact of annexation. In them only the "fundamental" provisions of the Constitution applied. A formal effort to list such provisions has never been made.

While the Court was thus at work, Congress had been legislating regarding the territories without being aware of this distinction. The Court now had to retrace the steps of Congress and, in a long series of cases, to decide when Congress had unintentionally conferred incorporated status on the territories. Eventually the jurists decided that only two territories had been unintentionally incorporated, Alaska and Hawaii.

The entire constitutional process ultimately turned out to be a successful, if tortuous, method of enabling the United States to acquire territory without undue embarrassment. Such embarrassment could arise from prematurely conferring rights upon her subjects, or from the difficulty of ever separating newly acquired possessions from American sovereignty, should this become desirable. Under the conception then becoming prevalent, the United States could grant rights and transfer land at its discretion so long as these areas did not enjoy constitutional protection. Whether they were in such status was determined by Congress.

Had the Constitution followed the flag? No one seemed quite sure, but it was clear enough that Americans were doing what they wanted to do. As Mr. Dooley put it, "Some say it laves the flag up in the air and some say that's where it laves the Constitution. Anyhow, something's in the air. But there's wan thing I'm sure about . . . No matter whether the Constitution follows the flag or not, the Supreme Court follows the illiction returns."

DISILLUSIONMENT WITH EMPIRE

Long before all these developments, American attitudes toward colonial possessions began to shift noticeably. Without an explicit change in ideology, the public gradually came to doubt that colonial expansion was the sole road to great-power status and to world recognition of America's new station. The seeds of disillusionment had been sown before the turn of the century at the peak of the campaign for expansion.

Opposition to overseas expansion had been organized and highly vocal from the beginning. Shortly after the end of the Spanish-American War it coalesced in an Anti-Imperialist League, which included prominent leaders of both political parties, industrial tycoons, and literary men. Two ex-Presidents, Benjamin Harrison and Grover Cleveland, gave the League respectability, and Mark Twain lent it his mordant pen. A dedicated rank and file echoed the attacks of a talented leadership with the result that advocates of expansion were held to narrow victories in a series of critical votes in Congress. Once the thrill of conquest had worn off and the country had settled down to the dull task of colonial administration, the Anti-Imperialist League won more recruits. When the zeal of the Leaguers threatened to flag, the rising Progressive movement took over the cause, focusing on the "undemocratic" aspects of colonialism. The conflict gradually subsided. The United States would keep what it already possessed but henceforth would rely on new ways of showing its expanding power.

In future years Americans would be able to look back on the election year of 1900 and say of their budding disenchantment with the consequences of becoming a colonial power, "We didn't know the half of it." The by-products of conquest included a wide assortment of ills which have been constant from that time to the present. Philippine "pacification" was not fully achieved for years. Administration created difficulties everywhere, and not only between Americans and the local population but between departments of the "mother country's" government. Local patriots never seemed satisfied; either they were such enthusiastic Americans that they wanted to be incorporated into the Union, or they were such ardent separatist-nationalists that they demanded independence. Unforeseen diplomatic problems multiplied in the aftermath of war and annexation; for instance, as we have already seen, the United States was before long negotiating with the Holy See.

Not the least of America's discomforts was the feeling of strangeness about what she was doing. In terms of fundamental national drives, the novelty of policy was much overdone by its critics. Yet many felt none the less strongly that they had abandoned valued traditions, and some even thought that America had lost her moorings. Even with allowances for the distortion of politics and emotionalism, it must be agreed that there were important departures from the past, though not often in the manner pictured. Up to this time Americans had not been greatly interested in imposing their own pattern of life upon the native populations, as some colonial powers had done. Neither had they, like others, left the original society largely intact. Traditionally they had simply fought such peoples, demolished their way of life, replaced them, and thus eliminated them from consideration. Now some of the societies they encountered were so advanced, so populous, and so remote that any effort to evict or supplant them was neither practical nor desirable. So in a sort of chain reaction following the Spanish War, the United States emerged almost automatically as a colonial power. For the first time, if Americans wished to expand territorially, they had to do so on terms similar to those that had always confronted the great colonial-imperialist powers of the past. This situation was new to a people hitherto able to expand into adjacent territory which was either fairly empty or unfairly emptied. The pursuit of one tradition was leading to the abandonment of another. The fact that Americans were so addicted to expansion as not to abandon it did not mean they were happy about all the concomitants of their new program. They found that they, who had built the political life of the nation on the principle of federalism, were now moving toward a limited colonial system. Others, who had begun as world powers with a colonial system, seemed to be moving toward federalism. There was something incongruous and, they vaguely felt, unwholesome about this.

The mild ironies noticeable up to this point in the Philippine episode are only the first of a long series. It had not been enough that Americans should claim that they were benefactors to the Filipinos. They had to fight the Filipinos because they did not agree. Again, while some Americans had no doubt been interested in the humanitarian aspects of American penetration into the Far East, the fundamental motives were those of American interests, as then conceived: strategic, economic, and political. The first saw the islands as a great American base in the Orient. The second divided its interest among the prospects of investment, the usual desires of growing industrial states for raw materials and markets, and dreams of making the islands the springboard to the exaggerated profits of the lucrative "China trade." The third visualized the presumed direct gains in prestige and the more indirect power advantages in keeping the prize out of the hands of rapacious competitors. The paradox of the position as it eventually developed, however, was that such hopes and aspirations as these, which motivated Americans most strongly, never materialized, while the humanitarian delusions with which they had sugar-coated the lure of their selfish interests for themselves and others were to a considerable degree realized.

The great expectations of economic returns were fulfilled in only a very limited way. American Peace Commissioners in 1898 had said: "The policy of the United States in the Philippines will be that of the open door to the world's commerce." Notwithstanding this declaration of principle, the United States soon converted the Philippines into a typical colonial dependency. Substantially free trade was established between the conqueror and the conquered, while the products of foreign competitors were admitted only under the handicap of import duties. Such a system was intended to create a protected market and develop the area as a source of raw materials. But even if successful to some degree, it was a mixed blessing, with the bitter kernel of truth that what made it "mixed" could probably have been avoided by not taking the Philippines, and what made it a "blessing" could probably have been had without resorting to that same device. Especially as a market for American goods the Philippines came along very slowly. In 1899 the proportion of Philippine imports coming from the United States was about what it had been in the days of the Spanish rule — 7 per cent. Nine years later it had risen by only an additional 10 per cent. That such modest gains justified the venture was highly doubtful; that they disappointed the hopes of the sponsors is certain. America's best customers by far continued to be the very European countries whose competition apparently could be met on their own soil but not in their Far Eastern possessions.

Theoretically the Philippines provided an area to which to export American surplus capital. But no spectacular advantage was taken of this opportunity. In the years before World War II, investments in the Philippines amounted to about 1.2 per cent of total United States capital abroad. It is obvious that the investor was less interested in whose flag was flying over the area into which he sent his dollars than in the percentage of returns he got. The emergence of this practical attitude further complicates the assessment of economic returns from conquest, for the suspicion is that the 1.2 per cent was not a result of the occupation but merely represents what Americans found it profitable to invest in the area.

At the outset there had been those who argued that American territory in the Far East would provide a lever for applying strategic pressures in the local struggle for position. It failed to work out that way. America's presence in the Philippines did not seriously modify the intensity of the competition among the great powers nor enable the United States to engage in it more successfully. These harsh facts invited rationalization. Some Americans justified landholding in the Orient on the ground that it would retard this same practice by others. A few admitted their enthusiasm for an annexationist policy. Whatever they said, other powers simply regarded America as a participant in the game. These rival states had no intention of allowing conquests by the United States to halt the process of expansion if they could help it. They were likely to accept such a situation only if an annexationist policy conferred enough power on the United States to destroy the regional balance. Acquisition of the Philippines did not give America that kind of leverage in the Far East. Moreover, she was in no mood to develop it from such an insecure base of operations. A modest annexationist policy might work near the American seat of power and in a hemisphere blanketed by the influence of the Monroe Doctrine. It could not work half a world away and under quite different circumstances.

Only the humanitarian crusade remained. Into this the Americans now threw themselves with guilty fervor. "We come as ministering angels, not as despots," the proexpansionists had avowed. That their impulses would have been strong enough to make them come without more human attractions is doubtful. Irrespective of their motives, not only they but all other Americans were involved. Unable to achieve the purposes which had brought them to the Philippines, and unwilling simply to get out, Americans took up the white man's burden with the enthusiasm of belated converts.

SUGGESTED READINGS

1. Mahan, A. T., *The Influence of Sea Power upon History.*
2. Pratt, J. W., *America's Colonial Experiment.*
3. Sprout, H. and M., *The Rise of American Naval Power, 1776–1918.*
4. Strong, J., *Our Country.*

CHAPTER FOUR

THE PROGRESSIVE MOVEMENT

While America was expanding overseas, pressures for domestic reform accumulated. These expressed themselves through the Progressive movement — a bipartisan reform crusade which dominated political life at every level from 1900 until American intervention in World War I. The people who were the backbone of the movement until it began to split in 1909 gave Progressivism a unique character. Unlike the agrarian crusaders of the post-Civil War period, they showed an unselfish moral zeal for the purification of democratic institutions and refused to pursue group economic interests in the name of reform. No single term accurately describes the membership of the movement, because the customary terms classify groups on an economic basis. Progressives often referred to themselves as members of the middle class, by which they meant that they did not belong to any special class (i. e., plutocrats, workers, and so on). A modern sociologist would protest the use of the term "middle class" and contend that the Progressives possessed class interests of which they were unconscious. If the point is valid, it is also irrelevant for our immediate purpose. The term "middle class" will have to do service for the Progressives. Not only did they think themselves a part of it, but they wanted everybody to belong and directed their crusade against special privilege as the cause of class distinctions. They fought political corruption, monopoly, the protective tariff, and all other devices designed to confer advantages on a particular group. By so doing, the Progressives hoped to restore equality of opportunity, smash political bosses, and return government to the hands of the people. Their method was to proceed by education and persuasion rather than by government supervision. They feared legislation would centralize power in Washington and thereby increase the incentive for various economic interests to seek control of political institutions.

Although Progressivism started out as an idealistic urban movement, it was gradually infiltrated by farmers, organized labor, and other pressure groups who thought that elimination of privilege would lead to improvements in their respective economic positions. When these benefits failed to follow the Progressive victory over political and economic corruption, they tried to take over the movement between 1909 and 1912. In the process, they split it, as well as traditional political alignments. As a result, two conflicting groups emerged — each professing to speak for Progressivism. The original group clung to its program of disciplining the new industrial forces within the traditional framework, and lost the election of 1912. Its victorious opponents paid lip service to the ideal, but advocated individual measures to modify institutions so that they would be more responsive to emerging pressure groups. This tactic led to a redefinition of Progressivism. Thereafter it did not aim at the preservation of the old democracy, but at its adjustment to changed conditions. The movement can best be approached by examining its original sources and its subsequent infiltration by groups with hostile ideas.

THE LITERATURE OF EXPOSURE AND REFORM

Progressivism fed on indignation, and the turn of the century witnessed a revolution in journalism and literature which made it easy for conscientious people to stir up indignation. Improvements in printing techniques, the use of cheap woodpulp paper for periodicals, and the appearance of the one-cent or two-cent daily newspaper reduced publishing costs and prices and thus enlarged the market for the printed word. Publishers succeeded in appealing to the new audience in developing the literature of exposure. The cumulative changes of the preceding twenty-five years had altered familiar landmarks just enough to disturb the average man and interest him in finding scapegoats.

The heralds of the new journalism were William Randolph Hearst and Frank A. Munsey. Applying the principle of consolidation which had worked so well in other areas, they bought up independent newspapers throughout the country and turned out a standardized product. Munsey did not sustain the hysterical tone so consistently as Hearst because he lacked the political ambitions of his rival. Hearst showed a special flair for building newspaper circulation on sensational news stories. The technique worked well during the Spanish-American War, and when that prolific source of headlines dried up he turned to politics. Headlines and editorial columns exploded with accounts of the iniquitous activities of trusts. His most important success was the publication of a series of letters from John D. Archbold of the Standard Oil Company to Senator Joseph B. Foraker of Ohio. This private correspondence, which indicated that the Senator was a tool of the unpopular oil trust, produced a great public outcry against dishonest politicians.

The two pioneers soon attracted a score of imitators. E. W. Scripps built up a large newspaper chain by serving his readers a diet of sensation and indignation; he championed every movement of the common man from a "street riot to an excess profits tax." W. G. Bonfils and James Tammen made a national reputation with the *Denver Post;* its crusades occasionally involved

"Chee, Annie, look at de stars — thick as bed-bugs!" (Cartoon cavalcade, *edited by Thomas Craven,* Simon and Schuster, 1943.)

the publishers in physical scuffles with subscribers. Many papers such as the *Emporia Gazette* supported reform in a more restrained and conscientious way; William Allen White, its editor-publisher, fought the special interests with a conviction that was not always apparent in the frothy columns of the big newspaper chains.

Magazines also played an important part in generating reform sentiment. Appearing at less frequent intervals than newspapers, they could investigate a topic exhaustively before publishing articles about it. *McClure's* set the highest standards of accuracy and objectivity. The publisher, S. S. McClure, was a brilliant but erratic thinker who had three hundred ideas a day and an efficient editor, John Phillips, to tell him which one of the three hundred wasn't mad. Both of them demanded articles based on careful research and presented with a spirit of scientific detachment. They kept Ida M. Tarbell on their payroll for several years looking up factual material about the Standard Oil trust before she produced a single installment on the subject. Her series was followed by one equally spectacular on political conditions in American cities written by Lincoln Steffens, an author who towered above contemporary journalists with his uncanny instinct for digging out the facts and his rare spirit of detachment toward the victims of his investigations. Starting with "Tweed Days in St. Louis," he went on to expose the political machines in Minneapolis, Philadelphia, Cleveland, Cincinnati, and other cities. His findings fell into a common pattern: behind the average city administration lurked the unofficial government of the boss who controlled appointments to office, passed out public contracts to his friends, and protected organized vice for a fee. Steffens discovered that boss government habitually cut across party lines and that the political opposition usually received enough favors to neutralize its militancy. He also traced the close three-way relationship among states bosses like Senator Matt Quay of Pennsylvania, municipal bosses like Iz Durham of Philadelphia, and their satellites in the business world. He guided the reader effortlessly through the maze of boss government, dramatizing the gap between political ideals and political practices.

The theme around which *McClure's* built its hard-hitting articles on corruption was American defiance of law. An editorial introducing the series pointed out the discrepancy between the reverent lip service paid to law and the systematic way in which its spirit was evaded. The simultaneous attacks on the monopolistic tactics of the Standard Oil trust and the New York Building Trades Union protected *McClure's* from being discredited by charges of bias or favoritism. Besides articles exploring dark corners of American life, the magazine featured short stories by popular novelists like Robert Louis Stevenson, Jack London, and Joseph Conrad. It also introduced a scholarly note with mildly popularized but competent accounts of the latest developments in medicine, physics, and biology.

McClure's achieved such tremendous success as an arbiter of public morals that a host of imitators followed suit. The readers with an insatiable appetite for revelations of wrongdoing in business and politics could choose between *Collier's Weekly, Everybody's, Pearson's,* and the *American Magazine.* Even the *Arena,* a venerable reform journal of the Populist era, copied the techniques of *McClure's.* These magazines managed to maintain a reputation for veracity until Hearst entered the field by launching the *Cosmopolitan* in 1906. His opening editorial sneered at the others for serving up "indiscriminate masses of arid facts." This statement introduced a sensational series by the distinguished Indiana novelist, David Graham Phillips, on "The Treason of the Senate." A half-dozen elderly senators were charged with "treason," which Phillips loosely defined as adherence to special economic interests rather than to the interests of the American people. The introduction of yellow journalism into the reform journals provoked Theodore Roosevelt to refer to them as "muckrakers." The name stuck, and although the more responsible magazines extracted private apologies from Roosevelt, he refused to issue a public statement labeling the "muckrakers" more specifically.

The reform journals never recovered completely from this episode, which had been precipitated by the irresponsible conduct of Hearst. Yet they exercised a decisive effect on national politics from 1908 to 1912, even while their influence was waning. Large numbers of corrupt officials had to retire from politics. Individual articles often produced very specific results. The careful study of life insurance companies by Burton J. Hendricks, for instance, cast enough light on questionable manipulation of policyholders' funds to cause an investigation and the punishment of offenders. Phillips's exciting and exaggerated series of articles on the Senate undoubtedly built up public pressure for the direct election of senators, while the constant drumfire of *Collier's Weekly* against the Payne-Aldrich tariff seriously damaged the Taft administration.

After 1912 magazines rapidly abandoned their "muckraking" character. Publishers responded to pressure from their advertising departments, which complained of business losses from plain-speaking articles. Subscribers dulled their appetites by overindulgence in reform literature and turned their interests in new directions. However, the "muckrakers" had performed a vital role in stimulating and educating the voters on public issues at the peak of the Progressive movement.

The novel was a supplementary source of popular restlessness and dissatisfaction at the turn of the century. The average reader, it is true, was addicted to the historical romance, the sentimental tale, the dime novel, and the Horatio Alger stories. He eagerly read Lew Wallace's *Ben Hur* about Christian persecution and martyrdom in the Roman Empire; Helen Hunt Jackson's *Ramona,* which recaptured the atmosphere of Spanish California; G. B. McCutcheon's *Graustark,* featuring a red-blooded American adventurer who turns up in a mythical European kingdom to rescue a princess from effete aristocrats; and numberless robust yarns about cowboys and Indians. On the other hand, the new realistic novels, hailed by the critics, considered contemporary problems with accuracy and objectivity and performed a distinct educational role. Hamlin Garland won passing popularity with *Main-Travelled Roads* (1891) and *A Spoil of Office* (1892), which vividly described the suffering of farmers during the Populist era. Brand Whitlock, who had already begun to climb the political ladder in Toledo, provided a fictionalized treatment of municipal government problems called *The Thirteenth District* (1902). The American novelist Winston Churchill turned away from historical fiction long enough to produce *Coniston* (1906) and *Mr. Crewe's Career* (1908), both drawn out of his own experience with boss government as a state legislator from Cornish, New Hampshire. David Graham Phillips used part of the material he had gathered as a muckraker for *Cosmopolitan* to write a political novel called *The Plum Tree* (1905).

Other authors laid emphasis on the class struggle and the heroic efforts of the common man to overcome his exploiters. In his *The Industrial Republic: A Study of America Ten Years Hence,* Upton Sinclair forecast the victory of the plutocratic class in the 1908 election and their smashing defeat by an indignant, upright citizenry four years later. Since he was not averse to using living public figures in his novels, he introduced William Randolph Hearst in *The Industrial Republic* as the incorruptible tribune of the people who would smash class rule and depression by inaugurating government ownership of the railroads. Sinclair was more successful with *The Jungle* (1906), a shockingly realistic description of the terrible conditions prevailing in the Chicago stockyards. His avowed purpose in writing the book was to create public sympathy for stockyards workers, but he succeeded only in stirring up public sentiment for federal inspection of meat.

Socialistic overtones were clearer in the writings of Jack London. His fame justly rests on *The Sea Wolf* and *The Call of the Wild,* but he also wrote a political novel, *The Iron Heel,* which predicted two unsuccessful working-class revolutions in 1917 and 1932 before a triumphant victory in 2212.

Colonel E. M. House, subsequently a confidential adviser to Woodrow Wilson, strayed into political fantasy in *Philip Dru: Administrator* (1912). Opening with a description of resistance to a dictatorial president "in 1928," the novel came to focus on Philip Dru, a sort of Platonic philosopher-king who emerged as leader of the oppressed masses. House has his hero take office with the title "Administrator of the Republic," and retire "in 1935" after seven years of successful reform.

The political novels were realistic in a very limited and specialized sense. They did deal with contemporary problems of society from the standpoint of the participants. Their leading characters, however, were essentially public figures who promoted causes, rather than individuals with emotions, interests, and ambitions. This unrealistic habit of ignoring personal motivation was coupled with the venerable practice of ending the novel on a happy note: in defiance of the political facts, honesty usually triumphed and the machine politicians usually lost their power.

These deviations from consistent realism did not bother the public, but they annoyed a whole school of authors who responded by writing novels that did bother the public. This group was called the Naturalists, primarily because they regarded nature, including the human environment, as a Darwinian arena of struggle for survival and emphasized the sordid, brutal elements of life. When their outlook was injected into a novel, it took the form of emphasizing hitherto unmentionable subjects like sexual drives or venereal disease, dwelling on the animal appetites of men, and proclaiming the futility of existence. The Naturalists gloried in the inversion of traditional hopes, insisting that nature sponsored the triumph of the strong over the weak, the unscrupulous over the honest, the passionate over the restrained. Their outlook implied that man could reform neither his environment nor himself. But the characters in their novels more often displayed the indignation of the rebel than the passivity of the fatalist. This tacit intrusion of value judgments in the bleak philosophy of the Naturalists assured varying interpretations of their work.

Because they introduced the note of pessimism which became the theme of many writers in the 1920's, the Naturalists seemed much more important to subsequent generations of writers and critics than to some of their contemporaries. The bulk of the reading public either ignored the Naturalists or denounced them as vulgar. Stephen Crane's depressing account of slum life in *Maggie: A Girl of the Streets* (1893) was treated indulgently after the author had won acclaim with his psychological novel on the Civil War, *The Red Badge of Courage* (1895). But the publication of Theodore Dreiser's Naturalistic novel *Sister Carrie* provoked widespread demands for its suppression because many people believed that Dreiser was condoning amorality.

Some portrayals of the grim aspects of American life gave unintentional impetus to the zeal for reform. The handful of Progressives who read Stephen Crane, Dreiser, Jack London, or their contemporary, Frank Norris, accepted the facts as described in their books, but not the implied philosophy of futility. The Dreiser trilogy, *The Titan,* traces the rise and fall of the brutal, sensuous capitalist, Cowperwood, a fictional counterpart of the traction magnate, Charles Yerkes. Jack London makes Wolf Larsen, the leading character of *The Sea Wolf,* spokesman for the pessimistic interpretation of the Darwinian struggle. London was more popular and less orthodox than Frank Norris, who indicted the Southern Pacific Railroad in *The Octopus.* In a vivid metaphor, Norris compared the Railroad to a kind of primitive killer: " . . . it was as though the state had been sucked white and colorless, and against the pallid background the arteries of the monster stood out swollen with life blood."

No inventory of the forces which stimulated the zeal to reform would be complete without reference to the moving picture and the sermon. During the decade after 1904, the cinema performed an educational service never subsequently duplicated. Edwin S. Porter, who directed film production for the Edison Company, released several fourteen-minute silent movies dealing with serious social and economic issues. *The Agitator* sketched the story of a ranch foreman who organized his subordinates so effectively that they were able to secure a larger share of profits from their employer. *Capital v. Labor* concerned the constructive activity of a clergyman who settled a strike by securing concessions for the workmen. As the titles indicate, *Lily of the Tenements, The Grafters,* and *The Money King* covered topics dear to the heart of the Progressive.

Increasing numbers of ministers became preoccupied with social and economic problems. This trend was especially marked among proponents of the Social Gospel who denied the traditional Christian doctrine of original sin. They insisted that sin was rooted in the environment rather than in human nature and regarded higher living standards as the key to salvation. Sermons on secular problems lashed out at exploitation, corruption in government, gambling, prostitution, and other forms of vice. Some Protestant denominations fretted over the political influence of brewers and distillers, organizing (1895) the Anti-Saloon League of America to fight them and to agitate for prohibition. All these groups stimulated reform zeal, but they also made Progressivism attractive to farmers, workers, and others with special interests to pursue.

AGRARIAN PROTEST

Farmers were especially eager recruits to the reform movement. From the close of the Civil War until the end of the nineteenth century, they had provided the momentum for successive Granger, Greenback, and Populist waves of discontent. During those rare periods when prices were high and weather was good, they held the orthodox political and economic view of the petty capitalist. The low prices that prevailed in most of the years after the Civil War, however, provoked demands for currency inflation, extension of credit facilities, and regulation of railroad rates. Indeed, when conditions reached rock bottom during the depression of 1893, there were proposals for government ownership of banks and railroads.

Although the revival of prosperity after 1896 moderated such demands, the superficial political calm meant that the acute edge of rural unrest had been blunted rather than removed. Farmers continued to complain about the costs of industrial consumer goods, which rose faster than the prices of farm commodities. They also objected to the rising production costs of traditional one-crop wheat farming. Even those who met this problem by diversifying production faced several painful transitional decades of reduced earnings, and this period was characterized by persistent agrarian agitation. It was no accident, therefore, that corn belt states like Iowa, Indiana, and Missouri, and dairy states like Wisconsin and Minnesota became strongholds of the Progressive movement. Farther north where the climate was too cold for corn, farmers resisted diversification more stubbornly, with the result that wheat yields dropped and tempers grew ugly. The Dakotas and northern Minnesota remained poor and fiercely Progressive even after the start of World War I when farm prosperity elsewhere abated the crusading fervor. Agriculture in the South seemed to suffer from different problems: tenant farming, excessive reliance on cotton, and serious soil erosion in the uplands. There as elsewhere, however, rural distress found expression in the Progressive movement.

Opinions differ regarding the role which resistance to diversification played in the economic distress of agriculture before World War I. The farmers understandably attributed their troubles to other groups; their diagnosis had not changed much from the one offered by militant Populists like Ignatius Donnelly, "Sockless Jerry" Simpson, and "Bloody Bridles" Waite. They blamed the trusts for high prices, the railroads for charging excessive rates, and the banks for not extending sufficient credit at reasonable interest. Hostility to industrial integration was reinforced by the rising price level after 1896, by a sudden increase in steel prices immediately after the formation of the United States Steel trust in 1901, and by the irresponsible duel of the railroad monopolists which precipitated a stock market panic the same year.

The protective tariff became a more conspicuous target of rural criticism than it had been in Populist days. Agrarian reformers blamed it for sheltering a wide range of manufactured products from foreign competition and hence for encouraging the formation of trusts. This outbreak of tariff heresy in traditionally protectionist territory was politically dangerous to the Republican party because it made cooperation possible between middle-western and southern farmers. Although the former never took the extreme position that all protective tariffs were iniquitous, they felt that the protective principle had degenerated into a system of favoritism for eastern manufacturers. For the moment they were prepared to join the southerners in a fight to reduce industrial tariff rates, although they wished to retain protection for northern agricultural products.

Sectional variations in agricultural production, land tenure, and soil fertility produced corresponding differences in the attitude of farmers regarding specific grievances, but in general they felt that the economic institutions of business were rigged against them. Immigrants of Scandinavian origin, who settled in Wisconsin and Minnesota, sought to combat the trusts by organizing rural producer and consumer cooperatives. These units grew in strength and effectiveness during the Progressive era but failed to capture the bulk of dissident farmers. This was due partly to the fact that cooperatives were slow to produce results, and partly to the fact that they ran counter to the deeply ingrained native tradition of individualism.

At all events, the main current of agrarian protest flowed into the Progressive movement. Farmers wholeheartedly endorsed its program for eliminating political corruption and favoritism in government because they thought such steps would smash the economic interests that oppressed them. They also saw that participation in the Progressive movement would create support for agricultural legislation among groups hitherto hostile or indifferent to farm problems. The importance of such an alliance was reinforced by their recollection that Populism had collapsed because it had relied largely on dissatisfied farmers.

WORKING-CLASS UNREST

American workingmen also hoped for great benefits from the Progressive movement. It would be an overstatement to say that they did anything as a disciplined class group; in fact, many of them remained under the spell of the nineteenth-century credo of individualism. They believed that plentiful opportunities still awaited the alert, hard-working citizen and took their membership in the middle class for granted. Most of those who joined a union regarded the relationship as a marriage of convenience to be abandoned as soon as their individual economic situation had been improved. Antagonism toward the wealthy was mingled with admiration and tempered by an instinct for imitation. Consequently, whenever labor solidarity developed, it was not so much a response to doctrinaire convictions regarding the necessity of class war as an effort to secure redress of specific grievances. Successive labor movements lost their effectiveness partly because the rank and file showed indifference toward them during prosperous periods. They also suffered because the temper of public opinion in post-Civil War America was even more individualistic than the temper of labor itself. The average citizen regarded the labor union as a sinister organization operating in a twilight zone between legality and illegality. It was feared as a promoter of violence and disorder, resented as a threat to the individual's right to pursue economic activity without hindrance, and condemned for sapping the self-reliance and independence of the citizen. These ideas often represented the sincere conviction of middle-class Americans who neither knew nor cared to know anything about submarginal wage scales prevailing in many industries. Unfortunately the same arguments were habitually amplified by unprincipled employers who realized that successful labor unions would force them to pay higher wages.

In such a mental climate, organization had proceeded slowly after the Civil War. Several false starts were made before the Knights of Labor emerged in 1869 as the result of a serious dispute between garment cutters and their employers. Under the dynamic leadership (1879–93) of Terence V. Powderly, the Knights dominated the labor movement for nearly twenty years. They tried to organize a nationwide network of lodges that would include all producers, white-collar workers as well as manual laborers, and the skilled as well as the unskilled. To supplement their vast organizational drive, the Knights formulated an elaborate program of legislative demands for the benefit of labor. They preferred political action, but this did not prevent them from using economic weapons like the strike and the boycott to secure their objectives.

The public disliked these tactics and became positively hostile to the Knights when they employed violence and sabotage in the railroad strike of 1886. Powderly officially denounced both practices, but the damage had already been done. Many citizens linked the Knights of Labor with the more violent and irresponsible elements behind the movement for the eight-hour day. As a result, employer denunciations of strikes and the use of court injunctions to prevent or terminate them won increasing popular support.

These developments in addition to a series of ineffective strikes demoralized the Knights of Labor in 1886–87. Their followers either drifted into the ranks of the unorganized or transferred to a new organization, the American Federation of Labor. The philosophy and program of the A. F. of L. differed sharply from that of the discredited Knights. Under the leadership of Samuel Gompers, who served as its president for nearly forty years, the A. F. of L. officially repudiated the policy of soliciting government legislation to improve working conditions. Gompers breathed fresh life into the nineteenth-century view that wages and hours of labor should be settled by direct negotiation between employers and workers. He had an extravagant faith in the potency of sheer economic power and believed that if labor was properly organized, it could force employers to grant favorable working conditions. His preference for collective bargaining between gigantic management and labor units reflected the fear that government aid for workers would be a prelude to government control of workers.

Although Gompers sought to convince the public that the objectives of organized labor were synonymous with social and economic justice, the A. F. of L. behaved like an ordinary pressure group. It fought big business monopolies by trying to create an equally strong labor monopoly. Unlike the Knights of Labor, which promoted a union of all producers, the A. F. of L. attempted to protect craft workers from the competition of unskilled laborers by means of exacting membership rules and long periods of apprenticeship. Whenever possible, employers were required to accept the closed shop, which prohibited them from hiring workers outside the craft union. Such tactics limited the size of the skilled labor force and strengthened the monopolistic position of union members.

This dual warfare against employers and against unskilled competitors undermined the illusion that union leaders were fighting for the public welfare. Not only did they attempt to push wage scales for craft workers as high as possible, but they showed little concern over the fact that employers habitually passed increased costs on to the consumer. In San Francisco, for instance, which the A. F. of L. dominated from the late 1880's until 1912, wage scales were raised far above the level prevailing elsewhere, and employer compliance was enforced by the labor-controlled municipal administration which took its cues from Abe Reuf, the astute political boss of the local trade-union party. Other cities also had brief experiences with collusion between the craft unions and management at the expense of the public: in New York the contractors and the building-trades union cooperated to raise prices and wages, and in Chicago coal dealers made a similar arrangement with the miners' union to assure a stable labor supply. Big business, however, fought the A. F. of L. more frequently than it cooperated. Even worse, most weapons of the employers could not be opposed by economic pressures. Gompers was obliged to seek federal legislation that would strengthen the bargaining power of labor and also to bid for Progressive support by joining the great crusade against the special interests.

The grievance which bothered organized labor most at the turn of the century was the national policy of unlimited immigration. Coupled with technological developments which rapidly substituted power-driven machinery for the operations of skilled workers, immigration exposed the craft unions to increasing competition from unskilled labor. Many of the immigrants had left rural communities in southeastern Europe where laborers were paid in goods. Unaccustomed to cash income, they were initially willing to work in America for the most niggardly cash wages. Skilled workers regarded them as a menace to the living standard of native labor and resented employers who habitually used them as strikebreakers. The A. F. of L. sought to meet the problem by demanding drastic restrictions on immigration, but businessmen were understandably opposed to this policy because they wanted a cheap labor supply. Despite repeated efforts by Gompers, the proposal never became a part of the Progressive program because most Progressives believed that America should always remain a land of opportunity for the underprivileged masses of Europe. Bills to exclude illiterate immigrants passed Congress twice before World War I, but on both occasions presidential vetoes prevented them from becoming law.

The A. F. of L. found the Progressives much more sympathetic toward legislation clearly designed to equalize bargaining conditions between labor and management. They conscientiously supported the efforts of the A. F. of L. to clear up the legal uncertainties surrounding the strike and to eliminate the use of the injunction in breaking strikes. These issues were of crucial importance to organized labor because the strike offered the only effective means of exercising pressure on employers. The courts had outlawed a number of nineteenth-century strikes on the ground that they violated the old common law prohibition of conspiracies in restraint of trade. The status of the strike had become still more doubtful after the passage of the Sherman Act in 1890. Originally designed to clear the way for prosecuting monopolies, the Act was interpreted by the Supreme Court to apply to all combinations that restrained trade, including labor unions. This led to a particularly devastating setback for organized labor in 1902 when the United Hatters Union tried to support striking employees of D. E. Loewe and Company in Danbury, Connecticut, with a nationwide boycott. The company retaliated by filing suit in Federal District Court for damages of $240,000 against officers and members of the union. In the supporting brief, the company asserted that the boycott had violated the Sherman Act. The final decision was not handed down for fifteen years, but the union suffered a catastrophic defeat in February 1908 when the Supreme Court sustained the company contention. To make matters worse, the majority opinion of the Court indicated that individual union members might be held responsible for the policies of their leaders and might suffer attachment of their property to meet damage charges.

The legal advantages of employers were not exhausted if they failed to invoke the Sherman Act successfully. In fact, the most convenient way to break a strike was to secure a federal injunction or court order. The injunction was an equity proceeding which usually took the form of a blanket order requiring the strikers to cease or desist from activities that would produce damage or impair property rights. If the union ignored the court order, it could be cited for contempt and forced to pay a substantial fine.

Attorney General Richard Olney had used this technique with such success in breaking the Pullman strike of 1894 that the injunction was employed with increasing frequency after the turn of the century. How severe a threat this was to labor became clear in 1907 when the Buck Stove and Range Company used it to break an A. F. of L. boycott. The controversy reached the courts when the A. F. of L. tried to support local foundry workers in a strike against the company by putting the company's name on a list of firms to be boycotted for unfair labor practices. The company promptly sought and obtained an injunction from the Supreme Court of the District of Columbia ordering the A. F. of L. and its affiliates to suspend all boycott activities either by written material or by word of mouth. This decree came so close to denying free speech that Samuel Gompers and two other A. F. of L. officials defied it. They were cited for contempt of court and sentenced to jail in 1909. Although they managed on a technical count to escape serving their sentences, the case dramatized the legal handicaps of labor in industrial warfare. It also convinced many Progressives of the necessity for legislation restricting the use of injunctions in such disputes and exempting unions from the operations of the Sherman Antitrust Law.

The incorporation of these planks into the Progressive program brought the movement substantial labor support, especially from the unskilled workers. A few of the latter entered various wings of the Socialist party. A picturesque remnant, which believed in an industrial union embracing skilled and unskilled alike, formed the Industrial Workers of the World in 1905. This new group regarded its normal relationship with employers and political authorities as one of total war. Strikes were called repeatedly and involved sabotage, violence, and destruction of property. In fact, the I. W. W. refused to sign contracts with employers or tie its own hands in any way.

The guiding spirit of the I. W. W. was the grim, one-eyed William D. ("Big Bill") Haywood, who had served his apprenticeship in the bloody miners' strikes at Coeur d'Alene, Idaho, in 1893 and Cripple Creek, Colorado, in 1903. He led the drive to organize the unskilled workers, winning his greatest success among the lumberjacks, miners, and migratory fruitworkers of the Far West. The immediate result of Haywood's feverish organizational drive was a rash of strikes in 1906 and 1907 by the silkworkers of Paterson, New Jersey, the loggers of Eureka, California, the miners of Goldfield, Nevada, and the foundry workers of Detroit, Michigan. With the exception of a partial victory in Goldfield, all these strikes collapsed, and the I. W. W. receded rapidly from its peak strength of 50,000 members. Internal quarrels also deprived it of supporters, although it returned to the limelight briefly in 1912 when Haywood directed a successful strike of textile workers at Lowell, Massachusetts. A handful of the old-timers kept the organization going until after the end of World War I, but its influence was confined to a scattering of miners and migratory workers, whose activities periodically provoked fits of alarm among employers.

THE SPLIT IN THE PROGRESSIVE MOVEMENT

Internal conflict in the Progressive movement increased as it was infiltrated by various economic groups unsympathetic with its original purpose. By 1909 a showdown impended because the founders of the crusade had accomplished their objectives: the purification of political life and the ouster of representatives of special interest groups from power in Washington. They did not propose to relax their vigilance, but opposed any tinkering with American institutions. Farmers, workers, and other groups who had joined the movement with concrete expectations of economic benefit were disappointed and angry. They demanded additional legislation to achieve the objectives that the elimination of special privilege had failed to give them. Neither side yielded, with the result that the movement gradually disintegrated into two antagonistic wings in 1912.

The political aspects of the split in the Progressive movement will be considered in Chapters Six and Seven; the conflict over principles will be our immediate concern. In effect, the rebel wing that demanded a positive legislative program was repudiating the original Progressive concept of government as an umpire between economic groups. It sought to substitute the concept that government was an agent of underprivileged economic groups. There was nothing new about organizations of all sizes and descriptions descending on Washington to wrench special favors from the government. What created indescribable confusion between 1909 and 1912 was the spectacle of such groups claiming to be authentic Progressives.

EVOLUTIONARY THOUGHT AND THE REDEFINITION OF PROGRESSIVISM

The objectives of the rebel Progressives, who tenaciously clung to the label after the split, were dignified by an appropriation of evolutionary thought. Rank-and-file members did not participate in the process of redefinition because they were concerned primarily about results. The specific promises in political platforms satisfied their intellectual curiosity. The work was done by a small but highly influential group of thinkers who justified reform on the general evolutionary ground that society was changing and that institutions ought to undergo corresponding adjustments. Usually they added the corollary conclusion that government planning was necessary to control evolutionary forces intelligently. This viewpoint borrowed from a variety of thought systems, including Darwinism, Pragmatism, and Socialism. The contributory sources must be examined because in aggregate they provided the working philosophy of the victorious rebel wing of Progressivism and re-emerged a generation later in the New Deal.

We have already noticed the skillful use of evolutionary theory by Lester Ward, who urged man to dominate the constantly changing natural environment through large-scale government planning. His plea was echoed by Americans who received doctoral degrees in German universities and who returned as advocates of the evolutionary approach to institutional problems and of the scientific method as an analytical tool. Two of the most eminent, Richard T. Ely and John B. Clark, insisted that ideals, beliefs, or assumptions formulated during earlier evolutionary stages should be tested by careful statistical studies and rejected if found wanting. They clothed "the fact" with new authority and believed that the accumulation of sufficient data would guarantee objectivc results.

Enthusiasm for the German type of training was contagious. During the 1880's Johns Hopkins University introduced the graduate seminar and the scientific method in the field of social studies. One of the first Ph.D.'s granted under the new system was to Woodrow Wilson, who applied the evolutionary analysis to political institutions in his famous book *Congressional Government* (1885). Elsewhere academicians accumulated facts designed to expose the provisional character of American beliefs and institutions. At Columbia University, James Harvey Robinson marshaled impressive evidence to debunk the moral approach to history. His colleague, Charles A. Beard, painstakingly investigated the financial resources of the Founding Fathers, and concluded that they had framed a Constitution to protect the interests of their class rather than to safeguard rights of absolute or universal application. Thorstein Veblen, who was too unorthodox to find a permanent university post, made a searching analysis of the capitalist system in *The Theory of the Leisure Class* (1899). He argued that America's economic institutions were based on irrational psychological habits of long standing rather than on eternal self-adjusting economic laws. In a companion piece, *The Engineers and the Price System* (1921) he demanded recognition of the evolutionary character of the productive system and urged that control over it be transferred from the anachronistic, quasi-parasitical businessman to the engineer-technician. Even William Graham Sumner, the Yale sociologist who had championed rugged individualism so extravagantly in the 1880's and 1890's, conceded that the personal characteristics blessed by his philosophy were suitable only to a particular stage of development. In a ponderous volume called *Folkways,* he pronounced the democratic credo to be a provisional ethic compounded of irrational myths and symbols. Gloomily he concluded that the whole nineteenth-century value structure would be swept away as soon as the environment changed enough to make it inappropriate.

In the kindred field of legal theory Oliver Wendell Holmes, the distinguished scholar and Supreme Court judge, reached a similar conclusion. His tightly knit treatise, *The Common Law* (1881), marshaled formidable evidence to substantiate the generalization that law owes its content to chance and change. He thought the legal system at any given moment was in the process of evolving toward correspondence with the social and economic needs of the era. Law reflected the shifting sentiments of the community rather than a fixed body of eternally valid principles; it was a guide which helped the analyst to forecast what kind of conduct society would currently accept.

The evolutionary analysis was cross-fertilized by Pragmatism. In theory, Pragmatists opposed all philosophies that made conformity to system the test of truth. Their chief spokesman, the Harvard philosopher William James, taught that the consequence flowing from a particular belief or line of action provided the sole standard for judging its correctness. Whatever produced beneficial results or had "cash value" was true, and nothing else possessed objective meaning. Although this method of establishing truth conflicted with that of evolutionists, the differences between the two were more apparent than real. Whether environment or practical consequences became the criteria for testing developments, both groups believed that the universe was flexible and plastic. The evolutionists headed by Ward agreed with James and the Pragmatists about man's dominant role in directing the processes of nature. The convergence of the two schools at the practical level strengthened the hand of all groups who wanted to tinker with hallowed institutions so that the latter would meet new conditions.

NATIVE VARIETIES OF SOCIALISM

The demand for large-scale government action to improve economic conditions was deeply rooted in the thinking of several militant but unsuccessful post-Civil War reform movements. The theories behind the demand had been stated so often that their socialist implications were neither so obvious nor so offensive as similar proposals advocated by Marxists. For example, the Knights of Labor and the Populists of the 1890's had taken the novel position that government ownership of banks, railroads, and the monetary system was necessary to strengthen competitive capitalism. They argued that government operation of the monetary and credit system at cost would keep small enterprises in business, whereas private management of key services for profit would freeze out the little fellow. Thus they sponsored the paradoxical formula of checking economic centralization by adding a new centralizing unit.

Quasi-socialistic proposals were also familiar, because the American environment had long been hospitable to voluntary Utopian experiments. Indeed, all through the nineteenth century small religious or secular groups of self-confessed idealists had founded cooperative communities in protest against what they regarded as the greedy, exploitative character of conventional society. Some regarded themselves as Christian saints who deserved to live apart from their erring brethren; others practiced new religions;

a few deserved to be called Utopian Socialists. Similar enterprises were still being launched at the end of the century. For instance, Julius A. Wayland founded a community at Ruskin, Tennessee, and Ralph Albertson another twenty miles east of Columbus, Georgia; the Socialist leader, Eugene V. Debs, talked of organizing a cooperative commonwealth in one of the western territories after the failure of the Pullman strike in 1894; Richard T. Ely praised the unselfish group spirit of the Mormons in turning the Salt Lake Valley into a blossoming garden. The multiplication of all such groups accustomed Americans to the practice of voluntary socialism and provided a leavening of theory for other reformers.

In 1889 socialism received a tremendously powerful presentation of its case in a best-selling novel by Edward Bellamy, *Looking Backward.* The plot revolved about Julian West, who fell asleep in 1887 and awoke in the midst of a prosperous socialist society one hundred and thirteen years later. The book owed its special charm to the author's assumption that the new society would arise out of peaceful revolution. He anticipated voluntary acquiescence in government planning and thought that the middle class would take the initiative in abolishing itself. Bellamy fans formed clubs to discuss implementation of his program, and a few proposals eventually found their way into platforms of the Populist party. It was characteristic of people responsive to Utopian Socialism that they wanted extensions of government authority without sacrificing the blessings of capitalistic society. Their hearts rather than their heads provided the point of departure for political thinking. Most of them would have stoutly denied that they were socialists, while insisting that some Bellamite measures were necessary to strengthen private enterprise. The popularity of *Looking Backward* encouraged imitations, and the public fed on a diet of Utopian novels during the 1890's.

Just as Utopian Socialism in its various manifestations produced sentiment for governmental paternalism, so did Christian Socialism help make such sentiments respectable. Sometimes called the Social Gospel, Christian Socialism was one by-product of the dissension in Protestant churches over evolution, biblical criticism, and the role of the Christian in industrial society. A denial of the doctrine of original sin was the theological point of departure for Christian Socialism. It led directly to the conclusion that the environment, rather than human sinfulness inherited from Adam, was responsibility for evil in the social order. This viewpoint, which received clearest statement in the books, lectures, and pamphlets of Walter Rauschenbusch, inverted traditional Christian doctrine by attributing poverty, greed, and strife to corrupt institutions rather than to the egocentric appetites of man.

Rauschenbusch was prepared to exploit the implications of his lofty estimate of human nature. He asserted that the Kingdom of God promised in the New Testament would materialize on earth as soon as men utilized their power to remake the environment. Convinced that the family, education, and political life had already been Christianized, he denounced capitalism as the sole remaining barrier to the advent of the Kingdom. He blamed it for institutionalizing acquisitiveness, for exploitation, and for disregard of neighborly needs, and he contended that only a socialist economy would nurture the spirit of brotherhood and cooperation enjoined in the Sermon on the Mount. His experience as a social worker in the slums of New York City reinforced his belief that a suitable social and economic environment was essential to spiritual growth. Hence he regarded the socialization of society as a prerequisite for the saving of souls. He systematized these views in *A Theology for the Social Gospel* (1917), but he is best remembered for sermons and political campaigns advocating municipal ownership of public utilities.

The drastic reinterpretation of theology undertaken by Rauschenbusch to provide a foundation for Christian Socialism reflected the growing tensions within evangelical Protestantism which reached the breaking point in the Fundamentalist-Modernist controversy of the 1920's. The more immediate significance of the new theology was that it endowed socialistic economics with a kind of religious and moral sanctity. Many Christians resented this trend; they regarded the attempted identification of their religion with a particular economic system as the degradation of a purely spiritual message. Nevertheless, the able advocacy of Christian Socialism by such eminent professors as Rauschenbusch, Ely, and Shailer Mathews took some of the weight out of objections to enlarged government services.

As the various ideological strains of native radicalism converged in the left wing of the Progressive movement, they provided it with strong humanitarian overtones. Individuals whose position could not easily be identified by conventional political labels either joined the crusade or acted as friendly critics. The distinguished Americans falling into the broad category included Jane Addams, the social worker who founded Hull House in Chicago; John R. Commons, Wisconsin professor and historian of the American labor movement; Clarence Darrow, the colorful criminal lawyer; and the philosopher John Dewey, who lent his name to innumerable reform projects.

CRITICS OF THE PROGRESSIVE MOVEMENT

Progressivism had few open critics except radical foes of democracy. Political bosses, corrupt businessmen, and other custodians of special interests nursed their wounds silently and waited for a relaxation of public vigilance. Occasionally a disgruntled industrialist denounced Roosevelt's warfare on trusts as harmful to prosperity, but an organized conservative opposition to Progressivism as a creed did not exist.

Extreme radicalism likewise found few supporters. Marxism, the noisiest and most militant of such movements, was resented because it was a foreign doctrine and advocated violence as well as class war. Many who were well disposed toward radicalism in general, opposed Marxist thinking. Its exclusive emphasis on a revolutionary working class as the vehicle of social and economic justice was a serious handicap in a country where farmers still constituted a majority of the underprivileged. To make matters worse, the Marxists dissipated so much energy quarreling with each other that little remained for the class struggle against the capitalists.

The orthodox Marxists exercised the least influence on Americans and may be dismissed most quickly. Their preoccupation with theoretical formulas clouded their sense of reality. They repelled the workers by trying to interpret all developments in terms of the class struggle and by employing an abstract sociological terminology to deal with practical problems. Under the leadership of Daniel de Leon they wasted their energy in the hopeless project of organizing unskilled laborers for revolutionary activity and street fights with employers.

A far more effective political and educational force was the group that gathered around Eugene V. Debs, Victor Berger, and Morris Hillquist. These men possessed a more practical approach to problems and diluted Marxian theory with the agrarian radicalism and Utopian Socialism of the American frontier. Despite individual differences in outlook, they agreed that any socialist experiments ought to be undertaken selectively and only after voluntary approval by the electorate.

During the 1890's Debs and De Leon managed to resolve their disputes within the framework of the Socialist Labor party. But in 1900 Debs left the parent organization and launched the Socialist party. Most of the rank and file followed him, leaving De Leon with a corporal's guard of unskilled workers and doctrinaire middle-class radicals. The new Socialist party reached its high-water mark in 1912, giving Debs 900,000 votes for President and sending Victor Berger to Congress as a representative from Wisconsin.

The party tried to achieve respectability by including all the Progressive proposals for reform in its platform. However, the divergent character of Socialist objectives was exposed by additional planks for public ownership of basic industries, government relief for the unemployed, social security, and a shorter work week. Such a program could not command widespread support even in a reform era, and the Socialist party subsequently split over the question of American participation in World War I. The ineffectiveness of critics before World War I is eloquent testimony to the strength of the Progressive movement.

SUGGESTED READINGS

1. Baker, R. S., *An American Chronicle.*
2. Chamberlain, J., *Farewell to Reform.*
3. Howe, F. C., *Confessions of a Reformer.*
4. Kazin, A., *On Native Grounds.*
5. Nye, R. B., *Midwestern Progressive Politics.*
6. Rauschenbusch, W., *Christianity and the Social Crisis.*
7. Regier, C. C., *The Muckrakers.*
8. Steffens, Lincoln, *Autobiography of Lincoln Steffens.*

CHAPTER FIVE

PROGRESSIVISM CAPTURES THE WHITE HOUSE

THE EARLY CAREER OF THEODORE ROOSEVELT

"I told William McKinley it was a mistake to nominate that man in Philadelphia. . . . Now look, that damned cowboy is President of the United States." With this expression of disgust Senator Mark Hanna, chairman of the Republican National Committee and leading conservative spokesman for the party, greeted the accession of Theodore Roosevelt to the Presidency. Part of Hanna's bitterness was due to the death of his close friend, President McKinley, who had been assassinated by a half-crazed anarchist, Leon F. Czolgosz, at the Buffalo Exposition in September 1901. But the old Senator was also giving vent to a kind of black despair, for he had a strong premonition that the new President would represent forces alien to his generation and way of life. His worst fears were quickly realized. The transfer of executive powers to Roosevelt marked the debut of Progressivism on the stage of national politics.

The new President conducted his administration with one eye cocked on the nomination of 1904. History did not offer him much basis for optimism. Both Chester A. Arthur and Millard Fillmore had succeeded to the Presidency in midterm, only to be subsequently denied the nomination for a full term by their respective parties. For a time Roosevelt was threatened with a similar fate. His aggressiveness, unpredictability, and outspoken Progressivism irritated influential Republican leaders. They intended to form around Mark Hanna of Ohio, for a last-ditch fight against Roosevelt's nomination, but their champion died unexpectedly on February 15, 1904, leaving them without a candidate of the requisite stature. Thereafter there was nothing for the malcontents to do but make their peace with the triumphant Roosevelt. Not only did he win an uncontested nomination from the June convention, but he also took complete control of the Republican organization. The platform conformed to his wishes, containing a forthright condemnation of trusts, a qualified endorsement of reclamation, and a routine statement praising the party as the guardian of prosperity. The conservatives salvaged a small consolation prize when they secured Charles W. Fairbanks of Indiana as the vice-presidential candidate.

The selection of Roosevelt as the Republican standard-bearer in 1904 climaxed a stubborn twenty-year fight for political preferment. He had launched his political career against a background of childhood luxury and of aristocratic education at Harvard, supplemented by cattle-punching in Wyoming and doorbell-ringing for the district Republican organization in New York City. Fortified by this training he went on to serve three terms as an assemblyman in the New York legislature, where his squeaky voice, pince-nez glasses, and fawn-colored vests produced something of a sensation. Contemporaries occasionally laughed at him but they could not ignore his energy, conscientiousness, and truculent independence which sometimes skirted the edges of party regularity. In 1886 he sought political advancement by running for mayor of New York City before he was thirty. Defeated by the efficient Tammany machine, he promptly accepted an appointment from President Benjamin Harrison on the newly created Civil Service Commission. At first he enjoyed the secure routine of the administrator, but by 1895 the novelty had worn off and he eagerly accepted the post of Police Commissioner in New York City. The opportunities to war against corruption and graft were virtually unlimited and there followed a picturesque interlude during which he tried to communicate a high sense of duty to apathetic Irish policemen. With characteristic energy, he participated personally in the struggle against vice. He roamed the streets at night, sneaking up on drunken patrolmen, disrupting the customary beats of pickpockets, and lecturing to saloon brawlers. However, the sinkholes of New York City vice were bottomless and after the Republicans had captured the Presidency in 1896, he was happy to take a more sedentary post as Assistant Secretary of the Navy. Even in this relatively quiet job, he managed to create a commotion. He zealously threw himself into the fight for a larger fleet and used his official authority to aggravate the controversy with Spain on the theory that war offered the best opportunity to increase the Navy. Most of his activities were carried on in partial defiance of his superior, John D. Long, the Secretary of the Navy, who sought to follow a peaceful policy.

The outbreak of the Spanish-American War gave Roosevelt his first opportunity to achieve a truly national reputation. Without hesitation he resigned as Assistant Secretary of the Navy and organized a regiment, the Rough Riders, to fight in Cuba. Although the military operations in that theater turned out to be rather desultory, he and his cowboy regiment won wide acclaim for a charge up San Juan Hill. Critics tried to minimize his exploitation of this comic opera affair, but the Chief Rough Rider produced the unanswerable response: "It wasn't much of a war, but it was all the war we had."

One of Mr. Roosevelt's quiet days. (McCutcheon, The Chicago Daily Tribune, *1905.)*

Rightly or wrongly, Roosevelt was regarded as a conquering hero when he returned to New York in the summer of 1898, and he found himself widely discussed as a possible gubernatorial candidate for the Republican party. The wily state boss, Senator Thomas C. Platt, did not want to nominate a man who, he realized, would be hard to control. But the incumbent Republican governor, F. S. Black, had earmarked a good deal of money for canals two years earlier, and there were still no canals. At any rate, there was no water in the depressions called canals. Since the Democrats intended to ask some embarrassing questions about misappropriation of funds, Black could not be renominated without courting party defeat. In the end Platt reluctantly supported Roosevelt, who was untouched by the canal scandals and was a party idol besides. The erstwhile Rough Rider won the governorship by an overwhelming majority, and Republican control of the state was preserved.

The ensuing two years were very painful for Platt. Roosevelt did not openly defy him, but he showed independence just often enough to keep Platt chronically in a state of anxiety. Platt did not dare deny Roosevelt a second nomination for the governorship in 1900, but he conceived the brilliant scheme of removing him by putting him on the national ticket with McKinley. Party leaders like Mark Hanna objected, considering the Vice-Presidency an excessive price to pay simply to help Platt get the governor out of New York. Meanwhile Roosevelt had a fairly distinct notion and a much clearer dislike of what Platt intended. But eventually all opposition, including his own, was overcome and he was nominated and elected Vice-President of the United States. Before the year was out death struck McKinley, prompting the despairing remark of Hanna which opened this chapter.

The Roosevelt who succeeded McKinley as President had shed the squeaky voice and effeminate manners of his early days in politics for a manly bellicosity, emphasized by cowboy hats, toothy grins, and a picturesque slang vocabulary. He had also developed a flair for dramatization that captured the popular imagination. He proceeded so noisily that the public could no more look the other way than a small boy could "turn his head away from a circus parade followed by a steam calliope." He embraced clean government, conservation, and trust-busting with the gentle enthusiasm of a cave man. Even in matters where his views proved to be perfectly orthodox, he managed to create the impression that he was taking the courageous path of the rebel and reformer.

He did not possess a very wide or original stock of ideas. Indeed, much of his political strength stemmed from the fact that he shared the prejudices and preferences of the average citizen. In common with other members of aristocratic families as well as indignant middle-class consumers, he disliked the brash, acquisitive capitalists who presided over the new industrial economy. He considered their monster trusts to be a perversion of the traditional competitive system.

He viewed the labor movement with the same deep suspicion. He had originally regarded the organization of the trade unions as the prelude to class conflict and had actually proposed that the Pullman strikers of 1893 be shot, if necessary, to ensure industrial peace. His attitude underwent considerable modification when he assumed the responsibility of political power. He was to treat the anthracite coal strikers with conspicuous fairness in 1902. Later in his career, Roosevelt was to sponsor legislation to raise the living standards of workers in the hope of sidetracking the labor movement and arresting class stratification.

Labor was so grateful for the political sponsorship of Roosevelt that it did not recognize his underlying hostility to class activity. By contrast, many businessmen looked upon him as an enemy. They assumed that his hostility toward monopolistic property rights was simply the first phase of an attack on property rights in general. This myopia led them to denounce him as a dangerous radical. The label was ironic because he regarded himself as a better defender of free enterprise than his critics on the right. He thought a plutocratic class of monopolists as dangerous to the free enterprise system as an impoverished class of urban workers. Consequently, he believed that history had marked him for a role as preserver and defender of American institutions from attacks by class-conscious groups on both the left and the right. He expressed this concept succinctly in his famous political slogan, "the Square Deal." Only on the basis of such a philosophy do his simultaneous condemnations of the "criminal rich" and "unruly labor leaders" become comprehensible. To the average citizen he seemed like an honest broker who had preserved public welfare from irresponsible class appetites. His behavior delighted the Progressives and they enthusiastically claimed him as their own.

TRUST-BUSTING

Despite a routine pledge to carry out the policies of McKinley and a cautious series of recommendations to the conservative Fifty-seventh Congress, Roosevelt quickly introduced a new tone into the Republican administration. The initial departure from orthodoxy took place abruptly on February 18, 1902, when he rocked the business world by instigating a suit against the Northern Securities Company, a newly created railroad trust. In this unexpected foray against special privilege Roosevelt selected an ideal test case and showed a superb sense of timing. Since the Grange movement of the 1870's, the railroads had been the most chronically unpopular symbols of monopoly. The Northern Securities Company was particularly offensive to the public because its formation had been preceded by an irresponsible war between two western railroad kings, James J. Hill and Edward H. Harriman. The first phase had involved a struggle for the control of the Chicago, Burlington, and Quincy, which was essential to connect either Harriman's Union Pacific or Hill's Northern Pacific–Great Northern System with Chicago. Hill, in alliance with J. P. Morgan, the investment broker and railroad consolidator, managed to win control of the C. B. & Q. The victors failed to anticipate the vindictiveness of Harriman, who quietly began buying up Northern Pacific stock. Since Hill-Morgan control of the Northern Pacific was based on a minority of the stock, they also began to bid desperately for fresh offerings of stock. The price of Northern Pacific common rose from $110 to $1,000 in a few days. Speculators were elated by the unexpected turn of events and accommodatingly offered to sell stock which they did not possess, thinking that they would pick it up at a lower price a few days later. When the financial sharpers proved unable to deliver the certificates at the specified time, a financial panic ensued, which bankrupted a number of small and presumably innocent investors. The public censured Wall Street and howled for justice. Hill and Harriman ostentatiously ended the titantic struggle by pooling their resources in the Northern Securities Company.

Such manipulations exposed the tremendous power of a few individuals and the cynical self-assurance with which they pursued private objectives irrespective of the effect on national prosperity. The revelation brought to a boiling point public indignation against the ten-year orgy of consolidation which had produced trusts in tin plate, sugar, dressed beef, wire nails, steel, and many other industries.

Roosevelt's challenge to the Northern Securities Company was delivered with apparent indifference to the probability of failure. Successive Supreme Court decisions had narrowed the application of the Sherman Antitrust Law, and McKinley had ignored it altogether. Now Attorney General Philander C. Knox used an unprecedented amount of time to prepare what he hoped would be a watertight case for the government. Additional months were consumed before the Supreme Court reached a decision. Nevertheless public interest remained at fever pitch, and in the spring of 1904 the Court sustained the government's suit by a 5 to 4 vote, declaring that the Northern Securities Company constituted an illegal monopoly of transportation in the Pacific Northwest and ordering its dissolution.

Handed down on the eve of a presidential election, the decision greatly enhanced Roosevelt's prestige. It made him the champion of the average man, who had hitherto felt powerless against the exactions of the trusts. It also endowed his bellicosity with a kind of wholesome, moral quality. The nickname "trust-buster" became a badge of honor and affection. This apotheosis of Roosevelt as an urban Jefferson was instrumental in removing the stigma of conservatism from the Republican party and making it a haven for ever-increasing numbers of Progressives.

Subsequent developments hardly justified the optimism felt on the morrow of the decision. Roosevelt followed up his victory by prosecuting the more vulnerable economic giants like the Standard Oil and the dressed beef trust. But court orders compelling the physical dissolution of trusts did not prevent the separate units from reaching "gentlemen's agreements," fixing prices, and dividing markets. To make matters worse, new trusts formed faster than the government could dissolve them. The number increased from 149 in 1900 to 10,020 when Roosevelt retired from the Presidency eight years later. The act of 1903 which established the Department of Commerce with a subsidiary fact-finding Bureau of Corporations did not speed up the preparation of cases appreciably. A companion law, giving antitrust suits a priority on court calendars, also fell short of public expectations.

The unsatisfactory results of trust-busting gradually convinced Roosevelt that he was breaking windows with silver dollars. So during his second term he groped his way toward a new policy. What finally crystallized in his mind was a program for government supervision of corporation activity on a scale sufficient to protect the public. He issued a number of trial balloons in 1905–1906 which took the form of complaints over the inadequacy of the Sherman Act. The President threw off the mask in his annual message of December 1907, proclaiming that industrial combinations were a fixed feature of the industrial landscape. Repeating previous assertions that the Sherman Act encouraged the persecution of corporations because of their size rather than their misconduct, he called for legislation requiring a federal license for corporations. Congress ignored the request, and further Roosevelt appeals failed to budge the legislators.

THE COAL STRIKE

Before Roosevelt had completed the remainder of McKinley's term, he strengthened his reputation as a Progressive by dramatically intervening in the great anthracite coal strike of 1902. Normally, industrial disputes stood outside the jurisdiction of the President or Congress. The federal Constitution had left such matters in the control of the states, and the original prohibition against action by the national government had been reinforced by a number of Supreme Court decisions. The only exceptions seemed to be disputes involving the obstruction of interstate commerce or essential government service like the delivery of mail. Otherwise state officials had to take the initiative and request federal intervention if they thought industrial peace jeopardized. The habitual response in Washington to such requests was to dispatch troops to the affected areas for a routine performance as strikebreakers.

These precedents did not provide Roosevelt with any promising clues for constructive action in industrial conflicts. Nor did the anthracite coal strike seem to warrant government intervention during the initial stages. When 140,000 miners walked off the job on May 12, 1902, citizens dismissed the strike as another incident in the turbulent industrial history of the eastern Pennsylvania coal fields. After the summer had elapsed without any coal being dug, the public became alarmed. Stock piles were seriously depleted, coal prices jumped from five dollars a ton in May to thirty dollars a ton in September, and numerous people faced a heatless winter.

The gravity of the situation not only produced demands for presidential action but focused more than customary attention on the miserable plight of the miners. They had been chronic victims of substandard living and working conditions for several decades. Part of their misfortune was due to the structure of the industry which featured cutthroat competition, wildly fluctuating prices, and frequent overproduction. The big coal magnates had never found it worthwhile to buy out the marginal operators and stabilize production. As a consequence the men were often limited to about 180 days of work a year and an annual wage of $400 to $600. To make matters worse, they had to purchase supplies, such as powder, oil, and fuses, out of their wages. Usually their only source for these items as well as food and clothing was the company store, which took full advantage of its monopolistic position.

The miners possessed almost no means of improving their status. Grievance committees were ignored by the operators. Terrorism provoked reprisals and produced no permanent relief. Even strikes had little prospect of success. The railroads owned most of the big coal mines and coerced the marginal operators into a united front by virtue of their control over freight rates. They also dominated the local law enforcement machinery in the mining communities and used it to smash labor resistance. If these techniques failed, the railroads hauled in carloads of unskilled immigrants and used them as strikebreakers. The price of an unsuccessful strike was black-listing by the operators. This meant permanent unemployment, since most miners lacked the skills to switch occupations in mid-career or the financial resources to emigrate from their native communities.

Only an extra turn of the economic screw could induce them to strike against such overwhelming odds. They had lost ground steadily in the price inflation after 1896, for a 10 per cent wage raise in 1900 did not cover increases in the cost of living. But they held back until the operators raised the prices of supplies at company stores. Driven now to desperation, the United Mine Workers' Union under the leadership of John Mitchell issued an ultimatum. The principal demands were: a 20 per cent wage increase, the eight-hour day, revision of the rules governing the weighing and grading of coal, and union recognition.

The operators had no intention of meeting these terms. The demand for recognition of the union filled them with alarm because they knew it would be the opening wedge for future demands. Moreover, they counted upon the traditional American suspicion of labor unions, the doubtful legality of a strike, and the fear of a heatless winter to swing public opinion against the miners. So they refused to negotiate about grievances, and the workers promptly walked off the job.

By mid-September the average citizen was upset over the strike, but contrary to the calculations of the operators he was more annoyed at them than at the miners. This unexpected attitude grew partly out of the publicity which the muckraking magazines and newspapers had given to the economic distress prevailing in mining communities and partly out of the arrogance of the operators whose sense of reality was clouded by their habit of victory. Particularly unfortunate was the attitude of George F. Baer, president of the Reading Railroad and principal spokesman for the operators. In a widely quoted letter on collective bargaining he gave substance to the union contention that management possessed a feudal mentality. According to him, the welfare of the workers would not be secured by "labor agitators" but by "the Christian men to whom God in His infinite wisdom has given the control of the property interests of the country."

The inflexible position on both sides gradually shifted the spotlight to Roosevelt and made his intervention seem natural and desirable. Even his conservative critics like Mark Hanna thought the operators had taken an extreme position, and urged him to settle the strike so that the voters would not rebuke the Republican party in the November congressional elections.

The President first attempted to bring the antagonists together through intermediaries, and when this failed he took a direct hand by convening a conference at the White House on October 3. John Mitchell took a conciliatory position, offering to accept the decision of a presidential commission; Baer and the representatives of the operators flatly rejected this proposal, tacitly casting doubt on Roosevelt's impartiality and integrity. They compounded the error by berating the President for his refusal to break the strike with federal troops as Grover Cleveland had done under similar circumstances during the Pullman strike of 1894.

Such tactlessness wounded Roosevelt's vanity and drove him into the camp of the miners. He employed various unofficial sources to inform the public that he regarded the operators as unreasonable obstructionists. He also let word leak out that he might order troops to take possession of the pits and mine coal with bayonets if necessary. The operators were not equal to the war of nerves and capitulated without waiting to see whether he was bluffing. They consented to the appointment of an arbitration commission, but almost precipitated a fresh crisis by insisting that it should include no representative of organized labor. Roosevelt scornfully met the objection with the selection of E. E. Clark, head of the Railway Conductors' Union, under the classification of "eminent sociologist."

The miners returned to work immediately, but the commission held such exhaustive hearings that it did not hand down a decision until March 21, 1903. The settlement fell considerably short of the miners' expectations. Wage increases were limited to 10 per cent, and maximum hours of work were set at nine rather than eight, as requested. The commission balked at union recognition, providing instead for a conciliation board to consider the grievances of both sides. Deadlocks were to be referred to the federal circuit judge of the district for final settlement. The whole range of questions connected with working conditions in the pits received no attention.

Judged against the background of long-standing public apathy toward labor problems, the settlement represented a victory for the miners. Unfortunately it was only provisional because neither the operators nor the government cared to do anything about the basic structure of the industry. Overproduction, surplus miners, and wild variations in the price of coal kept labor unrest close to the boiling point during most of the succeeding fifty years. Theodore Roosevelt emerged from the controversy with enhanced prestige. The operators and the more conservative businessmen condemned him for an interference which they would not have resented had it been in their favor. On the other hand, labor found special comfort in his departure from the traditional practice of employing troops for strikebreaking.

CONSERVATION

When Roosevelt wrote his autobiography, he recalled that conservation was the first project to absorb his attention as President. He might have added that his interest in this question never waned. In fact, the education of citizens to a sense of their responsibility for the preservation of the nation's resources was his most lasting achievement. It started during his first months in the Presidency and enlarged his stature as a Progressive. Like trust-busting and mediation in labor disputes, conservation gave him an area where he could formulate and carry out a program without too much reliance on Congress.

The official disappearance of the frontier, which had been proclaimed by the decennial census report in 1890, provoked a widespread demand for a review of policy governing the disposal of the public lands. The tracts best suited for agriculture had already passed into private hands, as well as countless others containing valuable timber and mineral resources. Discussion revolved around the rest of the public domain, which was located primarily in the western third of the country. Inhabitants of this region sought government-sponsored irrigation projects to convert deserts into productive farms; easterners desired legislation to preserve the remaining forests from ruthless exploitation and spoliation by private groups. From the outset, the western campaign for reclamation and the eastern campaign for conservation were separate ventures.

Roosevelt sought to guide developments by harnessing these distinct and sometimes discordant forces into a general program that would transcend regional lines. In his first annual message to Congress on December 3, 1901, he announced the shotgun wedding of irrigation and forestry, asserting that water for the arid West depended upon the preservation of the forests. Congress had already passed the Carey Act in 1894 to encourage the development of state and private irrigation systems. This law represented an effort to stimulate local effort by grants of arid public lands as soon as they were irrigated, settled, and occupied; but it resulted in so little activity that sentiment for direct federal support developed. Under the leadership of Roosevelt, Congress passed the Newlands Act in June 1902. This law provided that receipts from the sale of public lands in sixteen western states should go into a special fund for irrigation projects. The cost of constructing these was to be recaptured by assessments against the land benefiting from the irrigation. This provision reflected the bright hope that the projects would be self-liquidating and would be multiplied indefinitely by repeated use of the initial cash outlay. Needless to say, the perpetual motion machine did not perform as well as the proponents of the Act had hoped, nor did benefits develop rapidly. Survey of dam sites and actual construction took time, but applications for homesteads in the dry areas increased immediately.

Despite Roosevelt's contention that reclamation and conservation were complementary programs, bills for conservation received rough treatment in Congress. Presidential proposals to withdraw timber and mineral lands from settlement challenged the traditional policy of throwing them open for private development as quickly as possible. Westerners considered rapid settlement indispensable to economic progress. They regarded with suspicion all schemes to postpone transfer to private ownership or to keep the lands outside the jurisdiction of state government and local taxing units.

Generally speaking, westerners doubted Roosevelt's assurance that conservation involved only temporary withdrawal of land for classification purposes and would be followed by a program of orderly development. Congressmen from the public-lands states persistently opposed his requests for revision of the various laws that facilitated easy settlement of the public domain. Even the report of the Public Land Commission, which exposed the fraudulent accumulations of land under existing laws, left the westerners unmoved.

Meanwhile Roosevelt pursued his objective through other channels. Acting on the basis of a law of 1891, he rapidly enlarged the forest reserve by executive proclamation. Between 1902 and the end of his first term, he increased the number of forest reserves from 54 to 83, and the total acreage from 60,175,765 to 85,618,472. His opponents countered with loud protests, but Roosevelt mounted a new offensive in 1905 by transferring the Forestry Department from the General Land Office to the Department of Agriculture, and appointing Gifford Pinchot as Chief Forester. The latter had been concerned with problems of forestry from his earliest years. His father had provided the impetus for the establishment of a Forestry School at Yale and saw to it that Gifford received thorough training in silviculture at the best universities in Europe.

Coupled with Gifford Pinchot's knowledge of forestry was a fanatical enthusiasm for conservation that drove him directly toward his objective regardless of opposition. Immediately after his appointment he placed trained foresters on every reserve to enforce government regulations regarding tree-cutting, grazing, and fire prevention. These activities quickly made the Forest Service unpopular and filled the mail bags of western congressmen with violent complaints. Roosevelt not only refused to relax Pinchot's administration of the reserves, but between July and November of 1906 he withdrew for classification 66,000,000 additional acres of public lands believed to contain coal.

Congress retaliated by depriving the Forest Service of control over the funds from grazing fees and by passing a bill to prevent the creation of additional reserves in six western states. This did not quite end the controversy. While the bill was lying on Roosevelt's desk, he withdrew from entry all the remaining land that could possibly be used for forestry purposes. Then he signed the bill, leaving western congressmen to rage about executive tyranny.

During the ensuing months, Roosevelt sought to rally the country behind conservation. He devoted generous space to the problem in his annual message of December 1907. In the following May he convened a conservation conference at the White House, inviting state governors and distinguished citizens from every walk of life. Resolutions were drawn up endorsing government retention of subsoil rights on public lands subsequently sold, protection of watersheds of navigable rivers, and careful controls of timber cutting and grazing. A National Conservation Commission was also created to coordinate the activities of conservation agencies and to make an inventory of national resources. Roosevelt, with more courage than good judgment, appointed Gifford Pinchot to head the Commission. Congress reacted promptly by refusing to appropriate funds for the new organization. The upshot was that the Commission had to suspend operations until after Roosevelt retired from the Presidency.

Notwithstanding occasional setbacks Roosevelt thus managed to launch a conservation movement that retained its vitality during subsequent generations. His unflagging zeal encouraged both state and private agencies to set up commissions for the protection of national resources. The immediate costs were high, for out of the controversy there emerged a bipartisan bloc of congressmen who indiscriminately opposed all measures he recommended during the last year of his second term.

THE ELECTION OF 1904

The Democrats saw small possibility of beating the formidable Roosevelt in the 1904 election. Not only was he personally popular, but as a Progressive he had stolen several planks from their 1896 and 1900 platforms. Having so little to lose, the Democrats were therefore in an experimental mood. They had been beaten twice in a row by posing as the more radical of the major parties. To make matters worse their agrarian radicalism had alienated their traditional followers in the populous Atlantic seaboard states and had gained them only a few votes in the sparsely settled trans-Mississippi states.

Even the most unimaginative party wheelhorses saw the need for new strategy and a new campaign formula. They decided to sidetrack William Jennings Bryan, whose successive defeats in 1896 and 1900 entitled him to a rest. As a replacement they sought a candidate who would restore the party reputation for sane, flexible conservatism. The chief obstacle was Bryan's self-appointed heir, William Randolph Hearst, who had secured a wide hearing because of his newspaper chain and his impassioned attacks on big business. The regular Democrats regarded him as an unprincipled adventurer, half journalist and half fraud. Their control of the convention machinery proved to be decisive and they prevailed upon the listless delegates to nominate Judge Alton B. Parker for President.

The candidate was so dull and colorless that he made conservatism seem less attractive than usual. He had conditioned his acceptance upon the willingness of the party to purge itself of economic heresy. In deference to his wishes the platform planks of 1896 and 1900 on free silver were dropped. Most of the reform proposals associated with the turbulent era of the Populists were also dropped, leaving only the routine denunciations of Republican dishonesty and the routine affirmations of Democratic purity. To dispel any lingering impressions that the party stood for agrarian radicalism, it nominated a conservative, wealthy octogenarian, Henry Gassoway Davis of West Virginia, for Vice-President.

The cumulative effect of these preliminary maneuvers was a drastic political realignment. As the campaign opened, the parties resembled a couple of snakes who had exchanged their skins. The emergence of Roosevelt at the helm of the Republican party gave it a more authentic appeal to the common man than at any time since the death of Lincoln. This impression was heightened by the simultaneous retreat of the Democratic party from the militant radicalism of Bryan to the tenacious conservatism of Cleveland. All the benefits of these political acrobatics went to the Republicans. They held all their eastern supporters and picked up a number of erstwhile Democrats in the trans-Mississippi West. These gains were primarily due to Roosevelt, whose hearty, forthright indictments of corruption and indignant forays against the trusts won him many friends.

Parker was no match for Roosevelt on the platform. When all other tactics failed to arrest the campaign trend toward Roosevelt, Parker made a sensational last-minute attack on the Republicans. He accused them of extorting contributions from eastern corporations in return for pledges of immunity from antitrust suits. Roosevelt angrily branded the charges as a lie. He was doubtless technically correct in insisting that the party had not contracted improper obligations to big business; but the corporations, as usual, were making larger contributions to the Republicans than to the Democrats while the President was seeking to create the contrary impression. Parker's charges failed to enliven the campaign or affect its outcome. Only subsequently did they achieve notoriety by bobbing up repeatedly during Roosevelt's second term, especially after he had become a retired trust-buster.

The election on November 8 was a great personal triumph for Roosevelt. Except for the Solid South and a segment of the border states he carried every section of the country by top-heavy majorities. The margin in the electoral college was 336 to 140. He also won the popular vote by an unprecedented majority of 2,544,343.

PROGRESSIVISM IN THE STATES

Excitement over the national election partially obscured the fact that the Progressive victory was built on state and local units. Municipal governments were often the first to feel the impact of the reform wave. In Cleveland, Tom Johnson, who had dramatically given his life to reform after reading Henry George's *Progress and Poverty,* became mayor in 1901. Four successive terms enabled him to clean up the city government, reduce rates of street railway companies, and revise the system of property taxation. Neither Johnson nor his faithful successor, Newton D. Baker, ever succeeded in installing a single tax on the uncovered increment of land as advocated by Henry George, but they gave Cleveland fifteen years of uninterrupted clean government.

In neighboring Toledo, Sam Jones, a wealthy Tolstoyan anarchist who ran his factory, the Acme Sucker Rod Company, in conformity with the golden rule, was elected mayor of the city and applied the same philosophy to public administration. Like Tom Johnson, Jones trained a protégé, Brand Whitlock, to carry on his work. Moreover, both second-generation reformers played a prominent part in the Progressive administration of Woodrow Wilson — Whitlock as ambassador to Belgium, and Baker as Secretary of War.

Some variations developed in the pattern of municipal reform. A number of cities adopted the Galveston Plan, named after the municipal institutions which Galveston, Texas, had devised in cleaning up after the destructive hurricane and tidal wave of September 8, 1900. The key change provided for the division of the mayor's powers among a board of commissioners. This innovation was intended to increase honesty and efficiency. The fact that Galveston moved with great alacrity to construct a massive concrete sea wall gave the commission plan of government tremendous prestige and publicity. Subsequent experience with the plan or the closely allied city-manager plan indicated that permanent improvement in the tone of municipal government could not be guaranteed by structural tinkering. The graph of morality in civic administration continued to show peaks and valleys, varying directly with the alertness and interest of citizens.

Often the cleansing of municipal government was the prelude to a state-wide reform movement. Conviction of grafting St. Louis aldermen paved the way for the triumph of Progressive Governor Joseph W. Folk in Missouri; and exposure of the crooked Minneapolis government contributed to the success of John A. Johnson, who was elected three times as reform Governor of Minnesota.

Progressive victories were not confined to states with a predominantly urban population, but elsewhere success tended to depend more upon adroit manipulation of economic issues. Self-styled Progressive governors in the rural South, like James K. Vardaman of Mississippi and Hoke Smith of Georgia, sought to break the economic domination of the post-Civil War Bourbon aristocracy by sponsoring legislation that cleared the way for the transfer of political power to the poor whites and hence for the improvement of their economic status. Farther north, in Iowa, the administration of Governor A. B. Cummins took up the old Populist war against economic domination by the railroads.

The most striking achievements of the Progressive movement at the state level during the decade from 1900 to 1910 occurred in Wisconsin and New York. The work of Robert M. La Follette, who served three terms as Governor of Wisconsin from 1901 to 1906 has always received more attention because after 1906 he moved on to the national stage as a militant Progressive senator; whereas his New York counterpart, Charles E. Hughes, moved from the governorship in 1910 to the obscurity of the Supreme Court. Hughes re-emerged briefly as the Republican nominee for President in 1916, but by that time the great victories of Progressivism had been won and the attention of the country had turned to other matters.

Both men won their governorships only after epic fights against strongly entrenched political machines, and both pioneered in gaining more equitable conditions for industrial workers. Although the details of their labor legislation differed, La Follette and Hughes secured laws regulating wages, hours, and child labor, and providing compensation for workmen injured in industrial accidents. All told, Hughes signed fifty-six model labor laws during his two terms as Governor of New York from 1907 to 1910. Both men also waged active fights to conserve the natural resources of their respective states. La Follette was more successful in the fight for political reforms, securing a direct-primary law that transferred the nomination of party candidates from conventions to the voters. He also climaxed the traditional hostility of the Midwest toward railroads and corporations by sponsoring laws stringently regulating the former and levying heavier taxes on the latter.

Not all the effective Progressive leaders held public office. William S. U'Ren led a twenty-year campaign for direct government in Oregon as head of the People's Public Power League. A succession of Democratic and Republican governors responded to the voters' pressure mobilized by U'Ren, securing legislation for the initiative, referendum, and recall as well as a direct primary. Initiative permitted the voters to pass laws directly without recourse to the legislature; referendum permitted them to review and disallow certain categories of laws already passed by the legislature; and recall provided them with a procedure to secure a special election and retire unworthy state or local officials from public office before the expiration of their terms. These measures carried direct government about as far as it could be carried and were widely imitated in other Progressive states. The reform movements in New York, Wisconsin, Oregon, Iowa, Mississippi, and elsewhere provided not only laboratories for local testing of Progressive legislation but an indispensable base for Roosevelt's political success at the national level.

THE SECOND TERM

Roosevelt interpreted his impressive victory in the election as a mandate to expand the Progressive program. With unrestrained gusto he shed his responsibilities as executor for McKinley and became a militant spokesman of the people. From the White House he dispensed advice on a great variety of questions: corporal punishment was advocated to discipline wife-beaters, rules revision was urged to take unnecessary roughness out of football, and simplified spelling was demanded to streamline the ponderous English language. He reveled in public controversy, arguing with Senator Foraker of Ohio over the punishment of riotous Negro troops at Brownsville, Texas, and with the Reverend W. J. Long about the latter's descriptions of animals in schoolbooks for children.

Roosevelt's first term had been barren of legislative achievement. So when the new Congress met in December 1905, he made up for lost time by bombarding it with recommendations. Most controversial was his proposal for stringent regulation of rail rates. In the past, Congress had made efforts to protect farmers from exorbitant shipping charges, particularly in the law of 1887, which outlawed railroad pools, drawbacks, or rebates, and created an Interstate Commerce Commission to make investigations and recommendations regarding rates. This legislation had not measured up to the expectations of farmers because the federal courts, which were designated to enforce Commission orders, tolerated the delaying tactics of the railroads. To make matters worse, the Supreme Court handed down a decision in 1897 denying the I.C.C. authority to set maximum rates. The Elkins Act of 1903, which was aimed specifically at rebates, had only partially rectified the situation. Shortly after the 1904 election, Bryan proposed government ownership of the railroads.

It was against this background that Roosevelt requested Congress to enlarge the power of the I.C.C. over railroad rates. The House of Representatives promptly passed the Hepburn Bill in February 1906, embodying the bulk of the President's recommendations. Developments were less favorable in the Senate, where conservative Republicans led by Aldrich of Rhode Island and Elkins of West Virginia drastically amended the bill. Since he could not control his own party, Roosevelt had to form an alliance with Senator Benjamin R. Tillman of South Carolina and the Progressive Democrats. Even so, Senate action was slow and the Hepburn Bill reached the White House in mutilated form. It extended the jurisdiction of the I.C.C. to other types of transportation, and it also empowered the I.C.C. to reduce railroad rates upon complaint by shippers but denied it the power to initiate such action as Roosevelt had originally demanded. Worse still, the bill provided for judicial determination as to the reasonableness of rates. The sting of the provision was partially mitigated by a clause which permitted I.C.C. rate changes to take effect immediately and transferred the burden of initiating litigation to the railroads.

Roosevelt had expressed hostility to the Senate amendment granting the courts broad power to review rates set by the I.C.C., but he signed the bill and professed pleasure over the outcome. Shippers did secure some reductions under the Act. A number of Progressive senators, however, refused to be satisfied with half a loaf. Under the leadership of La Follette, they fought for what they called scientific rates based on a physical valuation of railroad property. The railroads responded with a fierce counterattack against what they considered an invasion of corporation privacy. The antagonists remained deadlocked until 1915, when Congress finally adopted the principle in the Physical Valuations Act. Unfortunately, no amount of legislative magic could cure the chronic squabble between carriers and shippers.

Other Roosevelt recommendations to the Fifty-ninth Congress encountered less opposition. Early in 1906 a Pure Food and Drug bill sailed through both houses on an irresistible wave of Progressive sentiment. Top-heavy majorities partially concealed the fact that the law had been blocked for twenty-seven years by states-rights Democrats and eastern Republicans representing industries using harmful preservatives. The Act specifically outlawed these practices, besides prohibiting the manufacture, sale, or transportation of misbranded or adulterated products, and requiring accurate labels on medicine bottles which contained dangerous drugs.

A companion measure, the Meat Inspection Act, was passed in the same session. Public attention had been focused on the unsanitary conditions in the Chicago stockyards by Upton Sinclair's muckraking novel, *The Jungle.* This made it easier for Senator Albert J. Beveridge, the Progressive Senator from Indiana, to expose and discredit the packers' lobby which fought the bill. In final form the Act provided for federal inspection of slaughterhouses and of meats shipped in interstate commerce. The packers avoided a complete defeat by securing an amendment which required the government to bear the cost of inspection.

WARFARE BETWEEN PRESIDENT AND CONGRESS

The 1906 session of the Fifty-ninth Congress marked the high tide of Progressive legislation under Roosevelt's leadership. Thereafter relations between the President and Congress steadily deteriorated until they reached the point of open warfare. Important legislative casualties were Roosevelt's recommendations to restrict the use of injunctions in labor disputes and to remove legal obstacles against the formation of labor unions.

The conflict of Progressives and Conservatives disordered party alignments, but other factors helped to produce virtual deadlock. Roosevelt had irreparably weakened his control over Congress and his party by announcing immediately after the 1904 victory that he would not stand for re-election in 1908. He took this position out of deference to the third-term tradition, counting the three and a half years which he served for McKinley as a full term. The result of his decision was not immediately apparent, but when the patronage had been passed out and his ability to give or withhold favors had been diminished, Congress grew defiant. His impotence toward the close of his second term was an object lesson for later Presidents.

A still more important source of friction was Roosevelt's determination to broaden his program by executive action in the fields of conservation and business regulation. He frequently asserted and exercised power in the disputed zone between the executive and the legislature, thus provoking hysterical cries of dictatorship from congressional opponents. Both sides settled down to a grim battle in 1908, during which Roosevelt bombarded Capitol Hill with special messages and the legislators retaliated with hostile resolutions. The most dramatic result of the controversy was a Senate resolution censuring Roosevelt for his action during the Panic of 1907. The President had intervened in a short, severe financial crisis which broke out when a number of New York banks failed. Other institutions called in their loans without warning, and the suddenness of the contraction produced a rash of bankruptcies. The effect of the panic was not immediately felt outside the financial centers of the country but Roosevelt, fearing that it might spread, was quite responsive to George W. Perkins, a partner in the firm of J. P. Morgan, when the latter dramatically demanded his help.

Perkins told Roosevelt that another large New York bank would fail unless it could dispose of sizable holdings in the Tennessee Coal and Iron Company. He also stated that the United States Steel Corporation with the financial cooperation of J. P. Morgan was prepared to make this altruistic purchase provided the government would not consider it a violation of the Sherman Antitrust Act. Roosevelt indicated that he would offer no subsequent objection to the transaction. The Steel Corporation promptly bought the Tennessee Coal and Iron Company stock at a fraction of its potential value and thereby integrated another large unit into an already swollen vertical monopoly.

The panic evaporated as suddenly as it had appeared, but the controversy lingered. Roosevelt possessed no satisfactory means of proving that his tacit approval of the merger had materially shortened the life of the panic. Conservative critics accused him of precipitating the whole crisis by his unsound financial policies. Others whispered that he had played favorites in the business world, busting the trusts of the Rockefeller interests but letting the Morgan interests go unscathed. Whatever the truth of the matter, senatorial critics of the President used the incident as an excuse to censure him for approving the enlargement of a trust.

Because of executive-legislative friction the only constructive legislation passed by the Sixtieth Congress was a Railroad Liability Law and the Vreeland-Aldrich Currency Act. The former established the liability of railroads engaging in interstate commerce for injuries sustained by their employees. The second was a stopgap measure designed to prevent a recurrence of the financial stringency that had produced the Panic of 1907. Since Congress recognized the inadequacy of emergency currency loans to banks as a permanent solution, it created a National Monetary Commission under the leadership of Senator Aldrich to make a comprehensive study of monetary and banking problems.

THE ACHIEVEMENTS OF ROOSEVELT

The feud with Congress that embittered Roosevelt's last years in the White House failed to damage his popularity with the people, but it does complicate the problem of bringing his achievements into focus. Contemporaries, influenced by the contagious quality of his personality, regarded him as a militant crusader for social and economic justice. Many later historians have judged his contributions in terms of the more sweeping New Deal program of the 1930's and have pronounced him an engaging but ineffective trimmer. A conflict of verdicts was further encouraged by his momentary conversion to advanced radicalism in the presidential election of 1912. Some have interpreted his program in that year as a farsighted anticipation of the future; others have regarded it as an unimportant deviation from his basic philosophy motivated solely by his desire to get even with Taft.

Despite the confusion surrounding those evaluations of Roosevelt, certain conclusions seem clear. His principal contribution to Progressivism was as an educator rather than as a legislator. For nearly eight years he appealed tirelessly to the conscience of the nation, demanding honesty in government and self-restraint in private affairs. Although frequently ridiculed for his "original discovery of the ten commandments," his forthright demands for moral behavior produced concrete results. The tone of public life improved perceptibly. The government bureaucracy functioned more efficiently and civil service was extended into new areas. More important still, national, state, and local officials under the domination of political machines began to be thrown out by the voters. Starting as a trickle in 1904, the drive reached tidal wave proportions by 1912. Roosevelt did not remain in office long enough to reap the spectacular legislative victories of Progressivism, but he deserves chief credit for arousing the American public, particularly on the question of conservation. That is why Alfred Kazin has said that Roosevelt performed his greatest service simply by being alive.

Roosevelt's record as a legislator was less clear cut and consistent. He refused to consider tariff revision even though most Progressives demanded it. He did not insist upon comprehensive railroad regulation when additional pressure on his part might have secured it. His serpentine path through the thicket of monopoly suggests that he approached the problem more as a canny politician than as a forthright crusader.

His tentative approach to reform revealed the practical man satisfied with half a loaf. It also revealed the lover of nineteenth-century institutions who believed the good society could be restored without basic change. Despite a certain dogmatism, pride, and adolescent self-assertiveness, which led Cecil Spring-Rice, the British ambassador, to caution a correspondent that the President "was about six years old," Roosevelt dominated his generation. As one contemporary said after an interview with him, "You go home and wring his personality out of your clothes."

SUGGESTED READINGS

1. Josephson, Matthew, *The President Makers.*
2. La Follette, R. M., *La Follette's Autobiography.*
3. Pringle, H. F., *Theodore Roosevelt, a Biography.*
4. Roosevelt, Theodore, *Autobiography.*

CHAPTER SIX

THE SPLIT IN THE REFORM MOVEMENT

TENSION WITHIN THE REPUBLICAN PARTY

As Theodore Roosevelt's second term drew to a close in 1908, his Republican critics grew more vocal and bitter. The ferocity of their attacks raised grave doubts whether the dynamic forces of Progressivism could be contained within the framework of the Republican organization.

As usual the party astrologers cast horoscopes loaded with assurances of victory, but the more realistic strategists knew that success depended upon the maintenance of a delicate balance of sectional forces. This search for equilibrium revealed that the party was suffering from a handicap common to successful American parties. It could produce majorities only by patching together an alliance of sections with varying objectives. For the Republicans such a feat was unusually difficult because only one effective combination would unite under their banner — the East and the Middle West. Though the Rocky Mountain and Pacific Coast states could be successfully wooed, they contributed few electoral votes; whereas the South possessed plenty of electoral votes but could not be won under any circumstances.

Historical developments were primarily responsible for limiting the geographical base of the Republican party. Although it had been founded in 1854 as the result of a spontaneous moral outburst against the extension of slavery to the territories, it could not win national elections on that issue alone. It quickly decided to pay the price of victory by multiplying its interests. Within six years it had framed a program broad enough to carry the East and the Middle West. Since it did not drop the original plank opposing the extension of slavery, its victory in 1860 led to secession and to the Civil War. The humiliation of the South in the ensuing conflict left that section with a lasting hostility toward Republicanism and all its works.

This political misfortune produced compensations elsewhere. In the North the war effort plus the economic program of the Lincoln administration had created emotional ties between eastern and western Republicans strong enough to overcome sectional economic differences. An unprecedented spirit of teamwork lingered long after the conflict, clothing the party with a kind of sanctity as the conserver and transmitter of the patriotic tradition. Second-generation Republicans capitalized on this reverence by repeatedly reminding the voters of past accomplishments. It helped them to victory in five out of seven presidential elections between 1872 and 1896. During this period depressed agricultural prices drove western farmers to repeated demands for currency inflation, tariff reduction, and regulation of monopoly — a program that alarmed the bankers, businessmen, and industrialists dominating the eastern wing of the party. Although the latter would probably have made concessions to agriculture, they gleefully discovered that when the farmers cast protest votes, they preferred to waste them on short-lived third parties like the Greenbackers or the Populists, rather than to support the Democrats who bore the historic stigma of having championed slavery and secession. This refusal to throw in their lot with the Democrats reduced the farmers' bargaining power and enabled the easterners to ignore their demands without serious consequences. Of the ten presidential elections between 1860 and 1900, the Republicans lost only two.

The relative stability of the coalition made the leaders of the dominant eastern wing even more careless. They had obtained the better end of the original sectional alliance. The protective tariff and subsidies for business had given them greater long-range economic advantages than free homesteads and railroads had given the farmers. Moreover, they had successfully withstood all efforts by westerners to modify the terms of the contract. If the latter applied pressure from within, they were ignored; if they bolted to the Greenbackers or Populists, they were solemnly disowned, the sectional aspects of the dispute being concealed behind fierce denunciations of the West as a hotbed of radicalism.

The last vestiges of caution left eastern businessmen when they smashed the Populist revolt and elected McKinley in 1896. This proved unfortunate because the generation of farmers with unlimited gratitude toward the Republican party was gradually passing away. The youngsters reaching maturity in the twentieth century could no longer be counted upon to vote contrary to their economic interests merely because Lincoln had saved the Union or had given away free homesteads thirty-five years earlier.

Republicans continued to represent the party to the new generation as the only reliable guardian of prosperity. Preservation of the "full dinner pail" was the formula devised to command wide support, but it had ceased to possess magical properties. As in the past, the manufacturers, as well as the workmen whom they employed, gained more from the protective tariff and sympathetic treatment of business than did the farmers. The latter felt that the benefit from rising agricultural prices was more than counterbalanced by the increase in the cost of industrial consumption goods. They also believed that they would continue to lose ground to the East unless the administration dealt energetically with trusts, railroad rates, and credit conditions. In fact, they were just as much dissatisfied with their subordinate

The return of the dove. (The Philadelphia Inquirer, *1909.*)

position during the period of McKinley prosperity as they had been during the depression years of the early nineties.

The party received momentary respite from its dangerous internal struggle when Theodore Roosevelt unexpectedly became President and put himself at the head of the Progressive crusade. Earlier chapters have already emphasized the character and content of the reform movement. Its idealistic appeal had the happy effect of making it seem like all things to all men. The ex-Populist farmer and his sons did not always experience moral anxiety over boss government, but Progressive propaganda did convince them that the current alliance between politics and business was responsible for official indifference to their economic interests. If the new movement would smash the power of the businessmen and their price-raising trusts, the farmers were prepared to become enthusiastic Progressives. At the same time the eastern wing was willing to extol the virtues of Progressivism, but it was not talking about the same thing as its western brethren.

As a consequence, the Roosevelt administration became a kind of uneasy interlude during which each of the sectional opponents sought to employ Progressive principles for the improvement of its own position. Each tried to conceal the game by periodically identifying Roosevelt with its opponent and attacking him. Sincere eastern Progressives kept their peace, but industrial groups who dominated that wing of the party accused Roosevelt of hostility to business. Westerners were more temperate in their criticism because he wore a cowboy hat, hunted bears, and superficially cultivated the manners of the Great Plains. On the other hand, they found fault with him for accepting such weak railroad legislation as the Hepburn Act and for refusing to revise the Dingley tariff of 1897.

The skirmishing between these opponents, both of whom professed devotion to Progressive principles, ended with the disillusionment of the westerners. Perhaps this was inevitable — the Progressives regarded government as an umpire between rival economic groups, while the West could not improve its position without converting government into its agent.

For better or for worse, historical developments during the preceding fifty years had favored the emergence of an urban industrial society. This process had generated a great deal of natural momentum apart from the legislative favors granted to businessmen during the Lincoln administration and thereafter. Even a hostile national government would have found it impossible, to check the concentration of economic power in the industrial East. A Progressive government under Theodore Roosevelt, which was unwilling to do more than launch a campaign for the curtailment of special business privileges and the elimination of corrupt officeholders, would leave the eastern domination of the Republican party unimpaired. As the 1908 election approached, it became increasingly clear to the farmers that nothing in the Progressive credo assured the transfer of economic or political control to their own section. The reform movement emphasized moral preachments more than legislation in the pursuit of its objectives, and most of what could be accomplished by an aroused public opinion had already been done.

One great item of unfinished business could, however, still be tackled under the auspices of Progressivism. This was the protective tariff, which had long been a source of special privilege. Unfortunately, western farmers did not want a general tariff reduction but a selective reduction on a sectional basis that would favor them. This was a stand based not on principle but on economic interests. Unless the East gave ground, the farmers were prepared to split the party. The issue as they defined it did not involve Progressivism, but they ignored the fact and posed as reformers. Some of the muckraking magazines also played their game. The problem came to a head just as the canny Roosevelt was retiring from the White House. Meanwhile, the Democrats waited hopefully for an opportunity to capitalize on the sectional quarrel within the G.O.P. Progressive elements had begun to take over their state organizations, but the national leadership was still in the hands of the embattled agrarian, William Jennings Bryan. Although he called himself a Progressive, Bryan pitched his appeal to a sectional audience in the South and Midwest.

TAFT AND THE 1908 ELECTION

The leader on whom Roosevelt's mantle descended was William Howard Taft. Born of a distinguished Ohio family in 1857, he had taken his undergraduate work at Yale University and completed his education at the law school of Cincinnati College in 1880. He was admitted to the bar the same year and shortly thereafter made his debut in public life as Assistant Prosecuting Attorney of Hamilton County, Ohio. During the ensuing decade he held various judicial posts and was brought to Washington as Solicitor General by President Benjamin Harrison in 1890. Almost immediately he struck up an acquaintance with Theodore Roosevelt, then a young Civil Service Commissioner, who lived in the same section of Washington. Their paths momentarily separated while Roosevelt was working his way up the ladder of New York politics, but they converged again in 1901 when Roosevelt became President and found Taft serving as head of the Philippine Commission. Roosevelt was so pleased with Taft's performance in easing the transition from military to civil government in the islands that he brought him back to Washington as Secretary of War in 1904.

Bound by his own pledge not to seek a third term in 1908, Roosevelt decided long before the election that Taft was best suited to carry on Progressive policies. In reaching this conclusion, he passed over the claims of Elihu Root, his able Secretary of State, and of Charles Evans Hughes, the Progressive governor of New York. A large corporation law practice diminished the political appeal of the former, and an unwillingness to accept the political tutelage of Roosevelt weakened the otherwise strong candidacy of the latter.

Roosevelt's control of the party organization and the convention machinery was so complete that no serious opposition could be organized. The Chicago convention dutifully nominated Taft on the first ballot and then made an illusory gesture of independence by selecting James S. ("Sunny Jim") Sherman of New York, an uninspiring party hack, as the vice-presidential candidate.

Taft fulfilled many of the requirements of a good candidate. Although his membership in Roosevelt's cabinet identified him with Progressivism, he had been sufficiently sheltered from party controversies to escape the enmity of conservatives. He had also managed to avoid involvement in sectional quarrels, since he had never held an elective office or compiled a voting record. He was sufficiently unknown to provide an effective symbol of unity for a badly torn party.

His personal bearing also produced a favorable impression on the voters. He had learned to capitalize on his tremendous bulk by cultivating the overflowing geniality expected of fat men. His laughter was a monumental display of good will, starting with a convulsive tremor in his midriff and subsiding ten seconds later in a series of infectious chuckles. To watch him campaign was to be convinced that he was genial, tactful, broad-minded, and flexible. During his subsequent career as President he showed stubbornness, indiscreet frankness, and undue sensitivity to criticism, but none of these weaknesses was exposed in 1908. Party orators sold him to the country as "good old Bill."

As was to be expected, the principal source of friction at the convention was the tariff. The westerners demanded a plank which would categorically pledge revision. They pressed their case with a grim determination bolstered by the conviction that the Progressive creed could be invoked in their behalf. Efforts to eliminate special privilege had hitherto brought little change in the balance between the East and the West. Tariff revision now provided the farmers a new opportunity for reopening sectional politics — with perhaps more chance of success. If the West had really stood for the elimination of all special privilege, it would have advocated dropping the tariff entirely. But nobody suggested abandoning protection as a principle; instead, the demand was for downward revision of certain schedules. It promptly became plain that such modification was to apply only to industrial and not to farm goods.

Concessions came easily for easterners at the convention because they recollected that tariff legislation in the past had seldom coincided with party pledges. Since the need for unity was immediate and the prospect of trouble was distant, they agreed to a plank for revision. No qualifying adjective was inserted to indicate that it would be downward. Not even the most suspicious westerner considered the possibility that upward revision would be attempted.

The only other serious dispute at the convention revolved about the demands of organized labor for a plank on the use of the injunction in labor disputes. After some discussion the delegates approved a qualified endorsement of the injunction, whereupon Samuel Gompers, president of the A. F. of L., complained that labor had been "thrown down, repudiated, and relegated to the discard by the Republican party." He subsequently secured a more satisfactory plank from the Democrats and repeatedly attacked Taft for his generous issuance of injunctions as a federal judge. Nevertheless the A. F. of L. did not formally take sides in the election, nor did the workers desert the Republican party.

The Democratic convention met two weeks later in Denver. The altitude did not elevate the tone of the transactions or the prospects of the party. William Jennings Bryan received his third nomination for President and John W. Kern of Indiana was selected as his running mate. The choice of Bryan temporarily wrested from the Democratic party the chance to go before the country as a Progressive party. His sole chance of victory seemed to depend on his effectiveness in shedding the stigma of sectional radicalism. But he had already thrown away his opportunity on August 30, 1907, by advocating government ownership of the railroads in a speech at Madison Square Garden. His subsequent attempts to undo the damage failed. His blunder made it possible for the Republicans to assume their customary role as defenders of American institutions from an immediate socialist menace.

Under the circumstances the campaign was formal and dull. Bryan denounced the trusts, the protective tariff, and corporation contributions to his opponents. With a fine disregard for genealogy, he claimed to be both the father and the heir of the Roosevelt reform movement. Taft had originally intended to conduct a dignified front-porch campaign in Cincinnati, but he got nervous in September and took the stump. Skillfully parrying the charges of Bryan, he promised to make the trusts live within the law and to revise the tariff equitably without abandoning the protective principle. By refusing contributions from the United States Steel trust and the railroads he also took the sting out of attacks on the party as the pawn of big business. Most important of all, he identified himself with the Roosevelt administration and engaged to continue its policies.

The outcome of the election was never in doubt; Taft carried only three less states than Roosevelt had won in 1904. On the other hand, the popular vote gave him less cause for rejoicing, for the plurality of 2,544,343 in 1904 dropped to 1,269,606. Much of the loss occurred in the Mississippi Valley. Ohio, Indiana, North Dakota, and Montana gave their votes to Taft but elected Democratic governors for the first time since the Populist revolt. Plainly, the Middle West was giving warning that solid agrarian support could no longer be taken for granted. Some Republican farmers in that area had taken the extreme step of voting Democratic when their own party was flying the flag of Progressivism. Others would soon split their party by redefining Progressivism. Whatever they had done or were to do, the election served notice that henceforth farmers would judge Progressivism by its practical economic results rather than by its principles.

THE PAYNE-ALDRICH TARIFF AND ITS AFTERMATH

Charles Francis Adams once observed that there were only two kinds of tariff men — thieves and hogs. President Taft was to learn the profound truth of that statement when he called a special session of the new Congress to redeem his campaign pledge of tariff revision. Superficially, the Sixty-first Congress resembled its predecessors with a sizable Republican majority in both houses and a strongly entrenched eastern leadership. The eight-year reform crusade had, however, gradually changed the character of the western delegations, replacing party wheelhorses with fierce, defiant agrarians who spoke the Progressive tongue. They trickled into the House in twos and threes. Victor Murdock of Kansas and George W. Norris of Nebraska had been elected in 1902, A. J. Gronna of North Dakota in 1904, and Charles A. Lindbergh of Minnesota in 1906. The same pattern developed in the Senate, where Moses Clapp of Minnesota appeared in 1904, followed by Robert M. La Follette of Wisconsin, William E. Borah of Idaho,

Jonathan Bourne of Oregon, and Joseph M. Dixon of Montana in 1906; and Joseph Bristow of Kansas and Albert B. Cummins of Iowa in 1908. These new members comprised only a fraction of the Republican majority, but their aggressive spirit carried others along with them. Their attitude on the tariff was uncompromising, and they had no intention of capitulating to the easterners simply to preserve party unity.

No sooner had Congress assembled than the determined band of Progressive Republicans in the House took the offensive by trying to block the re-election of Joseph G. Cannon as Speaker. Although he came from Danville, Illinois, in the heart of the farm belt, Cannon possessed the economic outlook and interests of an easterner. His voting record showed such undeviating regard for the *status quo* as to provoke the comment that "if he had attended the caucus on creation, he would have remained loyal to chaos." He was vulnerable on other grounds also, for he had alienated the Methodists by his solicitude for the liquor interests and had infuriated organized labor by his defense of injunctions. Although his own constituents were beguiled by his untidy clothes, incessant tobacco-chewing, and odd mixture of profane and pious expressions, many Republicans considered him responsible for the reduced party vote in the West.

If Taft had placed himself at the head of all these discontented forces, he might have secured the ouster of Cannon from the speakership. But he refused to gamble, and the revolt failed. Cannon repaid Taft's forbearance by refusing to lead the House fight for lower tariff rates. The House bill was primarily the product of the Ways and Means Committee headed by Sereno Payne of New York. It revised practically all the tariff schedules, but most of the reductions were modest. Some of the western Republicans disliked the bill, but the rules of the House limited their opportunity to alter it in any systematic way. Cannon held the waverers in line with covert threats to deprive them of choice committee posts and rammed the measure through in record time.

When the Payne bill arrived in the Senate, Nelson Aldrich of Rhode Island, who was chairman of the Finance Committee, rewrote it completely. Dignified, arrogant, and convinced that the interest of big business and those of the country were identical, Aldrich reported a bill to the Senate which actually raised many rates above those prevailing in the Dingley tariff of 1897. When Senator Bailey of Texas accused him of repudiating the Republican platform, Aldrich coldly replied that the platform called for tariff revision without specifying the direction. His statement was technically true, but neither Taft nor the Republican campaigners in 1908 had interpreted the plank to mean anything but downward revision.

Confronted by the insolent challenge of Aldrich, who cared nothing about the economic interests of the West, ten Republican senators under the direction of La Follette fought back. Even with Democratic support they lacked the votes to block passage of the new law. Since the Senate rules did not provide for any limitation on debate, they now decided to educate the public on the intricacies of tariff-making. Each of the ten senators took responsibility for a major schedule and exposed all the hidden subsidies and favors lurking in seemingly harmless clauses. Dolliver of Iowa turned his sardonic wit on the wool schedule, describing it as "the offspring of a marriage between the shepherds and weavers." And when Senator Warren of Wyoming interrupted to defend the schedule, Dolliver called him "the greatest shepherd since Abraham."

The muckraking magazines gave the rebels substantial documentary support for their repeated charge that eastern Republicans had betrayed the 1908 platform. *Collier's Weekly* featured regular articles by Mark Sullivan on the fortunes of the struggle. It also offered to mail to subscribers, free of charge, a simplified digest of votes by the individual senators on each of 117 schedules. By midsummer the western Republican senators and muckraking magazines between them had managed to convince the voters that tariff reduction was the acid test of Progressivism.

Taft should have sensed that his reputation as a Progressive depended on his tariff stand, but when the final revision was sent to the White House on August 5, 1909, he decided to sign it. He felt that the provision which he had sponsored for an impartial commission to dig up data on the various schedules would convert future rate-making into a scientific operation. He also managed to convince himself that he was fulfilling his campaign pledge for downward revision. He reached this conclusion because the bulk of the changes which constituted an increase were on expensive manufactured items beyond the reach of the average consumer, whereas the less numerous reductions were concentrated on raw materials like newsprint, hides, lumber, leather, and iron ore, which would directly affect the cost of living.

To defend the bill as a well-balanced revision of schedules was to court political reprisal; to defend it as a downward revision was to insult the intelligence of the dullest voter. Political inexperience drove Taft into both traps. He had no conception of the emotional intensity behind the popular conception that the tariff was responsible for high prices. He was accustomed to a broadly objective rather than a narrowly sectional concept of the content of Progressivism, and to the rational arguments of the courtroom rather than the florid phrases of senatorial debate. Consequently, he grew bewildered and then angry when his analysis of the tariff failed to silence his critics.

Matters did not improve when he embarked on a 13,000-mile tour in September 1909 to explain his stand to the people. Habitually tardy and careless in the preparation of speeches, he made a number of extemporaneous statements that were politically damaging. The worst blunder occurred at Winona, Minnesota, where he praised the Payne-Aldrich bill as the best tariff ever adopted by the Republican party. Newspapers reproduced the statement in screaming headlines, and the West denounced him as the betrayer of

Progressivism. Redefinition was now proceeding at a more rapid rate. To Taft's critics Progressivism had become synonymous with the economic interests of the Mississippi Valley.

THE BALLINGER-PINCHOT CONTROVERSY

As the quarrel reached a crescendo in the summer of 1909, a violent controversy over conservation shook the administration. This development could not be dismissed lightly, since conservation occupied a place in the Progressive hierarchy second only to tariff reform. It demanded a loyalty which Taft gave but which the public mistook for hostility. He had inherited that fanatical conservationist, Chief Forester Gifford Pinchot, from the Roosevelt administration. Not only was Pinchot a devoted personal follower of the ex-President but he had encouraged Roosevelt to take arbitrary action in behalf of conservation. Another enthusiast, James R. Garfield, Secretary of the Interior, jointly worked out with Pinchot a policy of mass withdrawals of land from settlement beyond the intent of congressional law. Garfield, who was also an attorney, justified this action on the ground that the Executive possessed a general supervisory power over the public lands.

Pinchot hoped for further withdrawals without the authorization of Congress, but Taft refused to act on such a dubious legal basis. He replaced Garfield as Secretary of the Interior with Richard A. Ballinger, who had been Commissioner of the General Land Office and who shared Taft's doubts. Ballinger had already collided with Pinchot in 1907 over the disposition of coal lands in Alaska, favoring the sale rather than the lease of these properties. Pinchot considered Ballinger hostile to conservation. His suspicions deepened when Ballinger's first act as Secretary of the Interior was to restore to public entry a number of power sites which had been hastily withdrawn by the Roosevelt administration.

Pinchot took the matter up with Taft, who then reviewed the whole question. It became apparent from the resulting study that Ballinger had not acted out of hostility to conservation; he began withdrawing sites again as soon as the Geological Survey furnished accurate data on the public lands involved. On the basis of the information he withdrew 421,129 acres. Although this action involved less acreage than the 3,450,460 acres which had originally been withdrawn by Garfield, it covered more actual power sites than Garfield's withdrawals, which had in many cases encroached on private land or on public land not bordering on streams. This review of land withdrawals for power sites by Ballinger brought administrative policy in closer harmony with the intent of congressional law. It also enraged Pinchot, who regarded opponents of indiscriminate withdrawals as opponents of conservation. He immediately began a campaign to discredit Ballinger.

Pinchot found a most helpful ally in young Louis R. Glavis, who had been a subordinate of Ballinger when the latter headed the General Land Office. In those days, Glavis had investigated the claim of Clarence Cunningham and others to coal lands in Alaska and had concluded that Cunningham was a front for a Morgan-Guggenheim syndicate attempting a gigantic land grab. When Ballinger ignored his evidence and approved the so-called Cunningham claim, Glavis suspected Ballinger of collusion with the looters of the public domain. On August 5, 1909, he communicated his suspicions to Pinchot, who indiscreetly sent the young man to Taft. After hearing the Glavis charges, receiving an indignant denial from Ballinger, and examining the evidence for three days, Taft fired Glavis. He could not have pursued any other course of action without reflecting a lack of confidence in his Secretary of the Interior.

The President did not anticipate the storm of criticism provoked by the firing of Glavis. The well-oiled publicity machine of the Forest Service, which had generated substantial backfires against anticonservation congressmen, released parts of the Glavis testimony to newspaper correspondents and national magazines. The muckraking journals enthusiastically took up the theme, because there had been nothing very exciting to expose since the spectacular fight over the Payne-Aldrich tariff. Norman Hapgood, the editor of *Collier's Weekly,* fired the first shot at Ballinger on November 6, 1909. The ensuing four issues of the magazine devoted vast amounts of space to the controversy, including an article by Glavis himself. Citizens who did not subscribe to *Collier's Weekly* found substantially the same information in *McClure's* and *Hampton's.*

Matters took a grave turn when the crusading Pinchot spurned Taft's repeated assurances of cooperation and wrote a letter to Senator Dolliver full of intemperate accusations against Ballinger. Dolliver read the letter on the floor of the Senate, and on January 7, 1910, the unlucky Taft had to fire Pinchot for insubordination.

Rebellious western senators, who felt that Taft had betrayed them on the tariff, were looking for an opportunity to embarrass him, but their opposition to conservation had thus far disqualified them for a role as sincere critics of Taft. The discharge of Pinchot provided them with a perfect excuse to turn the investigating machinery of Congress loose on the President. A special committee of six senators and six representatives was created on January 10, 1910, to consider the evidence against Ballinger; it conducted hearings for four months. Louis D. Brandeis, clever free-lance attorney and later Supreme Court Justice, presented the case against the administration. He dug out evidence that Ballinger had once accepted a retainer fee from the Cunningham group. He also embarrassed Attorney General Wickersham by proving that the latter had predated the reports which were used by Taft as a basis for firing Glavis.

Notwithstanding the exposure of these sensational facts, the evidence against Ballinger was inconclusive. The investigating committee exonerated him, but he had been tried and convicted by the muckraking press. His public reputation was ruined and he resigned as soon as he could do so without appearing to quit under fire. Recent research makes it clear that Ballinger suffered from exaggerated, if not irresponsible, attacks. Pinchot appears to have been sincere but wrong in his charges that Ballinger handled the Cunningham claims in a corrupt or dishonest manner. His distrust of Ballinger as an opponent of conservation was also based on insufficient evidence. In fact, their quarrel stemmed primarily from a difference of method rather than of objective. Pinchot wanted to withdraw land from settlement whether Congress authorized it or not, and Ballinger wanted to remain within the law. Neither saw the necessity of a policy for using the land withdrawn from entry. This next step in conservation was not taken until after World War I.

The most important effect of the Ballinger-Pinchot controversy was not felt in conservation policies but in the political fortunes of President Taft. Deservedly or not, Pinchot was a symbol of conservation, and his ouster reinforced the popular belief that Taft repudiated the conservation program.

By assuming, at no extra cost to themselves, the defense of conservation which they hitherto had opposed, the western Republicans broadened their policy of reinterpreting Progressivism for sectional advantage. As the 1910 election approached, they blamed the rising cost of living on the Payne-Aldrich tariff. Taft tried to retaliate by employing federal patronage against these critics in his own party. His efforts were unsuccessful and served only to widen the gap between the two sections.

Victory for the Taft forces in the congressional elections might have forced the West to employ other tactics than revision of the reform credo in unseating eastern leadership. However, the voters were confused about Progressivism and indignant about the tariff. The western Republicans suffered only one serious casualty, Senator Albert J. Beveridge of Indiana, but the party as a whole sustained heavy losses. The House of Representatives passed to the control of the Democrats for the first time since 1892, and the Republican majority in the Senate was reduced from twenty-eight to ten.

The unmistakable rejection of the administration by the voters in 1910 increased the bargaining power of the western Republicans within the party. If they could continue to capitalize the popularity of Progressivism by selling their economic program under its label, they could force the East to choose between accepting a western candidate for President or facing a party split.

THE ACHIEVEMENTS OF THE TAFT ADMINISTRATION

The unfortunate controversies over the tariff and conservation obscured the very real contributions of Taft to the Progressive cause. In his speech accepting the nomination he had asserted that his aim would be "to complete and perfect the machinery" for the preservation of Progressive reforms.

As President, therefore, his legislative program was designed to close the circle of law which still permitted special privilege or wrongdoing on the part of any selfish economic group.

His first step, taken during the special session of Congress, was the proposal of a graduated income tax for the dual purpose of equalizing tax burdens and raising revenue. Eastern Republicans headed by Aldrich promptly protested that an income tax was unconstitutional. So Taft maneuvered them into accepting a flat one per cent tax on the income of corporations above $5,000 and submitting the income tax to the states for ratification as a constitutional amendment.

His second step in consolidating Progressive reforms was a series of recommendations to the regular session of Congress in December 1909 for (1) enlargement of I.C.C. authority over railroads, (2) extension of executive power to classify the public lands, (3) mandatory federal charters for all corporations engaged in interstate commerce, (4) establishment of postal savings banks, (5) exemption of labor unions from suits under the Sherman Act, (6) legislation redefining the injunction power of the courts and modifying procedure so that labor would be given a hearing before an injunction was granted. Roosevelt had never asked for more.

Congress refused to act on the proposals regarding labor unions, injunctions and federal charters for corporations. Conservation fell into a more acceptable category. In fact, the Picket Act of 1910 clarified the status of presidential powers over the public lands, giving the President the authority to withdraw from all forms of entry land for water-power sites, irrigation projects, or general classification.

With considerably more reluctance Congress established postal savings banks. The measure had been assailed by the American Bankers' Association as socialistic, administratively unworkable, and destined to withdraw funds from normal sources, especially in times of panic. It turned out later that the two per cent interest rate of the postal savings banks did not attract money that normally flowed into private institutions, although they did provide a safe depository for the funds of small investors frightened by the rash of failures during the Panic of 1907.

Most important of all was the passage of railroad legislation to plug up the many loopholes in the Hepburn Act of 1906. That law had granted the I.C.C. jurisdiction over railroad rates. Roosevelt, in his determination to get a railroad law of some sort, had accepted a series of crippling amendments. The crucial clause granting the I.C.C. outright authority to bar unreasonable rates had been modified so that the Commission could take action only on the complaint of the shippers. The power of the I.C.C. had been further hamstrung by a provision allowing the courts to issue injunctions against its rulings, thus permitting the railroads to postpone or block rate charges with litigation.

The Mann-Elkins Act, passed in June 1910, embodied most of Taft's recommendations for remedying the defects of the Hepburn Act. It gave the

I.C.C. authority to establish rates on its own motion, to suspend railroad-initiated increases for ten months pending an investigation of their reasonableness, and to change freight classifications, which the railroads often manipulated for concealed increases. The law also transferred jurisdiction over I.C.C. orders from the district and circuit courts to a special commerce court. Although Congress eliminated this court three years later, other provisions prevented the railroads from using judicial filibuster to suspend the operation of I.C.C. rates. Senator La Follette managed to secure adoption of an amendment directing the I.C.C. to undertake a physical valuation of the railroads. This was the first step in the fulfillment of his dream for scientific rate-making which would limit the railroads to a fair return on their investment — an objective that he finally achieved when Congress passed the Physical Valuations Act of 1913. The railroads managed, however, to eliminate several recommendations from the Mann-Elkins Act. The most prominent would have permitted I.C.C. supervision of railroad securities in order to protect investors, and another would have authorized it to supervise railroad construction jobs in order to assure the safety of the workers.

In advocating such stringent regulation of railroads, Taft strengthened the trend toward the transfer of control over big business from private hands to government commissions in Washington. Nevertheless, he condemned Roosevelt two years later as a dangerous radical for advocating an extension of government regulation. He sought to avoid inconsistency by drawing a sharp line between businesses affected with a public interest, like railroads or public utilities, and businesses wholly private in character. He thought that the former category should be subject to regulation, but the latter should not. That distinction had traditionally been used by the courts in passing on the constitutionality of regulatory legislation and had been relatively serviceable during the nineteenth century. By 1910, however, the evolution of the American economy in the direction of business consolidation and increased interdependence was blurring the distinction between private and public business at the very time Taft was reaffirming it.

The trend of the times was pushing Taft, despite his attachment to the original concept of Progressivism, in the direction of those critics who advocated positive government action in behalf of underprivileged economic groups. It also pointed up the great practical dilemma of the Progressives described in Chapter Four. If they recognized the irreversible movement of industrial development toward ever-larger units and thereby toward the status of public enterprise, they would be obliged to put the business giants under government bureaus. Unfortunately, this response would destroy the basic character of the private enterprise system they were pledged to preserve. If they tried to avoid the dilemma by continuing the original policy of breaking up monopolistic combinations, they had to find a way to prevent the reunion of the fragments. Experience had indicated that the artificial monsters could defy extinction and function as a unit to choke off competition. With the advantage of present perspective one can see that neither solution was likely to preserve the traditional private enterprise system. One path would lead to government control, the other to domination by variously disguised corporate giants unresponsive to public opinion.

Except for the special category of business affected with a public interest, Taft doggedly followed the policy of breaking up trusts instead of subjecting them to regulation. At his instigation, Attorney General Wickersham instituted over seventy suits under the Sherman Act. Some of these misfired, but Taft won two spectacular victories in 1911, when the Supreme Court ordered the dissolution of the Standard Oil Company of New Jersey and the American Tobacco Company. The ensuing roar of Progressive approval was short-lived. The four fragments of the Standard Oil trust continued to follow common production and price policies, while the defunct tobacco trust still possessed the vitality to wage successful war against competitors.

The unsatisfactory results of trust-busting brought Taft under increasing fire during the closing months of his administration. Ironically enough, Theodore Roosevelt swelled the chorus of criticism by calling for government regulation of monopoly and by casting doubts on Taft's Progressivism. But it was Roosevelt, rather than Taft, who had changed his position. Taft steadfastly maintained the original Progressive view that laws should be amended to restore equality of opportunity, and should be enforced impartially against violators of all categories. When Roosevelt advocated positive supervisory action by a government commission it was he who had advanced to new ground.

Such a shift in Roosevelt's position was not surprising. He possessed a kind of political divining rod which enabled him to record all changes in public opinion. Not only did he hear the rising note of protest in the speeches of western congressmen, but he knew that it expressed the disillusionment of farmers who had dutifully re-echoed Progressive sentiments for eight years without reaping any economic benefits. The successive steps he took to put himself at the head of the discontented in the name of Progressivism were to become important milestones in the triumph and collapse of the reform movement. But at the time of the Republican defeat in 1910, his conversion had gone only far enough to encourage the contemporary verdict that western Republicans were the true defenders of Progressivism and that Taft had betrayed reform.

Unfortunately the personality of the President did much to encourage this viewpoint. He did not provide a heroic symbol for crusaders. Waverers were often alienated by his carelessness and bluntness. In fact, he often seemed to lumber through the political forest like an elephant, completely unconscious of the obstructions in his path. He surprised realistic politicians with his curious indifference to the value of sustained favorable publicity and to the methods of securing it. He allowed the all-important muckraking magazines to fall by default under the influence of his midwestern sectional opponents. For this blunder, he paid the full penalty, because these magazines convinced the voters that Progressivism was synonymous with downward revision of the tariff and other legislative manifestations of economic sectionalism.

THE PARTY SPLIT WIDENS

The Republican losses in the 1910 election, complicated by the widening rift within the party, caused inaction in Congress and dead-center government during Taft's last two years in office. He should have used this breathing spell to heal party wounds, but his political acuteness did not grow with experience. He promptly aggravated the intraparty conflict when he reopened the slumbering tariff controversy by making a reciprocity agreement with Canada. Since treaties had to receive a two-thirds vote of the Senate, Taft took the precaution of drawing up the agreement as an ordinary legislative measure, which would require a simple majority in Congress and in the Canadian Parliament. It was signed January 21, 1911, and provided for a free list of well over one hundred items and for reduced rates on four hundred others.

The President believed that reciprocity would appeal to all groups in the country: midwestern Republicans and southern Democrats who thought the Payne-Aldrich tariff was too high, and eastern Republicans who wanted to expand the market for manufactured goods. As usual, nobody knew exactly what the effect would be. Taft had approached the problem at a national level, but the various sectional representatives in Congress reacted with their traditional economic reasoning.

Neither the Democrats nor the eastern Republicans found reciprocity objectionable. The entire Midwest, however, regarded it as a vicious piece of legislation which would open the section to competition from Canadian grain, meat, and dairy products. As if to substantiate their fears, the price of wheat dropped in Minneapolis and rose in Winnepeg when the agreement was announced. Accordingly the midwestern Republicans now fought against reciprocity as hard as they had fought for tariff reduction two years earlier. What they really wanted was a tariff that would protect their own commodities and at the same time open eastern industry to competition. Such an issue did not involve Progressive principles but sectional economics, and it was gradually tearing the old East-West coalition apart.

The initial uproar over reciprocity in the Midwest prevented the Senate from taking a vote before the short session of Congress expired on March 4, 1911. Taft would have been well advised to let the issue ride until the new Congress met in December 1911, or to drop it altogether. Instead he poured salt in the party wounds by calling a special session of Congress in April. After two months of bitter debate the Senate passed the House-approved measure, June 21, 1911, by a vote of 53 to 27, with Democrats and eastern Republicans supporting the President.

Ironically, the legislation for which Taft had paid such a high political price was rejected by Canada. Sir Wilfred Laurier, the Liberal Prime Minister, had staked the fate of his administration on the agreement, which seemed likely to bring Canada substantial economic benefits. Unfortunately he had not taken sensitive national pride into account. The victory-starved Conservative party was looking for a winning issue and found it by exploiting Canadian fears that reciprocity would be the prelude to annexation. The Democratic Speaker of the House of Representatives, Champ Clark, gave this kind of reasoning a generous assist by announcing that he favored reciprocity because it would hasten the day "when the American flag will float over every square foot of the British North American possessions." Laurier found that he could not carry the agreement through Parliament, so he called a general election on the issue. His Liberal party suffered overwhelming defeat and the Conservatives returned to power, killing all prospects for ratification.

Back in the United States, midwestern Republicans cheered the Canadian verdict and sneered at Taft. The President promptly retaliated by vetoing the Farmers Free List — a bill reducing the tariff rates on key rural consumption items.

Elsewhere on the legislative front deadlock prevailed. Taft vetoed the Joint Enabling Act passed by Congress to confer statehood on Arizona and New Mexico, because the Arizona constitution provided for the recall of judges. In his veto message of August 22, 1911, he declared that such a provision struck a deadly blow at the integrity of the judiciary and made possible "the tyranny of a popular majority." Western Republicans greeted this message with howls of rage as a fresh betrayal of Progressivism. The President's stand, however, was perfectly consistent with the original Progressive objective of preserving the integrity of democratic institutions, which certainly included an independent judiciary. Once again the western Progressives, rather than the President, had shifted position. In less than a year Arizona deleted the objectionable provision in order to secure admission along with New Mexico, but won the last round by restoring the original constitution as soon as she had entered the Union, where she was beyond the reach of Taft.

The only important measure upon which Congress and the President could agree was the submission of the Seventeenth Amendment to the states for ratification. It called for the direct election of United States Senators and received the approval of the necessary number of states just as Taft was leaving office.

THE REBEL PROGRESSIVES ORGANIZE

While Taft was struggling to secure congressional approval of reciprocity, a new organization, the National Progressive Republican League, was launched on January 21, 1911, with Senator Jonathan Bourne, Jr., of Oregon as president. It immediately became apparent that the chief objective was to prevent the renomination of Taft in 1912. Joined by this negative bond of unity were prominent midwestern senators like La Follette of Wisconsin and Cummins of Iowa, disgruntled conservationists like Gifford Pinchot and James R. Garfield, and a miscellaneous assortment of Progressives, including the muckraking journalist Lincoln Steffens, the labor lawyer Louis Brandeis, and the millionaire industrialist Medill McCormick.

Although the members of the League knew what they did not want, they experienced difficulty in finding positive points of agreement. The objectives of the midwestern Republican congressmen were clear. They sought to use the League as a medium for wresting control of the Republican organization from the eastern wing of the party. This was not so much a revolt against sectional dominance as it was a protest against dominance by the wrong section. It was also the tip-off that not only Republican solidarity but Progressive integrity was in danger. For these people were out, from here on, to secure special advantages for their area and their class. Unless Progressivism would dutifully contort itself to fit into the new mold, its days were numbered. The leaders of this group had already made substantial progress in Congress, where George W. Norris organized a surprise coalition of Democrats and midwestern Republicans to strip Speaker Cannon of his autocratic powers. Until they managed to change the rules in March 1910, Cannon had dominated the Republican majority by virtue of his power to appoint the Republican members of House committees and to establish the rules of debate for a particular piece of legislation. The first power enabled him to reward the regulars and chastise the rebels, while the second forced representatives to secure private permission from him if they wanted House action on legislation. The bills of hostile congressmen seldom got out of committee, and the rebels themselves seldom got permission to address the House. The successful Norris resolution excluded the Speaker from membership on the Rules Committee and transferred to the House membership the selection of that important group. The Democrats completed what Norris had started when they got control of the House in 1911, depriving the Speaker of his power to appoint the members of any committee. Over in the Senate, midwestern Republicans had made life so miserable for the haughty Aldrich that he resigned his leadership and retired in 1911.

The next step for the rebellious midwesterners was to throw the weight of the National Progressive Republican League behind an acceptable presidential candidate. The political leader marked for this honor was Senator Robert M. La Follette. No individual in public life possessed stronger Progressive antecedents. He had broken with the Republican leaders in Wisconsin over the question of corruption in 1893, and had fought an epic seven-year battle against the most discouraging odds to capture the governorship and control of the state party organization. After spending three terms transforming Wisconsin into a model Progressive commonwealth, he had been elected to the Senate in 1906 and there he continued to promote reform legislation with tireless zeal. His approach to problems was scientific and analytical. Unlike Roosevelt, who tackled railroad monopoly by denouncing "bad" railroad men, La Follette dug out the facts on rebates, profits, and capitalization as a basis for legislation. His speeches were laden with statistics and were educational in tone. This does not mean that he lacked the moral conviction or crusading fervor that characterized so many Progressives; he glowed with righteous indignation, yet his passion had an odd, impersonal quality which inspired respect rather than warmth or affection. He was much too honest and statesmanlike to play the kind of politics that would satisfy the anti-Taft faction.

The midwestern Republican congressmen, who had endorsed La Follette for the Presidency in both April and October of 1911, began to squirm uneasily at the end of the year when his candidacy failed to generate widespread support. Other groups in the National Progressive Republican League had not wanted him in the first place. Some of them feared him as a kind of Republican William Jennings Bryan, who would smear the party with an undeserved reputation for extremism; others opposed him for no more complicated reason than that they thought the eastern Republicans would not accept him. A few, like Amos and Gifford Pinchot, did not want a western candidate at all, and thought Theodore Roosevelt was the only Republican who could avert a party split.

The twofold problem for the League was to find a graceful way of sidetracking La Follette, whom they had been booming for a year, and to substitute Roosevelt. Even those who disliked the ex-President saw the necessity of accepting him, since no one else possessed the status to challenge Taft with only six months remaining for a build-up.

A sheer accident made it easy to jettison La Follette. The Senator was scheduled to address the banquet of the Periodical Publishers' Association at Philadelphia on February 2, 1912. It was highly desirable for him to put on a superior performance because an appearance before this critical audience had often made or broken a presidential candidate. Unfortunately, the dice were loaded against La Follette. Pushed to the verge of a nervous breakdown by overwork and starved for sleep as a result of spending the preceding night at the bedside of an ailing daughter, he was in no condition to speak before such an audience. He lost his place in the manuscript on the second page and started to repeat what he had said. When a few of his listeners got up to leave, he lost his temper, shook his fist at them, and threw away his manuscript to deliver an extemporaneous tirade against newspapers. He rambled on for two hours to an ever-shrinking audience and finally sank into his chair, an utter wreck.

Within a few days he recovered completely, but the members of the League had found the excuse they wanted. Most of them, professing to believe that he had suffered an irreparable physical breakdown, switched their support to Roosevelt.

ROOSEVELT CHALLENGES TAFT

The collapse of the La Follette candidacy removed the last restraints on Theodore Roosevelt, who shortly thereafter took the momentous step of challenging his former protégé, William Howard Taft. There were three important reasons for his entry into the contest. First, he saw the drift of sectional politics in the party and believed he could put himself at the head of the rebellious farmers without destroying his following in the East. Secondly, he realized that the Progressive movement had accomplished about all that it could on the basis of its original principles, and he therefore assumed the job of restating the program so that it might meet the requirements of dissatisfied pressure groups. Lastly, he was motivated by a complex of personal factors, which included deteriorating personal relations with Taft, love of the limelight, an insatiable hunger for politics, and boredom.

Historians are not quite sure just what started the disintegration of the friendship. Certainly no trace of a rift was visible when Roosevelt sailed from New York City, March 9, 1909, on his great hunting expedition to Africa. He remained abroad nearly fifteen months and, after exhausting his appetite for disturbing the jungle residents, made a triumphant tour of Europe. His return was postponed an additional week so that he could serve as official American representative at the funeral of Edward VII. When he landed at New York on June 16, 1910, amidst enthusiastic displays of affection from his fellow countrymen, he refused an invitation from Taft's special messenger to visit at the White House. Although the two men met a few days later, the country soon learned that a distinct coolness had developed between them.

An early source of friction seems to have been Taft's refusal to retain a few intimate friends of Roosevelt in government jobs after having authorized Roosevelt to assure them of their reappointment. Mrs. Taft enlarged the area of misunderstanding by making frequent uncomplimentary remarks about Roosevelt which sometimes got back to him. The discharged Chief Forester, Gifford Pinchot, added his bit by taking the first available boat for Africa and delivering his highly colored version of the conservation controversy to Roosevelt as soon as the latter emerged from the jungle.

Although Roosevelt heard a forceful defense of Taft's position from Elihu Root in London, he showed little inclination to accept it at face value. The most Root could extract from him was a promise not to comment on the party quarrel until he had been home long enough to make his own assessment of the situation. He managed to maintain complete silence for four full days after his return. A press conference broke the jam of words, and thereafter politicians from both camps streamed to Oyster Bay for conferences. Roosevelt became still more involved when he met Governor Hughes of New York at a Harvard reunion and gave him an impulsive pledge of help in the campaign for a state direct-primary law.

Before Roosevelt knew it, he was knee-deep in the 1910 campaign, speaking for Republican candidates all over the country regardless of their voting records. He endorsed eastern Republicans who had voted for the Payne-Aldrich tariff and western Republicans who had voted against it. His pointed refusal to endorse Taft was an unmistakable gesture of hostility, although he ingeniously explained it away as reluctance to take sides within the party. In a speech at Osawatomie, Kansas, on August 31, 1910, he gave additional evidence that he had separated himself from the administration. Abandoning the original Progressive concept of government as an umpire to enforce the law, he demanded an enlarged, aggressive central authority which would harness the dynamic forces of industrial society for the benefit of the people. He indicted the courts for being primarily interested in property rights rather than in human welfare and designated the executive as the steward of the people who should mobilize the machinery of government for their purposes. He called this modified Hamiltonian philosophy the "New Nationalism." In its name he demanded the graduated income tax, workmen's compensation, child labor legislation, and a variety of measures in behalf of discontented groups.

The drastic departure from orthodox Progressivism in this speech would have received more attention if the voters had known that he was going to give numerous repeat performances two years later. Although for the moment the new doctrines were drowned out by the great party quarrel over the tariff, the always vigilant *Nation* gloomily observed that the Osawatomie speech opened up "an endless vista of legislative and administrative interference with business affairs and personal activity."

Roosevelt continued to campaign strenuously until the eve of the 1910 election. When his efforts failed to avert a Republican defeat, he decided that the voters had repudiated him as well as the party. He declined to sponsor the National Progressive Republican League or to participate in politics during 1911. He freely predicted the renomination of Taft and the defeat of the Republicans in 1912.

Characteristically, Roosevelt's mood of black pessimism was succeeded by a fit of unquenchable optimism. During the last weeks of 1911 Republican politicians, looking for a winner, made a fresh pilgrimage to Oyster Bay. Midwesterners promised to deliver convention delegates; and even eastern businessmen, who had criticized him bitterly in 1908, favored him over the trust-busting Taft. His shift in viewpoint became pronounced in the autumn when Taft brought a suit for the dissolution of the United States Steel Corporation. Roosevelt responded with an article in *Outlook* magazine, advocating sane regulation of the trusts by government commission.

This new enunciation of policy hopelessly confused the political and personal factors in the break with Taft. Roosevelt probably intended to produce this effect, because his public status was bound to suffer less if he could convince the voters that insurmountable differences in political philosophy rather than personal antagonism had forced the split. As we have already seen, he had by now moved away from his own political position of 1904, which Taft continued to occupy. The transition had been eased by the writings of Herbert Croly and Brooks Adams, the philosophers of the "New Nationalism."

A vitality extraordinary for a 54-year-old man was one of the personal factors that drove Roosevelt, against his better judgment, to private admissions of his availability in January 1912 and to open declaration of his candidacy shortly after the La Follette boom collapsed. He decided that the best vehicle for his announcement would be a letter from seven Progressive Republican governors, requesting him to run. He took the precaution of drafting the letter for them and made the text of his reply public on February 24, 1912. It announced that he was receptive to the nomination and would remain in the race "until the convention had expressed its preference."

The Roosevelt decision to challenge Taft was a dangerous gamble despite the Rough Rider's popularity with the rank and file. The Republican national organization, and most of the state organizations, except in the West, were under the control of Taft by virtue of his power over patronage. His grip was unshakable in the Solid South, where the party included only federal postmasters, judges, tax collectors, and their immediate satellites; yet these groups were apportioned delegates to the national convention on the basis of total population and had as much weight in nominating a presidential candidate as states normally won by the party. Elsewhere the control of the national administration was not so tight, but Taft appointees had little incentive to change their allegiance because the election of Roosevelt would mean their replacement by other Republicans.

Taft's control of these various layers of the Republican organization seemed likely to be decisive, because they selected most of the delegates to the nominating convention. Even in states where the warfare provided two sets of delegates, the National Committee and the convention Credentials Committee were almost certain to select the Taft delegates.

Roosevelt's sole hope lay in capturing the delegates from those states which, in response to Progressive demands for direct government, had passed laws establishing presidential primaries. There were only thirteen such states, with an aggregate of 388 delegates. This figure fell far short of the total necessary to nominate, but Roosevelt believed that if he won the primaries by a spectacular margin he would generate a band-wagon movement and jar loose some of the organization delegates. Accordingly, from February to June he campaigned strenuously, indicting Taft as a conservative and a defender of machine politics. The President retaliated in a series of speeches denouncing Roosevelt as a dangerous radical who proposed to destroy American institutions and break the third-term tradition. As the preconvention campaign warmed up, a bitter personal note crept into the speeches of the former friends. When Roosevelt invaded Taft's native Ohio in May, the President spoke of the Rough Rider's "egotism and vanity," sarcastically suggesting that Roosevelt be put in the White

House for life. The latter replied with sulphurous references to Taft as a puppet of the bosses.

The President took an unmerciful beating in the primaries. North Dakota, which voted first, established the trend by giving Taft 1,659 votes, or only 16 votes more than the total number of federal officeholders in the state. In other primaries he did somewhat better, but Roosevelt was the overwhelming choice of rank-and-file Republicans.

Notwithstanding the popular verdict, the band-wagon rush failed to materialize, and the National Committee refused to seat the Roosevelt delegates who challenged 252 Taft delegates as being illegally and irregularly selected. Most of the contests were frivolous, but the Taft-dominated committee showed no inclination to decide cases on their merits when they made up the temporary roll of the convention. The Roosevelt supporters made a new attempt to change the composition of the convention at the initial session, June 18, by proposing that 72 Roosevelt delegates be substituted for 72 Taft delegates. When this maneuver failed, they adroitly supported Francis E. McGovern, the Progressive Governor of Wisconsin, for permanent chairman of the convention in order to win the support of the La Follette delegates. Elihu Root, the Taft candidate, beat McGovern 558 to 501. This vote represented the high-water mark of the opposition to Taft and unquestionably ratified his control of the convention machinery. There was one more attempt to break his grip in the Credentials Committee, which disposed of the contests between contending delegations but the committee seated the Taft delegates to cries of "theft" and "fraud."

In the meantime the ex-President had taken the unprecedent step of entraining for Chicago to lead his supporters in person. He arrived two days before the convention and told reporters he felt "as strong as a bull moose." In a mass meeting at the auditorium the same night, he condemned Taft for trying to steam-roller the nomination and pledged himself to fight for the principles of righteousness and justice, whatever the cost. In a final dramatic phrase, he proclaimed: "We stand at Armageddon, and we battle for the Lord." The effect of this speech on Republican politicians was impaired by their recollection that he had used the same tactics to nominate Taft in 1908. Biblical metaphors also seemed less imposing when ten thousand handbills were distributed the next day announcing that Roosevelt would walk on the waters of Lake Michigan at 7:30 P.M.

The miracle did not materialize, but Roosevelt continued his preconvention skirmishes with evil so that he would have a moral basis for rejecting all compromises with the opposition. Accordingly, when it became clear that Taft would receive the nomination, Roosevelt ordered his followers to bolt the convention. Most of them obeyed, leaving the battlefield in the hands of the Taft forces, who promptly renominated the victorious Taft-Sherman ticket of 1908. Sherman died during the campaign and Nicholas Murray Butler, the president of Columbia University, replaced him as vice-presidential candidate. The platform made no concessions on the tariff. Otherwise it was an orthodox Progressive document, advocating maximum-hour laws for women and children in industry, workmen's compensation legislation, the broadening of antitrust laws, the streamlining of judicial procedure, and complete publicity on campaign contributions.

While the convention was completing its business, Roosevelt spent two uneasy days trying to decide whether sufficient support would be forthcoming to justify a national third-party ticket. The cruel blow to his political and personal prestige generated a desire for revenge, but he did not dare succumb to it until Frank A. Munsey had promised the backing of his journalistic empire and George W. Perkins of the International Harvester trust had pledged his millions to the campaign.

Fortified by these indispensable assurances of support, Roosevelt convened a meeting of his bolting delegates the night of June 22. In another fiery speech he denounced his foes for stealing the nomination and contended that the party had forfeited the confidence of the people. Continuing in the vein of a crusader, he called for the organization of a new Progressive party that would enforce the commandment, "Thou shalt not steal." The delegates were urged to return home for a sounding of local opinion and to reconvene August 5 in order to launch the new party.

During the interval the prospects of success were diminished by the fact that the Democrats nominated Woodrow Wilson, an avowed Progressive, for the Presidency. This meant that the new party would be built on a hard core of midwestern farmers, equally hostile to the blanket low-tariff policy of the Democrats and the reciprocity scheme of the eastern Republicans, which favored industry at the expense of agriculture. Beyond this rebellious half of the old East-West Republican coalition, reliable sources of support were not visible. But Roosevelt, the perennial optimist, hoped to entice the bulk of the urban Progressives and social reformers by means of an elaborate social security program.

THE NEW PROGRESSIVE PARTY

The most fanatical segment of Roosevelt's following was well represented at the August 5 convention, which launched the Progressive or Bull Moose party. There was a religious air to the proceedings. "The Battle Hymn of the Republic" and "Onward, Christian Soldiers" were sung by the delegates at the slightest excuse. The keynote speech by former Senator Albert J. Beveridge and Roosevelt's speech accepting the nomination intensified the mood of apocalyptic zeal. The delegates were compared by the more lyrical and imaginative newspapermen to the Pilgrim Fathers, Cromwell's Covenanters, and the crusading army of Peter the Hermit. The only reformer who lacked the passionate demeanor and bone-crushing handshake of a crusader was Hiram Johnson, the Governor of California and vice-presidential nominee.

Since the new party was primarily the creation of Theodore Roosevelt, its platform necessarily gave expression to his redefinition of Progressivism, which ostensibly had caused the break with Taft. The plank on corporations repudiated the old remedy of trust-busting and proposed a federal administrative commission to regulate industrial corporations. A still more controversial plank called for a referendum that would enable the voters to override those decisions by state courts which invalidated state laws on social and economic questions. This was a rephrasing of Roosevelt's proposal for the recall of judicial decisions, which he had enunciated in the so-called Charter of Democracy Speech in February 1912, to the alarm of orthodox Progressives. He felt strongly on this question because the New York State Supreme Court in the Ives case had just declared a workmen's compensation law unconstitutional. This plank, sought to prevent a judicial veto of social and economic legislation that had been passed by the states in pursuit of their police powers. It seemed all the more important to maintain the effectiveness of the states on this point because constitutional authority to enact such laws rested with them rather than with the federal government. For this reason, among others, the platform did not propose the recall of either the judges or the decisions of the federal courts, as the opposition professed to believe.

With these exceptions, the platform advocated the same broad program as the Republican one; where additional differences occurred, they were matters of degree rather than of kind. The Progressive platform, for instance, had a more detailed listing of the reform measures for which it stood. It denounced the Payne-Aldrich tariff in an obvious bid for the support of western farmers, but like the Republican platform it endorsed the protective tariff as such.

REPERCUSSIONS OF THE REPUBLICAN SPLIT

Developments in the summer of 1912 marked not only the end of Republican ascendancy and of a spectacular political friendship, but the end of an era. On the eve of its greatest triumph at the polls, Progressivism, as it had been known for ten years, was dying. Perhaps the formidable new problems of the opening twentieth century could not be solved by the purification and restoration of traditional institutions. Only the comforting insistence of Progressivism that the disintegration of treasured social, political, and economic landmarks could be arrested had been strong enough to stimulate some genuinely unselfish cooperation between groups that possessed selfish objectives. The honeymoon was bound to end. Much of the enthusiasm of the Bull Moosers stemmed from an unconscious ennoblement and rationalization of their economic appetites. With a kind of childlike guilelessness, they considered justice and equality of opportunity to be the same as the satisfaction of their economic objectives. This led eventually to disillusionment as they discovered that there were several definitions of justice, often incompatible.

Like all movements which operate at the idealistic level, Progressivism found it hard to draw up a profit and loss statement at the end of each day's work. The elimination of boss government, the dissolution of trusts, and the conservation of national resources did not produce lower prices for consumer goods or reduced costs of government. The warriors of Progressivism never reached Valhalla because clean government, conservation, and the preservation of equal opportunity required continuous vigilance rather than a single titanic battle that would destroy the forces of darkness once and for all. The genuine Progressives were willing to continue the crusade to preserve the gains they had made. The rest lacked the patience to fight a perpetual war for ideals; so they kept the Progressive label but pursued their interests.

In the process, the rebels wrecked the Republican party. Some drifted over to the Democrats. Their successful infiltration of the latter organization was easy because original Progressive principles had never taken firm root. Besides, the Democrats had been out of power since 1896, and hence did not have the embarrassment of a Progressive record to defend. Under the circumstances they could accommodate the various pressure groups with less friction than the Republicans. After 1912, sponsorship of the larger, rebel wing of the Progressive movement passed to the Democrats.

SUGGESTED READINGS

1. Bowers, C., *Beveridge and the Progressive Era.*
2. Croly, H., *The Promise of American Life.*
3. Mowry, G. E., *Roosevelt and the Progressives.*
4. Pringle, H. F., *The Life and Times of William Howard Taft* (2 vols.).

CHAPTER SEVEN

WOODROW WILSON AND THE "NEW FREEDOM"

THE RISE OF WOODROW WILSON

Election of a Democratic President for the first time since 1892 was virtually assured by the split in the Republican party. Moreover, the victory of Democratic governors and senators in several pivotal states east of the Mississippi in 1910 had given the party sufficient presidential timber to end its reliance on Bryan. The most hopeful candidates were three governors, Judson Harmon of Ohio, Thomas R. Marshall of Indiana, and Woodrow Wilson of New Jersey; one congressman, Oscar W. Underwood of Alabama; and the Speaker of the House of Representatives, Champ Clark. Although the selection of a dark-horse candidate was a distinct possibility in Democratic conventions, where a two-thirds majority rule often produced a deadlock, the race soon narrowed down to Clark and Wilson.

Their contest was complicated by the growing strength of Progressivism in the party. Speaker Clark did not take a clean-cut stand on current issues but he received the support of the older Democrats and the urban bosses, who regarded him as an unimaginative, reliable party wheelhorse. Governor Wilson, by contrast, represented the steadily growing Progressive faction. His career, indeed, resembled that of the improbable heroes of Winston Churchill's political novels. Like Taft, he entered the White House with little experience in the art of practical politics. Until he was suddenly catapulted onto the national stage by his spectacular victory in the New Jersey gubernatorial election of 1910, most Americans had never even heard of him. He had done nothing for the reform movement in his own state. He had not worked for the local organization which nominated him for governor and had shown such indifference that there was some question whether he had bothered to vote in the 1908 election.

This relatively obscure citizen was born in Staunton, Virginia, 1856. His father, the Reverend Joseph Ruggles Wilson, was a devout, conscientious Presbyterian minister, who passed on to young Woodrow both the attractive and the repellent characteristics of the Calvinist faith. As fixed elements of personality they proved to be a double-edged sword. The line separating perseverance from stubbornness, conviction from arrogance, and idealism from dogmatism was always thin and uncertain in Wilson.

He received a liberal education at Princeton University, studied law at the University of Virginia, and hung out his shingle in Atlanta, Georgia. His temperament was not suited to the legal profession, and he abandoned it almost immediately to prepare himself for a teaching career by enrolling at the Johns Hopkins University, where he earned a Ph.D. degree (1879).

After completing his graduate work, he held two minor teaching posts before returning to Princeton as Professor of History and Government in 1890. In the meantime he had won his academic spurs by writing a memorable thesis on *Congressional Government*. In it he analyzed the defects of congressional procedure so lucidly that the book went through many editions. Other competent volumes followed, although none of them attracted as much attention as the first. Had his talents been limited to teaching and scholarly research, he would probably have remained a college professor, but his outstanding ability as a public speaker introduced him to wider fields. He showed an instinct for clear and stimulating presentation of ideas and developed for illustrative purposes a vast repertoire of witty dialect stories and of jingles. He was greatly in demand as an after-dinner speaker for academic, business, and social groups. In this capacity he quickly extended his contacts and was elevated to the presidency of Princeton in 1901.

His administration at Princeton started off well enough, as was subsequently the case with both the governorship of New Jersey and the presidency of the United States. He won almost unanimous applause for instituting a preceptorial system which reduced the size of classes and brought students into more intimate contact with the faculty. Unfortunately his autocratic spirit and inflexibility soon brought him into an epic dispute with Dean Andrew F. West over the development and location of the graduate school. He also alienated many alumni by trying to abolish the social fraternities or "eating clubs" as they are called at Princeton. He was on the verge of being forced to sever his connection with the university when the boss of the corrupt New Jersey Democratic party, former Senator James Smith, Jr., offered to support him for governor.

The idea of launching the middle-aged educator on a political career had occurred first to Colonel George Harvey, publisher of *Harper's Weekly* and close associate of powerful businessmen in the party. What attracted Harvey to Wilson was the latter's eloquent and disarming defense of middle-class interests. His speeches seldom strayed from the path of political and economic orthodoxy. Even his original objection to Princeton's eating clubs was based on the fact that they contaminated the academic atmosphere rather than that they were undemocratic. As early as 1906 Harvey had come to regard him as the white hope of businessmen who disapproved

A leader at last. (The Minneapolis Journal, *1913.*)

of Roosevelt, and the publisher had begun to boom him for the Presidency.

During the summer of 1910 Harvey decided that the governorship of New Jersey would provide an excellent springboard to the higher office. Boss Smith cooperated enthusiastically because his candidates had not won a state-wide election in eighteen years, and he needed a victory to retain his grip on the party organization. Wilson looked more like a winner than anyone in the Democratic stable; so Smith passed the word along to his well-disciplined delegates at the Trenton convention in September 1910. Over the opposition of outraged Progressive Democrats, Wilson was nominated by a typical political machine. For a rookie politician, he waged an unusually effective campaign. He made vigorous attacks on the bosses who had nominated him, but they refused to be alarmed by what they regarded as a good political trick.

They received a rude and unexpected awakening as soon as he had been elected. Not only did he block Smith's effort to return to the Senate, but he used his patronage power to smash the machine and push a series of Progressive measures through the legislature. Overnight New Jersey was turned into a model Progressive state. A direct primary law, an employers' liability act, and a measure establishing a public utilities commission received quick legislative approval in 1911. Wilson even secured revision of the notoriously lax New Jersey laws governing the chartering of corporations, which had made the state famous as "the mother of trusts." This burst of reforming zeal stunned his conservative mentors. The platitudes that sounded so harmless in his after-dinner speeches had left them unprepared for his political program. It was not so much that he had deliberately misled them as that they had failed to anticipate the reaction of an honest but politically naïve educator, withdrawn suddenly from his world of neat abstractions and syllogisms. This performance had made Wilson a full-fledged Progressive.

George Harvey terminated his campaign for Wilson in December 1911, when the Governor indicated that the support of a journal as close to Wall Street as *Harper's Weekly* was damaging his presidential prospects in the West. Harvey did not immediately join the opposition camp, but some of his friends regarded Wilson as a kind of Frankenstein who had broken out of the control of his creators. During the winter of 1912 they launched a systematic newspaper campaign to discredit him. He was criticized for ingratitude to his political supporters and for using his office as a "traveling scholarship" to further his presidential ambitions. The opposition delivered a more damaging blow when the hostile *New York Sun* published a 1908 letter from Wilson to Adrian Joline, a Princeton trustee, expressing the hope that Bryan would be "knocked into a cocked hat." The barrage did some damage to Wilson but not enough to stop him. He had captured the popular imagination by his dramatic fight against the bosses and by his steady orientation toward Progressivism, which became more apparent every month. The attacks of eastern newspapers responsive to big business interests strengthened his reputation as a reformer at a time when such a reputation was a solid asset. Even Bryan forgave him the indiscretion of 1908 and welcomed him into the fraternity of Progressive Democrats.

THE CAMPAIGN OF 1912

When the Democratic convention met at Baltimore on June 25, 1912, Wilson was stronger with the voters than with the delegates. Out of a total of 1,088 delegates only 248 were pledged to him, whereas more than four hundred, including Bryan, were pledged to Clark. As at the Republican convention, the selection of a temporary chairman provoked the first test of factional strength. Bryan challenged Judge Parker, the choice of the National Committee, and was beaten 579 to 510. This vote did not provide a true measure of Progressive strength, because a number of Democrats were anti-Bryan rather than anti-Progressive. With some reason, they feared that Bryan had executed the maneuver and had introduced a resolution to expel the Tammany Hall delegates, representing big business interests, because he hoped to turn a deadlock into his fourth nomination for President. Whatever his real motives, Bryan did produce an inpasse on the second day of balloting by deserting Clark for Wilson when the ninety Tammany delegates switched from Harmon to Clark. Thenceforward it was impossible for Clark to secure the two-thirds vote necessary for nomination. Although his strength slowly dwindled, it took four more days and forty-six ballots to swing the convention to Wilson. By this time most of the delegates were eager to go home and agreed quickly to the nomination of Governor Thomas R. Marshall of Indiana as Vice-President.

The platform contained all the orthodox Progressive proposals. It would have been hard to differentiate it from the Republican platform but for the planks advocating downward revision of the tariff, presidential preference primaries, and limitation of the Presidency to a single term. The official adoption of a Progressive program guaranteed the triumph of the reform movement regardless of which candidate won. In fact, the Democrats had become converted to Progressivism just in time to preside over the redefinition that killed it.

The fall campaign was something of an anticlimax after the exciting preconvention warfare. The voters' almost unbounded enthusiasm for political activity had been dulled by continuous volleys of oratory since January. No amount of verbal pyrotechnics could cast any fresh light on either the personal or the political aspects of the Roosevelt-Taft feud. Even Roosevelt sensed the exhaustion of the electorate, because he began to respond to questions about Taft with the laconic reply, "I don't discuss dead issues." The only novel personality was Woodrow Wilson, whose views had hitherto commanded the attention of a narrower audience. He did little to convince the voters that there was any reason for the Progressives to be divided into more than two camps. Except for routine references to Democratic heroes of the past and a demand for a low tariff, his statements resembled those of Taft.

Although Wilson expressed thoughts clearly, his thoughts were not always clear. His tendency to develop ideals in a manner that did not place much reliance on consistency proved particularly noticeable because he was going through a transition from the defense of the old-style Progressivism to a kind of Democratic version of the "New Nationalism" which he called the "New Freedom." In a series of speeches devoted to a description of the "New Freedom" he repeatedly expressed the philosophical view that institutions evolved and that the old principles did not fit present problems. Such statements were at war with the more concrete Wilsonian assertions that the Democrats would dissolve unfair monopolistic combinations, clean up government, and undo the evolutionary changes in our institutions. Later his legislative program was to make clear his affinity for the concept of a positive government envisioned by Roosevelt in the "New Nationalism" rather than for the concept of limited government on which he campaigned. What he really wanted in 1912 was change — but not very much change. Thus he occupied a political position which was attractive from the standpoint of getting elected but hardly from the standpoint of constructing a logical and consistent line of thought.

Translated into practical terms, the confusion enabled him to reach partial agreement and partial disagreement with both his opponents. Like Roosevelt but unlike Taft, he thought the corporation had become a permanent feature of the economic landscape. Like Taft but unlike Roosevelt, he proposed to destroy this feature if it grew too large or broke the law. Elsewhere he had to work harder to find a distinctive interpretation of the Progressive credo. He came out flatly for a low tariff and a Jeffersonian decentralization of authority; the tariff, however, was a matter of sectional economics upon which Progressives had never agreed, and states' rights was the perennial theme of the party out of power. Most of the issues he raised were good politics and could be justified as such. Unfortunately, he always made his appeals for action on the basis of principle, creating for himself all the political problems which such a procedure was bound to produce.

The only question to be settled in the November election was the size of the Democratic victory, and the answer depended on the ability of Roosevelt's new sectional Progressive party to win the support of the businessmen and industrial workers of the East. Substantial success would have meant the reintegration of the old Republican East-West coalition under a new name. Roosevelt was especially optimistic about the labor vote because Taft, with characteristic ineptness, had alienated Samuel Gompers, president of the A. F. of L., and had thus picked up an undeserved reputation for hostility to labor. The Progressive platform sought to capitalize on this situation by advocating an elaborate legislative program for the workers.

The election returns demonstrated anew the difficulty of launching a successful third party and the unwillingness of the East to accept Roosevelt's leadership so long as he was the spokesman of midwestern agriculture. Roosevelt got 4,100,000 popular votes and 88 electoral votes. He ran strongest in the wheat and dairy states opposed to Canadian reciprocity, carrying Michigan, Minnesota, Pennsylvania, and South Dakota, and making a good showing in Wisconsin, North Dakota, and upstate New York. Elsewhere, except for the Pacific coast, where he carried California and Washington, the voters deserted Roosevelt. The business interests gave him little support, and he did not get enough labor votes to affect the outcome in the East.

Taft carried only two states, with eight electoral votes; but received a popular vote of 3,400,000. Had either of the former friends been willing and able to deliver his supporters to the other, the Republicans would have won by just over 50 per cent of the ballots cast. As it was, the Republican split enabled Wilson to win 40 states and 435 electoral votes with only 6,300,00 popular votes, or 42 per cent of the total. Eugene V. Debs, the Socialist candidate, got most of the remaining 8 per cent.

THE WILSON ADMINISTRATION AND ITS OPPORTUNITIES

The inauguration of Woodrow Wilson, on March 4, 1913, launched the final phase of Progressivism. Within a year and a half, a docile Congress was to complete virtually all the unfinished business left over from the Roosevelt and Taft regimes. At least a dozen major objectives of the reform movement won legislative approval — most of them from the Sixty-third Congress, which sat without serious interruption from April 1913 to October 1914. Never before, except in wartime, had executive leadership emerged so aggressively or the legislative mill ground out laws so rapidly.

This extraordinary situation was produced by a combination of circumstances. A decade of ceaseless agitation for Progressivism, capped by the conversion of the three major parties to its principles in the 1912 campaign, deprived the opposition of an organized following and of respectability. The public mood for action was whetted by the investigations of the Pujo Committee, a subcommittee of the House Banking and Currency Committee, which made headlines by exposing the tremendous concentration of financial power and credit in the hands of a few investment bankers. On the eve of Wilson's inauguration, the Pujo Committee was extracting from George F. Baker, the chairman of the First National Bank of New York, a description of interlocking directorates and techniques for corporate merger, as well as the ruinous admission that no enterprise could succeed without the confidence of J. P. Morgan and his associates.

Simultaneously the necessary states ratified the Sixteenth Amendment to the Constitution, authorizing the levy of an income tax, and the Seventeenth Amendment, providing for the direct election of United States Senators. The incorporation of these key Progressive principles into the Constitution created a robust optimism about the fulfillment of other objectives, since the amending process was a difficult one and had not been successfully employed since the Reconstruction period.

The task of translating public opinion into legislation was simplified by the willingness of the Democratic majorities in both houses of Congress to accept presidential leadership. The fact that the party had been out of power for sixteen years paved the way for a genuine "honeymoon period" between the Executive and the Congress until all the jobs had been distributed. An equally compelling reason for cooperation was that the Democrats had taken office as a minority and needed to compile an impressive legislative record in order to retain power four years later. Moreover, a number of the 290 Democrats in the House came from districts that would not have elected them but for the Taft-Roosevelt split. They were almost certain to lose in 1914 if the Republican opposition reunited. This possibility of short tenure as congressmen made it easier for marginal Democrats to defy the economic pressure groups of their own districts and to support Wilson. They had little to lose by cooperation and might be appointed to federal judgeships or other desirable political offices by a grateful President.

A final factor in the extraordinary legislative success of the Democrats was the type of guidance offered by President Wilson. As a professor of political science he had always praised the British form of government.

He preferred the parliamentary system, which vested both executive and legislative authority in the leadership of the majority party in the legislature, to the American presidential system. In fact, he liked to think of himself as a sort of American prime minister who would overcome the separation of powers despite the constitutional provisions obstructing a union of functions.

Whatever the shortcomings of the British system or the barriers to its application here, Wilson did the best he could to function both as executive and as leader of the legislature. He delivered his messages to Congress in person, reviving a practice which had been in disuse since the time of Thomas Jefferson. He used vigorously every weapon at his disposal to enforce party discipline. This novel interpretation of presidential functions was later to expose him to charges of dictatorship and executive usurpation, but in 1913 it produced results without provoking effective criticism. He showed great ability in converting public enthusiasm for Progressivism into pressure on Congress. Using his gift for framing issues appealingly, he often broke legislative obstruction by direct appeals to the people.

As important to success as his concept of leadership was his realistic decision to place his program in the hands of the party wheelhorses rather than obscure politicians carried to sudden fame by the Progressive tidal wave. He adopted this policy partly on the advice of Colonel E. M. House, a practical Texas politician who emerged as his confidential adviser and a sort of minister without portfolio in the administration. House's adroit political touch could be detected in the selection of Wilson's Cabinet, which was balanced with due regard for party seniority, geography, and sectional economic interests.

William Jennings Bryan, the Democrat with the oldest following and the most intimate knowledge of internal party politics, became Secretary of State. The South received adequate representation and attention to its patronage requirements when Josephus Daniels, a North Carolina newspaper editor, was appointed Secretary of the Navy; Congressman Albert S. Burleson of Texas, Postmaster General; and David F. Houston of the same state, Secretary of Agriculture. The border states were recognized in the selection of James C. McReynolds of Tennessee as Attorney General. As usual, the populous Northeast placed several men: William G. McAdoo, Secretary of the Treasury; W. C. Redfield, Secretary of Commerce; and Lindley M. Garrison, Secretary of War. The Department of the Interior went to a westerner, Franklin K. Lane of California. Organized labor received specific representation when the President chose Representative William B. Wilson, a former official of the miners' union, to be Secretary of Labor.

WILSON'S LEGISLATIVE PROGRAM

The first job Wilson assigned Congress was to give that venerable political football, the protective tariff, a good healthy kick. By arguing that the tariff sheltered trusts, Progressives had adroitly concealed the sectional malice that underlay all discussions of it. This had led them to advocate downward revision for items which their particular area consumed and to insist upon continued high protection for items which their particular area produced. Growing interest in overseas markets had, however, helped to bring about a reorientation in public thinking. The Republicans — who advocated both high tariff rates and expansion overseas — found it increasingly difficult to contend that American manufactured goods could compete successfully in foreign markets but could not compete successfully in the home market without protection. Logic also cast doubt on the argument that tariffs could be framed scientifically to compensate for the differences in the cost of foreign and of domestic production, when the cost of production varied from year to year and from business to business. Such considerations did not convert rank-and-file Americans into advocates of free trade, because McKinley had done too effective a job of selling the idea that prosperity depended on the tariff. On the other hand, it did produce a genuine sentiment for reduced rates, and upon this Wilson intended to capitalize. The chief danger to general downward revision was the usual congressional practice of logrolling, or trading votes for the protection of pet items. States like North Carolina and Louisiana even threatened to breach the traditional low-tariff southern bloc, because their increasing diversification gave them industries and raw materials to protect.

The administration bill sailed through the House of Representatives under the direction of Oscar W. Underwood, chairman of the Ways and Means Committee, whose tactics in silencing critics were worthy of old Joe Cannon himself. In the Senate the Democratic majority was smaller and the pressure for logrolling greater. Party discipline threatened to break, until Wilson combined the patronage weapon with a great appeal for public support against the lobbyists and special interest groups. Eventually the Underwood-Simmons tariff cleared Congress in substantially the form demanded by the President. The over-all reduction in rates was approximately 10 per cent, but more important was the fact that the law imposed the highest cuts on items constantly used by consumers. Many food products were placed on the free list, along with lumber, paper, raw wool, shoes, and iron ore. The few items singled out for boosts were either luxury goods or products of infant industries.

Historians are so fond of pointing out that the Underwood-Simmons Act was the first general tariff reduction since 1857, that they often fail to stress the retention of the protective principle. Duties on the thousand-odd protected items still averaged 27 per cent. Economists, with a variety of theories, hoped to make accurate measurements of the effect of lower rates on manufacturing and trade, but as usual their analysis was disturbed by a variable — in this case, World War I. Republicans did not attempt to judge the reduction by such detached standards. They proclaimed that it would destroy prosperity — and business conditions obligingly deteriorated in 1913 and 1914, before European war orders intervened to restore prosperity. The data on the economic effects of the tariff were inconclusive, as in the past.

To counterbalance the expected loss of revenue from the reduction of tariff rates, a graduated income tax was incorporated in the Act. Authorized by the recently ratified Sixteenth Amendment, the initial rates were modest. Unmarried citizens making less than $3,000 a year and married citizens making less than $4,000 a year escaped entirely. Those with higher incomes were subject to a normal tax of one per cent and graduated surtaxes which reached a maximum of six per cent on income in excess of $500,000. The revenue raised from the tax was inconsiderable.

Wilson did not permit the special session to end after the passage of the tariff bill but kept Congress at work on monetary legislation until action was completed on the Federal Reserve Act, December 13, 1913. Congress had recognized the necessity for overhauling the financial system of the country when it set up the National Monetary Commission under the chairmanship of Senator Aldrich after the Panic of 1907. The Commission held hearings for four years and studied banking systems outside the United States. It made some valuable recommendations that found their way into the final law despite Progressive suspicions of anything bearing Aldrich's approval.

Most of the problems tackled by the Monetary Commission grew out of the fact that the United States government possessed no effective system for regulating the volume of currency in circulation. Every autumn money was in short supply, and interest rates were high when farmers needed loans to tide them over until crops had been marketed. During other seasons money piled up in banks and frequently became concentrated in financial areas where it was used for speculation. This not only aroused agrarian wrath but, to make matters worse, the average bank experienced considerable difficulty in mobilizing reserves during periods of recession or panic. Either the bank was able to call in loans, which often ruined borrowers and their businesses, or else it was forced to close its doors, which ruined depositors. This unhappy situation developed partly because the reserve system under the old National Bank Act of 1863 never really operated to make funds available for banks that were experiencing runs. Furthermore, the system made no distinction between long-term investments and short-term commercial loans, with the result that an individual institution seldom concentrated on the type of operation it was best suited for.

The most promising solution for these problems appeared to be a central bank which would expand or contract the currency in accordance with the needs of the economy and assist individual banks in mobilizing liquid resources during periods of crisis. As a matter of fact, the Commission advocated a central banking association under the control of private bankers. This proposal seemed like a grim sort of joke to farmers, who had been trained to hate central banks since the time of Andrew Jackson. It was also unacceptable to urban Progressives, who distrusted the concentration of financial power as a source of special privilege and had found striking confirmation of their fears in the findings of the Pujo Committee.

The great problem for Wilson lay in devising a central bank that would not be under the control of New York financiers and would not open the administration to effective charges of trying to socialize the banking system. The bill introduced by Carter Glass, chairman of the House Banking and Currency Committee, went a long way toward meeting the wishes of bankers although they disliked government supervision as a matter of principle. The Senate version, introduced by Robert L. Owen, who headed the corresponding committee in the upper chamber, pleased Bryan and the western farmers.

The compromise law that emerged was far better than the usual product of congressional horse trading. A single central bank was avoided, but the essence of centralization was achieved by setting up a Federal Reserve Bank in Washington which coordinated the activities of twelve semiautonomous regional Federal Reserve Banks. The public character of the new system was partly diluted and partly concealed by a series of ingenious devices. The Central Bank became an independent government agency, although political considerations were allowed to intrude in the selection of its members. The latter consisted of the Secretary of the Treasury, the Comptroller of the Currency, and five other members appointed by the President with the consent of the Senate for terms of ten years. The Regional Banks also had governing boards, but the method of appointment left the members under less pressure and control from the government. Of the nine directors on each regional board, only three were selected by the Central Board, and the other six were selected by the member banks — private institutions. The most reassuring concession to the financial groups was the provision that the stock of the Federal Reserve Banks should be wholly owned by the private member banks. The agrarian opponents of centralized power over credit took some comfort from the fact that the large reserves which the law required the member banks to deposit in the Federal Reserve Banks would not move in speculative channels.

If the structure resulting from this series of reciprocal compromises reflected any principle, it was the division of powers. The authority over the banking system seemed to be divided between the Central Federal Reserve Board and the twelve Regional Banks, just as political authority was divided between the federal government and the states. The twelve Banks received enough powers to exercise substantial influence on money and credit. They could buy high-grade commercial paper and government securities from banks that joined the system. Payment was to be made in Federal Reserve notes, a new type of currency redeemable in gold and established both as legal tender and as a direct obligation of the United States government. By feeding the new currency into the financial system, the Federal Reserve Banks enabled a member bank to meet sudden demands for cash. Stated simply, the Federal Reserve Banks accepted the high-grade commercial paper or securities which customers had turned over to a member bank as collateral for loans and issued to it Federal Reserve notes in return.

Such a procedure is known as rediscounting. It became one of the devices for making the currency more flexible, because the Federal Reserve Banks were granted the authority to change the rate or fee for the service within certain limits. A lowering of the rate tended to expand borrowing and note-issues, while a raising of the rate tended to produce the opposite effect. Even if the rate remained untouched, the routine operations of the Federal Reserve System guaranteed a kind of automatic expansion and contraction of the currency. During periods of prosperity commercial paper of various types became more plentiful and accumulated in the Banks. There it provided the base for the issuance of an increased volume of Federal Reserve notes and for further credit expansion. Conversely, when business activity declined, less commercial paper flowed through the banking channels and fewer notes circulated. The only statutory check on the elasticity of the new notes was the requirement for the maintenance of a 40 per cent gold reserve.

Before turning to a discussion of the powers of the Central Board, it is worth while to note that the twelve Banks did not accept the accounts of individual citizens. They served primarily as the depository of member banks. Included in the latter category were all national banks plus the state banks and trust companies willing to purchase the stock of the Federal Reserve Banks and accept their standards for conducting business.

One additional service provided by the Banks was to act as the financial agent of the United States government and the custodian of its funds. The assumption of this function foreshadowed the abolition of the independent treasury system, which had featured an inconvenient dispersal of government funds.

Under the Federal Reserve Act most of the initiative in day-to-day policy decisions rested with the boards of the twelve Regional Banks. The primary function of the Central Board in Washington was to enforce honest operational standards and to review bank policies. It possessed wide inquisitorial authority, being empowered to examine the books of Federal Reserve Banks, to remove ineffective or dishonest bank officials, and in exceptional cases to close banks temporarily. The Central Board was also vested with power to review and modify the rates fixed by the Banks. This power became increasingly important after World War I, when the federal government engaged in more ambitious efforts to control the business cycle.

The Federal Reserve Act corrected a number of flaws in the American banking system and partially fulfilled the Progressive desire to curb the so-called "money trust." Its greatest immediate service was to provide a suitable agency for financing American participation in World War I, although this development could hardly have been anticipated in 1913.

From a number of other standpoints, however, the Act fell short of expectations. By making the membership of state banks in the system optional, it permitted many small and poorly managed banks to operate without supervision. In fact, twice as many state banks remained outside the system as entered it. Even membership was no guarantee of solvency and good management, because the Central Board lacked the authority to enforce uniform practices. Worst of all, the Act failed to require the separation of commercial and investment banking. The cumulative effect of these omissions was the catastrophic series of bank failures in the Great Depression from 1929 to 1933. No one could have been expected, however, to forsee all the interim developments.

Dearer to the hearts of old-style Progressives than either the tariff or currency legislation were the special recommendations which Wilson made to an overworked Congress on January 20, 1914, for dealing with the perennial problem of monopoly. Despite widespread enthusiasm for a strengthening of the Sherman Antitrust Law, nearly eight months of legislative maneuvering and debate followed. Opponents pointed to the deepening economic recession as evidence that the Wilson program was dangerous and unsound. When the huge Clafin Dry Goods Company failed in midsummer of 1914, they blamed the Federal Reserve Act and predicted that still more bankruptcies would follow the enactment of a new antitrust law. Businessmen bombarded Congress with circular letters protesting against the impending legislation. Their campaign reached such formidable proportions that Wilson denounced it as a conspiracy to create a psychological depression. Eventually Congress approved a pair of complementary measures: the Federal Trade Commission Act in September 1914, and the Clayton Antitrust Act in October 1914. These embodied most of Wilson's recommendations.

The Clayton Antitrust Act reflected the original Progressive conviction, which had again been enunciated by Taft and Wilson in 1912, that the power of monopoly could be broken by legislation. The law attempted to ban all the devices and techniques which had been used by businessmen to centralize economic control without explicitly involving them in a violation of the Sherman Act. Drawing heavily on the findings of the Pujo Committee, the Clayton Act outlawed interlocking directorates in banks and industrial corporations, spelling out in detail what constituted violations. For example, no individual could be a director of more than one corporation if such responsibilities involved competing firms or if a single corporation possessed capital, surplus, and undivided profits of more than a million dollars. The Act also prohibited price discrimination, special trade agreements, and other practices "designed to lessen competition." It tried to discourage violations by making the individual, as well as the corporation, subject to suit and criminal penalties. Where the Sherman Act restricted prosecution to cases involving clear proof of conspiracy or monopoly, the Clayton Act envisaged automatic prosecution for all practices specified as illegal.

Most of the provisions in the Clayton Act aimed at the complete destruction of the "money trust." In this context it could be considered a supplement to the Federal Reserve Act. Sections 6 and 20 attempted to remove what Wilson and Progressives of all persuasions deemed to be unfair burdens on labor. Section 6 stated that labor and agricultural unions were not illegal organizations to restrain trade. Samuel Gompers hailed this provision as labor's Magna Charta, because he thought it exempted labor unions from prosecution under the antitrust laws. He took particular comfort from the explicit recognition of laborers' rights to strike and picket peacefully, provided they used lawful and orderly methods to pursue their objectives. His enthusiasm proved to be premature. Representative C. C. Carlin, who had helped to write Section 6, said it simply safeguarded unions from being prosecuted for existing but did not give them immunity from prosecution for restraint of trade. Subsequent Supreme Court decisions accepted Carlin's interpretation of legislative intent and stripped trade unions of the protection they thought they had secured.

The benefits of Section 20, which sought to curtail the use of injunctions in labor disputes, also evaporated through judicial interpretation. The key clauses amounted to little more than a redraft of Taft's proposals, which an uncooperative Congress had failed to pass. Now it was stipulated that federal judges were not to grant such injunctions unless industrial warfare threatened irreparable damage to property. Contempt cases were not to be tried without a jury unless the contempt had been committed in court.

The Federal Trade Commission Act, which cleared Congress a month before the Clayton Act, was Wilson's tacit admission that "busted" trusts failed to stay busted and instead needed perpetual supervision. Congress granted the Federal Trade Commission extensive inquisitorial and regulative powers. It could not only compile information concerning the organization and business practices of corporations engaged in interstate commerce, but it could investigate the manner in which violators of antitrust laws carried out court decrees. On its own initiative, the Commission could issue orders requiring corporations to refrain from procedures it deemed unfair or contrary to law.

Some limits were placed on the power of the Commission, doubtless to ease the conscience of those Progressives who disliked the growth of central bureaucracy and had condemned Roosevelt for advocating it. Commission orders were made subject to court review, and it possessed no power to punish violators. The penalty clauses appeared in the Clayton Act, indicating that Congress hoped the Commission would limit its activities to fact-finding and exposure. The structure of the Commission followed that of other independent agencies. It was composed of five members appointed for overlapping terms of seven years on a bipartisan basis by the President with the consent of the Senate.

The legislation of 1914 did not solve the trust problem. What it did was to set up dual machinery that successive administrations could employ either to regulate the trusts or to dissolve them. The Federal Trade Commission provided a weapon for making the industrial giants behave, and the Clayton Act strengthened the procedures for achieving their formal extinction. After World War I both policies were pursued, sometimes simultaneously. Needless to say, recent generations have been less optimistic than the Progressives that the great corporations can actually be broken into competitive units, or that government commissions can police business without directing it. Consequently the modern integrated corporation, like a weather vane, has been blown in a new direction by every shift in the election wind.

The passage of the Underwood-Simmons Tariff Act marked the completion of the unfinished business of the older Progressivism. Both measures fundamentally represented the older idea of eliminating special privilege. On the other hand, when Wilson found it necessary to supplement the safeguard against a privileged status for big business by means of a supervisory Federal Trade Commission, he was abandoning the older principles and adopting the new idea of positive government. Implicit in Wilson's policy was the belief that the original program had failed and that the values of the older society could not be restored. However, by refusing to spell out this admission, he got people to support specific measures under the impression that they were still backing Progressivism.

Roosevelt was forced, unfortunately for himself, to work through the party that had sponsored the original Progressivism and had split over the difficulty of accommodating the old principles to the new ideas. Wilson faced no such problem. Both he and his party had adopted Progressivism at the eleventh hour, a fact which made their acceptance of redefinition simpler. Moreover, the Democrats had not held power long enough to develop the sectional antipathies which complicated the problems of transition for Roosevelt. In fact, the Democrats did not possess a following of eastern businessmen with sectional economic objections to a legislative program for distressed agrarian and labor pressure groups. Such measures could be passed by a combination of southern and western congressmen, who could be generous to farmers because they came from farm districts and generous to workers because labor legislation would have little effect on their own areas.

Wilson was happy to take advantage of this situation. His acceptance of the Progressive credo had been somewhat superficial because its emphasis on fixed values conflicted with his faith in progressive evolution. His status as a minority President, who needed the support of new economic groups in the impending election, reinforced his enthusiasm for championing underprivileged groups. A most conspicuous example of the new policy was the Federal Farm Loan Act, which went beyond the general measures to ease the flow of credit in the Federal Reserve Act and established special terms for agriculture. The desire of farmers for cheap credit and the unwillingness of bankers to grant it had always been a feature of American economic history. Generally speaking, financial institutions hesitated to load their portfolios with farm mortgages, because such assets could not be mobilized quickly in time of emergency. They took a very dim view of long-term loans with amortization features that allowed the farmers to pay interest and fractions of the principle simultaneously. Such a system was particularly unsuited to banks with limited resources, which could not profitably reinvest the small driblets of principle that came in from year to year over a long period of time. Inevitably when the smaller country banks took farm mortgages they tried to safeguard their investments by limiting loans to a three- or five-year period and charging rates of interest varying from 6 to 8½ per cent. An estimated $3.5 billion were tied up in farm mortgages in 1916 but practically none of the contracts for repayment included an amortization plan.

The suspicions of the farmers made it only natural for them to believe that a sinister design for exploitation explained the cautious behavior of the bankers. Currency inflation, which was the rural formula for cheap credit, had been rejected so decisively in the Populist era that farmers saw the necessity for adopting a more orthodox financial scheme. The Federal Farm Loan Act, which received congressional approval by top-heavy majorities and was given Wilson's signature on July 17, 1916, was a by-product of this shift in strategy. It sought to establish a government-supported system of farm banks that would reduce interest rates on mortgages and lengthen the period of repayment without abandoning the sound business methods of ordinary banks.

To set up machinery capable of administering loans and insuring the solvency of these farm credit institutions, Congress had ground out a law of twenty-five pages and thirty-five sections. Despite the complexity of its financial arrangements and operations, it provided a relatively simple structure. It established twelve regional Land Banks, each of which was required to start operations with a minimum capital of $750,000. In the event that private investors refused to furnish the entire amount, the government was to make up the deficiency.

The Land Banks did not lend money directly to farmers but to cooperative farm-loan associations composed of as few as ten farmers who wanted to borrow. Mortgage contracts on real estate, after clearing the local farm-loan association, were forwarded to the Land Bank, which reviewed the character and economic prospects of the applicant before granting the loan.

A responsible attitude on the part of farmers composing the local association was encouraged by the provision requiring the borrower to invest five per cent of the face value of his loan in stock of the Land Bank. This gave him a stake in the enterprise and an opportunity to share in the profits. It also increased the capital of the Land Banks. Their greatest source of additional funds came from the sale of tax-exempt bonds secured by the mortgages in the portfolios of the Land Banks. A large degree of uniformity of Land Bank policy was assured by a legislative provision for a five-man Federal Loan Board with supervisory powers. Private investors were not entirely reassured by the businesslike arrangements of the system, and the government had to subscribe about 95 per cent of the initial stock issue. Nevertheless the conservative administration of the Land Banks during the 1920's eventually coaxed private investors into purchasing all the stock originally held by the government.

Any government credit institution operated on a sound financial basis was bound to fall short of fulfilling the demands of the many farmers who wanted unsecured loans that no solvent institution could grant. So the Federal Farm Loan Act did not provide any permanent solution to the problem of long-term farm credit. It merely whetted rural appetites for an extension of the system on a basis that would make it a subsidy rather than a loan.

The administration did not exhaust its benevolence toward the farmer with credit legislation. The services of the Department of Agriculture were extended, uniform standards were established for the grading of staple crops, and federal funds were made available to supplement state funds for road building under the Highway Act of 1916. Still more important in terms of long-range consequences was the Agricultural Extension Act of 1914, which provided two agents for each of 2,850 rural counties, to instruct and assist farmers in developing better production methods. The county-agent system became the foundation upon which local farm organizations were built and ultimately expanded into powerful pressure groups.

Organized labor, with Samuel Gompers as its principal spokesman at the White House, demanded and received legislative favors beyond the removal of legal disabilities on unions already covered by the Clayton Act. Most of these concerned only categories of workers operating under special disadvantages, because Gompers was committed to the proposition that labor in general should extract concessions from management by its own efforts rather than through government help.

The first of these categories was covered by the La Follette Seamen's Act of 1915. This set up standards designed to protect American merchant sailors from substandard working conditions and degrading forms of discipline at sea. A subsidiary effect of these improvements was to make the cost of employing American merchant crewmen so high that native shipping lines could not afford their services without a government subsidy.

A second category inspired the Keating-Owen Act (1916) which sought to outlaw child labor. Inasmuch as the Constitution did not grant Congress specific power to legislate regarding labor conditions, the law was enacted under the power to regulate commerce. It excluded from interstate commerce goods produced in factories by child labor. The Supreme Court promptly declared the measure unconstitutional in *Hammer* v. *Dagenhart et al.* (1918). It also invalidated a second law which aimed at the same objective by using the taxing power to destroy the profit in products made by child labor. Still later a Constitutional amendment covering the subject fell short of securing the support necessary for ratification.

A more spectacular example of Wilson's support for the special demands of labor was the Adamson Act, granting the eight-hour day to railroad workers. Congress passed the measure after three days of debate, on September 2, 1916, to avert a strike scheduled for Labor Day. The controversy had started the preceding March, when a few railroad brotherhoods demanded an eight-hour day and time and a half for overtime. The employers had rejected these demands and both sides had ignored the efforts of the United States Board of Mediation and Conciliation, set up by the Newlands Act of 1913. When the deadline approached, Wilson secured quick congressional action by assuring the lawmakers that a strike would seriously damage the nation's armament and preparedness program. This kind of appeal did not exempt him from severe criticism as a tool of organized labor. Even the Progressive Republican Senator Borah said the administration had "crawled and cringed" before the labor unions. Whether or not this verdict was accurate, nobody could question the fact that Wilson had espoused the cause of the workingman and thus gained recruits for the Democratic party.

WILSONIAN DEMOCRACY AND PROGRESSIVISM

Wilson's successful appropriation of the Progressive label for the farm and labor legislation of 1916 completed the redefinition of reform ideology launched by Theodore Roosevelt six years earlier. Neither the President nor the rank and file who supported his program explicitly repudiated their original objectives. They simply sponsored a series of legislative measures contrary to the stated purpose of their movement without examining the cumulative effect. What started out as a crusade to free government from the control of all special interest groups wound up as a drive to make government the agent of hitherto ineffective groups like agriculture and labor. In the process, Progressives also accepted a concentration of regulatory authority in Washington that was at odds with their earlier intention of keeping government small. This shift in emphasis was a tacit admission that they had failed to arrest the centralization of economic power and to restore the small, competitive, free enterprise system. Whether the architects of the "New Freedom" admitted it or not, they had changed the goals of the Progressive movement by endorsing big government to supervise big business.

Inasmuch as the original purpose of the reform crusade was to purify democratic institutions, the redefinition of Progressivism involved a corresponding change in the concept of democracy. Hitherto, popular allegiance to a common set of political and moral principles had been regarded as the indispensable foundation of democratic society and the successful functioning of institutional devices for self-government. If such was the case, democracy could not be imposed on any society but had to develop from within. The redefinition of Progressivism in terms of the doctrines mentioned in Chapter Four weakened this faith: Darwinism undermined the idea that democratic principles were absolute and unchanging; Socialism denied that such principles had ever been valid and substituted economic ones; and Pragmatism insisted that the only reality was process. People borrowed just enough of this heady brew to fall into the habit of equating the democratic way of life with technological progress and material prosperity.

Legislative proposals in the final phase of Progressivism reflected this theoretical trend. Roosevelt as a third-party leader appropriated bits of Pragmatism and Darwinism. Wilson possessed a greater sympathy for evolutionary thought and incorporated it in his "New Freedom" program. The resulting emphasis on economic progress instead of agreement on ideals as a core of democracy had far-reaching implications. It encouraged Americans to believe that democracy could be imposed abroad by exporting the structure of self-government even if the intended beneficiaries did not profess devotion to democratic principles. This dubious assumption was to motivate the abortive Wilsonian crusade in 1917. It was to nurture the faith that America could democratize the world. On the home front it paved the way for the frenzied conservative-nationalist reaction in the 1920's. As we shall see, the leaders of that movement expressed their frustration over the collapse of democratic ideals by compelling the public to worship the structural shell of self-government. In the postwar decade only the form of the old institutions remained.

Whether or not Wilson and his followers saw clearly in 1916 that the equating of change and democracy would drain the latter of fixed content, their program ended the old Progressive crusade. The next reform movement, in the 1930's, was destined to embrace the Wilsonian style of Progressivism enthusiastically and to regard economic progress as the keystone of democracy. In retrospect, one can see that the New Freedom was the bridge between the older democracy based on principles and the New Deal based on enthusiasm for experimentation. Meanwhile, the outbreak of World War I provided Wilson with an ideal opportunity to bury the old Progressive movement which he had abandoned. His fellow countrymen shared his desire to blame failure on the distractions of the Great Crusade in Europe. They had already tired of the effort to sustain a movement generated by moral indignation. Their desire to restore nineteenth-century society and its values was at war with their desire to retain the benefits of industrial technology. Progressivism represented the last effort of this generation to force the new urban-industrial society into old institutional molds so that both could be enjoyed. Thereafter twentieth-century reform movements were to approach their problems with the assumption that the traditional institutional pattern could not be preserved in its original form.

SUGGESTED READINGS

1. Hibben, P. and Grattan, C. H., *The Peerless Leader* [Bryan].
2. Link, A. S., *Woodrow Wilson and the Progressive Era.*
3. Wilson, Woodrow, *The New Freedom.*

CHAPTER EIGHT

THE UNITED STATES AND THE WESTERN HEMISPHERE (1900-1917)

A REGIONAL APPROACH TO FOREIGN POLICY

It is customary to treat foreign policy from the inauguration of Theodore Roosevelt to the American entry into World War I by presidential administrations. This method of presentation breaks the diplomatic history of the United States into four- to eight-year segments: the "Big Stick" of Roosevelt, the "Dollar Diplomacy" of Taft; and the "Anti-imperialism" of Wilson. The result is that a continuous chain of developments is arbitrarily divided into a series of separate episodes. The reader emerges with the misleading impression that each President makes a sharp departure from the policy of his predecessor. In reality, the basic interests of the United States in various areas of the world remained relatively constant. What changed were the methods for protecting those interests rather than the interests themselves, although these aspects of policy were often confused. Since — as already noted — Americans did not consider it good form to acknowledge the existence of interests, the latter were pursued instinctively. It is necessary to analyze these unstated objectives in their international setting in order to understand the various responses to which they gave birth.

The best way of getting the proper perspective is to substitute a regional treatment of foreign policy in the Western Hemisphere, the Far East, and Europe for the conventional history of administrations. An organization of material on a regional basis will enable the reader to comprehend (1) the major goals of the United States in each theater, (2) the successive maneuvers of the great powers which America regarded as a threat to her position, and (3) the various countermoves by Washington. We shall start with the Western Hemisphere; move to the Far East; and conclude with Europe.

THE POSITION OF THE UNITED STATES IN THE WESTERN HEMISPHERE

Two connected facts shaped the pattern of American relations with other states in the Western Hemisphere during the opening decades of the century. The first was preponderance of power in the Hemisphere and the second was determination to preserve it.

The dominant position of the United States in the Western Hemisphere enabled her to exclude the operation of the balance-of-power principle from that area. Accordingly, all hemispheric republics had to adjust relations with nonhemispheric states through Washington. The most novel and perplexing feature of this dispensation was the refusal of the United States to exercise her domination by outright extinction of the sovereignty in areas where she was most interested. Had she converted them into colonies, their status would have been obvious. Instead, she evolved an empire system which defied precise description in the traditional terms of imperialism. As a result, millions of people in the Western Hemisphere lived in a sort of no-man's land. Although they did not enjoy all the rights of citizens of sovereign states, they exercised considerably more of them than the normal victims of conquest.

No single term describes the variety of arrangements prevailing between the United States and other hemispheric states which came directly under her supervision. One step removed from outright annexation was the legal fiction of "perpetual lease," which was confined to the single case of the Panama Canal Zone. Next came the "protectorate" — a designation often applied to countries where the United States established naval bases, controlled financial policy, or ousted unfriendly governments. Such intervention might be periodic or on a long-term basis. Usually it was covered by treaties forced on Latin-American states to give American interference an air of legality. No two cases were exactly alike. The term "protectorate" is useful only if one remembers that the phrase reflected a condition of dependence on the United States rather than an American guarantee to help defenseless states. At one time or another Cuba, Panama, the Dominican Republic, Nicaragua, and Haiti found themselves in this status.

South of the areas where the protectorate was in vogue, the states enjoyed a precarious independence. They escaped American intervention except when they tried to pursue foreign policies at odds with American sponsorship of the Hemisphere. Like the European powers, they were not always able to anticipate what action would displease the United States. The over-all pattern of domination without annexation suited the ideological tastes of Americans. It enabled them to believe sincerely that they had abandoned the policy of conquest and empire-building associated with the Spanish-American War and that they did not covet Latin-American territory. Nevertheless such pronouncements did not protect hemispheric states from

The man behind the egg. (The New York Times, *1903.*)

periodic intervention which often forced them into as much cooperation as conquest would have assured.

Completeness of domination enabled the United States to enforce demonstrations of solidarity unknown in regions where the balance of power prevailed. The agency through which these demonstrations took place was the Pan-American Congress. Customarily, "pan" movements grow out of a real or fancied ethnic similarity among states which makes possible an unusual degree of political cooperation. Depending on the circumstances, advocates of such movements proposes alliances, customs unions, or some type of federalism. The largest groups that could have sought a closer hemispheric association on such a basis were the republics in South and in Central America with their common Latin background. Several tentative efforts in this direction were made by various combinations of Latin states before the Civil War, but they met with repeated failure. Americans also lacked enthusiasm for closer cultural ties because they regarded Anglo-Saxon institutions as vastly superior to those of their southern neighbors. Moreover, the United States had no intention of joining any organization that she could not dominate. A hemispheric union based on states with an equal voice in making decisions would have tried to interfere with American expansion.

As might have been predicted, American interest in hemispheric unity soared in the 1880's when the prospects of dominating such an organization had improved. By that time, hemispheric organization looked like a good vehicle for enlarging trade with Latin America. The new interest, however, was accompanied by a paternalistic attitude that irritated the proud and sensitive Latin-American peoples. Appropriation of the term "Pan-American" seemed particularly ironic because there were none of the common interests associated with "pan" movements. Yet the instinct to resist was tempered by the reflection that there could be no escape and that conferences were less likely to involve a change of status than any other technique.

Accordingly, the republics south of the Rio Grande agreed to the first proposals from Washington for a Pan-American Congress in 1889–90. They did so with the secret hope that the assembly would do nothing but talk. At the meeting the United States proposed a customs union but would have been happy to settle for a broad program of reciprocity agreements; the Latin-American states politely resisted this poorly concealed effort to jockey Europeans out of the Hemisphere's southern markets. Other items on the agenda, including a scheme for the settlement of international disputes by arbitration, fared no better. Later conferences were held at Mexico City in 1901–1902, at Rio de Janeiro in 1906, and Buenos Aires in 1910. The Latin-American states participated without cooperating. Highhanded American action through the Caribbean undercut the northern republic's protestations of good will.

During the first world war and for five years thereafter, Pan-American machinery rusted. In the 1930's, however, the self-interest of the two groups began to converge. A second world war made it evident that there was a fate worse than following United States leadership.

THE STRATEGY OF HEMISPHERIC DEFENSE

Both as an experiment in regional association and as a method of bending the hemispheric states to the purposes of the United States before World War I, Pan-Americanism was a failure. Washington resorted to more direct methods when it was really intent on accomplishing something. What it wanted at any given time was usually related to the objective of preserving America's position in the Hemisphere, though occasionally it reacted violently to situations which by no stretch of the imagination could be regarded as threats to this objective.

Before considering in their specific contexts the methods the United States employed to impose her will on the Western Hemisphere, we must say a few words about how she viewed her security problem. In a general way, she felt that the maintenance of her position required (1) insulation of the Hemisphere strategically and politically from nonhemispheric influences, (2) tight physical control of the entire area and a determined effort to make this control stronger. Americans might argue about the methods for implementing these purposes but never about the purposes themselves.

Geography was an important factor in shaping America's grand strategy for the Hemisphere. It dictated different approaches in the Pacific and in the Atlantic. Any attempt to throw up defenses west of the United States would put America well out into the Pacific. That ocean was nearly void of offshore islands on the eastern side but contained potential strong points at mid-ocean: the Aleutians and Midway to the north; the Hawaiian chain and Wake in the center; and the Samoan group to the south. The great prizes of economic exploitation lay several thousand miles farther west in the islands off the Asiatic coast or on the China mainland. By the end of the nineteenth century, America had occupied the island chains in the central Pacific; expansionist fervor had indeed carried her beyond to Guam and the Philippines. During the decade following the Spanish-American War she found cause for uneasiness. Germany purchased the Carolines, the Pelew Islands, and the Marianas with the exception of Guam, and thereby stood athwart the American path to the Philippines. Simultaneously, the spectacular rise of Japan posed an additional threat to the position in eastern Asia. Advocates of American naval build-up in the Pacific soon learned that the Philippines were in an exposed location and that a proper defense would require virtual control of Japanese home waters. Lacking the strength for such an enterprise or the prospect of acquiring it soon, the United States fell back on the Samoan-Hawaiian-Alaskan line. As enthusiasm for empire-building waned, she accepted this as the hemispheric defense line in the West.

In the Atlantic, all the prizes were on the American side. Only a few offshore islands (Iceland, the Azores, the Canary Islands, and the Cape Verde Islands) lay close to Europe. They belonged to second-rate powers and were strategically unimportant at the time. Since the United States has generally regarded her Atlantic security system as depending upon the central region between North and South America, the focal point of her diplomatic activity was to be there. It included Colombia and Venezuela, Mexico and Central America, and the islands of the Caribbean. During the nineteenth century Great Britain had warded off intruders in this area. Her own interest as the strongest Atlantic naval power had caused her to throw up a protective screen for America. For reasons which we shall examine later, she now, at the moment when America emerged as a world power, was less able to maintain her commitments. Long-standing resentment of Britain's superior strength made the United States eager to take over the defense of the Atlantic frontier.

This strategic objective commanded more general support from the public than did the economic objectives of businessmen. Tighter supervision of the internal affairs of the Latin-American republics was periodically demanded by commercial groups in search of markets and investment opportunities. Their clamors for help grew in volume whenever local revolutionaries created disorder or repudiated debts contracted by earlier regimes. Washington, in turn, solicited the investment of American capital south of the border just as often as the businessmen sought help from the government. The State Department welcomed American capital as a method of minimizing the interference of nonhemispheric states in the affairs of the New World. Under President Taft the policy received an official blessing as "dollar diplomacy." Yet the task of persuading capitalists to do their patriotic duty was not always easy; their occasional reluctance illustrated how economic and strategic objectives could be inextricably tangled.

Neither the over-all design of insulating the Hemisphere nor the manipulation of financial interests as a method for achieving it was clearly understood. The United States utilized a bewildering variety of methods in implementing her program. Some were employed consistently; others, occasionally. The list that follows will help the student understand the diplomacy of the period:

1. A build-up of naval strength.
2. Establishment of peripheral defense lines in the Atlantic and the Pacific.
3. Improvement of continental defenses, especially the building of a canal controlled by the United States.
4. Intervention through the acquisition of territory or protectorates or by other methods.
5. The revision of old principles and the formulation of new ones to justify whatever the United States decided to do:
   a. Redefinition of the Monroe Doctrine.
   b. Expanded use of multilateral conferences (i.e., Pan-Americanism) to demonstrate hemispheric solidarity or Latin "equality."

ENLARGEMENT OF THE NAVY

The naval program started well in advance of canal construction and intervention in the Caribbean. Sentiment for a stronger navy grew rapidly in the 1880's — a decade when British domination of the seas was becoming more irksome to patriots. Simultaneously, Admiral Mahan was engaging in his tireless propaganda. Political leaders responsive to his arguments accepted the thesis that without maritime strength the United States could not project her power into areas beyond her continental limits. They recognized that the decline of the merchant marine and the failure of the Navy to grow as rapidly as the country precluded aggressive ventures overseas. The same group also saw that the mobility of the American Navy could be increased by the construction of a canal in Central America.

The first steps were taken in 1883 and provided for the addition of steel vessels. Six years later, Secretary of the Navy Benjamin F. Tracy recommended the creation of twenty first-class battleships, twelve for the Atlantic and eight for the Pacific. Although this proposal seemed modest by comparison with the recommendation of his policy board, which advocated a navy of two hundred ships at an estimated cost of $350 million, it was too much for Congress. The legislators grudgingly authorized three battleships, the *Indiana,* the *Massachusetts*, and the *Oregon*. Together with the *Iowa* these ships formed the nucleus of the fleet that defeated Spain.

After the war naval strategists began to think in terms of an armada which could destroy the navy of any potential enemy. Younger Republican politicians like Senator Henry Cabot Lodge and President Theodore Roosevelt embraced the "capital ship" theory. After 1903 a Navy League kept up a steady agitation for a two-ocean navy. By that time new responsibilities overseas and the construction of the Panama Canal provided persuasive arguments. The Canal was demanded to increase the effectiveness of the Navy, and a larger Navy was demanded to defend the Canal. Both were represented as indispensable for the protection of distant possessions like the Philippines.

All this agitation bore fruit in the decade after 1898 when the United States passed Germany in the naval race and moved into second place behind Great Britain. In 1907, on the eve of Roosevelt's decision to send the Navy round the world, the United States possessed an Atlantic fleet of sixteen battleships and a Pacific fleet of eight armored and eight light cruisers. The President felt his way toward a demonstration of naval power by announcing on July 9 that all the battleships of the Atlantic fleet would move from the East to the West Coast on a "practice cruise." Protests against stripping the Atlantic coast of its defenses and political opposition to presidential policy prompted congressional threats to withhold the necessary appropriations. Roosevelt's reply was that he possessed the funds to send the fleet to the Pacific Coast and that Congress could leave the ships stranded if it wished. The outmaneuvered legislators eventually capitulated, and the fleet departed from Hampton Roads in December 1907. After a cordial reception at South American ports, it arrived on the West Coast in April 1908. Thereupon Roosevelt announced that the cruise would be continued around the world. Japan and Australia cooperated by extending invitations to the fleet. From Pacific waters, the ships swung northward through the Indian Ocean, the Red Sea, and the Mediterranean and arrived home on February 22, 1909. Domestic criticism throughout the cruise was prompted largely by the fact that Roosevelt presided over the operation. Whether or not his foes misjudged his motives, he did make a considerable contribution to American prestige, demonstrating the nation's growing naval strength without focusing a "show of force" on a particular issue or area of the world.

THE PANAMA CANAL

In the midst of the naval program of the Roosevelt era, America began construction of the Panama Canal. Interest in a canal had first developed as a consequence of the westward movement in the 1840's. The United States had signed a treaty with New Granada (later Colombia) in 1846 assuring the government and its citizens "the right of way or transit" across the Isthmus of Panama. Enthusiasm for a canal lagged, however, and did not revive until the Spanish-American War, and the consequent acquisition of Caribbean and Pacific possessions. Then Americans realized that their hands were still tied by the Clayton-Bulwer Treaty of 1850 with Great Britain. The treaty had stipulated (1) that neither of the signatory powers would seek exclusive control of any canal route, and (2) that any canal subsequently constructed would be internationalized and receive joint Anglo-American protection.

Tentative steps toward abandoning joint action with the British had been taken in 1881. The excuse was provided when a French company, headed by Ferdinand de Lesseps — the builder of the Suez Canal — and operating under a concession from Colombia, began to construct a canal across the Isthmus. Beyond a routine protest about violation of the Monroe Doctrine, the United States did not actively interfere. Instead, she began exploring the possibilities of a Nicaraguan route without paying much attention to the British. When the French company went bankrupt a decade later without having achieved more than a good start, American interest also dwindled momentarily.

During the Spanish-American War, Congress showed signs of authorizing construction of a route through Nicaragua regardless of treaty obligations. To forestall such a deliberate affront to the British, Secretary of State John Hay opened negotiations for the modification of existing commitments. England was in an unusually tractable frame of mind because current problems elsewhere in the world made her eager to reach an understanding with the United States. Even so she conceded little in the first Hay-Pauncefote Treaty, signed on February 5, 1900. It authorized the United States to proceed with the construction of a canal but retained the neutralization features of the old treaty.

This situation was intolerable to the dominant nationalistic and expansionist groups in America. Reflecting their viewpoint, the Senate gave its "approval" to the Hay-Pauncefote Treaty on December 20, 1900, but in so doing declared that the Clayton-Bulwer Treaty was superseded and that the United States was exempted from its neutralization provisions. Senate action left the British in an impossible position. If they adhered to the treaty as negotiated, they would be bound by neutralization, whereas the United States and other powers would not. Convinced of America's determination to build and control a canal, the British resigned themselves to negotiating a new treaty.

The second Hay-Pauncefote Treaty, signed on December 16, 1901, gave the United States a virtually free hand with regard to the construction, fortification and regulation of a canal. In return, the United States pledged herself to grant all states equal shipping rights and to maintain neutralization of the canal in time of war. She did, however, reserve the right to close it to enemy vessels if she herself were a belligerent.

Meanwhile the problem of selecting a route came up again. The earlier French company, which had been reorganized and was now operating under a concession in Panama, was plagued by lack of capital and slow progress and so was ready to sell out. An American company which had been considering a route in Nicaragua had not lived up to its contract and had lost its concession from that country. Both Colombia and Nicaragua were ready to negotiate new terms with some state. Their interest grew when it became apparent that the American government itself proposed to undertake construction.

As might have been expected, rival factions favoring alternate locations developed quickly. The advantage of penetrating the Isthmus through Nicaragua was that much of the route could pass through rivers and lakes; the disadvantage was that it would be considerably longer than one through Panama. The estimated time for transit was thirty-three hours in Nicaragua compared to twelve hours in Panama. Furthermore, the work already done by the French company in Panama, which represented about two-fifths of the necessary excavation, would go with a concession.

At the outset, American opinion had inclined strongly to the former route, partly because the French company was operating in Panama. This consideration had led Congress to establish several commissions which were authorized to report only on the feasibility of a Nicaraguan waterway. As a result, the public thought primarily in these terms. In 1899 Senator John T. Morgan of Alabama pushed a bill through the upper house for the construction, operation, and fortification of such a canal. The Panamanian faction blocked passage of a similar bill in the House of Representatives under the leadership of two astute lobbyists, William Nelson Cromwell and Philippe Jean Bunau-Varilla. The former was a member of the New York law firm of Sullivan and Cromwell and counsel for the new Panamanian company; the latter was chief engineer of the old French company and a stockholder in the new.

The upshot of the deadlock was legislation providing for an investigation of all potential routes. This decision represented a temporary victory for the Panamanian faction but matters took a less favorable turn for them when the French company set a valuation of $109 million on its properties and rights. The congressional commission thought $40 million a reasonable figure, and on November 16, 1901, recommended the Nicaraguan route. The Panama company promptly brought its figure down to the commission's estimate, whereupon the recommendation was changed to the Panama route.

The ensuing battle in Congress slowly swung in favor of the Panamanian faction. The blow that finally spelled defeat for the other route was the eruption of several volcanoes in the Caribbean area. The groundwork had already been laid by propaganda stories about the numerous active volcanoes of Nicaragua. Some of the current eruptions were as far away from the proposed site as the island of Martinique, but the press obliged with accounts of an eruption of Mount Momotombo in Nicaragua, complete with earthquake. The Nicaraguan government inadvertently damaged its own cause by issuing a stamp with a picture of a smoking volcano rearing its head out of Lake Nicaragua, a segment of the proposed route. Bunau-Varilla thoughtfully placed one of these stamps on the desk of each senator. The result was that Congress passed the Spooner Amendment to the original Hepburn Act giving the rights to Panama and authorizing payment of $40 million. The entire measure became law on June 28, 1902.

Only the necessity of reaching an agreement with Colombia, which owned the Panamanian isthmus, stood between the United States and its coveted canal. Eventually Dr. Thomas Herran of the Colombian legation and Secretary of State Hay signed a treaty on January 22, 1903. It gave the United States a hundred-year lease of the proposed canal zone with the option of renewal for similar intervals as well as the necessary construction rights. The sovereignty of Colombia over the Isthmus was reaffirmed, but the treaty empowered the United States to protect it should Colombia prove unable to do so. Provision was also made for mixed courts in the zone and neutralization of the waterway in accordance with the Hay-Pauncefote Treaty. In return, the United States agreed to pay $10 million in gold upon ratification and $250,000 annually beginning nine years thereafter.

The Senate promptly approved the treaty on March 17, 1903. Colombia, which had been in no hurry to negotiate, temporized. President Marroquin noncommittally referred it to his senate in June. Opposition to several provisions developed, but it soon became clear that none of the objections would prove insurmountable if the American government agreed to pay a higher price. Hints were made to Washington that $25 million would be more acceptable than the $10 million offered in the Hay-Herran draft. The American government balked, and the Colombian senate voted the treaty down, 24 to 0.

Rejection did not pose the alternatives of resorting to coercion or abandoning all efforts to build a canal. Although it would have been easy to resolve the impasse by reverting to the Nicaraguan route, the United States refused either to tolerate temporary delay on an enterprise that had been considered in a leisurely manner for two generations or to build in a location favored by most Americans until the Panamanian propagandists had gone to work. What she decided to do was foment a revolution in Panama and make a treaty with the "independent" state. President Roosevelt stirred up the proper pitch of indignation by broadsides against the Colombian legislators. He succeeded in visualizing them simultaneously as "homicidal" and as "jackrabbits." He also announced that an isthmian canal constituted a "necessity." The revolution entered the planning stage in May 1903; it was openly predicted by the New York press a month later. Bunau-Varilla contributed $100,000 to encourage dissident groups in Panama. By prearrangement, United States naval units were stationed in strategic spots to prevent Colombia from sending troops to Panama. Bribery assured the immobilization of the small Colombian contingent already there. These precautions assured the prompt success of the revolution, which took place on November 3, 1903. The only casualties were a Chinese, killed by fire from a Colombian gunboat, and American good faith in dealing with her less powerful neighbors.

Belated offers by Colombia to make amends and to approve the treaty, if the United States would allow her to put down the revolt, were rejected with a show of moral indignation. Instead, the United States extended *de facto* recognition to the "Panamanian government" on the third day after the insurrection had started. Within another week Roosevelt received Bunau-Varilla, one of whose rewards for services rendered was the post of the first Panamanian Minister to the United States. Operating on a fast timetable, John Hay and he managed to negotiate a new treaty by November 18, 1903. It offered the new republic exactly the same financial terms that Colombia had rejected, but it so enlarged American powers in the ten-mile strip across the Isthmus that the United States would exercise *de facto* sovereignty over the area. Most ironic of all was a provision which pledged the United States to "protect" the independence of Panama. The Senate ratified the treaty on February 23, 1904. Panama gave her approval shortly thereafter, and the United States was at long last able to go ahead with construction. Operations began immediately, but the waterway could not be opened for business until 1913.

The incident exposed the discrepancy between American protestations of idealism and American conduct. Serious questions can surely be raised about the prudence of Colombia's conduct. Three days after Dr. Herran had negotiated the treaty with Hay, his government had ordered him to withdraw it. Unfortunately, he had not bothered to notify Washington of this decision. This error was followed by the unedifying spectacle of the Colombian senate stalling on the treaty in an effort to extract more money from the United States. But whether Colombia behaved wisely or not, she was a sovereign state and possessed the power to accept or to reject treaties. She had violated no American rights but merely asserted her own. Talk about Colombian violations of international law and treaty agreements was lofty but irrelevant. Actually America had asserted her dominance after the manner of great powers in similar circumstances elsewhere. She firmly rejected Colombia's request for the submission of the issue to an international tribunal.

Successive Secretaries of State strove to soften Colombian bitterness. In 1914 Secretary Bryan signed a treaty expressing regret and providing for payment of the $25 million originally asked. Enough Roosevelt admirers still remained in the Senate to block ratification. Then in 1921, with Colombian oil concessions in the offing and with the old Bull Moose silenced forever, the United States finally paid the money. Washington did not have the good grace to apologize, nor did Bogotá have the courage and consistency of purpose to refuse the money.

THE VENEZUELAN CRISIS

While the United States was pursuing the tactics that led to acquisition of the Canal Zone, she pushed ahead with other policies to insulate the Western Hemisphere from outside influence. Her action in the second Venezuelan crisis of 1902–1903, as well as her intervention in Santo Domingo in 1903, demonstrated her growing power. In neither case did a nonhemispheric state challenge America's dominant position in the New World. Hence both incidents provided the occasion for a reinterpretation of the Monroe Doctrine. Originally enunciated to assure the independence of hemispheric states from European aggression, it was now used to assist the impairment of such independence by an aggressive United States.

Whatever might be said about the merits of controversy with Germany over Venezuela, it was not one which involved the Monroe Doctrine as originally understood. America had pushed Great Britain, the last European power, out of the New World in 1895. On that occasion Britain had yielded in a boundary dispute with Venezuela (the First Venezuelan Crisis) rather than jeopardize her good relations with the United States. Thereafter, America was free to reinterpret the Monroe Doctrine without interference from a great power. The first opportunity to do so was provided by the behavior of Cipriano Castro, an irresponsible adventurer who headed the Venezuelan government. His regime protected neither peace nor private property. His subjects were accustomed to this kind of government, but foreign businessmen complained repeatedly to their governments. Castro paid little attention. Several European states wanted corrective action but were reluctant to offend the United States.

On behalf of her investors, Germany offered to submit their claims against Venezuela to the Hague Court of Arbitration. After Castro had rejected this proposal, Berlin began to consider intervention. The tenor of statements from Washington indicated that the United States would not object to measures designed to assure the collection of debts. Roosevelt had repeatedly indicated his distaste for hemispheric governments that defaulted on their obligations and expected America to protect them from the normal consequences. Specifically he had stated that if a South American republic "misbehaved," he was satisfied to see a European country "spank" it. Just to be on the safe side, the German government inquired if Washington objected to intervention in Venezuela for the collection of debts. Roosevelt and Hay responded with the assurance that the United States would tolerate such action as long as it did not lead to the acquisition of territory.

On the basis of this statement Berlin decided to go ahead, and Great Britain associated herself with Germany in a joint policy of intervention. Neither power intended to challenge the Monroe Doctrine as it had been formerly understood or recently restated by Roosevelt. The modest Anglo-German plans contemplated seizure of a number of ports and the appropriation of customs receipts as security for the satisfaction of claims. As the project matured, Italy was also permitted to join the other two powers. Units of the three fleets blockaded Venezuela in December 1902. This operation led to the shelling of two forts and the destruction or capture of several Venezuelan gunboats.

Castro promptly sought the help of the United States, proposing arbitration by the American Minister to Venezuela. Great Britain and Germany were officially informed of the overture on December 12, and both accepted in principle within a week. The blockade was continued until February 17, 1903, while the details of the negotiation were being hammered out. During the interval the Germans bombarded the Fort of San Carlos and destroyed the adjacent village. This action was unnecessary and unwise. It could serve no purpose in January when Berlin had agreed to arbitration in December.

The rest of Latin America remained calm. The only proposal of consequence was made by Luis M. Drago, the Foreign Minister of Argentina, who urged that the payment of public debts should not be enforced by armed might or occupation. Before the great powers accepted the principle set forth in the "Drago Doctrine," the Venezuelan Crisis was over. In weakened form the principle was eventually adopted as a convention at the Second Hague Conference (1907). Neither when Drago proposed his formula nor later was it regarded as any great innovation by states like Germany or as any source of comfort by evaders like Venezuela.

The reaction to the bombardment was more explosive in the United States than in Latin America. Roosevelt said nothing publicly, but privately he bristled with indignation. He had become convinced that the Kaiser intended to stir up trouble in the Western Hemisphere at the first opportunity. The press, for the most part ignoring the role of Great Britain in the affair, proclaimed the German bombardment an outrage against public morality and international law. The average citizen, who took his cue from the newspapers, became violently exercised. Notwithstanding the inflamed state of public opinion, Roosevelt could not find any excuse for either diplomatic or military action. He contented himself with an unnatural silence when a statement from him would have made it clear that Germany was in Venezuela with Washington's permission. Eventually all the claims against Venezuela were settled peaceably. The episode emphasized the fact that America was still enforcing the Monroe Doctrine, but would not say what she was enforcing. Plainly the need for redefinition was growing.

SANTO DOMINGO

American intervention in Santo Domingo helped pave the way for Roosevelt to enunciate the new version of the Monroe Doctrine. Santo Domingo, which covered the eastern half of the Caribbean island of Hispaniola, had won its independence in 1844. During the next seventy years it had a remarkable record of political instability, enjoying nineteen constitutions and fifty-three presidents. Of the latter, only three managed to complete the terms for which they were elected. The rapid turnover and accompanying disorder did not disturb the United States unduly until 1903, when Santo Domingo's debt reached $32 million and the government refused to heed its creditors. Some of these were American and British citizens who had invested in the San Domingo Improvement Company of New York. Washington bestirred itself in their behalf, with the result that the company was permitted to collect customs revenue in two ports.

Other creditors, represented by their respective European governments, proposed to satisfy their claims in the same way. There was no evidence that nonhemispheric powers intended to occupy the little republic or to do more than the United States was doing. But the latter had reached the point where she intended to treat the Hemisphere as a sphere of influence. A declaration of this intention had been urgently needed since the Second Venezuelan Crisis. Roosevelt chose the friction over Santo Domingo as the occasion for a clarifying statement. Known as the Roosevelt Corollary to the Monroe Doctrine, the new policy first received expression in the annual message to Congress in 1904. In essence, it asserted the responsibility of the United States for the collection of debts owed by hemispheric states to nonhemispheric states in cases where the former evaded their obligations. Other amplifications proclaimed the determination of the United States to punish wrongdoing anywhere in the Hemisphere.

Roosevelt's preliminary statement of the corollary was a combination preview, trial balloon, and softening-up process directed primarily at Santo Domingo. Execution of the program resembled a melodrama with the United States Minister to Santo Domingo acting as official prompter for the production. President Morales issued a declaration of national incompetence and invited the United States to take over. Next, President Roosevelt, the powerfully built leading man of the New World, entered from the wings and frightened off the stage the European villains, who apparently were about to steal what they were rightfully entitled to. He then promised to pay the national mortgage with Dominican money which he would collect. This accomplished, he stepped in front of the curtain to accept the double applause due him as both author and hero of the piece.

The entire performance took only about a month. Santo Domingo faced reality much more quickly than Cuba had done under similar circumstances, and signed an agreement on January 20, 1905. It opened with the customary guarantees of territorial and political integrity. The core was a provision whereby the United States established a kind of national receivership and undertook to collect all customs, with 45 per cent going to the Santo Domingans and the balance to creditors, after the deduction of collection charges. An additional clause pledging help for Santo Domingo to "restore credit, preserve order, and increase the efficiency of the civil administration" kept the United States involved intermittently in the republic for ten years.

Roosevelt first tried to circumvent Congress by assuming that commitments of the type made to Santo Domingo were executive agreements rather than treaties. Consideration of domestic politics caused President Morales to make the agreement public. This step inconvenienced Roosevelt, who then sent the agreement to the Senate for ratification after minor changes. His accompanying message again referred to the Monroe Doctrine as a justification for action. Senate Democrats prevented the treaty from being brought to a vote; so Roosevelt reverted to his original plan of supervising the republic under an executive agreement. Matters went on in much the same manner except that customs revenue had to be collected by a private citizen rather than by an American official.

Meanwhile, President H. H. Hollander of the Johns Hopkins University negotiated so successfully with the creditors of Santo Domingo that the country's indebtendness was scaled down from $32 million to $17 million. United States investors digested enough Dominican bonds to raise $20 million. This loan was used to pay off indebtedness to other countries. It resulted in the substitution of the dollar for the pound and the franc as the major source of foreign investment in Santo Domingo.

Two years after the submission of the first treaty to the Senate, Roosevelt tried again. The basic provisions were the same, except for the inclusion of two important clauses. The first called for definite termination of the American customs collectorship when Santo Domingo had paid off the bond issue. The second pledged the Dominican government not to incur further indebtedness without the consent of the United States until existing obligations were liquidated. Whatever scruples had induced the Democratic senators to block the treaty of 1905 deserted them in 1907, and the agreement was ratified on July 25. By implication the Roosevelt Corollary to the Monroe Doctrine had won the day in Santo Domingo. She had been protected from European customs collectors because the United States considered their intervention tantamount to the acquisition of territory. On the other hand, she had fallen prey to American customs collectors, though she received a Rooseveltian assurance that such an arrangement would protect her independence and territorial integrity. Thus the revered name of Monroe provided the only link between the older American policy of safeguarding the independence of hemispheric states and the newer one of supervising it.

Judging from the absence of repercussions, the financial protectorate worked well for about four years. Customs collections rose. President Caceres, who replaced Morales in 1905, used the surplus funds to provide schools, public works, and improved governmental services. Some of his countrymen, nevertheless, felt that his extended term of office — 1905 to 1911 — was not in the best national tradition, and in the latter year he was assassinated. Santo Domingo quickly reverted to a chaos compounded of revolution, civil war, political confusion, and mounting debt.

FROM BIG STICK TO DOLLAR DIPLOMACY

The opening phase of American intervention in Panama and Santo Domingo had fallen chronologically within Roosevelt's administration and had owed its character primarily to his methods. His corollary provided a useful rationalization of the "Big Stick" diplomacy at which he excelled. The transfer of the Presidency to Taft was marked not by any abatement of American determination to dominate the Hemisphere but by an emphasis on different methods. Although on occasion he employed force just as his predecessor did, he preferred to rely on financial pressure.

Taft used the phrase "Dollar Diplomacy" to describe his favored method. It was not novel. American diplomats had long recognized that a policy of economic investment in a particular country may lead to political control if pursued on a large enough scale. Before the Taft administration, however, cooperation between government and investor had been largely unplanned and informal. Washington had done nothing more than encourage businessmen to export capital into the Caribbean and the Far East; and sometimes the investors moved in without prompting and then clamored for help if local disorders created an unfavorable climate. Roosevelt heralded a change in this informal relationship by seeking to replace foreign with American capital in Santo Domingo. Taft broadened and systematized the tendency by consciously employing American economic resources to achieve foreign policy objectives. Utilization of the technique exposed him, it is true, to partisan charges that he was a tool of Wall Street. Such criticisms were politically effective then, but times have changed. After World War II the use of the taxpayer's dollars to implement the goals of diplomacy became commonplace.

NICARAGUA AND HONDURAS

The Taft approach became evident in Nicaragua, where America's repeated protests that defense considerations motivated intervention in the Caribbean were really true. Washington had several reasons for concern. In 1903 Nicaragua abrogated American transit rights for a canal through her territory. Then rumors began to circulate that she was trying to sell these rights to either Great Britain or Japan. Worse still, General José Santos Zelaya, dictator from 1893 to 1909, was repeatedly at war with his neighbors around the Canal Zone.

At first, the United States had sought to produce stability by getting the "banana republics" to give up wars and revolutionary plots against each other. A conference under the joint auspices of the United States and Mexico at San Jose in 1906 extracted appropriate pledges from the diminutive states. General Zelaya promptly showed his contempt for the transactions by waging war with Honduras. America and Mexico tried again a year later at Washington by sponsoring a sort of miniature League of Nations in the area. Provision was made for compulsory arbitration of disputes, and a Court of Justice was established to make awards. The conferees did not try to abolish revolution but pledged themselves not to recognize revolutionary regimes until free elections had been held. Again Zelaya paid little attention. Hence, when revolution broke out against him in 1909, American cruisers appeared in Nicaraguan waters and contributed materially to the success of the rebels.

The ouster of Zelaya precipitated demands by the great powers for the payment of the large debts accumulated during his regime. As a stopgap measure Taft instituted a customs receivership under Thomas C. Dawson and also a commission to consider all the claims. The commission succeeded in cutting these obligations to less than one-seventh of the original figures. More permanent arrangements were envisaged by the Knox-Castrillo Convention of June 6, 1911. It called for a loan to the new regime of Adolfo Díaz which would permit it to pay off all foreign claims immediately. American investors who had been coaxed by Secretary of State Knox to put up the capital for the loan were to be protected through a financial receivership until liquidation of the debt.

This convention was never brought to a vote in the Senate because of the vigorous public reaction against Dollar Diplomacy. The President and his Secretary of State had sought to substitute American for European funds in Nicaragua to minimize the prospects of instability near the strategic Canal Zone. Opponents contended that America had intervened in order to protect investments, though as a matter of fact her financial stake in Nicaragua was only about $2.5 million — less than that in any other Latin-American republic save one. Behaving like a man of conviction, Taft saved the convention by negotiating it on a private basis. As a result, an American banking firm participated in the financial receivership and took over some of the responsibilities that would otherwise have been exercised by the State Department. This arrangement lasted well beyond World War I.

Dollar Diplomacy was also employed in Honduras after the familiar preliminary developments had taken place. Years of borrowing money without repaying it had enabled the government there to run up an impressive debt. When its obligations reached $110 million in 1909, foreign creditors, headed by the British, insisted upon some definite funding arrangements. Washington promptly invoked the Roosevelt Corollary to avert the "danger" of British control of Honduran finance. Secretary Knox embarked on a new quest for American capital to replace the British funds. It took him until 1911 to convince American bankers of their patriotic duty. In the end, dollars were substituted for bullets. As arranged by the Knox-Parades Convention, United States investors took over the debt of Honduras, and agents approved by the American government as well as by the interested financiers supervised the administration of the customs. As in the case of Nicaragua, the nearness of Honduras to the vital Canal Zone provided a reason for intervention.

WILSON AND THE CARIBBEAN

When Woodrow Wilson entered the White House on March 4, 1913, the public expected a drastic change. The new President was an idealist and an accomplished phrasemaker. Not only did he denounce Dollar Diplomacy and the use of force south of the border, but he sounded as if he intended to reverse our basic policy in that region. Presumably the era of "financial imperialism," as he called it, was over and would be replaced by a new dispensation featuring democracy, good will, and respect for international law. Circumstances, indeed, favored such a shift. After the almost effortless displays of United States predominance during the preceding decade, it was impossible to continue believing that outside powers threatened the Hemisphere. Of course, neither Wilson nor the voters looked forward to the liquidation of America's dominant position. Although he talked like a citizen of the world, he was really no more capable of repudiating traditional policy than his predecessors who moralized less. This was especially true in his case because there was an inescapable contradiction between his intentions and his deeds, and it grew out of his fundamental point of view. As a political scientist Wilson had been preoccupied with governmental process. A corollary faith in the efficacy of structure led him to believe that he could export democracy by forcing outsiders without experience in self-government to accept American institutions. He simply could not see that selling democracy abroad by destroying the free choice which is its essence is a self-defeating enterprise.

Wilson's outlook reflected that of the typical American in this transitional period. Earlier generations had also been convinced of the superiority of their institutions and had longed to export them, but philosophical wisdom and limitations of power curbed their missionary fervor. By the second decade of the twentieth century, both restraints had begun to disappear. First of all, the United States now possessed power to burn and was disillusioned with conquest and empire building. The dissemination of democracy seemed an appropriate project for people who had always believed in their own superiority — a superiority based not on race, culture, and similar ethnic characteristics but on ideals worthy of export. Secondly, the content of democracy had begun to be redefined in the later phase of the Progressive movement in a manner which encouraged its export. The criterion for measuring American dedication to democracy was shifted from a fixed body of moral and philosophical principles to enthusiasm for experimentation and change. The infection of American political thought with Social Darwinism and Pragmatism placed the emphasis on social and economic progress. As a result, the essence of democracy came to be equated with the evolutionary process and the manifestations of democracy to be identified with the eight-hour day, improved living standards, technological efficiency. Redefinition of democracy in economic terms tempted Americans to disseminate it abroad, because the export of economic techniques is always easier than the export of principles. This trend in popular sentiment, interacting with the Wilsonian faith in the effectiveness of structural change in government, promoted a burst of crusading zeal.

The fruits of Wilson's evangelism were initially most apparent in Santo Domingo, where his methods showed a considerable contrast to those of his immediate predecessors. The merry whirl of revolutions on the tiny island affronted his "democratic" sensibilities. The political habits of the Santo Domingans had also annoyed Roosevelt and Taft, but principally because their behavior bred disorder and financial instability. Both Republican Presidents had concerned themselves less about the procedures used by Santo Domingans in recruiting chief executives than about the desirability of installing cooperative ones. Wilson insisted not only on democratic elections but upon uniformly friendly administrations, which such elections were not likely to produce.

In 1914 Wilson forced Santo Domingo to hold a general election which brought Jiminez to the presidency. All might have gone well had not Wilson insisted that Santo Domingo also accept a treaty expanding American financial control beyond the terms of the 1907 agreement. His demands got Anti-imperialism off to a conspicuously bad start. The natives retaliated with a revolution under the leadership of Desiderio Arias, the Secretary of War. Determined to teach the citizens a lesson in self-government, Wilson dispatched marines to occupy the capital in May 1916. Jiminez resigned, and the legislature democratically selected a successor whom Wilson would not recognize because he refused to sign the treaty. This experiment in educating Santo Domingans for self-government came to an abrupt end on November 29, 1916, when their country was placed under American military government. For the ensuing eight years the United States Navy Department ran the country with officers of the Marine Corps in cabinet posts.

American control over Nicaragua was also tightened and extended by Wilson despite ideological statements that pointed to a contrary policy. He had inherited a series of negotiations between the Taft administration and Nicaragua whereby the United States was to pay $3 million in return for a long-term option on canal rights. Since the Senate had not ratified the agreement before Taft left office, President Wilson and Secretary of State Bryan renegotiated it. At the suggestion of Nicaragua's President Dias, whose government desperately needed cash, new provisions were added that would have made his state a protectorate like Cuba. Only the mulishness of the Senate saved Wilson and Bryan from engaging in a policy they had previously denounced. A third draft of the treaty omitted the provision for a protectorate. In final form the agreement gave the United States perpetual and exclusive rights to build a canal through Nicaragua; a ninety-nine-year lease of the Great and Little Corn islands; and the privilege of establishing a naval base on Nicaraguan territory on the Gulf of Fonseca, also for a ninety-nine-year period. A final provision granted the United States an option to renew both the lease on the islands and the fortification privileges for an additional ninety-nine years. In return for these concessions, the United States was to pay the Nicaraguan government $3 million and supervise the expediture of the money. Wilson's interest in this treaty suggested that he possessed the same excessive concern about American security in the isthmian area as his predecessors. He presented the instrument to the Senate on August 5, 1914, and shortly thereafter the legislators acted favorably on it.

Costa Rica complained that the treaty disregarded her interests in the San Juan River portion of the proposed canal. El Salvador and Honduras made similar objections about the violation of their rights in the Gulf of Fonseca. The three republics refused to be placated by an amendment, graciously added by the Senate, which asserted that their rights were not impaired. They then took their case to the Central American Court of Justice. That body handed down a verdict against Nicaragua. The latter, with the backing of Washington, ignored the award. The defiant attitude of the United States killed the Court in 1918, just at the time that Wilson had begun to advocate the establishment of similar judicial procedures on a world-wide basis.

WILSON AND MEXICO

In both Santo Domingo and Nicaragua Wilson had inherited an interventionist policy that would not have been easy to reverse. There was, however no prior pattern in Mexico that would justify the divergence between his theory and his practice. The fact that his avowedly Anti-imperialistic policy produced three years of intervention in Mexico can be explained only in terms of his theoretical point of view. He was determined not only to export democratic institutions to Mexico but to be the judge of whether the Mexicans used them properly. In the process he was to unite the habitually quarrelsome Mexicans against the United States, and to undermine the already precarious position of American investors, whose interests he made a point of ignoring. Since Mexico possessed too large a territory and population to be democratized by a detachment of marines and since Wilson shrank from a policy of conquest, his intervention was bound to fail. In the futile pursuit of doctrinaire objectives, he also damaged American strategic and economic interests.

The point of departure for American interest in Mexico was the revolution of 1910 that ended the dictatorship of Porfirio Díaz. The latter had held power for over three decades, and his ruthless eradication of political opposition had created unusual political stability. He had also encouraged the investment of foreign capital and on the eve of the revolution a sum of approximately two billion dollars — half of it American — had found its way into a variety of enterprises. High returns for investors deprived the Mexican people of benefits from the development of native resources. Resentment of foreign exploiters was one of the ingredients of revolutionary sentiment, although the Catholic Church and the large landholders also provided conspicuous targets for the masses.

The victorious revolutionaries initially vested power (1911) in Francisco Madero, who attempted to establish a constitutional democracy. In accordance with normal usage in the international community, the Taft administration immediately recognized the Madero government. The political complexion of the new regime appealed to Americans and seemed unlikely to disturb their economic interests. Unfortunately, the new government did not have an opportunity to become firmly seated. The complex machinery of democracy was about as useful to the illiterate Mexican masses as a disassembled and nicely crated tractor would have been to their Aztec ancestors. They clamored for more drastic reforms than the scrupulous Madero was willing to sponsor. Moreover, some of the ambitious Mexican politicians who had put Madero in power soon deserted him. As a consequence, the government was overthrown in February 1913 and the chief executive was murdered. His successor, Victoriano Huerta, had been involved in the plot. Huerta's emergence from the snake pit of Mexican politics inaugurated a decade of disorder, civil war, and factionalism.

Taft, whose term was to expire within a month, turned the problem of recognizing the Huerta government over to Wilson. The latter promptly attempted to achieve the downfall of Huerta by withholding recognition. With this end in view he dispatched John Lind, a former Governor of Minnesota, to Mexico. Lind could serve as nothing more than a personal emissary since his mission was to survey the several factions and to pick one which would meet the standards of Wilson.

This procedure broke sharply from the accepted practice of the international community. Hitherto the United States itself had taken the view that a state was entitled to recognition if it possessed a functioning government. The revolutionary origin of the American government and the effect of nineteenth-century Latin-American revolutions in ousting European powers from the Hemisphere argued for immediate recognition of such regimes. The practice was, moreover, an indispensable rule of the Western State System. Known as *de facto* recognition, it involved several important corollaries: (1) the internal affairs of a country are not the legitimate concern of its neighbors; (2) changes in government do not justify interference by other states; (3) ideological resemblances or differences between governments should not affect the question of recognition. When Wilson reversed this traditional policy he committed the United States to a long, unprofitable intervention in Mexican affairs.

At first he thought that American diplomatic pressure would destroy Huerta. When this move failed, he resorted to the Dollar Diplomacy he had repeatedly denounced. Politicians hostile to Huerta were told that if they organized a new government, American bankers would be induced to provide the loans necessary to keep it in power. The Mexicans did not take the bait, and the Huerta government showed every sign of durability. At this point, John Lind ended his mission on a note of failure and frustration. Exasperated by the quality of Mexican politics, he recommended that the United States occupy Mexico City. This proposal for armed intervention was the only logical step open to Wilson if he intended to persist in his determination. But since he recoiled from military operations, he devised more pinpricks which not only failed to overthrow the Huerta regime but actually increased its popularity. He induced several European governments to withdraw the *de facto* recognition they had granted. He removed the embargo on shipments of arms so that weapons would reach Huerta's enemies. When the General purchased arms in Europe, the American fleet virtually blockaded Vera Cruz to keep them out.

While engaging in these maneuvers, Wilson informed Congress in his annual message (December 1913) that the United States had no intention of intervening in Mexico. Matters reached a climax in April 1914, when several United States sailors, who went ashore at Tampico to buy gasoline, were arrested and taken to local military headquarters. The commander promptly released them with profuse apologies. Nevertheless Admiral T. H. Mayo, commander of the American naval forces, chose to make an issue of the incident although the United States had sustained no injury to life or property. He sent an ultimatum to the Mexican general in Tampico demanding: (1) "formal disavowal of and apology for the act;" (2) "severe punishment for the officer responsible;" and (3) a public ceremony in which Mexico would "hoist the American flag in a prominent position and salute it with twenty-one guns."

Desirous of avoiding further trouble, Huerta complied with the first two demands immediately. He also expressed his willingness to order a salute provided that the Americans responded with a gun-for-gun reply in honor of Mexico. Mayo, who had exceeded his authority in issuing the ultimatum, refused the offer and was supported by the State Department. Wilson threatened war by referring the matter to Congress. When Huerta still refused to yield, the President made a formal request on April 20, 1914, for authorization to use armed force in Mexico. The following day the House of Representatives gave the necessary authority by a vote of 323 to 19, and the Senate took similar action on April 22 by a vote of 72 to 13. The day before, however, the administration had instructed Admiral Mayo to occupy Vera Cruz, and he did so after a short bombardment. The pretext for this action was that a German merchant vessel intended to unload a shipment of arms destined for the Huerta government.

Inasmuch as Huerta had neither used arms against the United States nor given any intention of doing so, the propriety of American behavior was open to serious question. The legal position would not have been materially better even if there had been proof of hostile Mexican intentions International law allowed states at war to blockade each other's ports and confiscate shipments of arms, but did not countenance blockades — to say nothing of naval bombardments — by states formally at peace with one another. The action at Vera Cruz created additional perplexities because the United States seemed to be seeking satisfaction from the Huerta government which it did not recognize.

The administration could have simplified its legal position by declaring war, but this the President was unwilling to do. His entire policy had been predicated on the assumption that the Mexicans cherished democracy and would welcome help in overthrowing a dictator. The successive failures of diplomatic pressure, embargo, and military bluster to undermine Huerta's standing with his own people had made undemocratic government popular, If Wilson persisted in the present policy, it seemed likely to end in the imposition of a democratic government that was unpopular. The President had wound up in a blind alley. Aside from war, his only alternative was retreat.

Wilson's distress gratified dictators all the way from Mexico City to the Straits of Magellan. They were fearful of more hemispheric crusades in behalf of democratic government, but they saw the wisdom of encouraging Wilson to retreat by helping him to save face. Accordingly, Argentina, Brazil, and Chile offered to mediate. Wilson accepted promptly. Mediators and principals met at Niagara Falls in May 1914. It quickly became apparent that the United States would accept any settlement which provided for the elimination of Huerta. Within a month a formula had been worked out which called for the establishment of a provisional government in Mexico "avowedly and sincerely in favor of . . . agrarian and political reforms." In effect, this meant a government headed by Huerta's leading rival, Carranza. The provisional agreement also called for the settlement of the financial claims of foreign powers by a commission. As part of the compromise, the United States waived all claims to an indemnity for its operations.

The whole scheme almost foundered on the refusal of Carranza to cooperate. His following had begun to gain strength in the multifactional struggle and he refused to jeopardize his position by receiving help from foreign powers. However, American acceptance of mediation deprived Huerta of the sympathy of other Latin-American states, and the combination of outside pressure and internal dissidence proved too much for him. In July he fled the country and was succeeded by Carranza.

The aftermath in Mexico was neither democracy nor stability but contention and civil war. Although Carranza invited American businessmen to return and operate their concessions, he could not protect those who accepted his offer. As the revolution developed, it became more violent and was aggravated by foreign interference. Forty-seven Americans lost their lives between

1910 and 1912; seventy-six perished during the next three years, most of them after the flight of Huerta; and the mortality rate was to double during the period from 1916 to 1920. On January 10, 1916, Francisco Villa, Carranza's rival, massacred eighteen Americans operating a mine in Santa Isabel. Protests from Washington elicited nothing but promises from the feeble Carranza government. Villa showed his contempt for both Washington and Mexico City by crossing the border and killing seventeen more during a raid on Columbus, New Mexico.

This defiance was more than the United States could bear. Wilson, with the consent of Congress, organized a punitive expedition. Under General John J. Pershing fifteen thousand American troops began to play bloody, dusty, and hopeless tag with Villa in his own back yard. The latter raided Texas several times in May 1916, and American counterraids brought increasing friction with the Carranza government. It was only a matter of time until American armed forces should clash with Mexican regulars. The incident occurred in June at Carrizal, where seventeen American soldiers attached to the second punitive expedition were captured. Carranza freed them after strong protests from Washington. A series of conferences between the two governments ended in deadlock. With Villa unpunished, Carranza unfriendly, American citizens unrevenged, and American hopes unfulfilled, Wilson withdrew troops during February 1917. The imminence of United States involvement in the European war provided him a welcome excuse to terminate an unsuccessful policy. In March 1917 the Mexican Congress confirmed Carranza's title to the presidency and adopted a new constitution. The timing of the move suggests that the Mexicans were determined to defer all governmental reforms until the Wilson administration could not possibly receive credit for them.

Neither American guidance nor native initiative could make Mexico democratic in the opening decades of the century. Carranza was overthrown and murdered in May 1920. His successor, General Obregón, took office immediately and was elected president four months later. He wore a bulletproof vest, but it did not protect him from assassination in 1928. Another decade elapsed before Mexico settled down to selecting her rules in honest elections and abiding by the results of the ballot box.

THE "DEMOCRATIZATION" OF HAITI

Like Mexico, the Caribbean island of Haiti escaped direct American intervention until Wilson became President. As in Santo Domingo, the turnover of governments was rapid and led to political instability, loose financial practices, and inconvenience for foreign investors. The turbulence came to the attention of Theodore Roosevelt, but he lacked a good excuse for intervention. Subsequently the Taft administration — reflecting its preoccupation with Dollar Diplomacy — played a part in the reorganization of the

National Bank of Haiti. The French, who had hitherto dominated the Bank, were forced to make room for American and German investors. Thereafter both political disorders and the complaints of investors mounted. The Bank pursued policies which helped to intensify the crisis. German demands for a large voice in Haitian finances were brushed aside by the United States in the name of the Monroe Doctrine. In the summer of 1914, the Wilson administration landed American marines to transport about half a million dollars' worth of funds to New York.

An uneasy period followed during which Secretary of State Bryan attempted to negotiate a treaty establishing the customary American direction of customs and fiscal policy. He also sought to extract pledges from the Haitian government that it would not permit other powers to establish naval bases in its waters. A kindred concern over political conditions took the form of a recommendation that the United States supervise an election. These proposals indicate that America had found more reasons than usual for Caribbean intervention. Aside from the protection of the Monroe Doctrine and American investors, there was a brand-new security phobia growing out of World War I. Wilson had come to crave stability in the America sphere of influence even at the sacrifice of Anti-imperialism.

Progress on the treaty was delayed for nearly a year because no Haitian president remained in office long enough to sign it. American patience became exhausted when another revolution broke out in July 1915. Wilson ordered a detachment of marines under Admiral Caperton to occupy the island, and the United States took over on July 26, 1915. Washington insisted on a democratic election but made its preference for Philippe Dartiguenave unmistakably clear. The National Assembly obliged on August 12 and elected him by a 4 to 1 majority.

The new American Secretary of State, Robert Lansing, promptly drafted a treaty. It envisaged such sweeping American controls that the Haitian legislature balked and Dartiguenave tried to resign. Slight revision coupled with Washington's hint that full government by the United States was the only alternative produced the compliance of the native legislators on November 15. Anticipating delay and opposition in the Senate, the State Department took the precaution of putting the essential provisions in operation immediately by executive agreement. The upper house in an unexpected fit of cooperation approved the arrangements without public debate in February 1916. Formal ratification took place seven months later.

In commenting on the treaty, Julius Pratt observed that "it went further in establishing American control and supervision than the Platt Amendment treaty with Cuba or the Dominican treaty of 1907 or both of them combined." The individual provisions bear out his conclusion. They conferred on America complete control of fiscal policy and the right to appoint key officials in the fields of civil works and internal security. They also provided that the United States might intervene in the future at its discretion. These terms were to be binding for ten years, and renewable for ten more at the option of Washington. Relaxation of American control did not begin until 1930, and troops were not withdrawn until 1934; final extrication from Haiti's internal affairs took place in 1941.

Under American control the Haitians sacrificed little democracy, for they had never possessed much of it. Neither Admiral Caperton's marines nor a new constitution granted by the Wilson administration in 1920 stimulated self-government. In fact, the constitution was never permitted to go into operation.

PURCHASE OF THE VIRGIN ISLANDS

The increasing reliance of the Wilson administration on security considerations to justify extensions of American power in the Caribbean is illustrated by the purchase of the Danish West Indies in 1916. After the outbreak of World War I, European military power was pinned down on the Continent. Nevertheless, between 1915 and 1917 Washington began to display alarm over the threat of German intervention in the Caribbean. As we have already seen, such considerations played a part in American intervention in Haiti. They also did duty in the purchase of the Danish West Indies, although America had long coveted the islands because of their strategic location on the Anagada Passage into Caribbean waters. Secretary of State Seward had tried to purchase them in 1867, only to be blocked by a recalcitrant Senate. John Hay had offered Denmark $5 million for them in 1902, but on that occasion the Danes refused to sell. Secretary of State Lansing renewed the offer and supported the bid with some old-fashioned shotgun diplomacy. Early in 1916 he told Copenhagen that America, fearing a German attempt to take the islands, would occupy them herself if the threat materialized. Inasmuch as Lansing made it perfectly clear that the United States would be the judge of what constituted a threat, Copenhagen decided that it would be prudent to sell. The United States offered $20 million, Denmark asked for $27 million and accepted a very satisfactory $25 million. The treaty of purchase for the Virgin Islands, as the Danish West Indies would henceforth be called, was signed on August 4, 1916, and ratified on January 17, 1917.

RESULTS OF AMERICAN HEMISPHERIC POLICY

The foregoing survey of the relations between America and the states within her sphere of influence points to the conclusion that the United States treated them in a more enlightened and humane way than the European powers treated their dependencies. In general, the United States relied upon periodic intervention in the affairs of hemispheric republics and avoided turning them into colonies. Whenever she interfered in internal operations, she improved sanitation, education, and governmental services. If she took over fiscal administration, it always became more efficient. Usually financial reforms resulted in more revenue for the local government even after deductions for debt payments to foreign investors. None of these improvements, however, reconciled the Latin Americans to paternalistic supervision. Domination by the United States on any terms was an affront; the citizens of the Latin-American republics would willingly have sacrificed all material progress for complete freedom from the "Colossus of the North."

The empire system had some unfortunate effects on Americans, notably in feeding their self-esteem and self-deception. The fact of American domination of the Hemisphere was so well concealed from most citizens that they simply did not believe their empire existed. With characteristic self-righteousness they ascribed the cooperation of Latin-American states to a recognition of the superiority of American ideals. If they were aware of the role of force in securing compliance with United States policy, they assumed that it was used only on rare occasions. The unwillingness of Americans to see the relationship between their power and their ability to market their ideals left them unprepared for the frustrations of World War I. They were to embark on the Great Crusade with the erroneous notion that their principles would be as acceptable in areas where the United States did not possess preponderant power as in the Western Hemisphere where she did.

SUGGESTED READINGS

1. Bemis, S. F., *The Latin-American Policy of the United States.*
2. Hill, H. C., *Roosevelt and the Caribbean.*
3. Perkins, Dexter, *Hands Off: A History of the Monroe Doctrine.*

CHAPTER NINE

THE UNITED STATES AND THE FAR EAST (1900-1917)

THE FAR EAST BEFORE 1900

If John Hay did not always know what the trouble was, he at least knew where it was. On the eve of the Boxer Rebellion (1900) he proclaimed: "The storm center of the world has shifted . . . to China." American eyes needed to shift only slightly; they were already focused on the Far East. Victory in the Spanish-American War had recently given the United States possession of the extensive Philippine island chain off the Asian mainland. It had also raised popular expectations that the archipelago would serve as a springboard for penetration of the lucrative China market.

Yankee interest in the sprawling Manchu empire had first been aroused nearly a century earlier. Adventurous Salem merchants had dispatched their clipper ships to China before the War of 1812; after commercial supremacy had passed from New England to New York, the trade was conducted on a still larger scale. American Far Eastern policy during most of the nineteenth century concerned itself with the protection of commercial privileges. The device relied upon to secure this objective was a series of "most-favored-nation" treaties. China accepted such an agreement in 1844, and Japan followed suit in 1854 and again in 1856. Under these treaties the United States assured herself of all the concessions extracted from weak Asian powers by European states without assuming commitments or responsibilities. Until the closing years of the century the policy worked satisfactorily. The European states had been strong enough to establish important commercial privileges and contemptuous enough of American power to tolerate Washington's transparent strategy of stealing a free ride. China had also given an unintentional assist to American policy by remaining just strong enough not to collapse and just weak enough not to resist the encroachment of outside powers effectively.

This unstable equilibrium broke down just as the United States was acquiring the Philippines and preparing to expand operations. The development took place against a background of regional power relationships different from those in the Western Hemisphere and in Europe. The Far East had not entered the Western State System as a single unit dominated by a pre-eminent state, as the New World had done. Neither had it come onto the international stage with the restraints of a balance of power operating among its members, as in Europe. On the eve of its full-scale involvement in world politics in 1895, it was a hybrid system that defies easy classification. It featured one resident great power (Japan), an absentee great power connected by a land bridge (Russia), an aspirant to great-power status (China), and a complex of colonial possessions and spheres of influence. An equilibrium of sorts existed among the European powers with oriental possessions, and between them and the resident powers.

The inherent instability of such an arrangement was aggravated by several factors. For one thing, the diplomacy of balance had not been clearly established and stylized by centuries of use. The resulting uncertainty about the rules of the game tended to thwart the crystallization of the balance at the normal point where great-power interests intersect. Second, the European states with Asian possessions assigned a higher priority to developments on their own continent than in the Far East. Some of them, like Great Britain and France, tried to compensate for losses in their relative power elsewhere by strengthening their position in the Orient. Germany followed the reverse procedure of trying to distract her troublesome rival Russia from European questions by encouraging the involvement of the Tsarist empire in eastern Asia. The pursuit of either policy by nonresident powers subordinated the Orient to European considerations and added external sources of instability to those already existing in the area.

The immediate cause for the explosion of the oriental powder keg was the spectacular collapse of Chinese power in the Sino-Japanese War (1894–95). This event climaxed a century of slow disintegration of the Manchu empire, demonstrated to the world that China was a vacuum area, and invited the resident and nonresident powers to contend for the possessions of the victim. China had been drawn into the fatal trial of arms by a quarrel with Japan over the control of Korea. Her defeat cost her the Pescadores Islands and Formosa. She also gave up all claims to Korea, which promptly became a bone of contention between Russia and Japan. Only the intervention of a European triumvirate composed of Germany, France, and Russia enabled China to withstand Japanese demands for economic concessions and railroad leases on the Liaotung peninsula. This action did not reflect a determination to arrest dismemberment of the Chinese Empire but a desire to prevent Japan from taking the lion's share of the spoils. Consequently it was the prelude to the most vigorous period of alien penetration. After its diplomatic victory over Japan in 1895, the triumvirate promptly placed the Chinese under political and financial obligations. Russia

The Chinese puzzle. (Inter-Ocean, *Chicago*.)

improved her position most during the ensuing three years. Neither her European ally (France) nor her European rival (Germany) tried to curb her appetite for a Far Eastern empire. In fact, Berlin actually encouraged the Tsar's government in the hope that it would get too involved to interfere in the Balkans and in the Middle East. The upshot of this policy was that in 1898 Russia extracted from China a twenty-five year lease of the southern Liaotung peninsula, the ports of Dairen and Port Arthur, and railroad rights from Harbin to those cities. Fresh demands by other European powers followed immediately. Relying on the traditional policy of compensation, the British secured a similar lease on the port of Weihaiwei across the bay from Port Arthur. France took Kwangchow, and Germany secured Shantung on roughly the same terms.

Two states that had not participated in the leasing arrangements viewed them with dismay. The Japanese were infuriated to see the Russians take over the concessions from which they had been ousted by diplomatic pressure in 1895. The Americans had lost nothing directly but were apprehensive about the future. Trade with China represented only two per cent of their entire foreign commerce but that modest proportion seemed likely to shrink further if the Manchu government proved unable to enforce the most-favored-nation treaties. Concessions already granted had seriously weakened China's prospects of remaining in control of her own house, and America faced the prospect of eventual exclusion unless she took positive steps to protect her position.

The simultaneous intensification of the China crisis and of American expansionist sentiment in 1898 eliminated any possibility that the United States would suffer the loss of her interests by default. Always sensitive to infringements on commercial rights, she was in an especially adventurous mood after the Spanish-American War. Dreams of Americanizing the Pacific in the near future assured public approval of an energetic policy.

At the outset Washington was much more clear about the need for action than it was about the type of action needed. Official irresolution found expression from 1898 to 1903 in a vacillating policy that was rooted in misconceptions about the relative importance of the two principal interests. Broadly speaking, these were (1) strategic and (2) commercial. In the long run the protection of the second would depend on the first.

The United States, however, mistook the vanishing stability of the Orient for a permanent equilibrium. As a result, she assumed that strategic interests would take care of themselves, and she concentrated therefore on the protection of commercial interests. This choice also reflected a hope that America could create a Pacific empire comparable to her New World empire. Accustomed to operating in the Western Hemisphere, where she possessed preponderant power, she expected to proceed on the same basis in the Far East. The plan envisaged a direct plunge into the China market from her Philippine base. The great powers were supposed to welcome American initiative and accept any rules that Washington might devise for safeguarding American commercial interest. On the contrary, no prospect existed for general acceptance of such a program. Had America thought about the Far East in terms of the power relationships prevailing in a regional balance, she would have recognized the futility of a narrow commercial policy. As it was, she commenced operations with her customary disregard for the stabilizing principles of the Western State System. The resulting collision between her objectives and the realities of the situation caused a rapid change in her policy at the end of the century.

THE OPEN DOOR NOTES

The first opportunity for the United States to take a larger role in the Orient came in the form of an invitation from England. In March 1898, British Ambassador Sir Julian Pauncefote suggested to Secretary of State John Sherman a joint Anglo-American declaration on policy. Specifically, Pauncefote proposed that the two powers cooperate to protect (1) the political and territorial integrity of China against further encroachments and (2) the equality of trading privileges and other economic opportunities.

The bid anticipated by a few weeks the wholesale demands on the Manchu empire for concessions and represented an effort to forestall them. America promptly rejected the offer. She had not yet acquired Far Eastern possessions from Spain nor had she become convinced that her interests in China were endangered. By the end of 1898, however, American opinion had sufficiently altered to encourage a fresh approach from the British. The new proposals, made in January 1899, again envisaged joint Anglo-American action. John Hay, who had recently replaced Sherman as Secretary of State, harbored pro-British sentiments and a flair for international intrigue. President McKinley also took a larger view of American responsibilities after he had assumed leadership of the expansionist movement in 1898. Even so, neither McKinley nor Hay wanted British cooperation badly enough to risk the hostility of both the American public and the Senate. Popular suspicion of Britain was deeply rooted, and senatorial obstruction of any proposal for an entangling alliance was a foregone conclusion. These formidable obstacles caused the administration to reject the second British bid for cooperation.

Unaccustomed to thinking in terms of a power context, Washington missed the significance of the offer. The century-old Pax Britannica was ending, and Britain was finding it impossible to cope on equal terms simultaneously with Germany in Europe, France in Africa, Russia in the Middle East, Japan in the Far East, and her own colonial peoples elsewhere. In the process of a strategic retrenchment on several fronts, she had already written off the Western Hemisphere and was about to give up sole responsibility for the Far East. Nevertheless she hoped to preserve her huge investments and markets by easing the United States into a joint defense. She assumed that interest in Far Eastern commerce would encourage Washington to cooperate in blocking further subdivision of China into spheres of influence. Her only miscalculation was that she saw the importance of China's integrity to America long before the Americans themselves. When the United States finally understood where her interest lay, she went beyond the modest British proposal for joint defense of China and became holder of the balance of power in the Far East.

Meanwhile the condition of the Manchu empire continued to deteriorate. The Italians, who had been frozen out of the scramble for leases in 1898, made demands on Peking in February 1899. Farther north, the Japanese and Russians stepped up the tempo of their duel for exclusive control of Korea and Manchuria. By midsummer it had become apparent that Great Britain would no longer defend the integrity of China singlehanded but would make the best possible terms with the partitioning powers. This left the United States with the unpleasant prospect of being excluded from Chinese markets altogether unless she shared in the partition or took steps to prop up the Manchu state. These developments as well as the activity of various pressure groups created the proper atmosphere for vigorous measures to protect American interests.

The initiative was provided by W. W. Rockhill, a State Department official and trusted adviser of John Hay, who had spent some time in the diplomatic service in the Far East. Acting on the advice of a retired British customs official, Alfred Hippisley, Rockhill drafted a memorandum recommending that the United States act independently of Great Britain. This proposal was approved with minor modification by Hay and placed before McKinley, who accepted it on August 28, 1899, as a basis for policy. It has never been determined whether Hippisley acted with the knowledge of the British Foreign Office when he suggested unilateral American intervention. If Hippisley operated on his own initiative, his achievement was indeed remarkable because he helped to involve the United States in China after two unsuccessful attempts by London. Immediate American action did not go so far as London had envisaged in official proposals, but it was sufficiently entangling to assure further steps when the crisis deepened. From the British standpoint, the disadvantage of not having the policy cleared through Whitehall was more than counterbalanced by the prospect that the responsibility for stability would pass to America. Her wholehearted support of unilateral intervention was to be sustained by a fear of helping England attain her own objectives and by a feeling of moral superiority to all the contending powers. Notwithstanding her acceptance of colonial burdens as a result of the Spanish-American War, she intended to proceed on the assumption that she was not an imperialist state.

The implementation of the Rockhill memorandum took the form of a series of communications directed by Hay to the governments involved in China. Between the first week of September and the middle of November 1899, notes were sent to Great Britain, Russia, France, Japan, Germany, and Italy. Washington asked each to subscribe to the position set forth in the notes and to promote the general concurrence of all the powers. Known as the "Open Door" notes, they proposed the following rules of conduct:

1. That no power interfere with the interests of other powers in an area controlled by it either as a formal leasehold or as an unofficial sphere of influence.
2. That in such spheres of influence the existing Chinese treaty tariffs should apply to the ports of all powers alike and that the Chinese government should collect such tariffs.
3. That in such spheres of influence harbor dues and railroad charges should be the same for the nationals of the controlling powers and for the citizens of other states.

The Open Door notes fell considerably short of British proposals a year earlier, which had sought to enlist American support for preservation of the political and territorial integrity of China. They said nothing about calling a halt to great-power encroachments on the sovereignty of that empire. In fact, the notes applied only to relatively small areas and to limited aspects of economic penetration. Plainly, the McKinley administration had not made up its mind whether the United States ought to join in the partitioning of China or to take steps to prevent such a development. So she simply asked the great powers which had already carved out special advantages not to exclude the United States from the opportunity for similar profits. In effect, the proposal for the Open Door was a "wait-for-me-while-I-catch-up" policy. Unable to compete on equal terms, America hoped to settle for the principle that future inequalities among exploiters should not be allowed to develop on the basis of past gains.

The recipients of the notes reacted adversely to the thinly disguised suggestion of America that she be excused from the handicaps of a tardy arrival at the partitioning. Only Italy accepted unequivocally, thereby making a virtue out of her inability to extract a leasehold from China the preceding February. The British agreed after excepting Hong Kong and Kowloon. Germany, France, and Japan made adherence conditional on the affirmative action of the other powers. Russia replied in such evasive language that no reasonable interpretation could construe her answer as acceptance.

With five of the six great powers either lukewarm or hostile, Hay ought to have retreated. Instead, he pretended that his circular letter had been unanimously accepted. On March 20, 1900, he informed each of the powers that it was now committed inasmuch as all the others had concurred. Only Japan bothered to challenge his arithmetic. The silence of the rest did not, however, lead to any alteration of their policies. The sole immediate result was to place American prestige behind a policy that would be repeatedly violated and hence guarantee further involvement in oriental affairs. Nevertheless, the Open Door enjoyed considerable popularity in the United States. At the time most Americans did not understand its real meaning, to say nothing of its inadequacies. They thought of it as symbolizing American championship of fair play. Some of them even imagined that it pledged disinterested protection of China from her tormentors. A few years later when the United States actually did become the guardian of China's integrity, the phrase "Open Door" came to be associated with a new policy and tended more and more to serve as a blanket designation for whatever America was doing in the Far East at any given time. Since changes in content did not result in corresponding changes in nomenclature, the evolution of American policy must be explained in other terms.

THE BOXER REBELLION

The original Open Door policy stood the rough wear of international usage barely six months. The crisis which led Hay to enunciate a new position was caused by the Chinese themselves. Pushed beyond endurance, they turned on their uninvited guests in the spring of 1900 and attacked them all simultaneously. Responsibility for this "man-bites-dog" development rested largely with the members of a semimilitary patriotic society whom the westerners dubbed the "Boxers." Growing nationalist sentiment intensified Chinese bitterness against the encroachment of the imperialist powers and made recruits for the Boxers. When this infection spread to the Peking government, an antiforeign faction clustering around the Dowager Empress encouraged the Boxers to make direct assaults on the lives and property of the intruders.

Violence broke out in an attack on the Fengtai railway station near Peking on May 28, 1900. Uncoordinated aggressions on foreigners mounted in the next few weeks, with the result that by mid-June approximately five hundred legation guards and a similar number of non-Chinese civilians were sealed off in Peking. A relief column of more than two thousand men composed of the naval forces of the western powers and Japan stationed in the Tientsin area failed to reopen communications. Heartened by the success of the Boxers and angered by enemy seizure of the Taku Forts (June 17), extremist elements forced the government to declare war on June 20. Elimination of foreign influences by the liquidation of foreigners now became official policy. In the following month over two hundred were killed, most of them missionary families, including wives and children.

The unreasoning ferocity of the Chinese horrified the entire world and provoked prompt reaction. An international force of twenty thousand was rapidly dispatched. It took Tientsin on July 24, and exactly one month later rescued compatriots trapped in Peking. The government fled from the capital the following day. Extensive territory around both cities was occupied, and mopping-up operations continued for nearly a year. Meanwhile the Chinese capitulated in December 1900. The twelve powers which had crushed the rebellion dictated peace terms, which the demoralized government accepted on September 7, 1901. Known as the Boxer Protocol, the settlement revised tariff rates, strengthened the security arrangements of the foreign legations, and provided for the punishment of officials who had directed the action. The most important feature concerned indemnity payments. The great powers set a total of one-third of a billion dollars, payable in installments spread over a forty-year period. Interest charges and other costs eventually doubled the bill. After agreeing to these humiliating terms, the hapless Manchu court returned to Peking and belatedly launched a series of reforms. However, its days were numbered and an unstable coalition of democratic and nationalistic forces overthrew the dynasty in the revolution of 1911.

Notwithstanding her physical remoteness from the site of the crisis and her modest stake in China, America had taken a conspicuous role in the suppression of the rebellion. During the siege of the legation in Peking, she became the first to re-establish telegraphic communication with her minister in China and to inform a nervous world of the safety of the beleaguered. About one-eighth of the combined forces which pushed from Tientsin to Peking in the summer of 1900 were Americans, and before the intervention ran its course five thousand American troops had been engaged. Nevertheless the United States managed to emerge from the incident with Chinese good will by declining to accept the full indemnity of $25 million awarded under the protocol. A sum of $6.5 million was retained to satisfy claims for damage to American life and property, and the rest was returned in two installments (1907–1908 and 1924). The Chinese reacted to this unexpected act by establishing a trust fund for the education of students, many of them in American schools.

MORE OPEN DOOR NOTES

The United States matched her energetic intervention with a new declaration which superseded the Open Door. Fearful that the powers would get out of hand, Hay enunciated the American position on July 3, 1900, before the completion of military operations. He again wrote circular notes to each of the intervening powers. These required no answer and were a unilateral assertion of policy. In straightforward language, they committed Washington to the proposition that the final solution of current difficulties required the preservation of Chinese "territorial and administrative entity" and that all the world should enjoy "equal and impartial trade with all parts of the empire."

Taken at face value, John Hay's second set of notes constituted a diplomatic revolution. They committed the United States at this early date to full-fledged support of Chinese independence from the threats of partitioning powers. In fact, they seemed to say everything on a unilateral basis that America had twice refused to assert jointly with Great Britain in the preceding eighteen months.

Subsequent action indicated that Washington was not quite prepared to accept the full implications of its position. The announced determination to oppose the encroachments of the great powers did not apply to similar behavior on the part of the United States. In November 1900, only five months after the declaration, she tried to lease a naval coaling station at Samsah Bay in Fukien Province from the Manchu government. Since Samsah Bay was already in the Nipponese sphere of influence, Japan thwarted Washington's effort to violate its own declared policy.

The contradictory impulses exhibited in 1900 indicated that American thinking was transitional. In 1898 the United States had regarded all the great powers in the Pacific as expansionist and had proposed playing the game under the favorable rules embodied in the Open Door notes. A few years later she was to adopt the position that no powers should expand at the expense of China. During the Boxer Rebellion and the months immediately thereafter, she showed the split personality of the stabilizer and the competitor. She wanted to establish a peaceful *status quo* that would tie all hands but her own. Expectations of success were geared to her experience in the Western Hemisphere, but the Latin-American formula could not be successfully applied in Asia.

Two more years were to elapse before the United States settled down to a consistent policy of defending Chinese integrity against all comers. The reactions of other states to the notes made the extrication of the United States from Far Eastern politics more difficult. Great Britain, France, and Germany responded favorably to the American attitude, which minimized the likelihood of military and financial reprisals. Heavy commitments in other areas increased the enthusiasm of all three for the *status quo* in the Far East and reduced their capacity for maintaining it. Hence they were inclined to give America as much responsibility as she would take for the preservation of regional stability.

The two powers fronting on the Pacific, Japan and Russia, viewed the activity of Washington with poorly concealed hostility. Neither of them intended to permit America to improve her position while imposing the *status quo* on others. Both contemplated further gains at the expense of China. Japan was the more cautious. Recently industrialized and untested in a major war involving the great powers, she hoped to reach an understanding with Russia. She was willing to acknowledge that Manchuria lay within the Russian sphere of influence in return for a reciprocal statement regarding the Japanese position in Korea. The Tsarist government, however, refused all proposals for an informal partition of North China. Instead, its troops crossed the Amur River and occupied South Manchuria in the fall of 1900. This defiant attitude was emphasized by Russia's refusal to sign the Boxer Protocol or to withdraw the troops. Further, the Tsarist government extracted more secret concessions in Manchuria from the unhappy Chinese.

The varying responses of the United States, Japan, and Great Britain to Russian encroachments in North China had the cumulative effect of making the United States the holder of the Far Eastern balance. Americans were not entirely conscious of the interaction between developments from 1901 to 1905 which conferred on them the custodianship of China's integrity. Nor would they have acknowledged acceptance of their new responsibility in terms of America's relation to the Western State System. On the contrary, the State Department continued to deliver sermons on great-power deportment in China. What distinguished the new policy from the old was not the pronouncements but the specific action taken to check Russian expansion. On February 1, 1902, Secretary Hay protested against a Chinese grant of exclusive mining and railroad privileges to the Tsarist government. Fourteen months later he objected to further Russian attempts to secure a favored position in North China through diplomatic and administrative restrictions on all non-Russians. On October 8, 1903, Washington actually seized the initiative from Moscow; it signed a treaty with China making the Open Door the subject of mutual agreement, and then promptly invoked the formula to forestall Russian closure of Mukden and Antung. These steps indicated that the United States was drifting from a doctrinaire preoccupation with its trading privileges to a concrete concern about the preservation of Far Eastern stability. This gradual reorientation coincided with the abatement of popular enthusiasm for an overseas empire; the incentive to extract concessions from China died with the discovery that the possession of Pacific colonies did not improve commercial opportunities.

THE ANGLO-JAPANESE ALLIANCE

Meanwhile Great Britain and Japan had responded to the Russian threat by signing an alliance on January 30, 1902. This event climaxed a four-year withdrawal of Great Britain from her role as holder of the Far Eastern balance. Initially London had unsuccessfully sought to persuade America to share the burden, but the subsequent willingness of the United States to take responsibility for stability on a unilateral basis left Britain with more freedom of action than she had hoped. The simultaneous multiplication of threats to the British Empire in other theaters hardened her determination to end her isolation in the Orient. An understanding with Japan would provide maximum protection with minimum friction. For the moment, no conflict of interests divided the potential allies in the Orient, for Great Britain did not intend to increase her holdings and Japanese ambitions were pointed toward Korea and Manchuria. Both powers also faced a common enemy. The British feared Russia as the principal disturber of the *status quo,* and the Japanese regarded her as their chief rival in northern China. On the basis of this temporary convergence of interests and animosities, the two countries formally became allies for a five-year period. The treaty opened with a routine avowal of interest in the maintenance of the *status quo,* the independence of China and Korea, general peace, and equal commercial opportunity for all states. Parts of this declaration were half true and others were wholly untrue. Each had to be understood in the context of the times. The second section of the treaty recognized the rights of both signatories to take such measures as they might see fit to protect their interests in the Far East; the specific purpose was to assure advance British approval of any Japanese action in Korea. The following clause provided for the neutrality of either ally in the event that the other went to war with a third power over the protection of its interests; and if a fourth power joined the enemy in a war on one of the signatory powers, then the other was bound to enter the conflict in support of its ally. The final section pledged both powers to consult each other before making a separate agreement with another state. These or similar stipulations continued to constitute the essence of subsequent treaties renewing the alliance.

At the outset the Anglo-Japanese alliance offered substantial advantages to both parties. Great Britain secured (1) diplomatic support for her exposed Far East holdings from the only resident power; (2) a reassurance against exclusion from future Japanese territorial acquisitions (i.e., a sort of private Open Door); and (3) a military ally in case of a general Far Eastern war. Reciprocal benefits for Japan included (1) a free hand from the

British in Korea; (2) insurance against the coalescence of another multi-power alliance like the one that had deprived Japan of her gains in China in 1895; and (3) a stronger position from which to negotiate with the Russians or wage war against them. In brief, Great Britain could concentrate on Europe without critical concern about the Far East, while Japan could concentrate on the Far East without critical concern about Great Britain. No single power in the Pacific was a match for the new allies, and no effective combination was likely to develop because the European states had to assume heavy commitments on the home continent. Until World War I, Great Britain and Japan could count upon being confronted by isolated powers in a weaker position than their own. Under these circumstances Great Britain was to conduct a holding operation, whereas Japan was to exploit her opportunity and improve her position at the expense of Russia. Both consequences assured deeper involvement by the United States in Far Eastern affairs. Britain's abandonment of her role as holder of the balance for a less vulnerable position as a member of the balance left her former responsibility to America. A Japanese attack on Russia created a situation which compelled America to exercise this new responsibility.

THE RUSSO-JAPANESE WAR

Although the Anglo-Japanese alliance encouraged Tokyo to take a stronger stand against Russia, the latter did not adopt a more conciliatory line. Throughout 1902 and 1903, she stepped up the simultaneous infiltration of Korea and of Manchuria. Japan finally lost her patience and broke diplomatic relations on February 6, 1904. Two days later a Nipponese squadron sealed off the Russian fleet in Korea, and a declaration of war followed on February 10. From the beginning, military developments favored Japan. A decisive victory at the Yalu River on May 1, 1904, inaugurated a series of successes on land and sea that filled the Japanese with pride, the Chinese with envy, and the rest of the world with amazement. Port Arthur fell after a seven months' siege on January 2, 1905. Not even the belated arrival of the Russian European squadron made any difference; it was destroyed in the battle of Tsushima Straits on May 27–29.

Damaging as these reverses were, they would not normally have brought the huge Russian empire to its knees. The Tsar, however, was disposed to end the war because of serious internal unrest produced by governmental blunders and by the activity of revolutionary groups. On the other hand, the Japanese, already overextended financially and fearful of getting bogged down in interminable continental warfare, were willing to take their profits and call it a day.

If it had been true that the Orient was a subordinate department of European diplomacy, the Russo-Japanese War would have been subjected to a European solution like the Sino-Japanese War a decade earlier. But times had changed and the canny Japanese in the spring of 1905 began asking the United States to mediate. Russia could not be induced to associate herself with the invitation until after her defeats in May. Upon receiving informal assurance that both parties would accept, the United States made a tender of good offices on June 8, 1905. Negotiations began at Portsmouth, New Hampshire, on August 9, 1905.

America's acceptance of the role of mediator heralded her unconscious capitulation to the compulsions of the balance of power. She possessed the qualifications to function as the holder of the balance in the Far East: (1) adequate power to make its application decisive; and (2) sufficient geographical detachment and political aloofness to function as "an honest broker." Theodore Roosevelt made a pretense of indecision before accepting the formidable responsibility, but American policy had already shaken off the last remnants of a disqualifying ambivalence. Upon the outbreak of hostilities, the United States had exhorted the belligerents to deal moderately with China, on whose soil they were fighting. Subsequently she had participated in a general declaration by neutrals that they would not enrich themselves with further Chinese territory while the war was in progress. The climax had come on January 13, 1905, when Hay had proclaimed United States determination to maintain the "integrity of China and the Open Door in the Orient." Thus in six years America had moved from willing participant in the division of China to defender of China from the partitioners. Thereafter her emergence as custodian of the Far Eastern balance was only a matter of time.

Before the peace discussions opened at Portsmouth, the Japanese insisted on settling the Korean question. Tokyo had established the legal basis for a protectorate a week before the war began by signing a treaty with Korea guaranteeing its territorial integrity. Hay had taken cognizance of Japanese wishes by exempting Korea from the application of the Open Door in his statement of January 13, 1905. Tokyo wanted American acquiescence in writing, but Hay died on July 1, 1905, before the matter could be settled. Although the United States possessed no real bargaining power on this issue, Roosevelt, who had become in effect his own Secretary of State, managed to extract a Japanese pledge of noninterference in the Philippines in return for formal acceptance of Korea's status. The two governments exchanged mutual assurances on July 29, 1905, because Roosevelt did not think he could work a treaty through the Senate. The agreement was subsequently known as the Taft-Katsura Memorandum.

Japan also improved her bargaining position at Portsmouth by renewing the alliance with Great Britain for a ten-year period three days after formal talks had begun. As a result, she pressed Russia for a large indemnity and the cession of Sakhalin Island. Since no third party was present at the negotiations, the United States did not mediate in a strict sense. When the Japanese demands became known, Roosevelt urged moderation on the victors. At the same time he sought to enlist German cooperation in coaxing further concessions from the Russians. The latter felt that they had yielded enough but eventually agreed to give up the southern half of Sakhalin Island. In return the Japanese dropped their demand for an indemnity.

The compromise on Sakhalin enabled both parties to complete and sign a draft of the peace treaty on September 5, 1905, exactly four weeks after the opening of negotiations. Besides the clause covering Sakhalin, the treaty provided for (1) Russian recognition of Japanese predominance in Korea; (2) withdrawal of both countries from Manchuria, which was to be restored to China; (3) the transfer of mining and railroad concessions in South Manchuria and the Liaotung peninsula from Russia to Japan.

The events culminating in the Treaty of Portsmouth demonstrated that a vast redistribution of power had taken place. An oriental power had defeated a European one, and American soil had been utilized for the first time to settle disputes involving states in other continents. Henceforth the Far East would be an independent power complex moving in an orbit of its own, and the center of gravity in world politics would be in the United States rather than Europe.

The new power structure in the Orient bore little resemblance to the balance of forces that had prevailed on the eve of the Boxer Rebellion. The most striking novelty was the substitution of Japan for Russia as the greatest potential threat to the Far Eastern *status quo*. Sole resident great power in the Orient and adept at learning the ways of the West, Japan prepared to enlarge her oriental holdings. The disposition of the Japanese to advance was matched by a reciprocal willingness on the part of the European powers to retreat under pressure. As tensions on the home continent mounted in the decade after 1905, they felt increasingly obliged to transfer their burdens in the East to Uncle Sam.

Although the United States did not foresee the magnitude of her involvement in 1905 nor consciously accept her role as holder of the balance, her instincts were sound. As behooved the honest broker, she modified her attitude during the Russo-Japanese War as the fortunes of the belligerents changed. Initially sympathetic to the underdog Japanese, she wound up trying to limit their gains at the Portsmouth Conference. She recognized that Japan had replaced Russia as the chief disturber of the *status quo,* and promptly revised her policy to block her erstwhile protégé.

THE GENTLEMEN'S AGREEMENT

Increasing American determination to defend the integrity of China would have been sufficient to assure a deterioration of relations with Japan. In addition, the ripening of the controversy over Oriental immigration into the United States sharpened tempers in both countries.

The problem was not new. Chinese had been encouraged to enter in the 1860's because of the critical need for laborers on western railroads. The

Burlingame Treaty of 1868 granted Chinese immigrants all the privileges normally accorded under "most-favored" agreements, except naturalization. During the next decade the influx into California was so rapid that by 1879 they comprised approximately 10 per cent of the population of the state. Local agitators organized a campaign of hate and violence, and Congress responded with an exclusion law which President Hayes vetoed. Subsequent efforts to regulate the matter by treaty culminated in an agreement in 1894. Provision was made for the admission of certain classes of Chinese immigrants, but laborers were excluded, as in an earlier treaty, for a ten-year period. When the terms of this treaty expired, Congress simply re-enacted the exclusion clauses and other pertinent regulations as domestic legislation. This general plan was followed until 1943, when Congress permitted a negligible number to enter under the quota system governing immigration from other nations.

In 1894 Congress also negotiated a treaty with Japan permitting the immigration of her nationals. History repeated itself and within a decade there was agitation for exclusion, based on a variety of grounds. It was asserted that the Japanese resisted cultural assimilation and exhibited a frugality and willingness to work for low wages that native competitors regarded as un-American. These traits led the Japanese to concentrate in clannish fashion in certain sections of California and to dominate a few occupations — notably agriculture and fishing. Nativist groups also professed alarm because an antiquated Japanese law required allegiance from American-born descendants of emigrants until they had rendered military service to the Emperor.

The Japanese government tried to head off the insult of an exclusion act by refusing passports to laborers desirous of emigrating directly to the United States mainland. Adopted in August 1901, this policy did not cut off those who came via Hawaii, Mexico, or Canada. Lax administration also enlarged the eastbound trickle of emigrants. Official friction was avoided until October 1906, when the San Francisco school board ruled that henceforth all Japanese children should attend a separate school for Orientals. Few people really believed that white pupils would be crowded out of their own educational facilities if Japanese youngsters in San Francisco — all ninety-three of them — were allowed to enroll. Some parents, however, worried because the so-called Japanese "schoolboys" were often several years older than American children in the same grade. The immediate repercussions touched off by such a trivial incident indicated that academic segregation was not an issue but an excuse for quarreling about a much bigger question.

National pride and resentment over American superciliousness assured a violent reaction from all sections of the Japanese press. On this and later occasions the implication that Orientals were inferior did a great deal to poison the relations between resident and nonresident powers in the Far East. Fortunately, the Japanese government took a more reasonable view of the problem than did the Japanese public, and Roosevelt saw also that some face-saving gesture was imperative for Tokyo. He assumed that the Japanese would settle for some formula which protected their nationals from being discriminated against by name. Thereupon he acted with customary vigor. First he sent a Cabinet member to the Pacific Coast to coax the school board out of its stand for segregation. When this deferential attempt failed, he denounced the Californians as troublemakers and made vague threats of coercion. An unproductive pilgrimage of the eight school-board members to Washington followed in February 1907. By this time Roosevelt had begun to describe the obstructers as "infernal fools" and to accuse them of "wicked absurdity" and "criminal stupidity." What started out as a controversy between America and Japan became a heated struggle between Washington and California.

The deadlock was eventually broken when the school board rescinded its action in return for a presidential promise to exclude all Japanese immigrants. Tactful implementation of the new policy required several steps. An amendment to the Immigration Act of February 20, 1907, empowered the President to bar the entry of immigrants with passports "to any other country than the United States." Roosevelt showed a fine disregard for the conventional meaning of the amendment by treating Hawaii as a country and stopping Japanese emigration from the islands to the mainland. The practical effect of this maneuver was to exclude the Japanese without discriminating against them specifically. Tokyo showed its gratitude by refusing to issue passports to laborers or their relatives except in certain acceptable categories. This informal arrangement came to be known as the Gentlemen's Agreement of 1907. It lasted with minor modifications until superseded by the legislation of 1924. The Japanese carried out their part of the bargain so efficiently that even immigration to Hawaii was curtailed, though the long-range effect was negligible because the Japanese birth rate exceeded that of other ethnic groups on the islands. By 1940 the Nipponese constituted 37.3 per cent of the Hawaiian population.

Notwithstanding the Gentlemen's Agreement, friction continued. As in Hawaii, the Japanese on the mainland increased much more rapidly than did other racial groups, largely through the practice of selecting wives in Japan from picture post cards, marrying them by proxy, and then bringing them into the United States. Even so, the Japanese population in California and other western states amounted to slightly less than 9,000 by 1924. The existence of this insignificant but growing minority, however, continued to stimulate Nativist anxiety over social and economic problems.

THE ROOT-TAKAHIRA AGREEMENT

While Japan was feuding with America about the status of her nationals in California, she made methodical preparations to improve her Far Eastern position. First she proposed to strengthen her hold on Korea and envelop the remainder of Manchuria. Once these bases on the Asian mainland had been consolidated, she intended to convert China into a protectorate. So far as possible she tried to proceed without violating American interests. Before the Treaty of Portsmouth she had taken the precaution of securing from both the United States and Great Britain the admission that her dominant position in Korea was not contrary to the Open Door. Her diplomacy from 1905 to 1908 aimed at securing similar assurances regarding Manchuria. British acquiescence had been part of the price for renewal of the Anglo-Japanese alliance in 1905. China followed by confirming Japanese possession of Manchurian leaseholds and concessions which had formerly belonged to Russia, and also secretly promised Tokyo that she would not permit any other power to acquire or build competing railroad lines in China. Both France and Russia recognized the special position of Japan in Manchuria in 1907. Only the United States held out, and her resolve was undermined by the capitulation of the European powers. When it became apparent that she would have to stand alone, America made the same concessions as the others in the Root-Takahira Agreement (November 30, 1908). The usual affirmations of virtue predominated. Both parties disclaimed aggressive intentions; they pledged themselves to maintain the *status quo* in the "region of the Pacific Ocean"; they promised to respect each other's territorial possessions in the area; they took vows to preserve the Open Door in China as well as China's "independence and integrity." A final provision obligated Japan and the United States to consult one another on the appropriate steps if their mutual interests were threatened.

As in the case of most contemporary documents spelling out great-power relationships in the Far East, the omissions in the Root-Takahira Agreement proved to be more significant than the assertions. Though the key issue was Manchuria, it was not directly covered. The negotiations prudently refrained from stating whether the phrases "independence and integrity of China" or "region of the Pacific Ocean" applied to Manchuria. The deliberate emphasis on ambiguity meant that the United States had reconciled herself to the presence of the Japanese in Manchuria. Henceforth America would accept Japanese domination there as part of the *status quo*. Theodore Roosevelt knew better than to submit to the Senate any treaty explicitly writing off American interests in Manchuria. He embodied the Root-Takahira terms in an executive agreement and thereby avoided the obstacle of senatorial ratification. Japan accepted the vague phraseology in return for getting the substance of what she wanted.

Roosevelt's policy ended on a mixed note of conciliation and firmness. He had negotiated the Gentlemen's Agreement to avoid a needless affront to Japanese nationalism, and the Root-Takahira Agreement to concede gracefully what America could not prevent. Simultaneously he had called the attention of Japan to growing American power by sending the fleet around the world (1907–1909). Looking back on the preceding decade, America had grounds both for satisfaction and for alarm. In this period she had moved from preoccupation with matching others in the penetration of China to a settled concern with preventing such penetrations. In 1898 China had seemed ripe for exploitation; a decade later its preservation seemed essential to safeguard American interests. This rapid evolution of policy involved hazards as well as responsibilities. The growing determination to preserve stability coincided with the weakening of European powers hitherto interested in maintenance of the *status quo* and with the strengthening of an expansionist Japan. Retreat in the Root-Takahira Agreement was an indication that the Nipponese position in the Far East was improving in relation to America's position.

DOLLAR DIPLOMACY IN THE ORIENT

This unfavorable prospect confronted the new foreign policy team of President William Howard Taft and Secretary of State Philander C. Knox which took over in Washington in March 1909. The more legalistic outlook of the incoming administration foreshadowed a greater rigidity of policy and a decreasing reliance on force. Roosevelt had recognized what was happening, accepted part of the Japanese program, and tried to counteract the rest with a combination of diplomacy and power. Taft was to ignore reality and to attempt to reverse the advance of Japan with a policy based wholly on pacific means.

The new approach was first applied to Manchuria. Secretary Knox assumed that whoever controlled the railroads would control the area. Accordingly he proposed to break Russo-Japanese domination of the railroad system as a prelude to giving it back to China. In a memorandum of December 14, 1909, he addressed the interested governments, recommending a collective policy of foreign loans which would enable the Chinese to acquire gradual control of all railroads in their country. The same memorandum outlined an alternative loan scheme whereby the Manchu government would be given funds to build railroads that would parallel those under alien control and thus neutralize their advantage. The plan was amazingly forthright by customary standards of Oriental diplomacy but took no account of political realities. Only the British accepted it categorically. China and Germany were not in a position to support Knox although both took a favorable view of his proposal. Because of alliance commitments to Moscow in Europe, France made her agreement contingent upon Russo-Japanese acceptance. This made her stand tantamount to a rejection, because neither Russia nor Japan could be expected to relinquish advantages over which they had been willing to fight. Despite her losses in the Treaty of Portsmouth, Russia still held substantial railroad concessions in North Manchuria, and besides, she had never concealed her opposition to the Open Door. The Japanese had always treated American policy pronouncements with more consideration, but now the Knox memorandum provoked Tokyo to unusual bluntness because she felt that the United States was repudiating her recognition of Japan's special position in Manchuria.

The immediate effect of the loan proposal was to drive the erstwhile rivals in Manchuria — Japan and Russia — into each other's arms. Both rejected the proposal in such unmistakable language that Knox could not resort to the Hay formula of 1899 and interpret polite refusal as acceptance. They also concluded a treaty on July 4, 1910, for joint defense of their interests in Manchuria and adjacent portions of Mongolia. A supplementary agreement on July 25, 1912, freed Russia and Japan for railroad building, economic penetration, and a military build-up in their respective spheres of influence. Thus the net result of the American effort to strengthen the Chinese position was disappointing. As holder of the balance the United States ought to have kept Japan and Russia apart but instead had frightened them into active cooperation, further weakened the position of China, and lowered America's influence in the area.

The preference of the Taft administration for the use of economic methods in the conduct of foreign policy survived the fiasco. The emphasis now shifted from loans aimed at the restoration of China's control over her own resources to an oriental version of Dollar Diplomacy. In effect, Taft accepted the thesis that if the great powers did not take their fingers out of the Chinese pie, American and presumably Chinese interests would be served by having the United States keep her fingers in also. The increased tempo of the contest over the privilege of financing railroad construction and other economic enterprises in China reinforced this conclusion. Specifically it looked as if Taft's determination to participate was a reversion to the Open Door policy of an earlier decade. But American motives had changed. The initial concern over Chinese independence as the best guarantee of the Open Door was now replaced by a new concern for the Open Door as the best guarantee of Chinese independence.

Accordingly the administration attempted to shoulder its way into great-power investment projects in hope of controlling them. State Department pressure on American bankers to invest funds in China did not succeed as well as solicitations for a similar purpose in Latin America where risks were smaller. Nevertheless, two years of maneuvering bore fruit on May 20, 1911, when British, French, and German investors permitted the United States to join in financing a Chinese railroad known as the Hukuang project. American participation quickly lost its point because a year later the Japanese and Russians were also admitted. Undaunted by this turn of events, Taft spent the last weeks of his term promoting a six-power consortium to loan China $125 million.

WILSON AND FAR EASTERN ANTI-IMPERIALISM

The policy of propping up China through participation in great-power loans was doomed at the outset by the unfavorable distribution of power in the Far East. The conduct of the French and Russians, who had supported the Japanese in defiance of their long-range interests, simply strengthened the destructive power of Tokyo. The final blow to the policy was delivered by the incoming President, Woodrow Wilson. On March 11, 1913, he fired an opening salvo against the economic orientation of his predecessor's diplomacy. A week later he specifically condemned Taft's China policy.

The diplomatic revolution in Washington would have been more helpful if it had reflected a realistic appraisal of Far Eastern politics. Unfortunately, Wilson's objections were made on doctrinaire grounds and were factually incorrect. He believed that America had aquired an imperialistic stake in China and that Taft's foreign policy had been dominated by self-interested bankers and businessmen. The figures actually show that America's participation in the railroad consortium had not enlarged her economic stake in China to a significant point. Of the total American foreign investment in 1913, only $59 million had found its way to China, and approximately 16 per cent of this figure represented funds tied up in missionary enterprises. Even if the Taft administration had joined in the six-power loan which Wilson vetoed, the United States would have held only slightly more than $7.3 million of the $835 million public debt of China. On the basis of such evidence, it is difficult to sustain Wilson's thesis that the Taft administration was a tool of imperialist groups. The obvious satisfaction of the bankers at being relieved from pressure to pour funds into the disorderly Chinese Republic suggests that they were unhappy tools of the government. Escape from such a risky enterprise more than compensated them for the accompanying misrepresentation of their motives.

Although the administration continued to cherish the goal of preserving Chinese independence, it did not immediately substitute any new method for the one it rejected. The closest thing to Far Eastern policy evolved during the next four and a half years was a combination of noninvolvement and verbal rebukes to challenges to the *status quo*. This formula would have been unproductive enough between 1905 and 1914, when the European powers exhibited a decreasing inclination to check Japanese expansion. It became completely untenable in 1914 because the outbreak of World War I focused all their energies on the home continent, leaving the United States as the only policeman on the beat.

Encouraged by the American policy of noninvolvement, the Japanese used the excuse of their alliance with Great Britain to overrun German Far Eastern possessions in the fall of 1914. By the close of the year they had occupied the naval base at Tsingtao, other German holdings in the Shantung peninsula, and the Kaiser's insular possessions in the Marshalls, the Marianas, and the Carolines. Except for Wake, Guam, and a few other minute American-held islands in the Gilberts, the Japanese now controlled the entire area of the Pacific north of the equator between the Philippine and the Hawaiian groups. If the Philippines had been hostages before, they were captives by December 1914.

The European states demonstrated their helplessness by acquiescing in Japanese action. The British even assisted in the operation on the Shantung peninsula, violating Chinese neutrality while fighting elsewhere to defend Belgian neutrality. The only note of restraint which accompanied these transactions was a four-power (British, French, Russian, and Japanese) agreement on September 5, 1914, pledging the signatories not to make a separate peace — a guarantee that was of small comfort in view of the prospect that the Japanese would fix its eventual terms with the sword.

THE TWENTY-ONE DEMANDS

Having completed their mopping-up operations in the East Pacific, the Japanese were ready to complete the envelopment of China. On January 18, 1915, they peremptorily confronted the helpless revolutionary government of Sun Yat-sen with twenty-one demands. Acceptance in the aggregate would have turned the Chinese Republic into a Japanese protectorate. Tokyo recognized that diplomatic pressure alone would not produce compliance if China received even token encouragement from the United States. Hence, it tried to keep the demands secret. The Chinese president made an identical diagnosis of the situation and let the terms leak out. The reaction of the American public was unfavorable, as both sides had anticipated. Washington began to consider some sort of action beyond its hopeful suggestion at the outbreak of the war that the combatants preserve the *status quo* in the Pacific. Japan sought to forestall intervention by forwarding an expurgated version of the terms to Washington on February 8, 1915. She explained that the demands were only requests, but at the same time she informed the Chinese that the requests were really demands.

Japanese double talk did not entirely reassure Washington. Secretary Bryan was convinced that the *status quo* envisaged by the Root-Takahira agreement had been endangered. Relying on the provision for consultation under such circumstances, he communicated the view of the American government to Tokyo and sent a carbon copy to the Chinese. The content of the note was perplexing. It accepted the Japanese argument that the proposed action would not impinge upon Chinese territorial integrity, disavowed American political interest in China, and recognized that Japanese "territorial contiguity" to Manchuria, Shantung, and parts of Mongolia created "special relations." Having granted the validity and legality of what Japan proposed to do, the note concluded by denying what it had conceded. Tokyo was warned that the United States "could not regard with indifference the domination of China by any other power" and that it favored the maintenance of the Open Door.

The confused tone of the protest reflected the uncertainty of the administration, which stood for the integrity of China but had not yet developed any policy for protecting it. In a vague way Wilson and Bryan sensed that only the United States stood between Japan and a defenseless China. They would have understood her responsibility more clearly had they realized that the exit of the European powers from the Far East left America alone to confront Japan in a simple balance, but ideological considerations prevented them from appraising the position in such terms. As a result, they still hoped that Japan could be stopped by diplomatic protests.

The reaction of Tokyo to the Bryan note was threefold: it modified some of the demands and withdrew others; forwarded the remainder to China in the form of an ultimatum which would expire within forty-eight hours; and bolstered its diplomatic position by agreements with other powers. This partial revision of the twenty-one demands, as well as the abrupt insistence on Chinese acquiescence, indicated respect and fear of America. Washington however, merely won a breathing spell for China, which accepted the modified demands on May 25, 1915. As usual, the Russians cooperated most enthusiastically with Japanese efforts to weaken American diplomacy in the Far East. For the third time in five years both countries renewed their pledge to cooperate in maintaining their oriental holdings. The clauses of the new treaty (July 3, 1916) which were made public contained the usual jargon about the preservation of "permanent peace in the Far East" and the safeguarding of China from "any third power whatever." The other European powers, after additional months of fighting in Europe had further weakened their position, subscribed to these pious sentiments and to secret pledges accepting Japanese arrangements in China.

Bryan had tried to forestall some of these arrangements with another note on May 11, 1915. He informed the Japanese that the United States could not recognize any agreement that impaired its ill-defined trilogy of interest in the Far East: treaty rights, Chinese integrity, and the Open Door. This statement did not mean that America was prepared to use armed force in defense of her position; neither the administration nor the rank-and-file citizen thought in such terms. They were unlikely to do so unless Japan made a direct attack, and Tokyo had no intention of resorting to military action as long as peaceful expansion paid off.

THE GROWTH OF FAR EASTERN TENSION (1917–1920)

As usual, developments in other areas affected the nature and timing of Japanese moves. The resumption of unrestricted submarine warfare by Germany on February 1, 1917, put the foes of the Central Powers in a desperate mood. They were willing to make fresh concessions to Tokyo in return for quick support against Germany and Austria-Hungary. The basis for a bargain arose out of Japan's desire to secure advance approval for all claims which she would make at the next peace conference. What she wanted was blanket acceptance of gains secured since 1914.

Russia gave the requisite pledge of cooperation on March 5, 1917, but it meant little because she was verging on disintegration. More significant was a British promise, on February 16, of support for Japanese claims to Shantung and to the German islands north of the equator; the French associated themselves with this promise two weeks later. In repayment Tokyo gave Great Britain convoy assistance in the Mediterranean and obliged the French by prodding China to break relations with Germany. The pressure on the Chinese was probably unnecessary because on August 14, 1917, they took the next step voluntarily and declared war on Germany. This bellicose gesture established the right of China to sit at the peace table and defend interests in Shantung and elsewhere which her prospective allies were bargaining away.

Washington stirred uneasily and suggested that Japan, Great Britain, and France join the United States in guaranteeing Chinese integrity and unity. This proposal was politely ignored by the powers concerned. Nevertheless Tokyo, still hoping to secure American recognition of its gains during the war, took the initiative in June 1917 and sent a mission under Viscount Ishii to Washington. Three months of negotiations with Secretary of State Robert Lansing ended in an exchange of notes on November 2, 1917, known as the Lansing-Ishii Agreement. America had the cold consolation of not conceding as much to Japan as the British and French had done. She avoided a pledge of support for territorial claims either on the Asian mainland or in the Pacific. Otherwise the terms favored Tokyo. In the first paragraph, America made the key concession: it took the form of recognition of the principle that "territorial propinquity creates special relations between countries." This statement cleared the way for the corollary admission that Japan had "special interests in China, particularly in the part to which her possessions are contiguous." The phrases were similar to those employed by Bryan two and a half years earlier, but the import was different. Bryan had used conciliatory language to conceal the harsh fact of American opposition to a policy at odds with American interests; in the context of the Lansing-Ishii Agreement the borrowed phrases conceded Japan's position and denied that America's traditional interests had suffered. The impact on the public was cushioned by the usual joint pledges to respect Chinese integrity and the Open Door.

The Lansing-Ishii Agreement marked the low point of America's influence in the Orient since the turn of the century. Wilson recognized that something new was needed to escape the consequences of his policy. His first step in December 1917 involved an attempt to pull the consortium out of the moth balls. The policy of safeguarding China through investment in her industrial development had not worked well even before Wilson had shelved it in 1913. Prospects were still less favorable in 1917 because of continued Japanese encroachments during the interval. The President consumed nearly three years coaxing first the bankers and later the Japanese into permitting the revival of the consortium. He gave American business interests the same offers of protection he had denounced his predecessor for giving some years earlier. Final agreement on terms acceptable to all the interested parties was reached on October 15, 1920. The delay prevented the policy from having any effect on the Far Eastern balance during the crucial period from the armistice to the Treaty of Versailles.

Only the joint pressure of the United States and the European allies of Russia discouraged Japan from seizing control of Siberia immediately after the revolution of March 12, 1917, which toppled the Tsar's government. When the Bolsheviks successfully staged a second revolution on November 5, 1917, the Entente Powers could no longer restrain the Japanese from landing troops at Vladivostok. The ensuing chaos in Russia and the inability of the Bolshevik government to establish its authority in Siberia encouraged Tokyo to expand its operations. British marines joined the Japanese on April 5, 1918, after the Bolsheviks had turned their backs on their erstwhile allies and negotiated a separate peace with the Central Powers at Brest-Litovsk. Woodrow Wilson also contributed a detachment of American marines to the mixed army which took control of Vladivostok on July 6, 1918.

The ostensible excuse for the occupation was to protect the retreat of the Czech and Slovak soldiers who had fought with the Russians against the Central Powers. The withdrawal of Russia from the war necessitated a long journey for these forces across Asian Russia and two oceans before they could fight again on the western front. Moreover, the unsympathetic attitude of the new government toward these foreigners lent some plausibility to the precautionary measures of the joint British-American-Japanese troops.

Behind this display of concern for the retreating forces was the determination of Japan to dominate the area, and of Great Britain and America to prevent her from doing so. Since the two powers could not keep Japan from intervening, they sent token forces along as a reminder that Siberia was not Korea. Other nonresident powers also joined the operation on a nominal basis. The participation of the United States annoyed Japan and cramped her style. Viscount Ishii tried to secure American acquiescence in an extension of the "special interests" formula to Siberia, but acting Secretary of State F. L. Polk stubbornly refused. He even managed to vest control of the Siberian portions of the Chinese Eastern Railroad in an Interallied Railway Commission. This maneuver kept the line out of Japanese hands.

The termination of World War I in November 1918 added the sentiment of war-weary peoples to insistent Japanese pressure on non-Asian states to withdraw their forces from Siberia. Wilson followed the example of the other powers and pulled the marines out of the Soviet maritime provinces, although the United States possessed a greater stake in the Pacific than the Entente did. All foreign troops were withdrawn from Russian territory by April 1920, except for those of Japan. The latter stayed on in Vladivostok until October 25, 1922, and were rewarded for their perseverance with an opportunity to overrun the remainder of Sakhalin Island.

Wilson left office in March 1921 with little to show for his efforts in the Far East. He had relied successively on verbal warnings, economic measures, and temporary military intervention in Siberia. None of these devices stopped Japanese penetration of China. The most they achieved was a kind of negative success by forcing Tokyo to slow down its timetable. As a result, America's position was considerably worse in 1921 than in 1913 but was not hopeless. Wilson operated under more trying conditions than had either Roosevelt or Taft. Nevertheless, his policy merits a harsher judgment because of the discrepancy between his pronouncements and his performance. He denounced the program of his predecessor, abandoned it momentarily, and then revived it under circumstances that precluded success.

The termination of the Wilson administration also coincided with the end of a twenty-year period in the Far East during which the westerners had retreated steadily in the face of a rising Asian power. In the process the United States had moved somewhat inadvertently from the role of interested bystander to that of holder of the balance and finally to an unhappy position as the principal antagonist of Japan in a simple balance. During the early 1920's she was to attempt to extricate herself from such an exposed situation. However, two lessons learned in the hard school of oriental politics assured her continued involvement in the area: (1) that Far Eastern stability depended upon forestalling the rise of a single dominant regional power, and (2) that the emergence of such a power could be thwarted only by preventing any state from controlling China or the bulk of her resources. Americans were to succeed in preventing other powers from dominating China in the 1920's and 1930's but were to wind up in an untenable position at the end of the 1940's by trying to prevent the Chinese from dominating China.

SUGGESTED READINGS

1. Dennett, T., *Roosevelt and the Russo-Japanese War.*
2. Griswold, A. W., *The Far Eastern Policy of the United States.*
3. Langer, W. L., *The Diplomacy of Imperialism.*

CHAPTER TEN

AMERICAN RELATIONS WITH EUROPE BEFORE WORLD WAR I

THE POWER STRUCTURE IN EUROPE

Notwithstanding the expansion of the Western State System to globe-circling proportions in the last quarter of the nineteenth century, the center of gravity remained in Europe. The emergence of Japan in Asia and of the United States in the Western Hemisphere foreshadowed momentous changes in the structure, but at the outset of the twentieth century both were on the periphery. Whatever action they might take raised a lesser threat to world stability than the maneuvers of the six great powers in Europe. In each hundred-year period following the crystallization of the State System in the seventeenth century, disruption of the balance in Europe had led to world wars, in every one of which America had become involved either as a colonial appendage or as an independent state.

Participation in the later stages of the Napoleonic wars had been prompted by the interference of the belligerents with American trade. After the establishment of peace at the Congress of Vienna in 1815, Europe had enjoyed a century free from general war. During this extended period, the stability of the Old World had created such a favorable environment for the conduct of American-European trade that the United States tended to take the safety of her transatlantic economic interests for granted. All that American businessmen had to worry about were the tariff barriers, which remained low until the 1860's and rose at only a moderate rate thereafter. The one serious dispute between the United States and the European powers in the nineteenth century occurred over the status of South and Central American republics. From time to time, Old World colonial powers tried to retain or expand their holdings in the face of a United States drive for hemispheric domination, but in the 1880's and 1890's they accepted the Monroe Doctrine and recognized American preponderance in the Western Hemisphere.

At the turn of the century, when America's unconcern with Europe reached its maximum, developments were occurring in the Old World destined to threaten her interests. At the same time her appearance as a world power multiplied her contacts with similarly constituted European states. To some degree her experience in Europe was to duplicate her Far Eastern experience of an earlier decade. She began by assuming that stability in Europe was self-sustaining and that she could protect her commercial interests without involvement in power politics. This initial attitude disappeared after further contact. The key to stability in Asia was the protection of China from two great powers, whereas the key to stability in Europe was the establishment of an equilibrium among six great powers. Aside from the greater complexity of the European structure, rapid modifications in the strength of individual members heightened the task of preserving a balance after 1870. In addition, the rapid development and outward projection of industrial power by Europe posed a serious threat to nonresident states if the Continent ever fell under the sway of a single power. Considered in such a context, one-power domination of Europe would be a greater menace to America than a similar Japanese hegemony over a relatively nonindustrialized Asia. Indeed, a state strong enough to master the Old World and appropriate its resources might well aspire to rule the entire globe.

In Washington the relative importance of developments in Europe and in Asia was sensed rather than understood. The United States ignored the threats to stability in the Old World longer than in the Far East. In the end she assigned a higher priority to Europe by intervening in World War I without being attacked, while avoiding military action in the Orient.

THE BREAKDOWN OF THE BALANCE IN EUROPE (1870–1914)

The European conflict, which ultimately involved the United States, arose out of a complex interaction of forces fatal to the political equilibrium of the Continent. As we have already noted in Chapter Two, the stability of any regional state system depends upon the maintenance of a balance of power. Threats to any given balance always exist in the form of changes in the relative strength of member states. Recognition of these changes and appropriate adjustments must be made periodically; otherwise, states entitled to revision of their status will seek it by resorting to war. Therefore, preservation of a balance requires a dynamic rather than a static relationship between powers. Obviously a balance can best be preserved when the members of a state system exhibit a high degree of flexibility in dealing with each other and when change takes place slowly enough to encourage adjustment. This fortunate combination of circumstances prevailed in Europe from 1815 to 1870. The balance consisted of a number of Continental

In barracks at The Hague. (Papagallo, *Bologna, 1907.*)

powers functioning more or less independently. Adroit operations by Great Britain as the holder of the balance discouraged any state from attempting to seek sole domination of the Continent. The inherent flexibility of these arrangements minimized the disruptive effects of industrialism, nationalism, and other forces promoting change. It was even possible for the system to absorb two new states — Germany and Italy — in the 1860's without a general European war.

The era of flexibility drew to a close in the seventies. Nationalism became a greater source of instability as it moved from Western Europe, where the distribution of national groups coincided roughly with the boundaries of existing states, to Eastern Europe, where such groups were scattered and intermingled. Furthermore, the Industrial Revolution began to alter sharply the relative strength of individual states as the emphasis shifted from the production of textiles to the production of steel. Those states possessing ample power resources, raw materials, and technological skill pulled ahead of neighbors less fortunately situated. The process, which created an imposing industrial system in some states, automatically increased their capacity to wage effective war. This development in turn encouraged them to seek changes and rearrangements in the balance of power that would take account of their greater strength. As a result of the swift and uneven character of industrial growth, the need for adjustments in the equilibrium now occurred more frequently than states cared to make them. Members of the system which favored change and stood to benefit from it were known as revisionist powers, while those in the reverse position were known as *status quo* powers.

Germany, the most important revisionist power, joined the European community as a federal state after Prussia broke French power in the war of 1870–71. The unification of the Reich had been thwarted for over two hundred years by France, which feared a dangerous rival would emerge out of any consolidation of "the Germanies." The correctness of the diagnosis quickly became apparent. In a world that soon came to measure great-power status by industrial output, Germany forged rapidly ahead. Within thirty years she pulled abreast of Greater Britain in steel production, and on the eve of World War I was turning out twice as much as the erstwhile "workshop of the world." The twin developments of unification and industrialization made Germany the strongest single power on the continent of Europe.

Notwithstanding her spectacular rate of growth, Germany did not immediately behave as a revisionist power. Although she had seized Alsace-Lorraine from the French as a spoil of victory, she took no more than others in similar circumstances and showed little appetite for fresh adventure. With Chancellor Bismarck at the helm from 1871 to 1890, she built an alliance system that was manifestly defensive. His program aimed at the isolation of France by maintaining close ties with Austria and Italy and by immobilizing Russia with fair words and diplomatic pressure in Eastern Europe. The cornerstone of the intricate German treaty network was an alliance with Austria negotiated in 1879 and enlarged to include Italy in 1882. A series of supplementary short-term agreements with Russia and an informal understanding with Great Britain completed the Bismarck system. The Chancellor showed considerable ingenuity in holding his Continental allies together because Austria-Hungary faced the revisionist demands of Italy in the Trentino and the rivalry of Russia in the Balkans.

The fluid system of Bismarck broke down when the youthful Emperor William II fired him in 1890 and refused to renew the three-year "Reinsurance Treaty" with Russia. Four years later, the isolated French and the jilted Russians signed a dual alliance. Inasmuch as Germany maintained the Triple Alliance with Austria and Italy, the great powers on the Continent were divided after 1894 into a pair of rival coalitions. The replacement of a multiple balance by a simple balance reduced the flexibility of the system and assured the involvement of all in a clash between any two powers from opposing camps. It inaugurated a period of increasing instability and frequent collisions between states.

Despite the fact that the Franco-Russian alliance of 1894 raised the specter of a two-front war for Germany, the policy of the Reich in Europe remained essentially nonrevisionist. However, Berlin began to use its strength on the Continent to force concessions elsewhere in the world where Germany was not so strong. This policy took the form of stepped-up activity in the colonial areas of Asia and Africa, aggressive commercial penetration of the Middle East, and a naval race with Great Britain. Kaiser William II made these moves seem still more reckless by injecting an element of intrigue, bluster, and caprice into his conduct of foreign affairs. The prospect of gains in areas of secondary importance hardly justified Berlin's hazardous policy of upsetting the stability in Europe where her vital interests lay. Even so, the increasingly revisionist orientation of German behavior after 1900 was matched by a similar trend in French and Russian policy. If the Reich bore graver responsibility for threatening gestures than her neighbors, it was because she possessed greater power to make trouble. None of the Continental states exhibited much capacity for self-restraint in the decade before the war.

France had more reason than Germany to behave like a *status quo* power. After her defeat in 1870–71 she fell behind rapidly in the race for population and industrial might. Instead of pursuing an unadventuresome foreign policy, however, she sought to compensate for her weakness on the Continent by building an overseas empire in Asia and Africa. Further, she clung to the avowedly revisionist objective of recovering Alsace-Lorraine. Her determination to retrieve the lost provinces gradually made her lose touch with political reality. National pride, an appetite for revenge, and a burning desire for the restoration of her pre-1870 status drove her into a policy that could end only in general war. Germany could neither be coaxed out of the provinces nor defeated single-handed. What France needed was allies with sufficient grounds for disliking the Reich to join in a war for Alsace-Lorraine. It took her forty-four years of methodical planning to assemble a coalition and to find an incident over which all the members were willing to fight.

Italy showed no more devotion to the *status quo* than did France. She possessed a revisionist appetite that was absurd in the light of her limited resources. It was whetted by dreams of past and future glory, a virulent nationalism, and a habit of regarding pageantry as a substitute for power. Her most specific objectives were the annexation of Trieste and the Trentino, which belonged to Austria and contained a substantial Italian-speaking minority. Beyond that she wanted enough of the Dalmatian coast to convert the Adriatic into an Italian lake, and a large but ill-defined Mediterranean empire. In a ceaseless quest for help in these enterprises, she flirted at one time or another with all the European great powers. Rome renewed the Triple Alliance at regular intervals, but never reconciled herself to genuine cooperation with Austria-Hungary. After 1900, however, she made separate agreements with Russia and France inconsistent with all her obligations under the Triple Alliance. The great powers treated these infidelities with amused tolerance because Italy had nothing to offer but her availability. Economically backward, strategically vulnerable, and devoid of the resources necessary to create a strong military establishment, she gained little from incessant diplomatic maneuvers except a reputation for irresponsible revisionist ambitions.

Austria-Hungary occupied a much more important role in the Triple Alliance and the European balance than did Italy. The Dual Monarchy was a sprawling, ramshackle state which owed its structural arrangements to a six-hundred-year accumulation of historical developments. Austrian Germans in the north and Hungarians in the south shared the responsibility for governing a realm composed of over a dozen ethnic groups. This federalism based on two dominant nationalities suffered from many shortcomings, but it would be difficult to demonstrate that any regional organization which preceded or followed the Hapsburg monarchy was more stable or more conducive to the general welfare. In any event, the heterogeneous character of the population made it especially vulnerable to the growing agitation of nationalistic minorities for autonomous status after 1870. Another source of weakness was economic backwardness. Despite the rapid technological progress of states farther west, Austria-Hungary continued to resemble an inverted pyramid with a huge agricultural superstructure resting on a flimsy industrial base.

Such handicaps would not have been serious a hundred years earlier when people gave their primary loyalty to a dynasty rather than to an ethnic group and when great-power status was reckoned in terms of large territorial holdings. Unfortunately for Austria-Hungary, states with more homogeneous populations and smaller possessions began to outstrip her in power and importance. This development confronted the Dual Monarchy with a pair of unpleasant alternatives: if she pursued a *status quo* policy, she had no prospect of keeping up with her more dynamic neighbors; if she embraced a vigorous revisionist policy, she faced the threat of a revolution from her dissident minorities in time of foreign crisis. Expansion into the Balkan peninsula seemed to offer the way out of the dilemma. The gradual collapse of Turkish power in the area made it a suitable target for old-style imperialism; while the desire of the little nationalistic Balkan states to reclaim their brethren under Austrian rule provided Vienna with added incentive for offensive operations. Thus expansion south and east would serve the double purpose of increasing Austrian power and preventing the growth of the Balkan states to the point where they could successfully champion the cause of Austrian minorities.

The Austrian drive for domination of the disorderly Balkan vacuum area converged in the 1890's with German economic penetration of the Near and Middle East. Inasmuch as the development of Asian markets and sources of raw materials awaited the construction of adequate transportation facilities, Germany focused her attention on the promotion of a Berlin to Bagdad railroad. This program was referred to as the "Drang nach Osten." It assured German-Austrian cooperation and self-aggrandizement in the Balkans.

The attempted German-Austrian penetration of southeastern Europe collided with a similar thrust by Russia. The old Tsarist monarchy was the largest of the great powers, territorially speaking, and the least advanced, industrially speaking. Landlocked and thwarted repeatedly by the major states of Europe in her effort to reach the Mediterranean through Turkey during the nineteenth century, Russia temporarily switched her attention to East Asia in the 1890's. The collapse of this drive in the Russo-Japanese

War (1904–1905) led to redirection of the thrust toward the Balkans and Constantinople. Thus, during the decade before 1914, Austria (backed by Germany) faced Russia (backed by France) in the Balkans, which came to be known as "the powder keg of Europe."

The Russians held the advantage in the ensuing propaganda warfare that preceded the World War. Moscow emphasized the Slavic character of the Russian empire and posed as the protector of the small Slavic states in the Balkans, although there was little to choose between the Russian intentions and those of the German-Austrian combination. Sympathy for the Balkan states developed in democratic countries which confused their frenzied nationalism with a zeal for popular self-government. Far from being defenseless, peace-loving kingdoms, they were irresponsible revisionist powers and useful tools of bigger states which hoped to upset the *status quo.*

The most reckless offender in the Balkans was the miniature mountain kingdom of Serbia. Peopled mostly by Serbs living south of Belgrade, it lived on chauvinistic dreams of becoming the nucleus of a great South Slavic Empire with a secure outlet to the sea. Pursuit of such a program was certain to produce a war with Austria, because the Dual Monarchy possessed two of the coveted provinces — Bosnia and Herzegovina. The wisdom of provoking a conflict would have been open to question even if the Serbs had occupied an unassailable moral position. However, a substantial percentage of the non-Serbian South-Slavs, such as the Croats, did not wish to be governed from Belgrade. Pockets of non-Slavic minorities in the disputed provinces also disliked the prospect. Hence Serbian success was not likely to terminate the problem of minorities. At best it would change some of the oppressed into oppressors and provide the remainder of the oppressed with new masters.

Notwithstanding the dubious character of Serb nationalist aspirations and the systematic preparations of Belgrade for war with Austria, Serbia appeared to much of the world to be an innocent victim — an impression that was not dissipated even when irresponsible Serb nationalists assassinated the heir to the Austrian throne and thereby started the chain reaction that exploded in war.

THE OUTBREAK OF THE EUROPEAN WAR

Meanwhile developments in Western Europe had undermined the stabilizing forces that might have cushioned the shock of Balkan rivalries. The most important casualty was Great Britain, who abdicated her traditional role as holder of the balance just after the turn of the century. Her position had become increasingly difficult in the mid-nineties when the major Continental powers divided themselves into a pair of hostile coalition systems. It became completely untenable when Germany began a naval race with her in 1898 and cut her off from diplomatic support during the Boer

War (1899–1902). The success of the Kaiser in promoting a Continental bloc to press Great Britain in Africa and Asia eroded the British reserve of power which had been used to stabilize Europe. As we have already noted, London's initial response was to abandon her role as holder of the balance in Asia and to reduce her commitments in the Western Hemisphere. She might still have weathered the storm in Europe had it not been for the continued hostility of Germany, and for the fact that, like France and Austria-Hungary on the Continent, she was losing ground in the balance by not increasing her political and economic power rapidly enough. To safeguard herself against further loss, she yielded her position as arbiter by making agreements with France in 1904 and with Russia in 1907. At first the contracting parties did nothing more than agree not to quarrel about matters which had traditionally separated them. Repeated German efforts to drive wedges between the allies, however, only drew them closer together. As a result the Triple Alliance balanced the Triple Entente after 1907, with London using what had hitherto been reserve power to maintain her place in a precarious equilibrium. Aside from an eleventh-hour Anglo-German understanding, the sole hope of stability and orderly adjustment of the balance depended upon American acceptance of the role recently vacated by Great Britain. Neither development materialized. The Germans continued the naval race with England and methodically pressed their revisionist claims overseas, while the Americans declined to take responsibility in Europe on any terms. A series of recurring crises followed, culminating in the assassination of the Austrian Archduke on June 28, 1914. With the position of holder of the balance vacant, the indispensable stabilizing operation could not be performed.

A month of inconclusive maneuvers followed as the rival coalitions sparred for position. The subsequent intervention of America was based in part upon judgments which she made about the responsibility of various powers for the breakdown of negotiations during this period. Some months after the war started, each participant also made elaborate efforts to establish the purity of its motives and the unworthiness of its enemies. The behavior of the individual powers during the crisis was conditioned, however, primarily by changes in their prospects over the preceding forty-five-year period instead of by moral considerations. They made decisions as *status quo* and revisionist powers rather than "good" and "bad" powers. A narrative of the tangle of ultimatums, abortive peace plans, mobilizations, and countermobilizations that consumed the last weeks of July does not answer the question of who was guilty of starting the war. It simply confirms earlier evidence that some revisionist states pursued objectives incompatible with orderly adjustment of the balance.

The worst offenders in this respect were France and Serbia. France had single-mindedly sought the restoration of Alsace-Lorraine for two generations. She had little incentive to settle the dispute in the Balkans, because it assured her of allies for the war of revenge. With her strength decreasing in comparison with other states, she ought to have been a *status quo* power rather than a revisionist one. Serbia likewise pursued objectives that could not be achieved short of war. The little Balkan state had systematically provoked her northern neighbor. Indeed, the assassination of the Archduke was only the last in a series of anti-Austrian plots inspired if not directed by the Serbian government. Russia had encouraged the reckless behavior of Belgrade and bore heavy responsibility for the sequel, but the Tsar apparently hoped to start nothing more than a local war. His revisionist program was ambitious but not especially urgent. Austria fell into a similar category. She knew that Serbia would have to be dealt with ultimately. Her instinct to proceed with caution was shaken by the assassination, which provided an excuse to settle scores with Serbia under circumstances that minimized the prospects of great-power interference.

Both Great Britain and Germany made some effort to restrain their respective allies. The English possessed a *status quo* mentality and sought nothing more than the preservation of their current position in the balance. The Germans were less satisfied. They did not feel that they possessed the holdings to which their growing strength entitled them. Nevertheless their revisionist aspirations were neither urgent nor concrete enough to preclude a compromise. Eventually the two states followed their allies into the conflict rather than risk isolation and possible deterioration of their respective positions. The reluctance of the kingpins in each coalition to fight suggests that if a holder of the balance had been on the job he could have forced limited revision without war.

THE HAGUE CONFERENCES

Meanwhile the conviction that European stability was self-sustaining kept America aloof from the deepening crisis on the Continent. Between 1905 and 1914, Washington wavered between three types of noninvolvement: (1) ignoring European politics altogether, (2) recognizing the reliance of European states on a balance of power and denouncing it, (3) participating in various noncommittal demonstrations of international solidarity.

Most of the prewar diplomatic relations between the United States and Europe fell into the latter category and drew nourishment from peace societies organized on both sides of the Atlantic. Foundations financed by philanthropic capitalists had stimulated much unrealistic optimism in the United States about prospects of permanent peace. This sentiment resulted in American participation in the Hague Conferences of 1899 and 1907 which were devoted to disarmament discussions. On both occasions the calculations of the great powers preparing for war prevented effective action. Disarmament was popular only with states that felt no need for arms or could not afford them. Russia was among the latter at the first Hague Conference and took the initiative in proposing arms limitations. Both her potential friends and foes suffered less from financial stringency than she did, and thought they had more to lose than to gain by a general agreement. Hence the sole concrete achievement of the conference was the establishment of a Permanent Court of Arbitration for the voluntary and pacific settlement of disputes. States accepting the jurisdiction of the Court could draw on a distinguished panel of international lawyers to make awards. The United States saw nothing entangling in this proposal and associated herself with the Court as well as with the resolutions of the great powers proclaiming their peaceful intentions. Washington accepted the services of the Hague Court in disputes with Mexico in 1902 (Pious Fund), Venezuela in 1903 (Claims Case), and Britain in 1910 (Newfoundland Fisheries).

Although Theodore Roosevelt had advocated a second Hague Conference as early as 1904, it did not meet until 1907 because of the Russo-Japanese War. By that time the defeated Tsar was a stronger apostle of peace than ever and issued the call. The intensification of the Anglo-German naval race since the first conference complicated the problem of disarmament. The British strongly favored a limitation on the construction of capital ships because the recent development of the Dreadnaught by naval designers had made older categories obsolete and hence had cut the British lead over the Germans. The opportunity to start a new naval race from scratch delighted the Kaiser and gave Berlin the incentive to block disarmament and compulsory arbitration. German truculence distracted world attention from the fact that disarmament was opposed by other important powers, including the United States, which were also engaged in naval building programs. In the end, the second conference settled for an enlargement of the voluntary arbitration procedures established by the first; a series of agreements covering blockade, contraband, and other aspects of maritime warfare; and miscellaneous protocols aimed at abating petty contemporary irritations. A follow-up conference met in London during 1908 and 1909 to resolve legal disputes over interpretation of the provisions dealing with maritime warfare and to codify international law. These deliberations produced the Declaration of London, which liberalized the regulations governing neutrals with small navies in time of war. Much to the disappointment of the United States, the British torpedoed the Declaration because it would neutralize their naval superiority in wartime.

ARBITRATION WITH CANADA

Besides these vague gestures of international cooperation, Roosevelt and his successors showed increasing interest in arbitration treaties for settling disputes. Their advocacy of such procedures was intended to demonstrate the pacific intentions of the United States and to set an example for the

European states, which Americans considered quarrelsome, militaristic, and alliance-ridden. Proposals for arbitration procedures, however, were usually made to powers involved in the Western Hemisphere where the United States possessed such overwhelming strength as to run little risk of an adverse award. Moreover, Washington avoided committing itself in advance to awards concerning vital American interests.

A long dispute between Canada and the United States over the slaughter of seals in the Pribilof Islands off the coast of Alaska was settled by arbitration in 1892–93. The issue had become complicated because, although the islands belonged to America, Canadian sealers operating offshore slaughtered the herd so systematically that it was threatened with extinction. During the 1880's the United States had picked up Canadian schooners engaged in the business outside the three-mile limit of American national waters, and Great Britain in Canada's behalf had protested the illegality of this action. The award went against the United States, which paid damages for the seizure of schooners in 1896. Since the slaughter of seals continued with the Japanese and others participating, the once mighty herd of four million had by 1910 been reduced to 100,000. A year later Russia, Japan, Great Britain, and the United States signed a North Pacific Sealing Agreement to stop the senseless butchery. The Americans gained the right to protect the herds and agreed to pay the Japanese and Canadians a percentage of their annual take. The seals showed their appreciation by multiplying in commendable fashion.

The United States was more interested in securing a favorable award out of the Alaskan boundary dispute. The issue might never have arisen but for the discovery of gold in the Klondike in 1896. The best access to the gold fields for the Canadians was across the Alaskan panhandle owned by the United States. Ottawa tried to establish a claim to this area by reinterpreting the boundary clause of the Russo-British treaty which had been negotiated in 1825 when Alaska belonged to Russia. At first the United States declined the British offer to arbitrate, but in 1903 Theodore Roosevelt agreed to accept the award of a six-man commission. The decision was to be by majority vote, with the President selecting three members of the Commission and the King of England selecting a like number. Neither side appointed "impartial" persons or "jurists" as the preliminary convention had stipulated. The three Americans and two Canadians prepared to vote their national interests. Only the single British appointee, Lord Alverstone, was even vaguely impartial. The tribunal met September 3, 1903, and continued its deliberations for nearly a month and a half. After a week Lord Alverstone made up his mind to support the American position in principle. Roosevelt, however, made the position of the English Lord Chief Justice difficult by threatening to take physical possession of the area in the event of an unfavorable award. Finally it was awarded to the United States by a vote of 4 to 2. Alverstone claimed that his decision was made on judicial grounds, while the Canadians charged that he had been browbeaten by Roosevelt.

ARBITRATION TREATIES

Despite his curious notions as to how arbitral procedures should operate, Roosevelt sent a bundle of arbitration treaties to the Senate for approval in 1905. Ever-jealous of its prerogatives, the upper house amended them to require Senate ratification of each award. Roosevelt in disgust withdrew the treaties, but when Elihu Root replaced John Hay in 1905 as Secretary of State the President agreed to try again. The Senate eventually approved twenty-five in 1908 and 1909, but protected its powers by requiring a separate treaty to implement each settlement. American acceptance of the arbitration principle was seriously qualified by the exemption of all issues involving "vital interests," "independence," or "honor."

When Taft succeeded Roosevelt, arbitration won an even firmer friend. The background and temperament of the new President predisposed him in favor of the judicial approach in foreign affairs. His Secretary of State, Philander C. Knox, wholeheartedly supported his views. Unfortunately, the administration tried to get more than the Senate would grant. In August 1911 it negotiated treaties with Great Britain and France for the arbitration of all "justiciable" questions and reserved to the President the determination of whether a case was "justiciable." The upper house balked at these arrangements, and when Taft appealed over its head to the people the Senate amended the treaties beyond recognition (March 7, 1912). Instead of trying to secure British and French consent to the emasculated version, Taft prepared for another fight with the legislature. Before it could take place, he was defeated in the 1912 election.

The succeeding administration carried on the fight to win Senate approval. Nomenclature was shifted slightly from arbitration to conciliation, but the approach was the same. It envisaged the submission of quarrels between states to standing commissions after other peaceful methods had failed to produce a solution. Disputants were not to be legally bound by commission recommendations but were pledged to refrain from using armed force until such recommendations had been made. The process of investigating disputes and formulating solutions could take up to a year.

This proposed method for settling quarrels was the brain child of William Jennings Bryan, the first Secretary of State in the Wilson administration. Known as the "cooling-off" treaty, it drew inspiration from the theory that delay would tend to discourage resort to violence. Neither President Wilson nor the press showed very much interest in the treaties. True to its traditions, the Senate greeted them with obstructive tactics. Nevertheless Bryan negotiated thirty of them in 1913 and 1914 and eventually worked twenty-two through the Senate.

The outbreak of World War I provides the ironic answer to the question whether American participation in disarmament conferences and American negotiation of arbitration and conciliation treaties made a significant contribution to peace. All three techniques ignored the basic fact that states regard their unity, prosperity, and security as more important than peace. If devotion to peace had been the overriding concern of states, they would have transferred their sovereign power voluntarily to a world organization. But neither the European states nor America showed any inclination to accept such a drastic cure. On the contrary, the United States threw its influence against the modest disarmament proposals at the second Hague Conference and exempted all questions involving vital national objectives from the jurisdiction of arbitration or conciliation commissions. The unwillingness of America to surrender sovereign power in the cause of peace indicated how little other states would be bound by peace agreements that ran counter to their own interests.

AMERICA AND THE ALGICIRAS CONFERENCE

American zeal for multiplying agencies to settle disputes offered some insurance against impulsive war declarations triggered by wounds to national pride. Americans seemed to regard these vague gestures of international good will as effective substitutes for participation in the balancing operations of the state system. They could have taken more constructive action in behalf of peace by accepting responsibility as holder of the European balance. The Kaiser had visualized the United States in some such role when he invited Theodore Roosevelt to use his good offices in the Franco-German dispute over Morocco in 1905. After some hesitation, Roosevelt agreed to participate, and chose Henry White, the American ambassador to Italy, as his representative at the ensuing Algeciras Conference. German hopes faded rapidly; instead of backing a settlement to promote European stability, the United States consistently supported the French. This policy ignored the claims of a revisionist Germany that was growing stronger, and it put American influence behind the claims of a revisionist France that was growing weaker. Deserted by all the great powers except Austria-Hungary, Germany accepted the verdict which aggravated the instability of Europe.

America retired from this single involvement in European power politics during the prewar decade, unaware of why she had been invited to participate. Some inclined to the view that the Old World had belatedly recognized the superiority of American ideals and wanted instruction in the conduct of foreign relations. Others dismissed the incident as another irresponsible Rooseveltian adventure. The refusal of European states to issue additional invitations to Washington in a period of mounting tensions suggested the contrary interpretation: they had excluded America from their calculations. In any event, the sequel of the Algeciras Conference demonstrated the tremendous influence of American prejudices against the balance of power and entanglements of American policy in Europe. Although an instinctive appreciation of interests gradually drew the United States into the position of holder of the balance in Asia, ideological objections blocked similar action in the Old World. This attitude was unfortunate because America possessed a greater stake in Europe than in the Far East and a better prospect of successfully manipulating the stable Old World balance than the volatile oriental one.

History cannot employ the experimental method and reassemble the great powers of an earlier era to determine what their reactions to a different policy might have been. Because of this limitation, it is impossible to assert that America could have prevented World War I by recognizing her membership in the Western State System and utilizing the generally accepted stabilizing rules. However, the operation of cause and effect in this period unfolds clearly enough to suggest that American participation in the balance before 1914 would have altered the calculations of all the states in the prewar crisis. The fiction that the United States had no interests in Europe did not eliminate those interests but prevented her from defining them realistically and taking the appropriate steps. Similarly, the assumption that she stood apart from the Western State System did not affect the obligatory character of her membership but deprived her of benefits from the system to which her power entitled her.

SUGGESTED READINGS

1. Brandenburg, E., *From Bismarck to the World War: A History of German Foreign Policy (1870–1914)*.
2. Fay, S. B., *The Origins of the World War* (2 vols.).
3. Schmitt, B. E., *The Triple Alliance and the Triple Entente*.

CHAPTER ELEVEN

THE BREAKDOWN OF AMERICAN NEUTRALITY

IMMEDIATE REACTIONS TO WAR

"Extra!" shouted the newsboy in September 1914. "Germans and Giants lose! Extra!" With gamin shrewdness he had sensed the casual attitude of his customers toward the war in Europe. The assassination of the Archduke at Sarajevo two months earlier had been good for only one day's headlines. When the hectic events of July and August turned the war threat into a reality, the initial reaction was a surge of revulsion against the inhumanity and senselessness of organized violence. A kindred feeling of relief over the remoteness of America from the war theaters followed quickly. The universal expectation was that America would remain aloof and continue to conduct business with the belligerents as usual. Not a single responsible leader voiced the opinion that the war would affect the United States vitally enough to justify participation. Hence Wilson spoke for a united people when he issued a formal declaration of neutrality on August 4. His fellow countrymen also approved his prompt offer to mediate, which the belligerents politely turned down.

The developments of the succeeding two and a half years that drew the United States step by step to involvement arose out of her determination to pursue contradictory policies simultaneously. A position of noninvolvement would have been easy enough to maintain if it had constituted her sole aim. Neither side could oblige the United States to enlist under its banners, nor could it risk driving her into the enemy camp for trivial reasons. What doomed the policy of aloofness was the fact that America had at stake all the interests of great powers as well as a few distinctively her own. Like other states, she would fight for interests seriously threatened, notwithstanding her repeated declarations of an overriding devotion to peace. Events were soon to reveal her determination to preserve the same commercial privileges during the war that she had enjoyed for the preceding hundred years — especially the right of her nationals to trade and travel anywhere. She also wanted a power position after the war that would be at least as favorable to her as the one prevailing earlier.

AMERICAN VIEWS OF NEUTRAL RIGHTS

America was to experience the difficulty of pursuing all these aims simultaneously. Eventually a choice would have to be made, but for the moment Americans thought they could avert it by a policy of neutrality. This policy held out the prospect of conducting business as usual, making profits from trade with the warring powers, and displaying a partisan interest in the outcome at no cost or inconvenience. The specific magic relied upon to impose this remarkable formula on the belligerents was something called international law. Presumably Americans could invoke its protection by a simple proclamation of nonbelligerency. They were vague about its character and coverage but confident that it safeguarded their rights, which they tended to equate with the rights of mankind.

History offered scant grounds for believing that the belligerents would accept the American view as to what rights the legal status of neutrality conferred. International law had always been subject to two crucial limitations: (1) its enforcement depended upon sovereign states who recognized no superior authority and who seldom felt bound by provisions contrary to their own interests; (2) its content depended upon a shifting body of rules which were usually amended by the great powers in peace treaties following major wars. The first limitation had special relevance in 1914 because international law had not been recodified since the Peace of Paris in 1856 and it contained outmoded rules that invited violation. The provisions governing such matters as contraband and blockade assumed the continued existence of the uncomplicated relationship between neutrals and belligerents that had prevailed before the industrial era. As a matter of fact, however, the half century after the Peace of Paris had seen the rise of states whose prosperity and warmaking power depended upon the functioning of a far more complex and vulnerable economy. Now the loss of access to a critical raw material or the deterioration of morale in a labor force could paralyze an entire war effort. Furthermore, the logic of combat under industrial conditions required states to besiege the entire country of an enemy rather than a few of his cities. This would assure the breakdown of the older distinctions between combatants and noncombatants as well as between shipments of contraband and of innocent goods. In other words if the belligerents violated international law to facilitate victory, neutrals were bound to suffer.

The contraction of neutral rights seemed probable precisely at the moment when America proposed to place maximum reliance on them. However, her new status as a world power made it more difficult for her to remain neutral than for smaller states to do so. Whatever action she took would be decisive because her power represented the difference between victory and defeat for the two European coalitions. This generalization applied even to commercial policies that America might choose to pursue. Since each side intended to strangle the economy of the other, it made a vast

Your uncle gets it coming and going. (The Philadelphia Inquirer, *1915.*)

difference whether Washington tried to trade with both coalitions, with one, or with neither. All three of these courses were legally possible for neutrals. Only the third opened up the prospect of combining impartiality with neutrality. Individual belligerents might be handicapped in varying degrees if America adopted a blanket policy of refusing to trade with them, but they would have no grounds for accusing her of intervention or favoritism. Any other policy was certain to involve her in the manipulation of armaments and supplies and hence in a murderous crossfire from the rivals.

The traditional way of viewing foreign affairs left America unprepared for the fact that her commercial policies would be judged elsewhere in terms of their effect on the prospects of belligerents. She assumed that as long as she preserved the legal status of a neutral, she could engage in partisan behavior without fear of retaliation. She steadfastly refused to recognize that by insisting on the maintenance of certain economic activities she was in effect trying to name a winner.

AMERICAN FAVORITISM

If misconception of neutral rights made America's eventual participation in the war probable, her favoritism in the administration of policy was to clinch it. From the outset her sympathies were with the Allies. After a hundred years of chronic mistrust, Britain's systematic cultivation of American friendship during the decade before the war was beginning to bear fruit. The establishment of cordial diplomatic relations also brought to the surface a residual good will based on the cultural and institutional affinities of the two peoples. France likewise benefited from revived American recollections of sentimental ties that dated back to the Revolutionary War. Even the chauvinistic Serbs were idealized as a nation of sturdy, peace-loving democrats fighting self-government.

Conversely, the popularity of Germany had been on the wane since the 1890's. The sometimes indiscreet statements of the Kaiser helped spread the impression that his government was arbitrary, unprincipled, and militaristic. More important, Germany was unwilling to indulge in the deferential behavior America had come to expect from Great Britain. Although by conventional standards of international conduct Berlin gave little reason for complaint, America sensed that the dynamic, expanding Germany of the early twentieth century was a rival, and fell into the habit of treating her with suspicion.

On the whole, the pattern of opinion among immigrants and first-generation descendants of immigrant parents was much the same as that for the older elements of the population. These "new" Americans numbered approximately 32 million or 35 per cent of the total, but only 9 per cent of them were German and 3 per cent Austrian. Few others sympathized with the Central Powers. Sentiment for the Allies did not preponderate among the foreign-born, however, until Italy changed sides in 1915. Enthusiasm grew steadily after America entered the war and Caruso began singing "Over There" in Italian.

The government shared and encouraged the popular prejudices with regard to the various belligerents. Starting with Theodore Roosevelt, successive Presidents had exhibited a pro-British and anti-German orientation. From the outset, Wilson held the view that strong sympathy for the Allies was not incompatible with an official policy of neutrality. Most of the members of his administration at diplomatic posts abroad either echoed or exceeded him in expressing a pro-Ally bias. Walter Hines Page, the American ambassador to England, deserves passing attention because of his uncontrollable enthusiasm for the British. His attachment to his hosts was so great that he sometimes helped them frame replies to outraged protests from

Washington about British interference with American shipping. Although Wilson soon recognized that the dispatches of his ambassador were little better than London propaganda handouts, he stubbornly refused to replace Page. Other ambassadors at important listening posts besides being pro-Ally were also without diplomatic training. Brand Whitlock, who served in Brussels, had been a reform mayor of Toledo, Ohio, while James W. Gerard in Berlin had been a Democratic politician from a fashionable New York district. The prejudices of such men and their deficiencies as observers deprived Wilson of the objective information he needed.

A similar unanimity of opinion and lack of experience in foreign affairs prevailed in the Cabinet. Only Secretary of State Bryan exercised independent judgment, but his earlier record as a supporter of unpopular causes encouraged the press and the public to discount his assertions. When he resigned in the summer of 1915 as the result of a quarrel with his chief, the last voice of dissent at the policy level was eliminated from the administration. Thereafter the President gave full rein to his inclination to be his own Secretary of State. He replaced Bryan with Robert Lansing, a counselor in the State Department, who later boasted in his memoirs that he had been unneutral from the start. Whatever influence Wilson's unofficial adviser, Colonel E. M. House had was also exercised in behalf of the British.

Neither the administration nor the public felt a strong enough devotion to the Entente Powers in 1914 to consider armed intervention in their behalf. However, with key government officials and the bulk of the articulate citizens and the press avowedly pro-Ally, an impartial policy was out of the question. Reaction to events would be colored by passionate prejudgment. The behavior of Germany would appear more objectionable than it was, and that of her enemies less reprehensible than the facts indicated. Against this background, American policy displayed a double aspect: neutrality for Great Britain, and neutrality against Germany. Such a formula could end only in war.

BRITISH INTERFERENCE WITH NEUTRAL RIGHTS

Sparring over neutral rights began shortly after the outbreak of hostilities. The problem for the rival coalitions was not whether to observe American rights but how to violate them most usefully. They hoped to keep violations from annoying the United States so seriously that her power would be applied in a decisive manner. The first offender was to be Great Britain rather than Germany. The former had many advantages, including superior geographical position, the largest navy in the world, and ready access to strategic materials outside of Europe. It would, however, take time to capitalize these assets. Germany, on the other hand, had entered the war better prepared and so the British were forced to employ emergency measures at once to avert a knockout in the opening round. These included a concerted drive for war supplies overseas and an equally determined effort to withhold them from the Germans.

On August 6, 1914, Secretary Bryan served notice on both sides that the United States expected to conduct business as usual. He asked the belligerents to accept the Declaration of London which the British had evaded signing in 1909. As already noted, the Declaration was an ambitious attempt to extend the coverage of international law to certain current practices in maritime warfare. Among other things, it envisaged a reduction in the types of contraband or war goods that belligerents blockading enemy ports could confiscate. This proposal favored powers with small navies and neutrals who hoped to trade with belligerents who were being blockaded. The Germans enthusiastically accepted the Bryan note because it opened for them the prospect of receiving goods that the British Navy would otherwise confiscate. Conversely, London regarded it as a legal device to neutralize her naval superiority. Accordingly Sir Edward Grey, the British Foreign Secretary, rejected the Declaration a second time. He pointed out that in the absence of general agreement — by which he meant British agreement — the Declaration did not have the status of international law. By Orders in Council of August 20, September 21, October 29, and December 23, Great Britain lengthened the contraband lists so that she could intercept most categories of goods headed for Germany. This step was an essential part of her over-all plan to wage war against the entire German population — a plan that involved a definition of contraband contrary to recent interpretations of international law and that foreshadowed severe encroachments on neutral shipping.

Interference with American shipments to Germany began in early September. On the 26th of that month the State Department drafted a note for Wilson's signature specifying violations and calling upon Britain to abide by the Declaration of London. The President consulted Colonel House, who thought that the State Department was proposing too strong a stand. Next, House talked the matter over with the British ambassador, Sir Cecil Spring-Rice, and found that the latter thought so too. Together the two men redrafted the note, removing the clauses which dwelt on British violations. When Wilson signed it, all that remained was a warning to London about the adverse effects of such behavior on American opinion. Fearful lest this assertion appear too harsh in print, Wilson permitted Ambassador Page to communicate the contents verbally to Sir Edward Grey instead of delivering the actual text. In this gentlemanly manner the United States dropped its fight for British adherence to the Declaration of London. The piecemeal encroachments on neutral shipping were promptly stepped up and before long everything from war weapons to cotton was treated as contraband.

Simultaneously London made other unilateral modifications of international law which hampered her effort to wage total war. One of the casualties was the time-honored practice of conducting on the high seas the visit and search for contraband. Under pretense of guiding American ships through German mine fields, the Royal Navy now brought them into British ports where they could be searched in leisurely fashion. This novel procedure defied all precedent. There had always been a certain vagueness about the definition of a blockade in the sense that it was difficult to specify the amount of naval strength necessary to seal off enemy ports. But since the right to confiscate contraband depended upon the establishment of a blockade, it was generally agreed that a blockading power should be able to implement her proclaimed intention. In the past, several states, including the United States, had instituted unenforceable blockades in the hope of bluffing neutrals, but none had hauled neutral ships into port without prior search and establishment of the fact that they were carrying contraband. After the Germans had denied the charges of sowing mines illegally, the British announced on November 3, 1914, that the whole North Sea was a military Zone and sowed retaliatory mines. Thereafter neutrals could travel in the area only at their own risk or by leave of the British.

Other British action stemmed from her determination to stop the shipment of goods to neutral countries for transshipment to Germany. The existing rule of "continuous voyage" permitted a blockading power to intercept cargoes ostensibly bound for neutral ports if the character of the shipment indicated that the ultimate destination was an enemy port. London arbitrarily redefined "continuous voyage" to include overland journeys. This device aimed at cutting off the transshipment of overseas goods from Scandinavia and the Low Countries to Germany. When London had worked out all the details, the United States was compelled to trade with Western European neutrals through special corporations organized by the British.

The cumulative effect of these measures was to choke off virtually all American trade with the Central Powers and the neutral states of Europe by the summer of 1915. Cargoes destined for the Continent either piled up on American docks or else were detained in British ports. Sometimes London responded to protests by paying for goods thus held; on other occasions she simply ignored complaints. Whether they got paid or not, American shippers suffered long and costly delays. Cotton exporters were especially wrathful because they found that their large German market was now abruptly cut off. Notwithstanding the pro-Ally sentiment in America, a substantial group would have favored strong measures against London during the first nine months of the war if the administration had offered any leadership in this direction.

The only action likely to compel British observance of international law was an embargo. Allied orders for munitions and other military supplies in 1914 were negligible, but in 1915 they increased rapidly enough to create a modest war boom. With a half billion dollars' worth of business in the offing for 1916, Wilson felt reluctant to choke off prosperity by slapping an embargo on the Allies. Furthermore he had the strongest political incentive to refrain from drastic action: his re-election in 1916 hinged in part on economic conditions, which would probably have suffered from such a daring gesture.

These considerations made it easy for Wilson to follow a pro-Ally policy.

On December 26, 1914, Washington delivered another note to Sir Edward Grey requesting that the rights of neutrals be interfered with only when necessary for British national safety. This statement amounted to a tacit admission that there were no objective standards for judging neutral rights since any action could be defended as "necessary." Had Washington been willing to accept the provisional character of neutral rights as a general principle, the position would have coincided more nearly with the realities of international politics. Since she was not prepared to do so, the note encouraged further assaults by the British and deprived the United States of adequate grounds for protesting the retaliatory German violations that impended.

The Allies were not willing to let matters rest when they had secured American acquiescence in their interpretation of international law. They wanted positive help in the form of financial aid. This need developed quickly because the British and French had sharply curtailed the production of goods for export which were normally relied upon to provide credit balances to finance foreign purchases. As a temporary arrangement they paid for American goods by liquidating investments abroad and depleting their gold balances, but the demands of the war machine were too great for prolonged operations on that basis. What the Entente wanted to do was to raise funds by floating huge loans in the American money markets.

The Wilson administration rejected initial feelers on August 10, 1914, from the house of Morgan which proposed to act as agent of the French government in floating a large bond issue. On that occasion the views of Secretary Bryan prevailed. He conceded that loans to both sides would be legal but would lead to an economic involvement incompatible with the American policy of avoiding participation in the war.

The United States stuck to this position barely two months. The same concern about prosperity which motivated the rejection of an embargo caused the administration to reverse its stand. In mid-October 1914, Wilson after some prompting from Lansing overrode his Secretary of State. The President informed the bankers personally and privately that the administration no longer viewed such transactions with disfavor. A few months later Bryan agreed. With a green light from the White House, dollar credits and the traffic in war goods mounted steadily. Between 1914 and 1916 the dollar volume of American trade with Allied countries rose nearly 400 per cent. The Morgan firm took the lead in promoting the loans which lubricated the flow of commerce. Eventually its transactions in behalf of the Allies amounted to nearly $3 billion.

For some time a tenuous distinction was maintained between credits from private banking firms and loans raised by public subscription. As soon as the former source had been exhausted, Lansing and Secretary of the Treasury W. G. McAdoo persuaded Wilson to permit the floating of loans on the open market. This decision was made in September 1915, and before the year ended the public absorbed loans of $500 million to the Allies and $27 million to Germany.

A generation later it became fashionable to echo the contemporary charge of Socialists that the United States entered World War I solely because her loan policy created a stake in the outcome. No evidence exists to substantiate this theory of economic causation. The bankers and arms manufacturers did not dominate administration decisions, although sentiment and long-standing associations made them pro-Ally. On the contrary, Wilson, the chief policy maker, had strong prejudices against business groups. Nevertheless economic considerations influenced both him and the public, to whose views he was sensitive. As a contributory cause of involvement, they deserve notice. The loan policy strongly emphasized American preference for an Allied victory and aroused the resentment of the Central Powers. The assertion that Germany was not excluded from raising loans on the American market is true but misleading. As long as Great Britain controlled the seas and prevented German access to American supplies, Berlin's theoretical opportunity to float bond issues in New York could not lead to any practical consequences. The persistence of this situation and of Wilson's complacency toward Allied loans left the United States in compliance with the technical requirements of neutrality but not with normal standards of impartiality.

GERMAN RETALIATION AGAINST THE BRITISH BLOCKADE

Paralleling the American policy of neutrality for Great Britain and France was the policy of neutrality against Germany. During the first six months German-American relations remained comparatively tranquil because Berlin declined to interfere with British encroachment on neutral rights and American acquiescence in this action. It hoped for a quick and decisive victory which would eliminate the necessity for inconclusive diplomatic sparring with the United States. It avoided controversy on the theory that an America stunned by a sudden German victory would be more willing to negotiate than an America previously antagonized by extended argument.

Germany's initial attitude evaporated along with her prospects for early success. By the end of 1914 her attempt to deliver a knockout blow had failed, and both sides settled down to siege warfare. Trenches were dug in the west from the North Sea to the Ardennes Forest and in the east from the Black Sea to the Gulf of Riga. Except for occasional break-throughs, the fighting front stabilized along these lines during the next two years. Although the Germans had been far better prepared at the outset than the Allies, their advantage disappeared when the war of movement turned into a war of attrition. Under these new circumstances, the problem of supplies became crucial. Unless Germany could regain access to overseas sources of nitrates, key metallic ores, fibers, and other raw materials, her superior military and industrial machine was likely to break down within a couple of years. Aside from the remote prospect of a complete victory by her surface fleet which would clear her path to the markets of the world, her only alternative was a counterblockade. Since Great Britain received 90 per cent of her food supplies and most of her raw materials from abroad, she occupied a vulnerable position which invited Germany to attempt her economic strangulation.

The only weapon at the disposal of the Reich for implementing such a blockade was the submarine. Invented after the last general codification of international law in 1856, the submarine could not be fitted into the conventional framework of rules governing surface vessels which intercepted contraband goods. Ordinarily, units of a blockading fleet were expected to search merchantmen suspected of carrying contraband on the high seas and to haul the offending vessels into port, where prize courts could condemn the cargo. Belligerent ships on the prowl for neutral craft carrying illegal goods were within their rights in sinking those that resisted search. In such instances, however, international law required the attacking vessel to provide for the safety of the passengers, crew, and papers of the ship which had been sunk.

The submarine dared not comply with these regulations. If it surfaced to search a merchantman, it ran the risk of being rammed by the larger vessel or raked by its guns. This danger was not merely theoretical, because once Germany started using submarines, the British admiralty fitted merchantmen with defensive armaments and gave them standing orders to ram the underwater raiders on sight. Hence, for the submarine to function effectively, it had to deliver its torpedo, sink the enemy vessel, and depart. In such an operation the passengers and property of neutrals were also going to be destroyed. Unless neutral states agreed to keep their citizens and property off Allied surface vessels, they were certain to become involved in quarrels with the Germans if the latter instituted large-scale submarine warfare.

The United States was the only important neutral state that Berlin needed to consider in weighing the advisability of submarine attacks on Allied shipping lanes in the North Atlantic. The charitable attitude of Washington toward British assaults on neutral rights during the first six months of the conflict suggested that the Americans would absorb further punishment without resorting to war. On the other hand, any hope Berlin nourished on this score was counterbalanced by knowledge of the American bias for the Allies; the United States was placing her whole productive capacity at the disposal of the Allied Powers and was indifferent to the exclusion of Germany from the same privileges.

What Germany had to decide was whether the benefits of keeping America out of the conflict exceeded the benefits of unrestricted submarine warfare. The answer would have been easy if Germany had possessed enough submarines to force an immediate decision. In January 1915, however, her U-boat fleet was composed of only twenty-eight vessels. Worse still from her standpoint, about two-thirds of these had to be tied in drydock for maintenance and repair at all times. Unable to strike a decisive blow until more had been built, she settled for a temporizing policy which called for activity on a scale that would cut the flow of American goods to the Allies without provoking a declaration of war.

Germany launched the policy on February 4, 1915, by proclaiming a war zone around the British Isles. She stated that after the eighteenth of the month enemy ships sighted within the area would be sunk. She also warned neutrals that they entered the zone at their own risk because they could not always be identified and because the British had begun to fly neutral flags on their ships. In justification, the Germans repeated the phrases employed by the British two months earlier: retaliation, new conditions, and necessity.

Although Wilson had tolerated British violations of international law, his note to Berlin on February 10, 1915, made it clear that America would judge Germany by different standards. Proposed German action was termed "unprecedented," and the Reich was informed that it would be held to "strict accountability" for American losses of life and property. The submarine was novel enough to justify the phrase "unprecedented" in anticipating the effects of its use, but the President also seemed to imply that it was illegal because it was new.

Wilson was hardly on stronger legal ground when he proposed to hold Germany to "strict accountability" for violations of international law. Existing usage did not cover the submarine any more than it did the airplane. Nevertheless, Wilson accepted the clear British violation of international law but challenged the German violation that had not been legally established. His response was an emotional one echoed by a majority of his fellow countrymen. Since Wilson regarded any position that he took to be a moral one, he felt obliged to act on it and defend the "law of nations" from the threat of German subversion.

After initially agreeing to the note of February 10, Bryan experienced misgivings about the wisdom and impartiality of the policy. He was especially uneasy about the provocative implications of "strict accountability." Wilson and Lansing ignored his objections but he was correct in thinking that a crisis would develop. Six weeks after the Germans had established the war zone, one American lost his life in the sinking of the British liner *Falaba* in the Irish Sea (March 28). On May 1, an American tanker, the *Gulflight,* was torpedoed during a fight between a British naval patrol and a submarine. Two Americans were killed, and the captain died of heart failure. These incidents aroused the resentment which had been slumbering since the invasion of Belgium. Berlin knew that worse would follow because the Wilson administration had ignored appeals to keep its citizens off belligerent vessels. So on the very day of the *Gulflight* incident, German officials in the United States took the extraordinary step of placing an advertisement in the New York press warning Americans against taking passage on munitions-laden British ships. Nevertheless a substantial number of American travelers left for Europe the same afternoon on the British Cunard liner

Lusitania. Besides its passengers, the *Lusitania* carried 4,200 cases of rifle cartridges, as well as other cargo of a nonmilitary character which had been confiscated when headed for German ports.

On May 7, 1915, the *Lusitania* encountered a submarine off the Irish coast, was torpedoed, and went down in eighteen minutes. Of the 1,198 persons who lost their lives, 128 were Americans, including 37 women and 21 children. Abnormal circumstances surrounded the sinking. The captain had neglected his orders, failing to take the elementary precautions necessary in a war zone. He was either unreliable or else had deliberately courted disaster. Those who favored the latter explanation thought that the British had exposed the ship to unnecessary danger in the hope of precipitating an incident that would bring the United States into the war. The indignant outcry of the American public against Germany caused the questionable aspects of the affair to be quickly forgotten. The chorus of condemnation was universal on the eastern seaboard. The pulpit joined the press in deploring German barbarism. Isolated voices screamed for war against the "Huns." The British sought to capitalize this turn of events by hastening the publication of the Bryce Report on German "atrocities" in Belgium. Released on May 11, 1915, when American anger was at fever heat, it presented some highly questionable conclusions drawn from a deplorable core of truth.

Notwithstanding the uproar, the vast majority of Americans still did not want war. In the Mississippi Valley and the Far West indignation had been more restrained than on the Atlantic coast. Even among the pro-British elements in the East there was little sentiment for following bellicose utterances with military action. President Wilson put himself at the head of the moderate forces. Three days after the tragedy, he said that the United States was "too proud to fight and so right that it does not need to convince others by force that it is right." In his Flag Day address, June 15, 1915, he reiterated his stand: "I sometimes wonder why men take this flag and flaunt it. If I am respected, I do not have to demand respect."

These utterances could hardly be taken at face value from a President who had almost started a war with Mexico over alleged insults to American honor at Tampico. At the time he meant what he said. Later developments made it clear that they were not generalizations about American policy but reactions to a particular crisis. In their contemporary context they indicated that America would not go to war over the *Lusitania* incident. He refused to back down from the position of February 10, 1915, when he had announced that he would hold Germany to "strict accountability." He also clung to his earlier policy of neutrality without impartiality. Thus he left the door open for war. The significance of his omissions escaped most people because chronic German-haters like ex-President Roosevelt launched such intemperate attacks on him that he looked more than ever like a man of peace.

The *Lusitania* controversy subsided in a sharp exchange of notes between the American and the German governments. Washington led off with a stiff protest on May 13, and Berlin's reply of the 28th was regarded as so unsatisfactory that Wilson called a Cabinet meeting on June 1. He presented it with his draft of a new note so truculent in tone that Bryan took exception to several passages. In a conversation with the President three days later, Bryan insisted that the only way to maintain peace was to curtail American travel and administer economic policy impartially. Wilson stuck with his view that Americans could enjoy not only peace but unrestricted travel and trade if they insisted firmly on their rights. The most the President offered to do was to reword the note to read that Americans should not take passage on ships carrying munitions. Bryan felt this concession was inadequate and resigned on June 7, 1915, to cries of "traitor" from the more rabid Germanophobes. Wilson replaced him with Lansing and sent the second *Lusitania* note in its original harsh form on June 9.

The verbal battle between Washington and Berlin continued until February 1916, when Germany agreed to pay an indemnity for the loss of American life. This gesture did not mean that Berlin had accepted Washington's interpretation of international law. The retreat was temporary and for tactical reasons. At the time of the incident, the submarine construction program had added only ten U-boats to the original fleet of thirty. This increase was not large enough to permit a systematic destruction of Allied shipping and hence did not justify an open break with the United States. So while the Reich was arguing with Washington, she issued secret orders to submarine commanders in June 1915 to spare the larger passenger vessels. These instructions failed to prevent a U-boat from sinking the British liner *Arabic* on August 19, with a loss of two American lives. Germany forestalled a fresh crisis by revealing the secret orders on September 1, 1915, and making a conciliatory reply five weeks later to an American protest. Known as the "*Arabic* pledge," the German note of October 8 promised that submarines would not attack unarmed passenger ships unless the latter struck the first blow or tried to escape. During the next few months, Berlin showed exceptional restraint. When a German submarine sank the Italian liner *Ancona* on November 7 with loss to American life, the Reich prodded Austria-Hungary into a confession of guilt and a promise of indemnity payments.

Americans were soon involved again when a submarine torpedoed the armed British passenger ship *Persia* in the Mediterranean on December 30, 1915. Matters reached still another of their periodic crises when several Americans were injured in the sinking of the French passenger ship *Sussex* on March 24, 1916. The German government had tried to prepare neutrals for such a development by announcing on February 10, 1916, that after March 1 enemy merchant ships armed with cannon would not be regarded as commercial vessels. The *Sussex,* however, was a passenger liner, and Wilson made the most of this violation of the *Arabic* pledge. On April 18,

1916, he threatened to break diplomatic relations with the Reich unless it observed American rights on the high seas. By this time Germany had run its string of submarines up to fifty-two, but this number fell far short of the total required to stop an American invasion armada from reaching Europe. So Germany yielded for the final time. On May 4, 1916, by the so-called "*Sussex* pledge," she promised not to sink ships without warning, but only if the United States convinced other belligerents to behave in equally humane fashion. This was another way of saying that Germany would reserve her freedom of action unless the British relaxed the blockade.

Wilson had no intention of allowing the equivocal German statement to stand without challenge, but he was equally reluctant to break relations with Berlin on the eve of the presidential election. He accepted the German promise but rejected its reservations. He glossed over its provisional character in his reply on May 8, 1916: "Responsibility in such matters is single, not joint; absolute, not relative." Once more he had asserted the double standard of neutrality.

Simultaneously the British were being allowed to violate American conceptions of international law. Just prior to the *Sussex* controversy, in January 1916, Lansing had seemed to recognize the connection between submarine activity and British arming of ships which carried American lives and property. On that occasion he had asked the British to stop arming merchant vessels and requested the Germans to observe the usual rules of search and seizure. When the former refused, he had quickly conceded that they possessed the right to arm merchantmen "defensively." His partiality was evident if it is considered that submarines could not distinguish between the two types of armament unless they surfaced and exposed themselves to being rammed.

If Wilson and Lansing failed to see the risks of such a policy, a substantial bloc of congressmen were aware of them. This group considered peace to be the paramount objective of American policy and believed that Wilson's insistence on the rights of American travelers was creating incidents which kept the public in a warlike mood.

Rebellion developed first in the House of Representatives among members of Wilson's own party. Speaker Champ Clark and Majority Leader Claude Kitchen had repeatedly advocated an embargo in 1915, and the latter believed that it would have won legislative approval but for White House opposition. The concern of rank-and-file members was expressed in a flurry of resolutions introduced shortly after Congress had convened in December 1915. Most of these proposals envisaged steps that would make American neutrality more impartial. When the Germans served notice on February 19, 1916, that merchant ships armed with cannon would not be treated as commercial vessels, congressional sentiment crystallized behind the Gore-McLemore resolution. Introduced in the House on February 17 by Jeff McLemore of Texas and in the Senate eight days later by Thomas P. Gore of Oklahoma, this resolution proposed a twofold policy. The first part called for positive action to protect American trade from Allied restrictions, and the second part urged the government to deny passports to American travelers on belligerent vessels.

The President met challenges to his leadership by appealing to national honor, denouncing the submarine as a barbaric and illegal weapon, and reaffirming his moral duty to defend international law. In a letter of February 24 to Senator W. J. Stone, chairman of the Senate Foreign Relations Committee, he asserted that he could not consent to "any abridgement of the rights of American citizens in any respect" nor could he "accept a single abatement of right." He concluded that insistence on rights had "made America a sovereign nation" and that yielding such rights would "surrender her independent position among the nations of the world." A conference with congressional leaders followed on February 21, 1916. The transactions are shrouded in controversy. Irrespective of what took place, the President successfully reasserted his leadership, and the Gore-McLemore resolution was tabled. Congressional intervention had failed, and Wilson was free to pursue the policy that culminated in the *Sussex* pledge of May 1916. The Reich could be counted upon to honor it only until the rising curve of German desperation over the blockade coincided with the calculation that the submarine fleet was large enough to clear the Atlantic of enemy shipping. Fortunately for Wilson, Berlin postponed the decision long enough to permit the Democrats to re-elect him on the slogan, "He kept us out of war."

BRITISH PROPAGANDA AND GERMAN SABOTAGE

The dispute over submarine warfare which dominated American-German relations in 1915 and 1916 made numerous recruits for the President's policy. Long before the beginning of the controversy, London had launched a twofold campaign to influence American opinion by preventing direct contact between the United States and Germany, and by bombarding Americans with British propaganda. The first objective was achieved during the initial week of the war when the British cut the transatlantic cable. Thereafter, virtually all war news and background stories came from British sources. The effort to create enthusiasm for the Allied cause was directed from Wellington House in England. A ceaseless flow of pamphlets, posters, cartoons, and edited documents carried the British message to America. Material was sent to influential citizens throughout the country. Propaganda officials at Wellington House also arranged for American lecture tours by popular Englishmen like Sir Arthur Conan Doyle and Lord Bryce. They even promoted correspondence between acquaintances in the two countries.

Conditions in America assured a favorable response to British efforts. Sentimental, ethnic, and literary ties predisposed some to accept London's version. The pro-British policy of the Wilson administration influenced others. The Germans also gave their foes an unintentional assist by using the submarine. Because the submarine took human life more quickly and spectacularly than the ruthless British blockade, it aroused the greater resentment in America. After the sinking of the *Lusitania,* German attempts to influence American opinion were futile.

Popular hostility deepened when Berlin resorted to sabotage in an effort to check the flow of supplies to the Allied powers. Franz Bopp, the German consul general in San Francisco, engineered the explosion of a munitions barge at a Seattle dock on Memorial Day, 1915. A similar plot produced the Black Tom tragedy near Jersey City in July 1916, when several lives and $40 million worth of property were lost. The personal and official improprieties of Captain Franz von Papen and Captain Karl Boy-Ed, who were respectively German military and naval attachés in Washington, led to their expulsion from the country on December 1, 1915. A similar fate had overtaken Dr. Constantin Dumba, the Austrian ambassador, three months earlier because of his efforts to incite strikes in munitions factories.

The policy of promoting sabotage in a neutral country was indefensible by any standard of international conduct. It was also futile, because German agents had no real prospect of organizing destruction on a large enough scale to disrupt deliveries to the Entente Powers. They could accomplish nothing by irresponsible acts of violence except to increase the effectiveness of Allied propaganda, which represented the Germans as a barbarian horde bent upon the overthrow of western civilization. The cumulative insult of the policy made Americans take a more severe view of submarine warfare, and it whipped up sentiment in 1915 and 1916 for the "preparedness" campaign and the pro-Ally orientation of Wilsonian diplomacy. In fact, progress toward preparedness was to provide another standard for measuring the successive stages by which the President and the country approached belligerency.

THE AGITATION FOR PREPAREDNESS

The initial agitation for preparedness was launched in October 1914, by a small but articulate group of citizens. Leading figures in the movement included several prominent politicians like Theodore Roosevelt, Elihu Root, and Senator Henry Cabot Lodge; a popular author, Booth Tarkington; a respected educator, ex-President Eliot of Harvard; and a controversial editor-publisher, Colonel George Harvey. What drew these men together was the common conviction that the United States ought to fight Germany as quickly as possible. They owed their opinions to a variety of sources, but it is safe to say that they had come to regard the Germans as unprincipled barbarians even before the Reich launched submarine warfare or the sabotage program. Some feared that Germany was bent on world conquest. Others felt that she practiced a cynical statecraft incompatible with membership in a moral and law-abiding international community. In either case, the object of their resentment was the same and could be destroyed only by war. Fearful that the Allies lacked the strength to do the job alone, they sought American participation.

Since public opinion overwhelmingly favored neutrality at the outset of the war, the advocates of preparedness prudently concealed their ultimate objective behind patriotic pleas for an enlargement of the armed forces. This strategy did not bear fruit immediately because Americans were no more willing to arm against an imaginary or unidentified foe than against the Germans. Wilson spoke for the majority in his annual message of December 8, 1914, when he asserted that there was no threat to the territorial integrity or the independence of the United States. He had added incentive to take a stand against a larger military establishment because the principal proponents of preparedness were Republicans. With a heavily Democratic Congress taking its cues from him, all attempts to increase the size of the armed forces were blocked in 1914. Senator Lodge and his son-in-law, Representative Augustus P. Gardiner, did, however, manage to launch a congressional investigation into the state of the country's preparedness.

The inconclusiveness of the first moves left the impression that an unbridgeable gulf separated the President from his opponents. Subsequent developments point to the inference that he was not opposed either to preparedness or to war against Germany once he found the issue to convert his bias into a call to arms. He revealed his idealistic fervor when he said: "I will not cry 'peace' so long as there is sin and wrong in the world." This statement cleared the way not only for a crusade but for placing war on a semipermanent basis.

The issue that finally jolted Wilson into a revision of his policy was the submarine. Within a few months he came to regard it as a symbol of all the evil forces loose in the world. The same reasons he had advanced for staying out of the war — respect for morality, humanity, international law, righteousness, and peace — were to be used for justifying involvement once Germany launched unrestricted submarine warfare. He gave concrete evidence of a change on July 21, 1915 — the day he sent the third *Lusitania* note — by giving the go-ahead signal for a "wise" preparedness. The first beneficiary was the Navy. Congress authorized a half-billion dollars for a three-year building program in October. Encouraged by this beginning, the admirals requested three times as much money for 1916.

Several factors helped to conceal the magnitude of the shift in Wilson's position in 1915. For one thing, he was subjected to a steady drumfire of bitter criticism from the original advocates of preparedness because he wrote notes to the Germans over submarine warfare instead of retaliating with force. The fact that the intemperate Theodore Roosevelt spearheaded the attacks left people with the impression that the President was still a pacifist. Whatever his ultimate intentions toward Germany, he refused to fight her in 1915 against the overwhelming opposition of the public. His determination to postpone a showdown was also strengthened by his lingering hope that the United States could avoid a clear-cut decision about Europe. This expectation fed on his faith in his power to dissuade the Kaiser from using the submarine.

While the rival commitments to neutrality and a military crusade against Germany struggled for supremacy in Wilson's mind, he made a bid to take over control of the preparedness movement during the winter of 1915–16. With a re-election campaign approaching, he was anxious to neutralize opposition charges that he had neglected the welfare of the armed forces. He relied on a speaking tour of the Midwest in January and February of 1916 to sell preparedness to the voters. He stressed the superiority of American ideals and the imminence of opportunities to export them as justification for enlarging the military forces. In a speech at St. Louis he took the extreme position that the United States should have an army and navy second to none. This proposal made no impression. Since the German government had just agreed not to sink passenger liners, crusading fervor was at a low ebb. Bryan, La Follette, Jane Addams, and other prominent Progressives expressed fear that the President would give up his domestic reform program for an expedition to save the British Empire, while Roosevelt and the extremists chided him for not arming forthrightly against the Germans.

THE HOUSE-GREY MEMORANDUM

The coolness of the popular response embarrassed the President because it coincided with his first major effort to affect the outcome of the war. He had sent Colonel House to Europe in January 1915 to explore the possibilities of mediation. On that occasion nobody had given the Colonel much satisfaction, but everybody had tried to keep him happy. In England, Sir Edward Grey had even taken some time off to discuss Wordsworth with his American visitor. The contrast between the objectives of the first House mission in 1915 and the second one about a year later reflected the shift in Wilson's attitude. What he offered to do for the British was to call a general peace conference after a prearranged cue from the Allies. If the Germans accepted the bid, Wilson would help the Allied coalition to secure an advantageous settlement irrespective of the current military situation. If they balked, he would undertake to bring America into the war. Known as the House-Grey Memorandum, this extraordinary proposal showed how definitely Wilson had committed himself to an Allied victory and why at the same time he was pressing so hard for enlargement of the armed forces. His threat of American intervention was belated recognition that the United States was affected by developments in Europe. Unfortunately, he did not intend to operate as the holder of the balance and intervene in behalf of stability.

The memorandum never got beyond the discussion stage. The British found a good excuse to back out when Wilson inserted the word "probably" in front of his pledge to bring America into the war. The qualification was intended to reflect the limitations on his constitutional powers rather than uncertainty about his personal attitude. Grey found the contingency unacceptable. The real reason for his reluctance was his unwillingness to state Allied war aims and risk the loss of Wilson's support. Chances were better that America would intervene on the side of the Allies if she knew nothing about their annexationist objectives. Moreover, the British had little to lose by a polite refusal. The postponement of American entry seemed likely to facilitate the re-election of Wilson, which would in turn assure the Allies of help later on. Meanwhile London could count on continued indulgence toward British violations of international law.

PREPAREDNESS AND WAR AIMS

Wilson reacted to his setback by throwing himself with renewed vigor into the preparedness campaign in May 1916. Besides wanting an enlarged army, he hoped that his identification with preparedness would kill it as an election issue. Nothing had happened since his midwestern tour to increase the popularity of an armament program. On the contrary the good behavior of the Germans after the *Sussex* pledge (May 1916) weakened sentiment for preparedness. Yet Wilson launched a campaign to stir slumbering Nativism by casting doubt on the loyalty of the foreign-born and their children. He began to call critics of his pro-British policies hyphenated Americans and to imply that the country needed armed protection against them. The prevailing climate of opinion favored this kind of appeal. A year earlier a revived Ku Klux Klan had received an encouraging response in the South to its attack against Negroes and foreigners. Isolated attempts at sabotage by German agents gave added momentum to the campaign.

Meanwhile, Wilson's vigorous tugs on the alarm bell had put new life in the faltering preparedness movement. Congress passed the National Defense Act on June 3, 1916, to strengthen the Army. It followed with a gigantic Naval Appropriations Bill which received the President's signature on August 29. By early fall, the forerunners of later wartime agencies and boards were being created. These developments took place amid impressive evidence that Wilson was joining hands with the original proponents of preparedness who had ridiculed him for two years as a cowardly pacifist. He began to speak well of the National Security League, hitherto an object of his aversion. He also appeared on the same platform with Lodge and Roosevelt on May 27, 1916, when all three endorsed a new organization called The League to Enforce the Peace. Three weeks later he and his Cabinet celebrated Flag Day by marching in a monster "preparedness parade" in Washington. Thus the country was moving toward mobilization without satisfying its need to have somebody to arm against. Disloyal immigrants did not justify such extensive preparations, and the President refrained from identifying the state that he wanted to fight. Nothing existed to sustain popular interest but a vague feeling that America ought to prepare for war in a world at war.

These demonstrations of solidarity between two such bitter foes as Wilson and Roosevelt were deceptive. They agreed only about the desirability of intervention. A wide gulf separated them on the question of what American war aims ought to be and hence on the related question of what kind of peace the projected league ought to enforce.

The preparedness advocates for whom Roosevelt and Lodge spoke were militant nationalists with a pro-Ally orientation. They believed that all sorts of benefits for both America and mankind would surely follow a German defeat. They expected a radiant new world to emerge based on the hegemony of the English-speaking peoples, with the French assisting in a number of areas and providing local color. To safeguard and perpetuate this postwar dispensation, Roosevelt and his supporters advocated the creation of an international association of states. They envisaged it as an organization of good states that would keep the bad ones in their places.

The Wilsonians wanted to defeat Germany for a different reason. They thought of her as the major obstacle to a world dispensation based on peace, democracy, and international law. They did not believe, however, that victory would assure the triumph of these principles unless there was created an international organization to override the narrow national interests of the winners. Their enthusiasm for a league blinded them to the durability of national interests and to their unconscious identification of ideals with American power objectives. It never occurred to them that the United States would have to conquer her potential friends as well as her potential enemies in order to make the projected league function as they intended. In any event, they favored a type of international organization, under America's disinterested leadership, which would dominate the victor states, whereas the Roosevelt-Lodge group favored one which would be an instrument of the victor states including the United States. The cleavage in outlook between the two wings of the preparedness movement was sufficient to account for the great postwar squabble over peace terms and the League of Nations. In the summer of 1916 differences were ignored because of a common determination to fight the Germans.

Each side pressed for intervention without recognizing either the position of America as holder of the balance or the need for action of a type that would preserve stability. Roosevelt wanted to make the world safe for the Anglo-Saxon states; Wilson wanted to make it safe for the establishment of moral principles as he defined them. Starting from somewhat different premises, both demanded a crusade against evil as embodied in the German state. Since the destruction of evil precludes compromise settlements, this outlook committed them to a policy that was self-defeating. Each elimination of an offending power would create a vacuum and thereby tempt the nearest great power to fill it. As soon as the latter succumbed to temptation, it would in turn be regarded as evil and become the victim of a fresh crusade. In the process, wars would become longer and more costly while an ever-diminishing number of states fought for survival. Hence the fruits of crusades were to be an aggravation of the instability and insecurity which they were supposed to correct.

Perhaps the United States might have avoided involvement in such a futile policy if the opponents of preparedness had offered a workable alternative. Unfortunately, they were as oblivious to the need of an American contribution to stability as the President was. When he and Roosevelt unveiled the German bogy, they retaliated by unveiling one of their own — the international banker who intended to trick America into saving the British Empire. They denied that America was a member of the Western State System or vulnerable to developments occurring withing it. Thus the foreign policy dispute revolved about the question of whether the United States could continue to enjoy peace and democracy at home without exporting those principles to other areas. Wilson thought that Germany threatened the existence of such ideals, while the advocates of neutrality disagreed with his conclusion.

THE ELECTION OF 1916

Preparations for the presidential election took place in an atmosphere of controversy over preparedness and American rights on the high seas. Popular devotion to peace was still unmistakable. Submarine warfare, sabotage, and pro-Ally propaganda had excited horror against Germany but not sentiment for war. The average American regarded himself as a spectator experiencing a sensation of fright in safety.

Although foreign policy issues dominated the political foreground, preconvention maneuvering revolved about the effort of both parties to capture the allegiance of the Progressives. Over four million of them had joined Theodore Roosevelt in the unsuccessful third-party crusade of 1912. It was a safe assumption that the bulk of this group was normally Republican. Political arithmetic indicated that the latter party would win in 1916 if the Progressives returned to the fold. Roosevelt was willing to do his part to heal the schism. His earlier interest in domestic reform had been completely overshadowed by his hatred of Germany. In the process he buried the hatchet with Taft and cultivated a new and more spectacular feud with Wilson over foreign policy. As the convention drew near, he dreamed of leading a reunited party to victory on a platform which called for the restoration of American power and prestige abroad. His expectations were tied to the hope that the party would nominate him if he brought the Progressive dissidents back. In an effort to further his scheme he arranged for the Progressives to hold their convention in Chicago at the same time that the Republicans were meeting.

This transparent strategy backfired because in presidential primaries the western Republicans showed a marked preference for peace. When the Republican convention met on June 8, 1916, Roosevelt's prospects were all but dead. Rather than lead another futile third-party crusade, he rejected the nomination of the Progressive convention and urged his erstwhile comrades to rejoin the G.O.P. His ill-concealed appetite for war had already alienated part of his Progressive following, and others resented his bland proposal that they support the arch-conservative, Senator Henry Cabot Lodge. The upshot was that the Progressive party organization merged with the Republicans but lost part of its following in the process. The G.O.P. convention tried to ease the return of the dissidents by giving the presidential nomination to Charles Evans Hughes, who had sat on the Supreme Court since 1910 and hence had taken no part in the intraparty strife of 1912. Former Vice-President Charles W. Fairbanks of Indiana was chosen as his running mate. The platform indorsed Progressive principles but criticized much of the "New Freedom" legislation. It bore down particularly hard on the Underwood tariff and Wilson's proposal to subsidize the construction of merchant ships. Planks on foreign affairs denounced the Mexican policy of the administration and promised full-scale preparedness.

One week later the Democratic convention went through the routine motions of renominating Wilson and Marshall. The delegates enthusiastically ratified planks praising Wilsonian Progressive legislation already enacted and promising more. On the other hand, their stand on foreign policy issues contradicted their expressions of sentiment on the convention floor. They wildly applauded keynoter Martin H. Glynn when he reviewed the successive occasions on which the administration had refrained from going to war despite the violation of American "rights." Yet they endorsed Wilson's foreign policy which made American involvement in war dependent upon German observance of "rights" as defined by the President. This equivocation reflected the tension between the devotion of the delegates to peace and the undeclared but bellicose intentions of their standard-bearer.

With the delegates at both conventions echoing grass-roots demands for peace, Republican hopes of victory hinged on the ability of the party to convince the electorate that Hughes opposed involvement more than Wilson did. This issue commanded top priority because of the outspoken antiwar sentiments expressed by members of the defunct Progressive party who constituted the largest bloc of uncommitted voters. The situation cried for a Hughes campaign which would exploit popular fears of Wilson's unneutral policy while muzzling the preparedness faction in the G.O.P. A more experienced and aggressive politician might have made such a formula work, but the mild-mannered Hughes could not control Roosevelt's extravagant pro-Ally utterances or his tirades against Wilson. In frenzied accents Roosevelt pictured the President as surrounded by ghosts: "the shadows of men, women, and children who have risen from the ooze of the ocean bottom and from graves in foreign lands; the shadows of the helpless whom Mr. Wilson did not dare protect lest he might have to face danger." This kind of campaign oratory, reaching a crescendo in mid-October, left the voters with the impression that the Republican party was the war party.

From the outset, the Democrats tried to advertise Wilson as the defender of peace. Vance McCormick, the chairman of the Democratic committee, plastered billboards all over the country with the slogan, "He kept us out of war." This tribute to Wilson was supplemented by vivid posters depicting the carnage of war and bearing the caption: "He has protected me and mine." The President took a more realistic view of his achievement, observing privately that "any little German lieutenant can put us into the war at any time by some calculated outrage." He ought to have stated his real position publicly, but he allowed the misleading slogan to stand. He spent most of the fall at Shadow Lawn, New Jersey, and made few formal speeches. Most of these dwelt on the domestic successes of his administration. He reminded farmers of the Agricultural Credit Act; organized labor, of legislation to strengthen unionism; and consumers, of measures to restore business competition and to lower prices. The dignified tone of the pronouncements was marred only by an exchange between him and Jeremiah O'Leary, who headed pro-Irish agitation in the United States.

In his fourfold role of social reformer, apostle of peace, architect of preparedness, and custodian of patriotism, Wilson was a difficult target to hit. The Hughes campaign went from bad to worse. The candidate was one of the ablest men in public life but did not appear to good advantage in a political campaign. He possessed a solemn, humorless platform manner and a full beard to match. Professional advice might have improved his technique, but he chose a political amateur, W. R. Willcox of New York, to manage his election. A series of blunders followed. Hughes alienated Governor Hiram Johnson, the leader of the California Republican Progressives, by failing to call on him when both men were staying at the Virginia Hotel in Long Beach. Critical labor votes were lost in Ohio because he failed to correct the impression that he was opposed to the eight-hour day. Worse still, he neither silenced nor repudiated the reckless Roosevelt who stormed about the country pursuing his feud with Wilson.

If Hughes had avoided any one of these errors, he might have been elected. As it turned out, the vote on November 7 was so close that the result remained in doubt for three days. Late returns from the West indicated that Wilson had shaded Hughes by a margin of 277 to 254 in the electoral college, and by 9,129,606 to 8,538,221 in the popular vote. The President carried the Solid South and the Border except for West Virginia, all but two states west of the Missouri River, plus Ohio and New Hampshire. The rest of the north-central and eastern states went to

Hughes. The distribution of the vote indicates that Wilson had drawn his decisive bloc of supporters on the "peace" issue, from the ailing Socialist party and the defunct Progressive party.

The Democrats did not fare so well in the congressional elections as in the presidential contest. Republican candidates for the Senate and the House won several hundred thousand more votes in the aggregate than the Democrats. The administration majority in the Senate was cut from 16 to 10 and disappeared completely in the House where the Democratic Speaker, Champ Clark, won re-election only by securing the vote of a dozen-odd Independents. For practical purposes the electorate had turned down the Democratic party and had accepted Wilson because of a misconception about the goals of his foreign policy. His mandate was for the maintenance of peace, but several years of pro-Ally diplomacy had carried him to the verge of war.

FINAL EFFORT AT MEDIATION

With the election out of the way, Wilson resolved to offer his services as mediator once again. This new approach was doomed from the outset because it ignored the conventional objectives of warfare. Wilson had in mind a monster peace conference of warring and neutral powers to effect a compromise settlement and to create an international organization. Germany occupied too good a military position to make the kind of concessions that would satisfy Wilson, while Great Britain had just replaced the indecisive Asquith government with a coalition headed by the chauvinistic Lloyd George.

Before Wilson could reveal his utopian plan, the Germans stole the initiative on December 12, 1916, with an announcement that they were willing to discuss a general settlement. Reluctantly Wilson abandoned the idea of a general conference and addressed identical notes to both parties asking them to state their terms. As might have been expected, neither was willing to do so in advance of a meeting. Behind the polite expressions of evasiveness was an unbridgeable gulf: the Central Powers intended to consider a negotiated peace only on the basis of current holdings, which included Belgium and much of southeastern Europe, whereas the Allies refused to talk unless Germany disgorged her gains and paid an indemnity.

During the uneasy month between the breakdown of the mediation offer and the German decision to resume submarine operations on February 1, 1917, foreign policy became more ambivalent and confused. On January 4, Wilson said that United States entry in the war would be a "crime against civilization" and reaffirmed his determination to keep America from being involved. Simultaneously he occupied himself with the formulation of American postwar aims, which he revealed for the first time in an address to the Senate on January 22, 1917. After asserting that the participation of the United States in postwar arrangements was "inevitable," he pleaded for "peace without victory." According to him, this required: (1) settlements consistent with "the political faith" of "the people of the New World," (2) the creation of a postwar organization to guarantee the peace so strong "that no nation" or "probable combination of nations could withstand it," (3) equality of rights among small nations, (4) general acceptance of the principle of self-government, (5) a direct outlet to the sea for "every great people," (6) freedom of the seas, (7) "limitation of naval armaments." He represented this program as the will of the American people and "forward-looking men and women everywhere."

UNRESTRICTED SUBMARINE WARFARE

Berlin ended the interlude of indecision in Washington by giving twenty-four-hour notice that unrestricted submarine warfare would be renewed on February 1, 1917. This momentous change in policy had been decided upon a month earlier. It constituted a victory for the strategic plan of the German High Command and a defeat for the Chancellor and the Foreign Office. The military planners imposed their viewpoint on the government with full knowledge that resumption of submarine warfare would bring the United States into the conflict. They counted on their underwater fleet, which by this time had been built up to more than a hundred U-boats, to knock the Allies out of the war before American military power could become effective. The timing of the High Command was tied to its estimate that unless Germany conquered her foes by August 1917, she would be slowly strangled to death by the blockade. Ambassador von Bernstorff received information about the new strategy on January 19 and worked unsuccessfully until the day before the deadline to alter the decision.

The delivery of the German note obliged Wilson to break relations with the Reich or to repudiate his earlier position on the submarine. He chose the first alternative without hesitation and announced his decision in a speech before Congress on February 3. He also served notice on Germany that when she sank American ships he would take more decisive action. The same day von Bernstorff was given his papers, and Ambassador Gerard was recalled from Berlin.

To the surprise of Washington, weeks passed without the anticipated encounter on the high seas, because American ships remained in port. When it became evident that shippers did not wish to expose their cargoes to the hazards of the submarine, Wilson sought to encourage them by seeking congressional authorization on February 26 for the arming of merchantmen. This proposal passed the House quickly, but a dozen senators under the leadership of La Follette made a last-ditch effort to block it. The President promptly denounced them as "a little group of willful men representing no opinion but their own." However, the foes of the bill killed it by filibustering until the session of Congress expired on March 4, 1917. The President fought back by announcing on March 12 that an eighteenth-century statute permitted him to do what the stubborn senators had refused to authorize. As a result, merchantmen armed and ready to shoot were moving through war zones before the end of the month. Meanwhile, incidents had finally begun to occur. The day after the President asked for the authority to arm merchant ships (February 27), two American women were drowned in the sinking of the British passenger liner *Laconia*. A submarine torpedoed the unarmed American ship *Algonquin* on March 12.

Other developments besides the submarine sinkings helped to stir up popular indignation. One of these was the publication of the Zimmermann Note — a message from the German Foreign Secretary Alfred Zimmermann to the Reich's ambassador in Mexico authorizing the latter in the event of war with America to offer the Mexican government an alliance plus the states of Arizona, New Mexico, and Texas. The ambassador was also urged to bid for Japanese adherence to the coalition. This dispatch had been intercepted by the British on January 16, 1917, and turned over to the State Department on February 24, but Wilson did not release it until March 1. The revelation of the contents had the desired effect on public opinion since Americans were sensitive to interference by outside powers in the Western Hemisphere. Denunciations of German treachery filled the air. In the heat of the moment Americans forgot that the Zimmermann proposals to Mexico were contingent upon the outbreak of war. As such they were precautions against a probable development and no more treacherous than earlier Wilsonian proposals aimed at Germany, such as the House-Grey Memorandum. Yet even if the action of Berlin did not violate prevailing standards of international morality, it showed both ingratitude and stupidity. The note had been transmitted over State Department facilities, which had been offered to the Reich because it claimed it could not otherwise communicate confidentially with German officials in North America. Mexico, moreover, possessed no military establishment worthy of the name and was cut off from German supplies by a vast ocean dominated by hostile fleets; the potential nuisance value of such an ally hardly justified the risk of annoying the Americans.

The popular furor created by the note and by the resumption of submarine activity was probably sufficient to assure favorable congressional action on a war resolution in early March. While Wilson cautiously tested public opinion, an unexpected event removed what he regarded as the last obstacle to his cherished crusade for democracy. A revolution in Russia toppled the Tsarist regime on March 12, 1917. Although the internal upheaval seemed likely to knock Russia out of the war, it enabled Wilson to proclaim that the major Allied governments were democratic. Since he equated democracy with disinterested idealism, the overthrow of the Romanoff dynasty cleared the way for him to believe that the war aims of the Allies were lofty even though the latter refused to state them.

The President recognized the provisional government in Moscow on March 18, and two days later received the unanimous approval of his Cabinet for a declaration of war against Germany. On March 20 he issued a call for a special session of the newly elected Congress to convene on April 2 and to receive his war message.

WILSON'S WAR MESSAGE

When the legislators assembled, it was a foregone conclusion that they would honor Wilson's request irrespective of the grounds on which he made it. Several considerations shaped the character of his appeal. First, he regarded himself as the spokesman of a just and upright America which was about to become the champion of the rights of all mankind. Second, he was mindful of the need to demonstrate the purity of America's motives to the skeptical groups — the Germans, the neutral states, and the substantial antiwar element within the United States. He wanted to convince friend and foe alike that beyond the inevitable defeat of Germany lay the eventual triumph of democracy and with it the assurance of a progressively brighter future. Third, he cherished the hope that the peoples of the world would force their governments to participate in the crusade in spite of previous commitments. He even attempted to distinguish between the German people and the German government, thus paving the way for his later assertion that the people could best serve their country by denying support to their government. Nothing short of a few quotations from the message can adequately reveal the manner in which he interwove the conflicting themes:

> Because submarines are in effect outlaws when used as the German submarines have been used against merchant shipping, it is impossible to defend ships against their attacks as the law of nations has assumed that merchantmen would defend themselves against privateers or cruisers, visible craft giving chase upon the open sea.
>
> The present German submarine warfare against commerce is a warfare against mankind . . . against all nations.
>
> We . . . fight thus for the ultimate peace of the world and for the liberties of its peoples, the German peoples included; for the rights of nations great and small and the privilege of men everywhere to choose their way of life and obedience. The world must be made safe for democracy. Its peace must be planted on the tested foundations of political liberty.
>
> We have no selfish ends to serve. We desire no conquest, no dominion. We seek no indemnities for ourselves, no material compensation for the sacrifices we shall freely make. We are but one of the champions of the rights of mankind.
>
> We are at the beginning of an age in which it will be insisted that the same

> standards of conduct and responsibility for wrong done shall be observed among nations and their governments that are observed among individual citizens of civilized states.
>
> We have no quarrel with the German people. We have no feeling toward them but one of sympathy and friendship. It was not upon their impulse that their government acted in entering this war. . . . we know that in such a government, following such methods, we can never have a friend. . . . We are now about to accept gauge of battle with this natural foe of liberty. . . . We must put our excited feeling away. Just because we fight without rancor and without selfish object, seeking nothing for ourselves but what we shall wish to share with all free peoples, we shall, I feel confident, conduct our operations as belligerents without passion and ourselves observe with proud punctilio the principles of right and of fair play we profess to be fighting for.
>
> It will be all the easier for us to conduct ourselves as belligerents in a high spirit of right and fairness because we act without animus, not in enmity towards a people or with the desire to bring any injury or disadvantage upon them, but only in armed opposition to an irresponsible government which has thrown aside all considerations of humanity and of right and is running amuck. We are, let me say again, the sincere friends of the German people, and shall desire nothing so much as the early re-establishment of intimate relations of mutual advantage between us.
>
> I have exactly the same things in mind now that I had in mind when I addressed the Senate on the twenty-second of January last. . . . Our object now, as then, is to vindicate the principles of peace and justice in the life of the world as against selfish and autocratic power and to set up amongst the really free and self-governed peoples of the world such a concert of purpose and of action as will henceforth assure the observance of those principles.

In the message the President excluded Germany's allies, Austria-Hungary and Turkey, from his indictment and did not ask for a declaration of war upon them. He justified this distinction on the ground that neither had employed the illegal and immoral submarine warfare against the United States. A more practical reason was the hope that he could convince both states to make a separate peace with the Entente Powers. Wilson's message made little direct reference to America's prospective allies except Russia, which was hailed as having always been "democratic at heart" and as "a fit partner for a League of Honor."

The concluding sentences restated America's commitment and proclaimed it a privilege for her "to shed her blood and her might for the principles that gave her birth and happiness and the peace which she has treasured." The final words, "God helping her she can do no other," paraphrased Luther's famous defiance of the Papacy at Worms. These words gave a thumbnail sketch of the President as he viewed himself at this moment of history: Woodrow Wilson, the Reformer, taking his stand at Washington to defy the Germans. The chamber thundered applause. Wilson wept.

The ensuing debate was fervent but relatively brief. Lodge spoke for a large Senate majority when he endorsed the resolution, but refrained from comment on the plans for the postwar world. Borah echoed the views of an undetermined number of nationalists when he conceded that a declaration of war was unavoidable but coupled his reluctant support with a denunciation of the internationalist crusade. La Follette and Norris were the spokesmen of the small and preponderantly Progressive minority that opposed the war. Undismayed by a hostile gallery, La Follette blamed the presidential policy of neutrality without impartiality for the deterioration of American-German relations. After contending that the administration ought not to have tolerated the unlawful establishment of war zones by either Germany or Great Britain, he concluded that the war was "being forced upon our people without their knowing why and without their approval." Norris spoke in a similar vein, charging the bankers and munitions makers with a plot to traffic in human lives for their own selfish ends. In the House Wilson's own majority leader, Claude Kitchen of North Carolina, insisted that America "could keep out of this war with Germany." He anticipated charges of disloyalty and cowardice with the scorching reminder to his colleagues that it took "neither moral nor physical courage to declare a war for others to fight."

The foes of the resolution possessed strong voices but few votes. The Senate ignored their protests on April 4 by a vote of 82 to 6, and the House concurred on April 6 by a vote of 373 to 50. The endorsement reflected popular sentiment only in the sense that Americans had acquiesced in what they regarded as inevitable. The *New Republic* described this widespread feeling when it observed that a great democratic nation had been "gradually forced into war, in spite of the manifest indifference or reluctance of the majority of the population."

The least understood of the motives which drew Americans unwillingly down the path to involvement was national interest. A century-old tradition conspired against any explicit recognition that the United States possessed concrete objectives. This self-imposed censorship did not eliminate the objectives but doomed her to pursue them in a subconscious and hence unsystematic way. She showed little knowledge of how to protect her position in the world balance but increasing awareness of the fact that it would be affected by the outcome of the war. Between 1914 and 1917 an ever-growing number of Americans also recognized the necessity of doing something to preserve their ill-defined interests. Having failed to do so by preventing war or staying aloof from it, they drifted unhappily to the conclusion that they would need to enter it.

THE REASONS FOR AMERICAN ENTRANCE

Among the most immediate of the reasons for participation was the illusion that an uncomplicated prewar world could be restored. This led to resentment against Germany for having disturbed the settled order, and also fostered the belief that America would have remained neutral if an unprincipled state like the Reich had not shouldered her way into the family of nations. The pro-Ally policy of Wilson, submarine warfare, the British propaganda campaign, and the behavior of the Germans contributed to make this picture plausible. These irritants provided individual Americans with a wide choice of reasons for fighting Germany. Some felt a personal interest in fighting — particularly exporters and businessmen harassed by the submarine. Still others either idealized international law as a world-wide code of behavior and thought it jeopardized by Teutonic militarists or regarded German warfare on the high seas as a defiance of all standards of human decency. No inventory of reasons can fully account for the way each citizen made his decision. One point, however, is clear: whether the citizen based his acquiescence on national, personal, or ideological grounds, he believed that if America smashed the militaristic Prussian state, she could go back to being her usual, isolated, civilized self.

Wilson himself went further than the rank and file. He wanted to set up a new world-order based on democracy and international law. This objective competed in his mind with other objectives, but it provided the basis for his claim that war would be a great crusade. The mass of Americans, on the other hand, envisaged nothing but the physical defeat of Germany and thought the whole job would be done when that had been brought about. This fundamental divergence between the presidential and the popular view of war objectives deserves emphasis here because it casts light on the whole series of developments in subsequent years.

The President and the voters achieved temporary solidarity on the middle ground of resentment against Germany. Was this burst of emotion cause enough to risk a war? In the heat of the moment, the majority agreed with the President. Both had groped their way instinctively to the proper decision despite the confused and contradictory character of their reasons. Wilson was right in thinking that the United States possessed a stake in the war and a function to perform with reference to the European State System. He misconstrued his mission by regarding it as a mandate to destroy the System and rebuild it, rather than as an obligation to stabilize it. He was probably right, too, in thinking that military intervention would be the best way of retrieving a situation that he had allowed to deteriorate. Finally, he was probably right — conditions being what they were — in deciding that the United States would be better off if it produced a victory for the Allies instead of for Germany. He was wrong in thinking that European power relations could be forced back into an 1870 mold and that his allies possessed the virtues and his enemies the vices which he attributed to them.

In general, Wilson's World War policy proceeded from false premises, through undesirable but unavoidable methods, to a striving for unattainable goals. In the light of harsh post-World War II realities, Samuel Flagg

Bemis once succinctly summarized the situation of a previous generation in these words:

> As we look back on the First World War it would seem that the real motive for our entrance into that conflict should have been a clearly discerned *raison d'état:* to prevent Germany and her allies from overturning the balance of power against us. . . . We would like to believe that he [Wilson] finally brought the United States into the war on the Allied side in order to prevent Germany from upsetting the balance. . . . There is no satisfactory evidence that he did. . . . Fortunately he took his country into the conflict on the right side.

Speaking from the rather different context of his *Murder in the Cathedral,* T. S. Eliot gave poetic expression to a very similar idea, when he wrote:

> The last temptation is the greatest treason:
> To do the right deed for the wrong reason.

SUGGESTED READINGS

1. Morrissey, A. M., *The American Defense of Neutral Rights, 1914–1917.*
2. Millis, W., *Road to War: America 1914–1917.*
3. Seymour, Charles, *American Neutrality, 1914–1917.*

CHAPTER TWELVE

THE WAR ON THE HOME FRONT AND ABROAD

THE IMMEDIATE EFFECT OF THE AMERICAN WAR DECLARATION

The American declaration of war on Germany did not start a stampede of neutrals into the Allied camps. Those in Europe ignored Wilson's call for a crusade against militarism and autocracy. In the Western Hemisphere eight states, headed by Brazil, joined it; five others broke off relations with Germany; Argentina, Chile, Colombia, El Salvador, Mexico, Paraguay, and Venezuela remained neutral. In the Far East, China waited until August 1917, when she reluctantly joined because of concern over her deteriorating regional position.

At first the United States refrained from declaring war on Austria-Hungary although the latter broke off diplomatic relations on April 9, 1917. For a time hopes of driving a wedge between the Dual Monarchy and Germany were encouraged by the Hapsburg Emperor Charles, who put forth peace feelers. Wilson tried to promote a negotiated settlement by offering a guarantee against dismemberment. When the soft approach failed, he threatened on June 24 to support a policy of self-determination for all the minorities in the multinational state. By this time America's European allies had begun to plan the partition of the Dual Monarchy, and this killed all lingering prospects of a separate peace. The collapse of negotiations led to a declaration of war in December 1917.

THE SECRET TREATIES

The United States became a member of the Allied coalition long after the original participants had decided what they were fighting for. Their aims had been spelled out in a series of formal agreements between March 1915 and March 1917. Such arrangements were customary among members of a war coalition to protect their individual interests and to reduce the tension arising out of their conflicting objectives. Because the contents were not published, they came to be known as "secret treaties." It is incorrect to find overtones of impropriety in this term; secrecy was not used primarily to conceal something sinister but to avoid goading the enemy into a last-ditch fight.

Three considerations had motivated the negotiation of most Allied treaties: (1) the necessity of promising specific spoils in advance to purchase the support of wavering neutrals; (2) the desire to promote cooperation among members in executing operations that had become desirable as a result of previous successes; (3) the fear that unless tacit understandings were put in formal terms an unpredictable United States might try to overturn them. Agreements of the first type included the Treaty of London (April 26, 1915), which brought Italy into the war on the Allied side, and the Treaty of Bucharest (August 8, 1916), which bribed Rumania into taking similar action.

Both the Anglo-French-Russian Treaty of March 11, 1915 and the Sykes-Picot Treaty (May 1916) fell into the second category. The earlier of these called for a partition of some Turkish provinces among the contracting parties and thereby cleared the way for the Dardanelles campaign. Although the Allies failed to take Constantinople, they achieved enough military success the next year to warrant negotiation of the Sykes-Picot agreement which divided much of the Near and Middle East into spheres of influence.

The third group of treaties were all hurriedly drawn up after America had broken with Germany but before she had entered the war. This precaution seemed wise because Wilson had recently served notice on the world that the United States would seek a "peace without victory." Accordingly in February and March of 1917 Japan extracted written pledges of support from Great Britain, France, Russia, and Italy for her claims to Far Eastern territory taken from Germany. The same documents confirmed in more ambiguous language her special position in China. On March 11, 1917, Russia and France granted each other a free hand in determining their respective postwar frontiers with Germany. Great Britain remained aloof from this agreement because she disapproved of French intentions to push their eastern frontier to the Rhine.

In the aggregate, the secret treaties and their supplements proposed to divide the bulk of enemy empires. German colonial possessions were marked for distribution among the Japanese, British, and French. The Ottoman Empire faced complete destruction, its possessions being assigned as follows: (1) Constantinople, the Asiatic side of the Straits, Armenia, and portions of the southern Black Sea coast to Russia; (2) Syria and the hinterland eastward as far as the Mosul oil fields to France; (3) Palestine, Transjordan, and the southern Tigris-Euphrates area to England; (4) the Dodecanese

"And, by ginger, he can play 'em all!" But it keeps Uncle Sam busy these days. (The Cleveland Plain Dealer, *1918.*)

islands to Italy and Greece. Similar arrangements pointed to the dismemberment of Austria-Hungary, with Rumania, Serbia, Russia, and Italy slated for the lion's share of the spoils.

Besides the explicit awards the treaties contained conflicting promises that were to be sources of future trouble. Smyrna had been offered to both the Italians and the Greeks, while Dalmatia had been dangled as bait alternately to the Italians and to the Serbs. Palestine fell into the same classification; the British had promised it to the various groups of Arabs in return for their help against the Turks and had left the French with the impression that the Holy Land would be placed under an international administration. Foreign Secretary A. J. Balfour was to deepen the confusion in November 1917 by a public endorsement of Zionist aspirations for a Jewish national state in Palestine. Conscious duplicity seldom motivated the major Allied Powers in assigning a piece of enemy territory to more than one junior partner; more often the propaganda and military needs of the moment encouraged the practice.

The foregoing summary of treaties does not cover all the agreements concluded by the Allies, but it is representative enough to reveal the character of their aims. With unlimited help from America they could look forward to winning the war. The big question from their standpoint was whether Wilson would consent to full-fledged American participation without insisting that the Allies scale down their aims. In an effort to strike a bargain that would facilitate the flow of urgently needed supplies, they promptly dispatched missions to the United States. At the end of April 1917, a British delegation headed by Balfour and a French delegation headed by former Premier René Viviani came to Washington. They were followed by representatives from the smaller states.

On their arrival, the Old World diplomats were surprised to discover that America showed much more interest in getting into the fight than in spelling out her objectives. The administration possessed some information about the secret treaties, but House urged Wilson to postpone discussion of them. This advice was curious, because if the United States hoped to extract concessions from the Allies it would have to do so while they needed help rather than after the war had been won. The Colonel proposed to throw away a strong bargaining position on the ground that the gulf between American and Allied war aims was too vast to be bridged by discussion. House even visualized the possibility of the Allies fighting each other if Wilson took up the question immediately.

When it became apparent that Wilson intended to act on House's advice, Balfour took the initiative and showed the American government all the secret treaties involving Britain. By so doing he took a long step toward absolving his country from responsibility for later conflict and confusion. The record indicates that American officials expressed little criticism of British commitments and made no demands beyond those that might have been inferred from Wilson's earlier public statements. Balfour offered to repudiate British agreements with Russia on the theory that the establishment of a new government in Moscow relieved London of obligations contracted with the Tsarist regime. The other missions, concluding from the experience of Balfour that American aid would be forthcoming without concessions on their part, made little serious effort to discuss war aims. As a result, this crucial issue was shelved until the eve of victory.

Why Wilson conducted wartime diplomacy in such careless fashion will probably never be explained satisfactorily. He was so distressed two years later by the fruits of his action that he told the Senate Foreign Relations Committee (August 14, 1919) he had not known about the treaties before the peace conference. This statement tells us more about his subsequent embarrassment than about his original motives. Perhaps he at first overestimated his powers of persuasion and imagined that he could write his own terms by appealing over the heads of rulers to their people. Perhaps he identified "right" with his own views and believed that their triumph was inevitable. He once said: "I believe very profoundly in an overruling Providence and do not fear that any real plans can be thrown off the track."

If either estimate of his thought processes is correct, he would have had little incentive to negotiate over war aims. The probability that he acted on some such combination of beliefs is high.

THE MILITARY SITUATION IN 1917

Once the Allied missions discovered that America did not intend to demand a revision of the secret treaties in return for military aid, they presented Wilson with a list of their most urgent needs. They required both credit to finance purchases of supplies and naval assistance to get the supplies safely across the Atlantic. Items in demand included raw materials, food, and certain types of armament that American factories had already begun to produce. There was less interest in the services of American soldiers. Viviani cautiously asked for 500,000, but he wanted them to replace casualties in existing regiments rather than to function as an independent army on the western front.

The extensive character of the Allies' demands indicated their desperate situation in the spring of 1917. On the eastern front the Germans had overrun Rumania the preceding winter and were advancing steadily against the demoralized Russian armies. In the west, they had just completed a planned withdrawal to the fortified Siegfried line, relinquishing a thousand square miles of French territory. From this shorter and more easily defended position they repelled a massive nine weeks' French offensive and inflicted heavy losses on the attackers. General Nivelle, who had directed the unsuccessful drive, was relieved of his command on May 20, 1917, and replaced by General Pétain. Pétain wisely spent the rest of the year trying to rebuild the dispirited and mutinous French army.

Meanwhile German strategy called for defensive operations on the western front and an all-out attack on Allied shipping which Berlin relied upon to end the war. The limited U-boat activity of 1916 had destroyed about 300,000 tons of Allied shipping per month, and the High Command hoped now to double the rate. According to its calculations British merchant tonnage would be reduced by 40 per cent if the U-boat fleet could sink 600,000 tons a month during the next half year. Presumably this rate of destruction would paralyze the Allied war effort before American help became effective enough to turn the tide. The Germans fell just short of their target for February and March of 1917 by destroying approximately 570,000 tons of shipping in each month. During April they sank 881,000 tons, which meant that they were torpedoing ships twice as rapidly as the Allies could build them. As a result the grain reserves on the British Isles dwindled to a six weeks' supply, and starvation became a real possibility.

THE CONTRIBUTION OF THE AMERICAN NAVY

The intervention of the American Navy turned the tide although submarines continued to sink over 600,000 tons in both May and June. The principal American contribution at the height of the crisis was a small fleet of destroyers to detect and hunt down the U-boats. With these on the job, the rate of sinkings turned downward in July and dropped to 289,000 tons in November 1917. The use of the airplane and other new weapons for submarine destruction led to steady cuts in Allied losses during 1918.

The Americans also attempted to restrict the activity of the submarines by mining the entire northern entrance to the North Sea. With some help from the Allies, they laid a mine barrage 245 miles long and 20 miles wide. The project had not been completed when the war ended, but by June 1918 the area was closed to submarines for all practical purposes. Even during the early stages of construction the barrage destroyed one out of every ten U-boats that tried to slip through it. It damaged many others and greatly lowered German morale.

The third effective technique to combat the submarine menace was a convoy system for troopships and merchantmen. An earlier British effort along the same lines had failed because of inadequate naval forces. With more seapower at his disposal Admiral Sims now revived convoying on a larger scale. Fortunately his responsibilities were limited by the range of the German submarine which did not extend more than a few hundred miles beyond European waters. Employing a shuttle service, the American Navy convoyed approximately 90,000 vessels through the danger zone and lost only one-half of one per cent.

Simultaneously America sought to tighten the naval blockade of Germany. Contraband lists were extended to cover virtually all commodities, and firms in neutral countries which dealt with the Germans were blacklisted. If the American Navy did not actually win World War I, it prevented the Allies from being beaten in 1917 and assured them of a breathing spell to regroup their forces for the knockout blows of 1918.

BUILDING AN ARMY

Washington was better prepared for an immediate contribution to the war on the high seas than to that in the trenches. Congress had authorized a volunteer army of 175,000 in 1916 without the vaguest notion that a year later it would be needed in Europe. Military planners had failed to show much foresight. Hence the Army was completely unprepared for action overseas in April 1917. As already noted, the Allies modestly requested 500,000 men for service on the western front; but when General John J. Pershing, the newly designated commander of the nonexistent American Expeditionary

Force, arrived in France just after the collapse of the Nivelle offensive, he demanded a million men by May 1918. The planners in Washington expected the war to last a year longer than it did and insisted on a still larger military establishment. They not only got their way but sustained the American reputation for doing things on a big scale by putting four million men under arms in eighteen months.

Unfortunately it proved easier to make a decision about the size of an army than to raise one, equip it, and dispatch it to Europe. Months were consumed in these preparations, although a token force composed of the First Infantry reached France in late June of 1917. It paraded in Paris on July 4 to demonstrate the solidarity of America with her Allies. Other units were slow to arrive. Only 6,000 officers and 80,000 men had arrived by October, and the total did not reach 200,000 until the end of the year. A few battalions were moved to the front and traded volleys with the Germans for the first time on October 21, but most units did not receive their initial taste of combat until 1918.

Although Pershing did not have enough troops at his disposal to participate in the campaign of 1917, he was an astute observer and quickly reached some firm conclusions about Allied strategy. One of these was that the United States ought to have a separate army. Patriotism and the desire for an independent command undoubtedly played a part in his rejection of the proposal that untried "doughboys" be fed into existing regiments as replacements. But the major reason for his stand was the belief that the Allied strategists were too exhausted either to devise new strategy or to execute it. Wilson backed Pershing over the protests of the French government. His decision cleared the way for a major offensive by American units once they reached France in sufficient numbers. Pershing was not a brilliant strategist, but he had solid qualities of leadership as well as complete confidence in himself and his troops. He also showed wisdom in his choice of subordinates. General Charles G. Dawes, whom he selected as Purchasing Agent, made some notable improvements in the supply services; others helped coordinate related aspects of the sprawling military machine. Thus, although the American expeditionary army was too small in 1917 to affect the deadlock on the western front, its commander laid the groundwork for the victories of the next year.

INDUSTRIAL MOBILIZATION

Meanwhile, Washington was concentrating its attention on organizing the country for war. The Civil War offered few useful precedents because during the intervening years the industrial revolution had complicated the problems of mobilization. The increasing interdependence of the economy opened the possibility of utilizing the resources of remote mines, forests, and farms and also put a premium on the coordination of raw materials, transportation, and manpower. The spontaneous character of peacetime productive activity could not be continued without seriously handicapping mobilization. The government thus faced the dual responsibility of persuading businessmen to manufacture military goods and consumer goods in proper proportions and on a larger scale than ever before. This task involved the further problems of creating new facilities, converting existing ones to new uses, and tapping new sources of labor to replace workers called up for military service. Logic dictated some form of government compulsion since industry was unlikely to give up established markets and profits voluntarily for the temporary and uncertain gains of war contracts.

Although most warring states had at the outset recognized the necessity for centralized control by regulating the use of food, raw materials, and manpower, the Wilson administration moved slowly in this direction. A long tradition of limited government and a widespread desire to wage war with as few sacrifices as possible stood in the way of rapid mobilization. Congressional jealousy of executive power also delayed the concentration of authority in Wilson's hands. The inertia of the legislators and of the rank and file was reflected to some degree in the outlook of the administration. Neither Wilson nor his advisers understood the complexity of the industrial system. They simply did not anticipate that the regulation of such areas as labor and raw materials would produce repercussions in the wage–price structure and necessitate further controls. As the history of mobilization will demonstrate, they eventually mastered all the ramifications of planning and regulated everything from food production to public expression.

WAR FINANCE

The order in which the United States tackled the problems of mobilization was affected to some degree by the requirements of the Allies. The various missions that converged on Washington in April 1917 made urgent demands for financial aid. Most of them had already exhausted the obvious sources of dollars by liquidating the investments of their nationals in American firms, selling bonds through the J. P. Morgan syndicate, and depleting gold reserves at home. Additional credit of some sort was necessary to pay for urgently needed American goods. An outright cash gift or a series of subsidies from Washington would have been most welcome. During earlier wars the British and others had adopted the practice of aiding their allies with financial contributions rather than with large numbers of soldiers. If the Entente Powers expected such a solution now, they were disappointed. Americans disapproved too much of unbusinesslike arrangements to propose them voluntarily, and the Allies prudently refrained from taking the initiative.

Congress preferred a more conventional arrangement and promptly passed an Emergency Loan Act which the President signed on April 24. The key provision authorized the addition of $5 billion to the national debt in the form of bonds bearing 3.5 per cent interest. Two billion of this was earmarked for war expenditure in the United States, but the remaining $3 billion was made available for loans at the same rate of interest to the powers fighting Germany. Great Britain and France immediately took advantage of this legislation and were followed by the lesser members of the coalition. Eventually Italy, Russia, Serbia, and Cuba received loans. So persistent was the need of the Allied nations to fuel their sputtering military machines with the seemingly inexhaustible resources of the United States that Congress repeatedly authorized new loans. During eighteen months of participation in the war America made more than $7 billion available to her allies. Even the Armistice did not immediately shut off the flood of credit. In a final gesture of international good will before the nationalist reaction, Congress provided $3.25 billion in relief and rehabilitation loans for which some twenty nations qualified.

As usual Congress showed more enthusiasm and haste in authorizing the expenditure of money than in providing ways to collect it. Since the government's new obligations were larger than the tax revenue, Congress provided for short-term borrowing by the Treasury through the Emergency Loan Act. It then supplemented this stopgap arrangement by specifying that funds should be raised on a long-term basis by selling bonds to the public.

Congressional insistence that citizens rather than banks should hold the national debt was a concession to popular prejudice rather than an endorsement of a specific monetary theory. By permitting a bankers' syndicate to market government bonds at a handsome profit, President Cleveland had provoked such general resentment that no responsible official dared repeat the procedure. But Congress was so uncertain of the outcome of a fund-raising drive based on popular subscription that it prudently omitted from the Emergency Loan Act any specific instructions for the Treasury Department. This left the dates of issues and the amounts to be raised by each loan in the hands of William Gibbs McAdoo.

Professional bankers doubted that McAdoo could raise more than a billion dollars on a single call, but the Secretary decided that patriotic citizens would absorb two billion at once. In exploiting the notorious susceptibility of Americans to a high-pressure campaign, he named his promotion "The Liberty Loan of 1917," promised it would be spent to the last dollar in defense of democracy, and launched an intensive seven weeks' drive on May 2. Local committees sprang up as if by magic to push sales; bankers unselfishly served as private solicitors and salesmen; newspapers devoted generous space to the project; and purchasers wore patriotic buttons. McAdoo stumped the country and had able assistance from the "four-minute men," who interrupted public entertainments to give brief speeches for the drive. Actors and idols from the sports world added their endorsements.

When the campaign closed, the public had exceeded McAdoo's target by $1.035 billion. Three more Liberty Loans, and a Victory Loan launched after the Armistice, were equally successful. Citizens who could not raise a lump sum of fifty dollars to buy the smallest bonds outright, purchased War Saving Certificates and Thrift Stamps — the latter for as little as twenty-five cents. Altogether the Treasury was able to borrow over $22 billion from the American people to finance the war.

The repeated use of Liberty Loans exposed the unwillingness of Congress to pay the bulk of war costs out of current revenue. In fact, the United States had been a belligerent for six months before the legislators could agree on a war revenue measure. The instinctive reluctance of congressmen to jeopardize their tenure by raising taxes found reinforcement in the solemn warnings of bankers and manufacturers. Both groups used the traditional arguments against increases, predicting that production would be disrupted, individual initiative destroyed, and the war machine paralyzed. They strongly backed the revival of Civil War fiscal policy that had extracted only one dollar by taxation for every five dollars borrowed.

At the other extreme was a smaller group of citizens who organized the American Committee on War Finance under the leadership of Amos Pinchot and advocated the payment of war costs from current taxation. The most effective champion of this viewpoint in Congress was the truculent old reformer, Senator Robert M. La Follette. Neither he nor the other supporters of "pay as you go" anticipated the disruptive effect of inflation on prices and wages. They were equally unaware of the role which abundant money or credit would play in redistributing wealth to the advantage of wage earners and to the detriment of fixed-income groups. Reflecting their Progressive antecedents, they sought to make war finance a vehicle of social reform. Their targets were big business and "war profiteers."

In the end, Congress steered between the two extremes and followed the recommendation of McAdoo, who proposed that approximately one-third of the war cost be met by taxation. The least painful and most obvious method of securing additional revenue was to increase excise taxes, particularly on old favorites such as alcohol and tobacco. The levy was also extended to miscellaneous articles ranging all the way from railroad tickets to chewing gum.

Although excise taxes continued to be the principal source of revenue, Congress raised additional funds through an income tax. First used to help finance the Civil War, the income tax had been declared unconstitutional by the Supreme Court only to be revived in 1913 by the Seventeenth Amendment. The Progressives had regarded great wealth as a sign of wickedness and the income tax as a whip to chastise the wealthy. This view presisted in the Revenue Act of 1917. Only citizens with what was then the very comfortable income of $3,000 felt the tax. Exemptions of $1,000 for unmarried persons and $2,000 for heads of families further restricted the numbers affected. The tax started at 2 per cent and reached 67 per cent on all incomes in excess of $2 million. Later acts increased the base rate and the graduated surtax on larger incomes.

The final noteworthy source of revenue tapped by the legislation of 1917 was the tax on the net profits of corporations. Like the income tax, this had originally been enacted to recover for the public what the Progressives regarded as ill-gotten wealth. Congress saw that a flat rate which was high enough to siphon off the abnormally high profits of war industries would work a hardship on firms less favorably situated. So it levied a general tax of 6 per cent on net profits, plus a special tax on excess profits graduated from 20 to 60 per cent, the latter computed on the basis of prewar earnings as well as invested capital. Businessmen did not know how to calculate this tax and lacked the incentive to learn. It produced much litigation but a disappointing amount of revenue. This did not prevent Congress from raising the rates again in 1918.

Taken all together, the various war revenue measures produced about one-third of the $32 billion spent over a three-year period either directly on the conflict or in the form of loans to the Allies. Practically all the remaining funds were raised through the Liberty Loans, which meant that the United States borrowed heavily from her own citizens. It is difficult to avoid the conclusion that this policy was not based on a definite fiscal theory. Congress created a patchwork of measures, partly from habit and partly because it did not see the close relationship of finance to other phases of the war economy.

SELECTIVE SERVICE

Congress showed more promptness in raising an army than in raising taxes. Wilson forwarded Pershing's recommendation to the legislators in mid-April of 1917. Nearly two months of debate followed, with most of the opposition directed against the provision for recruiting by conscription. Some denounced conscription as a violation of the guarantee provided by the Thirteenth Amendment against slavery and involuntary servitude. Others objected on the ground that it was an implied slur on American patriotism. A few recalled the protest riots in New York City against the draft during the Civil War and feared a repetition of such incidents. To the embarrassment of the President, the Democratic leaders in the House led the fight against conscription. Speaker Champ Clark observed that there was "precious little difference between a conscript and a convict," and Stanley H. Dent of Alabama, chairman of the Military Affairs Committee, flatly declined to sponsor the legislation.

Even so, conscription was inevitable. Congress knew that a million-man army could not be raised without some element of compulsion. It also learned from the British experience with volunteering that enlistment drives often enticed patriotic citizens from key industrial jobs to a position in the army where they functioned less usefully. As a result, the real issue before Congress was not conscription, but the kind of conscription system that would be needed to supplement the volunteer army. The administration wanted to feed all volunteers into units already activated, while Wilson's critics wanted to permit the formation of new units outside the existing military structure. The controversy took on distinctly political overtones because the advocates of wide-open recruiting linked their cause with the military aspirations of Theodore Roosevelt. The aging Rough Rider had been seriously enfeebled by his strenuous explorations in South America, but he wanted to relive his youth by organizing a regiment of volunteers to fight on the western front. His popularity was so great that he would have had little trouble doing so. But he needed Wilson's authorization, and after spending the first week of the war on a preliminary enrollment he dramatically called on the President. Wilson flatly rejected the offer. Republicans saw nothing but personal vindictiveness in this action, but sound reasons existed for the decision. Lives had been needlessly lost in both the Civil War and the Spanish-American War because of the monumental incompetence of political line-officers and generals. Regular army officers wanted the war fought on a professional basis. They had already decided not to commission young businessmen without special instruction in officers' camps. Whether such short courses actually qualified the graduates to be officers was doubtful, but the attitude of the War Department reinforced Wilson's determination to prevent the infiltration of the Army by semi-autonomous political adventurers. The only effect of the Roosevelt-Wilson encounter on conscription legislation was the adoption of an amendment which authorized the President to accept or reject volunteer units.

The final subject of controversy concerned the age limit for registrants. The War Department wanted a range from nineteen to twenty-five years, because younger men made the best soldiers. Congress, which was more sensitive to parental pleas to protect teen-agers from the influences of army life, finally settled on ages twenty-one to thirty. It also prohibited the sale of liquor in the vicinity of army camps or to soldiers in uniform.

On May 18, 1917, the bill finally reached Wilson's desk for signature. Because it exempted the physically unfit, conscientious objectors, certain categories of key civilians, and citizens with large numbers of dependents, the term "conscription" was replaced by the more euphemistic phrase "selective service." Another device to soften the appearance of compulsion was the creation of local draft boards for registering and calling young men to the colors. Army officers remained in the background. The decision to conscript an individual ostensibly rested with his friends and neighbors. The strongest advocates of registration at draft boards likened it to registration at the polls and to similar duties of citizenship.

The mechanics of the draft were simple enough. President Wilson designated June 5 as registration day, and over nine and a half million young men reported to 4,557 local boards and filled out the appropriate blanks. Each registrant received a serial number. His order of classification was determined in a great lottery on July 20. Secretary of War Baker drew the first number, which happened to be 258 and affected all registrants so assigned. Later drawings established the call numbers of the other registrants, who were classified in order. The draft boards placed 3,706,544 men in Class I, as immediately available for military duty. Four other classes were set up to cover various deferments.

Within a year the twenty-one to thirty age-group was nearly exhausted and Congress on September 12, 1918, reluctantly authorized the registration of all men between eighteen and forty-five. The war ended before many were affected by the new regulation. Altogether 24,234,021 men registered under selective service legislation. Of this total over three and one half million were drafted, two million were shipped overseas, and approximately one million saw action on the battlefield. Only the Army relied on the draft. Other branches of the service, including the National Guard, the Navy, and the Marine Corps, filled their quotas by enlistments, which the government did not discontinue until August 9, 1918.

THE MOBILIZATION OF LABOR

The withdrawal of several million young men from the labor force, coupled with the wartime drop in immigration, created a dangerous shortage of workers just when greater production was needed. The administration had no formal plan to deal with this problem. Political considerations ruled out any type of solution which would have frozen workers to their jobs or set up compulsory recruitment for the labor force. Patriotic appeals were bound to lose force without more substantial inducements. Hence the remaining alternative was to raise wages high enough to attract a new labor supply as well as to satisfy workers already on war jobs.

The administration found this policy easy to implement because it became the ultimate customer for most industrial production during the war. In government-owned war plants it could establish any wage scale it pleased. It could secure the same standards in private plants doing war work through the "cost-plus" contract, which enabled employers to pass the cost of all wage increases on to the government.

Wilson used this power to make an informal but firm bargain with labor. He undertook to establish the principle of union recognition in government plants and to secure wage increases as rapidily as prices rose. In return, he extracted a no-strike pledge from organized labor in basic industry for the duration of the war.

Although no single individual in the labor movement could speak for the great body of workers with the same authority as the President could employ in committing the government to a particular policy, Samuel Gompers emerged as labor's leading spokesman and worked wholeheartedly for the no-strike pledge. Already grateful to Wilson for the Clayton and Adamson acts, he became additionally indebted for his appointment to the

Advisory Committee of the Council of National Defense and other mobilization agencies. The resulting prestige made it possible for him to rally most American workers behind his policy. Only the I. W. W. and a few socialistic groups refused to accept his leadership and the no-strike pledge.

On the whole the bargain operated in the interest of efficient production. Most of the interruptions to work during the nineteen months of the war were brief and were ended on terms acceptable to labor. The government established several wartime agencies to handle specific problems as they came up. Especially noteworthy were the War Labor Conference Board, which formulated a code of fair labor practices, and the National War Labor Board, which tried to settle industrial disputes peacefully. The latter agency performed with distinction under the joint chairmanship of former-President William Howard Taft and Frank P. Walsh, an eminent labor lawyer.

Not only did the attractiveness of war work ensure steady production; it also drew manpower from hitherto untapped sources. Large numbers of Negroes, perhaps as many as 400,000, migrated from the South to work in war plants. Many women left the shelter of the home for the first time to take jobs in defense plants or less essential industries. The administration's policy of attracting civilian workers by high wages rather than by coercion was so effective that it was broadened to include farmers, businessmen, and other groups. It had the special merit of being familiar because the achievement of cooperation by the grant of concealed government subsidies was as old as American history. In fact, the granting of subsidies within the existing institutional framework went far to conceal or to make palatable the centralized planning and operation of the economy. On the other hand, it strengthened the tendency of all pressure groups to look to the government for help whenever they wanted anything they could not get themselves.

THE EVOLUTION OF WAR AGENCIES

The most complicated phase of mobilization was the harnessing of raw materials, food, and power resources. Key commodities had to be located, processed, and distributed so that essential civilian and military needs were met. This required the conservation of critical materials and the establishment of a system of priorities, as well as the conversion of existing manfacturing facilities to the production of essential goods and the creation of additional plants when needed. Each segment of the economy had to be drawn into the web of regulation. Wilson and his advisers understood this elementary proposition but did not realize that industrial interdependence had reached the stage where almost every area of economic life was affected.

The creation of a serviceable industrial machine was further slowed by the casual attitude of the administration in the period before hostilities began. Although Congress had passed and Wilson had signed a preparedness measure in 1916, neither the legislators nor the President had wanted to discuss military problems realistically. Public opinion supported them in the delusion that it was desirable to enact legislation which contemplated involvement in the war but unsportsmanlike to make any preparations before the country was actually in it. Even the War Department did not indicate what preparedness was supposed to accomplish. Nor could economic planners foresee what equipment the armed forces would need when the War Department itself did not have a file of plans against potential enemies in the Western Hemisphere — much less in Europe.

The first agency to tackle the problem was the Council of National Defense. It had been created by the Army Appropriations Act of August 29, 1916, and given advisory powers to harmonize the needs of civilians with the enlarged military requirements under the preparedness program. The same legislation empowered the President to appoint an Advisory Commission of seven specialists, serving without pay, who would furnish important data on mobilization problems. Two hundred thousand dollars was appropriated for investigations which would presumably end in "recommendations to the President and the heads of Executive Departments" for the coordination of economic activity. Wilson promptly appointed a well-balanced team of experts: Daniel Willard of the Baltimore and Ohio Railroad for transportation; Julius Rosenwald of Sears, Roebuck and Company for supplies, particularly clothing; Samuel Gompers of the American Federation of Labor for labor relations; Howard Coffin, an automotive engineer, for manufacturing; Dr. Franklin H. Martin, a leading physician, for medicine; Bernard Baruch, speculator and market analyst, for raw materials; and President Hollis Godfrey of Drexel Institute for education.

Despite the assembling of this galaxy of talent, the President did not encourage the Advisory Commission or its parent to do more at the outset than hold conferences. He lacked a sense of urgency in 1916 and ignored the Commission until resumption of submarine warfare by Germany forced his hand. Congress was equally suspicious and refused to give the Commission any authority. Other groups criticized the practice of having government business transacted by experts who remained on the payrolls of private corporations, and insinuated that their advice would not be disinterested. The Commission also suffered because the responsibilities of various agencies overlapped and because military officials ignored or defied civilian planners.

Under the circumstances it was amazing that the Council of National Defense accomplished as much as it did. But by the spring of 1917 it had spun a web of committees staffed by volunteer specialists in almost every field of economic activity affected by war demands. The Council was unique among government agencies in that it did not seek to centralize power in itself. With the broadest spirit of disinterested public service, it tried to set up agencies that would perform specific jobs and considered its responsibilities over as soon as those jobs were under way.

This period, during which the various offspring of the Council tried to secure cooperation with advisory authority, might be called the first phase of industrial mobilization. Whenever any agency reached the limits of what it could achieve on this basis, Congress ordinarily met demands for more efficiency by granting the group specific regulatory powers and then withdrawing it from the jurisdiction of the Council. Both the Food Administration and the War Industries Board emerged by this process.

Because the mobilization agencies matured at an uneven rate, the second phase cannot be fixed by date, but it falls generally into those months when most of them enjoyed independent status. This stage was short. Since congressional grants of power were made sporadically, there was a large administrative no-man's land between the various areas of specific authority. As Wilson became more aware of the extreme interdependence of the economy, he pressed for powers to coordinate and direct all aspects of mobilization. Congress had been reluctant to grant even limited regulatory power to the agencies whose personnel was controlled by the President, and it thoroughly disliked the idea of concentrating more authority in his hands. In the winter of 1918, however, he cleverly parried complaints of inefficiency by ascribing the shortcomings of his administration to the fragmentary nature of its authority and by making a public plea for greater power over mobilization. Congress had to capitulate or face the charge of obstructing the war. It chose the less daring course and in April passed the Overman Act giving the President practically a blank check.

Thus the third and last phase of economic mobilization began. By the terms of the Act, Wilson could create agencies, abolish them, or redistribute their functions as he saw fit. So sweeping was the dictatorship conferred on him that his bitter foe, Senator Brandegee of Connecticut, sarcastically proposed an amendment: "If any power, constitutional or not, has been omitted from this bill, it is hereby conferred." Wilson used his new authority to concentrate control in six great agencies which were either surviving committees of the Council of National Defense or government corporations chartered by Congress.

THE WAR INDUSTRIES BOARD

One of the first offices to be set up, and the agency destined to exercise the widest authority, was the War Industries Board. It emerged as a distinct organization on July 28, 1917, and was designed to consolidate the functions of the Council's advisory committees on raw materials, finished products, procurement, priorities, and prices. At that time the Board, like most mobilization agencies in their second phase, was hamstrung by limited grants of authority. It could neither enforce a priorities system nor prevent purchasing agents of the Allies and the United States from bidding against each other for the same scarce items. Wilson did not move to end the chaos until he was certain that Congress would accept the ultimate concentration of authority embodied in the Overman Act. On March 4, 1918, he reorganized the Board for the final time, granting it specific power to establish priorities for all types of materials used in war, to convert existing facilities to new uses, and to create new facilities or sources of supply. Final determination of policy on all these matters was left to the discretion of the chairman. The only area exempted from his control was the establishment of prices, which required the consent of a price-fixing committee.

The delegation of so much authority to the chairman of the War Industries Board made it necessary for Wilson to select a specially qualified individual. The newspapers called for a superman or, as one commentator put it, an administrator able "to look any man in the face and tell him to go to hell." Bernard Baruch, who was chosen for the job, satisfied on both counts. After a year of hard work as head of the Raw Materials Committee of the Council of National Defense, he knew the location and quantity of practically all strategic materials in the United States. He had also tracked down the necessary information on key minerals like manganese and chromium that were not available in North America. Furthermore, in his successful career as a Wall Street speculator he had built up an encyclopedic knowledge of American business. He spoke the language of the businessman and showed a refreshing contempt for red tape. Above all, he had a talent for focusing his attention on large objectives and leaving the petty details to others.

The elastic powers conferred on Baruch as chairman of the War Industries Board made him a dictator over large areas of the war economy. His authority to establish priorities on all materials except agricultural commodities gave him life-and-death power over business. If a manufacturer refused to convert from the production of horseshoes to trench shovels, Baruch could cut off his supplies of iron and shut down his assembly lines. He could even commandeer the plant for the government and operate it. In cooperation with the price-fixing committee, he could exercise further leverage by setting the prices of raw materials at wholesale.

Despite his impressive authority, Baruch tried to proceed by negotiation rather than coercion. Usually, democratic discussions with businessmen preceded decisions on the distribution of raw materials and the fixing of prices. On occasion he resorted to a naked display of power, but for the most part businessmen cooperated voluntarily. Patriotism, enhanced by cost-plus contracts with guaranteed profits, induced them to give the war effort the same wholehearted support that labor was already providing. Consequently the unprecedented amount of central economic planning seldom expressed itself in crude compulsion at the production level.

Because of the tremendous powers of the War Industries Board, it was logical for it to dominate peripheral areas. Baruch took over the additional responsibility of coordinating procurement for businessmen, government agencies, and members of the Allied coalition. In his effort to prevent different groups from bidding for the same scarce items and raising prices, he turned the Board into a clearinghouse for all war purchases.

Subordinate divisions of the Board exercised still more authority by launching a program of standardization and substitution to conserve strategic materials and shipping space. They reduced automobile tires to three types, shoes to three styles, and cloth caps to a single style. They took the whalebone out of corsets and replaced cardboard cartons with paper ones wherever possible.

THE FARMER AND THE WAR

The success of the war depended as much on effective use of food as of industrial resources. It was therefore natural that the second major wartime agency should deal with this problem. No controls would have been necessary to assure enough food for the American people, but the United States was now forced to assume much larger responsibilities. European agriculture had been badly disrupted, and many areas producing surpluses had passed under the control of the Central Powers. Plagued by severe shortages, the Allies greeted American entrance into the war with urgent pleas for food.

Most eagerly sought was wheat, long a staple in the European diet and convenient to transport because it did not deteriorate if kept away from moisture. Ordinarily the wheat deficit of our European allies could have been made up by Argentina or Australia, but submarine warfare had created such a serious shortage of merchantmen that Great Britain and France dared not tie up shipping space for the forty-five days necessary to haul a cargo of wheat from Australia. Hence the United States became a desirable source of supply just at the time when rising population was cutting down the surplus available for export.

To increase shipments of wheat to Europe, an organized effort would be needed. American citizens would have to adopt systematic measures for food conservation, consume more of the perishable and fewer of the nonperishable commodities, and plant more grain than before. The Council of National Defense authorized an Advisory Food Committee, and on May 20, 1917, Wilson appointed Herbert C. Hoover as Food Commissioner. Hoover brought to the job a tremendous reputation gained as head of the Commission for Belgian Relief. A native of Iowa, a graduate of Stanford University, and a distinguished mining engineer who had spent half his forty-three years outside the United States, he had turned to relief work at the outset of the war. His experience in Europe had convinced him that food was the key to an Allied victory, and he immediately launched a drive to make Americans food-conscious. Despite a shy and solemn manner, he knew how to organize programs and to secure sustained favorable publicity. He quickly assembled a volunteer staff that preached "the gospel of the clean plate" all over the United States. Citizens were urged to "Hooverize" by using less sugar in their coffee and less butter on their potatoes. In some areas, local committees made door-to-door canvasses to secure pledges of compliance with food regulations. Dietary propaganda extolled the virtues of fish, fruit, vegetables, and warmed-over gravy. The nation was asked to observe meatless and wheatless days. Even the home vegetable patch became a badge of enlistment for food conservation.

But there were limits to the amount of wheat that could be released for export by voluntary changes in dietary habits and by victory gardens. Acreage would have to be increased substantially to meet the requirements of Europe. Unfortunately, Hoover lacked the authority to fix prices or guarantee the farmer the minimum return necessary to stimulate additional production of wheat or any other commodity. Fearful that the whole program would collapse, he requested broad regulatory powers over the production, processing, pricing, and consumption of agricultural commodities. Although a bill embodying his main demands was presented to the House of Representatives in May, nearly three months elapsed before it emerged as the Lever Act, August 19, 1917. Some congressmen opposed it as a dangerous and unprecedented dictatorship of agricultural life; others had heard rumors that Hoover manipulated grain supplies in Belgium to break speculators and feared he would use his power to reduce prices in the United States; a few, as usual, disliked independent agencies under the control of the President.

The final version of the Lever Act gave Hoover about what he wanted. All foods, feeds, fertilizers, and fuels were brought under the control of the President — which meant Mr. Hoover. The Act also authorized a comprehensive licensing system to cover all economic groups that processed any of the enumerated commodities, thus providing the Commissioner with an effective weapon against speculators and hoarders. Prohibitionists secured a clause prohibiting the use of food stuffs for the manufacture of alcoholic beverages. Farm congressmen, suspicious of Hoover, fixed the minimum price of wheat at two dollars per bushel for the 1918 wheat crop and authorized the President to set in advance the minimum price for ensuing years.

Although the Lever Act gave Hoover dictatorial power over food nine months before the War Industries Board received comparable authority over industry, he used coercion sparingly. The original volunteer organization he had set up functioned as before. Conservation was urged by appeal rather than by rationing. The most important effect of the Act was to stimulate wheat production. The President, at Hoover's advice, fixed the price at $2.20 a bushel and established a government-owned grain corporation to stabilize the market. This decision was consistent with the general policy of sugar-coating economic planning with subsidies. Agriculture, like labor and management, accepted centralized direction through the combined appeal of patriotism and financial gain.

FUEL, RAILROADS, AND SHIPPING

Although the gradual concentration of power in the War Industries Board and in the Food Commission gave those offices final responsibility for mobilizing all material resources, effective control of important marginal areas was held by four independent or semi-independent commissions.

One such separate area was fuel, which Congress, by a special provision of the Lever Act, turned over to a Fuel Administration. Wilson appointed Henry A. Garfield, son of a former President, to head this agency. Since fuel generated power to drive machinery and locomotives, policy decisions governing its use affected industrial mobilization. Nevertheless, the problems of fuel were more similar at some points to the problems of agriculture. Specifically coal, like wheat, did not reach the market in the volume required by industry. To stimulate production, the price of coal would have to be raised and then stabilized at a level that would make marginal mines profitable. Garfield took the necessary price-fixing measures and supplemented them with the usual public appeal for conservation. Notwithstanding these efforts, a severe shortage developed in January 1918 and prevented the departure of thirty-seven ships with munitions from New York harbor. Garfield reacted energetically, shutting down for five days all plants east of the Mississippi that were not producing essential goods. He followed this unexpected gesture with an order for "heatless Mondays" during the ensuing nine weeks. By early spring the crisis had passed, but the Fuel Administration ran a gauntlet of severe criticism.

With debatable logic the shortage was blamed on the railroads and thus precipitated government seizure of the carriers on December 26, 1917. Wilson appointed his tireless Secretary of the Treasury, McAdoo, as Director-General of the Railroads, thereby extending government control to a fourth great area of the economy.

Even before America entered the war, the railway system had repeatedly been condemned for inefficiency. Divided into thirty-two separate lines and forced by legislation to compete in a specified manner, the roads provided uneven and wasteful service. They possessed two and a quarter million freight cars, which eventually proved inadequate to carry wartime freight. The shortage of rolling stock was aggravated by the natural unwillingness of the individual railroad companies to cooperate at the sacrifice of revenue. They did not ship over the shortest route or move war goods ahead of less essential commodities that carried higher rates. Worst of all, they refused to pool freight cars and terminals.

Congress responded to the situation by giving the President authority to take over the roads in an emergency. Into the hands of the Interstate Commerce Commission the lawmakers gave the threatening weapon of authority to pool the use of boxcars without reference to ownership. The railroads moved to forestall public control by organizing a Railroads War

Board (April 11, 1917) to coordinate the thirty-two systems. It made substantial progress during the summer and fall in eliminating bottlenecks, but the roads could not give up the habits of half a century in a few months. As a torrent of war goods began to flow from the factories toward the ports of embarkation in the last months of 1917, the congestion at the key terminals increased. The ensuing confusion, coupled with the coal shortage at the ports, gave Wilson a plausible reason for taking over operation of the railroad system. McAdoo now instituted a policy of pooling coal supplies, terminals, freight cars, and ticket offices and sought to enforce the shipment of freight over the most direct route. Congress took care of the financial problems associated with seizure by guaranteeing each railroad a standard return based on its earnings from 1914 to 1917.

The authority of planners over the war economy was extended to a new area when Congress passed the Trading-with-the-Enemy Act on October 6, 1917. This Act authorized a War Trade Board, under Vance McCormick, to regulate all imports and exports. The agency choked off American trade with the Central Powers, limited the categories of shipments that could be sent to neutrals adjacent to the Central Powers, and implemented its policy by licensing or black-listing firms in neutral countries.

Companion legislation created an Alien Property Office to administer the property of enemy citizens — particularly American branches of German firms manufacturing chemicals and dyes. Wilson appointed A. Mitchell Palmer as head of the Office.

Consideration of the United States Shipping Board, which was actually the first of the six great mobilization agencies, has been deferred until last because it functioned almost independently of the other five. Created by Congress on September 7, 1916, as part of the preparedness program, it was intended to spearhead the expansion of the merchant marine. It started almost from scratch, because during the quarter-century preceding World War I the United States had habitually relied upon ships of foreign registry to carry American cargoes. The increased demands of the war upon Allied shipping space, plus the staggering losses through submarine attack, now made American construction of merchant ships all the more urgent. In the crisis Congress showed an experimental mood and authorized the Shipping Board to set up an Emergency Fleet Corporation to buy, lease, build, and operate ships. The creation of a corporation wholly owned by the government with a capital stock of $50 million represented an effort toward speed and flexibility of production characteristic of private enterprise.

The advantages of the government corporation were not immediately realized. A feud quickly broke out between William Denman, the chairman of the Shipping Board, and General George W. Goethals, famous for his part in the construction of the Panama Canal, who was appointed manager of the Emergency Fleet Corporation. The two administrators cooperated harmoniously in taking over 105 enemy ships interned when war broke out, and in foiling attempts at sabotage by the crews. They also agreed to commandeer over four hundred ships under construction in American yards for foreign purchasers. But they disagreed violently on the type of merchantmen the Emergency Fleet Corporation ought to build. Denman thought wooden ships could be turned out most quickly and cheaply. Goethals was equally positive in favor of steel ships. After six months of controversy Wilson removed both men and concentrated authority in the hands of Edward N. Hurley, a prominent Chicago businessman. Thereafter the shipbuilding program proceeded harmoniously.

The chief problem was to increase the supply of ships, which in turn required the construction of shipyards, the design of a standard vessel suitable for mass production, and the opening of fresh sources of lumber, steel, and labor. Before their retirement Denman and Goethals had set a target of 2,700 ships — 1,000 wood and 1,700 steel. But nearly a year passed before mass production was under way. During the last months of the war, new yards from the Gulf Coast to Hog Island below Philadelphia were turning out 150 ships a month. Such a rate of production was a tribute to the Emergency Fleet Corporation and to American inventive genius.

THE MOBILIZATION OF PUBLIC OPINION

The effectiveness of all the war measures depended largely on the attitude of the American people. Without their enthusiastic cooperation in the trenches, on the farms, and in the factories, all the paper calculations of the mobilizers would have come to naught. Although large-scale government management of the economy was unfamiliar to most Americans, it could be attempted more easily during a crisis than in normal times. By its very nature, wartime planning focused public attention on victory, whereas peacetime planning lacked a single goal capable of evoking such widespread support.

Even so, the people did not rally single-mindedly behind the banner of victory in 1917. During the three preceding years there had been an inconclusive debate over participation. In the 1916 election substantial numbers had voted for nonintervention and favored that policy as long as Germany did not attack the United States. Most of the 585,000 voters who had supported the Socialist party that year agreed with Debs and Berger that the war was a conflict of imperialistic powers over spoils and that Americans should have nothing to do with it. In North Dakota, where the Nonpartisan League had won control of the state with a program of agrarian socialism couched in Populistic terminology, many Leaguers resented the war for distracting public attention from reform. Elsewhere sentiment was more evenly divided than the vote on the War Resolution in Congress indicated.

Hence the federal government had to find some way to mobilize public opinion behind the war; otherwise it might have a lukewarm army, and passive resistance to economic planning at home. The most obvious resources for strengthening solidarity were its official media of publicity, which could be used to justify war objectives, and its police powers, which could be used to suppress criticism.

Ten days after the declaration of war the President established a Committee on Public Information to publish and disseminate news about the conflict. He provoked bitter attacks on the new agency from many sources by appointing an argumentative free-lance journalist, George Creel, to direct its activities. Much of the time Creel worked diligently to pry stories on war developments from government bureaus and turn them over to the newspapers. But more important than his effort to inform the public was his determination to bias it. He organized brigades of four-minute speakers, briefed them with favorable information, and arranged for them to talk at movies, amusement parks, and other centers of public entertainment. In this way the administration viewpoint was widely disseminated. Creel estimated that 75,000 four-minute men addressed 7,555,190 audiences during the course of the war. To support the speakers he produced many pamphlets explaining and defending Wilson's viewpoint. He did not directly exploit atrocity stories, but he did reinforce the stereotyped opinion that an irresponsible German autocracy was solely responsible for the war.

The official view presented by the Committee on Public Information became still more familiar as propaganda for the Liberty Loan drives. Private organizations, like the National Security League, also reworked the basic theme, emphasizing hatred of Germany and advocating her destruction.

The propaganda of various official and unofficial committees was sufficiently emotional to undermine the traditional American respect for civil liberty and fair play. Professional patriots tormented citizens with German names, denounced them to the authorities as spies, and occasionally painted their houses or barns yellow. If German-Americans became a ready target for charges of disloyalty, sabotage, or espionage, the persecution of native radicals and pacifists was not quite so easy to explain, but they also became victims of intolerance. The ominous attitude of local citizens was frequently enough to scare nonconformists into silence. A number of states even established Public Safety Commissions which enforced political orthodoxy, prohibited public speeches by critics of the war, and sometimes jailed the defiant.

Even if one assumes that the propaganda helped to create a national spirit hostile to civil liberties, it is hard to estimate how great this effect was. The use of war legislation to suppress criticism can be more easily traced. The Espionage Act of June 15, 1917, provided the legal basis for most government action. It set fines as high as $10,000 and imprisonment up to twenty years for those who wilfully caused or sought to promote insubordination and the obstruction of recruiting in the armed forces. Fewer citizens were prosecuted under this clause than under its successor (the Sedition Act, May 16, 1918), which applied the same penalities to persons who wilfully made false reports and statements with intent to interfere with the operation or success of the armed forces. This Act was so broad that it could be construed to include anyone who conspired to violate the law, whether his actions had dangerous consequences or not. It also gave the Postmaster General formidable powers of censorship by authorizing him to bar from the mails any publication which violated the provisions mentioned above or advocated treason, revolution, or forcible resistance to United States laws.

Attorney General Gregory and Postmaster General Burleson ruthlessly disregarded civil rights in exercising their new authority. The Department of Justice arrested 1,532 persons for disloyal utterances. Eugene V. Debs was prosecuted, convicted, and sentenced to a ten-year prison term for a speech made at Canton, Ohio (June 16, 1918) in which he denounced war as the supreme curse of capitalism. While his case was still pending, the Department of Justice raided the national headquarters of the Socialist party and carried off membership lists. The government dealt as severely with the I.W.W. and its leaders. One hundred of them were convicted and sentenced to terms varying from five to twenty years for trying to use the war crisis for the overthrow of capitalism. Many lesser fry were sent to prison for statements which government prosecutors and juries construed as efforts to obstruct the war effort: L. B. Nagler for criticizing the Red Cross; O. C. Enfield for advocating repeal of the draft law; and Pastor C. H. Waldron for saying that Christians ought not to fight. After the end of the war, most of them were pardoned.

The Post Office Department put on a supplementary campaign to muzzle the press. Twenty-two Socialist publications were banned from the mail along with German-American newspapers like the Philadelphia *Tagenblatt* and Irish-American newspapers like Jeremiah O'Leary's *Bull.* Later legislation, including the Sabotage Act of April 20, 1918, and the amended Espionage Act of May 16, 1918, conferred more sweeping powers on the administration for the suppression of free expression, but the war ended before the new laws could be tested.

The administration's double-barreled campaign of propaganda and coercion to eliminate criticism was partly hidden by Wilson's masterly and moving speeches in behalf of civil liberties. By pleading preoccupation with more weighty problems, he created the impression that he was not responsible for the policy of persecution so zealously pursued by his subordinates. It would be easier to explain his campaign for solidarity if he had assumed, like the European dictators of the 1930's, that a docile population would mobilize economic resources more efficiently, but there is little evidence that he held a clear view of the interdependence between various elements in an industrial society at war. He certainly did not realize that the dragon teeth of intolerance sown during the war would blossom into the hysterical "Red scare" and the blatant nationalist reaction of the 1920's. He regarded the wartime suspension of democracy as a sacrifice necessary to preserve it — an opinion that blinded him to the possibility that the experience would permanently damage democracy itself. It was easy for Wilson to deceive himself because he imagined that all his actions stemmed from moral motives.

DISSATISFACTION WITH THE WAR EFFORT

The account of mobilization on the home front has carried us at some points beyond the year 1917. Many citizens were exceedingly critical of the administration's accomplishments after nine months of participation. Except on the high seas where the Navy was gradually winning the crucial but unspectacular battle against the submarine, the United States had no victories to her credit. Shortages of crucial items, waste motion, and confusion continued to hamper production. Dissatisfaction boiled over in December 1917 when draftees were arriving at training camps in advance of adequate clothing, blankets, and arms. Senator George E. Chamberlain, chairman of the Senate Military Affairs Committee, led the attack with a blunt assertion: "The military establishment of America has fallen down. There is no use to be optimistic about a thing that does not exist." Roosevelt echoed his complaints and proposed that Congress create a War Cabinet to take control over mobilization out of Wilson's hands.

Opinions differ as to whether such complaints were premature and unjustified. The President had his defenders who attributed delay to the complexity of mobilization problems and to the uncooperative attitude of various pressure groups. The rapid improvement of production in the spring ended the argument on an inconclusive note. The most significant result was Wilson's reaction to the criticism. As usual he countered by demanding fresh powers, which — as already noted — Congress felt obliged to grant. This behavior created a fatal breach between him and the legislature. Congressmen of both parties waited for the victory which would deprive him of his invulnerable armor and abnormal stature.

THE WITHDRAWAL OF RUSSIA

While the government was wrestling with problems of mobilization in the fall of 1917, important developments occurred on the diplomatic and military fronts in Europe. Great Britain had forced Greece into the war on the Allied side in June 1917, but this advantage was more than counterbalanced in October when the Austrians achieved a massive break-through at Caparetto on the Italian front. Within a matter of weeks the Italians lost all the ground gained in two years of hard fighting. They finally managed to re-form their battered lines at the Piave River. Fearful of a fresh disaster, the Entente Powers rushed up reinforcements from their slender pool of manpower.

Between the Greek entry into the war and the Allied reversal at Caparetto, peace sentiment had revived in Berlin and Vienna. Discouraged by the failure of the submarine campaign to knock the British and French out of the war, the Reichstag passed a resolution in July calling for peace without annexations or indemnities. Although its action was not binding on the government, the resolution indicated that exhaustion impended. The situation in Austria-Hungary was still more precarious because of the growing discontent of various minority groups. These and other symptoms of weariness encouraged Pope Benedict XV to offer his services as mediator in mid-August. The Central Powers were willing to settle for a draw; but the Allies, with the prospect of massive American aid in the offing, rejected a negotiated peace.

With slow strangulation facing them, the Central Powers experienced a sudden and unexpected revival of their fortunes when a second revolution on November 6–7, 1917, knocked Russia out of the Allied coalition. This development lengthened the war nearly a year. The overthrow of the inefficient Tsarist regime the preceding March had been hailed by the United States as the prelude to a democratic crusade against Germany. Her more realistic allies feared that this first revolution would hasten the collapse of the Russian military effort. The events of the summer and fall confirmed this gloomy forecast, but at the outset the provisional government headed by Prince Lvov promised to continue the war. His predominantly middle-class cabinet fell before the spring thaw on the eastern front, and the Prince was replaced by Alexander Kerensky. Although the new prime minister brought more radical elements into the provisional government, he honored the pledge of his predecessor and launched an attack against the Austrians in June. The initial phase was successful, but the Germans turned it into a major disaster with a counterattack in July. Thereafter the Russian army slowly disintegrated. Entire regiments shot their officers and deserted. Even loyal units refused to fight because strikes and riots behind the lines cut off the movement of virtually all supplies and equipment to the front.

Meanwhile the moderate socialist regime of Kerensky was losing supporters to more extremist groups which demanded the termination of the war so that social and economic reforms could be implemented. The most ruthless and energetic of the radical parties were the Bolsheviki — a faction of Marxian socialists who plotted a second revolution to bring the working class to power. These doctrinaire leftists regarded war as the last stage of capitalism and were quite willing to purchase a class victory at the price of a national disaster. They justified their treasonable activities on the ground that defeat and humiliation would be temporary. This conclusion was based on a belief in the imminence of world revolution which would destroy capitalistic states and cancel their harsh peace treaties.

Needless to say, the Tsarist regime had imprisoned or driven into exile most of the Bolshevik leaders, but immediately after the March revolution the provisional government announced an amnesty for all political prisoners. As a result, revolutionaries of every stripe began to trickle back into Russia from the United States, Europe, and Siberian prisons. The German government assisted exiles stranded in Central Europe with funds and transportation, on the theory that their return would further hamper the Russian war effort. The most important beneficiary of this policy was Nikolai Lenin, the leader of the Bolshevik party, who arrived in Petrograd in mid-April from Switzerland. Although the Bolsheviks had only 200,000 members, they were effective in undermining the Kerensky government. Throughout the summer and all of 1917 they exploited the dissatisfaction of the masses with their threefold slogan of "bread, peace, and land." Committed to the doctrine that the demoralization of the capitalistic state is a necessary prerequisite for a proletarian revolution, the Bolsheviks systematically promoted strikes, riots, and mutinies. They carried out their assignment so well that Russia was on the verge of collapse when Lenin seized power in the November revolution.

With the army reduced to an undisciplined rabble and with industrial production virtually at a standstill, it would have been impossible for the new regime to continue the war. Instead of opening peace negotiations immediately with the Central Powers, Lenin issued a "peace decree" on November 7. He proposed everything from the evacuation of conquered territory to the freeing of colonies, on the theory that the war-weary masses would revolt against their governments. Two days later the new Soviet Foreign Commissar, Leon Trotsky, broadcast an appeal to all the belligerents for an immediate armistice. Petrograd detonated another propaganda bombshell on December 5 by publishing the secret treaties between the Allies and the Tsarist government. The Allied governments were outraged by the prospective defection and by the Bolshevik breach of etiquette in releasing the secret agreements. After a few ineffective protests, they began to support counterrevolutionary adventurers with money and troops. The United States associated herself with the policy of Allied intervention and contributed six thousand soldiers to a joint Anglo-American expedition which landed at Archangel in September 1918. An attempted push south to Petrograd failed and the troops were withdrawn in May 1919. Later efforts to overthrow the Soviet regime fared no better, although the Allied governments subsidized counterrevolutionary activities until 1921. Except for the American landing at Vladivostok in Siberia to watch the Japanese, Washington refrained from direct intervention against the Bolsheviks after the abortive Archangel campaign.

The Central Powers made a more cautious response to the Soviet peace proposals and after some delays negotiated a truce on December 5, 1917. Formal conversations began December 22 but broke down in January because the Germans demanded the evacuation of more territory than the Bolsheviks were willing to give up. The visionaries in Petrograd threatened Berlin with a revolutionary war and were answered with a new attack.

Proletarian slogans failed to bluff the advancing Germans or to improve the fighting qualities of the weaponless Russians. Confronted with the alternatives of yielding to Berlin or jeopardizing the existence of his regime, Lenin chose to save the revolution. On March 3, 1918, he signed the Treaty of Brest-Litovsk with the Central Powers, accepting less favorable terms than he could have obtained in January. The territorial provisions deprived Russia of Finland, the Baltic provinces, Poland, the Ukraine, and Bessarabia. In effect Germany gained control of a vast slice of Eastern Europe stretching from the Baltic to the Black Sea. She intended to annex part of it and to grant semiautonomous status to the remaining provinces. Rumania accepted proportionately severe terms from the Central Powers in the Treaty of Bucharest, May 1918.

The Russian revolution was to have greater repercussions than any other development in the first half of the twentieth century. It inaugurated four decades of class conflict, war, and subversion on an international basis. The long-range effects fall beyond the scope of this chapter. If the German High Command had foreseen even a part of them, it would certainly not have helped Lenin and other Bolshevik leaders return to Russia. The immediate results, however, justified such a course. Russia left the war and cleared the way for the Central Powers to concentrate their entire military effort on the western front. By the same token, they gained access to the vast agricultural resources of Eastern Europe. Whether these advantages could be capitalized quickly enough to counterbalance the effect of the Allied blockade and the entry of America into war, remained to be seen. In any event, the Central Powers were nerved for a new effort.

The ideological by-products of the Bolshevik revolution were nearly as serious for the Allied coalition as the loss of a military partner on the eastern front. Lenin's peace decree, his publication of the secret treaties, and his subsequent inauguration of peace talks at Brest-Litovsk had a profoundly unsettling effect on neutrals as well as on public opinion within the Allied countries themselves. The exposure of the annexationist war aims of the Entente Powers and their determination to continue the war belied their protestations of devotion to peace and justice. It reduced the incentive of exhausted workers and soldiers to continue making sacrifices.

THE FOURTEEN POINTS

The attempt of Lenin to pose as the spokesman of humanity and as the architect of a new world order would have been sufficient to arouse Wilson. The President received further encouragement from the Entente governments to make a statement about war aims, because the United States was the one major belligerent untainted by participation in the secret treaties. Simultaneously, British Prime Minister Lloyd George, who had become head of a Liberal coalition after the negotiation of the secret treaties, undertook to remove the "imperialist" label that Lenin had pinned on the "democratic crusade."

Lloyd George spoke first on January 5, 1918, in the properly proletarian setting of a trade-union meeting; Wilson chose Congress as the vehicle for his remarks on January 8. Neither speaker had formally cleared his remarks with the other nor were the contents in complete agreement. Wilson covered many matters about which Lloyd George was silent. On a number of issues treated by both, an arbitrary kind of interpretation is required to reconcile their viewpoints. The context of their statements regarding "self-determination" suggests that the phrase did not mean the same thing in England and in America. Lloyd George's guarded endorsement of "some international organization to limit the burden of armaments and diminish the probability of war" could hardly be construed as approval of Wilson's views about a League of Nations. Similarly, when the Prime Minister referred to the "legitimate interests" of Italy and "justice" for Rumania, his remarks fell far short of repudiating the "secret treaties."

Wilson's statement commanded the greater attention because of his worldwide prestige. Unfortunately it did not represent a long-planned or careful formulation of war aims. There were several reasons for its inadequacy. As we have already noted, Wilson pursued more lofty and remote aims than most Americans, who saw their mission in the narrow context of stopping certain objectionable German actions. The gap between the President and his fellow countrymen was sufficient to discourage him from specific statements that might disrupt wartime solidarity. Similiar fears about the divergence between his views and those of the Entente Powers gave him an added incentive to be vague. Finally, he had neglected to inform himself about many of the disputed areas in Europe and had postponed the discussion of Allied plans for disposing of them by secret treaty. As a result, his statement of January 8 was prepared on the spur of the moment. The only specific data available to him were supplied by a five-man committee of experts dubbed "The Inquiry." The President had created it to deal with the formidable task of translating his vague, nebulous statements into practical war aims. It was under the chairmanship of Colonel House and had made nothing better than a good start when it was called upon to help Wilson formulate a reply to the Russian propaganda barrage. Hasty discussion produced a short preamble reaffirming the purity of America's intentions, six statements of a general nature which had appeared in previous presidential utterances, and eight others about territorial and related questions. Taken together, the so-called Fourteen Points constituted an effort to blunt the criticism of Allied war aims:

> . . . What we demand in this war, therefore, is nothing peculiar to ourselves. It is that the world be made fit and safe to live in; and particularly that it be made safe for every peace-loving nation which, like our own, wishes to live its own life, determine its own institutions, be assured of justice and fair dealing by the other peoples of the world as against force and selfish aggression.

All the peoples of the world are in effect partners in this interest, and for our own part we see very clearly that unless justice be done to others it will not be done to us. The programme of the world's peace, therefore is our programme, and that programme, the one possible programme, as we see it, is this:

I. Open covenants of peace, openly arrived at, after which there shall be no private international understandings of any kind but diplomacy should proceed always frankly and in the public view.

II. Absolute freedom of navigation upon the seas, outside territorial waters, alike in peace and in war, except as the seas may be closed in whole or in part by international action for the enforcement of international covenants.

III. The removal, so far as possible, of all economic barriers and the establishment of an equality of trade conditions among all the nations consenting to the peace and associating themselves for its maintenance.

IV. Adequate guarantees given and taken that national armaments will be reduced to the lowest point consistent with domestic safety.

V. A free, open-minded, and absolutely impartial adjustment of all colonial claims, based upon a strict observance of the principle that in determining all such questions of sovereignty the interests of the populations concerned must have equal weight with the equitable claims of the government whose title is to be determined.

VI. The evacuation of all Russian territory and such settlement of all questions affecting Russia as will secure the best and freest cooperation of the other nations of the world in obtaining for her an unhampered and unembarrassed opportunity for the independent determination of her own political development and national policy and assure her of a sincere welcome into the society of free nations under institutions of her own choosing; and, more than a welcome, assistance also of every kind that she may need and may herself desire. The treatment accorded Russia by her sister nations in the months to come will be the acid test of their good will, of their comprehension of her needs as distinguished from their own interests, and of their intelligent and unselfish sympathy.

VII. Belgium, the whole world will agree, must be evacuated and restored, without any attempt to limit the sovereignty which she enjoys in common with all other free nations. No other single act will serve as this will serve to restore confidence among the nations in the laws which they have themselves set and determined for the government of their relations with one another. Without this healing act the whole structure and validity of international law is forever impaired.

VIII. All French territory should be freed and the invaded portions restored, and the wrong done to France by Prussia in 1871 in the matter of Alsace-Lorraine, which has unsettled the peace of the world for nearly fifty years, should be righted, in order that peace may once more be made secure in the interest of all.

IX. A readjustment of the frontiers of Italy should be effected along clearly recognizable lines of nationality.

X. The peoples of Austria-Hungry, whose place among the nations we wish to see safeguarded and assured, should be accorded the freest opportunity of autonomous development.

XI. Rumania, Serbia, and Montenegro should be evacuated; occupied territories restored; Serbia accorded free and secure access to the sea; and the relations of several Balkan states to one another determined by friendly

> counsel along historically established lines of allegiance and nationality; and international guarantees of the political and economic independence and territorial integrity of the several Balkan states should be entered into.
>
> XII. The Turkish portions of the present Ottoman Empire should be assured a secure sovereignty, but the other nationalities which are now under Turkish rule should be assured an undoubted security of life and an absolutely unmolested opportunity of autonomous development, and the Dardanelles should be permanently opened as a free passage to the ships and commerce of all nations under international guarantees.
>
> XIII. An independent Polish state should be erected which should include the territories inhabited by indisputably Polish populations, which should be assured a free and secure access to the sea, and whose political and economic independence and territorial integrity should be guaranteed by international covenant.
>
> XIV. A general association of nations must be formed under specific covenants for the purpose of affording mutual guarantees of political independence and territorial integrity to great and small states alike.
>
> In regard to these essential rectifications of wrong and assertions of right we feel ourselves to be intimate partners of all the governments and peoples associated together against the Imperialists. We cannot be separated in interest or divided in purpose. We stand together until the end. . . .

The contents of the Fourteen Points were so general and ambiguous that the statement seemed to offer something to everyone including the enemy. It reaffirmed the justice of the Allied cause, invited minority groups — most of whom were in Austria-Hungary — to press their claims, made a bid for the cooperation of the defiant Bolsheviks, and offered the protection of American ideals to the exhausted peoples of the enemy coalition. It contained enough of an internationalist orientation to satisfy the supporters of the President, and enough proposed chastisements of the Germans to silence for the moment nationalists of the Roosevelt stripe.

At home and abroad George Creel tried to sell the Fourteen Points as deathless wisdom and their author as a New World messiah. Tons of leaflets were dropped on the Germans from the sky and shot at them across the no-man's land of the western front. Neutrals, Allies, and Americans also underwent a similar indoctrination. As a device for taking the ideological initiative away from the Russians the campaign was a sensational success. On January 24, Berlin and Vienna found it expedient to accept the first four and the last of the Points, but rejected the territorial ones detrimental to their interests. Allied governments made a guarded endorsement of some points and challenged others at once. Unfortunately their display of solidarity was not followed by repudiation of the secret treaties. Closer acquaintance with the President caused Americans to receive the Fourteen Points with fewer manifestations of awe. The proposal for a League of Nations attracted scant attention at the time. The principle of self-determination for racial minorities possessed a wider appeal because it sounded liberal and because the average American knew so little about the areas where Wilson wanted to apply the formula. The sweeping declarations produced the greatest display of enthusiasm. They were in keeping with the American tradition but they required no action until at the end of the war Wilson tried to commit his fellow countrymen to the practical implementation of the program.

Meanwhile the President followed up the Fourteen Points with fresh statements. On February 11 he again chose Congress as a forum for the enunciation of the Four Principles:

> First, that each part of the final settlement must be based upon the essential justice of that particular case and upon such adjustments as are most likely to bring a peace that will be permanent.
>
> Second, that peoples and provinces are not to be bartered about from sovereignty to sovereignty as if they were chattels and pawns in a game, even the great game, now forever discredited, of the balance of power; but that
>
> Third, every territorial settlement involved in the war must be made in the interest and for the benefit of the populations concerned, and not as a part of any adjustment or compromise of claims amongst rival states; and
>
> Fourth, that all well-defined national aspirations shall be accorded the utmost satisfaction that can be accorded them without introducing new or perpetuating old elements of discord and antagonism that would be likely in time to break the peace of Europe and consequently of the world.

The new statement added little of a specific character and omitted all reference to the League of Nations. Nevertheless the preoccupation of the President with a world organization revived in the summer of 1918, although he avoided discussing it or other matters in definite detail. Instead, he added two other general statements — the Four Ends and the Five Particulars. Taken together these amendments ran as follows:

> I. The destruction of every arbitrary power anywhere that can separately, secretly, and of its single choice disturb the peace of the world; or, if it can not be presently destroyed, at the least its reduction to virtual impotence.
>
> II. The settlement of every question, whether of territory, of sovereignty, of economic arrangement, or of political relationship, upon the basis of the free acceptance of that settlement by the people immediately concerned, and not upon the basis of the material interest or advantage of any other nation or people which may desire a different settlement for the sake of its own exterior influence or mastery.
>
> III. The consent of all nations to be governed in their conduct toward each other by the same principles of honor and of respect for the common law of civilized society that govern the individual citizens of all modern States in their relations with one another; to the end that all promises and covenants may be sacredly observed, no private plots or conspiracies hatched, no selfish injuries wrought with impunity, and a mutual trust established upon the handsome foundation of a mutual respect for right.
>
> IV. The establishment of an organization of peace which shall make it certain that the combined power of free nations will check every invasion of

right and serve to make peace and justice the more secure by affording a definite tribunal of opinion to which all must submit and by which every international readjustment that can not be amicably agreed upon by the peoples directly concerned shall be sanctioned.

(Address at opening of Fourth Liberty Loan campaign, September 27, 1918):

> First, the impartial justice meted out must involve no discrimination between those to whom we wish to be just and those to whom we do not wish to be just. It must be a justice that plays no favorites and knows no standard but the equal rights of the several peoples concerned;
>
> Second, no special or separate interest of any single nation or any group of nations can be made the basis of any part of the settlement which is not consistent with the common interest of all;
>
> Third, there can be no leagues or alliances or special covenants and understandings within the general and common family of the League of Nations;
>
> Fourth, and more specifically, there can be no special, selfish economic combinations within the League and no employment of any form of economic boycott or exclusion except as the power of economic penalty by exclusion from the markets of the world may be vested in the League of Nations itself as a means of discipline and control;
>
> Fifth, all international agreements and treaties of every kind must be made known in their entirety to the rest of the world.

Some of the liabilities arising out of the Fourteen Points were due to the fact that they were a prompt response to a wartime propaganda threat. It would be easier to excuse Wilson for the inconsistent and self-contradictory character of his program if he had corrected it in later statements, but he did not do so. The publicity given the original statement, as well as the continued elaboration of the basic theme, tended to give the impression that it was an Allied peace program. In the early months of the year the Allies had welcomed the unilateral declarations of Wilson as useful tactics. They became increasingly disturbed, however, as their suspicions grew that he not only believed what he said but intended to make peace by unilateral declaration. The Allies made no protest during the crucial summer battles on the western front but waited for the victory that would free them from the necessity of behaving deferentially toward the United States.

THE WESTERN FRONT IN 1918

Although the incessant bombardment of the enemy with the statements and restatements of American war aims weakened his will to resist, the outcome of World War I was settled on the western front in 1918. The succession of events set in motion by the Russian revolution gave the Central Powers an eleventh-hour reprieve, but still their over-all situation was grave. In January 1918, Russian propaganda had produced a crippling outbreak of strikes in Berlin, accompanied by demands for peace. The government resolutely put down the strikes and imposed martial law, but the incident demonstrated that the limits of endurance were being approached. The position of Austria-Hungary was even more desperate. As the year opened, the Czechs, Slovaks, and other Slavic groups within the Empire made open attempts to secede. These efforts were actively encouraged by self-appointed leaders of revolutionary groups operating from the major Allied countries and the United States.

Notwithstanding these handicaps, Germany launched a final spectacular campaign to save herself and her demoralized Austrian, Turkish, and Bulgarian allies. The effectiveness of the army had passed its peak, but for the first time since hostilities had begun, the High Command enjoyed the luxuries of a one-front war and a temporary numerical superiority on the western front. In an effort to capitalize the latter advantage before it disappeared, General Ludendorff opened the season on March 21 with a massive offensive. The fury of the "Friedensturm" fell on the British-held Allied left and was designed to take Paris and end the war. As before, the defense still possessed the advantage in the trench warfare, but now the Germans advanced twenty-five miles within a week. Their smashing attack gained more ground than any offensive on the western front since the lines had been stabilized in 1914.

German success drove the Allies to desperate countermeasures. After three and a half years of uncoordinated military operations, they decided on a unified command and appointed the French Marshal, Ferdinand Foch, to head the forces. Simultaneously, General Pershing shelved his demands for a separate American army and offered troops to help bolster the sagging British lines. The same month, the prime ministers of Britain, France and Italy issued a frantic plea for more regiments of doughboys and predicted the loss of the war unless reinforcements arrived. This step marked a sharp reversal of attitude on the part of the Allies.

As early as the first of March something called an American sector had been established, although it was manned by only 300,000 doughboys. During the month 80,000 more arrived, and 50 per cent more in April. A spectacular increase occurred in May when the arrivals jumped to 245,000. This pace was maintained or improved upon monthly until the end of the war. As a result, 1,750,000 Americans reached France between March and October of 1918.

Before the full effect of American manpower was felt, the Germans unleashed a second successful offensive against the British on April 9. Five weeks later they launched a major drive against the French-held center of the line opposite Paris. Beginning on May 27, they advanced thirty miles within three days. When the French fell back to Château-Thierry on the Marne River, the Reich's forces were only about forty or fifty miles from Paris and began shelling the city at a range of about seventy-five miles.

But by now American troops could be thrown into the breach in significant numbers. On May 28, 1918, they participated in their first serious fighting and acquitted themselves so well that they stopped the enemy thrust toward Montdidier. From this point on they made appreciable contributions to stopping the German general offensive. They repulsed the enemy decisively in the offensive and defensive successes of Cantigny, Château-Thierry, and Belleau Wood. Nevertheless, the fighting qualities of the predominantly untested American troops continued to be regarded skeptically by many Allies. Only after Château-Thierry did the London *Times* correspondent condescend to observe that "these are allies worth having."

Several times during this series of offensives the Germans had been so exhausted by their brilliant and furious performance that they were unable to capitalize on their gains. This was the way to ultimate defeat, as they knew well enough. One final, desperate drive therefore seemed imperative to them while they still had the strength for it. They were organized and rolling by July 15. Despite its shattering force, this attack failed to achieve the break-through which was essential for the capture of Paris and victory for Germany. In the engagements of July 15–18 which turned the tide, American manpower was probably decisive. In the second battle of the Marne, focusing on the Château-Thierry salient, 275,000 Americans were committed. On July 18, as soon as it was clear that the Germans had failed, the Allies began a sustained counterattack that lasted until August 6. From here on, the western front became a series of Allied successes.

With the crisis past, renewed United States demands for separate status could no longer reasonably be denied. On August 10 an independent command was established for the ever-larger number of American troops now participating in combat. Half a million of them shortly thereafter took part in the battle that reduced the St. Mihiel salient. Once on the move, Pershing wanted to keep up the pressure and drive all the way to Metz. If successful, this move might have ended the war six or eight weeks sooner. But Foch, preferring Haig's advice, directed his forces toward Sedan, which remained in German hands until the Armistice was signed. On August 30 Pershing took charge of the First American Army.

July had proved that the Germans would not win; September demonstrated that the Allies would. Multiple drives unleashed on several sectors were successful in varying degrees. At the same time Allied attacks knocked Bulgaria out of the war by the end of that month, and Turkey by the end of October. In Italy the Central Powers were on the defensive after the failure of Austria's final effort. In fact, Vienna had been dickering for terms since the middle of September.

By September 26 Foch began the Allied drive which was to end the war. It bogged down after a few days and had to be reorganized, but by October 4 it was moving again and kept gaining momentum until the Armistice. The principal American role in this effort was the famous Meuse-Argonne battle, which lasted forty days, involved 1,200,000 American soldiers, and featured appalling casualties. In these closing phases of the fighting the Germans continued to resist stoutly. But the remnants of the Reich's once-great armies were not equal to the task. Outnumbered, outclassed, and exhausted, the Germans continued to retreat. The Hindenburg line was broken. By October 8 United States troops under Pershing's command had cleared the Argonne forest, held a seventy-five mile front, and were moving toward Sedan. Within another month America held about one-fourth of the Allied line.

The Allies did not know how close they were to complete victory. Foch was planning next year's campaigns. Pershing was seeking to double his army. In contrast, the German General Staff knew that their cause was lost. The mercurial General Ludendorff, in fact, became pessimistic in August and desperate in September. The Reich's political leaders were steadier, but they too knew what needed to be done. When matters had reached the stage where Ludendorff undertook to inform the Kaiser in person at Spa on September 29 that the war was lost, the politicians set out methodically to try to save whatever could be salvaged from the military wreckage. A demand from Hindenburg on October 1, and another, more imperative, on October 3, that a peace offer be made, convinced everyone that the time had come. Germany prepared to capitulate.

ARMISTICE NEGOTIATIONS

In October 1918 the military struggle between the adversaries of World War I yielded in importance to the negotiations between them; diplomacy was in the limelight as it had not been since August 1914. For the first time propaganda had to become program — Allied and American propaganda, that is, since the Germans no longer had a program. The United States and its associates were forced to examine realistically a host of problems hitherto ignored. For a variety of reasons Berlin chose to open negotiations with Wilson: he possessed greater prestige than any other Allied leader, a reputation for moderation, and a novel unorthodoxy and naïveté in his approach to international politics. The Germans realized, of course, that in order to deal with him they would have to present a different political front than the one to which he had objected so often and so bitterly. It was easy to oblige him, since internal pressures were pushing in the same direction. Chancellor Hertling therefore resigned on September 30, and the beginning of October brought in a moderate government headed by Prince Max of Baden. The new leadership had as its primary task the conclusion of the war; a secondary and concomitant objective was to achieve this in such a way as to save the Hohenzollern dynasty and, if possible, the Kaiser himself. Accordingly, the next weeks were devoted simultaneously to negotiation with the victors abroad and to a liberalization of the government at home. While Prince Max was pushing the Reich toward a constitutional monarchy, he put out feelers to Washington on October 3. The following day both Germany and Austria-Hungary openly appealed for a cessation of hostilities. On October 5 the German government informed the United States that it was willing to accept a peace based on the Fourteen Points and Wilson's speech of September 27. On the 6th, Germany followed this proposal by requests for a general armistice, Austria-Hungary made a similar plea on the 7th.

The Germans soon found that instead of an easy dupe they had a stern judge and political mentor to deal with. Wilson used the communication of October 5 to initiate prolonged exchanges before he turned further negotiations over to others. During this time he established a number of essential stipulations regarding preliminary terms. This task, however, did not consume too much time, since Berlin's replies were affirmative and usually prompt. Such unwonted Prussian pliability was a result of the fact that while the correspondence was going back and forth, such severe military pressure was maintained that on October 12 Ludendorff did not think Germany could hold out more than another two days. Diplomacy of this kind did not require a great deal of finesse. In fact Wilson was not negotiating in the normal sense of the term. As he said to Sir William Wiseman, he had a different approach: "House and I have arrived at a formula which we think fairly sums up the position: If the Germans are beaten, they will accept any terms; if they are not beaten, we don't want them to accept any terms."

The last five weeks and five days during which the guns pounded on the western front were not consumed primarily in bargaining with an enemy who had anything to bargain with. They were divided almost equally between two other projects. The one was for Wilson to delay long enough, while he had the play to himself, so that political circumstances within both the major enemy countries reached a stage which would satisfy his ideological purposes. The other was to come to some sort of belated and makeshift agreement with the Allies on what everybody on their side was fighting for.

Perhaps the most transparent case of these tactics was that involving Austria-Hungary. Her suggestion of September 16 for a general discussion of peace terms went unheeded while crisis at home vied with crisis abroad. Separatist movements were launched by all her numerous minority groups, including the German Austrians, so that during October the Hapsburg Empire virtually disintegrated into its component national elements. The once-powerful state which had been, with all its faults, the greatest stabilizing force in southeastern Europe over a period of centuries was simply evaporating. Far from experiencing concern at its disappearance, Wilson and most of his countrymen welcomed the development. The most aggressive members of the wrecking crew were the Czechs. This nationality group had Wilson's unqualified support for recognition even before they announced the establishment of a provisional government for themselves, the Slovaks, and the Moravians on October 29. The Serbs, now posturing as spokesmen for a number of minority groups called the Yugoslavs, enjoyed their new power. The Poles were moving in a similar direction, although at this time somewhat less energetically. Austrian appeals were met with the reply that since the United States had recognized the Czechs, Vienna would have to deal with them. It also became unmistakable that Washington intended to press for the destruction of the Dual Monarchy as foreshadowed if not stated in the Fourteen Points. So Austria turned to the Allies and signed an armistice with the Italians who were representing them, on November 3, 1918. The break with the past was made complete when Emperor Charles, who had succeeded the octogenarian Francis Joseph two years before, abdicated on the day the Germans signed their armistice.

Meanwhile, on October 8, President Wilson had responded to the overtures of the Germans by asking whether they accepted the Fourteen Points without reservations and whether they were willing to evacuate all occupied territory. With Ludendorff's dire warnings to spur them, the Germans agreed on October 12. Two days later Wilson proceeded to lay down three further conditions. First, Germany was to surrender in a form satisfactory to the Allied military command; this was an indirection for announcing that the military would fix the armistice terms. Second, Germany was required to put an end to submarine warfare. Third, the government agreeing to the armistice was called upon to demonstrate that it represented the German people.

There was, of course, no practical way that the third requirement could be satisfied; and Wilson, in fact, seems to have been willing to treat it rather frankly as what it was, namely, a spur to the Germans to move farther in the direction in which they were going rather than as a new demand to be implemented in some new way.

On October 16 Wilson frankly stated that the German government had met his terms. The real difficulty was that he did not want to deal with them. "We do not want to discuss peace with them," he said, although he admitted that he thought "even the present German government wants peace." Already the Germans had got the point. If they had been disposed to overlook it, Wilson made the lessons to be learned in this costly period of ideological tutelage unmistakable. He implied that if he was obliged to deal with the German imperial government, even as it was now being refashioned, he would be obliged to demand "surrender," whereas if he were enabled to deal with something else he would find it possible to enter into "negotiations."

Berlin replied on October 22 that the reconstituted government of Max of Baden represented the German people and hence met Wilson's third condition. The President ignored the assertion and kept American armies moving until the Germans finally realized that they would have to sacrifice the monarchy in order to secure peace.

Wilson's policy contained disturbing implications because it harnessed raw military power to the service of political ideology. He had already used the technique to force structural changes in Latin-American governments that displeased him. He imagined that he was liberating the Germans by imposing self-government on them. He based his attitude on the assumption that all people possessed an innate desire for the Wilsonian form of democracy.

In the case of the Germans there was little evidence of a ground swell against the form of government. Dissatisfaction had existed for some time, but it fed on the operational faults of the regime rather than on the theoretical objections to a monarchy. What the majority disliked most about the Kaiser was not his undemocratic outlook, but his rashness and irresponsibility. Wilhelm II had turned out to be an ineffective poseur instead of an efficient "first servant of the state" like Frederick the Great. Left to their own devices, the German people might have taken gradual steps to democratize their state. Wilson had endorsed an evolutionary approach to the remodeling of institutions thirty years earlier in his book on *Congressional Government* but ignored his own advice in 1918. Instead he tried to hurry the process by refusing to arrange an armistice until the Germans ousted the Kaiser on November 9 and replaced him with the inexperienced Socialists. Whether the latter spoke for a majority was uncertain. In any event, Wilson's tactics brought them to power and relieved the imperial government from shouldering responsibility for the loss of the war. By so doing the President did not further the cause of democracy but encouraged the Germans to associate it with foreign dictation and their hour of humiliation.

Before the events leading up to the expulsion of the Kaiser had taken place, Wilson recognized the necessity of bringing the Allies into the armistice negotiations with Germany. So the day after Berlin replied to his note of the previous week, he turned all his correspondence over to the Allies. It immediately became apparent that the United States and the Entente Powers could no longer postpone a discussion of war aims. The Reich had already accepted the Fourteen Points as a basis for the cessation of hostilities without knowing what they meant. Incredible as it may seem, their author was also uncertain about the specific implications of the various Points. On the eve of Colonel House's departure for Europe, Secretary of State Lansing complained that there had been no clarification of American war aims. Wilson told Sir William Wiseman that House "knows my mind completely," but Wiseman was still uncertain after interviews with the President and House in mid-October. Because of the vagueness of his instructions, House found Allied diplomats angry over the unilateral declarations from Washington. They balked at "open diplomacy" if it meant negotiations conducted in public and at the "removal of economic barriers" if it meant free trade in Europe. The British flatly refused to subscribe to freedom of the seas, and the French opposed the provision which sought to deprive them of payments for damage done by German invaders. Differences over these points were symptoms of the basic disagreement between the United States and the Entente Powers about war aims.

THE CONGRESSIONAL ELECTIONS OF 1918

Simultaneously, domestic critics of the President found their voices. The imminence of victory and of the off-year congressional elections encouraged them to challenge him. Roosevelt opened the attack in late September by telegraphing Republican senators to oppose the Fourteen Points and soft armistice terms. He denounced the war aims of the President and demanded the election of a G.O.P. Congress to safeguard national interests. Others echoed his complaints about the vagueness and impracticality of Wilson's program. Fearful of the possibility that the voters might consider such criticism unpatriotic, Republican congressional candidates also insisted that they had supported war legislation more conscientiously than had the Democrats. For good measure they accused the administration of political favoritism — centering their fire on the War Food Administration for fixing wheat prices in the Republican North but not cotton prices in the Democratic South.

The G.O.P. drummed so effectively on these three themes that Wilson became alarmed and issued an appeal to the voters on October 24 for a Democratic Congress. He added that the election of a Republican Congress would be interpreted in Europe as a repudiation of his leadership. This statement was certainly unwise and invited the G.O.P. to obstruct his peace program if the voters gave it a majority, as seemed probable. Whether the appeal affected the course of the campaign is debatable. The party in power customarily loses ground in off-year elections and the Democratic edge was so thin that a slight shift in public opinion would turn both houses over to the Republicans. Actually the Democrats experienced a smaller than average loss for an off year. The voters returned 49 Republicans and 47 Democrats to the new Senate, and 237 Republicans, 191 Democrats, and 7 Independents to the new House. The outcome was a warning of future trouble for the President's peace program at home.

While the storm clouds gathered on Capitol Hill, Wilson was bargaining with the Allies over the Fourteen Points. They stoutly stuck to their original positions on freedom of the seas and reparations but yielded temporarily at other points. An agreement was reached on November 3 and the Germans were informed two days later that the Allied and Associated Powers would accept the Fourteen Points with these two reservations. The same communication referred Berlin to the Allied High Command for negotiations. General Haig favored mild terms, Pershing wanted to break off discussions and invade Germany, and Foch occupied a middle position with his insistence that the terms should be severe enough to disarm Germany. The view of the Supreme Commander prevailed, and he laid down conditions that precluded the renewal of hostilities by the enemy. The thirty-five clauses of the armistice agreement provided for German evacuation of France, Belgium, Luxemburg, and Alsace-Lorraine within two weeks, and all territory on the left bank of the Rhine within a month. French occupation was to include, in addition to the German portions of this area, the cities of Cologne, Coblenz, and Mainz east of the Rhine. The treaties of Brest-Litovsk and Bucharest were abrogated, and withdrawal of German troops from Austria, Rumania, Russia, and Turkey was provided for. The blockade of Germany was to continue. There was no guarantee of relief for the undernourished population of the Central Powers, the Allies merely observing that they "contemplated" sending supplies. Most of Germany's war-making potential was to be surrendered according to lists of munitions, materiel, ships, submarines, and the like, among which 5,000 locomotives and 150,000 railway cars were only items in a long agenda.

The German representatives passed through the Allied lines to receive these terms on November 7. A false alarm that an armistice had been concluded, set off wild celebrations in many parts of the world on that day. Actually, the Reich was given seventy-two hours in which to accept. Since the Germans had no real choice, they spent the next few days making their government acceptable to the conquerors.

Radical Socialist groups, which had been engineering giant strikes in Germany since January, came forward in October to proclaim a socialist republic in Berlin. By the 29th the Kaiser no longer regarded his capital as safe and fled to Spa. Important elements among his people had been talking of abdication since the beginning of the month.

The final blow came when the German naval command, faced with the certainty of defeat and the prospect of having to surrender its fleet, ordered it to steam out and fight. The sailors vowed their readiness to defend the country's coasts to the last. But they knew that armistice discussions were in progress, and they rebelled at sacrificing their lives in a gesture. By November 4 a mutiny, which had begun at Kiel, had flared into open rebellion that spread first to other coastal cities and then into the interior. There were Communist uprisings in Bavaria by November 7. Munich joined Berlin in revolt, and by the following day it had spread to other cities, including Cologne, Stuttgart, and Leipzig.

Still the Kaiser was reluctant to sign the abdication. Finally, on November 9 Prince Max simply announced it as a fact and turned the government over to the Socialists for formation of a "republic." That night the last of the Hohenzollerns found asylum on the other side of the Dutch border. Two days later, at five A.M. on November 11, in General Foch's private railway car in the Forest of Compiègne, the Armistice was signed. Firing stopped at eleven o'clock in the morning.

The war which was thus brought to a conclusion had been by far the costliest and bloodiest ever fought up to that time. Monetary costs are difficult to compute accurately and, though shockingly large, are overshadowed by the statistics of human destruction. Russia, Germany, France, Britain, and Austria suffered the heaviest losses in that order — together about

6,500,000 dead. The total for all belligerents has been estimated at nearly 10,000,000. Twice that number were wounded.

The United States had raised an army of over 3,500,000 men, more than 2,000,000 of whom had been sent overseas. About 1,300,000 were in actual combat. America had lost about 115,000 dead (of whom less than half were battle casualties); a little over 200,000 were wounded. These figures were modest indeed when compared to those for the European powers, but even at that they were greater than most Americans had bargained for. Now the people of the United States were interested in liquidating an unpleasant situation. "Bringing the boys back home" was how most of them oversimplified it. The postwar decade had begun.

SUGGESTED READINGS

1. Chafee, Z., *Free Speech in the United States.*
2. Clarkson, G. B., *Industrial America in the World War.*
3. Paxon, F. L., *American Democracy and the World War* (vol. 2).
4. Seymour, C., *American Diplomacy during the World War.*

CHAPTER THIRTEEN

THE QUEST FOR A WILSONIAN PEACE

POST-ARMISTICE MOOD

As far as most Americans were concerned, the war ended the day the Armistice was signed. Their feelings on this matter were firm and uncomplicated. They had set out to destroy the German menace and had accomplished their objective. The Kaiser was in exile, his autocratic empire in ruins, and his U-boat fleet at the bottom of the North Sea. Every objectionable act from the sinking of the *Lusitania* to the dispatch of the Zimmermann Note had been avenged. Texas was safe again, as well as American shipping on the high seas. Moreover, all the successor states emerging from the ruins of the German, Austrian, and Russian empires advertised themselves as "democratic." Citizens could not be expected to support other aims, since Wilson had not reduced wartime statements to a specific program.

With the helpless Reich under the watchful eyes of the Allies and with the world apparently destined for democracy, Americans hoped to call it a day. They had not asked for territories or indemnities and did not want them. They assumed that the collapse of Germany would automatically re-establish their cherished prewar position of aloofness from the frequent troubles of Europe. In short, they expected that permanent peace would be the product of their efforts and they did not anticipate fresh obligations stretching far into the future. George M. Cohan aptly expressed the mood of the average citizen in the last line of his popular war song: "We won't be back till its over, over there!" Once the clean-up job in Europe was completed, Americans intended to come home for good.

In an effort to arouse wartime patriotism, Wilson had encouraged public expectations that military victory would create a brave new world. The success of his appeal was to cost him dearly, because he regarded the destruction of Germany as a preliminary step to greater enterprises. In his Armistice Day message to the nation he dropped hints about his unfinished business. After reaffirming the popular belief that "everything for which America fought has been accomplished" he went on to say: "It will now be our fortunate duty to assist by example, by sober, friendly counsel, and by material aid in the establishment of a just democracy throughout the world."

In subsequent weeks, the gulf between the President and the majority of his fellow countrymen became apparent as he spoke more explicitly about his peace plans. Especially disquieting to them in view of what they had hitherto been told was his insistent advocacy of a League of Nations. It raised the specter of long-term intervention in Europe. Coming when it did, the proposal struck many people as unnecessary. Probably a majority favored some sort of international forum for the discussion of world problems, but only Wilson, a sprinkling of organization Democrats, and a dedicated band of idealists believed in a league to enforce peace. Peace now seemed secure enough without fresh commitments through a world organization.

During the weeks after the Armistice, signs multiplied that Wilson would suffer a serious defeat if he tried to force further projects on the weary country. He had already lost both houses of Congress in the off-year elections after announcing that he would regard a Democratic defeat as a repudiation of his leadership. Although he did not intend to acknowledge an adverse verdict by resigning, he ought to have regarded the results as a warning to proceed cautiously. His old enemy Theodore Roosevelt informed the nation and the world on November 25 that Wilson had no right to speak for the United States at the forthcoming peace conference. Henry Cabot Lodge, who was to head the Foreign Relations Committee in the newly elected Republican Senate, also served notice that ratification of a peace treaty would not be automatic. In a statement on December 21 he expressed the opinion that the treaty and the projected League of Nations should not be part of the same settlement. He also urged postponement of the League question until other issues were out of the way. In a similar vein he proposed that the European Allies be allowed to work out terms for Germany without interference from the United States. Over the years Lodge had accumulated many reasons for disliking Wilson, and his personality was such that he did not forget any of them. In his cold, malignant way he had fought the President with the same intensity as had Roosevelt. At the same time, his opposition was based on differences of principle which were a matter of public record. As a pioneer advocate of preparedness, Lodge had favored a war against Germany and a league of victor powers to keep her helpless. In the light of his earlier attitude, his desire to let the angry Europeans dictate a German treaty first and organize a league later was wholly consistent. He showed a greater understanding of power politics than many of his countrymen and approached the problem of a postwar settlement with vengeful spirit. Even so, his views about the proper order of business in peacemaking tallied closely with those of the majority. At this stage the issue was not whether America should join a League of Nations, but whether the organization of such a league should take priority over other matters and entail additional obligations for the United States.

In order to get the sugar.
(The Chicago Tribune, *1919*.)

PREPARATIONS FOR THE PEACE CONFERENCE

From the outset, Wilson ignored both his Republican opponents and the manifest desire of the voters to resume their normal pursuits with as little fuss as possible. On November 18, 1918, he announced that he would head the American delegation to the Peace Conference. In so doing, he was exercising an unquestionable prerogative of the Executive in a manner that has since become commonplace. Nevertheless, the decision provoked an outburst of criticism because no President had hitherto left the country during his term of office. Other factors, too, ought to have made him hesitate. His mandate had been clouded by the election of 1918 and his inexperience as a negotiator was likely to aggravate the consequences of this handicap. By the same token, his tremendous prestige in Europe seemed certain to be a greater asset if he avoided the give-and-take of the conference table. Public concern with demobilization problems also made it advisable for him to remain home. The principal reason that led him to brush aside these considerations was the belief he alone could represent his own position. Such logic was unanswerable, for nobody else possessed a clear idea about the meaning of the Fourteen Points or the appropriate methods for implementing them.

Unfortunately, the President did not appoint any members to the peace delegation who would dispute his stand on a major issue or represent the viewpoint of Republican party leaders. His selections, announced on November 29, were honorable and in some cases able men, but none had a large popular following. They included Secretary of State Lansing; Presidential Adviser House; the military delegate to the Allied Supreme War Council, General Tasker Bliss; and the retired career diplomat, Henry White. The President could not have been expected to appoint arch-enemies like Roosevelt or Lodge, but he ought to have included a prominent Republican with an internationalist orientation. Ex-President Taft, Elihu Root, and Charles Evans Hughes fell into this category. Taft also shared the general outlook of the President on foreign affairs and possessed sufficient independence to offer honest criticism. By passing over the claims of cooperative Republicans, Wilson increased the odds that the Senate would mutilate any treaty subsequently presented for ratification.

The same day that the President released the names of the delegation, he proposed Paris as the site of the conference on the theory that friendly influences would prevail. The other major participants, with the understandable exception of the French, favored the neutral city of Geneva but bowed to American wishes. As it turned out, the atmosphere in postwar Paris was hostile to Wilson's peace plans and was subsequently blamed for some of his setbacks at the conference. Unfortunately, he bore the principal responsibility for whatever adverse affects this factor had on American diplomacy.

Inter-Allied negotiations over the preliminary arrangements also revealed Wilson's determination to give top priority to the League of Nations. Mindful of impending quarrels over the secret treaties, the French approached him on November 29 with a compromise formula. They offered to wipe out all the wartime agreements and proposed that the peace treaty be drawn up by the Big Five (i.e., France, Great Britain, Italy, the United States, and Japan). They also expressed willingness to consult neutrals and other belligerents on decisions affecting them. The merit of the plan was that it would eliminate a number of secret treaties already outmoded by events and would vest the settlement in the hands of countries certain to have a determining voice in any event. Both Secretary Lansing and Colonel House favored the proposal, but Wilson opposed it. His principal objection was that the French wanted a quick peace settlement and a subsequent conference to create a world organization. Determined to invert the order of business and force immediate adoption of a League, Wilson killed the French plan by ignoring it.

Thus, as 1918 drew to a close, the main lines of conflict between Wilson and his countrymen as well as between Wilson and his allies were clear. He intended to force a League of Nations upon Americans who were dubious about assuming fresh obligations and upon Europeans who were anxious to settle peace terms first. The drama unfolded simultaneously in America and in Europe with the developments and responses on each continent affecting opinion on the other.

PROBLEMS OF DEMOBILIZATION

The initial phase of the estrangement of Americans from their President began when the latter sailed for Europe in December 1918. Popular indifference to the details of the European settlement would have protected Wilson from criticism of his activities in Paris if demobilization had proceeded smoothly on the home front. The manifold problems of reconversion, however, prevented a prompt restoration of normal conditions. The President would have been blamed for domestic problems in any event. The fact that he was in Paris, preoccupied with diplomacy, aroused special resentment and eventually generated a backfire against his entire program.

The post-Armistice atmosphere in America was not conducive to cooperation and tolerance. Victory had removed the patriotic incentives for individual and group sacrifice. Citizens were free to air an eighteen months' backlog of grievances against the President and lost no time in doing so. Republicans disliked him for what they regarded as his deliberate effort to make political capital out of American victories. Congress objected to the wartime enlargement of executive powers and was determined to curtail them. Many voters who had supported Wilson on a peace platform in 1916 were angry over his subsequent decision to take America into the war. Liberals in both parties blamed him for the ruthless suppression of minority opinion during the war.

Besides these well-defined grievances, nearly every economic pressure group felt that the Commander-in-Chief had made it bear a disproportionate share of mobilization burdens. As a consequence most of them were prepared to fight each other as well as the President. Businessmen wanted to throw off the irksome restraints of collective bargaining and put organized labor in its place. Workers were anxious to abandon the no-strike pledge because price inflation had reduced the purchasing power of wages. Egged on by stories about the swollen profits of big business, the farmers prepared to renew the fight against their old antagonist. Simultaneously, the architects of business consolidation were seeking a legal way to regularize the industry-wide trading agreements made during the war. The existence of so many crosscurrents blurred the lines of conflict, but the popular preoccupation with domestic problems boded ill for Wilson, who wanted to ignore them and concentrate on world affairs.

Superimposed upon popular resentments arising out of the war were fresh problems that aggravated them. The military machine had taken time to assemble and would take time to dismantle. The dislocations in production resulting from the diversion of food, raw materials, and finished commodities to military uses led to a rapid rise in prices as consumers bid for a diminished quantity of goods. Between July 1914 and November 1918 the dollar had shrunk 37.6 per cent in value, and during the year and a half after the Armistice its purchasing power dropped an additional 20.5 per cent.

Price inflation was intensified by pent-up consumer demand, reconversion bottlenecks which slowed the resumption of production, and reconstruction loans to European governments which sustained their purchases of American goods.

Demobilization was also accompanied by severe unemployment. The abnormal expansion of industry and the high wage scale underwritten by the administration had attracted a large labor force from rural areas that could not count on permanent peacetime jobs in the city. Even before the Armistice the newcomers had overtaxed housing facilities and public services. Since many of them were Negroes and immigrants, they roused the wrath of older residents and Nativist groups long before they became an economic burden.

Careful government planning could have softened the impact of reconversion. But the President adopted the orthodox view that wartime economic controls should be dismantled as rapidly as possible. All government contracts were abruptly terminated; the War Industries Board and its subsidiary agencies suspended operations in December 1918. The President set up a plan to return the railroads to private hands and lifted all restrictions on the use of food and fuel in the spring of 1919. A bill introduced in the lame-duck session of Congress by Senator William S. Kenyon of Iowa, to appropriate $100 million for road construction, was rejected. Other bills designed to give temporary employment on public works projects failed. The United States Employment Service also became a casualty of demobilization fever in March 1919. Congress refused an appropriation that would have kept that agency alive when it was most needed, and Wilson declined to intervene.

The sudden withdrawal of government from the economy while industry was retooling for peacetime production created acute distress in the spring of 1919. As late as November 30, 1918, there had been a balance between idle labor and open jobs. By the next February 262,000 were without jobs and the total increased at the rate of 100,000 a week for two months. Two factors aggravated the situation: the unwillingness of the unemployed who had tasted the pleasures of urban life to return to the farm, and the hasty demobilization of the Army. Congress had provided $60 discharge pay and a railroad ticket home for each soldier. But it set up no machinery to ease the personal adjustment of returning veterans or to help them find jobs. As a result, many ex-soldiers joined the ranks of the jobless with bitterness toward the government and toward noncombatants who had sat out the war safely while accumulating profits or entrenching themselves in secure jobs.

As both prices and unemployment increased in the spring of 1919, citizens fought back as best they could. Some consumers launched well-publicized but ineffectual buying strikes. Others demanded government action. In late June, twenty-six members of the Massachusetts legislature sent a peremptory telegram to Wilson in Paris: "The citizens of the United States want you home to help reduce the high cost of living which we consider far more important than the League of Nations." The President responded with a special message to Congress recommending legislation to force hoarded stocks into the market and to facilitate the prosecution of flagrant profiteers. The Republican majority blocked action and Wilson allowed his political position to deteriorate by showing no further interest in high prices.

LABOR UNREST

As might have been expected, organized labor tried to counter inflation by striking for wage increases. Starting in the textile centers of New York and New England in the winter of 1919, a wave of strikes engulfed the country. Seattle, Washington, was convulsed for five days in February by a general strike when sixty thousand workers of all trades walked off the job to support the demands of the shipbuilders. Midsummer saw the infection spread to the railroads, the building trades, and the cigar industry. Capitalizing on a shortage of farm hands, the I.W.W. did an unusually effective job of unsettling labor conditions during the harvest season. September brought strikes by the steelworkers and by the Boston police, which attracted nationwide attention. The coal miners rang down the curtain on a year of industrial warfare when John L. Lewis ordered them to leave the job on November 1. Altogether, more than four million workers were on strike at some time or other during 1919.

Most strikes backfired because of the basic weakness of the unions. They showed the greatest strength in defense plants, which were shut down after the Armistice, but they did not have a firm foothold in steel and other heavy industries. Only the traditional craft unions of the A.F. of L. survived the war intact and they were incapable of paralyzing plants which relied increasingly on unskilled workers.

Notwithstanding the failure of the strikes in 1919, public opposition to them was violent and hysterical. Ever since the Bolshevik revolution of November 1917, labor organizations all over the world had behaved more aggressively, and conservatives had grown correspondingly fearful that union activity was the prelude to revolution. The lurid tales drifting out of Russia about mass liquidation of capitalists and wholesale nationalization of property stirred up indignation. The fact that the revolutionaries were promoting worker uprisings in other countries created an indiscriminate fear that all labor unions were conspiratorial organizations.

The danger of a Bolshevik revolution in the United States in 1919 was negligible. The old Socialist party of Debs and Berger, which contained most of the potential recruits for a subversive movement, had already lost in the 1916 election about 40 per cent of the million votes it received in 1912. Further defections had occurred during the war when the party leaders denounced the European conflict as an imperialist squabble and urged the workers not to support the government. The victory of the Bolsheviks in Russia created a fresh crisis in American Socialism because a substantial faction wanted to abandon the peaceful methods of Debs for a militant revolutionary program. A majority of the 100,000 dues-paying members opposed the imitation of Bolshevik tactics in 1919 with the result that 45,000 seceded. Of this group nearly 35,000 accepted the jurisdiction of the Third International which had been established in Moscow in 1918 to coordinate revolutionary strategy all over the world. They pledged their loyalty to a twenty-one-point Bolshevik oath and thereby took on obligations incompatible with allegiance to the United States. The remaining 10,000 organized a Communist Labor party which was also committed to the violent overthrow of capitalism but refused to accept directions from Moscow.

The actual threat posed by 45,000 Marxist zealots was not so great as their numbers suggest. They fell victim to fresh schisms and lavished more energy on disputes over revolutionary strategy than on concrete efforts to organize the workers. Recruits came primarily from frustrated middle-class intellectuals and dreamers who were of little practical use. Speakeasies and artists' garrets seethed with rebellion against capitalism, but the industrial workers paid little attention to their self-proclaimed benefactors.

Nevertheless, Americans were obsessed with fear of a genuine Bolshevik revolution, and this apprehension blossomed out into a "Red scare" in 1918. Conditioned by wartime propaganda to regard alien nationalities as disloyal, they were confronted with a series of isolated incidents which seemed to fall into a revolutionary pattern. The speeches of Seattle's mayor, Ole Hanson, encouraged this view, while his strikebreaking activity made him a national hero overnight.

The Boston police strike six months later produced the same effect on the American public. It had been preceded by several unsuccessful efforts on the part of the policemen to secure a wage increase that would offset the rise in living costs. The incident that precipitated the trouble was the decision of Police Commissioner Edwin U. Curtis to suspend nineteen patrolmen who had urged their colleagues to form a union and apply for an A.F. of L. charter. The entire force defied the commissioner on September 9, 1919. All posts were abandoned for twenty hours, with the result that hoodlums roamed the streets of downtown Boston, smashing windows, looting shops, and terrorizing the population. Popular concern over the economic plight of the police gave way to fear that only unreliable patrolmen stood between society and the Bolshevik revolutionaries. Although Mayor Peters persuaded the patrolmen to return to work the following day, the nation learned with relief that Governor Calvin Coolidge had called out the State Guard and had asked Washington to make federal troops available in the event of a general strike. These precautions proved unnecessary, but the Governor remained in the limelight. When Curtis ignored the request of Samuel Gompers that the strikers be reinstated, Coolidge backed his Police Commissioner with a sharply worded telegram to the head of the A.F. of L.: "There is no right to strike against the public safety by anybody, anywhere, anytime." The incident led to a vice-presidential nomination for Coolidge in 1920. It also provided ammunition for foes of the A.F. of L. who were denouncing the craft unions as agents of Bolshevism. Gompers had already contributed to this impression by endorsing the Plumb Plan for permanent government ownership of the railroad systems taken over during the war.

The outbreak of a steel strike two weeks later seemed to confirm the charges that organized labor was part of a revolutionary conspiracy. Once again the public ignored the role of price inflation, poor working conditions, and employer resistance to concessions as motives for the strike. The greatest source of discontent was the seven-day work week, which averaged sixty-eight hours. To make matters worse, employers sometimes required the mill hands to work a twenty-hour shift without extra compensation. The A.F. of L. had long been reluctant to organize industries where the craft principle could not easily be applied, but in the summer of 1919 it set up a committee to unionize the steelworkers.

By this time the more panicky Americans believed that the Bolsheviks were behind all industrial disputes and would have denounced the activity of the A.F. of L. in any event. The popular attitude had some justification in the case of the steel strike because of the prominent role assumed by William Z. Foster. Whether or not he took orders from the Third International in Moscow, Foster believed in the overthrow of the existing American system. He concealed his ulterior motives from steelworkers who were interested only in economic objectives. The presence of Foster gave Judge Elbert H. Gary, Chairman of the Board of the United States Steel Company and spokesman for the industry, a patriotic excuse for rejecting the eight-hour day and other worker demands. From Gary to Buffalo 300,000 men walked off the job on September 22. Senator Atlee Pomerene of Ohio denounced the strikers and asserted that they were being promised "Soviet rule and nationalization of industry." Lieutenant D. C. Van Buren of Army Intelligence made headlines by telling a Senate Investigating Committee that he had seen un-American literature in Gary. Public hostility to the strikers strengthened the position of management. Although the strike dragged on until January of 1920, the men were forced to return on company terms.

THE "RED SCARE"

The hysterical popular response to the strikes of 1919 was encouraged by a wild series of bombing attempts against prominent foes of Bolshevism and by the frantic retaliatory measures of the government. Nobody ever found out who was responsible for the detonation of explosives, but the Communists, who tended to promote organized violence rather than isolated acts of terror, were blamed.

The fireworks started in April 1919, when an alert clerk isolated a suspicious package addressed to Mayor Ole Hanson of Seattle, which contained a bomb. What had seemed like the work of an isolated crank took on more serious proportions a month later when postal authorities in New York City intercepted sixteen similar packages intended for conspicuous capitalists and public officials, including J. P. Morgan, John D. Rockefeller, Postmaster General Burleson, and Attorney General Palmer.

When the bombs failed to reach their intended victims, more direct methods were employed. On the night of June 2 major explosions occurred simultaneously in eight cities near the homes of citizens hostile to radicals and immigrants. The resulting damage was negligible, but the public, prompted by the newspapers, connected the explosions with striking workmen. Only three years earlier eight persons had lost their lives from a bomb blast at the San Francisco Preparedness Day parade, and two radical union leaders, Thomas J. Mooney and Warren K. Billings, had been convicted for the crime. Against a background of domestic strikes and world-wide Bolshevist agitation the bombings were regarded by excitable citizens as the first stage of a working-class revolution.

The administration might have done something to dispel the growing sense of panic, but Wilson was preoccupied with the League and allowed Attorney General A. Mitchell Palmer a free hand. Far from minimizing the danger, Palmer added official sanction to public fears. He believed that a revolution was imminent, but did not relax his vigilance when an uprising predicted for July 4, 1919, by W. J. Flynn, chief of the Federal Bureau of Investigation, failed to materialize. Instead Palmer redoubled his efforts to smash Bolshevism by launching a series of raids on the headquarters of radical groups. Relying on a 1918 war statute which gave the Secretary of Labor authority to deport aliens who advocated revolution or belonged to organizations holding such views, Palmer systematically accumulated dossiers on radicals. By November 7, he was ready for a crackdown and raided the headquarters and branch offices of the Federated Union of Russian Workers. He bagged enough Bolshevik sympathizers in this loosely knit organization of Russian immigrants to round out a boatload for shipment to Russia. The Secretary of Labor was ill; subordinates willingly signed the deportation papers; and 249 unhappy radicals sailed December 21, 1919, on the *Buford*, which was nicknamed the "Red Ark."

Public applause exceeded Palmer's expectations and excited his presidential ambitions. So he continued to promote the "Red scare" with a second raid on a nationwide basis on January 2, 1920. Some five thousand members of various parties that had splintered off from the parent Socialist organization were rounded up. More than half of them proved to be citizens and hence beyond the jurisdiction of the Attorney General. Even their arrest had been illegal and most of them were released promptly. The aliens spent a longer time in jail but escaped deportation because the new Undersecretary of Labor, Louis F. Post, refused to authorize their expulsion.

Official expressions of alarm encouraged private citizens to vent their prejudices. The famous revivalist preacher, Billy Sunday, who had hitherto concentrated his venom on the liquor trade, dancing, and other "big city" vices, proposed that "every one of the ornery, wild-eyed I.W.W.'s, anarchists, crazy Socialists, and other types of Reds" be stood up "against a firing squad to save space on our ships." Others with no more ability than Sunday to distinguish between various types of radicalism heeded his call to violence. In New York City a group of ex-servicemen raided the offices of the *New York Call,* a conspicuous Socialist newspaper, and smashed the printing presses. A hot-tempered Indiana citzen who killed another man for saying "To hell with the United States," was promptly acquitted by the jury. Armistice Day of 1919 provided an occasion for considerable violence, particularly in Centralia, Washington, where four members of the American Legion were killed in a scuffle with the I.W.W. Each side blamed the other for starting the bloodshed, but local opinion ran heavily against the "Wobblies." Of the twelve implicated in the death of the Legionnaires, one was lynched by the mob and the others were convicted and sentenced to terms lasting anywhere from twenty-five to forty-five years. Elsewhere in the Far West the Centralia incident touched off vandalistic attacks on the property and meeting places of the I.W.W.

The hysteria reached its crest in the last months of 1919, overshadowing other problems and providing a ready explanation for their existence. Although the "Red scare" subsided rapidly in 1920, it left a permanent residue of intolerance behind. Throughout the next decade private organizations dedicated to the eradication of Bolshevism were to stretch the term to cover all sorts of unorthodox viewpoints. In the process they attempted to impose limits on free speech incompatible with prewar standards. The subsequent record of world Communism suggests that those who raised the alarm in 1919 were justified in fearing the movement but wrong in thinking of its adherents as an immediate threat to the *status quo.* The stereotyped postwar picture of the Bolshevik as an unshaven, wild-eyed bomb thrower eventually gave way to a more realistic recognition of his double role as underground revolutionary and soft-spoken infiltrater of democratic organizations. The grotesque cloak-and-dagger version of the Bolshevik conspiracy prevalent in 1919 made Americans look foolish and behave unfairly. This performance should not blind us to the fact that their instinct was sound: Marxism did offer a threat to traditional American institutions whether in its revolutionary or in its peaceful form.

RACIAL AND RELIGIOUS TENSIONS

On other sectors of the home front demobilization problems that could neither be solved nor ignored were dealt with in an angry intolerant way. One of the most explosive concerned the thousands of Negroes who had migrated northward for war work and were stranded without jobs when the government abruptly terminated defense contracts. Idle, rebellious, and conscious of their inferior bargaining power, they reacted violently to the taunts of whites. Isolated scuffles were converted into large-scale riots in Omaha, Chicago, Knoxville, and Washington, D.C., during the summer of 1919. Beyond brutal suppression of Negroes by local police authorities, no steps were taken to improve race relations. The public, which had acquired a taste for the persecution of Germans during the war, found no difficulty adjusting to the new situation. The *Chicago Tribune* spoke for the professional patriots when it observed that there were only ten million Negroes and dared them to rest their case on armed force. Simultaneously, organizers were beginning to circulate in the South and the Midwest, reviving the old Ku Klux Klan, which had coerced Negroes after the Civil War. Dormant since the Reconstruction, the Klan recruited nearly five thousand members in 1919 and broadened its defense of white supremacy with a program designed to chastise all minority groups.

Postwar urban conditions also alarmed many deeply religious citizens from the rural South and West. They shared the general indignation against striking workmen, rioting Negroes, and clannish immigrants, but their wrath was concentrated on drinking, gambling, dancing, and prostitution. These had always existed in big cities, but were especially attractive to idle soldiers and now flourished on a larger scale than ever before. Other activities objectionable to the religious community, like prize fighting and horse racing, enjoyed new popularity. This trend indicated that America was on the verge of redefining standards of respectability in recreation. It was one phase of a larger revolution that accompanied the transformation of the United States from a rural to an urban society. Unfortunately, the war had speeded up the process and stimulated change at a faster pace than the older generation could absorb. Unaware of the deeper forces at work, rural Americans fought back at immigrants, Catholics, and other urban groups identified with the new developments. Their voices swelled the chorus of mutual recriminations in 1919.

It is doubtful whether public opinion would have tolerated government action on the scale necessary to soften the impact of demobilization problems. Besides, nobody thought in such terms. Wilson proposed few legislative remedies but even these were too much for a Congress bent on dismantling war controls and curtailing executive power. With the election of 1920 in the offing, the Republican majority had little incentive to rescue the President from public wrath. So deadlock prevailed in Washington during the critical months after the Armistice, while the popularity of the President slowly eroded.

WILSON'S RECEPTION IN EUROPE

Long before matters on the domestic front had reached an impasse, Wilson had sailed for Europe with a staff composed of about three hundred officials, specialists, advisers, secretaries, and the like. His ship, the *George Washington,* docked at Brest on December 13, 1918. Since more than a month would elapse before the conference convened, Wilson busied himself with tours of Allied capitals and European battlefields. These ceremonial appearances produced tremendous ovations and were a tribute to Wilson's personal popularity. At that time his prestige was greater than that of any Allied spokesman — perhaps greater than any other man has ever enjoyed in Europe.

To some degree Wilson was the focus of thc spontaneous emotional gratitude which most Allied peoples felt for the timely rescue recently performed by the United States. His ringing appeals for peace, justice, and national self-determination also struck a responsive chord among war-weary Europeans. The attractiveness of these aims lay precisely in their vagueness. With the exhausted masses desperately wanting something to believe in, it was not surprising that they hailed Wilson as the custodian of their contradictory hopes. He promised them both perpetual peace and the realization of their conflicting national ambitions. In the intoxication of the moment, neither he nor his auditors seemed to see that the simultaneous fulfillment of all those objectives was impossible. Inevitably, disillusionment would set in on the day Wilson began to translate his ideals into practical terms that involved the drawing of boundaries and the distribution of human and material resources.

The hazards inherent in his position escaped Wilson. The wild applause drowned out the nagging voices of criticism from the other side of the Atlantic. It erased whatever lingering doubts he might have felt about the advisability of forcing immediate adoption of the League of Nations. He had already managed to convince himself that his views represented those of Americans and that opposition would melt when his program was adequately explained. With the applause of Europeans ringing in his ears, he assumed the role of spokesman for a world constituency. He imagined that he could surmount the opposition of Allied governments by appealing over their heads to the people themselves. Such an estimate of his position strengthened his sense of self-righteousness. It also weakened any lingering instinct to compromise that he might have.

THE ATMOSPHERE IN PARIS

When the conference formally opened on January 12, 1917, Paris reflected the mood of an exhausted and demoralized continent. Feelings of hatred, vengefulness, and greed were mixed with feelings of elation, hope, and magnanimity. These contradictory attitudes competed for supremacy in the hearts of victors and vanquished alike. An undercurrent of anxiety complicated the sentiments of the delegates because the tide of Bolshevism had begun to roll westward in the wake of destruction, hunger, and disease. The area most vulnerable to revolution was Central Europe, where the collapse of German, Austrian, and Russian power had cleared the way for both Communistic and Nationalistic agitators. A Bolshevist regime was temporarily in control of Hungary, while revolutionary movements threatened the shaky governments of Germany and Italy. With the ground crumbling under their feet, Allied diplomats recognized the necessity for a quick settlement, but the accumulated hatred of four years blocked relief in enemy areas. They continued the economic blockade of Germany and spurned discussions with the representatives of the Central Powers about peace terms.

Already it was clear that the Allies intended to dictate a settlement. The quarrels would be among themselves; most of their enemies, including the revolutionary Russians, would not even be consulted. Many neutrals were to receive the same treatment. Some Western Hemisphere states absented themselves by choice, while China and Japan participated on a limited basis. Thus the conference would not be a world conference.

The tense atmosphere in Paris encouraged intrigue, and the interested parties pursued it on a scale that set an all-time record. Seventy accredited delegates were present, representing twenty-seven states and five British Dominions. Besides the official representatives of the belligerents, states that had broken relations with the Central Powers, and neutrals, numerous emissaries of nationalistic minorities and other special interests groups set up shop in Paris. Hundreds of inquisitive newspapermen — including 150 from the United States alone — descended on the city and harassed the diplomats for information. Wives of delegates, tourists, sensation seekers, pickpockets and the international set also appeared in great numbers — attracted by the scale of the production.

THE ORGANIZATION OF THE CONFERENCE

The proceedings of the conference began with an informal meeting of representatives of the great powers on January 12. The ensuing deliberations fell into four distinct phases: (1) January 12 to February 14, when the chief business under discussion was the League of Nations; (2) February 14 to March 14, which was characterized by a lull because Wilson was in the United States; (3) March 14 to May 7, when the delegates hammered out the German treaty and handed it over to her representatives for comment; (4) May 7 to June 28, which was devoted to securing German acquiescence in the terms of the settlement and ended in the signing of the treaty at Versailles.

In deference to Wilson, who expected spectacular results from open diplomacy, plenary sessions were held on January 12 and January 25. At first the President even favored admitting reporters to the sessions and was dissuaded with difficulty by his more experienced colleagues. However, the meager accomplishments of the initial plenary sessions quickly converted him to secret negotiation. Only four more of them were subsequently held — principally for ceremonial purposes. Since the scores of delegates and thousands of experts were too unwieldy a group to conduct negotiations, responsibility devolved on the principal Allied states that would ultimately make the major decisions. For a time their agent was a Council of Ten composed of the chief delegate and the second-ranking representative, normally the prime minister and the foreign minister. This group included Lloyd George and Balfour (Great Britain); Clemenceau and Pichon (France); Wilson and Lansing (America); Orlando and Sonnino (Italy); and Saionji and Makino (Japan). The Council met in secrecy and concentrated its attention on the larger issues. Detail work was left to specialists from the staffs of the various delegations, which the Council organized into commissions. Eventually it created fifty-two such groups and received in return much useful information and many sound technical recommendations. Some of the latter were ignored by the parent organization because of political considerations. When the conference got down to serious work, even the Council of Ten proved to be too large. So the chief delegates, dubbed the "Big Five," began to meet alone. Later this number was reduced again, with the result that many key decisions were made by Wilson, Clemenceau, and Lloyd George.

PROPOSALS FOR A LEAGUE OF NATIONS

The concentration of decision-making in the hands of representatives from the five great powers established in effect the procedures recommended by France and rejected by Wilson in December. But there were two important differences. France had not sacrificed the secret treaties nor Wilson his insistence that creation of an "association of nations" be the first order of business. The President's fight for prompt consideration of the League dominated the first phase of the conference. Internal unrest in Europe and the urgent need for economic reconstruction made most of the delegates reluctant to postpone treaty making. However, Wilson possessed sufficient prestige to carry the day. At the session of January 25, 1919, the conference adopted a resolution making a League of Nations an integral part of the treaty and thereby assuring it immediate attention. The President paid a high price for his victory. He had drawn heavily upon his initial reserves of good will and had purchased Italian support by offering Rome a string of Alpine valleys up to the Brenner Pass which contained 250,000 Germans. This bargain violated the principle of self-determination and demonstrated Wilson's willingness to sacrifice other war aims for the League.

The day the conference cleared the resolution on the League, it appointed a commission composed of the representatives of fourteen governments under the chairmanship of Wilson to draft a constitution for the new organization. Several plans were available to choose from: (1) Theodore Roosevelt's proposal of 1910 for an association of states restricted to friendly powers "honestly bent on peace"; (2) a British version drawn up in 1918 by a Parliamentary Commission under Lord Phillimore which likewise envisaged limited membership but avoided provisions for specific political or territorial guarantees and stressed arbitration procedures — a formula in keeping with London's traditional role as holder of the balance of power; (3) a French plan of June 1918, which featured the familiar membership arrangements but also proposed an international armed force to preserve the territorial integrity of member states and to enforce their decisions. The latter provision reflected France's preoccupation with the *status quo*. All three of these proposals were based on the common assumption that a League would be used to safeguard the national interests of member states rather than to sponsor more idealistic purposes.

Colonel House and David Hunter Miller worked up an American plan in July 1918 which was more ambitious than its European counterparts. The House-Miller draft called for (1) a larger membership than earlier plans, (2) guarantees of the political and territorial integrity of members, (3) acceptance of the principle of self-determination, (4) establishment of a secretariat and of a permanent agency for compulsory arbitration, (5) the disciplining of recalcitrant states by economic sanctions. A similar plan produced by General Jan Christiaan Smuts of South Africa in December 1918 contained two distinctive features. The first provided for a council of great powers, and the second for a mandate system.

Wilson did not commit himself to a specfic plan until the fall of 1918, when he endorsed a version similar to the House-Miller proposals. With the help of Miller, who was now attached to the American delegation, and Sir Cecil Hurst, British legal adviser, Wilson hastily threw together a first draft of a constitution and presented it to the commission on February 3. This document incorporated the suggestions of Smuts and the President's own provision for the use of armed forces against defiant states. The latter proposal did not harmonize with a clause that envisaged drastic disarmament, but it reflected Wilson's belief in the use of force for moral purposes.

For the next ten days the League Commission was the center of conference activities, and Wilson dominated the deliberations. On February 14, he read the completed draft — henceforth known as the Covenant of the League of Nations — to a plenary session of the conference. The next day he left for the United States to explain his work and to act on whatever legislation the lame-duck Congress might pass before its adjournment on March 4.

THE LEAGUE: CONSTITUTION AND FUNCTIONS

The Covenant which Wilson carried home did not propose to make as abrupt a break with the past as either its friends or its foes were to contend. A few of the functions it would eventually undertake, such as arbitration and the standardization of postal regulations on a world-wide basis, had been performed by some kind of international body before. Earlier organizations, however, had usually been restricted in membership and purpose — in other words, confined to powers that possessed a real interest in furthering common objectives. The novelty of Wilson's League was that in theory it would admit all states as members and consider all questions at issue between two or more members. Moreover, it would be the first international organization of this character to operate under a permanent constitutional form. Whether the aspiration to universality warranted the inclusion of nonsympathizers was the most obvious practical problem.

The structure of the organization established by the Covenant provided for an Assembly, a Council, and a Secretariat. In the Assembly every member state had one vote even when the option was exercised of having as many as three delegates. The Assembly was to meet at regular intervals and was to be omnicompetent. The Council was to be composed of a single representative for each of the Big Five powers as permanent members, and four smaller states elected to temporary membership from time to time by the Assembly. The Council, too, was to have regular meetings, but not less than one a year. Its chief feature, in addition to concentrating most of the power of the organization in a small body, was the fact that it could be and was expected to be convened more quickly and hence could move efficiently in an emergency. Both Council and Assembly were empowered to hold special sessions in addition to their regular meetings; and in both all but procedural matters, which required only a majority, had to be determined by unanimous vote. The Secretariat was a collection of departments located in a permanent headquarters at the seat of the League in Geneva. It was to assemble and disseminate information, publish and act as a repository for treaties, and perform all manner of clerical and administrative services for members, and, for that matter, in many cases for nonmembers.

Long-range purposes were threefold: the achievement of peace, security, and international cooperation. These three were regarded as interrelated and inseparable. But peace clearly stood highest on the list, as *the* great objective. And security stood next, as the avenue through which peace must be approached.

Several immediate tasks were assigned to the new organization in the hope that their performance would further its stated purposes. It was charged with executing the terms of the treaty in which it was to be incorporated. It was also instructed to establish an agency that was supposed to settle disputes peaceably by discharging a "judicial" function at the international level if called upon by disputants or the League to do so. This agency was called the Permanent Court of International Justice and eventually it was located at The Hague. Another immediate task with semipermanent implications was the establishment of the mandate system. The theory behind this arrangement was that colonial territories, which would not be permitted to remain under the control of the defeated powers, should be administered by "advanced" states as a form of "tutelage."

There were other continuing functions of the body besides the supervision of mandates. All manner of desirable activities were to be furthered and developed for the future. Initially this meant that the League would act as godfather to a variety of functions that had been discharged effectively before it appeared. But improvement of world health standards and of labor conditions on an international scale, as well as the sponsoring of plans for disarmament, were now specifically enjoined on the new organization. Especially the last named was a most ambitiously conceived undertaking, as it envisioned even the control by the organization of the production facilities of the individual states. The League was to assist in keeping diplomacy "open" by publishing treaties. Much more delicate an assignment than that was the charge to "advise the reconsideration" of international agreements, including "treaties which have become inapplicable."

In the same vein but even more difficult was the League's obligation to settle disputes. It was supposed to concern itself about "any war or threat of war," whether it involved member states or not. It was empowered to take "any action that may be deemed wise and effectual to safeguard the peace of nations." This function was related to the most important of all League objectives, namely, the preservation of peace.

The list of obligations which was imposed on individual member states by all these and the many other provisions was an impressive one, by way of both the limitations on their freedom of action and the tasks to which each member pledged itself. Thus a state declared its readiness to make public all its treaties, reveal the status of its armaments and arms industry, reduce its armaments, and renounce all previous engagements which might be in conflict with the provisions of the Covenant. Furthermore, any member was to submit to inquiry and arbitration by Council or Court all disputes to which it became a party and which it "recognized to be suitable for submission to arbitration." This sounded as though it left the states far greater areas of discretion than it did, for immediately the Covenant went on to specify a list of matters which states agreed *a priori* to be suitable for arbitration, including such ample fields as the interpretation of treaties and international law. Members pledged themselves not to go to war until three months after a decision by arbitrators, which the latter were enjoined to bring in "within a reasonable time," or by the Council, which was allowed six months to arrive at its rulings. Indeed, in another article member states pledged to abide by arbitral awards themselves and not to go to war against any state that did.

More onerous than any of these obligations, however, was the task each state assumed of assisting in the enforcement of League decisions and the discharge of League functions. All members were bound to apply economic sanctions automatically against any member, or, for that matter, nonmember, found in violation of the Covenant or of the League's rulings. The resort to war was in effect such a violation no matter where it occurred or whom it involved. Upon recommendation of the Council, economic sanctions could be followed by military and naval action; under these circumstances contributions to the general effort, permission for passage through the territory of members by enforcing troops, and the like, were in order. The foregoing arrangements obviously contemplated a joint war against nonconforming states, although this kind of terminology was studiously avoided when referring to the activities of the League.

The scope of such obligations was most clearly indicated in Article X of the Covenant:

> The Members of the League undertake to respect and preserve as against external aggression the territorial integrity and existing political independence of all Members of the League. In case of any such aggression or in case of any threat or danger of such aggression, the Council shall advise upon the means by which this obligation shall be fulfilled.

Accordingly although the complicated web of stipulations and duties ran through many portions of the Covenant, this article became the focus of most of the criticism which centered upon what came to be called "collective security." This was the notion that peace could be guaranteed for everyone by threatening war against one on the part of all others. The President frequently insisted that this article was "the heart of the Covenant," and his opponents generally took him at his word and met him on that ground more energetically, frequently, and protractedly than on any other.

OPPOSITION TO THE LEAGUE DEVELOPS

When Wilson returned to the United States with the League Covenant, he was vulnerable on several counts. He had defied a number of key Republicans by forcing consideration of international organization ahead of a peace settlement. Thomas A. Bailey has said that the Covenant had been thrown together so hastily that it "bristled with defects." Anticipating some trouble with Congress, Wilson on the eve of his return trip had cabled invitations to the members of the House and Senate Committees on Foreign Affairs to confer with him. He also made a general request to the legislators to defer discussion until his return. The effect of this plea for silence until he had relinquished the floor can well be imagined. Opposition senators began firing at the Covenant while the President was en route. The lead was taken by Senators Borah and Reed, who were outraged by the prospect of a long-term entanglement in European affairs.

Few minds were changed at the famous White House dinner which Wilson gave for members of the Foreign Relations Committees on February 26. Although he answered questions on the Covenant for three hours, his foes either engaged in aggressive interrogation or remained frigidly silent. Senator Brandegee of Connecticut displayed the ugly temper of the irreconcilables when he told reporters that having a discussion with Wilson was like "having tea with the mad hatter." Even more friendly senators did not think that the President had presented the Covenant effectively.

The outspoken opponents of the League were far in advance of public opinion. The initial response in the country generally was favorable. Inveterate internationalists, many Protestant clergymen, and a high proportion of educators hailed the League. People responsive to pronouncements from pulpits and universities, as well as loyal Democrats and a few prominent Republicans, gave a nonpartisan flavor to the enthusiasm.

Closer analysis of the Covenant produced misgivings among some who had been disposed to cheer. One of the first defections was Oswald Garrison Villard, editor in chief of the *Nation* and spokesman for an articulate group of liberal internationalists. He feared that the peace would not be a "people's peace," and that the League and treaty together would constitute a cynical device of the victor powers to maintain the *status quo*. By February, Villard had begun to denounce "the new Holy Alliance misnamed the League of Nations."

More important were the objections of friendly critics. Some of their points seemed so obvious that Wilson promised to seek appropriate modifications at Paris. The changes most frequently demanded by the moderates were (1) that the United States should not pledge itself to employ sanctions or otherwise attempt to enforce the Covenant without authorization by Congress, (2) that all matters usually regarded as subjects of domestic legislation (e.g., tariffs and immigration) be specifically exempted from the jurisdiction of the League, (3) that provision be made safeguarding a state's right to withdraw, (4) that Western Hemisphere security arrangements (i.e., the Monroe Doctrine) be explicitly recognized by the great powers as falling outside the purview of the League, (5) that the United States not be obliged to accept a mandate except by its own choice. These amendments had the backing of earnest pro-League Republicans like ex-President Taft, Charles Evans Hughes, Elihu Root, and President A. Lawrence Lowell of Harvard. William Jennings Bryan also took the same position.

Past experience with treaties indicated that the upper house would not approve Article X or any substitute proposal for impairing legislative control over American foreign policy. Elihu Root was especially insistent about an amendment to prevent the League from committing the United States to intervention without the consent of Congress. However, this was precisely the issue on which Wilson refused to make concessions. As a result, he lost the active support of Root. The others were content with the President's pledge to report their remaining proposals for revision.

Unfortunately for Wilson, his eminent Republican sympathizers did not control party policy in the upper house. A handful of senators like Porter J. McCumber of North Dakota and Frank B. Kellogg of Minnesota shared their viewpoint, but they were not numerous enough to assure ratification. A slightly larger group of Republican irreconcilables headed by Borah of Idaho and Johnson of California were immune to argument. They cherished the nineteenth-century myth that America was unaffected by developments in Europe and they regarded the League as a challenge to the sacred principles of the Founding Fathers. Their votes were lost and Wilson had no alternative but to ignore them. The prospects of the Covenant rested with the remaining thirty-odd Republican senators. All of them wanted more extensive restrictions than Wilson cared to consider. Some came by their views honestly and favored a Roosevelt-type league of victor powers. Others were more concerned with administering a defeat to the President than with the fate of the League, but thought it politically unwise to join the irreconcilables. Their scheme was to propose reservations unacceptable to Wilson with the hope of goading him into killing the League. Whether they knew it or not, time was on their side. The pro-League sentiments of the public would evaporate as domestic problems piled up and as the President stubbornly ignored the deep-felt desire of the majority to end the crusade "over there."

Uncommitted key man among these groups was Henry Cabot Lodge, who would become Chairman of the Foreign Relations Committee after the lame-duck Congress adjourned on March 4. During the next year he was to lead the fight against Wilson without ever opposing the idea of a League. Lodge had been invited in February to state the amendments which he regarded as essential, but he refused to do so. Instead he rose in the Senate just before midnight on March 3 and asked unanimous consent for a resolution rejecting the League of Nations in its present form. When the Democrats objected, as Lodge had anticipated, he read into the record the names of thirty-nine senators and senators-elect who would have voted against the current version of the Covenant if they had been given the chance. Since this group was larger than the one-third necessary to defeat the League, the so-called Round Robin Resolution constituted a serious setback for Wilson. Coupled with the further demand that consideration of the League be deferred until after a peace settlement, it foreshadowed rough going for the Covenant if tied to a treaty. As a final gesture of defiance, the Republicans filibustered to death several appropriations bills so that Wilson would have to call a special session of the new and more hostile Congress.

The President replied in a speech on March 4 at the Metropolitan Opera

House just before he departed for Europe. Defiantly he announced: "When the treaty comes back, gentlemen on this side will find the Covenant not only in it, but so many threads of the treaty tied to the Covenant that you cannot dissect the Covenant from the treaty without destroying the whole vital structure." Despite these boastful words, the tides were beginning to run against the President. Two weeks later Taft, who had shared the platform with him at the Metropolitan Opera House, was urging fresh concessions to the opposition. Simultaneously Wilson faced a revolt against his program in Europe.

WILSON'S POSITION AT PARIS

Wilson's return to Paris on March 14 opened the third and most hectic phase of the Peace Conference. During his absence the commissions had continued their work, but Lloyd George had also gone home and Clemenceau had spent most of the time recuperating from an anarchist's attack. With the principals absent, little progress could be made. The sole major accomplishment after two months of intermittent sessions was the adoption of the League Covenant. Wilson still had thirteen points to go, and his prospects of success were not bright.

For one thing, the conference would be shifting its attention from the unfamiliar problem of international organization to conventional territorial, political, and economic questions. On the subject of a League Covenant, the European delegates were just as inexperienced as Wilson, whereas on the concrete issues connected with a peace settlement they knew far more than he did. In addition, they were quite clear about what they wanted and how to get it.

Second, Wilson's bargaining power was slowly diminishing. He had lost his principal asset when he committed American power to the Allied cause in 1917 without insisting on a full discussion of war aims and an adjustment of points at issue. By March 1919 the timely contribution of American power to victory was already history and the Allies did not need the United States any longer. They had capitulated to Wilson's urgent demand for a League partly because of gratitude and partly because of his unique standing with the European masses. But the negotiability of gratitude was diminishing and the people were beginning to sour on their idol as the weeks passed without visible improvement of world conditions. Voluntary concessions could no longer be expected, and the secret treaties were still obstacles to implementation of the Fourteen Points. Rapid demobilization of the American armed forces in Europe removed another incentive for cooperation, while Wilson's policy of granting devastated states badly needed economic aid without attaching conditions deprived him of his last trump card. Henceforth he would have to pay for the objectives he secured, including the badly needed amendments to the League Covenant.

Finally, Wilson was handicapped because he made assumptions about the objectives of other powers which none of their leaders shared. The latter expected all states to place paramount importance on the preservation of their sovereignty and took it for granted that each of them would place individual interests above larger considerations. This estimate of the intentions of neighboring states was not very lofty, but it tallied well with experience. No evidence existed during the war or in 1919 that any states were prepared to sacrifice their traditional interests for broad ideological objectives. Under the circumstances, any power that formulated policies as if a different standard of conduct prevailed was certain to be at a disadvantage. It would lose the game as surely as a football team which arbitrarily started to play "touch" in a league where the remaining teams played "tackle."

Wilson did not really want to destroy American sovereignty any more than the leaders of other states. It is doubtful that he ever faced the question in precisely that form. He preferred not to think about the problem. This tactic enabled him to reach the unwarranted conclusion that states would act on his definitions of international conduct to the detriment of their sovereignty. He expected them to give up their narrow interests after proper enlightenment and rescue from bad leadership.

We have already noted that Wilson expected the Germans and others to embrace democracy even when such a choice involved disloyalty to their governments. In so doing, Germany had not acted from conviction but to secure an armistice. The rest were less democratic than their structural arrangements suggested. Wilson, however, found it easy to believe that democratization had been voluntary and complete. Since most of the changes took place before the opening of the peace conference, his assumption about the universal enthusiasm for democracy had little direct effect on the deliberations but encouraged him to make the other assumptions that did.

The most important of these assumptions was that people preferred peace to all else and would sacrifice the conventional objectives of their respective states to obtain it. If he had been correct about the universality of the abhorrence to war, then his League of Nations was likely to work. States could then be expected to gang up 99 to 1 against one of their number who employed force whatever the cause. It is not necessary to deny the desirability of permanent peace to question the validity of his assumption.

Despite the universal lip service of diplomats to peace, it has always turned out that the concept is used in a relative sense and associated with particular objectives. This inevitable qualification gets us right back to the Western State System, because each power evaluates peace in terms of the security of its territory, its prosperity, and its way of life. In the event that these are challenged, it sacrifices peace. Evidence of this unpleasant fact was apparent even in the behavior of America, which regarded herself as more addicted to peace than others. If peace had been her paramount objective, she could have enjoyed it beyond April 1917 since the Germans made no move to wage war on the United States. The fact that America chose to fight indicates that she gave priority to other objectives over peace. This conclusion is not less true because Americans refrained from admitting that they possessed interests. Such self-deception was involved in America's paradoxical pronouncement of her intention "to fight for peace" — meaning to fight for her own interests.

Wilson recognized the need for a just and long-range settlement. In this regard, he was far ahead of the European statesmen who nursed vindictive sentiments toward their enemies. His subsequent frustrations at the conference were to stem from the unwillingness of other states to accept his conviction about the overriding importance of an abstract thing called "peace" or his corollary premise that a League would preserve it. Few of them objected to the League or even a number of world organizations for different purposes. They preferred associations of like-minded powers and feared that a League which included hostile powers would be ineffective. Furthermore, they knew that the aggressor seldom operates alone and they expected a balance of power to develop either inside a League or outside it. In short, they understood that Wilson's alternative to the stabilizing devices of the Western State System involved in effect the surrender of sovereignty to a world organization. Neither Wilson nor his former allies — to say nothing of the American people — were prepared to make such a sacrifice.

Under the circumstances, Wilson would have done well to make the establishment of a League secondary to peace terms that created a stable balance. Such a plan offered the best guarantee of lasting peace. Since it would have involved power politics and placed America in the role of honest broker or holder of the balance, he refused to consider it. He regarded the League as indispensable, and the European powers were to make him pay a high price for it.

Besides his assumptions about the overriding commitment of the world to democracy and peace, Wilson had one further presupposition that foreshadowed the quarrels ahead. It was a belief in "national self-determination." This principle dominated the territorial provisions of his Fourteen Points and had stiffened his determination to achieve the destruction of the multinational Austro-Hungarian state. He erroneously associated the aspirations of various nationalities to statehood with a craving for democracy. He also found it possible to imagine that the encouragement of nationalistic sentiments was compatible with the development of the internationalistic attitudes needed in a League of Nations.

Europeans had lived with nationalism for a long time and were well aware of its potency as a force in welding people together. They also knew from experience that it could be ignored only at the price of stability. Nevertheless they judged the capacity of nationalities to attain statehood on a pragmatic basis. If a group possessed the political and economic cohesiveness to survive, they usually recognized it. But the great powers felt no moral obligation to provide independence for every splinter nationality on the Continent. In the past, small nationalities had often been oppressed, but independence did not assure them of a better life unless they had other attributes of statehood. As pigmy states, they became pawns of their former oppressors or of somebody else. Moreover, if they took their nationalistic aspirations seriously, they were likely to feud with neighbors and aggravate regional instability.

Wilson exhibited a far greater preoccupation with the splinter nationalities of Europe than their oppressors or their neighbors did. Unfortunately, no easy solution to their plight existed and it is easy to see why his allies should regard his plan for a mosaic of petty Central European states as a worse remedy than their own. Underlying much of the opposition of the Continental diplomats to the novel schemes of Wilson was a personal dislike prompted by his attempted monopolization of virtue and morality. Not all his critics doubted the existence of principles or the desirability of applying them to the improvement of international relations. They were skeptical of his ability to define such principles in disinterested fashion because he was the representative of a national state with interests like their own.

THE POSITIONS OF THE OTHER GREAT POWERS AT PARIS

If Wilson was to deal in terms of the unattainable and to experience difficulty in balancing the books at the end of each day, Georges Clemenceau of France was to undertake the opposite task. A bent, dried-up shadow of a man in a black skull cap, the seventy-eight-year-old Clemenceau embodied the hopes of an exhausted and vindictive nation. Living on past glories and determined to seize the maximum advantage from helpless Germans, he emerged as the principal foe of Wilson and a soft peace. Long before the two men clashed directly in March, Clemenceau had announced his policy to the French Chamber of Deputies: "There is an old system of alliances called the balance of power — this system of alliances, which I have not renounced, will be my guiding thought at the peace conference."

Unfortunately, the Clemenceau brand of peace was not to offer any more constructive solution to the problems of Europe than the vague and sometimes conflicting principles of Wilson. Love of France and hatred of Germany were the consuming passions of the old man. They burned so fiercely in his soul that he lacked the power of rational judgment. He equated France with "civilization" and regarded her right to pre-eminence as self-evident. The painful suffering of his country in the war explained his attitude but did not justify it. If he had sought lasting stability through the balance of power, he would have favored a settlement that reflected realistic power relationships. Nothing was further from his mind. He ignored the pathetic weakness of France and refused to recognize that she had been rescued by America from almost certain defeat. His sole objective was the humiliation of Germany, and he intended to make it so complete that the Reich could never rise again. Since France lacked the capacity to enforce such a treaty over the long run, this policy pointed toward a new war. Wilson's opposition to Clemenceau's program, coupled with the divergence between the moralizing and the practical statements of the President, infuriated the old premier. On one occasion when he could no longer contain his annoyance, he snorted: "He talks like Jesus Christ, but he acts like Lloyd George."

Planted squarely between the main antagonists and determined to profit from their quarrels, was the bouncy Welshman, David Lloyd George. He was not a diplomat in the professional sense nor a genius in any sense, but he enjoyed a distinct advantage. Unlike his American and French counterparts, he had both feet on the ground most of the time. He was shrewd enough to see his openings, opportunist enough to exploit them, sufficiently shifty to avoid getting caught, and cynical enough to enjoy the performance. For the moment, he enabled Great Britain to wrench the role of holder of the balance from the indifferent Wilson, while acting simultaneously as a self-seeking member of the balance.

British aims were obvious: (1) colonial expansion, (2) rehabilitation of war-damaged trade, (3) elimination of the German naval threat, and (4) reparations to restore a badly worn industrial plant. Pursuit of these goals was not incompatible with a posture of moderation. Restrained treatment of Germany would restore the economic health of Europe and Great Britain's markets on the Continent. Opposition to the harsh program of France would prevent the latter from a foolhardy attempt to dominate the Continent. Mild modification of American ideas on international organization might result in a contribution to stability. This program was not disinterested and Lloyd George was not unselfish. Nevertheless, the role of Britain at the peace conference came the closest to being genuinely constructive.

Saionji of Japan and Orlando of Italy rounded out the Big Five. The former spoke for a power whose claims in the Far East had already been approved by Great Britain and France in secret treaties. His principal purpose was to secure formal confirmation of Japanese gains and a recognition of racial equality in international diplomacy. Otherwise he remained aloof from the deliberations. Orlando had the most difficult task of all. His country had large ambitions and little bargaining power. He participated as a suppliant but an able and effective one.

Besides the principals, the most aggressive diplomats at the conference were the representatives of the various nationalities — Masaryk and Beneš for the Czecks and Paderewski for the Poles. Other spokesmen appeared for the Jews, Armenians, Balts, Ukrainians, and additional groups. Focusing their attention on limited aims, they harassed the Big Five with increasing energy.

THE CONFERENCE MAKES DECISIONS

During the crucial third phase of the peace conference (March 14 to May 7), it quickly became apparent that the major decisions would be made by Wilson, Clemenceau, and Lloyd George with the help of Orlando. Sessions of the Council of Ten were discontinued on March 24 and the next day the world learned that the Big Four would meet separately. Thereafter treaty-making was carried on in secret. Other powers learned about decisions affecting them only through such official communiques as the Big Four chose to issue. The principals held 145 meetings — most of them without the presence of even a secretary — and hard bargaining was the order of the day.

The negotiations took a heavy toll on the physical resources of all the participants but were especially hard on Wilson. By this time he was at odds not only with Lloyd George and Clemenceau but with the members of his own delegation. Lansing and House had forfeited his confidence by exploring compromise proposals during his absence in the United States. Henry White continued to measure up to the President's exacting standard of loyalty. In fact, he rejected improper feelers from Lodge to serve as a contact man between Republican senators and the Allies. Nevertheless, Wilson kept White at arm's length and tried to do everything himself. The assumption of this staggering responsibility overtaxed his energies and he contracted a severe case of influenza on April 3. Illness in no way weakened his determination to carry on alone despite a temperature four or five degrees above normal. For several days he conducted negotiations from his sickbed with the other members of the Big Four who conferred in an adjoining room and transmitted their proposals to the invalid. The Allies tried to take advantage of his condition by seeking approval of several controversial items, but he met these unworthy maneuvers with a series of vetoes. On April 7 he even threatened to return home, and he ordered the *George Washington* to be put in readiness for the voyage. This gesture alarmed his aggressive colleagues and they beat a hasty retreat. No fair-minded person can question Wilson's sense of dedication, courage, or tenacity under discouraging circumstances. He gave a magnificent performance, but the incident exposed the danger to his health and to American interests arising out of his self-imposed isolation.

While the Big Four were redrawing the map of Europe, the League Commission held five sessions on the Covenant. Four changes of major importance were adopted at the behest of Wilson to make the League acceptable to his friendly critics in America. They provided for (1) the withdrawal of members, (2) the exemption of domestic questions from League jurisdiction, (3) the right of members to refuse mandates, and (4) the removal of the Monroe Doctrine and similar regional agreements from the provisions of the Covenant.

The conference formally approved the text of the Covenant with the proposed amendments on April 28. The first three dealing with withdrawal, domestic questions, and mandates aroused little opposition. Either the great powers agreed with Wilson on these issues or regarded them as inconsequential. However, the President was forced to pay for the provision which established the special status of the Monroe Doctrine. He bought British support with a promise to accept a future naval arms-limitation agreement and French support with a deal on the Saar basin which violated all his professed principles. He also made another personally distasteful concession to the Japanese. It was prompted by the fear that Tokyo would not otherwise ratify the treaty and hence would not be a League member. The dispute concerned the Shantung peninsula, which Japan had seized from Germany at the outset of the war and intended to keep. Since the area contained 35 million Chinese, Tokyo was challenging the cherished Wilsonian principle of self-determination. Her claims also ran counter to the President's policy of checking Nipponese expansion in the Far East. With Tokyo entrenched in Shantung and threatening to bolt the conference if challenged, Wilson capitulated. In return he extracted a promise from the Japanese to give up physical control of the peninsula. The Chinese were so incensed by the President's decision that they refused to sign the Treaty of Versailles. This action, however, did not keep them out of the League because they subsequently signed the Treaty of St. Germain with Austria, which also contained the Covenant. The entire transaction left the Chinese in the curious position of repudiating a treaty that denied self-determination in Asia but accepting one that violated the same principle in Europe.

The total damage inflicted by Wilson on his own ideals in order to get the League was negligible in comparison to the damage inflicted on them by others in the course of negotiating the peace treaties. He fought the trend, but his own early violations of principles set an unfortunate precedent. Log-rolling tactics by his more experienced colleagues did the rest. In the end the terms of settlement resembled those arranged by earlier conferences, with the stronger powers getting much of what they wanted and the weaker powers complaining of injustice.

The two major states that made the most determined attack on Wilsonian principles were France and Italy. Obsessed by their fears, the French sought terms that would render Germany physically helpless. They prevented the Armistice from being renewed on a long-term basis and each time it came up for extension they imposed new conditions on the Reich. General Pershing protested against these tactics as a breach of faith, but Paris ignored him.

A more important part of the French formula for eliminating Germany as a great power was the demand that all territory west of the Rhine be separated from the Reich. Paris would have liked to annex this area of 10,000 square miles which was inhabited by approximately 5.5 million Germans and contained about 80 per cent of the Reich's coal and heavy industry. Encountering stern opposition to this demand, France backed an alternate plan for a semiautonomous Rhineland buffer state plus demilitarization of the right bank of the Rhine.

Since the latter scheme envisaged French economic and military control of territory indisputably German, both Wilson and Lloyd George united against it. They recognized that the proposed arrangement would constitute an unmistakable breach of self-determination, create a new Alsace-Lorraine, and provoke a new war whenever Germany recovered. They were right by every standard of principle or practical politics, but this did not spare them from bitter denunciations by Clemenceau and the more nationalistic segment of the French press.

Eventually Paris had to settle for Alsace-Lorraine and economic control of the Saar basin on a fifteen-year basis. In return she demanded pledges that the United States and Great Britain would come to her aid in the event of a future German attack. Wilson and Lloyd George went through the motions of drawing up such a guarantee in treaty form. However, this face-saving gesture did little to improve relations because the French knew that neither the American Senate nor the British Parliament would accept a treaty of alliance. Wilson confirmed their analysis by making no fight for its ratification in the United States.

FIUME

The quarrel with Italy was less important but illustrated the fallacy of Wilson's assumptions about the common man's dedication to principles. Rome had been granted all the spoils at the northern end of the Adriatic promised to her by the Treaty of London. With the other victor powers committed to the creation of a greater Serbia (Yugoslavia), this award did not seem adequate to the Italians. Their cupidity was stimulated by a determination to dominate the Adriatic, which involved getting control of ports appropriate for naval bases on the Dalmatian (Serbian) side. Accordingly, Rome demanded that her boundary with Serbia at the head of the Adriatic be pushed eastward to include the port of Fiume. As matters already stood there were 400,000 Slavs within Italian frontiers. Fiume itself contained a mixed Slavic and Italian population, but the hinterland attached to the city was almost entirely Slavic. Furthermore, the proponents of a greater Serbia believed that their enlarged state would need an outlet to the sea, and Fiume was the only suitable port for the purpose.

The Italians were deaf to Wilson's pleas on the basis of principle. In fact, they contested his attempt to apply Point Nine to the issue on the ground that the Fourteen Points were not part of the armistice agreement between Italy and Austria. Rome was technically correct in her contention but would undoubtedly have demanded Fiume in any event. Needless to say, Wilson did not yield without a struggle. The British and French, who agreed with him on this issue, gave no outward sign of support and contentedly allowed him to carry the ball. On April 23 he issued a public appeal to the Italian people over the heads of their delegates in Paris. It was probably the most dramatic demonstration of his belief that he enjoyed closer contact with the thinking of a people than its own representatives.

As might have been predicted, the Italians turned on their former idol with indignation. Orlando and Sonnino, who had bolted the conference in protest on the day of Wilson's appeal, received a 10 to 1 vote of confidence from the Italian Chamber of Deputies. They sulked in Rome for a time, but returned to Paris on May 6.

Since neither side was willing to yield, the conference adjourned without taking action on the Fiume question. Several months later, Italy achieved a *de facto* solution. On September 12, 1919, a small group of Italians led by the superpatriot and poet, Gabrielle d'Annunzio, seized control of the city's government by a coup. Thereafter Fiume existed as a free city until 1924, when Yugoslavia recognized the Italian claim to it in a bilateral treaty.

FIVE TREATIES

Other issues debated by the Big Four were usually settled more conclusively than the Fiume question but principles seldom governed the solutions. Between June 28, 1919, and August 10, 1920, separate treaties were made between the Allies and each of the defeated states. Named after the places where they were signed, they appeared in the following order: (1) Versailles with Germany, June 28, 1919; (2) St. Germain with Austria, September 10, 1919; (3) Neuilly with Bulgaria, November 27, 1919; (4) Trianon with Hungary, June 4, 1920; (5) Sèvres with Turkey, August 20, 1920.

Although four of the five treaties went into effect after the adjournment of the Paris conference, they will be described as a unit because the Big Four were largely responsible for the principal features of each. The relationship of the United States to the treaties is curious. She did not become a party to a single one of them. In the case of those with Bulgaria and Turkey, she had little direct interest and no official reason for participation because she had not declared war on either country. Nevertheless, American representatives helped to write all five and bore some responsibility for the consequences.

THE TREATY OF VERSAILLES

The German treaty, the first to be completed, became available in early May 1919. The text filled 260-odd pages and contained 440 articles. It dealt with everything from the League Covenant to the precise number of sows which Germany was to deliver to her conquerors. The entire pattern was based on the assumption of Germany's "war guilt." This unprecedented pretext for harsh terms had received official sanction in the plenary session of January 25 which established a Commission on Responsibility for the War under the chairmanship of Lansing. No Frenchman could have discharged this responsibility with more zeal than the American Secretary of State. His commission found the war to be the result of premeditated acts by Germany and Austria-Hungary with modest assists from Bulgaria and Turkey. Subsequent historical research exposed the inaccuracy of this analysis. In any event, war guilt was an unsatisfactory basis upon which to erect a durable peace structure because it superseded rational considerations. Even a crude adherence to the formula of "making the loser pay" was not likely to create as much mischief as punitive terms on allegedly moral grounds. The Allies did not enhance the attractiveness of the formula by incorporating in Article 231 of the Treaty the statement:

> The Allied and Associated Governments affirm and Germany accepts the responsibility of Germany and her Allies for causing all of the loss and damage to which the Allied and Associated Governments and their nationals have been subjected as a consequence of the war imposed upon them by the aggression of Germany and her Allies.

The Germans accepted this article not because they believed it but because they were helpless.

Other articles specified the proposed manner in which the Germans would pay for their guilt. One group aimed at the destruction of military power. Although France did not succeed in separating the Rhineland from Germany, she of course got Alsace-Lorraine and was permitted to occupy the Rhine provinces for fifteen years. In addition, she got several important bridgeheads on the right bank, while that area was constituted a demilitarized zone to a depth of fifty kilometers, or about thirty-one miles eastward into Germany. The Reich was not permitted to have any air force. The army was reduced to a shadow and saddled with restrictions designed to render it innocuous. General conscription was abolished. The 100,000 officers and men which constituted its maximum strength had to enlist for terms of twenty-five and twelve years respectively. The number of officers was held to 4,000 and the general staff was abolished. The new German navy was limited to six heavy cruisers up to 10,000 tons (sometimes called battleships), six cruisers, six destroyers, twelve torpedo boats; its personnel was to consist of a maximum of 15,000, including the 1,500 officers allowed them. No submarines were to be permitted. The Imperial German Navy had been turned over to the Allies in November of the preceding year. While the treaty was being drawn up, it was interned at the British base at Scapa Flow. The intention now, of course, was to take it over. But a week before the treaty was signed, on June 21, 1919, the German crews scuttled almost all these vessels. The import and export of arms by Germany was forbidden, and the manufacture of materials of war was regulated.

All of Germany's overseas holdings and concessions of every description were taken away. The Allies reserved to themselves the right to dispose of these as they saw fit. Hence, principles such as those embodied in the Fourteen Points were quite frankly ignored for the most part, and distribution was made substantially in accordance with the secret treaties and such modifications as the victors decided that changed circumstances required. Much of the Ottoman Empire was treated in the same way. The one thing that received almost no attention was the wishes of the people being transferred. Some German colonies were annexed directly by the beneficiaries of Allied favor. But many portions of the German and Turkish empires were placed under "mandate." These grants of territory were divided into three classifications of A, B, and C mandates, grouped roughly according to what the treaty-makers regarded as the decreasing order of their readiness for self-government. Thus they ranged from Class A mandates like Syria or Iraq, which were autonomous, to Class C mandates that were simply governed as part of the territory of the mandatory power, like Japan's holdings of the German islands north of the equator.

No less thorough a job was done on Germany in the economic field. The determination to impose reparations was carried out. A large portion of these were to consist of payments in kind, such as huge numbers of livestock to be given to France and Belgium in consideration of the losses they had suffered in the invasion. France, for example, was to be enriched by the acquisition of 10,000 goats. Destruction of coal mines, principally in France, was to be made up by putting the Saar with its rich resources at France's disposal. This area of 723 square miles with a population of 660,000 Germans, one of the most highly industrialized regions in the world, was to be occupied by France for a period of fifteen years, after which a plebiscite was to determine its allegiance. In addition, and after also losing her second most productive mining area in Silesia, Germany was to deliver up to 40 million tons of coal annually to a number of Allied countries for a period of ten years after the war (7 million tons to France, 8 million to Belgium, and so on).

The question of financial reparations was one of the most troublesome. Britain and France succeeded in having included in the figure the novel items of military pensions and separation allowances. There was also agreement on presenting a bill of $5 billion for payment by May 1, 1921. This was to cover the costs of occupation and if, after Allied accounting had its way, there was any surplus, it could be applied to reparations. Beyond that not much was clear. Wilson had been successful in holding out for the principle that Germany should not be assessed for the total cost of the war. He proposed that the amount, whatever it was, should be definite, and that it should be based on the ability of Germany to pay. He did not get formal acceptance of these ideas, mostly because Allied statesmen had built up the expectations of their people with irresponsible promises and dared not set a reasonable figure. They temporarily ducked the issue by leaving final determination of the total to a commission.

Other provisions tightened control of Germany's economic life. Most private properties abroad were expropriated. All merchant ships above 1,600 tons were to be delivered to the Allies, as well as half of those between 1,000 and 1,600 tons. Thus her merchant marine was reduced from about 5.5 million tons to 400,000 tons. For five years she was to build 200,000 tons of shipping annually for delivery to the Allies. Her important rivers like the Elbe and the Rhine, and waterways such as the Kiel Canal, were placed under international control. In effect, the Allies proposed to take so much from Germany immediately that she would be able to pay nothing in the future. At the same time they wanted to collect so much in the future that they needed a prosperous and productive Germany. The self-defeating character of these provisions was recognized by the British economist, John Maynard Keynes. A decade later Winston Churchill branded the economic provisions of the treaty as "absurd" and "monstrous."

Besides the territorial losses and restrictions involving France, already mentioned in connection with military terms, Germany lost to Belgium in the west only the relatively small areas of Eupen, Malmédy, and Moresnet, the two former after a mockery of a plebiscite. Similarly a plebiscite on the Danish boundary returned 1,500 square miles of the province of Schleswig to Denmark, while the rest of the old Schleswig-Holstein elected to remain with the Reich. Memel and surrounding territory were taken by the Allies to provide Lithuania with a port.

By far the largest and most serious losses went to the resuscitated Poland. Posen and West Prussia were separated from Germany and given to the new state to the east of her. These provinces constituted a stretch roughly 80 miles wide and 260 miles long, with a population of about 3 million of mixed Polish and German nationality. Then the diplomats bestowed upon the new state both banks of the Vistula all the way to its mouth, thus creating the "Polish Corridor" which separated Germany from her East Prussian holdings. Thereby they achieved a strategic monstrosity, placed a considerable number of Germans within Poland, and fathered a new and especially plausible German irredentism. These grants gave the Poles control of both banks of the Vistula except in the districts of Marienwerder and Allenstein. Plebiscites in these overwhelmingly German districts during 1920 retained them for the Reich by majorities as high as 50 to 1.

When the boundary-makers had worked their way to the mouth of the Vistula in order to give Poland an outlet to the sea, they found that the only major seaport for many miles along this unprepossessing stretch of the Baltic coast was the wholly German city of Danzig. The Allies wished to make it available to Poland as a trade outlet yet could not quite stomach putting it under Polish sovereignty. Finally they compromised on a solution more reminiscent of the days of the Hanseatic League than of the League of Nations. They declared it and about seven hundred square miles surrounding it a "free city," whose foreign affairs were under Poland's control and where Poland had other special rights, but which was under the protection of the League of Nations and under the governance of a High Commissioner appointed by the League. Poland, backed by France, made one more gain at Germany's expense. Her demand for Upper Silesia was met by arranging for a plebiscite to be held later in this area. When in 1920 it went more than 7 to 5 in favor of Germany, a division of the region was decreed which gave Poland most of its resources and destroyed its economic unity. The transfer of a small but rich district of Silesia, Teschen, to Czechoslovakia, completed the list of Germany's losses.

These losses constituted one-eighth of her European territory and one-seventh of her arable land. Loss of over 6 million of her citizens reduced her population by about 10 per cent. With these areas went nearly half of her coal, two-thirds to three-fourths of her iron ore, and more than half of her lead and zinc. In order to be sure that she would not recoup any of her losses by annexing ethnically related territories, Article 80 forbade union with Austria.

The Allies carried the guilt theme outside the framework of the treaty by citing almost nine hundred Germans for offenses against international law and international morality. Singling out the Kaiser as guilty of the "supreme offense against international morality and the sanctity of treaties," they called upon the Dutch government to give him up for trial. Nothing much came of these efforts. The Dutch recognized the essentially political nature of the Kaiser's alleged offenses and stood on their traditional policy of granting political asylum. After a protracted series of maneuvers the trial of the other Germans charged was left to German courts, where, years later, the fewest of them received the lightest kinds of sentence. Meanwhile Wilhelm settled down to a well-heeled retirement devoted to raising fierce mustaches, chopping wood, and posing for photographs on his birthday.

What the treaty did not say, do, or provide for, was at some points as important as what it did. As noted, Japan had wanted a specific statement of the equality of all races incorporated into the League Covenant. Britain accepted the opprobrium of having her delegate turn down the demand. Although heavily freighted with principles, references to law, and the application of both, the treaty said nothing about the matter which was supposed to have been important enough to precipitate American entry in the first place, namely, submarine warfare — except, of course, that Germany would not be the one to engage in it, for she would have no submarines. While disarmament was imposed on the vanquished and pledged by the victors, no specific provisions were made for implementing it in the case of the latter. Finally, little or no consideration was given to how the provisions were to be made economically workable. This oversight alone made it unlikely that this peace would be a permanent one.

GERMAN REACTIONS TO THE TREATY

The Germans had not been represented at Paris nor consulted by the Big Four until the treaty was virtually completed. On April 25 the Allies notified Berlin that she should dispatch an envoy to "receive" the treaty. Offended by the implications of the message, the Germans actually considered ignoring it, but the helplessness of their position caused them to comply. After considerable debate they selected a delegation headed by Ulrich von Brockdorff-Rantzau, an able diplomat and Foreign Minister of the Provisional Republic. He appeared at a plenary session of the conference on May 7, received a copy of the peace treaty, and listened to a vindictive and humiliating attack from Clemenceau. If roles had been reversed, the Germans might have behaved as badly as the French, but the performance of Clemenceau certainly justified a re-examination of Wilson's contention that the United States had gone to war because of an essential difference between the Allies and the Central Powers.

Von Brockdorff-Rantzau replied to Clemenceau point by point. He denied that Germany was solely responsible for causing the war and asserted that the imperialism of all the European states had been poisoning international relations for fifty years. He also paid his respects to the idea of a League but warned that only a reasonable peace could endure. His weakest argument was that the Germans had been tricked by the Fourteen Points into disarming and were subsequently confronted with a different kind of peace. The fact was that the Reich had been beaten and would have faced a dictated peace irrespective of the Fourteen Points. The Allies did not behave straightforwardly, but von Brockdorff-Rantzau was in error when he insisted that Germany had possessed a real alternative to capitulation at the time of the Armistice.

The exchange of views before the delegates did not change the realities of the situation. The Germans were given fifteen days to file written objections. They uncovered so many that they requested and were given an extra week to prepare them. The Allied Powers received the reply on May 29 and took it under advisement. Only Lloyd George was disposed to grant concessions, and in the end the Big Four stood pat on their original terms.

The German representatives received the final draft of the treaty on June 16. The Provisional Assembly of the Reich voted to accept it with reservations on Articles 227 and 231, which covered the controversial statements about war guilt and war crimes. An ultimatum from Marshal Foch with a twenty-four-hour time limit convinced the reluctant German legislators to withdraw the reservation. They did so with an hour and a half to spare on June 21.

Some delay followed while the Germans searched for inoffensive representatives with the requisite stature to sign the treaty. Eventually they selected Herman Mueller and Johannes Bell to do the job. The ceremony took place in the Hall of Mirrors of the Palace of Versailles where the German Empire had been proclaimed in 1871. The date chosen was June 28 — the fifth anniversary of the assassination of the Archduke Francis Ferdinand at Sarajevo. Within about forty minutes, beginning at three P.M. the delegates of all the signatory powers affixed their names to the treaty while guns boomed outside. Of the original representatives of the great powers, only Orlando was absent. He had fallen from power on June 13 and Italy was represented by Francesco Nitti. Great Britain, France, Italy, and Germany exchanged ratifications on January 10, 1920; but as we shall see, the American Senate refused to accept the treaty.

THE PEACE TREATIES IN EASTERN EUROPE

While the Big Four were engaged in drawing up the treaty with Germany, they also worked out the settlements for the rest of the Central Powers. The formal principle invoked by Wilson for dealing with Eastern Europe was self-determination, but a number of factors blocked its application to the area. In the first place, the disorder resulting from the simultaneous collapse of Turkey, Austria-Hungary, and Russia encouraged the Eastern European members of the Allied coalition to take what they wanted from their helpless foes. The Entente statesmen and Woodrow Wilson bore the main responsibility for the chaotic situation in the area since their wartime propaganda had incited minority groups to rebel. After matters got out of hand, they were confronted with the painful alternatives of acquiescing in the territorial grabs of their allies or ousting them. In such cases, the great powers chose to sacrifice self-determination.

A second barrier to application of the Wilsonian principle was the unwillingness of the various Central European nationalities to accept it. They did not want the boundaries of their projected states drawn along ethnic lines but demanded the inclusion of provinces that their national group had once ruled. The Poles sought the reconstitution of the Polish state of 1772 although other nationalities would fall under their control. The Serbs cherished similar ambitions incompatible with self-determination. Such demands were fortified by a clamorous insistence on strategically defensible frontiers and outlets to the sea.

The final obstacle to the establishment of frontiers along national lines was the shameless determination of the French to exploit the aspirations of the minority groups for their own purposes. What Paris wanted was new states weak enough to be dependent on France and devoted enough to oppose her traditional enemies. To this end, she systematically encouraged extravagant territorial demands made at the expense of Germany, Russia, and the defunct Dual Monarchy. Her policy was intended to serve the twofold purpose of crippling her foes and loading the new states with hostile minorities which would increase their dependence on France. In the process,

Paris defied generally acceptable principles, sound practice, history, ethnography, and common sense. She invoked self-determination where it helped her and opposed the principle where it hurt her. Wilson knew little about the areas involved and was soothed by promises of plebiscites and by his own faith that the League would subsequently correct injustices.

The Big Four possessed least control over the boundaries of the new states of Finland, Latvia, Lithuania, and Estonia that broke away from Russia in the wake of the Bolshevik revolution. However, the Allied policy of blockading the Soviet Union and subsidizing counterrevolutionary armies hampered Bolshevik efforts to crush the independence movements. As a result the four fledgling Baltic republics enjoyed a sufficient breathing spell to consolidate their positions and form stable governments. The great powers at Paris granted them recognition in the summer of 1919 and the Soviet Union followed suit in 1920. The boundaries of the new republics adhered closely to national lines. Aside from the chronic quarrel between the Lithuanians and the Poles over Vilna, the area enjoyed remarkable stability in the postwar decade.

Of all the new successor states, only Poland enjoyed the dangerous distinction of being formed out of German, Russian, and Austrian territory. We have already noted that the Big Four detached extensive sections from the Reich and awarded them to Poland. The conference was not disposed to ignore nationalistic considerations as flagrantly on Poland's eastern frontier. A commission headed by Lord Curzon recommended a boundary that corresponded to ethnic realities. Unfortunately, the Curzon line did not satisfy General Pilsudski and other Polish nationalists who wanted to restore a medieval empire which had stretched from the Baltic to the Black Sea. They promptly invaded Russia and reached Kiev, but were later thrown back by the Bolsheviks. Only the hasty intervention of French troops under General Weygand saved Warsaw from destruction. Subsequent French military and economic aid eventually enabled Poland to push her boundary with the Soviet Union one hundred miles east of the Curzon line and gain control of 4 million White Russians. This violation of self-determination was formalized in the Treaty of Riga on March 18, 1921.

The provinces of the new Poland carved out of Austria contained mostly Polish-speaking peoples, but Warsaw managed to grab some Hungarian districts at the same time. She also launched a feud with the Czechs over Teschen and with the Lithuanians over Vilna. The result of these accumulations was a Poland with an area of 150,000 square miles and a population of 30 million — one-third of which constituted an indigestible lump of minority peoples.

The sixth of the completely new states in Central Europe was Czechoslovakia. Originally envisaged as a marriage of convenience between the Czechs and Slovaks, it mushroomed under the indulgent eyes of the Big Four into a much larger amalgam of nationalities. The Czech-Slovak union had first begun to take shape at a rally in Pittsburgh during May 1918. The tireless promoter of the projected state was Thomas Masaryk. With the help of Eduard Beneš he managed to get some sort of recognition from all the major Allied governments by the following September. Their efforts abroad were seconded by nationalists at home, and a provisional government emerged on October 29, 1918. Initially the revolutionaries sought to base the new state on the Austrian provinces of Moravia and Bohemia plus the Hungarian province of Slovakia. Encouraged by the French, they subsequently asked for the Sudetenland — a mountain district adjoining Bohemia which contained rich mines and forests as well as a population of 3.5 million Austrian Germans. Lloyd George objected vigorously to incorporating the area into Czechoslovakia but was unable to block the award. Clemenceau carried the day by arguing that Czechoslovakia needed the area for a defensible frontier against German aggression. Masaryk managed to pick up other fringe areas, including Ruthenia and a port on the Danube (Bratislavia) at the expense of Hungary.

Consequently, Czechoslovakia turned out to be a fair-sized state but hardly a monument to the principle of self-determination. Her 54,000 square miles of territory contained a population of 14 million, roughly one-third of whom were German, Hungarian, or Polish. The dominant Czechs and Slovaks had regarded themselves as separate peoples for a thousand years, and sufficient differences persisted to prevent effective cooperation between them. These handicaps were partly counterbalanced by French thoughtfulness which had resulted in the transfer of territory containing 80 per cent of Austria's heavy industry to Czechoslovakia.

Whether Yugoslavia qualifies as a successor state depends upon the definition of the term. Unlike the six already mentioned, she grew out of the small Balkan state of Serbia which had existed before the war. Thanks to Allied generosity the Serbs were allowed to realize their ancient dream of a South Slav empire. In the process, they created a multinational state similar to the Dual Monarchy which they hated. Besides absorbing the major South Slav groups (i.e., Montenegrins, Croatians, Bosnians, Herzgovinians, and Slovenes), they also annexed territory inhabited by Italians, Germans, Hungarians, Greeks, and Bulgarians. They quickly encountered difficulty in dominating this hodgepodge of 12 million people spread over an area of 96,000 square miles. The Croats and Slovenes had expected to be autonomous partners of the Serbs in a federated state, and resisted the centralization of power in Belgrade. Internal quarrels culminated in a reversion to the traditional Serbian practice of shooting the dissidents.

Even the pretense of self-determination was abandoned by the Big Four in distributing spoils to Rumania. She had entered the war late, signed a separate peace with the Central Powers in May 1918, and re-entered the conflict the day before Germany surrendered. For this modest contribution, Rumania received 31.5 per cent of prewar Hungary's territory, plus Dobruja from Bulgaria, Bessarabia from Russia, and part of Bucovina from Austria. As a result of these gains, she doubled her size and acquired national minorities of Hungarians, Germans, Russians, Bulgars, and smaller groups totaling about 4 million.

The transfers of territory summarized in the foregoing pages were mostly at the expense of Austria, Hungary, and Bulgaria. The Big Four treated them as severely as Germany. The terms imposed on Austria were the most indefensible. After blocking the effort of the Austrian Germans to exercise self-determination by joining their brethren in the Reich, the Allies reduced the size of the old Hapsburg monarchy from 135,000 square miles to about 32,000. Only 6.5 million Austrians remained in this pigmy state and more than half that many acquired new masters. Nothing was left to Austria but an oversized capital of 2 million people, a fringe of Alpine scenery, and the Salzburg musical festivals. These arrangements were formally embodied in the Treaty of St. Germain, complete with reparations provisions, war guilt clause, the League Covenant, and all.

Hungary was scaled down from an area of 125,000 square miles containing 20 million people to an area of 35,000 square miles containing about 8 million. She lost most of her forests and half of her arable land. The peace treaty contained all the familiar provisions noted above.

Bulgaria suffered comparable territorial losses and was saddled with a reparations bill that amounted to about $100 per head. Of the Central Powers, only Turkey managed to evade a dictated peace. Initially she was forced to sign the humiliating Treaty of Sèvres on August 20, 1920. However, a revolutionary government under Mustafa Kemal Pasha revived Turkish power so quickly that the Allies had to grant new and more favorable terms at Lausanne in 1923.

The cumulative effect of the settlements in central and southeastern Europe was the creation of seven new states, the replacement of Austria-Hungary by two small republics, and the severe crippling of three survivors — Germany, Russia, and Turkey.

EVALUATION OF THE SETTLEMENT

The settlement following World War I touched off the longest and most voluminous post-mortem in history. It has aroused recurring curiosity because historians have generally regarded it as a failure and have wanted to find out why. Defenders of the treaties seldom asserted that they were a success, but endorsed them as the best possible arrangements under the circumstances. Our task of summary is the twofold one of asking (1) whether Woodrow Wilson secured the bulk of American war aims as outlined in the Fourteen Points and (2) whether he and his colleagues produced a workable settlement even if America did not get exactly what she wanted.

The answer to the first question need not detain us long. All that the President was able to salvage from the Fourteen Points was the restoration of Belgian independence, the reconstitution of Poland, the return of Alsace-Lorraine to France, and the creation of a League of Nations. "Freedom of the seas" had been sacrificed before the Armistice; "open covenants" was an early casualty of the conference; "self-determination" and "free, open-minded, and absolutely impartial adjustment of colonial claims" perished later. The territorial points concerning Italy, Russia, Rumania, and Turkey were forgotten, while the over-all commitment to "impartial justice" did not restrain the victor powers from doing what they wanted.

The reasons why Wilson could not achieve his program have been suggested through our narrative of the peace conference. Perhaps a brief review will put them in focus: (1) the insistence of the President on making assumptions about the objectives and motives of other states which none of them shared; (2) the vague and occasionally conflicting character of his aims; and (3) his unwillingness to discuss American war objectives with his allies at a time when a major portion of them might still have been attained.

Historians disposed to minimize Wilson's failure at Paris as a spokesman of American interests contend that his fight for principles prevented the settlement from being worse than it would otherwise have been. They cast the President in the role of an idealist far ahead of his time who secured the best compromise available under the circumstances.

As far as the process of negotiations was concerned, compromise had taken place, but the total product did not constitute a compromise in the sense that it represented a harmonizing of interests. Enough has already been said about the difference between the views of Wilson and those of his opponents to indicate that they could not be blended. A durable peace might have been created by offering conciliatory terms to the defeated powers and by tying the settlement to a world organization capable of exercising a constructive role. The prospects of such an arrangement would have been good even if the vanquished paid the normal price for losing and if the world organization fell short of fulfilling Wilson's extravagant expectations. Conversely, the imposition of vindictive terms and their enforcement by a strong league of victor powers might have insured stability for a longer period than the Treaty of Versailles was to do.

Unfortunately, neither Wilson's view nor Clemenceau's prevailed at Paris. Each succeeded in clinging to the goal most important to himself, with the result that the settlement was compounded of conflicting parts. Wilson sacrificed the specific terms necessary for a just peace in order to get the League in substantially the form he desired. Clemenceau insisted on unrealistic material gains and gave up the kind of organization required to protect them. Thus the product was neither vindictive nor conciliatory. It was hard enough to infuriate the Germans but soft enough to permit them to challenge it again. It was drastic enough to turn Central Europe upside down but not drastic enough to stabilize the area.

The real casualty at the peace conference was the old stabilizing principle of the balance of power. Clemenceau had proclaimed himself its champion, but his frenzied nationalism drove him to flout it as defiantly as did Wilson. The power structure established by the treaties confirms this assertion. The two potentially strongest powers on the Continent — Germany and Russia — were avowedly revisionist. Between them lay an inviting vacuum where Austria-Hungary and the Baltic provinces of the Tsar had once existed. It stretched from the Baltic to the Black Sea and was crisscrossed by eleven new states, each one suspicious of her neighbors, stridently nationalistic, and incapable of standing on her own feet. Self-determination had been invoked to justify the division of Europe into these political and economic compartments. Its erratic application had resulted in the reduction of minority groups from 50 million to 30 million. This achievement was purchased at the expense of stability because the smaller postwar minorities had greater capacity for making trouble than the larger prewar minorities. The latter had usually been scattered under the jurisdiction of several powers and wanted to be unified as a state. On the other hand the postwar minorities were detached fragments of national groups like the Germans, Hungarians, and Russians which were already operating as states and were prepared to mobilize foreign policy in behalf of their separated brethren. Three or four million Germans looking to Germany for support in the 1930's were to be far more dangerous than 20 million Poles looking to the exiled Paderewski for sympathy in 1914. The practical objections to self-determination were not the only ones. Aside from the fact that the Big Four did not want to apply the formula, it could not be imposed on an area of hopelessly mixed populations nor solve its problems. The peacemakers sensed the inadequacy of their rearrangement of nationalities, for they forced the successor states to sign treaties pledging kind treatment of the new minorities. It is difficult to avoid the conclusion that the welfare of the people of Central Europe could not be achieved within the context of self-determination.

Often historians who concede the unworkability of the peace settlement insist that Wilsonian idealism exercised a wholesome influence on Europe. It seems more probable that his repeated emphasis on principles as a guide to peace terms made the practical decisions of the Big Four more difficult to accept. His statement on May 30 that standards of right and the interests of mankind now governed was typical of assertions which had an unfortunate psychological effect on the Germans and their fellow sufferers. His blindness to the defects of the treaty helps account for the intense hatred of the vanquished for the treaty.

The generalizations about the contribution of Wilsonian ideals would be easier to defend if his League of Nations had faced a more promising career. Linking this institution for preserving peace with Clemenceau's incompatible territorial and political settlement put it under a severe and perhaps fatal handicap at the outset. Many of its projects could be carried out only if it functioned as a universal organization, but treaty terms were certain to keep some states outside and in opposition. Similarly, its projected twofold function as enforcer and reviser of treaties envisaged the performance of contradictory responsibilities. Other perplexities revolved about its intended role as a promoter of collective security among sovereign states who could be expected to put national interests above collective ones. A final novelty that raised disturbing questions was the procedure for exploring issues through debate rather than through confidential discussion and settling them by votes rather than negotiation. Such arrangements seemed to imply (1) that states with no parliamentary traditions would abide by parliamentary rules, (2) that they would acquiesce more readily in decisions contrary to their interests if they were denounced publicly rather than persuaded privately. These assumptions were contrary to the traditional practice of the Western State System, and history offered little hope that the great powers would accept them. The more contemporaries thought about the League of Nations, the more skeptical they became. On both sides of the Atlantic the idealistic enthusiasm of February had begun to ebb by June. This development mattered less in Europe than in America, where the Treaty of Versailles and the attached Covenant were about to run a gauntlet of criticism in the Senate.

THE GREAT DEBATE

Wilson could not avoid a special session of the new Republican-dominated Congress because its predecessor had filibustered the appropriation bills to death. Anticipating criticism of his peace program from hostile senators, he postponed the call until May 17 and tried to keep the provisions of the treaty secret as long as possible. This strategy failed and on June 9 — a full month before he returned from Paris — the Great Debate started. His arch-enemy, Senator Borah, introduced an unofficial draft of the treaty in the upper house for discussion, and Senator Lodge followed with an announcement that the Covenant, even as amended, would not be acceptable. Wilson was unable to participate in the Great Debate from across the Atlantic, but on July 10 — the day after his arrival home — he appeared at the Senate chamber in person to present the treaty for approval. He reminded the legislators of their patriotic duty and predicted that America would "break the heart of the world" if she did not carry "her burden." Four days later the treaty was referred to the Foreign Relations Committee of the Senate, and the epic fight was on.

The division of sentiment in the United States had not changed very markedly since March. Probably a majority still took the view that the United States would have to sign some kind of treaty and were prepared to settle for Wilson's version with some modifications. An April poll of the *Literary Digest* reported that various groups favored a League of Nations. Newspaper editors also approved of an international organization approximately by a 4 to 1 margin. Thirty-two state legislatures had passed resolutions often cited as in favor of the League. All these endorsements were qualified in the sense that they accepted the principle of international organization rather than a specific League. Once Wilson presented his particular version some supporters would be lost. Others were certain to follow because of dissatisfaction with the treaty of which the League was a part. Furthermore, American illusions had been evaporating at an alarming rate. Reports from Paris about the quarrelsome, uncooperative attitude of Europeans had brought to the surface latent isolationist instincts. This trend was currently being strengthened by reconversion troubles on the home front.

Nobody knew exactly how these factors would influence the thirty-odd Republican senators destined to cast the decisive votes on the treaty and the League. However, elementary political strategy called for a conciliatory approach by Wilson: (1) frank recognition of weaknesses in the treaty for which he was only partly responsible, and (2) willingness to make concessions. If he had pursued this line, he would probably have outmaneuvered Lodge. The provisions of the treaty precluded a league of victor powers of the type sought by the nationalistic bloc for whom Lodge was the principal spokesman. Any reservations to the Covenant that they might propose would not alter the universalist character of the League. The most they could do was insist on prior congressional approval of League action designed to commit the United States to economic or military measures against aggressors. In such a situation, Congress was certain to exercise this power anyhow. Moderate Republicans like Elihu Root felt that it was wise for America to say so rather than to accept an obligation that she had no intention of honoring. Hence it seems probable that the President could have won the uncommitted bloc of Republican senators by accepting a reservation to Article X of the Covenant. In view of the fact that other states had no intention of accepting a League command contrary to their interests, they were not likely to quarrel with an American amendment.

Unfortunately, Wilson was constitutionally incapable of adopting a cautious approach. Instead he minimized the flaws of the treaty and claimed in sweeping terms that it fulfilled American ideals. He also insisted that Article X was "the backbone of the whole Covenant" and that any modification of it was tantamount to repudiation of the League. He expressed these views publicly and in a three-hour conference with the Senate Foreign Relations Committee on August 19, 1919, which left the opinions of everybody unchanged.

Meanwhile the opposition had begun to pick up support. Besides the shocked idealists of the Villard stripe and the irreconcilable isolationists who had been sniping at the President since February, a number of immigrant groups joined the attack They were more outraged by the provisions of the treaty than of the League but also disliked the latter because of its projected role in enforcing the treaty. German-Americans resented the severity of the terms imposed on Germany. Italian-Americans reflected the bitter disappointment of their homeland at Wilson's attitude on the

Fiume question. The numerous Irish in the United States found a new reason for hating the President because he had not supported self-determination for Ireland. American Zionists were disgruntled because the United States Commission to Syria and Palestine had reported unfavorably on the idea of establishing a national home for the Jews in Palestine. Every week more people joined the foes of the President because they resented his preoccupation with the League in the face of mounting unemployment and strikes. By far the most tragic defection was the loss of moderate Republicans who favored some reservations to the Covenant and found Wilson inflexibly opposed to them.

The combined efforts of all these groups produced a deafening assault on the League. Hearst contributed his extensive newspaper chain; the millionaire Pittsburgh industrialists, Henry Frick and Andrew F. Mellon, organized and financed a League for the Preservation of American Independence; the vengeful Colonel George Harvey, who had fought Wilson since their tragic break in 1911, donated his considerable talents as a wire-puller; and isolationists as well as personal foes of the President fired away in the Senate.

Senator Lodge was delighted with this turn of events. The fury of the opposition reinforced presidential stubbornness, which in turn reduced the likelihood that Wilson would accept reservations. Delay seemed likely to widen the gulf between the two sides and goad the President into killing the League. So Lodge adopted the dual strategy of stalling for time and loading the Covenant down with reservations. He made an excellent start by reading the entire treaty out loud — a procedure that took about two weeks. He consumed an additional month and a half by holding public hearings during which critics of the treaty were allowed to register protests. Self-appointed spokesmen for all dissatisfied groups — including the Egyptians and Ukrainians — presented their cases.

While the Foreign Relations Committee was conducting leisurely hearings on the treaty, it also harassed Wilson with a request for his notes on the Paris negotiations and drafts of other treaties. The President had refrained from submitting the French Security Treaty to the Senate, but he capitulated under pressure on July 29. Since the only intention of the Committee had been to publicize the unpopular treaty, it promptly buried the document without ceremony. Wilson was on better constitutional grounds in refusing to release the records of the Paris conference and countered by inviting the Committee to the aforementioned conference of August 19. He released little information at this meeting, but hostile senators scored more points by forcing him into an unwise denial that he had known about the secret treaties before the peace conference. At other points, close questioning pushed him into inaccurate statements. Article X of the Covenant came under repeated attack. After the session, Borah and Johnson told the press that their worst fears were justified. Considering their capacity for alarm, the assertion was a frightening one.

The evidence of mounting opposition to the treaty and the Covenant did not put the President in a mood to compromise but reinforced his stubbornness. Intent on securing ratification without revision, he made up his mind to stump the country. His decision was courageous but unwise. He had already drawn heavily on his physical reserves, and his doctors opposed the trip. Moreover, the advantages likely to be derived from such exertion hardly justified the risk. Even if he won additional popular support, he had no assurance that it would change any votes in the Senate, where long tenure encouraged independent action. Brushing aside these considerations, he left Washington on September 3 on a speaking marathon of twenty-two days during which he delivered thirty-seven speeches. He opened his campaign at Indianapolis on September 4, swung through the Midwest to the Pacific coast, and doubled back to the Rocky Mountain states. Everywhere he went, the President pleaded for a League of Nations without reservations. He represented it as an essential safeguard for the welfare of mankind and repeatedly expressed his belief that Americans would support it "to underwrite civilization." In general, his speeches were rambling, repetitious, and extravagant in their claims for the League, but they drew sympathetic crowds and carried a tremendous emotional appeal. What the large popular turnouts meant was difficult to say, because opposition senators followed the President from city to city and also attracted audiences of comparable size.

RESERVATIONS TO THE COVENANT

The battle of the handclap ended on a tragic note September 25 when Wilson collapsed shortly after delivering a speech at Pueblo, Colorado. The tour was abandoned; the President was rushed back to Washington. The day following his return he suffered a stroke which paralyzed his left side and incapacitated him for six months. With no leader of the necessary stature available to replace him, all chance of pushing the unmodified treaty through the Senate disappeared.

Two weeks before Wilson's breakdown, the Senate Foreign Relations Committee had finally reported the treaty to the floor with forty-five amendments and four reservations. These recommendations of the Republican majority were subsequently whittled down to fourteen "points." They were classed as reservations which — unlike amendments — did not require renegotiation.

1. Reservation to the United States in case of its withdrawal from the League of sole judgment whether it had fulfilled its international obligations under the Covenant.

2. Disavowal of any obligation to preserve the territorial integrity or political independence of any other country, or to interfere in controversies between nations, under Article X, or any other article of the entire treaty, or to employ the military or naval forces of the United States for any purpose except by act of Congress.

3. No mandate to be accepted by the United States without vote of Congress.

4. Exclusion of domestic questions from consideration of the Council or of the Assembly of the League.

5. Declaration that the Monroe Doctrine was "wholly outside the jurisdiction of the League of Nations" and entirely unaffected by any provision of the treaty.

6. Withholding assent of the United States to the Shantung settlement, and reserving complete liberty of action.

7. Reservation to Congress of the right to enact laws for the appointment of representatives of the United States to the League.

8. That the Reparations Commission should have no right to interfere with trade between the United States and Germany, without the approbation of Congress.

9. Necessity of an act of Congress for appropriation of expenses of the United States in the League.

10. Right to increase armaments of the United States, under any League plan of disarmament, in case the United States is threatened with invasion or engaged in war.

11. Right to allow nationals of covenant-breaking states, residing in the United States, to continue their normal relations.

12. Freedom to regulate private debts, property rights, and interests of citizens of the United States.

13. Withholding assent to the section of the treaty setting up an international labor organization, until Congress should have voted approval.

14. Protecting the United States against any unequal vote, in the League, of the entire British Empire, notwithstanding the votes of self-governing Dominions or Colonies.

Eventually a fifteenth reservation dealing with Ireland was added. It represented the only Democratic contribution to the list.

From the outset Wilson opposed all the reservations and never subsequently retreated from his position that they constituted "a nullification of the treaty." In the light of what the reservations actually said, the President's assertion is not very convincing. Some were unnecessary, and a few served accurate notice of how America would interpret her specific obligations. None seemed important enough to impede seriously the operation of the Covenant or the treaty if both functioned successfully at other points. Debate over the reservations was concentrated on Article X of the Covenant. Lodge took the view that America would be guided by her interests where League enforcement measures were concerned. He felt it best to say so, and to add that the proposed action would be subject to review by Congress whenever economic or military sanctions were involved. Such a reservation had been urged by the less partisan Elihu Root on the ground that America ought not to assume obligations that she did not intend to keep.

Since the United States would follow the procedure outlined in the second reservation in any event, Wilson had little to lose by yielding. He refused to do so because he did not want to admit that America's action in a given situation was likely to be governed by self-interest. He undoubtedly knew better but would not give Lodge the satisfaction of exposing the fact that interests of members were going to affect the operations of his idealistic world organization. Both before and after his illness, he steadfastly maintained that Article X was not a legal but a moral obligation.

With deadlock impending, a host of prominent people including Hoover, Taft, Bryan, House, and Cardinal Gibbons urged the President to accept moderate reservations. Their task was hampered by the fact that his physician and Mrs. Wilson kept him in almost complete isolation for seven months after his stroke. Cut off from virtually all contact with public opinion, he did not recognize the hopelessness of his position. As a result he clung single-mindedly to the view that reservations could not be considered because European states were bound to object. All the evidence pointed to a contrary conclusion. Lord Grey wrote a semiofficial letter to the *London Times* in January 1920 indicating that in his opinion most of the Lodge reservations would be acceptable to the Allies. The French policy of building an alliance structure in Central Europe suggested that Paris did not regard either the existing League provisions or the reservations as worth a quarrel.

Undoubtedly Wilson could have accepted enough reservations to assure ratification of the treaty with no serious loss except to his prestige, but he refused to pay the price. Instead, he further weakened his position by successively breaking with trusted friends and personal lieutenants who had already annoyed him in Paris. He cut off all contact with House in the spring of 1920 after the latter urged that he resign and let Vice-President Marshall carry on the fight for the League. Lansing was fired for holding unofficial Cabinet meetings. His break with his secretary, Joseph Tumulty, also occurred during this crucial period. Thus, as Lodge prepared for a vote on the treaty, he faced only a demoralized Democratic minority in the Senate with no leadership save an occasional letter from the White House.

THE VOTE ON THE COVENANT

Meanwhile the Massachusetts Senator had succeeded in uniting all Republicans but a handful of irreconcilables behind his reservations. Under the circumstances neither the Democratic proponents of an unmodified League nor the foes of any League could win the necessary two-thirds vote. The only possible outcomes were compromise or deadlock.

The Senate voted for the first time on the treaty November 17, 1919. The initial pair of votes were on the treaty with the Lodge reservations. The Democrats under written orders from Wilson joined the thirteen irreconcilables to block ratification of the compromise. The first vote was 39 for and 55 against. The second was 41 for and 51 against. Next the Senate voted on the treaty without reservations. This time the irreconcilables went over to the Lodge forces to vote negatively and defeat the administration 53 to 38.

Lodge would probably have been willing to call it a day, since he did not really like the League even with his reservations. The country was less willing to end matters on such an inconclusive note. The only people who had got their way were the small minority of irreconcilables. Prodded by insistent popular demands for a peace treaty, the Senate resumed consideration of the issue on February 16, 1920. During the ensuing month of debate, Wilson received urgent recommendations to let the Senate vote its own way and to accept whatever compromise it could devise. Once more he ignored all such pleas and wrote a second letter to the Democratic minority leader, Senator Gilbert M. Hitchcock, calling upon his supporters to stand firm. With a presidential election in the offing about twenty Democratic senators broke ranks. However, the remaining twenty-one, plus thirteen irreconcilables prevented ratification. The final vote on March 17, 1920, was 49 to 35 for approval of the treaty and the Covenant with reservations. The minority fell only seven votes short of the necessary two-thirds. The Republicans then made an effort to terminate hostilities by joint resolution, but Wilson blocked this maneuver on May 27, 1920. So the country remained technically at war for another year.

THE ELECTION OF 1920

The final stage of the League struggles lasted from March 1920 until the election in November. Because his invalidism kept him out of contact with the main currents of public opinion, Wilson was much more optimistic than he had any right to be. He took almost as much comfort from the deadlock on the League as Lodge, and confidently expected the voters to vindicate his stand. As was usually the case when elections approached, he began to think of himself much as a British Prime Minister who had just dissolved Parliament over a crucial issue to ask the country for a vote of confidence. He assumed that the election of 1920 would be a clear-cut test of public opinion — or, in his own phrase, "a solemn referendum."

Unfortunately for Wilson, the election of 1920 was like most American elections — neither solemn nor a referendum. All sorts of extraneous issues emerged in the campaign to rob it of the clarity which the President so ardently desired. Even without them, he would have been disappointed because the Republicans took an ambiguous stand on the League. Thanks to the guidance of Lodge, they had compiled a voting record which enabled them to pose plausibly as supporters of international organization but opponents of Wilson's particular version of it. They could probably have won the election on a straight anti-League platform, but they employed the classic strategy of straddling the major issues and sought to ride to victory on the wave of petty irritations against the administration.

The electorate was psychologically prepared to give this kind of campaign the maximum response. The eighteen months since the Armistice had completed public disenchantment over the war and all its by-products. The prevailing mood was compounded of irritation against both the quarreling, unreconstructed Europeans and the President. Many citizens thought that Wilson had opened a Pandora's box of domestic problems by sponsoring an American effort to save Europeans from themselves. Hence they slowly came to regard him with the indignation of the sucker who discovers the author of his humiliation. These feelings bred an unreasoning desire to eliminate Wilson and all the grandiose projects associated with his name — to wipe out the memory of the exhilaration and hardship of the war. What Americans wanted to do was to turn back the clock and return to the good old days before the European crusade. They saw the past through a rosy lens, and were prepared to follow any leader unimaginative enough to try to recapture it.

The Republican convention, which met at Chicago on June 8, 1920, addressed itself with real zest to the task of retreating into the past. The presidential sweepstakes were wide open, because the prewar Republican leaders had either passed away or grown old waiting for the call or slipped into obscurity. Theodore Roosevelt, who would probably have been the leading candidate for the nomination, was dead. Taft still possessed his old vigor, but could never be a serious contender after the debacle of 1912. Hughes, who had streaked like a meteor through the skies of 1916, took little share in party activities. Lodge was too old, and other senators lacked grass-roots support.

During the pre-convention maneuvering three candidates emerged as leading contenders. General Leonard Wood had accumulated the largest bloc of delegates. His chief attractiveness lay in the fact that he had made the proper enemies. After serving as Chief of Staff under Roosevelt, he had annoyed Wilson by joining the ex-Rough Rider in an outspoken campaign for preparedness that carried the General beyond the bounds of political neutrality. For this error, Wilson had condemned him to fight the war at Parris Island, South Carolina. Consequently, he presented himself in 1920 as an apostle of Roosevelt and a martyr to Wilson's vindictiveness. These assets were counterbalanced by public revulsion against the war and military men.

Crowding the favorite closely was Governor Frank O. Lowden of Illinois. Like all governors of large states who run for the Presidency, Lowden possessed considerable appeal because he lacked a voting record on national issues and had taken little part in recent controversies. His performance as a state executive had been outstanding, and he had endeared himself to the agrarian wing of the party by working diligently for farm legislation during several prewar terms in Congress.

Considerably behind the two leaders in delegate strength was Senator Hiram Johnson of California, another former Rooseveltian who had been the vice-presidential candidate on the Progressive ticket in 1912. He had built a political career on his overpowering capacity for indignation, which after the war he had diverted from big business to the League of Nations. A towering, solemn man with a flabby handshake, Johnson regarded himself as the representative of honesty and righteousness in the Republican party. It was a useful role because he had little in the way of campaign funds, and prodded a Senate investigating committee — the Kenyon Committee — into exposing the tremendous contributions made in behalf of Wood and Lowden. On the eve of the convention, the Kenyon Committee reported that the Wood forces had spent $1,773,303 while the Lowden backers had disbursed $414,000. The effect of this revelation was to damage the prospects of Wood and Lowden without materially improving those of Johnson.

During the first four ballots none of the three favorites showed substantial strength beyond what had been anticipated in pre-convention forecasts. A pooling of delegates would have created a sufficient band-wagon rush to assure the nomination of either Wood or Lowden, but they declined to cooperate. This left the decision in the hands of a large number of delegates nominally committed to favorite sons who had scattered their votes during the initial ballots. The irresolution of these delegates encouraged a lot of lesser aspirants like Governor Calvin Coolidge of Massachusetts, Herbert Hoover, President Nicholas Murray Butler of Columbia, and Senator Warren G. Harding of Ohio to hope that the presidential lightning would strike them.

The situation was disorderly enough to elate the professionals who saw a prospect of nominating one of their own number. So Lodge managed to recess the convention from four P.M. Friday until the next morning. During the interval the important work of selecting a President was completed in Room 404 of the Blackstone Hotel. Members of the senatorial cabal like Lodge, Brandegee, Curtis of Kansas, Watson of Indiana, and Smoot of Utah, plus a few peripheral figures like Colonel George Harvey and Murray Crane of Massachusetts, conferred for hours. Their task was simplified by the fact that Republican victory seemed certain and that competence would not, therefore, have to be a leading consideration. What they most wanted was a candidate with a pleasant manner, humble antecedents, a subdued record of party regularity, and a willingness to let Congress re-emerge from the shadows of executive domination. About two A.M. Saturday, the cabal decided that Harding best fitted the specifications, and passed the word to other vigilant Republicans in the corridors.

Despite the fact that the elders had spoken, many delegates needed time to disengage themselves from former commitments. So Harding was not nominated until the tenth ballot. In an effort to give the transactions a vaguely Progressive note, Hiram Johnson was offered the vice-presidential post. When he bluntly rejected it, Governor Calvin Coolidge received the honor on the first ballot.

The country was amazed by the selection of so obscure a figure as Harding. He had sat in the Senate throughout the war and the League fight without attracting any attention. People found it hard to identify him with any issue except Daylight Saving Time, which he had consistently opposed. Nevertheless he was genuinely attractive to a war-weary electorate. He had handsome features, a ready smile, and an informal, homespun manner that contrasted sharply with the aloof, professorial Wilson. An amiable air of bewilderment combined with just the right amount of conscientiousness and physical bulk to give him a kind of natural dignity. His orthodox rise from small-town newspaper editor to Lieutenant Governor and Senator heightened the impression that he was an ordinary but substantial citizen. In short, Harding emerged as a symbol of the plain, neighborly, unsophisticated American who had presumably populated the nation before the war.

The Republican platform promised that the party would resume its traditional role as the guardian of prosperity by extending the protective tariff, restricting immigration, and giving aid to the farmer. Several planks were strongly nationalistic in criticizing Wilson's policy toward Mexico and promising that the military forces would not be reduced to their former weak position. On the crucial question of the League the platform went out of its way to be ambiguous. It asserted that the party stood for "agreement among nations to preserve the peace of the world" and expressed confidence that this objective could be achieved without compromising national independence. This qualified concession to international organization was balanced by a denunciation of Wilson's League as incompatible with independence and destined to produce "the hostility and controversy among nations which it proposed to prevent." From such a formula both internationalists and isolationists could take comfort.

As usual, the Democratic convention was held after the Republicans had chosen their standard bearer. Wilson would have liked to stand for a third term, and wrote Carter Glass, the Secretary of the Treasury, a letter on the eve of the convention discreetly hinting at his availability. The President's illness gave the delegates a graceful excuse for passing over his name, but the real reason for ignoring the invalid was the rising popular hostility to all things Wilsonian. It threatened to engulf the party in November, and even though the President's record could not be repudiated, new faces were urgently needed.

Unfortunately, the San Francisco convention did not have a wide group from which to select. Outside of the Solid South, most of the vote-getters of the previous decade had been beaten in the 1918 elections. The one conspicious and politically available survivor was James M. Cox, the Governor of Harding's own Ohio. Since none of the victorious generals identified themselves as Democrats, only Cabinent members like Attorney General A. Mitchell Palmer and ex-Secretary of the Treasury William G. McAdoo, offered Cox competition. It took the convention forty-four ballots to reach a decision, but eventually Cox was nominated. The convention chose the Assistant Secretary of the Navy, Franklin D. Roosevelt, for Vice-

President, partly in the hope that voters from the remoter districts would confuse him with the deceased Teddy.

The Democratic standard bearer aroused little popular enthusiasm. A successful newspaper publisher before he entered politics, Cox made an honest but undistinguished record as governor. Like Harding, he was deficient in imagination and aggressiveness. However, he did not possess the compensating political charm of his rival, who made vague statements of policy sound forthright.

Because of the policy which Wilson had pursued since the Armistice, the Democrats were left with no alternative but an explicit endorsement of the League. The platform called for immediate ratification of the treaty without crippling reservations. It advocated independence for the Philippines and expressed sympathy for Ireland. The domestic legislation of the "New Freedom" was endorsed and the consolidation of its benefits pledged.

The conservative temper of the major party platforms stimulated the formation of a radical Farmer-Labor party which nominated Parley P. Christensen of Utah for President. It advocated government ownership of the key industries and natural resources, restoration of diplomatic relations with Russia, and the rewriting of the peace treaty. Although 1920 was a poor year for martyrs, the Socialist party could not resist a grandstand play. It nominated Eugene V. Debs, who was still serving a term in Atlanta prison for his outspoken opposition to the war. Demoralized by schisms and the defection of splinter groups, the Socialists failed to exercise any significant influence on the election.

Confident that mounting dissatisfaction with the Wilson administration assured victory, the Republicans took no chance of alienating important groups by a positive stand on any controversial issue. Harding was confined to his front porch at Marion, Ohio, where party professionals could supervise his activities and prevent any indiscreet pronouncements on policy. Accordingly, his campaign consisted of a series of general statements, usually to delegations of faithful party workers who made the pilgrimage to Marion.

Much more was said about Harding than by Harding. Party publicity glorified him as the embodiment of the honest, unspectacular virtues of an older America. Nostalgic dispatches from Marion described the town as having "the comfortable look of an old shoe." The public was assured that the candidate worked at an ancient flat-top oak desk and that there were "no jangling notes of liberalism" in his philosophy. Thus he emerged as a kind of Republican Jefferson who would lead his people out of a treacherous wilderness where the landscape was dominated by labor unions, international organizations, and city vices.

Harding did not allow the League issue to intrude in a way that would break the spell. He endorsed a world association that would "discourage or tend to prevent war" but made it clear that Mr. Wilson's League did not fit his specifications. The irreconcilables insisted that Harding was in their camp; and thirty-one pro-League Republicans, including Root, Hughes, and Lowell, issued a statement that Harding favored an international organization with proper safeguards. With the party cultivating confusion so carefully, it is difficult to guess how many individuals voted Republican in the belief that they were voting for a League. However, all indications point to the conclusion that the League had become a Wilson symbol and could have been denounced without loss to the Republican party.

While Harding conducted his front-porch campaign, Cox made the more conventional swing around the country. He took a strong stand on the League and tried to force some sober discussion of issues. But it was to no avail. The Republicans reflected the unreasoning demand of the electorate for change in their famous billboard slogan, "Let's be done with wiggle and wobble." Harding won by a landslide. He captured 61 per cent of the popular vote, 37 states, and every section of the country but the Solid South.

A POST-MORTEM ON THE LEAGUE FIGHT

The popular verdict was more of a defeat for Wilson than for Cox. It ended all hope of American participation in the League of Nations. Characteristically, Wilson continued to believe that he was right and his opponents misguided or evil men. He chastised them once more on Armistice Day, 1923, just prior to his death: "I have seen fools resist Providence before and I have seen their destruction." Rudyard Kipling replied for those who disliked Wilsonian dogmatism and self-righteousness with a sardonic epitaph shortly after the ex-President's death:

> He lies beneath the earth he made his own
> And God once more is running things alone.

Several legends persisted after the League fight and flourished in the 1940's when the United States again found itself at war. One was that if America had joined the League of Nations she would have been able to prevent World War II. A second was that a Republican conspiracy promoted by the malevolent Lodge prevented United States adherence to the Covenant when a majority favored such action. The disheartening result of American participation after World War II in a similarly constituted United Nations has done much to kill the first legend. This experience has also led historians to reappraise the "conspiracy theory" and to concede that many Republicans favored a League but opposed some features of Wilson's version from conscientious motives. The underlying purpose of Lodge continues to remain an enigma. He never went on record in opposition to the principle of a League, although he did more than anyone else to defeat the President. Some of his objections could have been expected in view of his earlier statements on international organization. Others were probably motivated by personal animus to Wilson. It is difficult to avoid the conclusion that Wilson could have secured ratification of a League with a few concessions. What effect American membership would have had on world peace is a matter of conjecture. Unless American ideas about foreign policy had undergone reorientation at some points where they were in conflict with the assumptions underlying the League, participation by the United States would not have been enough to avert World War II.

The election of 1920 also marked the culmination of the revulsion against the war and all the inconveniences it had wrought in American life. The new decade was to open with the conservative mood dominant. Many voters who helped return the Republicans to power desired a counteroffensive against the forces of change on a broader basis than a political party could launch. The ensuing years were to prove them able to dominate politics but powerless to control social, economic, and intellectual activity beyond the reach of legislation. In those areas, the disintegration of the old American value pattern continued apace.

SUGGESTED READINGS

1. Allen, F. L., *Only Yesterday.*
2. Nicholson, H., *Peace-making 1919.*
3. Bailey, T. A., *Woodrow Wilson and the Lost Peace.*

CHAPTER FOURTEEN

THE SETTLEMENT IN THE FAR EAST AND STATUS QUO DIPLOMACY

AMERICA AS A STATUS QUO POWER

Wilson's illness, growing popular revulsion against the League of Nations, and congressional opposition to the President forced the postponement of a general peace settlement until his retirement in March 1921. Meanwhile, the negative reaction to his program had indicated the probable direction of foreign policy. Out of the controversy one clear fact had emerged — the unwillingness of the United States to extend her commitments outside the Western Hemisphere by either annexation of territory or membership in an international organization. With the defeat of Germany she considered her job accomplished. This conclusion reflected her contentment with being a *status quo* power, although American policy makers would never have formulated her position in the terminology of power politics.

Analysts dispute the exact time the United States ceased to be a dynamic expanding power and settled down into role of a *status quo* power. Most of them would probably agree that the transition took place just after the beginning of the twentieth century when she became disillusioned with overseas empire building. The shift is most clearly marked in the Far East, where she switched between 1899 and 1904 from a policy of trying to grab spoils in China to a policy of trying to preserve China's territorial integrity. Wilson unsuccessfully challenged the trend with his European diplomacy, which sought to revive American dynamism on an ideological basis. At all events, by 1920 the change had occurred. Henceforth the United States would be content to maintain her preponderance in the Western Hemisphere and the position in Europe and Asia which she had enjoyed before World War I. Her commitment to the preservation of the postwar *status quo* was to dominate American foreign policy from Versailles to Pearl Harbor.

In general, the American estimate of the security of the *status quo* at any given time governed the tactics which were pursued. Reactions went through four distinct phases during the interwar period: (1) 1920–29, when the *status quo* was considered to be self-sustaining on the basis of existing factors and the United States therefore proceeded to disarm; (2) 1930–32, when the *status quo* was considered to be in danger and Washington engaged in limited action to save it; (3) 1933–37, when the *status quo* was collapsing but Americans convinced themselves that they would be unaffected by the changes and retreated into complete isolation; (4) 1938–41, when the disintegration continued amidst growing popular recognition that the power position of the United States was deteriorating in the process — a situation which made Washington determined to restore the *status quo* even at the cost of war.

Except during the third phase, America's response to developments elsewhere was based on the unconscious assumption that maintenance of the *status quo* would preserve her favorable power position. Translated into the customary moral terms, this policy identified her with respect for treaty obligations and peace. Revisionist powers were denounced as "aggressors," "lawbreakers," and "foes of human rights." It is true that the methods employed by Hitler in pursuing his revisionist objectives in the 1930's justified the use of these terms, but the majority of Americans revealed the overriding importance of their instinctive commitment to the *status quo* by ignoring Hitler until his challenge unmistakably threatened their power position.

Since the strength and prospects of states constantly undergo change, those committed to the maintenance of the *status quo* are likely to succeed only if they aim at the preservation of their relative position within the power configuration. Instead of indiscriminately thwarting all the aims of revisionist states, they must permit adjustments while taking steps to improve their own position proportionately. Such maneuvering requires participation in the balance of power and hence it was unsatisfactory to the Americans. They took the contrary view that the *status quo* was the perpetuation of a static relationship. As a result they sought to prevent change, pretend that it had not taken place, or ignore it. This concept was to work well enough in the 1920's when the revisionist urges of Germany and Russia were weakened by exhaustion and when Japanese dynamism was qualified by the desire to consolidate the gains of World War I. But during the depression decade the relative strength of states changed so rapidly that American insistence on the restoration of the post-Versailles *status quo* made a military collision with the revisionist powers inevitable.

AMERICA ACCEPTS THE EUROPEAN SETTLEMENT

Inasmuch as the Treaty of Versailles formalized the defeat of revisionist Germany and the ascendency of the *status quo* powers in Europe, most

"Everything depends on you, Sam!" (The Dayton Daily News, *1921.*)

Americans were willing to accept it once the provisions for United States membership in the League had been dropped. Rather than reconvene the peace conference to remove the offending clauses, the Harding administration revived the Knox Resolution which Wilson had vetoed in 1920. Passed by an overwhelming majority on July 2, 1921, it simply declared the state of war "to be at an end" and reserved for the United States all the benefits that would have been obtained from Senate ratification of the treaty. The new Secretary of State, Charles Evans Hughes, wisely insisted that the United States comply with international usage and spell out the peace terms in formal documents. Accordingly, in August 1921 separate treaties were drawn up with Germany, Austria, and Hungary reaffirming all the provisions of the Versailles settlement except those which might be construed as involving American commitments in Europe.

With these formalities out of the way, the United States completed the disarmament of her land forces and resumed her familiar aloofness from European affairs. For a time Washington even refused to acknowledge communications from the League. Determination to enjoy complete isolation was soon qualified by a number of developments that gradually drew the nation back into closer relations with the Continental powers. By the mid-1920's she was willing to make a cautious contribution to postwar recovery but continued to avoid any type of entangling alliance.

Although the supporters of Wilsonian internationalism repeatedly deplored the trend of American policy, it was appropriate under the circumstances. The victory of the Allied coalition had created temporarily a *status quo* that was self-sustaining without American help. Germany was defeated, disarmed, and burdened by economic disabilities that precluded rapid recovery. Russia and Italy, the other two revisionist powers on the Continent, likewise lacked the capacity to upset the Versailles settlement. The former was diplomatically isolated and internally weak as the result of civil war and Communist experiments, while the latter was economically exhausted and unable to function even as a nuisance. As long as these conditions prevailed, the *status quo* powers could police the Continent without outside help. They did so through the League of Nations, which became a sort of club of the victor states and of those revisionist powers which temporarily found membership useful. Until the Versailles settlement began to break down in the middle 1930's, a stable regional balance prevailed with the League as the focus of the *status quo* and those outside of it as the focus of the opposition.

The fact that equilibrium existed throughout the 1920's justified the aloofness of the United States. As holder of the balance she was correct to avoid joining either the static or the dynamic powers. Unfortunately she was right for the wrong reasons, because neither the isolationists nor their critics thought in terms of the balance. When the Versailles settlement plainly no longer coincided with the real distribution of power, Washington should have adopted a new policy.

TENSION IN THE FAR EAST

Harding inherited a stable situation in Europe, but one of his most pressing problems was to establish stability in the Far East where matters had gone from bad to worse since the conclusion of World War I. As already noted, the Paris peace conference had confirmed Japanese claims to German islands in the West Pacific and to German economic rights and leases on the Shantung peninsula. Not content with these concessions, the Japanese continued to occupy Vladivostok and the southern half of Sakhalin Island. Japan also persistently evaded a verbal promise to return political control of Shantung province to Peiping. Simultaneously she was engaged in tightening her financial grip on China.

The trend of events in the Far East emphasized America's exposed position as a counterweight to Japan in the simple balance. Nipponese occupation of the former German islands was a potential menace to American communications with the Philippines and reduced the value of Guam as a site for an American naval base. Theoretically Japan could not fortify the newly acquired islands because she held them as a mandate from the League of Nations. This restriction did not satisfy Woodrow Wilson, to say nothing of Americans with less faith in international agencies. Public opinion was especially exercised over the award of Yap Island in the Mariana group to Japan as a mandate. Naval strategists feared that it would be converted into a submarine base for future operations against Guam and the Philippines. The State Department was also concerned because Yap served as a link in an American submarine cable between San Francisco and the Far East. With the Japanese in control of the island confidential communications could be interrupted, censored, or suppressed.

During the last two years of Wilson's administration American policy had been uniformly hostile to Japan without being especially effective. The President had disputed Nipponese claims to Germany's Far Eastern possessions at Paris, refused to recognize Tokyo's mandate over Yap, and failed to support the inclusion of a clause for racial equality in the League Covenant. He had also kept American troops in Vladivostok for over a year to thwart Japanese designs on the Soviet maritime provinces. His unfriendly attitude was emphasized by repeated refusal to give up the American naval building program of 1916. In 1919 the United States possessed a sizeable lead over Japan in most categories of naval craft and if vessels under construction were completed on schedule in 1924 the gap would be widened. Despite the devastating role played by the submarine in World War I and the revolutionary potentialities of the airplane, most naval theorists continued to build their offensive strategy around battleships and heavy cruisers with sixteen-inch guns. With the United States building a fleet that would include forty-two such capital ships by 1924, the Japanese were fearful of American domination of the West Pacific. Handicapped by a belated start in naval construction, they had no hope of overtaking the United States. Still, they attempted to close the gap in 1920 by authorizing a building program that would give them a fleet of twenty-five modern capital ships by 1927.

Japan was not the only power disturbed by the American naval building program. Great Britain had become equally concerned when Wilson refused to discontinue it after the Armistice. Bitter words were exchanged over the issue at the Paris conference. The British stubbornly reaffirmed their pre-Armistice opposition to freedom of the seas. They felt that the security of both the home islands and the Empire rested on their naval supremacy and they therefore resented the American challenge. As matters stood in 1919, they had a greater number of capital ships in service than had the United States, but by 1924 the latter would enjoy a distinct advantage because sixteen of the heavy cruisers and battleships under construction incorporated improvements in design based on the tactical lessons of World War I.

At Paris, Lloyd George pressed Wilson for some kind of guarantee that the United States would not push naval construction to a point where it threatened British supremacy on the high seas. The President flatly refused to make such a commitment. By this time he had come to believe that a big American fleet was unnecessary because the League of Nations would protect freedom of the seas. So his refusal to end the naval race was motivated by the hope that the Senate would ratify the League Covenant if he made disarmament contingent upon favorable action. This strategy failed to avert deadlock on the League, with the result that the dispute with Great Britain over the naval building program dragged on throughout the remainder of Wilson's term.

PRESSURES FOR A SETTLEMENT IN THE PACIFIC

Several incentives operated simultaneously in the summer of 1921 to pave the way for settlement of Far Eastern problems and the related three-power naval race. For one thing, the United States was now willing to accept Nipponese gains in the West Pacific and settle for the new regional *status quo*. In return she expected other powers to help maintain it. Such an arrangement would enable her to retreat from her exposed position as sole stabilizing force in the Far East which she had occupied since 1914.

Japan was also disposed to settle for the *status quo*. Her revisionist program was not urgent and in any case she needed a breathing spell to consolidate recent gains. Signs multiplied that she would be willing to terminate the costly armament race provided she could do so without jeopardizing her position in the West Pacific. The principal obstacle to an agreement with Washington was the Anglo-Japanese alliance which was to expire on July 13, 1921. Its utility to both the British and the Japanese had diminished with the collapse of German and Russian power in the Far East. Neither needed protection against China, and London had no intention of trying to improve her own power position in the Orient. Under the circumstances Washington objected violently to a renewal of the alliance on the ground that it could be aimed only at the United States.

Other pressures were building up on Great Britain to drop the alliance. Canada understandably opposed an agreement that might have unpleasant repercussions for her in the event of an American-Japanese war. Australia and New Zealand supported Canada, and all three Dominions expressed their position forcibly at a London conference in late June of 1921. Prime Minister Lloyd George stalled for time by announcing on July 2 that the Anglo-Japanese alliance would automatically continue for another year unless denounced sooner. Plainly he regarded it as expendable but he wanted to soften the blow to Japan by coaxing the United States into sponsorship of a multilateral agreement. Harding rose to the occasion on July 10 and proposed a conference at Washington to discuss arms limitation and Far Eastern policies. Invitations were sent to the principal naval powers — Great Britain, Japan, France, and Italy — and to four other powers with substantial interests in the Orient — China, the Netherlands, Portugal, and Belgium. The Japanese delayed their acceptance until they had made an unsuccessful attempt to exclude some Far Eastern problems from the agenda, but the others accepted promptly and in some cases enthusiastically.

THE WASHINGTON CONFERENCE

The conference opened on November 12, 1921, in Continental Memorial Hall. Secretary of State Hughes headed the American delegation, Arthur J. Balfour led the group from Great Britain and the Dominions, and Premier Aristide Briand was the chief spokesman for France. Baron Takaakira Kato, the Japanese Naval Minister, and Dr. Wellington Koo, the Chinese Minister to Great Britain, rounded out a distinguished list of envoys.

From the outset the United States assumed leadership. Secretary Hughes recognized that the mutual willingness of the powers to accept a Far Eastern *status quo* made a multilateral political agreement probable. Therefore he concentrated his preliminary planning on disarmament. This was a more difficult problem for several reasons. Despite the widespread lip service to disarmament, few governments considered it a practical possibility. Unlike the United States, they had been accustomed to maintaining huge military establishments for several decades. Even in periods of general security, they were prone to regard disarmament discussions as futile, because nobody wanted to cut arms except on a basis that would put neighboring states at a disadvantage. Finally, their inability to check on each other's arms production deprived them of all incentive to attempt limitations in most categories of land weapons.

Bearing these factors in mind, Hughes devised an adroit disarmament formula and sprang it on the delegates as soon as President Harding had finished his address of welcome. In his "bombshell" speech, Hughes made the following proposals: (1) a ten-year holiday on the building of capital ships; (2) the scrapping of certain designated vessels already launched and others under construction; (3) the subsequent limitation of capital ship tonnage to approximately 500,000 for Great Britain and the United States; 300,000 for Japan; and 175,000 for France and Italy. The Hughes plan was unprecedented because he offered to commit the United States to far greater armament reductions than he expected of others. Specifically he proposed to scrap fifteen of the sixteen capital ships under construction and slated for completion in 1924, plus fifteen prewar battleships. In return he asked the British to scrap nineteen older ships and the Japanese ten. Both powers were also requested to give up post-1916 capital ships authorized or under construction. Since the British had none in the latter category and the Japanese only seven, the United States was making the key concession of the fifteen modern capital ships which had frightened the other naval powers in the first place. Stated in terms of total weight, the Hughes plan called for Great Britain to sacrifice 583,375 tons, Japan 448,928, and America 845,740.

By confining his specific disarmament formula to capital ships, Hughes avoided many objections that would have been raised to a broader proposal. Capital ships were so large and difficult to conceal that construction in violation of a treaty would be easily detected. Moreover, it took so long to construct them that no power could modify the projected ratio quickly. These considerations plus the fact that no naval strategists thought offensive action possible without a large battle fleet increased the attractiveness of the plan.

Hughes made the most of his dramatic plea by adjourning the conference over the weekend. Before the delegates reassembled, newspapers all over the world had endorsed the plan. Public opinion in Japan and Great Britain was so strongly in favor of it that the delegations of both states expressed qualified approval. In the ensuing weeks bargaining revolved around the effort of Japan to secure a 10–10–7 ratio instead of a 5–5–3. After some discussion, she intimated that she would accept the smaller allotment if America agreed to some limitation on the fortification of Pacific naval bases. This counterproposal reflected Japan's desire for an additional safeguard against offensive operations by the larger American fleet in the West Pacific. It was eventually incorporated in the naval limitation treaty.

While the delegates hammered out the details of an agreement on capital ships, a less successful attempt was made to extend the principle of arms limitation to auxiliary naval craft. Dissatisfied with her modest allotment on capital ships, France blocked tonnage restrictions on small cruisers and submarines. She also prevented any serious consideration of reductions in land armies and fortifications. The most that could be salvaged from this phase of the discussions was a vaguely worded agreement designed to prevent merchant ships from being armed and submarines from being used in the same fashion as in World War I.

THE WASHINGTON TREATIES

On February 6, 1922, the naval limitation treaty was signed. In final form it incorporated most of the provisions originally advocated by Hughes: (1) a list of capital ships to be scrapped by the United States, Great Britain, Japan, France, and Italy; (2) a ten-year ban on the construction of capital ships except as replacements for those twenty years old; (3) limitations on both the tonnage and the size of guns for replacement vessels; (4) restrictions on the number and weight of aircraft carriers; (5) maintenance of the *status quo* on fortifications and naval bases in the Pacific except for islands adjacent to the continental bases of the signatories. This restriction did not apply to the Hawaiian Islands and certain other groups. The ban on increased fortifications was to remain in effect until 1936 unless a signatory gave two years' advance notice of intention to terminate it.

While the delegates worked on the naval limitation treaty, they were also hammering into shape the related political agreements. One of these was the Four-Power Pact pledging the United States, Great Britain, France, and Japan to maintain the *status quo* in the Pacific. It made provision for joint conferences of the signatories to settle any difference that might arise during the ten-year life of the treaty. The Four-Power Pact was a logical by-product of the capital ship limitation which would presumably preclude offensive operations by a single power. A final clause, especially gratifying to the United States, provided that the new treaty would supersede the Anglo-Japanese alliance as soon as ratified by the principals.

The disproportionate American concessions on disarmament were used as levers to pry Japan out of Siberia and Shantung and to establish a Nine-Power Treaty reaffirming the Open Door in China. Signed by all the participants in the Washington Conference, the Nine-Power Treaty pledged them to respect the territorial and administrative integrity of China. The latter made a reciprocal promise not to discriminate against the nationals of any other state using her transportation and communications system. The treaty did not abolish the extraterritorial privileges of the colonial powers in China. It did, however, provide for the establishment of a commission to consider the problem. Just as the Four-Power Treaty superseded the Anglo-Japanese alliance, so the Nine-Power Treaty superseded the Lansing-Ishii agreement of 1917 by which the United States had made a damaging acknowledgment of Japan's special position in China. The retreat of Tokyo was further amplified in a clause that explicitly withdrew Group V of the Twenty-one Demands. A separate agreement safeguarded American access to Yap and her cable communications on the island. The Senate promptly ratified this bundle of treaties with only one reservation: an assertion that the Four-Power Pact was not an entangling alliance.

The Washington Conference was one of the most successful chapters in the history of American diplomacy. Under the canny leadership of Hughes, the United States made a contribution to stability without sacrificing her own interests. She retreated from her exposed position as sole counterweight to Japan in the Far Eastern balance and substituted a nine-power regional security system. She also managed to replace the Anglo-Japanese alliance with a four-power commitment to maintain the *status quo* in the Pacific.

Japan's successful resumption of expansion in the next decade touched off charges that the United States had paid an excessive price for stability by scrapping such a large portion of her capital fleet. However, it is unfair to criticize the arrangements of the Washington treaties in terms of the changed circumstances of the 1930's. By that time Japan had resumed her expansionist program and Washington needed a new policy long before she adopted one. The fact remains that in the 1920's Tokyo was willing to accept the *status quo,* and disarmament was a logical consequence of prevailing conditions. Public opinion in America would probably have forced the Harding administration to reduce naval armaments in any event. On the eve of the conference Congress had cut naval appropriations below the level required to complete the construction program of 1916, and Senator Borah was leading a fight for further reductions. Under the circumstances Hughes did well to drive as good a bargain as he did for the scrapping of the American fleet.

The sequel of the Washington treaties was ten years of stability in the Far East. President Coolidge made a new attempt in 1927 to extend the naval limitation agreement to light cruisers and other auxiliary craft. The five signatories of the 1922 treaty were invited to meet at Geneva on June 10. France and Italy boycotted the conference, while Great Britain, Japan, and the United States failed to agree on a formula that would suit their respective strategic requirements. After six weeks of discussion the conference adjourned in deadlock. Because of several bitter exchanges between the Atlantic powers at Geneva, Anglo-American relations were subsequently somewhat strained, but the temporary rift between the two had little effect on Far Eastern conditions.

WORLD COURT MEMBERSHIP REJECTED

As the extreme nationalist sentiment of the early 1920's subsided, the United States gradually resumed closer relations with Europe. She did not participate in any of the early postwar conferences convened to implement various provisons of the Treaty of Versailles. She also shunned official contacts with the League of Nations but took an active role in many of its humanitarian, cultural, and economic projects. Unofficial American observers were on duty continuously at Geneva. They often expressed opinions on nonpolitical questions and showed keen interest in the Preparatory Commission for Disarmament which under League auspices functioned intermittently from 1926 to 1931. When the general disarmament conference finally met at Geneva in 1932, the United States was officially represented.

Distrust of the League was persistent enough to prevent American membership in its judicial organization, the Permanent Court of International Justice, which had been established by separate statute so that non-League members could join. Since strong bipartisan support for an international tribunal to settle justiciable questions had existed in the United States since the turn of the century, both Harding and Coolidge urged Senate ratification of the World Court protocol. Isolationists prevented the issue from coming to a vote until December 1925, when the upper house authorized American membership by the wide margin of 76 to 16. However, foes of the protocol managed to attach a reservation which was unacceptable to League members. Efforts at compromise failed and Coolidge abandoned the fight to secure ratification in December, 1926. Both Hoover and Roosevelt subsequently urged the Senate to reverse its stand, but the proponents fell a few votes short of the necessary two-thirds on the final roll call in 1934.

LOANS, WAR DEBTS, AND REPARATIONS

The most tangible American contribution to European stability during the 1920's was in the form of reconstruction loans. These were not made by the government itself but by businessmen who pumped a steady stream of capital into anemic postwar economies. Washington would undoubtedly have given official encouragement to this revival of Dollar Diplomacy had such action been necessary. As it was, the businessmen went ahead enthusiastically on their own, saving postwar administrations the embarrassment that had accompanied Taft's effort to coax funds into Latin America a generation earlier. The indulgent attitude of the government toward reconstruction loans reflected the view that prosperous people are happy people and that economic recovery would soften the animosities of revisionist states. Only the avowedly anticapitalistic Russian regime was denied American recognition and loans.

Unfortunately, the stubborn insistence of the United States that her erstwhile allies repay their war debts partially canceled the good effects of her contributions to international economic recovery. The term "war debts" included both the $7,077,114,750 loaned to the Allies before the armistice and an additional $3,273,364,324.70 subsequently made available for relief and reconstruction. Included in the latter category were loans to former enemies like Austria and Hungary as well as to the newly independent states of Eastern Europe. As a result of the war or its aftermath, every major

European power but Germany and most of the smaller ones became debtors of America.

Uncle Sam had loaned slightly more than $10 billion before Congress created a debt-funding commission on February 9, 1922, to negotiate with debtors about the terms of repayment. Although the President was empowered to appoint the members of the commission, Congress expressed distrust of executive discretion by specifying that foreign debts be paid off completely by 1947 through bond issues bearing 4.25 per cent interest. The lawmakers also reserved the right to pass on each individual settlement. The passage of this legislation was a severe disappointment to the powers with large war debts. They had made interest payments during the war to maintain their eligibility for fresh credit but had discontinued them as soon as the United States had made some post-Armistice loans. Confronted with staggering reconstruction problems, postwar inflation, unbalanced budgets, and widespread unemployment, the European states needed a breathing spell for financial recuperation. They would have preferred not to pay their debts at all but were especially unhappy over Washington's haste in pressing them for definite funding arrangements.

Seven years of hard bargaining between the commission and the various debtor nations followed before the last schedule of repayment was drawn up and ratified by Congress in 1930. In the process the United States agreed to substantial reductions of the total indebtedness and of interest payments. Great Britain secured the first modification of the original terms in February 1923, when Congress authorized her to discharge her debt in semiannual installments over a sixty-two-year period at an interest rate of 3.3 per cent. France and Italy obtained still greater concessions, the former settling for an interest rate of 1.6 per cent and the latter for 0.4 per cent. Soviet Russia escaped funding arrangements in the 1920's because the Communists refused to acknowledge the debts of earlier regimes and the United States refused to recognize their government. A few smaller states that had received reconstruction loans also managed to evade their obligations on one pretext or another. In aggregate, the debtors agreed to shoulder about 50 per cent of the total — both the principal and unpaid interest — owed to the United States in 1923.

On paper these concessions were quite impressive. Nevertheless they not only failed to satisfy the debtors but left a residue of bitterness which poisoned relations between America and Europe on other issues. At home most citizens took the uncomplicated view that the Allies had borrowed the money and ought to meet their obligations. They regarded the proposals for cancellation as a transparent attempt to transfer a legitimate European war cost to American taxpayers. Disillusionment over the ingratitude of former allies was mingled with feelings that Old World diplomats were trying to make a sucker out of Uncle Sam. Europeans countered with sneers about Uncle Shylock and the worship of the almighty dollar in America. They insisted that the United States had grown rich off the war and had entered it so late that she could afford to cancel the debts as a compensatory contribution.

Behind the noisy controversy was the larger question of whether Europe possessed the capacity to pay without gravely damaging her financial stability. Subsequent developments suggest that the American effort to collect war debts aggravated the troubles of shaky postwar economies. Inasmuch as the belligerents had spent most of their gold to purchase war materials from America, they needed the remainder to stabilize their depreciating paper currency. Consequently the only feasible way for them to pay was through the sale of goods. Congress blocked this solution by raising the tariff rates in 1922 and again in 1930 so that European products could not compete successfully in the American domestic market. To make matters worse for the debtors, the United States had deprived them of another source of gold by taking over much of their export trade during the war and then refused to relinquish it in the 1920's.

These developments drove the Allies to various countermeasures. The most important was a concerted effort to extort from Germany the funds needed for debt payments. In the Treaty of Versailles the Reich had been forced to accept responsibility for damage done to civilian property in enemy countries. Reparations payments were to be made in both commodities and cash, but the Allied governments gave up any attempt to establish the total liability of Germany before the peace conference adjourned in 1919. Instead they created a Reparations Committee and required it to present the Weimar Republic with a final figure before May 1, 1921. In the interim the demoralized German government was to pay 20 billion gold marks on account. When the Reparations Commission reported, it set a total equivalent to $33 billion. Several factors accounted for the establishment of such a staggering bill and one of them was the desire of the Allies to make reparations payments cover their installments on the war debt. In fact, they would have liked to make the discharge of their financial obligations to the United States contingent upon German payments.

Successive American Presidents from Wilson to Hoover stoutly maintained that there was no connection between Allied claims against Germany and war debts. This attitude did not prevent the debtors from making persistent attempts to establish one. The first opportunity occurred after Germany had suspended reparations payments in the spring of 1923 and the French had retaliated by invading the Ruhr. A subsequent German sitdown strike led to a rapid depreciation in the value of the mark and threatened the stability of other currencies. With neither France nor Germany benefiting from the financial chaos, Secretary of State Hughes hinted that America would make a contribution to stability. Accordingly, the Reparations Commission invited a group of American financial experts headed by General Charles G. Dawes to work out a compromise schedule. The result was the so-called Dawes Plan which provided for (1) German resumption of reparations installments at a reduced rate, (2) French withdrawal from the Ruhr, and (3) an American-Allied loan of $200 million in gold to Germany so that she could stabilize the mark and make the initial payments. American participation in this scheme was partly motivated by a desire to hasten the negotiation of funding agreements. Hence it represented a tacit admission of a relationship between reparations and war debts. Four years later a second commission headed by another American financier, Owen D. Young, unofficially made this relationship more explicit. It again scaled down the size of the German burden and for the first time established a definite terminal date on reparations payment. The Young Plan spread the payments over a fifty-nine-year period and set each annual installment at approximately $153 million plus a variable amount which would depend on the level of prosperity enjoyed by Germany in a given year. The $153 million was almost exactly what the Allies had agreed to pay the United States each year on the war debt. Whatever denials Washington might subsequently make about the connection between reparations and war debts, the Young Plan of December 22, 1928, made it virtually certain that the Allies would suspend payment if the Germans defaulted.

Besides trying to saddle Germany with ultimate responsibility for payment of war debts, the Allies adopted a variety of restrictive trade practices designed to build up their respective gold supplies. At first they relied on higher tariff walls, but the outbreak of the depression at the end of the 1920's encouraged them to experiment with currency devaluation, exchange controls, and quotas on imports. Although these devices were employed sporadically at first, they developed into full-fledged weapons of economic warfare as the contraction of foreign trade dried up gold supplies. By the middle of the 1930's, tight government control of exports and imports was the order of the day in European dictatorships and democracies alike.

It is difficult to avoid the conclusion that the attempt of the debtors in the 1920's to pay the United States aggravated the economic problems of Europe. It prevented them from relaxing the financial pressure on Germany and hence slowed down German recovery, which was essential to the prosperity of the Continent. It also encouraged the revival of restrictive trade practices in a period when a free flow of commerce would have had a tonic effect. Lastly, it led to the erection of a complicated intergovernmental payment system which put fresh pressure on the already weakened Old World currencies. Perhaps in a technical sense the European countries possessed the capacity to pay war debts, but if the United States had anticipated the side effects of collection she would probably have followed a different policy. As it was, she helped create a financial structure that collapsed under the first impact of depression and sharpened tempers on both sides of the Atlantic in the process.

OUTLAWING WAR

The temporary economic revival of Europe in the middle 1920's encouraged the United States to make a contribution to stability in the form of the Kellogg-Briand antiwar pact. French fear of Germany stood in the way of a general disarmament formula for Europe along the lines of the Washington naval limitations treaty. Nevertheless, France was a *status quo* power and quite anxious to sign any political agreement that would help her conserve her gains of World War I. In 1925 she had negotiated the Locarno treaties whereby she and Germany agreed never to go to war over their common western frontier. Two years later the French Foreign Minister, Aristide Briand, proposed to extend the principle through a treaty with the United States in which both signatories would outlaw war between themselves. His invitation struck a responsive chord among American isolationists, who seized upon it as an ideal way for the United States to help preserve peace without making an entangling alliance. Senator Borah of Idaho urged that the Briand proposal be expanded into a multilateral treaty outlawing war. The idea quickly caught fire and developed a following outside isolationist circles. Various economic pressure groups and religious denominations endorsed it, and the metropolitan press gave it sustained publicity. Petitions poured into the White House by thousands soliciting presidential support.

Coolidge and his Secretary of State, Frank B. Kellogg, were initially cool to the scheme, but an enthusiastic public eventually converted them. In December 1927, Washington sounded out the French on the possibility of broadening the Briand proposal to include other states, and received an affirmative response. As a result, representatives of sixteen states, including Great Britain and her dominions, Germany, Japan, Poland, Belgium, and Czechoslovakia, gathered in Paris and on August 27, 1928, signed a declaration condemning "recourse to war as an instrument of national policy in their relations with one another." They also pledged themselves to settle all disputes by pacific means. The Kellogg-Briand Pact contained no termination date, and the obligation of the signatories was expected to be perpetual. The United States invited other powers to join the pact and all but five of them complied by 1935.

Most states attached reservations to their ratification. The American Senate exempted defensive wars and all measures that might be taken to safeguard the Monroe Doctrine. The absence of enforcement machinery encouraged Kellogg to buttress the pact with bilateral arbitration treaties. In all, eighteen such treaties were negotiated by 1931. Each of them contained a standard clause which pledged the signatories to submit all justiciable questions to some international tribunal — preferably the Hague Court. True to its traditions, the Senate in ratifying the Kellogg treaties reserved the right to determine what issues should be submitted to arbitration. Thus the coverage of arbitration procedures was not noticeably broader in 1931 than it had been a quarter of a century earlier.

Like the naval limitation treaty, the Kellogg-Briand Pact was an appropriate arrangement for the dominant *status quo* powers. It bound potential revisionist states except Russia, who was not a signatory, to repudiate war except for defense. The reservations served notice that the *status quo* powers would fight to defend their position. Under the circumstances prevailing in the late 1920's, the Kellogg-Briand Pact was a legitimate policy statement for America. Critics who subsequently condemned it as impractical and quixotic did so when conditions had changed completely. By that time the policy was out of date, but such a fate eventually overtakes all policy statements.

AMERICA AND THE WESTERN HEMISPHERE

The postwar quest of the United States for peace through disarmament and international agreements upholding the *status quo* had less effect on her relations with Latin-American powers than with nonhemispheric states. Her preponderance in the Western Hemisphere was so overwhelming that the reduction of her military establishment did not change her basic position. Nevertheless, her methods for dealing with her sister republics underwent substantial modification during the postwar decade. The general trend was toward liquidation of existing protectorates in the Caribbean and repudiation of the Roosevelt Corollary to the Monroe Doctrine which underwrote them. She wavered from time to time in her application of the new approach but by the mid-thirties it was firmly established.

Several factors help to account for the reorientation of policy. Most important was the decline of the unreasoning fear about the safety of the Panama Canal which had motivated much of the prewar intervention in nearby republics. Naval disarmament reduced the risk, while a changing trade pattern quieted old anxieties that European powers would dominate Latin-American markets. Between 1913 and 1919 the United States share of the total annual Latin-American imports jumped from 25.03 per cent to 47.79 per cent. During the same years American investment capital south of the Rio Grande increased on a comparable scale. Most of these gains were at the expense of the European belligerents, who were unable to recapture their position after the war. Lastly, the retirement of Woodrow Wilson from the White House ended the policy of intervention in Caribbean republics on purely ideological grounds. Thereafter, she gradually adopted the policy of supporting stable Latin-American governments irrespective of their ideological views.

The first tentative step toward a liquidation of Caribbean protectorates was an attempt to revive the ineffective Central American Confederation of 1907. The five member states (Honduras, Panama, Costa Rica, Nicaragua, El Salvador) were invited to Washington for a conference in 1922 and after some prodding adopted treaties to revive and strengthen the earlier union. New provisions included (1) a reorganization of the Central American Court of Justice designed to assure the selection of judges from a panel of qualified jurists, (2) a conciliation agreement modeled on the Bryan "cooling off" treaties, (3) a multilateral pledge by the signatories not to recognize the legal existence of governments installed by revolution.

Although America was a party only to the conciliation agreement, she threw her weight behind the other provisions to promote stability around the Canal Zone. Congress cooperated in 1922 by renewing a 1912 resolution which had authorized the President to ban arms shipments to revolutionaries. Coolidge invoked the embargo against rebel factions in Honduras (1924) and in Nicaragua (1926). Unfortunately these regional security arrangements did not end the chronic disorders in Nicaragua. Washington made a conciliatory gesture in 1925 by withdrawing the marines, detachments of whom had been stationed there since 1912, but matters failed to improve and Coolidge sent them back almost immediately. Hoover gradually reversed the Coolidge policy and pulled all American forces out of Nicaragua before he left office in March 1933.

Similar efforts to terminate American occupation of Santo Domingo in 1924 had a more satisfactory sequel. A treaty was negotiated with the native government which validated all the financial reforms and other measures undertaken by the United States authorities since Wilson had intervened in 1916. It also ended the military government but made the American withdrawal contingent upon the good faith of Santo Domingo in discharging her bonded indebtedness. The little republic escaped further intervention by meeting her obligations with unexpected regularity until the bond issue was finally paid off after World War II.

The United States also displayed restraint in her dealings with Mexico over the compensation claims of American citizens. The area of controversy included the title to property destroyed during the revolutionary era (1910–20) as well as the mineral rights of American oil companies subsequently threatened by Mexican land reform laws. After lengthy negotiations in 1923, Mexico agreed to settle outstanding claims. These amounted to a total of $573,649,267.17 against Mexico by the United States, and of $245,158,395.32 against the United States by Mexico. Progress was disappointingly slow because successive Mexican governments passed more laws which impaired the property rights of foreigners. Only 148 claims out of a total of 3,617 filed by both governments were adjudicated between 1924 and 1931. In an effort to speed up the settlement, the United States agreed to exclude certain agrarian claims in 1932. When further deliberations by the joint commission proved fruitless, the incoming Roosevelt administration negotiated a treaty whereby it agreed to accept a fraction of the total American claims. Under the new arrangement the United States was to receive $500,000 in annual installments beginning in January 1935. In view of the delaying tactics of Mexico and her continued efforts to curtail American property rights, the United States showed extraordinary patience during the long controversy. She refrained from making common cause with other governments engaged in the prosecution of similar claims against Mexico and finally settled for a pittance.

The cautious behavior of Roosevelt in his dealings with Mexico was one aspect of his general attempt to continue and broaden the policy of preceding administrations. He negotiated a treaty with Cuba in 1934 which abolished the Platt Amendment and ended all phases of the American protectorate except for the retention of the naval station at Guantanamo. The same year he withdrew troops from Haiti and liquidated the twenty-year-old American financial protectorate in 1935. These measures enjoyed substantial support at home and coincided with a wave of popular revulsion against empire building. The depression was instrumental in encouraging the new attitude. As export markets dried up and Americans lost money on the securities of defaulting foreign governments, overseas colonies and protectorates lost their appeal. Economic reasons were added to moral reasons for nonintervention in the affairs of other hemispheric states.

This gradual shift in policy toward Latin America was well received south of the Rio Grande. As distrust of American intentions subsided, Washington began to pull Pan-Americanism out of the mothballs.

We have noted in an earlier chapter that absence of the basic ingredients of "pan" movements doomed prewar Pan-Americanism. The Latin-American republics lacked the intimate ethnic, linguistic, and economic ties with the United States that normally provide the incentive for closer regional association. Moreover, they had feared that the United States was interested in Pan-Americanism as a vehicle for dominating the entire hemisphere and gave the proposal a chilly reception. Aside from the establishment of a permanent secretariat in Washington and the standardization of trade marks, copyrights, bills of lading, and other routine aspects of international intercourse, the three Pan-American conferences before 1914 accomplished nothing.

The dominant position of the United States in the Western Hemisphere was strengthened as a result of World War I. With the exhausted European powers obviously unable to interfere in the New World, she felt less obligated to demonstrate her power through tough talk and physical intervention in the affairs of Central American states. The reorientation of policy produced a corresponding willingness on the part of Latin America to accept American preponderance in the less menacing form of regional organization. The revival of Pan-Americanism in the late twenties and early thirties occurred against this background.

Inter-American conferences were held at Santiago in 1923 and at Havana in 1928. Inasmuch as the United States still had occupation troops in several Central American republics, the delegates shied away from any binding commitments. Former Secretary of State Charles Evans Hughes made more news in an unofficial speech to the American Chamber of Commerce in Havana than in his official capacity as a delegate. He created a mild sensation by asserting that the United States regarded independence and stability as "the pillars of Pan-Americanism" and would withdraw as soon as possible from areas currently occupied. The so-called Clark Memorandum drafted in the State Department in 1928 but withheld from publication until 1930 went considerably further. It denied in guarded language that the Roosevelt Corollary was a valid part of the Monroe Doctrine. Undersecretary of State W. R. Castle was more explicit in repudiating the Roosevelt Corollary in a speech on July 4, 1931, when he said that the Monroe Doctrine did not confer on the United States "a right to interfere in the internal affairs of other nations." These pronouncements, followed by preparations to terminate Caribbean protectorates, paved the way for the growth of Pan-Americanism during the administrations of Franklin Roosevelt.

Shortly after he took office, Roosevelt reaffirmed the new trend in policy by stating that Uncle Sam intended to be "a good neighbor." The other hemispheric republics grasped the proffered hand of friendship at the seventh Inter-American Conference at Montevideo in 1933. As a result the delegates adopted 114 resolves and recommendations to promote hemispheric solidarity. More important than these expressions of good will were the provisions incorporated in a protocol to the inter-American conciliation treaty of 1929. In Article 8 the signatories pledged themselves not to interfere in the internal or external affairs of another state, while in Article 11 they agreed not to recognize any acquisition of territory by force. The United States demonstrated its good faith by ratifying the protocol on June 29, 1934. A year later it also ratified the Saavidra-Lamas Antiwar Pact which had been launched by Argentina in 1933.

Before all the Latin-American republics had taken affirmative action on these treaties, they assembled for a special conference at Buenos Aires in 1936 at the request of Franklin Roosevelt. On this occasion additional machinery was established to assure peaceful settlement of disputes between American states. With an eye to the growing threat of a European conflict, the delegates approved a convention calling for consultation in the event of "an international war outside America which might menace the peace of the American republics." These treaties plus a convention for the promotion of cultural relations through the exchange of professors and students were ratified by the United States Senate on June 29, 1937.

Pledges of noninterference in the internal affairs of other American republics were put to a severe test in 1937 when Bolivia confiscated property belonging to a subsidiary of the Standard Oil Company of New Jersey. The Mexican government delivered a similar challenge the following year by expropriating all foreign-owned petroleum corporations, but the United States refrained from coercive action.

Two years elapsed before the eighth Inter-American Conference met at Lima in December 1938. The delegates produced 112 resolutions reaffirming the principles adopted at earlier meetings, but not a single treaty. Probably the most important was 109 which envisaged the establishment of a Permanent Inter-American Consultative Committee of Foreign Ministers. As spokesman for several states that feared the United States would exercise disproportionate influence in such a body, Argentina had blocked an earlier attempt to adopt mandatory consultative procedures.

Despite the fact that Resolution 109 was not binding, all the Latin-American foreign ministers answered the call for a conference at Panama immediately after the outbreak of the European war. The session, lasting from September 23 to October 3, 1939, was dominated by the United States, which coaxed her sister republics into following a parellel foreign policy with reference to Europe. The result was the Act of Panama — a multilateral executive agreement which did not require ratification by the states concerned but which spelled out obligations in the binding language of a treaty of alliance. The provisions of the document reflected Washington's belief that American states should pursue a neutrality policy favorable to Great Britain and France. Accordingly, the American republics agreed to open their ports to armed merchant ships and to close them to submarines. Their decision reversed the rules governing the treatment of belligerent vessels adopted by the United States and four other American republics in the Maritime Neutrality Convention of 1928. Coupled with the concurrent action of Congress in lifting the ban against arms shipments to belligerents, this portion of the Act of Panama was a real boon for the Allies.

The other noteworthy resolution that emerged from the Panama meeting concerned the transfer of sovereignty over territory in the Americas currently held by non-American states. It read as follows: "In case any geographic region of America subject to the jurisdiction of a non-American state should be obliged to change its sovereignty and there should result therefrom a danger to the security of the American continent, a consultative meeting such as the one now being held will be convoked with the urgency that the case may require." This resolution anticipated the possibility that a hostile Germany might conquer some of her European neighbors with colonies in the New World and seek to gain control of the latter. When the Nazi conquest of Denmark, the Low Countries, and France in the spring of 1940 turned this possibility into a real danger, Congress reaffirmed the principle by joint resolution on June 18.

The ostensible purpose of the Act of Panama was to keep the threat of war away from the New World. Whether the American-sponsored policy of redefining neutrality rules in favor of Great Britain and France was more likely to avert war or to hasten the involvement of the Hemisphere will be considered in Chapter Twenty-one. In any event the Panama Conference demonstrated the effectiveness of the good-neighbor policy in converting Pan-Americanism into a vehicle of United States leadership.

The foreign ministers met again at Havana in July 1940 to consider the situation created by German victories in Europe. Again the delegates put their decisions in the form of a series of multilateral executive agreements known as the Act of Havana. These included (1) a resolution prohibiting the transfer of territory from one non-American power to another and pledging joint action to prevent threatened transfers from taking place; (2)

a declaration that whoever committed an act of aggression against one American state committed it against all and that in such cases consultation for purposes of common defense would be instituted. The Act of Havana also provided for the establishment of an emergency committee made up of one member from every American state to take over the administration of territory that might be occupied in implementing the "nontransfer" principle. This latter section spelled out the responsibilities of the proposed committee in detail. It was put in the form of a treaty and was to become operative when ratified by two-thirds of the member states. Anticipating the probability that considerable time would elapse before ratification by the necessary fourteen states, the foreign ministers authorized one or more of the signatories to act first and consult later if an emergency developed. In effect this arrangement gave the United States a blank check to enforce the nontransfer principle. The treaty went into effect on January 8, 1942, when Honduras — the fourteenth state — ratified it.

The elaborate Pan-American machinery was put to the acid test when Japan attacked Pearl Harbor on December 7, 1941, and Germany and Italy promptly joined her by declaring war on the United States. Pursuant to the Act of Havana, a conference of Foreign Ministers was convened at Rio de Janeiro on January 15, 1942, to consider common action against the aggressors.

Before the foreign ministers assembled, nine Latin-American republics had declared war on the Axis powers, and three others had severed diplomatic relations. As a result of the conference five more states chose the latter alternative. Only Argentina and Chile remained aloof, and even they paid lip service to resolutions for cooperation in hemispheric defense. This display of solidarity paved the way for the participation of most Latin-American republics in a nonshooting war against the Axis.

SUGGESTED READINGS

1. Feis, H., *The Diplomacy of the Dollar: First Era* (1919–32).
2. Pusey, M. J., *Charles Evans Hughes* (vol. 2).
3. Sprout, H. and M., *Toward a New Order of Sea Power.*

CHAPTER FIFTEEN

THE NATIONALIST REACTION

FROM PROGRESSIVISM TO REACTION

Just as World War I changed the relationship between America and the rest of the world, so it changed political feelings at home. The dominant prewar Progressive movement gave way to a Nationalist reaction that was drastically different in outlook and spirit from the reform crusade. In its most familiar aspect the reaction was a protest against the rapid changes in the material and social environment that had been accumulating since the 1890's. Evangelist Billy Sunday reflected the mood of the postwar movement when he said, "To hell with the twentieth century."

The triumph of the Nationalist reaction was the sequel to the disintegration of the Progressive crusade. We have already noted that the first phase of Progressivism (1900–1910) was dominated by a spirit of moderation. Leadership was authentically conservative in the sense that it sought to preserve traditional ideals and institutions without stifling the new socio-economic forces seeking expression. We also saw that, although opponents became more numerous after 1910, the popularity of the Progressive label protected the movement from open attack. Radical critics who served as spokesmen for various pressure groups changed the character of the reform program by redefining its credo from the inside. It was impossible for reactionaries to employ the same technique because they had no confidence in moderation. They did not believe that a workable balance between the new environment and the old institutions could be effected, nor did they share the Progressive faith in the outcome of a moral crusade. Instead, they expected the forces that were producing change to become more aggressive and proposed to destroy them. In short, the reactionaries cherished the impossible goal of restoring *in toto* nineteenth-century institutions.

The reactionaries dared not express such views during the optimistic prewar period when a vast majority believed that Progressive goals were attainable. However, the war created an atmosphere more suitable to their purposes. It bred an intolerant spirit alien to Progressivism and aggravated all the evils that reformers had tried to eradicate by a moral crusade. Big corporations grew bigger. Class tensions multiplied as the unions organized war workers. Animosities between immigrant groups, Negroes, and native whites flourished in overcrowded cities. The fast pace of urban expansion strained traditional moral practices as well as recreational habits. Army life upset conventional behavior patterns. In the process, the central government steadily extended its regulatory functions.

The post-Armistice impact of these changes upon the country was all the more devastating because people had been preoccupied with the war and ignored them. Progressive leadership was discredited. The moderates could not cope with the angry spirit of the public, and the radicals became objects of suspicion as the fear of Bolshevism spread. Some of the radicals were to go off the deep end and embrace Marxism. The rest were to seem dull by comparison and to lose their following because prosperity took the edge off discontent. The only splinter of the radical group that subsequently attracted attention was a small but articulate band of rebels who ignored economic problems but denounced the artistic, ethical, and moral values of American society. Their activity will be considered in the next chapter.

The simultaneous collapse of leadership in both wings of Progressivism left an irresolute rank and file to drift into the control of the hitherto ineffective reactionaries. It has sometimes been said that the reactionaries sought to turn back the clock. This statement is not true in a literal sense because few of them desired a restoration of the simple agrarian life of their forefathers. What they really wanted was to enjoy the material benefits of industrial society without suffering the inconveniences of labor unions, mass immigration, dilution of Anglo-Saxon culture, and other by-products of technological change. Hence the reactionaries regarded the unskilled worker, the radical, the immigrant, the Catholic, and the Jew with undisguised hostility, and intended to enforce the compliance of these groups with an arbitrary definition of Americanism.

Inasmuch as the Federal Constitution and the Bill of Rights precluded uniform legislation about political, religious, and moral beliefs, the program of the Nationalist reaction had to be carried out primarily through private organizations like the Anti-Saloon League, the Daughters of the American Revolution, and the Ku Klux Klan. Methods varied according to the taste of the individual organization, ranging all the way from dignified propaganda campaigns to outright violence.

The spirit of the Nationalist reaction dominated the Democratic and Republican parties during the 1920's, just as the spirit of the Progressive movement had dominated the political life a generation earlier. The only challenge to the reaction was delivered in 1924 when Senator La Follette made an unsuccessful effort to reconstitute the old prewar Progressive coalition as a third party. The quality of leadership in the Nationalist reaction was not brilliant by most standards, but it did not need to be because it was so plentiful: the rural preacher condemning urban vice; the industrialist

The outcast in the Bryan zoo. (The Chicago Tribune, *1925.*)

fighting labor unions; the small-town politician and the Klan leader persecuting Negroes, Catholics, and immigrants. Scattered throughout the country, these people organized a mass movement for conformity. Warfare was conducted against three major groups: radicals, ethnic and racial minorities, and foes of nineteenth-century frontier Protestantism.

THE LEGISLATIVE DRIVE AGAINST BOLSHEVISM

One prong of the reaction aimed at the suppression of Bolshevism. It broadened out into a drive against all working-class movements. Reactionaries took this suspicious view of labor partly because Marxist theory singled it out as the vehicle of revolution, and partly because native labor groups, from the A.F. of L. to the I.W.W., had adopted a more militant tone after 1917.

As we shall see presently, the reactionaries tried to cope with the situation by curtailing free expression and breaking labor unions. Since every generation redefines the limits of liberty in terms of its own problems, the frontiers are being expanded or contracted at any given time. The reactionaries insisted on a sharp contraction because they believed that the ultimate objective of radical theorists or labor organizations was the subversion of the private property system. This conclusion erred on the side of severity. The alternative offered by liberals was not milder safeguards against radicalism, but no safeguards at all. Confronted with a choice of extremes, the average man joined the reactionaries because he thought the radicals threatened the existing structure of society.

The advocates of legislative curbs on revolutionary doctrine quickly tested the validity of this remedy. During the war Congress had made a beginning with the Espionage and Sedition Acts, but the restoration of peace destroyed the effectiveness of these measures. Simultaneously the Supreme Court restored the Bill of Rights as a barrier against federal legislation limiting free expression. In *Schenck* v. *U.S.* (1919), Justice Holmes vindicated the right of the individual to make statements with subversive implications provided such utterances did not create "a clear and present danger" of revolutionary violence.

The judicial veto of Congressional legislation which had set standards for exposing and punishing subversive utterances led reactionaries to exploit the possibilities of state laws. Some of the constitutional provisions restricting the federal government did not apply to the states. In *Barron* v. *Baltimore* (1833), the Supreme Court had handed down the opinion that the freedom of expression guaranteed in the First Amendment protected the individual only from arbitrary action by the federal government. This doctrine freed the states for legislation restricting individual liberties provided such laws did not conflict with Bills of Rights in their own constitutions. This power had not been used extensively until World War I when a number of states followed the lead of the federal government and passed Sedition Acts. Montana, which was a stronghold of the I.W.W., adopted a sweeping law to harass the unpatriotic. It established severe penalties for critical or abusive statements about the armed forces, the American flag, and the democratic form of government. To silence opponents of the war, Minnesota created a Public Safety Committee which soon became an instrument for persecuting the agrarian socialists of the Nonpartisan League.

Some of these restrictive state laws perished after the war, but often they were broadened to cover additional areas. In a number of instances the new legislation prohibited the advocacy of anarchy or Bolshevism and the display of red flags. A few states supplemented individual statutes with blanket criminal syndicalist laws forbidding the advocacy of sabotage to effect political changes or to transfer the ownership of industrial property. The reactionary Governor of Idaho, C. C. Moore, urged his legislature to define sabotage so that it would include "slowing down work on production." Right-wingers in the National Republican Club of New York wanted to go still further and adopt a law which would prohibit citizens from urging amendment of the state constitution or criticizing public officials.

SUPREME COURT DECISIONS ON FREE EXPRESSION

In the end the decisions of the Supreme Court rather than the self-restraint of the conservatives established the limits of statutory restrictions on free expression. Although the Court shifted position several times, it stood for a wider protection of civil rights than the majority of citizens did. The most important legal landmark of the decade was *Gitlow* v. *New York* (1925), a decision in which the Court overturned the century-old doctrine enunciated in *Barron* v. *Baltimore*. Justice Sanford wrote the majority opinion, contending that reasonable freedom of speech is part of the liberty which the Fourteenth Amendment prohibits the states from denying to the individual without due process of law. In effect, the decision forced state laws to meet the standards of free expression established in the federal Bill of Rights. The Court reiterated its new position in *Fiske* v. *Kansas* (1927), and four years later voided the red flag law of California (*Stromberg* v. *California*).

The trend of Supreme Court decisions did not halt the reactionary effort to stifle expression of radical opinions but deflected it into private channels. Numerous organizations came forward to make such expression an unpleasant experience even if it could not be made an illegal one. The Daughters of the American Revolution conducted a systematic educational and propaganda campaign against what it regarded as Bolshevism. Local authorities were encouraged to ban sales of subversive literature, and public school boards were urged to dismiss teachers with radical views. The D.A.R. also published an index of books which it regarded as unsuitable for the public. These efforts were supplemented by a flood of D.A.R. pamphlets. One called *The Common Enemy* described Bolshevism as a "world revolutionary movement which proposes to destroy civilization and Christianity." More obscure organizations like the Industrial Defense Association charged the Civil Liberties Union with sponsoring Communism, pacifism, and free love. Often the groups under attack did harbor subversives in their midst; often, too, the objectives of these subversives were correctly stated by patriotic organizations. Unfortunately, the guns of reactionaries frequently fired on the innocent as well as the guilty, making opponents of people whose chief crime was to question the imminence of the Communist menace or the appropriateness of the methods employed for dealing with it.

WARFARE ON LABOR UNIONS

The drive against labor unions proved to be a campaign where the popular fear of subversives and the economic interest of employers intersected. During the war the combination of a short labor supply and government policy had strengthened the hand of the unions. As the prospects of the unions improved, their aggressiveness increased. Since the Russian revolution had already publicized one possible goal of worker militance, many people viewed the growth of unions and the nationwide reconversion strikes in 1919 with genuine dismay. Employers often shared this attitude on exactly the same grounds, but they had other reasons also. With sound instinct they saw that the recognition of unions would be the prelude to demands for higher wages and better working conditions. The focusing of so many anxieties on the labor movement guaranteed a fierce campaign of union-busting. It also assumed public acquiescence in the use of spies, goon squads, state troops, and injunctions as legitimate methods for breaking organizations allegedly infiltrated by Bolshevism.

Postwar economic conditions tipped the scales still more decisively against labor. In the first place, the unions had never gotten a toe hold in the mass industries but only in war plants that were quickly shut after the Armistice. Second, the A.F. of L., which had spearheaded the organizational drives during the war, feared the unskilled worker almost as much as the employer and clung to a craft-union philosophy. Finally, the economic dislocations and unemployment accompanying reconversion created a large pool of potential strikebreakers.

The collapse of the steel strike in 1919 was the signal for a concerted drive to break unions and establish what was called "the open shop." In January 1921, representatives from twenty-two manufacturing associations met in Chicago to coordinate strategy on a nationwide basis. Calling their program the "American Plan," they solicited the cooperation of local trade associations and chambers of commerce. The results were nothing short of spectacular. Within two years the A.F. of L. had been dislodged from the building trades in San Francisco and reduced to helplessness in Chicago; the International Seaman's Union had lost two-thirds of its membership after a disastrous shipping strike; and the Railroad Brotherhoods had suffered a severe setback when Attorney General H. M. Daugherty secured an injunction forcing them to end a walkout on management's terms. Of the five million union members in 1920, only three and a half million still maintained their affiliation at the end of 1923.

Organized labor reacted bitterly to the open-shop drive that deprived workers of their bargaining power. Mr. Dooley expressed its sentiment accurately in his famous description of the open shop: "Sure 'tis where they kape the doors open to accommodate th' constant stream av' min comin' in t' take jobs cheaper than th' min what has th' jobs."

The Supreme Court, which took an increasingly strong stand on behalf of free expression during the 1920's, did not broaden the application of the principle to cover labor disputes. In the crucial case of *Truax* v. *Corrigan* (1921) it upheld the right of the courts to issue injunctions, although both federal and state courts often granted such sweeping "cease and desist" orders as to deny workers the privilege of expressing their viewpoints. In fact, Daugherty secured an injunction during the rail strike of 1922 so comprehensive that a striker was taken into custody for "deriding" a strikebreaker. Even opponents of labor unions admitted that the literal enforcement of the order would confine every striker to a life of "silent meditation and prayer."

The potency of the injunction as a weapon for employers was also displayed in upholding the "yellow dog" contracts which bound workers not to join labor unions during their term of employment. The existence of such agreements was accepted by the courts as valid grounds for enjoining all efforts by organizers to recruit union members. Coupled with Supreme Court decisions limiting the right of workers to picket and impairing the benefits conferred on unions by the Clayton Act, the injunction put labor at a serious disadvantage.

If the policy of the government during the war had conferred advantages on labor which it could not have secured by collective bargaining alone, the postwar reaction tilted the balance far in the other direction. All the legal disabilities against which the unions had fought during the Progressive era were restored by judicial decision in the 1920's. The Communists helped to make this development palatable in quarters previously sympathetic to labor by energetically infiltrating unions. They seldom won control of worker organizations, but their activity provided a plausible justification for the general antiunion campaign of the conservatives.

The A.F. of L., despite a consistent hostility toward all brands of radicalism, was the chief sufferer. Annual conventions repeatedly sidetracked inflammatory resolutions and just as often opposed the recognition of Soviet Russia by the United States government. Official A.F. of L. publications reflected an unqualified attachment to the private enterprise system. Proposals for the amalgamation of unions or for the chartering of mass industrial unions, which would have dismayed employers, were rejected as dangerous threats to the craft structure. The A.F. of L. also reacted vigorously against Communist tactics of infiltration sponsored by William Z. Foster, who openly joined the Communist party after the failure of the steel strike. The charters of local unions captured by the Communists were summarily revoked, and officials sympathetic to Foster were ousted from their jobs. However, the cost of stopping infiltration altogether was prohibitive since it would have involved such drastic modifications in membership qualifications as to change the A.F. of L. from a union movement to a group of secret fraternal orders.

Despite the vulnerability of unions to infiltration, the Communists attracted few supporters in the working class. They employed an unfamiliar terminology and wasted their energy in the pursuit of distant, abstract objectives. The noisy doctrinaire disputes over tactics and the ceaseless search for revolutionary situations gave an air of unreality to their activities. Rank-and-file American Communists of the 1920's were drawn from disillusioned intellectuals, unsuccessful artists, and bored college students rather than from the exploited workers for whom the *agents provocateurs* pretended to be speaking.

The popular view of the A.F. of L. as a Trojan horse which would disgorge its band of revolutionaries at the crucial moment ignored the more immediate menace of underworld efforts to control craft unions. Gangsters sought and in some cases achieved control of locals as a part of their program to monopolize key commodities and extort high prices from the public. The successful organization of all phases of the milk business by gangster Larry Fey set a pattern which threatened the integrity of several A.F. of L. unions.

Although fear of organized labor persisted throughout the decade, employers dealt more magnanimously with workers after their victory in the open-shop drive. Some of the grievances which had provoked post-Armistice strikes were adjusted voluntarily. The United States Steel Corporation, under considerable pressure from public opinion, eliminated the twelve-hour day in 1923, and a number of smaller firms followed suit. Many businesses set up company unions for the dual purpose of considering employee grievances and enlisting cooperation in cost reduction programs. The company union was seldom allowed to discuss or bargain about wages and hours on a plant-wide basis, but it did provide employees with a medium for ventilating individual complaints about working conditions and made them more receptive to management plans for achieving greater operational efficiency. The company union became so popular with employers that over four hundred corporations had adopted the device by 1926. Industrial relations also improved slowly in plants where the A.F. of L. still retained a foothold. Fearful of being supplanted by company unions, Gompers swung the A.F. of L. behind the policy of cooperating with management in cutting costs.

The revival of good feeling in the middle 1920's was stimulated by high employment and modest wage increases. Some members of top management tried to assume the role of industrial statesmen. President Mitten of the Philadelphia Rapid Transit Company received considerable publicity for his proposal to tie wages to the cost of a market basket, although he prudently refrained from listing the items on which his calculations were based. Owen D. Young of General Electric told a National Industrial Conference Board that business had already implemented the policy of paying labor a living wage and was moving toward the payment of a cultural wage. Optimistically he forecast a gradual improvement in working conditions which would provide labor with the money and leisure to enjoy recreational opportunities hitherto limited to the wealthy. The businessmen committed to showering blessings on the workers who did not strike, join labor unions, or espouse radical economic doctrines, spoke only for the industries participating in the boom of the decade. In those sectors of the economy which did not recover from the postwar slump, the industrial turmoil so alarming to reactionaries continued all through the period.

Unrest in the coal fields of the Pennsylvania–West Virginia–Ohio triangle was chronic. The industry suffered from overproduction, cutthroat competition, and a labor surplus. The abundance of coal and the existence of innumerable marginal mines had made the cost of monopolizing the industry prohibitive. Hence price fluctuations were wide and employment opportunities erratic. Union miners fought for their jobs against operators who practically owned the squalid coal towns and ran them like feudal fiefs. The basic problems of the industry were aggravated by the increasing use of natural gas, oil, and falling water as substitutes for coal in the generation of industrial power. Simultaneously, the introduction of new types of equipment such as the conveyor, the electric drill, and the loading machine produced technological unemployment. These developments reduced the average number of working days a year for coal miners from 226 days in 1890 to 195 days in 1925. The contraction of the work week did not spread the employment sufficiently to cover all the miners who wanted jobs. The problem was further aggravated by the fact that the unemployed miner had no way of improving his economic status. He lacked both the financial resources to give him mobility and the education or skill to seize new employment opportunities. Industry was reluctant to hire middle-aged laborers in general and unemployed coal miners in particular.

The combination of falling production, falling wages, and rising unemployment made for industrial chaos. John L. Lewis, the president of the United Mine Workers, believed that the salvation of the miners lay in an industrial union, while the coal operators were flatly opposed to such an organization. The incompatibility of their objectives led to the fiercest kind of industrial warfare. The United Mine Workers repeatedly struck for higher wages, better working conditions, and union recognition. The normal financial hardships of a walkout did not apply to miners as much as to other industrial workers, because their standard of living was so miserable that they had little to lose. With prospects of working only three-fifths of a year, they did not care much whether idle time was called a layoff or a strike. The operators usually retaliated against walkouts by recruiting scabs and strikebreakers from the great pool of the unemployed.

These tactics produced flareups of violence and bloodshed throughout the twenties. Turmoil occurred first in the bituminous fields of West Virginia between the Big Sandy and Kanawha rivers. Particularly in Boone, Logan, and Mingo counties, the home of feuding mountaineer families like the Hatfields and the McCoys, union miners fought a series of bloody battles in 1921 with detectives and scabs. Eventually Harding called in troops to establish an uneasy military peace.

The following year fresh violence erupted in the pits of southern Illinois when the operators tried to break a strike by importing scabs from Chicago. On June 21, 1922, the miners retaliated by storming a stockade where the strikebreakers were protected by company detectives and private police. Three men lost their lives in the battle before the strikebreakers surrendered the stockade. Nineteen more of the nonunion men perished at the hands of a bloodthirsty mob as they were marching from the stockade to Herrin, Illinois. The authorities indicted many local citizens, but the juries refused to convict. The *New York World* said of the incident that "bituminous mining in the United States hardly deserves the name of a business. It is chaos and a bloody one."

Although over 50 per cent of those digging coal were unorganized, the United Mine Workers sought to avoid a wage deduction by calling a strike on April 1, 1927. Reduced demand for coal and severe price wars had forced the miners to absorb several pay cuts during the middle 1920's. Seeking to preserve a basic wage of $7.50 a day, they now hung on until October 1 when the operators finally capitulated. The relatively peaceful character of this strike did not prevent violence elsewhere. In the Colorado coal fields, for instance, a wildcat strike called by the I.W.W. led to several scuffles between miners and law enforcement authorities; these encounters reached a dreadful climax when state troopers fired into a crowd, killing six and wounding twenty.

Each outbreak of bloodshed in the coal fields led to congressional investigations and official reports recommending some sort of federal regulation to stabilize an industry which could not solve its own economic problems. Congress, however, took no action, and economic warfare continued to smolder, repeatedly provoking solemn warnings as to the dangerous radicalism of American workers.

The textile industry likewise suffered from deteriorating economic prospects which drove management to wage cuts and labor to retaliatory strikes. The northern mills were hit particularly hard by competition from southern firms with lower labor costs. Mill workers in New Hampshire and Rhode Island went on strike in the spring of 1922 after being asked to accept a pay reduction of 20 per cent on top of a 22½ per cent cut the preceding year.

Although reviving prosperity reduced the friction for several years, the industry could not lower operating expenses enough to arrest the growing public demand for silk and other foreign goods. Repeated efforts to cut wage costs provoked a grim strike in the woolen mills of Passaic, New Jersey, which started January 21, 1927, and lasted for nearly fourteen months. The economic issues were quickly overshadowed by violent clashes between strikers and police and by the activity of Communists who had taken the initiative in launching the strike. Since the public outcry against the Communists jeopardized the prospects of the workers, a switch in leadership was effected from the Communists to the conservative United Textile Workers Union. The workers eventually settled on management's terms.

During the next two years, dissatisfaction spread southward in a spontaneous rash of strikes from Elizabethtown, Tennessee, to Thompson, Georgia. The principal causes of discontent were a series of wage slashes coupled with the introduction of an efficiency system which workers called "the stretchout." Operators who had tended forty-eight looms and made $19.00 a week before the stretchout, got as little as $17.70 for tending ninety looms under the new system. The strikes at Elizabethtown, and at Gastonia, North Carolina, were particularly bloody. Local mobs, who resented outside organizers, complicated the normal pattern of industrial warfare by hacking down the shacks which served as headquarters for the National Textile Workers' Union and the Workers' International Relief. Since the latter was a Communist organization, employers and local authorities felt justified in using extreme measures. They won such a complete victory that subsequent attempts to organize southern workers failed miserably.

THE SACCO-VANZETTI CASE

The ruthless suppression of strikes by employers and local police authorities did not go unchallenged. The Civil Liberties Union as well as less conspicuous organizations raised their voices in protest against the frequent encroachments upon civil rights during industrial disputes and against the persecution of individuals for their political or economic views. Usually the violations of free expression and legal justice were not sufficiently clear-cut to warrant a trial of strength between the defenders of unlimited civil liberties and the foes of radicalism. One incident, however, the Sacco-Vanzetti case, exposed so nakedly the temper and outlook of reactionaries that it was used to dramatize the menacing potentialities of the postwar movement. For nearly seven years the liberals fought what they regarded as a flagrant miscarriage of justice until the controversy, like the Dreyfus affair, became a symbol of differing philosophical outlooks.

The protagonists were a pair of obscure workmen, Nicola Sacco and Bartolomeo Vanzetti, who had been arrested in 1920 and accused of holding up and murdering the paymaster of a shoe factory in South Braintree, Massachusetts. The trial took place the following year, and both men were found guilty and sentenced to death. The defense attorneys fought for five years to secure a new trial on the ground that the first one had been unfair.

Sacco and Vanzetti embodied all the qualities that arch-conservatives feared and wanted to destroy at whatever cost. They were anarchists and had participated in strikes some years earlier. They were also products of the new immigration, with a cultural and social background different from that of native Americans. They had even fled to Mexico during World War I to avoid conscription. None of these facts had the slightest thing to do with the question of whether they had murdered the paymaster. But the presiding judge, Webster Thayer, helped to assure conviction by permitting — and in some instances encouraging — the admission of such evidence.

When Thayer refused all motions for a new trial and was sustained by the state Supreme Court, his critics applied to Governor Alvin T. Fuller for a commutation of the sentence. Prominent citizens, ranging from literary figures like Edna St. Vincent Millay and John Dos Passos to lawyers like Arthur Garfield Hayes and Dudley Field Malone, interceded on behalf of the accused. Professor Felix Frankfurter of the Harvard Law School even wrote a book summarizing all the evidences of unfairness in the trial. Governor Fuller responded to the pressure by appointing a panel of experts under the direction of President A. Lawrence Lowell of Harvard to study the case. Acting on the basis of their recommendation as well as his own review of the trial, Fuller refused to interfere. Sacco and Vanzetti were sent to the electric chair on August 23, 1927.

The very fact that the controversy had lasted seven years and received world-wide publicity guaranteed an explosive reaction. Outside the United States there was an almost unanimous feeling that Sacco and Vanzetti had been executed for their political views. In many countries the protest took the form of hostile demonstrations in front of American embassies and short-lived boycotts of American goods. At home the defenders of civil liberty loudly denied that the evidence warranted a verdict of guilty. They upbraided the Massachusetts authorities for committing what they regarded as judicial murder. For the most part, the self-appointed champions of Sacco and Vanzetti were artists, journalists, lawyers, and members of other groups whose professional work might be hampered by restrictions on free expression. In other quarters, however, the decision of the court received greater support. Those who wanted to restore part or all of the old America did not really object to trying Sacco and Vanzetti for their unorthodox viewpoints. On this occasion the partisans of tolerance and fair play suffered defeat. On the other hand, they defended Sacco and Vanzetti well enough to discourage the reactionaries from further contracting the frontier of free expression. The episode had distinct educational overtones, because thereafter the pendulum began to swing slowly in the other direction.

RESTRICTION OF IMMIGRATION

Generally speaking, the postwar drive against immigrants paralleled and supplemented the drive against radicals. Several organizations simultaneously pursued both objectives. As we have already seen, the one group considered the emergence of radicalism to be the primary problem. They were less concerned about who entered the United States than about what the immigrants believed after they arrived. By contrast, the second group thought that the incidence of radical thought was highest among immigrants and assumed that the exclusion of non-Anglo-Saxon ethnic groups would cut off subversive doctrine at its source.

Whether or not such a high correlation existed between the new immigration and the spread of political heresy as the nationalists supposed, their outlook reflected growing public concern over the problem of assimilating nationalities from southern Europe. The prewar immigration rate of a million a year had dwindled to a handful upon the outbreak of hostilities, but after the Armistice, the volume rose sharply. As in the preceding decade, most of the immigrants came from the Latin and Slavic countries of Europe. Opinion differed as to the success of earlier attempts at assimilation, but the "Red scare" and other turmoils of reconversion created sentiment for restricting immigration. Only a few clung to the nineteenth-century view that the United States could continue to permit unlimited immigration without jeopardizing the dominant position of Anglo-Saxon culture. They asserted either that assimilation would proceed rapidly in the future because it had done so in the past, or that native institutions were strong enough to force conformity on all immigrants. The first argument ignored the character of the old immigration from northern Europe. Absorption of such groups had been relatively easy since their customs and values so closely resembled those of Americans; southern Europeans diverged from our tradition at so many vital points that predictions about their impact on American society could not be safely made. The second argument was also open to question. Native institutions had been under attack for over a generation and were undergoing changes at some vital points; the most likely tentative conclusion seemed to be that they would be subject to modification themselves rather than that they would firmly grind into immigrants a uniform regard for Anglo-Saxon culture. The Nationalists probably overestimated the threat of the immigrants to American institutions just as the conservatives overestimated the threat of the radicals. But those who charged the Nationalists with destroying the dream of America as a land of opportunity usually overlooked the fact that assimilation was a greater problem than ever before.

The history of immigration legislation in the 1920's was a dreary chronicle of trial and error. During the war and the reconversion period, Congress had established a literacy test and provided for the exclusion or expulsion of alien radicals. Alarmed by reports that millions of Europeans sought to flee a devastated continent and establish a new home in America, the House in December 1920 had passed an emergency bill virtually cutting off immigration. A milder Senate version was sent to the White House two weeks before the lame-duck Congress adjourned on March 4, 1921, but Wilson killed it with a veto.

The new Republican Congress, which Harding called into special session in April 1921, promptly passed the Senate bill almost unchanged. Signed by Harding on May 19, 1921, the so-called Emergency Quota Act limited the admission of aliens to 3 per cent of the foreign-born belonging to each nationality group as determined by the census of 1910. In addition, the new law provided that not more than 20 per cent of the annual quota would be allowed to enter in any one month.

The Emergency Quota Act succeeded well enough in fulfilling its primary purpose, which was to reduce immigration. During the first year of its operation 309,556 entered as opposed to 805,228 the preceding year. The measure was not successful, however, in modifying the character of immigration. Slightly less than half of those entitled to enter under the quota for the "old immigration" areas of northeastern Europe took advantage of the opportunity; whereas 95 per cent of the allotment for the countries of southern Europe was promptly filled. Thus the majority of immigrants continued to be recruited from ethnic groups which American Nationalists regarded as less desirable than the older elements from northern Europe.

The Johnson Immigration Act, passed by Congress in May of 1924 to replace the Emergency Quota Act, discriminated pointedly against individuals from southern Europe. The 1890 census was substituted for the 1910 census in computing quotas because the representatives of the new immigration formed such a small part of the total population in the earlier year. Their prospects of becoming American citizens were further impaired by a reduction of the annual quota percentage from 3 to 2. As a result of these provisions only 15 per cent of the total allotment was assigned to the new immigration.

Nationalistic zeal also protruded in a clause which denied entry to those who could not become naturalized citizens. Since naturalization laws applied only to whites, the clause aimed an insulting blow at the Japanese. It excluded them when their quota would have permitted only 146 per year. By so doing Congress broke the informal Gentlemen's Agreement of 1908 in which the Emperor of Japan had pledged himself to prohibit his subjects from emigrating provided the United States government did not specifically exclude them. President Coolidge and the State Department opposed the inclusion of such a provision in the immigration law, and Japanese Ambassador Hanihara delivered a sharp protest to the American government, but Congress had its way.

Several provisions of the Emergency Quota Act which had created special hardships for immigrants were eliminated. Henceforth primary selection took place at the port of embarkation rather than at stations in the United States. The 20 per cent monthly quota system which sometimes compelled immigrants to return home if the quota for that month had already been filled was mercifully discontinued. Countries of the Western Hemisphere received a specific exemption from the provisions of the quota system. Finally, the Johnson Act established a new basis for computing the quota after July 1, 1927. Only 150,000 immigrants a year would be permitted. Each country would be entitled to a percentage of the total arrived at by computing the exact ratio of its nationals to the whole population in 1920. Each nationality, however, was assured a minimum quota of 100.

It proved difficult to give practical effect to the so-called "national origins" provision of the Johnson Act. The statistical data on the ethnic composition of the population in 1920 was so inaccessible and unreliable that until 1930 government statisticians could not work out the percentages necessary for implementing the new quota. This fresh departure in policy had little chance to bear fruit because the world depression sharply reduced the number of Europeans seeking entrance. Nevertheless, President Hoover took the precaution of lowering the annual quota from 150,000 to 48,500 in 1931 so that immigrants would not compete with the native-born for a shrinking supply of jobs. Simultaneously he suspended the immigration of Mexicans, who were exempt from the quota system and had moved freely into the United States as migratory workers.

The majorities for successive bills restricting immigration were drawn from as temporary and incompatible a coalition as were the opposing minorities. Nationalists and organized labor teamed up on this particular issue to defeat a hitherto unbeatable combination of industrialists, who wanted cheap labor, and idealists, who wanted unlimited immigration. On most domestic questions nationalists and workers took opposing stands.

The intolerant and coercive element in the Nationalist reaction did not operate as conspicuously in the drive to limit immigration as it did in the drive to assimilate non-Anglo-Saxon groups which had already arrived. Social Darwinism of one type or another was usually relied upon to justify harsh treatment of minorities. It often reached the man in the street in the form of an assertion that the struggle for survival in the animal world had its counterpart in the struggle between the Anglo-Saxon and other races for planetary domination. The attractiveness of this loose, unscientific analogy was due to its simplicity.

A more plausible version of racism was the eugenics movement. It popularized the idea that most important human traits were hereditary and transmitted to successive generations. The pioneer study of the Jukes, an illiterate, underprivileged family, published by Richard Dugdale in 1877, provided documentary basis for the theory that disease, pauperism, and immorality were inherited. A similar study of the Kallikaks by Henry Goddard put forward the hypothesis that feeble-mindedness bred prostitution, crime, and drunkenness.

The conclusion usually drawn from these data was that steps should be taken to weed out defective hereditary strains. The colleges and the medical profession, which were giving increased attention to the study of psychology and mental disease, did much to popularize this viewpoint. States responded by passing laws for the sterilization of the feeble-minded. Indiana started in 1907 and eleven other states joined her by 1915. A Eugenics Record Office was founded in 1910 to propagandize for legislation, and four years later a National Conference on Race Betterment was held. Shortly after the war the Supreme Court sustained the constitutionality of state sterilization laws. In *Buck* v. *Ball,* Justice Holmes upheld the Virginia law under which a woman with a record of feeble-mindedness in her family was sterilized. Speaking for the majority, he tartly observed, "three generations of imbeciles are enough."

The fact that feeble-mindedness seemed to be inherited did not warrant the extension of the theory to other mental characteristics or to physical and ethnic ones. Nevertheless, popular ideas of heredity and of biological evolution became the foundation for unsound books on race that provided the Nationalists with ammunition for their various schemes. *The Rising Tide of Color* by Lothrop Stoddard and *The Passing of the Great Race* by Madison Grant viewed with alarm the fertility of inferior dark-skinned races as compared to the falling birth rate of the masterful whites. Both regarded the multiplication of these lesser peoples as the most momentous development of the new century. W. C. Abbott in *The New Barbarians* (1925) complained about the assault upon American traditions by the hordes of immigrants from southeastern Europe. To check this threat to institutional integrity, he proposed special privileges for the Anglo-Saxon aristocracy that would protect it from the rootless masses.

H. W. Walter took a leaf out of Plato's *Republic* as well as the modern eugenics movement in a book called *Genetics* which advocated state control of human reproduction to improve the race. Dr. William McDougall, Chairman of the Psychology Department of Harvard University, proposed a caste society based on literacy tests. In *Ethics and Some Modern World Problems* he proposed that intermarriage between the two major castes be prohibited. However, his system made allowance for human variability to the extent of creating an intermediate caste for marginal individuals until their status was clarified.

What all these theories possessed in common was a fear that some minority — either the feeble-minded or the illiterate or the ethnically and racially inferior — would become a majority and destroy what currently passed for Anglo-Saxon culture. Antidemocratic in the extreme, these critics of existing institutions wanted to protect a white, Anglo-Saxon aristocracy from infiltration by Americans with a different ethos or culture pattern. To achieve this objective they were willing to endorse schemes that would even destroy equality before the law.

The area in which the public activity of the various Nationalist groups intersected most frequently was education. A beginning had been made during World War I to control education in the public school by means of various state laws which prohibited the teaching of the German language. After the Armistice the drive was conducted on a broader front. Patriotic organizations harassed state legislatures for laws that would prohibit the adoption of textbooks even mildly critical of American history or its makers. The statute passed by Wisconsin was a model in this respect. It specifically forbade the adoption of texts which falsified the facts regarding the War of Independence, defamed the nation's founders, or contained propaganda unfavorable to American government.

Public interest in the battle for antiseptic textbooks was kept at fever pitch by exploiting latent anti-British sentiment. Charles G. Miller, who had originally been appointed by Mayor F. Hylan of New York to investigate textbooks in the city schools, sounded the keynote in a famous magazine article. Published in 1921 and widely reproduced by various patriotic organizations, it charged that there was an organized conspiracy of textbook writers to create pro-British sentiment.

The American Legion promptly sponsored a program to write an acceptable seventh-grade text in United States history. The Knights of Columbus offered prizes to encourage the revision and rewriting of books so that they were less pro-British. The D.A.R. put on its "hate list" several books which examined the Revolutionary period critically. Scholarly works particularly singled out for attack were *The Life of George Washington* by Rupert Hughes and *The American Revolution* by Van Tyne. The former aroused the D.A.R. because it emphasized some of the unattractive qualities of Washington, and the latter because it contained statistics indicating that many colonial Americans had not favored the Revolution.

The campaign was effective with politicians looking for sure-fire issues. Mayor William Hale Thompson won a third term as Mayor of Chicago in 1927 when he not only denounced the Superintendent of Schools appointed by his predecessor as "a stool pigeon of King George," but promised the voters to make the English monarch "keep his snoot out of America." Mayor Thompson was backed by the *Chicago Tribune,* which denounced the Rhodes scholarships as an academic espionage system aimed at converting gullible American students into British spies. Outside of Chicago the political exploitation of the textbook issue was less spectacular, but in many areas it created a public demand for laudatory treatment of American history irrespective of facts.

THE KU KLUX KLAN

The educational and propagandistic campaigns organized by various nationalistic groups sometimes involved coercion and violence. The most spectacular exponent of the latter tactic was the Ku Klux Klan. The avowed purpose of the organization was to defend the whole cluster of values which it believed to be in jeopardy: Anglo-Saxon racial integrity, American culture, Protestantism, and traditional morality.

Founded on Thanksgiving night, 1915, by Colonel William J. Simmons and thirty friends who gathered under a fiery cross atop Stone Mountain near Atlanta, Georgia, the Klan copied the name, ritual, and practices of a defunct organization of the Reconstruction period. Like the earlier Klan, it concealed the identity of members, held secret meetings, and wore sheets at night to frighten Negroes. Ceremonials featured imposing uniforms, secret language, passwords starting with the letter "K," and grand hailing signs of distress. The impressiveness of ritualistic activities was heightened by the emphasis placed on rank in the organization. The Imperial Wizard presided over the "Invisible Empire." Immediately beneath him were Grand Goblins, who headed large territorial and administrative districts known as Dominions. They in turn supervised King Kleagles who were in charge of Realms. The rank-and-file Klansman belonged to a Realm and bore the dignified title of Kleagle.

The appeal of such an organization would have been small in a society which permitted titles of nobility or utilized the Army as a vehicle for the display of rank consciousness. It fascinated the average American who detested the Army, lacked the wealth to join an exclusive club, but wanted recognition and social prestige. The slightly furtive conspiratorial atmosphere surrounding the organization, the high-sounding ideals for which it professed to stand, and the exaggerated emphasis on hierarchy, were its strong drawing cards. As H. L. Mencken acidly said, "The Klan is as absolutely American as chewing gum, crooked district attorneys, or Chautauquas."

During the first years of its existence, the Ku Klux Klan attracted no more than four or five thousand members, but between 1920 and 1925 it enjoyed a phenomenal growth. Over four million belonged to it at its peak. Besides, its leaders exercised such great influence that it could make or break public officials in several states. During the middle 1920's the Klan dominated the governments of Oregon, Oklahoma, Texas, Arkansas, Indiana, Ohio, and California. Where it did not dominate, it often held the balance of power.

The sudden enlargement of membership was due partly to its appeal as a defender of 100 per cent Americanism and partly to the effective promotional activities of Edward Clarke and Mrs. Elizabeth Taylor. They helped to organize the incentive scheme of recruitment whereby thousands of local Kleagles were allowed to retain four dollars of the ten-dollar initiation fee for rounding up new members. The prospect of such a generous reward converted many Klansmen into supersalesmen. Higher ranks also received a share of initiation fees. One dollar went to the King Kleagle of the Realm, fifty cents to the Grand Goblin of the Dominion, and the remainder to the Imperial Wizard, who used it to finance the many activities of the Klan.

Despite the fact that all Klansmen were presumably bound together by a common set of principles, regional organizations emphasized different problems. Generally speaking those in the North and East tried to arouse the native-born against immigrants with different manners, recreational practices, and religions. Jews and Catholics were usually singled out as special objects of resentment. In the deep South, the Klan stirred up the smoldering antagonism of whites toward Negroes. Activity in rural areas was often focused on individuals who violated the conventional moral code or outsiders who sought to organize labor unions.

Klan methods of enforcing principles also varied. In some localities Kleagles were content to parade, burn crosses, and hold mysterious meetings. In others they sought to create a godly American society by sending threatening messages to bootleggers, prostitutes, radicals, and immigrants whose conduct did not reflect a recognition of their alleged inferiority. If warnings did not suffice, Klansmen often organized boycotts against the businesses of Catholics, Jews, or critical native-born citizens, and campaigns against schoolteachers and ministers who expressed unorthodox opinions.

The line between such activity and violence was a thin one which many local Kleagles crossed, notwithstanding the steadfast denials of Klan officials. In Birmingham, Alabama, local members attempted to close down Chinese restaurants by intimidating patrons. Elsewhere the property of immigrants or Negroes was subjected to vandalism. Still more reprehensible were the nocturnal forays of Klansmen in uniform who flogged, mutilated, and occasionally killed their victims. Frequently such crimes went unpunished where the Klan controlled local law-enforcement officials. In fact, other villainous elements of the population sometimes averted investigation by scratching a "KKK" at the site of the crime.

The Klan pursued its mission so zealously that it stirred up many respectable citizens to a pitch of hysteria reminiscent of the war years. Many Americans were led to believe that Catholics menaced the United States because they owed a dual allegiance to State and Church. Rumors circulated regarding the imminent departure of the Pope from Rome. It was assumed that he would come to the United States. The threat seemed so real to inhabitants of North Manchester, Indiana, that on one occasion they met a particular train in order to repel His Holiness. Citizens of other communities soberly pointed to watermarks on United States currency which they identified as papal insignia. Some insisted that the Catholics were storing ammunition in cathedral vaults preparatory to taking over the country. On one occasion Senator Thomas J. Heflin of Alabama dramatically ordered the Senate galleries cleared because, he said, Catholics were trying to assassinate him. In such an atmosphere it was easy to justify restrictions on immigration from the Catholic areas of southeastern Europe, and the harassment of native Catholics.

The Klan's reign as arbiter of the community's ethnic and moral standards was shortened by revelations of questionable moral behavior on the part of conspicuous Klansmen. In 1922, the *New York World* exposed the fact that the crack organizers, Edward Clarke and Elizabeth Taylor, had been arrested at an underworld resort in Atlanta. The Klan successfully weathered the ensuing wave of moral indignation by dropping Imperial Wizard Simmons, who was closely identified with both Clarke and Taylor, and appointing a respectable Texas dentist named Hiram Evans in his place. Four years later a more serious scandal developed. The leading Klansman in Indiana, Daniel C. Stephenson, was arrested in connection with the suicide of Madge Oberholtzer, whom he had kidnapped. Despite the fact that he had established a clandestine dictatorship in Indiana, Stephenson was convicted for murder. He promptly retaliated against his disloyal henchmen by releasing documents which ultimately sent the governor and a number of other officials to jail for corruption.

The sensational events in Indiana, where Klan domination had been complete, undermined public confidence and started an exodus from the organization. Conscientious citizens and opportunists alike hastened to disassociate themselves from it. Those shocked by the low moral standards of its officials were the first to leave. Even an order by Imperial Wizard Evans banning the use of masks failed to restore respectability. The Klan made a final bid to regain lost prestige in the 1928 election by closely identifying itself with Hoover. In the process ugly religious and racial issues were injected into the campaign, but such maneuvers failed to check the Klan's disintegration.

The rapid eclipse of the Klan's fortunes was not followed by a mass rejection of the principles for which it stood. During World War I and the ensuing decade, the constant harassment of minority groups, under the guise of patriotism, left a permanent residue of popular antagonism toward diversity. If nationalistic agitation took a less blatant form thereafter, it was because most citizens had grown ashamed of Klan methods. In the early 1930's embryo Fascist groups like the Industrial Defense Association, the Silver Shirts, and the Vigilantes filled the vacuum left by the Klan. Never as influential or effective as their predecessor, they provided rallying points for extremists who wanted to carry on the Klan program.

CHALLENGES TO CHRISTIANITY

Energetic support for the Nationalist reaction also developed as a by-product of the controversy over Darwinism and the Social Gospel in the larger Protestant denominations. As we have already noted, some of the people who accepted evolutionary theory turned their backs on Christianity. One group professed to find the ultimate truth in the cold, impersonal operations of natural law. Humanism provided a haven for others who wanted to believe that the universe depended on a Deity but were unwilling to accept a religious view of a Supreme Being. The latter group came to be called the "New Humanists" in the 1920's because two eminent classical scholars, Paul Elmer More and Irving Babbitt, were hospitable to the idea of a God as an underwriter of ethical absolutes and natural law, but refused to think of Him as a personal Saviour. Presumably their God guaranteed harmony and a rational order in the universe but left men complete freedom to shape their own destinies. Aristocratic in tone, the New Humanism set high standards of conduct. It proposed the doctrine of restraint or the "inner check" as a rational guide to conduct.

The philosopher-scientist, Alfred North Whitehead, borrowed from both the Naturalists and the Humanists in formulating his complicated mathematical analysis about the nature and structural characteristics of substance. His three much admired but seldom read treatises, *Science in the Modern World* (1925), *Religion in the Making* (1926), and *Process and Reality* (1929), make a place for God as a master organizer and physicist. But like the God of the Humanists, Whitehead's God was needed as a source of order rather than a redeemer intimately concerned with the problems of men. The Pragmatist John Dewey all but crowded God out of the universe by describing Him as the sum total of forces and conditions that further the realization of social ideals. According to his definition, God was nothing more than process oriented toward secular goals.

MODERNIST AND FUNDAMENTALIST RESPONSES

The Humanists, Pragmatists, and others who repudiated Christianity as a logical result of their assumptions about the nature of the universe did not start the struggle within the churches. The real crisis was generated by those who sought to reconcile the claims of science and of Christianity by trying to join the comforting teachings of the Bible with scientific theories which seemed to contradict the Christian position. The intellectual activities of this group — known as the Modernists — provoked a violent backlash which became part of the conservative-nationalist reaction of the twenties.

Since most Modernists accepted the Social Gospel and were awed by the practical achievements of the natural sciences, they wanted to treat the pronouncements of biologists and geologists as literal truth. Doctrinal problems grew out of this aspiration because the scientists often advanced hypotheses in conflict with the literal interpretation of the Bible as the word of God. Matters did not improve when the scientists insisted that all mysterious phenomena, including the miracles recorded in the Bible, could be explained only on rational grounds.

The Modernists took refuge in an unstable compromise by asserting that the Bible was symbolically rather than literally true. As Harry Emerson Fosdick, the distinguished Modernist theologian, put it, the Bible was inspired, not infallible. It offered general guidance rather than a comprehensive religious philosophy. Fosdick expressed doubt that the biblical authors foresaw, or should have been expected to foresee, the problems raised by evolutionary theory or machine-age technology. Whatever the commonsense merit of this view, it clouded the role of the Bible as revelation of Divine Will. If the supernatural elements of the Scriptures were invalid, then the greatest miracle of all — the saving work of Christ — would be reduced to nominal importance. Most Modernists willingly accepted the view that Christ was a moral example rather than a Saviour and hailed this revision as a much-needed refinement of traditional Christian dogma. In the same spirit they faced the fact that acceptance of Darwinian evolution involved the corollary proposition that man rose from a low estate rather than fell from grace, as the Bible taught. Optimism about the outcome of evolutionary processes led them to transfer the Kingdom of God from heaven to earth and to substitute secular ends for spiritual ones.

The Modernists did not become influential in the Catholic and Lutheran groups where doctrinal positions had been worked out with great clarity. A genuine cleavage developed, however, in the more populous Methodist and Baptist churches, which had always been tolerant of individual interpretations of Christian doctrine. The Baptists were especially vulnerable to controversy because the key position of the denomination was the refusal to make doctrinal conformity a test of membership.

Those most anxious to do battle with the Modernists were called Fundamentalists. Originally the name had been applied to Protestants who accepted the theological position expressed in *The Fundamentals,* twelve pamphlets financed and published (1909–12) by Lyman and Milton Stewart. In brief, *The Fundamentals* reaffirmed the positions abandoned explicitly or tacitly by the Modernists: (1) the authenticity and supernatural character of the Bible, (2) the indispensable role of Christ in salvation, and (3) the certainty of Christ's triumphant Second Coming.

Many who identified themselves with Fundamentalism were temperamentally conservative, disturbed by the rapid changes in their material environment, and prone to find relief from the complexities of life in the biblical message. Without knowing much about science, they regarded it as an enemy which was tempting their children from well-worn grooves of belief and conduct. Already the Fundamentalists had witnessed the infiltration of higher education by scientific subjects. Most denominational colleges had already capitulated, and science threatened to invade the churches themselves, eroding away faith in supernatural power, revelation, and biblical cosmology. Convinced that the crucial battle for the preservation of American as well as Christian values would be decided on the religious front, the Fundamentalists attacked the Modernists with an intensity sometimes amounting to fury.

The weapons for the counteroffensive had been forged in the three decades before World War I. They consisted primarily of educational agencies designed to train preachers and to revive religious zeal among worshippers. In the first category fell the Bible Schools, founded to offset the secularization of the denominational colleges. The Moody Institute, launched in 1886 by the famous evangelist, Dwight Moody, served as a model for others. Although it did not offer courses in the Bible at the analytical and scholarly level customary in the older theological seminaries, its graduates often felt themselves superior to ministers educated along more conventional lines. The Moody Institute also conducted missions among the foreign born and produced sectarian literature.

The Fundamentalists found a more effective way of reaching the ordinary citizen through regional Bible Conferences held for a few weeks every summer. They likewise managed to place some of their most prominent spokesmen on the platforms of the chautauquas, although the latter were primarily educational in character. This medium became especially important after 1904, when the chautauquas made an annual tour of some ten thousand villages.

Outside the formal educational framework but very influential in disseminating the Fundamentalist view were hundreds of evangelists or wandering preachers. As a rule, they preached from street corners or from a tent set up on the edge of a town. They also conducted revivals lasting anywhere from one to six weeks in the larger communities. Intended to stimulate religious interest and supplement the efforts of local ministers, the revivals often sharpened denominational controversies.

The staples of evangelistic sermons were (1) denunciations of human sinfulness, (2) exhortations to repentance, and (3) forecasts of the imminence of the Judgment Day. These topics were reworked in morbid detail because evangelists felt that the saving grace of Christ could operate only if the sinner recognized his own worthlessness and yearned for forgiveness. Often revival sermons were couched in picturesque language not usually associated with the pulpit. Billy Sunday, the most successful of the evangelists, used a large repertoire of slang expressions. He described Goliath as an "old stiff" who went "strutting up and down," and David as a hero who "socked the giant in the coco between the lamps." After condemning the Devil roundly, Sunday would delight the crowd by daring the Prince of Darkness to come up through the floor and take his medicine. He often vowed that after he had died his skin would be made into a drum and beaten regularly to scare the Devil. Sunday always pointed his sermons against big-city vices, particularly drinking, card playing, and dancing. He also lashed out repeatedly at godless scientists, Modernists, labor agitators, and Catholics. Not only did he put on a colorful performance, but he made evangelism financially profitable — a fact which his critics sourly referred to on every possible occasion.

Sharing the limelight in the 1920's with Sunday, Torrey, and the older evangelists was Aimee Semple McPherson. A deep-voiced blond woman who gave the impression of being perpetually in her middle thirties, she settled in Los Angeles after a decade of roving evangelism. An ever-increasing band of followers raised $1,500,000 to build her a church known as Angelus Temple which was opened January 1, 1923. The edifice housed a theological seminary, a radio station, several musical units, and a testimonial room full of trusses, crutches, and wheel chairs donated by beneficiaries of her faith healing. In the main auditorium she expounded the "Foursquare Gospel," promising salvation to those who repented their sins and believed in Christ. The devotion of her congregation was so great that her temporary disappearance under somewhat compromising circumstances failed to shake it.

Even before the war the strictures of the evangelists against sin and science had paid impressive dividends. Teamed up with the Anti-Saloon League, they had mobilized the extraordinary popular majority necessary for passage of the Eighteenth Amendment which outlawed the manufacture and sale of intoxicating liquor. After the Armistice their numbers and influence grew. They won a wide following among the angry, bewildered foes of machine-age culture. Comparing the turbulent reconversion years to the era of disorder which the Bible promised on the eve of the Second Coming, evangelists predicted the end of the world. They inspired audiences with zeal for eleventh-hour chastisement of the sinful. Acquiescent city councils passed ordinances prescribing standards for public entertainment. Cleveland prohibited noisy cabaret music, and Rochester regulated dancing steps and postures. A few rural communities outlawed such amusements altogether.

THE CONTROVERSY OVER EVOLUTION

A more ambitious effort of the Fundamentalists to ban the teaching of organic evolution in the public schools encountered stiff resistance. The ensuing skirmish was billed by leaders on both sides as a great battle between religion and science. It turned out to be something considerably less, for neither the Fundamentalists nor the Darwinists qualified as authentic spokesmen for the positions they were defending. The Fundamentalists regarded their definition of Christian doctrine as the only authoritative one. Their well-advertised contempt for theological training separated them from other Protestants and produced distrust of their interpretations of the Bible. Although many Christians believed that God helped the faithful to understand the meaning of scripture, they did not view higher education as a barrier to the free flow of Divine Inspiration. Billy Sunday's boast that he knew no more about theology than "a jackrabbit about ping pong" was certainly not typical of Christian attitudes on biblical interpretation outside of Fundamentalist circles.

Similar objections existed to the assertions of Evolutionists as spokesmen for the scientific viewpoint. Many of them talked glibly about the descent of man from apes and about "missing links" as if anthropologists and biologists had uncovered conclusive evidence on the subject. They claimed scientific authority for statements about the mechanism of evolutionary development which were only hypotheses. Thus, the controversy did not pit the laboratory against the Bible, but the Fundamentalist interpretation of the Scriptures against an extravagant version of Darwinism.

During the long-drawn-out quarrel, the supporters of evolution enjoyed a better press than the Fundamentalists. One reason was that some of the latter developed such hostility to scientific study that they refused to inform themselves about the simple facts in the field, and hence made statements which exposed them to ridicule. Secondly, the Darwinists managed to convince the public that they were carrying the banner of academic freedom and to identify some prominent liberals with their cause.

Notwithstanding their handicaps, Fundamentalists enjoyed phenomenal success in the opening round of their war over the content of the secondary school curriculum. Mobilizing the Anti-Evolution League, the Bible Crusaders, and other pressure groups, they got the legislatures of Tennessee,

North Carolina, and Arkansas to ban the teaching of evolution in public schools. Texas and North Carolina also banned textbooks accounting for the origin of the human race by theories contrary to Genesis.

The movement threatened to spread beyond the Fundamentalist areas in the South and West, alarming Modernist clergymen, self-appointed defenders of scientific freedom, and perennial opponents of this phase of the nationalist reaction. The American Civil Liberties Union announced that it would defend any schoolteacher who agreed to test an antievolution law. The offer was taken up by John Thomas Scopes, a biology teacher in the high school of Dayton, Tennessee, after some prompting from publicity-conscious members of the local chamber of commerce. He allowed himself to be caught red-handed, teaching organic evolution to a fourteen-year-old boy, and was brought to trial in July 1925.

As the boosters of Dayton had hoped, the trial took on epic proportions. The Civil Liberties Union contributed a brilliant trio: Clarence Darrow, famous criminal lawyer and acid-tongued skeptic; Arthur Garfield Hayes; and Dudley Field Malone. The prosecution presented as its star attraction William Jennings Bryan, who had launched a personal crusade against Modernism comparable to his earlier efforts against imperialism and alcohol.

The battle of the Titans inevitably thrust poor Scopes into the shadows but attracted nationwide attention. Reporters, photographers, and telegraph operators, as well as Fundamentalists, jammed the courtroom. The trial judge was John T. Raulston of Fiery Gizzard, Tennessee, who presided in purple suspenders. The streets of Dayton were thronged with vendors of balloons, "monkey medals," and books on Darwin. A wandering atheist exhibited a mangy chimpanzee. On the edge of town evangelists held long and noisy revivalist meetings. The situation was made to order for scoffing editors like H. L. Mencken, who referred to Dayton as the center of the "hookworm belt" and to local citizens as "gaping primates" or "homo boobiens."

The outcome of the trial was a foregone conclusion when Judge Raulston denied the motion of the defense to admit the testimony of expert scientists. By ruling that the only question before the court was whether Scopes had taught evolution, Raulston also denied Darrow a forum for ridiculing the Fundamentalist position. Bryan threw away this advantage by allowing Darrow to question him as an expert on the Bible. The latter cleverly avoided the formidable questions of doctrine essential to Christianity and goaded Bryan on trivial matters.

The partisan courtroom audience cheered Bryan's defense of what he regarded as literal biblical truth, but the world outside Dayton was equally partisan and critical. It dismissed the Fundamentalists as victims of superstition and applauded their opponents as disinterested searchers for truth. Christianity suffered unjustly because the Fundamentalists professed to speak for it.

The Bryan-Darrow debate was the prelude to the conviction of Scopes. The Supreme Court of Tennessee upheld the constitutionality of the antievolution law. On the other hand it set aside Scopes's hundred-dollar fine on a technicality, thereby blocking a test of the law in the United States Supreme Court. While newspaper editors were still debating the verdict, the Fundamentalists lost their champion. Bryan passed away suddenly on Sunday afternoon, a victim of exhaustion and old age.

After the Dayton trial the popular current ran strongly against the Fundamentalists. It killed their chances of dictating the manner in which the public schools should teach biology. In a larger sense, the trial was a defeat for all groups who sought to control the curriculum by legislation.

PROHIBITION

The Fundamentalists were more successful in their agitation for prohibition. One of their own organizations, the Anti-Saloon League, had led the battle which culminated in the passage of the Eighteenth Amendment (1920). But this legislative victory was only the beginning of a long fight to stop the consumption of alcohol.

Successive Congresses combined outward enthusiasm for prohibition with inward hostility. Most members disapproved of the policy but lacked the courage to defy the voter openly. Consequently they timidly obstructed by refusing to centralize the authority over prohibition or to grant the enforcement agencies sufficient funds for the discharge of their duties. The Coast Guard was supposed to intercept illicit cargoes headed for American ports, but the Customs Office was supposed to provide the same service along the Canadian and Mexican boundaries. To complicate matters still further, the suppression of the manufacture and sale of alcohol was entrusted to the Treasury Department. Even when offenders had been caught and prosecuted by federal attorneys, local juries did not always feel obliged to convict them. Some states passed laws for the concurrent enforcement of prohibition, but several states with big urban populations, like New York and New Jersey, refused to cooperate with the federal government.

The chaotic diffusion of responsibility made it easy for lawless elements to organize a traffic in bootleg alcohol. Talents hitherto lavished on prostitution, gambling, and other rackets, moved into this new field because of the dazzling profits. The El Fay Club of New York City was typical. It sold at fifteen dollars a quart champagne which was made of cider and grain alcohol costing fifteen cents a quart. When Texas Guinan greeted patrons at the entrance of the El Fay with "Hello Sucker," she spoke the literal truth.

Warfare erupted periodically between various gangs which sought to control the numerous speakeasies and other media for the sale of alcohol. Gradually Chicago became the headquarters of the liquor traffic and the battlefield of rival syndicates headed by Al Capone and Dion O'Banion. Capone managed to establish his supremacy after a nine-year contest, climaxed by the notorious St. Valentine's Day Massacre of 1929 when seven of O'Banion's men were lined up against a garage wall and shot. Despite a preference for solving problems with sawed-off shotguns and dynamite blasts, Capone also resorted to traditional methods of political manipulation. Judges, law enforcement officers, and politicians in several Chicago wards did his bidding. Speakeasies flourished, and public officials received substantial cuts for their cooperation. The profit reaped by Capone was estimated to be in the neighborhood of $20 million. Capone could not be successfully prosecuted for bootlegging and the allied crimes of extortion and murder which made him famous. But in 1931 he was convicted of income tax evasion and sent to prison. The pattern established by Capone in Chicago came to prevail with mild variations elsewhere. Control was gradually centralized and rival groups eliminated because the bootlegging of alcohol, like other businesses, functioned more efficiently and produced higher profits without competition.

Other leaks thwarted the efforts of the Anti-Saloon League and the Fundamentalist groups to keep America dry. In innumerable basements, private citizens produced home-brew of varying quality. Equipment costs proved to be negligible. Indeed, a loathsome tasting beer could be brewed with nothing more than a teakettle, a pound of oats, and an ordinary bath towel. Citizens lacking the imagination to work out their own recipes could write the Department of Agriculture for pamphlets describing the manufacture of alcohol from various fruits.

Still worse, many alcoholic commodities could be bought legally in drugstores and groceries. In 1927 the American Medical Association listed 235 such preparations, including everything from patent medicines to hair tonic. Witch hazel, which had hitherto been popular as a drink only with the Choctaw Indians, found other buyers after prohibition had put other Americans in the same status as those wards of the government. Doctors sometimes helped patients with a proclivity for strong drink by issuing them medical prescriptions high in alcoholic content. Industrial alcohol, which was supposed to have been rendered undrinkable, often reached people capable of restoring its properties as a beverage.

The political pressure of angry prohibitionists obliged the government to launch special drives and to shake up the enforcement agencies repeatedly. The exploits of two picturesque prohibition agents, Izzy Einstein and Moe Smith, who secured evidence of violations by disguising themselves as gravediggers, vegetable vendors, and streetcar conductors, provided an element of comic relief. Still, the three thousand agents employed by the Treasury Department could not do the job, and Congress refused to appropriate additional funds. By 1929 the Wets were calling for the outright repeal of the law that could not be enforced, while the Drys were demanding additional legislation to make the purchase as well as the sale of alcohol a crime. In May of the same year, Hoover established a commission under George W. Wickersham to canvass "the entire question of law enforcement and organization of justice." When the commission, after more than a year of study, finally issued an exhaustive report, the high tide of sentiment in favor of prohibition had passed, thus foreshadowing the end of the "noble experiment."

Several factors contributed to public disenchantment. The spectacular rise of lawless gangsters and their conspicuous identification with the illicit liquor trade was disquieting. The invasion of individual rights accompanying enforcement looked to some citizens like an opening wedge for further assaults on personal liberty. The zeal of many Drys was so excessive as to be self-defeating. W. E. (Pussyfoot) Johnson, a leading figure in the Anti-Saloon League, disillusioned some by admitting, "I had to lie, bribe, and drink to put over prohibition in America." Bishop James Cannon of the Methodist Church also helped to destroy the reputation of the Drys for superior moral qualities when his unsavory financial manipulations on Wall Street were exposed in 1930. Finally, the prohibitionists faced ultimate defeat because they tried to set legislative standards for an area of human life beyond the normal reach of government. Generous appropriations would have made the Volstead Act more effective but also more irritating. In fact, energetic enforcement might have led to public revulsion more quickly.

Just as the Wets exaggerated the role of prohibition in the rise of gangsters, so the Drys overestimated the blessings of the Eighteenth Amendment. Doubtless some citizens formerly accustomed to drinking, gave it up as a result of the law. Others felt challenged by the restriction on their liberty and consumed larger amounts of alcohol in sheer defiance. Statistics fail to provide any reliable information as to the relative size of each group.

What made the experiment important was the fact that it spearheaded the drive of resurgent Fundamentalists against twentieth-century urban society. There had always been a substantial temperance movement in America, but it was politically ineffective until taken over by the Anti-Saloon League, which in turn drew its strength from the Fundamentalists.

The movement exerted its maximum political influence before the fiasco at Dayton, Tennessee, in 1925. Thereafter its strength receded slowly, although cooperation with other units of the conservative-nationalist reaction concealed the decline until the end of the decade. Political eclipse did not end the importance of Fundamentalism as a religious force within Protestantism. After the Great Depression, the control of Methodists, Baptists, and several smaller denominations passed gradually into the hands of the Modernists. However, many congregations, particularly in rural areas, clung to their old Fundamentalist views. What made them seem more moderate was the abandonment of spectacular revivals for winning sinners to Christ. The door-to-door method slowly replaced street preaching, and practical church work drained off energy that had been lavished on doctrinal disputes.

Viewed in retrospect, the cumulative effort of the extremist nationalist organizations to revitalize old institutions must be termed a failure. The discouraging outcome of the movement was partly due to the fact that many of the leaders did not really desire rehabilitation of the whole structure but only of those parts that conserved their particular interests. Since common principles underwrote nineteenth-century institutions, they could not be saved selectively. They had to stand or fall together.

A still more important reason for failure was that the social, ethnic, and religious solidarity necessary for healthy institutions had already disappeared by the 1920's. The first cracks had developed in the middle of the nineteenth century when the attempt to harness the national spirit for territorial expansion had provoked social and economic particularism in the South. The ensuing Civil War produced a strongly centralized political state but failed to reactivate the old sense of nationality. Later trends superimposed the economic particularism of nationwide pressure groups on sectional particularism. Most damaging of all was the shattering impact on cultural and religious homogeneity of industrial technology, scientific thought, and clashing ethnic groups. The Progressives had tried to check these disruptive forces and failed. When the conservative-nationalist movement took up the job a few years later, the situation had deteriorated further. The only institutional symbol of unity still remaining was the Constitution of 1787. It no longer reflected the ideals of a unified society. Nevertheless the reactionaries tried to enforce a worship of the petrified structure that still stood. Theirs was the last such effort; and when the New Deal grappled with depression, it frankly modified the institutional shell which no longer served the purposes originally intended.

SUGGESTED READINGS

1. Allen, F. L., *Only Yesterday.*
2. Furniss, N. F., *The Fundamentalist Controversy.*
3. Leighton, I. (ed.), *The Aspirin Age.*
4. Merz, C., *The Dry Decade.*

CHAPTER SIXTEEN

THE CULTURE OF THE TWENTIES

THE COMPOSITION OF THE REBEL ARMY

The postwar decade has been referred to as "The Roaring Twenties," "The Aspirin Age," "The Era of Wonderful Nonsense," and "The Lost Generation," phrases which suggest that no ten-year span had hitherto seen so many social and intellectual trends working at cross-purposes. This extraordinary ferment expressed itself simultaneously in Fundamentalism, Freudian psychology, "Red" baiting, spectator sports, and petting parties. Such surface manifestations of diversity were fed by two distinct movements: the Nationalist reaction and the splinter group of radicals determined to defy the traditional code of moral behavior. A head-on collision between the two groups seldom occurred because the Nationalists concentrated their wrath primarily on political and economic nonconformists, while the rebels showed little interest in such matters. The latter were hostile to capitalism only because they thought it stifled creativeness and experimentation in art, music, literature, and the theater. Their unconventional religious and moral views aroused the ire of the Fundamentalist wing of the reaction. But, in general, the rebels' attacks on private institutional values, and the reactionaries' defenses of public ones, inflicted little damage on either antagonist.

The rebel army was smaller than that of the reactionaries. It had been recruited from people with nothing in common save their aversion to the values and ideals of contemporary America. Some were prewar Naturalists who regarded the democratic credo as a smokescreen concealing the brutal Darwinian struggle for survival. Their assertions about the amoral character of the universe and the pointlessness of human activity had shocked and annoyed the prewar generation. Their ridicule of ideals, however, made more of an impression on soldiers subjected to the frustrations of trench warfare and on civilians disillusioned by the post-armistice collapse of the Wilsonian program. Although the Naturalists said nothing new after the war, people listened to them more carefully.

Other rebel recruits were Greenwich Village bohemians, whose sneers at traditional standards of behavior sounded somewhat like the more serious criticisms of the Naturalists. Since the Progressive decade, a handful of these eccentrics had plotted a revolution in American culture and taste. New art forms had spread westward before the war, but the vast majority of Americans either did not perceive them or did not like what they saw. A number of the more restless prophets of the aesthetic revolution felt oppressed by the hostility of their fellow countrymen and migrated to Paris, where a more favorable atmosphere prevailed. The larger number, who could not afford transatlantic travel, got out journals like the *Little Review* and *Transition,* denouncing everything from the World War to the use of punctuation in sentences. They further affronted the majority by ostentatiously flouting accepted canons of dress, manners, and sex behavior. Their defiance stemmed from the belief that unconventionality released creative instincts, or, as Burton Rascoe put it, "The wages of sin is art."

The years of ostracism ended for the bohemians as for the Naturalists after the war. Their new style in art and literature attracted many imitators and became a vehicle for attacking the beliefs of the older generation. Even more important, their insolent attitude of defiance toward the contemporary moral code was enthusiastically adopted by postwar college students, who became the most conspicuous rebels of the time.

Often unaware of the bohemian view that unconventional behavior stimulated artistic instincts, the collegians practiced defiance for its own sake. Male students indulged in wild pranks, proclaimed themselves atheists, and ridiculed their elders. The coeds shortened their skirts, bobbed their hair, and talked in a manner that would have made their mothers blush. Courtship activities on the campus led to a spectacular pooling of resources for shocking the strait-laced. Young couples danced to jazz bands in dimly lit cabarets, drank bootleg gin, and went off on petting parties or midnight swims without chaperons.

The disconcerting behavior of college students was also inspired by the age-old instinct of the young to push their elders from the center of the stage and take over as quickly as possible. Seldom had the prospects for successful rebellion been so favorable. The war partially broke down the effectiveness of the family as a stabilizer of manners and morals. Young women had left the sheltered life of the home to take war jobs and quickly insisted on the same social privileges as men. Many boys who had experienced the long monotonies of army training punctuated by short bouts of feverish debauchery, found it difficult to accept a responsible role in civilian life.

Some suffered a powerful disillusionment after paying allegiance to Wilsonian ideals and finding them unattainable despite the grim exertions of trench warfare. Rightly or wrongly, they blamed the older generation for deceiving them and took a kind of perverse pleasure in repudiating the values of American society. Defiant in word and deed, these youngsters thought of themselves as a lost generation, smashing their tender, sensitive

"Mother, when you're dummy, will you hear my prayers?" (Alice Harvey, The New Yorker, *1928.)*

souls against a wall of outworn tawdry ideals. Nobody will ever know how many were really disenchanted by their experiences and how many adopted disillusionment as a pose to justify a prolongation of immature, adolescent behavior. At all events, bohemians, college students and prewar Naturalists, formed a loose but articulate coalition to destroy the authority of the traditional ethical and moral code.

THE LITERATURE OF DEFIANCE

The most effective medium for the expression of rebel views proved to be literature. Without prearrangement, the new generation of novelists drifted into an informal division of labor. Sinclair Lewis analyzed culture in a business-dominated society; F. Scott Fitzgerald and Percy Marks dealt with the wild, irresponsible collegians and socialites; Ernest Hemingway spoke for the disillusioned soldier; and John Dos Passos moved from an earlier preoccupation with the restless victims of the war to a massive indictment of contemporary society.

Redheaded, noisy Sinclair Lewis was the most sarcastic of the lot. He possessed a special knack for irritating the older generation. In his novels the unattractive mannerisms of Americans were blown up to point where their repulsiveness seemed overpowering. One way that he achieved this effect was by loading a vernacular style with descriptive details. His photographs were recognizable, but his lens exaggerated the defects of his subjects. Although Lewis did not limit his criticism to a particular segment of American society, he reached his peak of sneering eloquence in describing the aspirations and anxieties of life in the small midwestern town. *Main Street* (1920) dwelt on the intellectual stagnation and moral complacency of Gopher Prairie, a thinly disguised replica of the author's home town, Sauk Center, Minnesota. *Babbitt* (1922) revealed that Lewis did not like the acquisitive, boastful, small-town businessman any more than the drab, colorless midwestern community. He portrayed Babbitt as a typically ignorant and intolerant real estate broker, addicted to the use of clichés, gadgets, and cheap cigars. After a more restrained treatment of a physician in *Arrowsmith* (1925), Lewis castigated the religious go-getter in *Elmer Gantry* (1927). Some saw in Lewis's later novels a mellower attitude toward his enemies of the postwar decade. Whether the emphasis shifted enough to justify assertions that he really respected American ideals, there was no question about his corrosive cynicism and contempt for old-fashioned virtues in the 1920's. Almost gleefully he proclaimed the bankruptcy of American culture.

Percy Marks struck a less strident note in *The Plastic Age,* which described life on the college campus and the process of education so fatal to student faith in ideals. He was a more detached observer than F. Scott Fitzgerald, an ex-college student and war veteran who spoke for the restless, unhappy sophisticates of the twenties. In *This Side of Paradise* (1921) and *The Beautiful and Damned* (1922) Fitzgerald dealt with college students and the young married set struggling to conceal their sense of drift and inward emptiness behind a smoke screen of boisterous dissipation. He went on to write his masterpiece, *The Great Gatsby* (1926), which caricatured the American dream of success. Dancing through its pages are shallow, pleasure-loving heirs of fortunes, stock market speculators, polo players, and amiable drunks of both sexes. The only stationary figure in this cross-section of the time was the enigmatic young businessman, Jay Gatsby, who gave huge parties once a week. Gatsby had followed the old Horatio Alger formula, "Study electricity . . . work . . . study needed inventions," and it had brought him a mansion, a limousine swollen with chrome, and a closet full of pink suits. Despite the outward symbols of success, Gatsby is an unhappy man who moves inexorably to his doom. Death ends his career on a mocking note of futility. None of his fair-weather friends attends his funeral, except the drunken party-crasher, Owl Eyes. Speaking through Owl Eyes, Fitzgerald pronounces the obituary on Gatsby, "The poor son of a bitch." It was also the epitaph for his own rudderless generation.

The reader who turned from Fitzgerald to Ernest Hemingway left the glittering but empty world of parties and midnight swims for the crude but equally fumbling quest for some kind of unattainable peace through sexual lust, hunting, and bullfights. An ambulance driver on the Italian front during the war, Hemingway spoke for the soldiers who regarded American ideals and war aims as a sham to delude the stupid. In the light of his own war experience, he restated much of the naturalist philosophy of such authors as Crane, Dreiser, and Norris, but with a deeper concern for the personal tragedy of the lost generation. In two full-length novels and a series of short stories, he established the character whose basic sensitivity and fury at his world can find no outlet except through violence. Lady Brett, the well-groomed nymphomaniac of *The Sun Also Rises* (1926), and Frederick Henry and Catherine Barkley, the unwed lovers of *A Farewell to Arms* (1929), never stray far from the bar or the bedroom. But if they pursue pleasure with an improbable single-mindedness, it is becausc they despair of achieving the better things they dimly desire but cannot define.

John Dos Passos ends with somewhat the same despair for humanity but only after losing faith successively in Wilsonian ideals and in Communism. His initial postwar novels, *Three Soldiers* (1921) and *Manhattan Transfer* (1925), express the routine bitterness of the lost generation against its own society. These were the prelude to a more comprehensive indictment of American ideology and institutions in *U.S.A.*, a trilogy composed of *The 42nd Parallel* (1930), *1919* (1932), and *The Big Money* (1936). Although two of the three fall chronologically outside the decade, the dominant mood and subject matter entitles the trilogy to consideration along with other novels of the 1920's. In essence *U.S.A.* is a social novel that examines the broad sweep of American life from 1900 to 1930. On a canvas as broad as the country, it traces the vicissitudes of a dozen-odd characters whom Dos Passos regards as representative American types. He uses several ingenious and original devices to interrupt the flow of narrative and give the reader a sense of the *Zeitgeist:* the newsreel, which examines with clinical thoroughness various cross-sections of American life; the camera eye, which reports the blooming of evil forces with a dry ironic objectivity; and biographical sketches of famous Americans, which emphasize the less attractive ingredients of material success like greed, ambition, and ruthlessness. *The 42nd Parallel* follows the misfortunes of Mac, a member of the I.W.W. In this volume Dos Passos shows a real nostalgia for some features of prewar America, but the dominant note is one of outrage over the poisonous inroads of a capitalist ideology that destroys the prospects for genuine democracy. *1919* recreates the atmosphere of the months just before and just after the Armistice as a backdrop for an analysis of the collapse of Wilsonian ideals. A whole battery of characters, from shrewd businessmen to empty-headed girls who volunteer for the Near East Relief, are conscripted to sustain the mood of disillusionment and indignation. Nevertheless *1919* ends on the hopeful note that a revolution will change everything. The four years that elapsed between the publication of *1919* and *The Big Money* gave Dos Passos enough time to become disillusioned with Marxism — the last of his ideals. Hence in the final volume of the trilogy he describes American society in the 1920's in a tone of despair.

THE SYMBOLISTS

A second group of novelists also questioned the existence of absolute values in American society but reached the position of moral relativism by a somewhat different route than Dos Passos or Hemingway. Often referred to as Symbolists, this school contended that all experience was private and subjective, isolating each man with values incapable of being objectified or shared. The Irish novelist, James Joyce, had created a style intended to give the reader a sense of the jerky, discontinuous quality of human thought. He utilized long semicoherent soliloquies and clothed simple ideals with symbols or fanciful imagery. Gertrude Stein, an American expatriate who settled in Paris, went still further by stringing together repetitive phrase-patterns. Virtually incoherent, these patterns when read aloud produced a kind of rhythmic tongue dance which Miss Stein seems to have regarded as a faithful verbalized reflection of individual mental activities. Her technique influenced both the members of the lost generation that went to Paris and those who stayed home. Even Hemingway, with his predilection for earthy rather than idealistic symbols, owed his staccato sentence style in part to Gertrude Stein.

Generally speaking, the Symbolists wrote in language too obscure to interest the general public. James Branch Cabell and Sherwood Anderson were exceptions. The former wrote a best-selling novel, *Jurgen* (1919), which was more scandalous than meaningful. The hero, a middle-aged pawnbroker, forsakes the earth for the magical land of Poictesme where he enjoys a series of amorous and other adventures. Cabell employs a kind of surface symbolism throughout the novel to assert that insulation from reality in a private dreamworld is the best way of gilding the boredom of existence. However, most Americans bought *Jurgen* more for its ability to titillate than for its philosophy of life.

Sherwood Anderson was a more profound exponent of the view that irrational, subjective cravings motivate human behavior. In *Winesburg, Ohio* (1919), a volume of short stories, he brought individuals together for chance encounters which exposed their hopes, frustrations, and anxieties. He and other Symbolists found confirmation for their views about the sources of human action in current theories of psychologists and biologists. The widely quoted Viennese psychologist, Sigmund Freud, traced the origin of most behavior to subconscious anxieties, fears, and sex drives. The biological researches of Jacques Loeb led him to conclude that men like animals were machines responding to complex laws. John B. Watson, who founded the behaviorist school of psychology, added the corollary that the human machine was a nervous system which reacted in a particular way to outside stimuli.

Such hypotheses underlay much of the work of the Symbolists. They embodied their beliefs that men were driven primarily by irrational compulsions in stories whose every detail was focused on showing how their poor lives were shaped. In its extreme form, this view of human nature deprived the individual of responsibility for his own conduct and drained objective meaning from conventional concepts of morality.

The iconoclastic spirit dominated other art forms during the 1920's. Eugene O'Neill, the first significant American playwright, launched a revolution in stage production by employing unusual costumes, exotic scenery, and weird lighting effects. More important, he gave the drama revolutionary depth and meaning. The characters in his plays wore masks, spoke realistically, and reflected the absorption of the time in exposing the inner life. In *The Hairy Ape, The Dynamo,* and *The Great God Brown,* he spoke for the disturbed and disenchanted youngsters immortalized by the novelists. Like Cabell and Anderson, he partly shrouded his message in a cloud of symbols and allegory.

Poetry also dealt with disillusion and symbol, although the views of the poets defy easy classification. Edwin Arlington Robinson had been brooding over the infirmities of the human race since he published his first collection of poems in 1897, and so he antedates the lost generation. But the melancholy tone of *The Man Against the Sky* (1916) and *Tristan* (1927) compelled attention in the postwar generation. Edna St. Vincent Millay also won fame with casual little verses which were more widely quoted than her serious sonnets and lyrics. She maintained a somewhat frivolous attitude of despair which was re-echoed with satirical overtones by Edgar Lee Masters in his *Spoon River Anthology* (1915). The pessimistic outlook was stated in a harsh naturalistic context by Robinson Jeffers who from *Tamar* to *The Double Axe* guided the reader through symbolic labyrinthine horror of lust, brutality, and perversion.

The symbolism so pronounced in the nightmarish verses of Jeffers was developed in still more obscure fashion by T. S. Eliot. A Harvard graduate who made his home in London after the mid-twenties, Eliot wove his poems together out of rhetoric, slang, and veiled but immensely learned allusions to everything from English topography to classical mythology. Many critics hailed *The Waste Land* (1922), but the average reader found it unreadable. Except by his master, Ezra Pound, Eliot was unsurpassed in poetic allusiveness.

Subjectivism, abstraction, and symbolism likewise dominated bohemian experimentation in painting and sculpture. Canvases featured geometric designs, strange color patterns, streaks of interstellar fireworks, and grotesque figures. Statues bordered on shapelessness or took monstrous, distorted proportions. In both media, asymmetry and unconventionality were the frequent products of the perpetual search for new forms. Traditional aesthetic standards were subordinated to the effort to communicate the artist's private feelings. Outside the coterie of the initiated, few thought the results worth the expenditure of energy.

OTHER LITERARY TENDENCIES

The rebels owed their conspicious position in the cultural life of the 1920's partly to an extraordinary self-appointed press agent, H. L. Mencken. From the editorial chair of the *American Mercury,* a magazine with a bright green cover launched by A. A. Knopf in January 1924, Mencken lambasted the older generation on a variety of fronts. He denounced politicians as "barber-surgeons," college professors as "intellectual eunuchs," businessmen as "mountebanks," and farmers as "hinds" following "platitudinous messiahs." He paid his respects to the South by calling it as sterile "artistically, intellectually, and culturally as the Sahara desert." The success of William Jennings Bryan was attributed to the fact that he had been born with a roaring voice "which had a trick of inflaming halfwits."

The circulation of the *American Mercury* grew by leaps and bounds as Mencken systematically insulted every major group and its beliefs. Subscribers either assumed that they belonged to the exclusive circle of the Mencken elect or tolerated unmistakable digs at themselves as the price of enjoying insults showered on others. College students, unhampered by professional loyalties, regarded Mencken as their patron saint. They scuffled with one another to get the first look at each new issue delivered to fraternity and sorority houses. Like his defiant readers, Mencken and his co-editor, George Jean Nathan, cared relatively little about socioeconomic problems, and for the most part they kept them out of the *Mercury.* Aside from articles debunking American heroes, democracy, the jury system, and Fundamentalist religious sects, the editors devoted considerable space to the literature of rebels. The work of new authors was printed as well as analytical essays praising their outlook.

Despite the iconoclastic tone of the *American Mercury,* Mencken was more of an intellectual snob than a radical. As a young journalist at the turn of the century he had matured under the tutelage of James Huneker, a literary critic with a Continental manner and a contempt for American manners and traditions. Pride in his German ancestry, reinforced by enthusiasm for German music and philosophy, made it easy for Mencken to adopt the Huneker pose of regarding America as a cultural backwash. Voracious reading of Nietzsche, Shaw, and Ibsen built up the arsenal of immoderate and derisive adjectives which he habitually used to ridicule the tastes of his countrymen.

Behind the cosmopolite was a saucy, elfish Mencken who enjoyed outraging the respectable and discovered a formula for making his pleasure profitable. He simply stood for everything contrary to orthodoxy—atheism, alcoholic beverages, and government by the elite. On the eve of the publication of the *American Mercury* he confided to Sinclair Lewis that he hoped to "stir up the animals," and the technique worked beyond his fondest expectations. He was not a constructive thinker, but as a spokesman of the angry postwar generation he was without a rival.

To describe the activities and viewpoints of the rebels is easier than to measure their influence. For the most part, citizens of rural America were untouched by the noisy iconoclasm of Sinclair Lewis, the unconventionality of the bohemians, and the antics of college students. In the agricultural community, any echoes of controversies over art and morals met with indifference or the uniform hostility traditionally accorded to the city and all its works. Those farmers and townspeople who enjoyed reading continued to plow through prewar American favorites like Susan Warner's *The Wide Wide World* and *Queechy,* Gene Stratton Porter's *Freckles* and *A Girl of the Limberlost,* or Kate Douglas Wiggin's *Rebecca of Sunnybrook Farm.* These insipid but harmless novels celebrating rural virtue competed with perennially popular historical romances, the plays of Shakespeare, and the Bible. Willa Cather found a wide audience for the realistic portrayal of the Nebraska frontier in *The Song of the Lark* (1915) and *My Ántonia* (1918). A decade later, while the literary critics were acclaiming the novels of the rebels, she finished a best seller about the old Southwest, *Death Comes for the Archbishop* (1927). Like Willa Cather, Ellen Glasgow wrote about the old America with a warmth and nostalgia sharpened by realism. Her novels about the changing South, from *Barren Ground* to *In this Our Life,* gave pleasure to Americans who found the fiction of the lost generation repulsive or confusing. Thornton Wilder capitalized on the strong interest in religious themes with *The Bridge of San Luis Rey,* a novel which reformulated the quest for moral absolutes by examining the lives of several individuals engulfed in a common tragedy.

The city accepted the rebels more hospitably than the village or farm, but their audience was limited to intellectuals, professional sponsors of the arts, and college students. The salesman, the industrial worker, and the housewife sometimes read Hemingway or Cabell for a thrill, but rarely went beyond the narrative to savor the pessimism of the authors. If they encountered a modern play, painting, or statue, they did so by accident and hastily dismissed it as incomprehensible.

The narrow scope of the rebel appeal raises some doubt whether the lost generation justifies the generous space usually accorded to it in the conventional history of the 1920's. The irresponsible, amoral characters depicted in many postwar novels certainly did not mirror the beliefs or feelings of the average American. The credo of negation had little influence on the optimistic masses engaged in the pursuit of permanent prosperity. Even the widely applauded sneers of Sinclair Lewis and H. L. Mencken at the cultural poverty of America failed to arrest the aggressively materialistic and nationalistic trends of the decade.

If the rebels did not speak for the average American, they did faithfully broadcast the views of the articulate and intellectually curious youngsters whose war experiences sharpened their dissatisfaction with the older generation and its values. They also caught the mood of plain people who seldom read books or expressed themselves in philosophical terms but instinctively sensed the growing ineffectiveness of hallowed institutions. How many felt disillusioned in the 1920's without voicing their feelings will never be known. The number must have been sizeable because a substantial group abandoned old beliefs during the ensuing depression decade.

SPECTATOR SPORTS

The rebels of the lost generation have often been credited with launching the postwar revolution in manners and behavior, but they functioned more as conspicuous practitioners than as leaders of social change. Most citizens who embraced jazz, spectator sports, and other novel recreations did not do so out of a conscious desire to rebel but because a changing social environment favored such activities. The closing of the frontier a generation earlier had curtailed the routine opportunities for physical exercise, hunting, and wilderness sports, thereby increasing the popularity of archery, canoeing, tennis, golf, and boxing as well as team games. Simultaneously the rapid urbanization of America coupled with the war-born emancipation of women had opened a huge market for organized amusement. In addition, the techniques of yellow journalism and high-pressure advertising were available for campaigns to create heroes out of entertainers and hero-worshippers out of spectators. During the 1920's these ingredients fused to produce a revolution in public taste.

Probably the most conspicuous manifestation of the new spirit was the phenomenal rise of spectator sports. Boxing, baseball, and football were the most popular. Spectators achieved a momentary illusion of agility and power by identifying themselves with the almost superhuman feats of Jack Dempsey, Babe Ruth, or Red Grange. They reveled in the fast action, sudden reversals of fortune, and unpredictable endings of the games.

Boxing faced the greatest obstacles to popularity and respectability. Before the war, prize fights had been illegal in most states, and promoters were forced to hold them in barns, cellars, or athletic clubs. Sometimes even more ingenuity was required. The authorities had shown such diligence in thwarting various efforts to hold the James J. Corbett–Joe Choynski fight of 1889 that the two sluggers were finally brought together on a grain barge anchored in San Francisco Bay.

The serious hazards associated with sponsoring prize fights had made domination of the sport by underworld groups inevitable. Gamblers fixed fights as a routine matter, adding the taint of dishonesty to a spectacle already regarded by the general public as brutal and unrefined. Some religious groups fought boxing as zealously as they did the liquor trade and prostitution. Despite such handicaps, prize fighting came into its own in the 1920's. The successful drive for respectability was spearheaded by Tex Rickard, Yukon miner, stud-poker dealer, and promoter extraordinary. He brought prize fights out of cellars and back rooms into auditoriums and stadiums. He dressed ushers in uniforms, sold reserved seats, and started the fights on time. He also cracked down on the informal little fights that usually broke out among the customers before the main event. Most important of all, he managed to interest women in boxing.

These face-lifting operations would have accomplished little without Rickard's special talent for promoting spectacular fights. His resourcefulness and showmanship bore fruit in the Carpentier-Dempsey contest, July 2, 1921. Georges Carpentier was a French war hero and handsome boulevardier with a dimple in his chin. New York City sports writers, after some prompting from Rickard, began comparing him to a Greek god and Dempsey to a primitive jungle beast. As the date of the fight approached, journalists enthusiastically forecast an epic struggle between civilization and savagery. These metaphoric flights brought society women to Carpentier's training camp on Long Island and ultimately to the fight itself. At the last minute Governor N. L. Miller banned the fight from New York City, but the adroit Rickard built a wooden arena just over the New Jersey line on a swampy field known as Boyle's Thirty Acres. An appreciative crowd paid $1,789,238 to watch Dempsey knock out Carpentier for the heavyweight championship of the world.

Rickard's first million-dollar gate was followed by four more in the 1920's. All of them featured Jack Dempsey, a lethal slugger, whom Rickard alternately presented in the role of villain and hero as events required. The climax came at Chicago in 1927 when Dempsey, who had unexpectedly lost his title to a Shakespeare-reciting ex-marine named Gene Tunney, went down to defeat in a spectacular rematch. Gate receipts reached the staggering total of $2,650,000. If the amount of newspaper coverage was a reliable measure of public interest, the second Dempsey-Tunney fight rated as the most important single sports event of the decade.

For those who preferred to watch team sports, professional baseball had many attractions. It was organized into a hierarchy of leagues which observed a series of complicated rules designed to assure the flow of talent from the numerous minor leagues to the two major leagues. Especially important in determining the structure of the sport was the use of the "reserve clause," which made players the property of a particular club or team and prevented them from selling their talents to the highest bidder. As a consequence, if a particular player could not reach an agreement over the terms of employment with his owner, he was condemned to idleness for the season unless purchased by another team. This arrangement stabilized the structure of baseball but seemed to violate both the Sherman Antitrust Act and the old common law rights of free contract. The owners of clubs have on the whole been successful in preventing test cases from reaching the courts. Because of the doubtful legality of their position, they strove from the beginning to establish baseball as the national pastime. Each year they have linked the game with Americanism by inviting the President of the United States to throw the first baseball of the season. When gamblers bribed certain members of the Chicago Black Sox to throw the World Series in 1919, the owners promptly established the post of High Commissioner and appointed Judge Kenesaw M. Landis to it.

Although baseball had developed an enthusiastic following before World War I, the repeal of the ban against Sunday sports and the emergence of a new hero, Babe Ruth, won new converts for the game. Ruth's spectacular career made him a household name. After breaking in with the Boston Red Sox as a combination pitcher-outfielder he was bought by the New York Yankees in 1920. His new masters promptly converted him into a full-time outfielder, and the following year he hit fifty-nine home runs. This feat produced so many Ruth fans that the Yankee management opened a new three-decker stadium on the Harlem river in 1928 to accommodate them. The so-called "Sultan of Swat" improved his previous home-run record with sixty in 1928 and was rewarded with a salary nearly as large as the one paid to the President of the United States. By that time his popularity had become so universal that nobody questioned the appropriateness of the pay scale.

New York fans who got tired of watching a team win with such monotonous regularity as the Yankees, could cross the Gowanis Canal to observe the antics of the Brooklyn Dodgers. Under the management of the eccentric Uncle Wilbert Robinson, who often conferred with taxi drivers about the batting order, Brooklyn played colorful if not victorious baseball. Frenchy Bordagaray sometimes stopped to pick up a fallen cap in the course of pursuing an outfield fly, while the celebrated Babe Herman startled fans and sportswriters by pulling lighted cigar butts out of his pocket for a casual puff. On one occasion three members of this uninhibited team wound up on third base simultaneously.

The enthusiasm for spectator sports took a new and unexpected turn when college football games began to draw vast numbers of people who had never attended either of the opposing schools. Originally a monotonous variant of rugby which featured brutal contact work as well as indiscriminate kicking of both the ball and the opponents, football had become more interesting to watch after the legalizing of the forward pass in 1905. Crowds traveled hundreds of miles by special train or automobile to cheer pile-driving fullbacks like Ernie Nevers of Stanford, elusive running backs like Red Grange of Illinois, and breath-taking passers like Frank Carideo of Notre Dame. Nationwide interest was aroused over championship contests, and countless sportswriters wrote learned articles about the relative merits of offensive formations like the Single Wing, the Short Punt, and the Notre Dame Box.

College administrators, delighted by the turn of events, built huge coliseums to accommodate crowds for five or six Saturdays a year. Syracuse had opened Archibald Stadium in 1900, and a few Ivy League schools had followed suit in the ensuing decade. The great era of stadium building occurred after the war. Stanford University dedicated a vast coliseum which seated 93,000 in 1921. California followed two years later with a Memorial Stadium accommodating 82,000. In the mid-twenties the University of Illinois opened a large double-decker which Red Grange christened by running for touchdowns the first four times he got the ball.

The financial success of the colleges attracted competition. An American Professional Football League was organized in 1926, with Big Bill Edwards, a former Princeton star, as its president. Instead of challenging the colleges directly, the professionals played their games on Sunday. At first the public response was disappointing. In fact professional football had to undergo several reorganizations before it began attracting large numbers of spectators in the 1940's.

Meanwhile college football teams continued to occupy the limelight. Enthusiasm for the sport moved steadily westward. The prewar center of gravity had been New Haven, Connecticut, where the pioneer Yale coach, Walter Camp, turned out several championship teams. By the middle of the postwar decade, the football fever became most acute at Columbus, Ohio. Students and alumni alike possessed such an insatiable thirst for victory that Ohio State became a graveyard for unvictorious coaches.

The tremendous popularity of football was not an unmixed blessing for the academic institutions concerned. It usually provided profits to subsidize other sports and evoked from alumni a tribal loyalty which sometimes resulted in cash gifts to alma mater. But, it also introduced a distressing professionalism into college athletics and diluted academic standards. Most of the large universities recruited gladiators to play football and paid them by various ingenious methods. Special courses were devised to meet the needs of those whose athletic aptitude exceeded their capacity for absorbing the conventional academic subjects. Professor Andrew Kerr, the football coach at Stanford University, launched the new trend in 1923 by offering the first college course in cheerleading. At the end of the decade the methods of producing a successful football team had been so standardized that one out of seven college athletes received some kind of pay.

Although professors fumed over the lowered standards of scholarship and the well-publicized pretense that athletes played football for fun, the public was well satisfied. The only thing it demanded was more spectacular offensive battles. Consequently the forward pass came to be used with increasing frequency. In the early 1930's the rules were modified to lessen the penalties for unsuccessful passes. Also the short-axis diameter of the ball was reduced three-quarters of an inch so that the throwers could get a better grip on the pigskin. Coupled with the liberalization of the rules governing substitutions, these changes produced the desired avalanche of touchdowns.

MOVING PICTURE, RADIO, AND TABLOID

Competing with spectator sports for the patronage of an amusement-hungry public was the rapidly expanding moving picture industry. Even before the war the fourteen-minute shows in the "nickelodeons" had been replaced by longer pictures shown in more pretentious theaters. Press agents had also begun to create the stars whom audiences worshipped so slavishly a decade later. David Wark Griffith, destined to be one of the most famous directors, was experimenting with the fade-in and fade-out, the angle shot, the close-up, the vista, and the vignette. All these camera techniques were successfully employed in his *Birth of a Nation* (1915), an epic treatment of the Civil War and the Reconstruction era. A decade later movie-goers were purchasing an average of 100,000,000 tickets weekly for admission to more than 20,000 theaters. Before the popularity of the silent movie waned, the industry was able to synchronize sound and action in the "talkie." *The Jazz Singer,* starring Al Jolson, appeared in 1927 but it took more than two years to convert most of the theaters for "talkies."

Within limits the silent movie offered a varied fare. Tender love stories, torrid romances, swashbuckling adventures, wholesome comedies, and grandiose spectacles or extravaganzas were all available. Audiences thrilled to the innocent sweetness of Mary Pickford, the sophisticated glamor of Greta Garbo, and the provocative charms of Clara Bow, the "It" girl. John Gilbert and Rudolph Valentino possessed the handsome features and persuasive manners necessary to make their impersonations of ardent lovers convincing. For heroic exploits none rivaled Douglas Fairbanks, a combination of Robin Hood, Monte Cristo, and Paul Bunyan. Tom Mix was relied upon to shoot outlaws and cattle rustlers on the Great Plains, while Harold Lloyd convulsed spectators of all ages with his boundless zest for foolishness.

For citizens who wanted to be entertained without leaving their homes, the radio was the perfect answer. It emerged almost by accident out of scientific research directed toward the creation of private wireless communication service comparable to the telephone. Those engaged on the project were dismayed over the fact that messages transmitted by radio could be picked up on any receiving set. This technical difficulty, which doomed it as a medium for the transmission of confidential business information, led to much further experimenting by the Radio Corporation of America, which had been organized in October 1919 to market receivers. Confronted with a large and seemingly worthless investment in sets, Westinghouse Electric, one of the co-owners of R.C.A., began looking for a way to stimulate public interest. Vice-President H. P. Davis stumbled into the future by building a sending station on the roof of a Westinghouse plant in Pittsburgh. He got the Department of Commerce to assign it the call letters KDKA and broadcast the returns of the 1920 presidential election and of the Dempsey-Carpentier fight.

The experiment was an immediate success. Sales of receiving sets jumped from $3 million in 1920 to $650 million in 1929. By the end of the decade 40 per cent of all American families owned at least one radio. Like the moving picture, the radio benefited from a series of technological improvements which pleased consumers but bankrupted manufacturers and retailers unfortunate enough to be loaded with inventories of obsolete equipment. In 1923 the crystal set, which transmitted sound only through earphones, was supplanted by the tube set and loud-speaker. Stations multiplied so rapidly as a result of the prospects for large profits that some seven hundred were in operation by 1927. To prevent chaos on the airwaves, Congress created the Federal Radio Commission and gave it power to license stations, fix their wave lengths, and regulate the hours of operation.

Programs also underwent rapid change. The original stations stayed on only a few hours a day and presented a limited variety of entertainment. At first the novelty of occasional strange noises from distant cities satisfied the listener, but toward the end of the twenties the pressure for programs from dawn to midnight could not be withstood. The broadcasters soon discovered that such large-scale operations were beyond their resources, and delegated the programming to sponsors who purchased radio time. The latter, in turn, passed the job on to advertising agencies that specialized in radio shows. Although sponsors were happy to present outstanding sports contests as well as other events of nationwide interest, the backbone of the business was programs of recorded music, popular orchestras, comedy teams, serials, and news summaries.

The popularity of the radio made deep inroads on other types of home entertainment. The upright piano and the Pianola, or automatic player piano, were conspicuous casualties. The Victor phonograph, which had brought opera singers, symphony orchestras, and jazz bands into the living room, also retreated before the onslaught. Even the substitution of a more functional horizontal console for the traditional ugly humpbacked model in 1924 did not save the Victor Company. Unable to produce a radio within its patent rights, Victor eventually sold out to R.C.A., which promptly began manufacturing the combination radio and record player.

From their inception both the moving picture and the radio had been hailed as potentially superior media for the advancement of education. Neither subsequently justified such hopes. Producers, finding that the largest market was for films about romance, or adventure, made no real effort to elevate public taste. They also discovered that pictures dealing with significant issues offended various pressure groups and menaced the industry with government regulation. To prevent such a development, they instituted a self-censorship program in 1922. This doomed the moving picture as an intellectual force. Will H. Hays, Harding's Postmaster General, was prevailed upon to resign from the Cabinet and head the censorship activities of the Motion Picture Producers and Distributors of America, Incorporated. Known popularly as the Hays Office, it evolved a purity code which banned profane or obscene language, ridicule of conventional morality, sympathetic treatment of criminals, unsympathetic treatment of religious groups, and the portrayal of debatable social and economic issues. Additional provisions governed the shooting of love scenes and the wearing of clothing. Pictures without the seal of approval from the Hays Office were outlawed in all except a handful of independent theaters. Any film which ran such a formidable gauntlet of regulations and retained a substantial intellectual content was the exception rather than the rule.

The content of radio programs, like that of moving pictures, was governed to a large degree by the prospect for profits. Sponsors aimed their shows at a large, homogeneous audience in a mood to be persuaded of the need for purchasing certain products. They had nothing to gain by catering to the tough-minded or reflective who were immune to the persuasiveness of advertisements. Hence the soap opera, the serial, the comedy show, or the musical program unimaginatively adhered to a common formula year after year. Nevertheless the individual willing to spin the dial could frequently find relief. Churches presented provocative religious material; the networks carried both sides of major political controversies; and a few sponsors experimented with plays, symphonies, round tables, and lectures. Most of the latter were presented by noncommercial educational stations connected with universities. The mortality rate of such stations was exceedingly high. Of the ninety-four licensed during the twenties, only a few were still broadcasting at the end of the decade.

The trend in journalism likewise favored newspapers that entertained rather than those that informed. In the prewar "yellow journals" of Hearst and Munsey, it is true, political, economic, and foreign events usually dominated the front page but they were treated in a sensational and irresponsible manner. A new phase began with the tabloid, the first of which was the *Illustrated Daily News,* launched in the summer of 1919 by Joseph M. Patterson, a member of the McCormick journalistic clan. It devoted headlines and lead articles to murders, divorces, rapes, and the like, relegating cursory treatment of public affairs to the back pages. Aimed at the unreflective reader, the tabloid featured numerous pictures and a small page that could be conveniently handled on a crowded subway train. The *News* won such rapid public acceptance that a whole host of imitators quickly appeared. Many older papers copied its techniques even though they stuck to a more conventional size. Columns on astrology, diet, marital relations, and gardening diluted the news content in order to stimulate reader interest.

THEATRICAL ENTERTAINMENT

The various types of entertainment associated with music halls and theaters also felt the impact of changing public tastes. Some styles, like the variety show, continued to exist separately after being partially absorbed in musical comedy. In addition, the persistence of a time lag between the emergence of a new entertainment form on Broadway and its adoption by the hinterland prevented the development of uniform trends.

Musical comedy and vaudeville enjoyed the greatest popularity. The ingredients of both had been available in one form or another since the Civil War — the extravaganza with large-scale reproductions of famous spectacles; the pantomime relying primarily on grotesque gestures by the actors and plots from Mother Goose; the minstrel show featuring singers with burnt cork on their faces, plantation dances, and gags; and the variety show of the saloon.

Vaudeville owed most to the old variety show glossed over with respectability. This process was begun by B. F. Keith and E. F. Albee, who opened a family vaudeville theater at Boston in 1885. They banished from the show the broad-minded waitress and over-age chorus girls who had loped around the sawdust floor of the old saloon and relied instead on comedians, acrobats, singers, novelty dancers, and gifted animals. During this period certain popular actors worked out the gags and tricks which they were to repeat without substantial change for the next three or four decades. Herb Williams never stepped on the stage without his famous piano, which featured a spigot for beer and a hand that reached out to hit him on the top of the head. W. C. Fields always appeared with his pool-table props, and Leon Errol did a version of the turkey trot which owed its special charm to his collapsing ankle.

The exiled barmaids returned to vaudeville — or a thinly disguised variant of it — in *The Passing Show* (1895). Twelve years later Florenz Ziegfeld launched his Follies, which added shapely chorus girls to the routine. By the 1920's this innovation enjoyed such widespread public acceptance that Ziegfeld faced many competitors. George White lauched his Scandals on an annual basis in 1921, the Shuberts inaugurated a new series called Artists and Models in 1923, and Earl Carrol's Vanities were introduced the same year. Another show, known as the Greenwich Village Follies, tried to attract a more sophisticated audience with corrosive satire and lampooning. Even an all-Negro revue, the Blackbirds, was started by Lew Leslie in 1920 and attracted considerable comment because of its overemphasis on tap dancing. Outside of New York, local vaudeville companies imitated metropolitan productions to the degree permitted by local opinion.

Pressure of competition forced the Big Four to produce new shows every year but did not lead to much change in basic content. On the whole,

Ziegfeld cornered the best talent. Victor Herbert, Jerome Kern, Irving Berlin, and Rudolph Friml wrote musical scores to adorn his shows. Ed Gallagher and Al Sheen provided a comedy routine, and after 1921 Will Rogers, the Oklahoma cowboy, convulsed successive audiences with his homespun humor.

Depression, increasing competition from radio and films, and the inflexibility of the program killed vaudeville. Ziegfeld's last edition of the Follies in 1931 was a financial failure. The carefree, prosperous atmosphere which had nurtured vaudeville simply disappeared.

Musical comedy, maturing more slowly than vaudeville, also reached a peak of popularity in the twenties. Drawing on the songs, dances, gags, and novelties that had been staples of American entertainment, the musical comedy now added the distinctive unifying feature of a story. The narrative was usually developed by speaking, acting, and singing, punctuated by irrelevant interludes of dance numbers and comedy acts.

Until the 1890's, musical comedy relied almost exclusively on European plots. The prototype which set the fashion for many years was *The Black Crook*. Patterned on Gounod's *Faust,* this was an extravaganza or spectacle of the type later served up by Cecil de Mille in the movies. The climax came in the "Grand Ballet of Gams," followed by a scene in the Harz Mountains where beautiful girls "poured down the wild glens" in a hurricane of gauze.

The popularity of European-style musical comedy was reinforced by the extraordinary success of Gilbert and Sullivan's *Pinafore,* which reached New York in 1879. Even after the turn of the century, Americans overwhelmingly preferred Franz Lehar's *Merry Widow* to any native product. Opening in 1907, it took the country by storm. A craze for Merry Widow hats, dresses, and drinks quickly developed. On the eve of the war, over one hundred touring companies were organized to present the operetta simultaneously in various parts of the United States.

With Broadway committed to the lucrative formula of translating and producing musical comedies and operettas from London, Paris and Vienna, native composers did not easily win acceptance. Ivan Caryl's *Pink Lady* enjoyed extended popularity, and a transplanted Irishman, Victor Herbert, turned out a succession of hits with *Babes in Toyland* (1903), *The Red Mill* (1906), *Naughty Marietta* (1910), and *The Princess Pat* (1915).

After the war, composers with native themes began to dominate musical comedy. The most spectacular example of the new trend was Jerome Kern's *Showboat* (1927). Everything about it was authentically American from the river-boat captain to the blues singer. George Gershwin, after several false starts, scored a resounding success in *Strike Up the Band* (1930), a good-humored satire on war and politics. Sigmund Romberg utilized European settings for *Blossom Time* (1921) and *The Student Prince* (1924) but shifted to North Africa for *The Desert Song* (1926) in which the heroic Red Shadow behaved like an American cowboy. Before the decade was over, Cole Porter had launched his career with *Fifty Million Frenchmen,* and Vincent Youmans had begun to develop a successful musical comedy formula with *No, No, Nannette* and *Hit the Deck.*

As in the case of vaudeville, the primary function of musical comedy was to entertain. The stories for the most part revolved around light-hearted heroes and heroines who surmounted a series of improbable mishaps to unite in marriage. Depression did not kill musical comedy but encouraged experimentation with more serious themes.

While vaudeville and musical comedy flourished, grand opera languished. It had always been the plaything of the rich and did not widen its appeal in the 1920's. The Metropolitan Opera House in New York had been constructed in a way that gave the audience a clear view of the boxes and their occupants rather than of the stage. Such an arrangement discouraged enthusiasm for opera almost as much as the practice of singing parts in a foreign language.

The elder Oscar Hammerstein had tried to popularize opera by organizing his own company in 1906, but since he did not have wealthy patrons to make up the annual deficits, he went out of business four years later. So the "Met" regained its monopoly and carried on serenely indifferent to the public. Only after World War II when the Texas Company began broadcasting performances from the Metropolitan stage on Saturday afternoons did a genuinely popular audience for opera develop.

The legitimate stage deserved better of the public than opera, but ironically fell into financial difficulties just when it was becoming the vehicle of serious ideas. Between 1910 and 1925 the number of legitimate theaters dropped from 1,520 to 634. The contraction occurred almost entirely in the trans-Appalachian region; the number of theaters in New York City doubled during the same period. Behind these figures were rising costs of production, the competition of movies, and the abandonment of prewar farces and melodramas aimed at relaxing the tired businessman. The rebel generation, inspired by European iconoclasts like Shaw and Ibsen, inaugurated a burst of experimental playwriting.

A "little theater" movement composed of amateur devotees of the stage flowered in a number of communities, filling the vacuum left by the dissolution of the touring companies. The most important were the Washington Square Players, renamed the Theater Guild in 1919, and the Provincetown Players, who converted a wharf on Cape Cod into a theater in 1915. By producing unusual American and European plays both organizations encouraged authors to break away from orthodox forms. They were receptive to realism, poetic drama, fantasy, and comedy of manners. Recruiting audiences by subscription, they felt under no obligation to decide the merits of plays in the conventional terms of box-office appeal. Except for the works of Eugene O'Neill, few plays growing out of the movement found their way into the permanent repertory of the American theater. Broadway produced a few hits that utilized war themes; especially noteworthy were *Journey's End* by R. C. Sherriff and *What Price Glory* by Maxwell Anderson and Laurence Stallings.

JAZZ

A revolution of musical taste long in the making reached its height in the 1920's when jazz bands sprang up all over the country. This development marked the emancipation of native music from reliance on European forms. The early bands employed six or seven instruments — clarinet, cornet, and trombone to carry the melody, and banjo, tuba, and drums to provide the rhythm. After World War I the piano was frequently added to the rhythm section, the string bass was substituted for the tuba, and the saxophone emerged as a distinctive badge of the jazz band. Not only did the saxophone come to function as an all-purpose instrument but as a vehicle of comedy, surprise, and dismay. In the hands of an expert it could be made to chuckle, groan, wail, and snort.

Like ragtime, an earlier kindred musical form, jazz relied on a rhythm pattern of four beats to the measure and a tune syncopated or played so that an unaccented note is continued through the time of the following accented note. What distinguished it from ragtime was the introduction of syncopation into the rhythm as well as into the tune or melody. The rhythm instruments did not actually play out of time with each other, but the musicians utilized wide discretion in anticipating or delaying the exactness of the beat. They took the same kind of liberties with the tune, embroidering on it and improvising as they went along. Sometimes the improvising was confined to one player in the melody section, but just as often cornetist, clarinetist, and trombonist devised variations on the main tune simultaneously. In the early days, the performers made no effort to write down or score the products of their musical flights. In fact, they seldom played a composition the same way twice.

The eccentricity of syncopation led to rhythms within rhythms and improvisations that concealed the melody from the untrained ear. It also replaced the conventional skip from one musical tone to another with a glide which touched all pitch points between the tones. Coupled with an almost explosive accent pattern, these features created the impression that jazz was a sensuous, primitive type of music.

Except for cowboy songs and the ballads of mountaineers, farmers, and railroad workers, jazz was the only musical form based on unassailably native traditions. The Negro had brought the basic pattern with him from Africa and preserved it in his work songs through more than two centuries of slavery. The various mutations developed most rapidly in New Orleans, where French influence had permitted a greater tolerance toward members of other races. Even before the emancipation, Negroes were allowed to meet on Saturday nights and Sundays in a field adjoining Rampart Street for singing, dancing, and recreational purposes. After the Civil War their talents were in demand for the numerous parades, concerts, and marches sponsored by various fraternal organizations of the city. Enterprising merchants frequently employed a Negro band and hauled it through the streets in a wagon to advertise their wares. Funeral processions often included bands which jazzed the standard marches. This practice was not followed for lack of reverence or sorrow but to honor the deceased by playing music which he had enjoyed in his life.

Additional opportunities for the Negroes to work and develop their musical talents opened in Storyville, the notorious red-light district of New Orleans. Until the turn of the century the proprietors of bordellos had usually provided a piano player who banged out ragtime tunes to entertain customers. In 1910 Billy Phillips stole a march on his competitors by replacing the piano player with a jazz band in his establishment known as the 101 Ranch. Others followed suit, and jazz became a regular feature of the entertainment offered in Storyville.

The period from 1890 to 1910 when parades, concerts, funerals, and houses of prostitution in New Orleans drew on the musical talents of Negroes has often been called the golden age of jazz. During those years, pioneer jazzmen like Buddy Bolden, Manuel Perez, and Bunk Johnson were weaving together work songs, ragtime tunes, and blues ballads into the new musical form that swept the country after World War I.

Just as ragtime had been exported from New Orleans up the Mississippi River to Memphis and St. Louis by entertainers who worked the river boats, so jazz moved northward on the eve of the war. The big migration began in 1918 when the Navy closed down the red-light district of Storyville. Scattering in all directions, the unemployed musicians organized bands in the major cities. The new music caught on so quickly that the popular Paul Whiteman gave a jazz concert at Carnegie Hall on February 12, 1924. Substituting a huge brass section and all sorts of drums for the conventional sixty-piece string orchestra, he served notice on the country that the musical revolution had arrived. The acceptance of jazz by white cabaret bands like Paul Whiteman's did not steal the spotlight from talented Negroes. As the pioneer players died of overwork and dissipation, new stars like King Oliver, Jelly Roll Morton, and Louis Armstrong emerged. The second generation endowed jazz with a popularity that lasted well beyond the twenties and provided a base for experimentation in boogie-woogie and swing. The whole classical tradition of eighteenth-century composers was taken apart and re-examined.

Inevitably novel dance steps were contrived to fit the requirements of the new musical style. The vogue of ragtime in the 1890's called attention to the hoochie-coochie and turkey trot, which obliged the dancers to employ a convulsive shoulder jerk for each silent accent in syncopated melodies. The tango and maxixe replaced them but enjoyed only a brief prewar popularity because the steps were numerous and intricate. Both types of dances, as well as the more venerable Viennese waltz, gave way to the fox trot; devised for four-four time, it was simple to execute and easily adapted to the rhythmical eccentricities of the jazz band.

ART AND ARCHITECTURE

The experimental mood in popular taste was not quite so venturesome when applied to architecture and the fine arts. Public buildings had long been compounded of many styles, ranging all the way from Gothic to Moorish. The development of structural steel which could bear the weight of the largest buildings ushered in the age of the skyscraper and reduced the need for the heavy masonry characteristic of the Romanesque and Gothic styles. Louis H. Sullivan, a Chicago architect, sought to exploit technological improvements by designing buildings without superfluous ornamentation. On the principle that function rather than tradition should govern form, he drew up the plans for a graceful, slender skyscraper, the Wainwright Building, erected in St. Louis in 1890.

The public was slow to accept the ideas of Sullivan or his more illustrious successor, Frank Lloyd Wright. It did tolerate the cold, geometric design of the skyscraper but resisted the application of functionalism to residential construction. The next generation was more flexible and edged toward functionalism in the guise of a regional revival. The western ranch house, the native stone cottage, and the compact colonial mansion reappeared with the blessing of the functionalist when properly adapted to climate and topography.

Popular taste in painting, as opposed to that of the rebels, leaned mildly toward realism. George W. Bellows, who painted crude, vigorous prize fights and street scenes; Edward Hopper, who specialized in reproducing decayed mansions; and a triumvirate of middle-westerners — Grant Wood, Thomas Hart Benton, and John Steuart Curry — these received most attention.

To move from the description of various phases of life in the 1920's to larger generalizations is hazardous in the extreme. The era featured crosscurrents rather than clear-cut trends. Notwithstanding the noisy strictures of the lost generation against various aspects of American life, the overwhelming majority exhibited a conservative temper on political, economic, and moral questions. Running counter to this prevailing mood was a general willingness to experiment in matters of entertainment, dress, and social convention and a cautious desire to sample the unfamiliar in music, literature, and art. The 1920's did not always "roar," but they did always seem confused.

SUGGESTED READINGS

1. Fitzgerald, F. S., *The Great Gatsby.*
2. Gallico, P., *Farewell to Sports.*
3. Hemingway, E., *A Farewell to Arms.*
4. Kazin, A., *On Native Grounds.*
5. Lewis, S., *Main Street.*
6. Manchester, W., *The Incredible Mr. Mencken.*

CHAPTER SEVENTEEN

THE POLITICS OF PROSPERITY (1921-1929)

On the morrow of the 1920 elections, elated Republicans hailed their triumph as a mandate to restore normalcy. They were reluctant, however, to say how this was to be done because nobody quite knew what normalcy meant. Congressional leaders, ever distrustful of abstractions, thought that it could be achieved by repealing the remaining wartime economic controls and by a modest program to aid business. Successive Presidents thought so, too, because their legislative recommendations favored manufacturing and commercial groups, and ignored the interests of other pressure groups. Such a political formula would have encountered heavy resistance in the Progressive era, but public preoccupation with the drive for conformity and the revival of prosperity took the edge off prewar hostility to business.

BUSINESS CONSOLIDATION

The opening of the new era was heralded by a series of business consolidations comparable to those that had followed the Spanish-American War. The Radio Corporation of America was organized in 1919 to dominate the marketing of radio sets and equipment. E. I. duPont de Nemours and Company, which expanded enormously by profits from explosives and fertilizers, moved into the field of plastic, lacquers, and synthetic textiles. Simultaneously, various areas of retail merchandising were integrated into nationwide systems of chain stores by F. W. Woolworth, the Atlantic and Pacific Tea Company, and United Cigar Stores. Even criminal activity, like the numbers racket and the sale of bootleg alcohol, produced a few giant syndicates which operated everywhere. By the end of the period the two hundred largest corporations, exclusive of banks, possessed nearly half the corporate assets of the country. Fifteen of the giants had entered the billion dollar class.

Although the outright absorption of smaller firms by trusts continued, the holding company became the more characteristic method of consolidation, and "oligopoly" replaced "monopoly" as the favorite bugbear of those who decried the trend. The holding company developed so many mutations that it defies easy description. In general it was a management corporation superimposed on several producing corporations and empowered to issue its own stock on the basis of a small percentage of shares in them. It enabled small groups of businessmen to control the policies of large firms in which they held a negligible financial interest and also covered the activities of professional manipulators who unloaded many worthless stocks on the public.

The holding company was the popular device for unifying control and eliminating competition in the utilities field; the oligopoly proved to be more typical of heavy industry as a whole. It involved an informal arrangement whereby three or four large corporations amicably divided the main market for their particular product, leaving to lesser rivals a few customers with specialized demands. The formalities of competition were preserved by costly advertising wars, but all participants understood that these skirmishes did not go beyond heated claims and counterclaims about the superiority of the respective products and did not lead to price wars. The automobile field, for instance, was shared by Ford, General Motors and Chrysler; the tobacco field by Liggett and Myers, Reynolds, and the American Tobacco Company; the chemical field by DuPont, Union Carbide and Carbon, Dow Chemical, and Allied Chemical and Dye; and the moving picture field by Metro-Goldwyn-Mayer, Universal, and Fox. Without exception the practitioners of oligopoly extolled competition and equality of opportunity at patriotic gatherings. If the general public noticed any difference between theory and practice, it did not complain.

STIMULANTS TO CONSOLIDATION

Before picking up the thread of political developments, let us analyze the events which produced such a favorable atmosphere for big business. In the first place, the unprecedented requirements of war production had placed a premium on business cooperation, thereby transforming the practice from a vice to a virtue, from a conspiracy to a patriotic act. A vast governmental machinery had been developed to help standardize production, save storage space, utilize waste materials, and reorganize assembly lines. Industry-wide committees had taken up the task of enforcing improvements, while statistical agencies had made careful measurements of production progress. Since businessmen invariably preferred cooperation to competition, they utilized this opportunity to establish informal but permanent understandings with erstwhile rivals.

Gratitude to industry for wartime production would not by itself have reconciled the public to business collusion and the domination of political

Don't worry, he'll get around them! (Ireland, The Columbus Dispatch, *1928.)*

policy. More important was the fact that industry continued and broadened the policy of standardization. Corporations conducted time and motion studies, rearranged plant layouts, and installed laborsaving devices. Their enthusiastic adoption of efficiency engineering led to spectacular cuts in costs and phenomenal increases in output. How much of the savings was passed on to the public in the form of lower prices has always been a question. After the outbreak of the Great Depression in 1930 many economists contended that the lower costs of the 1920's had warranted reduction rather than maintenance of prices. Whatever the merits of such a retrospective analysis, the public took an opposite view at the time. It had never known a boom without a substantial price inflation and was genuinely grateful for a prosperity which featured stationary prices. Corporation executives, who had once ridiculed Frederick W. Taylor — the pioneer advocate of efficiency engineering before the war — repaid public confidence by proclaiming that scientific production practices provided the key to perpetual prosperity.

General postwar economic conditions, also, provided businessmen with a favorable opportunity to reap the benefits of efficient, low-cost production. The war boom, with only a brief post-Armistice interruption, had burned itself out in wild price inflation during the summer of 1920. A short but severe depression followed, throwing nearly seven million workers out of jobs in 1921 and drastically reducing the price level. The pent-up demand for housing and consumers' goods, the production of which had been suspended during the war, hastened an upturn in the spring of 1922. Operating from a lower price base, business found a huge and enthusiastic domestic market to exploit.

During the initial stages of the new boom the demand for replacement goods would in itself have been sufficient to keep activity high. But the extraordinary feature of the heightened economic activity from 1922 to 1929 was the fact that it drew nourishment from a whole series of new industries. In another connection we have already noted the rise of a multibillion dollar amusement and luxury industry based on the moving picture, the radio, and spectator sports. A second new field, and a most lucrative one, was the cosmetics industry, which took two billion dollars annually from the purses of American women. Forty thousand beauty shops ministered to their routine manifestations of vanity; and in the grimmer fight against advancing age, they tried everything from simple skin preparations to face-lifting. A third field, the tobacco industry, was converted from a relatively sleepy, stable business into a billion dollar enterprise. Between 1914 and 1927 the value of all tobacco consumed increased from $490,165,000 to $1,163,768,000 as a result of the rising popularity of the cigarette, which had previously been regarded as a badge of low morals. Not only did numerous men switch over from smoking tobacco, chewing tobacco, and cigars, but the more daring women began to use cigarettes. Although the number of workers directly employed in the industry dropped about 28 per cent during the decade, the loss was more than counterbalanced by the jobs that opened in advertising and sales.

In addition to these areas of expansion there was a group of new heavy industries. By all odds the most important one was the automobile. Before the war it was a curiosity and a luxury, as the production figure of five thousand for the year 1900 suggests. P. T. Barnum probably expressed the opinion of his fellow countrymen when he bought an early model for his circus and paraded it with the freaks and wild animals. Vermont reflected initial popular wariness by passing a law which required a motorist to employ "a person of mature age" holding a red flag to walk an eighth of a mile ahead of each automobile.

General public acceptance was tied to the production of a cheap car. The individual who did most to secure that objective was Henry Ford, the son of a small Michigan farmer. After experimenting with several types of engines, Ford began manufacturing the famous four-cylinder Model T in 1908 and selling it for $850. By 1924 he had managed to reduce the price to $290. Behind this achievement was a ruthless application of efficiency engineering and scientific techniques of production. He organized assembly lines with an eye to eliminating waste motion, and set up a vertical monopoly to assure himself control of all materials used in producing a car. Equally important, he concentrated on manufacturing a single model which was durable as well as cheap, sacrificing beauty for functional utility. The boxlike body stood high off the ground so that it could negotiate muddy country roads, while a powerful engine enabled it to back up the steepest hills.

Although nearly two hundred companies at one time or another tried to manufacture automobiles, Ford could ignore his competitors until the middle 1920's. Then, a series of bankruptcies and consolidations resulted in the emergence of two great rivals, the Chrysler and the General Motors corporations. The latter successfully invaded the low-price field with the famous Chevrolet, forcing Ford in 1928 to bring out the Model A, with a new engine and a more graceful body than the Model T. The following year Chrysler also made a bid for the same market with the Plymouth. Thereafter Ford had to share the limelight and the business with General Motors and Chrysler. The Big Three dominated more than two-thirds of the market, leaving the remainder to half a dozen smaller companies.

Ford had performed his greatest service before he was partially eclipsed by his huge rivals. More than any other business leader of the time he had implemented the credo of scientific management and had sold it to the public. He put the automobile on a mass production basis, reduced prices, raised wages, and made a fortune in the process. These achievements together with a fanatical conservatism and a colossal ignorance of facts outside his own field gave him unprecedented popularity. His career renewed faith in rugged individualism.

Besides the 375,000 workers who produced nearly 4,800,000 automobiles in the peak year of 1929, approximately four million more owed their employment indirectly to the motorcar. The industry used vast amounts of steel, plate glass, rubber, leather, and light alloy metals, to say nothing of gasoline. Once an automobile had been built, salesmen, chauffeurs, repairmen, and filling station operators were required. Even suburban real estate developments, summer resorts, and roadside motels owed their prosperity in varying degrees to the advent of the automobile.

Stimulus was also radiated outward to the construction industry by the irresistible demand for paved highways capable of handling the heavy volume of traffic. Just after the war the Army Motor Transport Corps had dramatized the need for three thousand miles of paved road by organizing a transcontinental trip of eighty vehicles which took two months to make the distance. It required three more years and tremendous political pressure from civilian motorists to obtain federal aid. The Townsend Act of 1922, which set the pattern for future highway legislation, made $75 million in federal funds available for road construction provided the states matched the appropriation and agreed to maintain the highways after completion. Before the decade was over, federal, state, and local governments had spent nearly $10 billion on road construction. The resulting use of highway-building machinery, cement, steel, and labor on such a large scale, provided one of the most durable props for the boom.

Another industry that continued to spread rapidly during the decade was electric utilities, which had already become a billion dollar business before the war. Just as the growth of the automobile industry stimulated the use of gasoline and oil, so the manufacture of washing machines, vacuum cleaners, radios, toasters, and other household appliances increased the demand for electricity. Even refrigerators, stoves, and clocks powered by electricity now became common. Industrial establishments as well as households underwent conversion on a large scale. Electricity made the operation of factory machinery safer and also permitted a greater variety of procedures for sorting and testing products on the assembly lines. More than twice as many factories ran machines by electrical power at the end of the decade as at the beginning.

The growth and consolidation of the power industry into twelve large systems, which controlled three-quarters of the electric power in the United States, provoked more criticism than other mergers. Perhaps the long prewar educational campaign carried on by the Christian Socialists for municipal ownership of public utilities had left a lasting impression on the country. At all events Senator George W. Norris of Nebraska, Governor Alfred E. Smith of New York, and other critics of Republican policies demanded public control of power resources. Norris kept up a steady agitation for government generation and sale of hydroelectric power at reasonable rates to municipal distributing systems. He argued that if such a policy could by carried out on a sufficiently large scale it would provide a yardstick for measuring the rates of private companies.

Two other elements of the boom deserve passing attention — the chemical industry and the packaged foods industry. Before the war the United States had manufactured a considerable quantity of chemicals, like saltpeter, sulphuric acid, and caustic soda, used in industrial processes, but had been dependent upon Germany for aniline dyes and various synthetic products based on secret formulas. The war not only cut off such supplies but stimulated Germany to produce a wide range of substitutes for commodities that could not be sneaked through the blockade. One of the fruits of the Allied victory was that the United States fell heir to the closely guarded secrets of the German chemical industry. Through the Alien Property Custodian this technical information as well as several thousand German patents reached the hands of American firms. The Fordney-McCumber Tariff Act provided high protection while the industry groped its way toward efficient production methods. Not only did industrial chemical firms like DuPont and Union Carbide and Carbon prosper but ethical drug firms, led by Squibb, Parke-Davis, Pfizer, and Merck, also expanded rapidly.

The tremendous boom in packaged foods was partly due to urbanization. As families moved into apartments with modest food-storage facilities and as women turned from housekeeping to office careers, a demand developed for the small packages and cans that produced quick meals. The trend was accelerated by a dietary revolution. The sedentary workers of the city required smaller quantities of food than their rural counterparts. Urban women discovered the calorie and its clandestine contribution to obesity. No longer willing to tolerate the illusion of slimness promoted by the whalebone corset, they launched a program of self-imposed dietary restrictions. Salads, soups, gelatines, and dry cereals were substituted for potatoes, hot cakes, and fat meats. Stokeley, Del Monte, and Heinz, which canned foods, and Standard Brands, Beechnut Packing, and Best Foods, which put them in everything from glass jars to cellophane wrappers, prospered as never before. The Kellogg company sold a diet-conscious public so thoroughly on the healthfulness of packaged dry cereal for breakfast that a permanent monotony was introduced into the morning meal.

THE CREDO OF BUSINESS

Not only did the businessmen take credit for volume and diversification of production in the 1920's but they assured the public that American industry operated on an ethical basis. The success of the moral appeal in marketing war bonds had suggested the tremendous potentialities of such a sales technique even under normal conditions. No doubt some businessmen did operate from lofty motives. In any event they all represented the modern corporation as an altruistic institution which had sublimated its acquisitive instincts. As Bruce Barton, the unofficial herald and philosopher of the new order, contended in *It's a Good Old World,* American business is unique because it is organized primarily for public welfare. The man at the top draws strength and power from his unswerving determination to serve others. Barton went on to expound the scriptural basis for the business principle of service in a best seller entitled *The Man Nobody Knows* (1925). He proclaimed Jesus Christ to be the author of the ideal of business service, and interpreted various incidents in the Gospel story as proof that Christ was a great executive, organizer, and salesman. According to Barton, Christ inferentially endorsed salesmanship by selecting twelve apostles and converting them into the most effective sales force the world had ever seen. The theme was accepted and amplified by a number of so-called business divines like C. F. Reisner and Samuel Parkes Cadman. Although most churchmen did not approve of the artificial union of spiritual values and sales commissions, protests did not get nearly so much publicity as endorsements.

Whether the salesman unselfishly ministered to public welfare or induced wants that consumers would not otherwise have had, he blossomed out as the chief executor of the corporate policy of service. J. H. Patterson, President of the National Cash Register Company, deserves the principal credit for the systemization of the sales organization. He produced manuals on sales technique and created special posts in his corporation for sales engineers and "pep" specialists. Methodically he blocked out territories for his salesmen and assigned them larger quotas each year, organized contests, and offered tempting bonuses to generate a fanatical pitch of enthusiasm. American business quickly adopted his methods and turned swarms of aggressive salesmen loose on a bewildered but tolerant public.

Consumer resistance was also undermined by advertisements and installment buying. Billboards, trolley cars, newspapers, and magazines drew attention to products with an insistence that verged on the hysterical. The favorites were candy, cigarettes, soap, and other items that consumers use up quickly. Three types of appeals were most prominent: products possessed some new and magical ingredient, preferably with a scientific name; they conferred on the purchaser a prestige associated with a higher socioeconomic group; or they were made of the finest materials in the world.

Installment buying provided a more insidious inducement for the consumer to purchase articles normally beyond his resources. By making a small down payment and agreeing to pay fixed installments on a monthly basis, he could obtain immediate physical possession of an item as expensive as an automobile. The exponents of this kind of buying hailed it as a humanitarian service that put a whole range of expensive products within reach of the common man. They also contended that it nursed the old-fashioned virtues because the buyer had to save money to meet installments. The actual functioning of the system was not, however, so utopian. Since most purchasers could offer no surety, they paid interest ranging from 10 to 20 per cent, although this fact was usually concealed in the schedule of payments. The need to save for large monthly payments often led buyers to default on small debts at the grocery or hardware store. Most discouraging of all was the fact that the item purchased had often worn out before the final payment could be made.

Notwithstanding the evidences of materialism and sharp sales practices that reduced the persuasiveness of the doctrine of service, most Americans accepted it at face value. Service clubs of businessmen sprang up as if by magic. At weekly intervals Rotarians, Kiwanians, and Lions met for a meal of chicken à la king and canned peas, followed by a good-natured razz session and an earnest discussion of community service projects. Universities, confronted by a rising demand for business training, organized business schools and correspondence courses.

To their intense gratification, businessmen replaced politicians as the leading citizens of the community. They presided over meetings on patriotic occasions, directed the activities of civic welfare groups, and held important local political offices. Their advice received respectful attention. As the creators and defenders of prosperity, who had put the Midas touch on a scientific basis, they commanded a veneration that was almost religious. Indeed, they became so much the victims of their own propaganda that they believed the doctrines of service and of scientific management would guarantee the economic well-being of the masses.

THE HARDING ADMINISTRATION

The general state of culture described in the foregoing pages dominated the political transactions of the 1920's. President Harding opened his administration with a large amount of good will. His simplicity of manner, natural kindliness, and blind loyalty to his friends were contrasted favorably with the aloof, haughty character of his predecessor. The pedestrian quality of his program might have caused misgivings under other circumstances, but for the moment it appealed to many who blamed current troubles on excessive thinking.

The mediocre tone of the new administration was first revealed in the selection of a Cabinet. Yielding to considerable pressure, Harding named two tested public servants, Charles Evans Hughes and Herbert Hoover, Secretary of State and Secretary of Commerce respectively. With more enthusiasm he selected the able but opinionated Pittsburgh banker and aluminum magnate, Andrew D. Mellon, as Secretary of the Treasury. These appointments represented the absolute limit of his concessions to the principle of efficiency in government. His desire to reward political cronies and his understandable reluctance to be surrounded by people brighter than himself governed most of the remaining selections. Of these Henry Wallace, the Iowa farm editor and Secretary of Agriculture, who challenged unwary political opponents to cow-milking contests, was the best. Albert B. Fall, the former New Mexico Senator and sheep rancher who was appointed to the Interior Department, qualified as the most dangerous. Harry M. Daugherty, close friend of the President, had a reputation as a corrupt, unblushing spoilsman long before he became Harding's Attorney General.

The most thankless task of the new administration was to complete the liquidation of wartime policies and controls. Neither Woodrow Wilson nor the Republican Congress elected in 1918 had shown the slightest inclination to compromise. The only piece of constructive legislation emerging from the two-year deadlock had been the Esch-Cummins Transportation Act (1920), returning the railroads to private ownership. This law went beyond the terms of the Hepburn Act of 1906 in giving the I.C.C. power to initiate railroad rates. Additional provisions specified the procedures for establishing reasonable rates. These included physical valuation of railroad property — a great victory for Senator La Follette — and the regrouping of the railroads into large systems with similar average earning capacities. Congress also anticipated the possibility that strong systems might earn excessive profits and that weak ones might operate at a loss. So it added a "recapture clause" which provided that carriers earning in excess of 6 per cent on the value of their property had to turn over half the surplus to the I.C.C. for the rehabilitation of weaker lines. Not so closely related to the rate problem were provisions authorizing financial help for railroads during the transition period, and creating a Railroad Labor Board with powers of mediation.

Practically all pressure groups found fault with the Esch-Cummins Act. Labor disliked it for returning the railroads to private ownership and for setting up a Railroad Labor Board that could infringe on the right to strike. Farmers showed their hostility by making the unwarranted assumption that the recapture clause guaranteed the railroads a return of 6 per cent. Businessmen saw a sinister precedent in the provision which forced railroads to open their financial records to the I.C.C.

Not only did the Esch-Cummins Act rain a bewildering assortment of blows and caresses on the railroads but it proved difficult to administer. Every provision from the physical valuation clause to the procedure for recapturing excessive earnings caused trouble. Eventually Supreme Court decisions made part of the legislation inoperative. Still, neither Harding nor his Republican successors saw fit to review railroad policy in any systematic way. The Railroad Labor Board, composed of nine representatives from management, labor, and the public, became a casualty. Because it had managed to offend both organized labor and the carriers, Congress abolished it in 1926 and substituted a five-member mediation board. Other changes at that time were not substantial: the idea of choosing board members from the principal interest groups was dropped but the appointing power was again lodged in the President; the new board, like the old, lacked the power to compel arbitration; when the parties to a dispute refused the board's services, the President could appoint an emergency investigating board if he concluded that a strike threatened interstate commerce, and both sides were forbidden to change conditions for thirty days after this board's report. Considering the superficial character of these changes, the new mediation machinery functioned surprisingly well. On all other fronts Harding either ignored or undid the work of the preceding administration.

He tried to consider the wishes of business in disposing of the 2,000-odd government-owned merchant ships built during the war by the Emergency Fleet Corporation. The Merchant Marine Act of 1920 had authorized the Shipping Board to sell these to private operators on easy terms and it had also provided the Board with a revolving fund of $25 million for loans to companies that would operate new routes. Unfortunately these inducements were not sufficient to attract interest in the purchase of government ships, which could not compete with ordinary freighters. To make matters worse, the protection of seamen provided by the La Follette Act had made the cost of operation under the American flag prohibitive for most properly constructed ships. As a result the Shipping Board was forced to retain ownership of many vessels which slowly rotted at their moorings. Even the privately operated companies, which had continued to lease some of the merchantmen from the Shipping Board on a cost-plus basis after the war, gave up during the depression of 1920–21.

Holding all the orthodox fears of government owned and operated enterprises, Harding wanted to put the Shipping Board out of business, but he was confronted with the undeniable need for a merchant marine as a measure of national defense. Accordingly he sought both objectives with a bill to withdraw the government from direct participation in the shipping industry and to subsidize private owners who would operate usable parts of the fleet. This measure, which passed Congress in the spring of 1923, cost the government anywhere from $12 million to $50 million annually. After his death the Coolidge administration broadened the subsidies to the merchant marine in the Jones-White Act of 1928, which increased the loan fund of the Shipping Board from $25 million to $150 million and made the money available to shipowners on easy terms for either renovation or construction. It also authorized long-term mail contracts with shipping firms at rates far in excess of the cost for such service. Despite these efforts to provide relief, the merchant marine languished until the eve of World War II. No administration dared to ignore it or to repeal the legislation which shielded it from operating on a competitive basis. In the absence of a constructive policy the subsidy provided the solution most congenial to shipowners and politicians and also set the pattern for treatment of the embryo air-transport business, which at the end of the decade was dependent on government air-mail contracts for 85 per cent of its revenue.

FARM LEGISLATION AND THE TARIFF

If Harding threaded his way slowly through the maze of demobilization problems, he showed more confidence in reviving traditional Republican policies. The protective tariff headed the list. Nearly every major economic group but the cotton farmers had come to regret the low rates established by the Underwood Act of 1913. Many citizens, whose outlook had recently been reoriented by the Nationalist reaction, regarded the depression of 1920–21 as divine retribution visited upon them for abandoning the policies of their fathers. In such a mood they favored passage of a protective tariff as both an act of penance and a concrete step toward economic recovery. Farmers confronted by lower agricultural prices and the rumors that Europeans intended to dump their surpluses on the American market, momentarily forgot their objections to Republican tariffs. Organized labor was easily won over by the feigned solicitude of the protectionists for the standard of living. Industrialists exploited patriotic sentiments with lofty assertions about the duty of protecting chemicals and other strategic industries from competition. In such an atmosphere the old Populist-Progressive argument about the tariff conferring special favors on business sounded unconvincing. By the time Harding moved into the White House, public support for a protective tariff had become so strong that he did not need to worry so much about providing leadership as climbing on the band wagon. Two weeks before his inauguration the lame-duck Congress had passed an emergency bill raising the rates on agricultural imports, but it was killed by a Wilson veto on March 3, 1921.

Harding promptly called a special session of the new Sixty-seventh Congress to repass the emergency bill and to start general revision. Despite top-heavy Republican majorities in both houses, Harding did not enjoy the congressional cooperation usually accorded a newly elected President. The old rift between the western agrarians and the eastern industrialists, which had presumably been closed in 1916, reappeared now that the party was to bear responsibility for formulating policy. The farm wing took the offensive at once because it spoke for constituents in acute distress as a result of rapidly falling prices.

Without actually issuing an ultimatum, the western Republicans made it clear that agricultural relief would have to precede general tariff revision, tax reduction, and other items dear to business. Thanks to the rule of seniority and heavy Republican casualties in eastern states during the Wilson era, the westerners controlled most of the congressional machinery. Even the crucial Senate Finance Committee, which would frame tariff legislation, fell into their hands when Chairman Boies Penrose of Pennsylvania died suddenly in 1921 and was succeeded by Porter J. McCumber of North Dakota.

As a consequence the Republican farm bloc with occasional assistance from the Democrats dominated the special session. Its legislative program was based on the assumption that agricultural prosperity would be revived by a protective tariff and some Populistic-type regulations of the grain trade. Since the farm bloc knew what it wanted, the legislative machinery turned rapidly. The emergency tariff, which sharply raised the duties on such key commodities as corn, wheat, meat, wool, and sugar was revived and passed on May 27, 1921. The Packers and Stockyards Act, which followed on August 15, 1921, sought to divorce the ownership of stockyards from that of retail outlets for meat. The Secretary of Agriculture was granted wide supervisory powers over the packing industry and could issue "cease and desist" orders to stop unfair trade practices. Within two weeks Congress produced the Futures Trading Act, giving the Secretary of Agriculture similar power over brokers who dealt in wheat and other grains. Before the session ended, a companion piece of legislation broadened the lending powers of the War Finance Corporation. The new measure authorized it to raise a billion dollars by bond sales and use the proceeds to assist in financing the disposal of agricultural products abroad.

A Cooperative Marketing Act sponsored by Senator Arthur Capper of Kansas and passed February 28, 1922, completed the immediate program of the farm bloc. Besides continuing the routine exemptions of agricultural organizations from the provisions of the antitrust laws, the Act authorized them to engage in interstate marketing operations under the supervision of the Secretary of Agriculture.

Harding and the industrial group made the best of this unaccustomed domination of party policy by the agrarian wing. The President found the adjustment rather easy because he took a narrow view of his constitutional responsibilities, but a larger element of calculation entered into the conciliatory behavior of the eastern Republicans in Congress. In the first place, the spate of marketing legislation did not threaten their vital interests nearly so much as the old Populist-Progressive trust-busting program had done. Second, the emergency tariff cost them still less and put the farmers in a poor moral position to resist increases elsewhere. Finally, the continuing preoccupation of the farm bloc with its elaborate legislative program left the industrial pressure-groups free to draw up new schedules with a minimum of interference. As a result of this unique situation, the eastern wing of the party was able to dominate the crucial process of tariff making more completely than when it had controlled the legislative machinery.

The House acted with habitual speed. Joseph W. Fordney, the chairman of the Ways and Means Committee, had a bill ready for consideration in mid-July. After a minimum of debate it was passed on to the Senate, where a more leisurely mood prevailed. In fact, the Finance Committee considered the requests of the industrialists at such length that the bill was not reported out until April 1922 and by this time it had been altered beyond recognition. Many rates had been raised and a host of commodities had been added to the dutiable list. On the Senate floor two thousand more changes were made, most of which raised the rates still higher. The industrial lobbyists circulated freely during the debate and got exactly what they wanted.

In the end the House accepted the majority of Senate changes. The final version, known as the Fordney-McCumber Act, was signed by President Harding on September 19, 1922. It established record rates on most agricultural and industrial commodities, singling out the infant dye and light-metal industries for specially generous treatment. In an effort to give its handiwork a scientific and flexible character, Congress added a clause authorizing Tariff Commission studies of foreign and domestic production costs. If the commission were to find sharp changes in the relationship between the two, it would be obliged to notify the President, who might in turn modify existing rates as much as 50 per cent in either direction.

The Fordney-McCumber tariff produced wider effects outside the United States than earlier protectionist legislation. This was due partly to the disruption of world export markets by World War I and partly to American insistence that Europe repay war loans. Some congressmen could doubtless see that a high tariff would reduce American imports from European nations and hence block the normal avenue for debt repayment, but they did not anticipate the magnitude of the retaliatory restrictions that American policy would ultimately provoke. The boom of the 1920's and the liberal investment of American capital abroad postponed for a time the worst international repercussions.

The only immediate complaints against the Fordney-McCumber Act came from the farmers who had withheld their usual criticism while it was under consideration. Failing to experience relief from the legislation upon which they had insisted, they exploded with the indignation of men who had made a bad bargain. W. O. Scroggs put their case most graphically: "[The farmer's] day begins when he is aroused by an alarm clock, and the new tariff bill raises the duty on this article 67 per cent. His first act is to throw off the bed covering on which the duty had been increased 60 per cent. He jumps from his bed, on which the duty is advanced 133 per cent, and dons a summer bathrobe with the duty up 60 per cent and slippers with the duty increased 33 per cent."

The Fordney-McCumber tariff was the sole legislative concession to business that Harding could extract from a recalcitrant Congress. Otherwise deadlock prevailed, particularly on the fiscal front. The President strongly urged a downward revision of wartime taxes, but the lawmakers ignored him. When they in turn attempted to increase the financial burdens of the government by passing a Soldiers' Bonus bill, Harding killed it with a veto.

The President had the better of the quarrel because he was able to give business sympathetic administrative policies. The new approach received quick expression in the Department of Justice, which reduced the volume of antitrust suits far below the prewar level. Herbert Hoover, the Secretary of Commerce, encouraged the creation of permanent industry-wide trade associations to replace the temporary organizations that had worked for standardization and cost-cutting during the war. Assuming collusion between business units to be inevitable, he believed it could be made socially useful if sponsored and supervised by government. He also thought small business would have a better chance of surviving through cooperation with other units in the trade association movement than by competition. At first, the Supreme Court regarded the exchange of statistical and technical production information by a member of a trade association as a violation of the Sherman Act. However, it began to take a more lenient view of this activity in the Maple Flooring case of 1925. The court also inferentially blessed the holding company form of organization by refusing to order the dissolution of the U.S. Steel Corporation in 1920.

Other departments in the administration, especially the Department of the Interior, showed little sympathy for conservation and opened up government resources to private exploitation whenever possible. Indeed, loose administration of the public lands was to lead to the worst scandal of the 1920's.

The President also created a more sympathetic atmosphere for corporation activity by appointing businessmen to regulatory agencies like the I.C.C. and the F.T.C. as the terms of old Progressives expired. He did not live long enough to recast these commissions completely, but his successor, Calvin Coolidge, continued this policy as well as others favorable to business.

Outside the area of partisan politics, Harding and the Sixty-seventh Congress collaborated to reform the fiscal system. Wilson, before his retirement from office, had recommended legislation which would have concentrated in the executive branch the responsibility of drawing up the budget. His proposal was designed to terminate the wasteful procedure whereby each department worked for the largest possible annual appropriation without regard to the needs of other departments. Congress responded with a Budget Act in the fall of 1920, but Wilson vetoed it because he thought it put unwarranted restraints on the executive. There the matter rested until Harding reopened it by asking a special session to pass the measure in the form originally requested by Wilson. The legislators complied in June 1921.

The new law, known as the Budget and Accounting Act, required each department to submit an estimate of its fiscal needs to the President, who was in turn required to present to Congress a consolidated budget on the opening day of every regular session. The law also made it mandatory for the President to accompany the budget with a report summarizing income and expenditures for the preceding year as well as estimates for the coming year. The Act also recognized the need of the President for competent advice by authorizing the creation of a new Budget Bureau and a Director of the Budget to be appointed for a fifteen-year term. Charles G. Dawes, a picturesque, tight-fisted Illinois banker, became the first to hold the office. Although the new fiscal system represented a substantial improvement over the old, nothing short of a constitutional amendment could have curtailed the ancient congressional policy of loading the budget with wasteful pork-barrel appropriations. In fact, the very nature of lawmaking in a democratic state militates against the establishment of efficient budgetary practices.

As the 1922 Congressional elections approached, it became clear that Harding had made only a beginning on his program. Tax revision, immigration legislation, and a settled policy for veterans were still pressing problems. Worst of all, the farm bloc had been given virtually a free hand, passed measures which brought agriculture little relief, and blamed Harding for the results.

The rural areas of the Midwest swung sharply against the Republicans. The top-heavy majority of 1920 shrank from 22 to 6 in the Senate, and from 167 to 15 in the House. The party suffered an even worse disaster than the official results indicated. Particularly in the Senate the majority was fated to disappear because several of the newly elected members were Republicans in name only. Men like Smith W. Brookhard of Iowa and Frank B. Howell of Nebraska owed their victories to rebellious state organizations. Senator Lynn D. Frazier of North Dakota was a member of the Nonpartisan League, which had captured the Republican party of that state from the inside by advocating a program of agrarian socialism. An even more violent upheaval took place in neighboring Minnesota where a new Farmer-Labor party elected Henrik Shipstead to replace the incumbent Republican, Frank

B. Kellogg. Six months later when the second Minnesota Senate seat fell vacant through the death of Knute Nelson, the voters sent a second Farmer-Labor Senator, Magnus Johnson, to join Shipstead in Washington.

Stunned by the ferocity of the agrarian revolt, Harding cooperated with the farm bloc to push the Federal Intermediate Credit Act through the lame-duck Congress on the last day of the session. The new measure built on the foundation of the Federal Farm Loan Act, adding twelve new banks which would extend credit to farmers on a broader basis than the original banks.

THE DEATH OF HARDING

Further measures of farm relief could not be undertaken until the new and more militant Congress met in December 1923. To strengthen his position against extremists who seemed certain to dominate that body, Harding lauched a transcontinental speaking tour on June 20, 1923. Although few people suspected it at the time, he was also seeking momentary escape from problems of a grave character. For a man whose personal code emphasized blind reliance on his friends, Harding had shown unusually poor judgment in making appointments from this group. Rumors were beginning to reach him about the misuse of funds in the Veterans' Bureau and of improper activities in the Alien Property Office and the Justice Department. A senatorial subcommittee headed by Thomas J. Walsh of Montana was investigating a series of oil leases made by the Secretary of the Interior. Just how much Harding knew about the details of the wrongdoing that became public property the following year is uncertain, but he did know that charges would soon be made against members of the administration who were close personal friends. The available evidence suggests that he left Washington brooding deeply over his betrayal.

Harding's conduct on the tour was that of a man trying to shut out problems beyond his power to solve. From St. Louis to Seattle he petted livestock, pitched hay, drove farm machinery, donned miners' lamps and cowboy hats, and joined Indian tribes. This routine, coupled with several major speeches in defense of his policies, reduced him to the verge of a breakdown in Seattle. A voyage to Alaska failed to revive him and after his return to Seattle he fell ill of ptomaine poisoning. He was rushed to San Francisco, and specialists were summoned to his bedside. His condition grew rapidly worse. Pneumonia set in on July 31 and was followed without warning by an embolism which killed him instantly on August 2, 1923. The progress of disease would probably not have been so rapid had he possessed the will to live. Subsequent developments suggest that death was a merciful solution to his problems.

The immediate reaction of an unsuspecting public was one of grief over the loss of a very human and lovable President. The large crowds that gathered respectfully along the route of the funeral train from San Francisco to Washington and then to Marion, Ohio, regarded him as the victim of an overexacting job.

THE NEW PRESIDENT

Political parties seldom select a vice-presidential candidate with the expectation that he will reach the White House. Election strategy rather than qualification for executive leadership normally governs the nomination. Consequently, good fortune rather than foresight led the 1920 Republican Convention to choose for Vice-President Calvin Coolidge, a politician whose political outlook was almost identical with Harding's.

As mayor of Northhampton, state senator, and Governor of Massachusetts, Coolidge had served an exacting apprenticeship. Although he lacked the good looks, appetite for sports, and Rotarian heartiness of Harding, he in his own way embodied the tastes and aspirations of those who had elected his predecessor. He dressed soberly, saved money, displayed an old-style Yankee canniness, and genuinely abhorred ostentatious social functions. He shared the prejudice of the average small-town American against the bohemian manners of the younger generation and disliked modernism in art, psychology, religion, or elsewhere.

Despite a limited stock of ideas, Coolidge achieved a status as a dispenser of folk wisdom comparable to that of Henry Ford. His commonplace statements seemed to possess an oracular dignity because they were delivered tersely and with an occasional touch of dry humor. A kindred streak of taciturnity contributed to his reputation for wisdom. By making public pronouncements as infrequently as possible, he guaranteed a respectful audience for anything he said. To Americans impatient of machine-age complexities, he seemed like a combination of Aesop and Ben Franklin.

The political philosophy that Coolidge brought to the White House was quite simple and straightforward. He admired American business as the source of national prosperity and intended to create a favorable environment for private enterprise. Beyond tax relief and the reduction of government expenditures, he saw no need for legislative activity. He regarded the various proposals of the farm bloc as costly and futile. As the son of a Vermont farmer who had little to show for a lifetime of hard work, he reached the conclusion that rural poverty was an immutable feature of the economic system. He recognized the political need of seeming to be doing something for the farmers but was deeply prejudiced against large-scale government action in their behalf. The demands of the lesser pressure groups, like organized labor and the veterans, he proposed to ignore entirely. What made this formula of aggressive inactivity so extraordinary was the fact that it succeeded politically.

Before Coolidge could get his belongings decently unpacked in the White

House, evidence of graft and corruption began hitting the front pages of the newspapers. A voluminous output of revelations, continuing until the eve of the 1924 presidential campaign, implicated high officials in the Republican party. Practically all had been close to Harding. Attorney General Harry Daugherty, who connived at the diversion of confiscated liquor from government warehouses into the hands of bootleggers, had engineered Harding's nomination. Two of his associates, Jesse Smith, a jovial clotheshorse and lobbyist, and Thomas W. Miller, who pocketed $50,000 in disposing of patents as Alien Property Custodian, were also charter members of the Ohio gang that followed him to Washington. Colonel Charles R. Forbes, Director of the Veterans' Bureau, did not belong to the original coterie but stood close enough to him to receive great publicity for milking the Bureau of $250,000. Miller and Forbes eventually went to prison, Daugherty escaped because of a hung jury but had to resign as Attorney General, and Jesse Smith committed suicide.

These disclosures produced only a mild sensation compared to the Teapot Dome scandal, which featured everybody from a crooked Cabinet officer to a playboy newspaper millionaire. The key figure was Albert B. Fall, the New Mexican with the granitelike face, the piercing blue eyes, and the bluff hearty manner of the westerner. As a United States Senator, he had been intimate with Harding. The selection of Fall as Secretary of the Interior was like the selection of a wolf to guard sheep, for Fall favored indiscriminate private exploitation of the public lands. His dislike of conservation dated from 1910 when the authorities had caught him trying to overgraze Almo National Forest by entering two thousand sheep under the name of an employee.

As Secretary of the Interior Fall made a systematic attempt to concentrate the administration of all the public lands under his jurisdiction. Although the Department of Agriculture successfully resisted his efforts to get control of the Forest Service, Edwin Denby, Secretary of the Navy, obligingly transferred to him the administration of oil lands. In the spring of 1922 he secretly leased the Teapot Dome field to Harry F. Sinclair, and Elk Hills to Edward L. Doheny, both of whom were large oil operators.

When the Senate heard of these transactions, the Public Lands Committee called Fall for questioning. He defended his decision to reverse the congressional policy of storing oil underground on the plea that private companies were draining government pools. He justified his policy of secret leases as a maneuver to mislead Japan. The senators were not entirely satisfied with these explanations. Chairman La Follette appointed a subcommittee under Thomas J. Walsh to investigate further, whereupon Fall contemptuously dumped a truckload of documents about oil leases on the Montana senator's desk. It took Walsh nearly eighteen months to plow through the material, most of which was irrelevant or unrevealing.

Meanwhile Fall's behavior gave the committee more reason to distrust his integrity. He resigned his Cabinet post, took a leisurely trip through Europe, purchased a New Mexico ranch for $91,000, and made immediate improvements on the property which brought the total cost up to $175,000. Walsh again called Fall for questioning about the sources of his new affluence. At first Fall stuck to his original story, but in the ensuing weeks other witnesses made this so untenable that he admitted receiving "loans" of $100,000 from Doheny and of more than $200,000 from Sinclair. This damaging testimony in January 1924 was the climax of the case.

On the basis of the evidence extracted by the subcommittee, Fall, Doheny, and Sinclair were indicted for conspiracy against the United States. The accused used every available legal resource to avert conviction with the result that the case dragged on for several years. Fall beat the charge of conspiracy but was eventually found guilty in October 1929 of accepting a bribe, fined a hundred thousand dollars, and sentenced to one year in jail. The verdict did not create a ripple because by that time citizens had other things to worry about. Sinclair and Doheny escaped conviction on both counts, although the former served a short sentence for contempt of the Senate committee. The only other inconvenience they suffered was the cancellation of their leases at Elk Hills and Teapot Dome.

Coolidge adroitly chose the role of bystander during the investigations. He felt that the newspapers were much more excited than their readers and assumed that the whole issue would disappear in the bottomless sink of public apathy if he did nothing to revive it. So beyond dismissing Daugherty and issuing a statement that the guilty would be punished, he took no official notice of the proceedings. This appraisal of public opinion was completely accurate. All the emotional indignation against crooks had been squandered on the bribery of major league baseball players during the World Series of 1919. Corruption in the national administration simply failed to incense citizens as it had done during the Progressive era.

Coolidge was almost as fortunate in his relations with the rebellious agrarian wing of his party. Most farmers disliked low prices rather than the capitalist system. Consequently their chief inducement to unrest disappeared as the prices of farm commodities rose steadily in the spring and summer of 1924. Those who thought in terms of the lush war years were still dissatisfied, but many farmers instinctively returned to their old place in the Republican party without a single promise from Coolidge.

The President's gradual consolidation of control over the Republican organization was a quiet professional job. To assure his nomination, he appointed C. Bascom Slemp, a former congressman from Virginia, as his secretary. Slemp promptly rounded up all the southern delegates. William M. Butler, a Massachusetts industrialist who had replaced Henry Cabot Lodge in the Senate, did the same job in the populous eastern states. Thus long before the convention a majority of the delegates were pledged to Coolidge. Western agrarians were forced to accept him or bolt the party.

Without any ground swell of popular enthusiasm he had become inevitable. Clinton Gilbert summarized the situation nicely when he said that Coolidge, "like the singed cat, is better than he looks."

THE SOLDIERS' BONUS AND TAX RELIEF

Only in his dealing with the refractory Sixty-eighth Congress did Coolidge receive a serious setback. He wanted to reduce expenditures and taxes, while Congress held out just as stubbornly for the soldiers' bonus. The two issues were connected only to the extent that appropriation of funds for a bonus would reduce the effectiveness of pleas for lower taxes. Other motives, however, played a larger role in generating sentiment for the bonus. A number of Republican congressmen, recalling that the post-Civil War supremacy of the party had been built partly on the support of pension-hungry veterans, hoped to revive the policy in the twenties and reap the same happy consequences. Other congressmen simply feared the result of defying the veterans in an election year, and there was ample justification for their attitude. Colonel Theodore Roosevelt, Jr., the son of the deceased President, had promoted an organization of all veterans called the American Legion, which received a congressional charter on September 16, 1919. Within a matter of months, the Legion had emerged in the forefront of the drive against radicals and aliens, launched a campaign for strong national defense, and sponsored awards to promote good citizenship. It rode the prevailing wave of nationalist sentiment so successfully that resistance to the demands of its well-organized lobby was regarded as unpatriotic. The law of August 9, 1921, had already set up a Veterans' Bureau to provide hospitals and rest homes for soldiers. Later legislation had gradually extended medical and compensation rights to veterans suffering from disabilities that might have been contracted during the war. Some eight thousand special cases were handled through private pension bills. The focal point of the Legion lobby was a bonus, or "adjusted compensation" as it was euphemistically called. Spokesmen for the veterans insisted that some retroactive pay increase was necessary to make up for the low wartime wages received by soldiers while civilians got rich on defense contracts.

Representative Fordney introduced the first bonus bill in May 1920. It sailed through the House by a huge majority, only to die in the Senate. The Legion redoubled its pressure, and two years later a slightly different version passed the House by 333 to 70 and the Senate by 47 to 22. Harding showed unexpected political courage by vetoing this piece of legislation on September 19, 1922. The House, with an eye on the impending elections, overrode his veto. But the Senate sustained it by four votes.

Nothing further could be done until the long session of Congress which started in December 1923. Ignoring Coolidge's objections, both houses again passed the bill by a lopsided vote and sent it to the White House on

May 7, 1924. In final form the measure called for twenty-year paid-up endowment policies to be given to veterans on the basis of $1.00 a day for home service and $1.25 a day for overseas service. The veterans were also authorized to borrow up to 22.5 per cent on the face value of their endowments, which averaged $1,500 and bore 4 per cent interest. The Act established a special category for those entitled to less than fifty dollars and permitted them to be paid in cash.

Coolidge, like his predecessor, vetoed the bonus bill. He labeled the measure as class legislation, described it as a deadly blow to government economy, chided the proponents for failing to pass a companion law that would raise the necessary funds, and accurately predicted fresh bonus demands in the future. Congress ignored these objections and overrode the veto by comfortable margins. The cost of this legislation was expected to reach $3.5 billion. Added to the payments made under successive acts providing hospital service and vocational rehabilitation for veterans, the total cost by 1932 had reached $17.5 billion. The magnitude of the program showed what a well-organized pressure group could accomplish and provided a model for the more numerous raids on the federal Treasury in the 1930's.

Although the passage of the Bonus Act reduced the effectiveness of presidential pleas for tax reduction, Coolidge's defeat on the latter issue was primarily due to Democratic solidarity in a closely divided Congress. The issue revolved around the question of eliminating the excess-profits tax and the high surtax rates on individual incomes which had been instituted as war measures. Neither produced large amounts of revenue. Since ninety-three out of every one hundred Americans did not receive the net income of $3,000 which obligated them to make an income tax return in 1920, high surtaxes clearly fell on the wealthy few. The excess-profits tax likewise reached only an inconsiderable number of large corporations after the war. Business found it hard to calculate and claimed that it penalized efficiency. The Democrats in Congress from the rural South and the farm bloc Republicans wanted to retain the wartime levies which cost their constituents nothing. Both sides professed concern over the public debt that had reached a high of $26,596,701,648 in August 1919, and defended their differing tax proposals as designed to lower it. Neither side understood that the great potentialities of the income tax as a revenue producer could be realized by lowering exemptions and broadening coverage.

The opponents of the administration had the best of the early fighting. Before Wilson left office, basic or normal income tax rates were reduced from 6 to 4 per cent on the first $4,000 of taxable income and from 12 to 10 per cent on the remainder, but the surtax rates were left untouched. Harding repeatedly sought the repeal of the excess-profits tax and the reduction of surtaxes. Congress responded by raising the former and ignoring the recommendation regarding the latter. Coolidge with the enthusiastic support of Mellon tackled the matter again in his annual message to the unruly Sixty-eighth Congress in December 1923. He proposed reduction in normal and surtax rates, sweetening the recommendation with the suggestion that the greatest relief be granted to those in the lower brackets. He reiterated Harding's plea for the elimination of the excess-profits tax and added his own plea for the repeal of the estate tax. He also asked Congress to start a constitutional amendment that would abolish tax-exempt securities.

When the Revenue Act of 1924 reached the President for signature in June, it followed his recommendation only to the point of granting a token reduction in the normal and surtax rates. The antagonistic temper of Congress was revealed in the provision for raising the estate tax from 25 to 40 per cent and for publishing the names of all persons making tax returns and the amount they paid. Coolidge criticized both the general spirit and the specific items of the new tax law but eventually signed it.

THE THREE-CORNERED ELECTION

The campaign of 1924 was one of the dullest on record. Generally speaking, public concern over policies decreases as prosperity increases, and 1924 was a prosperous year. Except for the coal and textile industries, the railroads, and some segments of the farm population, the level of economic activity pushed steadily higher. Nevertheless, even the routine complacency bred by prosperity does not entirely account for the extraordinary apathy. The uninspiring character of the candidates and the hollowness of the campaign issues stifled whatever interest was left.

The Republican Convention met at Cleveland in mid-June and gave Coolidge a first-ballot nomination with 1,065 out of a possible 1,109 votes. It tried to show a spark of independent enthusiasm by offering the vice-presidency to Frank Lowden, a conspicuous advocate of farm bloc policies. Lowden refused, several others also turned down the chance, and so the nomination finally went to the blunt-spoken Director of the Budget, Charles G. Dawes, who was a kind of midwestern Coolidge. The platform generously attributed the reviving prosperity to the meager legislative achievements of the administration. It also pledged the party to pursue the same successful course during the ensuing four years. There were orthodox endorsements of such policies as conservation, immigration restriction, and the eight-hour day. Corruption and child labor were deplored, and a constitutional amendment was urged to eliminate the latter. Farmers and veterans received a courteous reminder that the party had befriended them, as well as a hint of more blessings to come. Foreign affairs received cursory treatment, the most notable planks being devoted to an endorsement of the World Court and a sneer at the League of Nations. The Ku Klux Klan, which dominated several Republican state organizations, was ignored.

The Democrats met at Madison Square Garden, New York City, two weeks later in a state of disorganization induced by their poor prospects. The southerners had split into a series of state parties whose major interests were local enforcement of prohibition and white supremacy. Defense of the low tariff was no longer a potent rallying cry in a South that was undergoing substantial industrialization. Hence there was less reason than usual for Dixie to accept a candidate with views unacceptable to her. That was exactly what the northern Democrats wanted. In the years following World War I, their wing of the party had become the champion of the Catholic immigrant workingman who disliked the Ku Klux Klan and prohibition. This cleavage left the southerner closer to the conservative-nationalist wing of the Republican party in most respects than to northern members of his own party.

A strong leader might have redeemed the situation, but none emerged to replace the deceased Wilson. Bryan was still active and his ear was cocked to receive the call, but a long record of political indiscretions capped by the crusades in behalf of prohibition and Fundamentalism made him unacceptable. The freshman senators and governors produced by the 1922 elections were not taken seriously as presidential candidates by any one except themselves. Thus the field narrowed down to ex-Secretary of the Treasury William G. McAdoo and Governor Alfred E. Smith of New York, who had first been elected in 1918 when Democrats elsewhere were losing. The northeastern delegates coalesced around Smith; those from the South and West around McAdoo. A large bloc of favorite sons prevented either from getting the two-thirds vote necessary to nominate. After 102 fruitless ballots the delegates were so tired and short of money that they nominated John W. Davis of West Virginia. A conservative corporation lawyer, who had not recently been active in public affairs, his qualifications were two undistinguished terms in Congress, a short hitch as Solicitor General, and three years as Ambassador to Great Britain. By naming a standard-bearer as safe and colorless as Davis, the Democrats condemned themselves to defeat in November. They paid a tribute to William Jennings Bryan by giving the vice-presidential nomination to his brother Charles, who was also Governor of Nebraska. The platform contained an abnormal number of vague planks because the party could agree on nothing else. The Klan escaped denunciation by five votes, and prohibition was handled with caution. Aside from routine criticisms of Republican legislation and an indignant denunciation of corruption, the domestic planks in the two platforms were almost indistinguishable. Even in the section devoted to foreign affairs, the Democrats moved closer to their opponents by cutting the detrimental League of Nations from around their necks. When the convention adjourned, it was hard to predict what the orators would find to argue about.

Coolidge did not enjoy campaigning even under the most favorable circumstances. His determination to avoid the conventional swing around the country was reinforced by the tragic death of his younger son in midsummer. The grief-stricken father could not bear the carnival spirit of the speaking tour, so he worked quietly in the White House during most of the campaign. Whenever he did break his silence, he emphasized economy almost to the exclusion of other issues. His speech to one business organization was typical: "I am for economy; after that I am for more economy. At this time and under present conditions that is my concept of serving all the people."

While Coolidge was focusing his attention on governmental frugality, Davis urged the voters to be guided by higher moral considerations. He spoke indignantly of corruption and condemned the Republicans as unfit to provide honest or competent public service. Others amplified his theme, sometimes with more conviction; but the public remained uninterested.

The only excitement in the campaign was provided by Senator La Follette. The stormy petrel of Wisconsin politics, then in his seventieth year, decided to bolt the Republican party when the convention contemptuously ignored his bid for the nomination. He issued a call for a convention of Progressives at Cleveland on July 4. The delegates who assembled showed considerable militance. They nominated La Follette for President and a radical Democrat, Senator Burton K. Wheeler of Montana, for Vice-President. This ticket subsequently picked up endorsement from the Socialist party, the Farmer Labor party, and the A. F. of L. The Communists offered to help but were indignantly repudiated by La Follette. Thereupon they ran their own ticket with William Z. Foster as their candidate for President.

The platform adopted by the Progressive party was the handiwork of La Follette. It contained fourteen points and expressed the same concern over the welfare of underprivileged farmers and workers as earlier third-party platforms. In most respects it did not advance beyond the ground occupied by the Populists in 1892 and the Bull Moosers in 1912. What made it seem dangerously radical was the fact that socialistic implications were more evident than in earlier platforms. Many of the old Populist expedients for dealing with monopoly were endorsed. The Progressives' platform revived the plank for government ownership of railroads which had been dropped by the third party in 1912. It also extended to water power the principle of public ownership. Other natural resources were to be strictly regulated by the government. The platform likewise showed closer affinity to Populists than to Progressives in advocating direct election of judges and congressional authority to override judicial decisions. A whole section was devoted to condemnation of the Versailles peace settlement and its aftermath. Postwar foreign policy was labeled imperialistic. The solution urged was total disarmament and the outlawing of war.

La Follette hoped to become the spokesman for the great army of Progressives that had dispersed during the war, but the only groups to which he now appealed were a sprinkling of eastern intellectuals, a corporal's guard of erstwhile Progressives protesting the curtailment of free expression, a portion of organized labor, and an indeterminate number of disgruntled farmers. To make matters worse, the latter group shrank steadily while the campaign was going on. As the *New York Herald* put it cynically but accurately: "With wheat at $1.23 a bushel, keeping the 'discontented' farmer discontented becomes more of a problem." Still other difficulties dogged the grim, conscientious La Follette. Election laws prevented him from getting on the ballot in some states and forced him to run under the Socialist label in others. Where flourishing third parties already existed, as in Minnesota, his managers quarreled with the state organizations over the distribution of campaign funds.

Old "Fighting Bob" no longer cut an impressive figure in stump speeches. Never popular in the East, he had begun to lose his touch in the Midwest where the generation which enjoyed three-hour speeches crammed with statistics was rapidly dying out. Burt Wheeler did what he could to lighten the colorless tone of the campaign. He stormed about the country proclaiming that Coolidge and Davis were just alike, driving his point home by referring to them as the "Gold Dust twins." He also asked his opponents to debate and capitalized their refusal by dragging two empty chairs on the rostrum and addressing leading questions to the absent candidates.

The launching of a third-party ticket proved to be a godsend for the Republicans, who had always campaigned most effectively when they were saving the country from something. Even the most enthusiastic G.O.P. partisan could not represent Davis as a menace, but it was easy to picture La Follette as a kind of American Kerensky whose advent to power would be the prelude to revolution. Accordingly the Republicans ignored the semi-respectable Democrats and concentrated their fire on the Progressives. Not only were the latter condemned for harboring ideas abhorrent to the American way of life but for threatening a constitutional crisis. Republican orators speculated about the dreadful consequences that might follow if the Progressive vote was sufficiently large to prevent any candidate from getting a majority. According to their analysis the party strength in the House was too evenly divided for a President to be elected, in which case the choice of Vice-President would devolve on the Senate. By assuming that the two Farmer-Labor senators from Minnesota would vote with the Democrats, the Republicans predicted the selection of Charley Bryan as Vice-President and therefore *de facto* President.

The electorate was supposed to conclude from Republican speculations about constitutional probabilities that a vote for La Follette meant a vote for the paralysis of normal election machinery. Whether the citizens actually feared such a contingency or whether they decided to endorse prosperity, the President won a comfortable victory in November. Out of nearly 29,000,000 votes, Coolidge polled 15,726,016; Davis 8,386,503; and La Follette 4,822,856. As usual, the winner piled up a more lopsided advantage in the electoral college. The totals for the three parties were:

Republicans, 382; Democrats, 136; and Progressives, 13. With the exception of Wisconsin, which went to La Follette, and a couple of border states which changed sides, Coolidge carried the same states won by Harding four years earlier. In seventeen west central and north central states where agrarian disaffection ran high, the Progressives outpolled the Democrats 1,829,000 to 957,000. Previous indications of apathy were confirmed by the fact that only half the eligible voters went to the polls.

TAX RELIEF

Coolidge interpreted the election as a mandate for four years of inactivity. He gave the clearest expression of this attitude in the inaugural address of March 4, 1925, when he said, "Our most important problem is not to secure new advantages but to maintain those which we already possess." Translated into practical terms, it meant that he would accept no major legislative proposals except those that would cut government expenditures and ease taxes. Behind all this was his simple faith that prosperity for business assured prosperity for other groups. Thinking in such terms, he was bound to oppose laws which increased the burdens of business.

Theoretically the President possessed a comfortable working majority in the new Congress. The Senate was composed of fifty Republicans, forty Democrats, and six who had broken ranks to support La Follette. In the House, where about the same ratio prevailed, the Republicans held 233 seats, the Democrats 183, and the Progressives 20. If the La Follette group had included all the farm bloc dissidents, presidential leadership would have been easy to assert, but actually the Republican majority was honeycombed with party members regular in name only.

The administration Republicans had enough strength to exclude legislators who had supported La Follette from key committee assignments, but their margin was not sufficient to give them control of the Congress. Coolidge was handed a stunning defeat six days after his inauguration when the Senate rejected the nomination of Charles B. Warren of Michigan for Attorney General. Otherwise he was allowed to remodel his Cabinet as he chose. Ex-Senator Frank B. Kellogg replaced Charles Evans Hughes as Secretary of State. Other changes followed until the only members left from the Harding era were Mellon, Hoover, and James J. Davis, the Secretary of Labor.

Coolidge did hold Congress in line long enough to accomplish the tax reforms so dear to his heart. The Revenue Act of February 1926 reduced the normal income tax rates to 1.5 per cent on the first $4,000 and drastically cut the surtaxes which the Democrats and the farm bloc Republicans had resisted for so long. Citizens with incomes of over $100,000 would pay a maximum of 20 per cent under the new law. The estate tax was cut in half, and the clause of the 1924 Revenue Law requiring publicity of tax returns was repealed.

Opponents of the measure predicted that tax relief would prevent reduction of the public debt. When revenue continued to rise, they took the opposite tack and condemned the administration for not reducing taxes enough. So in 1928 Coolidge and Mellon prevailed upon Congress to cut the corporation tax to 12 per cent and abolish the automobile sales tax. Notwithstanding the successive rounds of reduction, treasury collections remained large, with the result that the public debt, which stood at $26 billion in 1920 was cut to $16 billion by 1930. Thus Coolidge accomplished his twin objectives — the relief of business from heavy taxation and the reduction of the public debt. Since prosperity prevailed under his program, Coolidge converted many doubters to the proposition that generous treatment of business would guarantee a high level of investment and economic activity. Fortunately he retired from office before the Great Depression shattered public faith in the adequacy of his policy.

COOLIDGE FIGHTS THE FARM BLOC

Once the Revenue Law of 1926 was out of the way the farm bloc seized the initiative from Coolidge and held it for the remainder of his term. The struggle ended in a deadlock, which was actually a victory for Coolidge, because the farm bloc possessed the votes to pass its program but not enough to override a presidential veto.

Despite some improvement in conditions during the middle of the 1920's, farmers were growing more of the basic crops than could be sold at a profit. A series of mechanical inventions starting with the McCormick reaper in 1847 had made possible the mechanization of almost every step in agricultural production by the beginning of the twentieth century. A majority of the farmers possessed neither the financial resources nor sufficiently large acreage to warrant full mechanization of their farms. On the other hand, those who purchased reapers, combines, or binders could raise a larger crop with less work. Louis Hacker has estimated that it took 183 minutes to produce a bushel of grain in 1830, and only 10 minutes by 1900. The widespread introduction of the tractor opened up vast new tracts because the machine could operate in areas of less water and fodder than could draft animals.

Time does not permit us to dwell on the sociological aspects of agricultural mechanization. The economic by-products were increase in production, decrease in the number of farmers, and acceleration in the consolidation of agricultural holdings. The outbreak of World War I encouraged these trends because it produced an unprecedented demand for American food. Wheat acreage alone increased 50 per cent. Much of the additional crop was grown on marginal land which justified cultivation only when prices remained high. A good portion of it lay in the arid states of the Great Plains where rainfall is irregular. Montana alone increased the amount of wheat land from 258,000 acres in 1909 to 3,417,000 acres in

1919. There and elsewhere the price of land rose from 100 to 300 per cent. Farmers sought to take advantage of the boom by mortgaging their property so that they could buy acres.

The abnormal European demand for American food products ended in the summer of 1929, leaving farmers with greatly expanded acreage and heavy indebtedness. Prices dropped sharply, dragging land values down with them; but property taxes, transportation rates, and interest payments on mortgages remained fixed. To make matters worse, the Federal Reserve Board pursued a deflationary policy, raising the discount rates and demanding additional collateral from rural banks, which were in turn forced to call in farm loans. Numerous country banks failed in 1921 and 1922, and large numbers of farmers lost their property.

As we have already seen, the Sixty-seventh Congress lashed back at the banks, the grain brokers, the packers, and sundry other enemies of agriculture with a legislative program worthy of the Populists. Enthusiasm for it evaporated quickly, however, because it provided little relief. The Government Intermediate Farm Banks loaned more freely than private institutions, but easier money simply enabled farmers to bury themselves more deeply in debt. Far from correcting the conditions which made farmers seek loans, the laws regulating middlemen and authorizing cooperative marketing did not improve prices. Even the close supervision of the railroads failed to bring any tangible benefits. The farm bloc therefore began to look for new remedies.

The most obvious cure for continued low prices was restriction of production. Manfacturers had discovered this some years earlier and had set up monopolies to limit output whenever necessary. Farmers, however, always resisted so elementary a solution. A strong sense of self-interest as well as the absence of any organizational machinery to enforce cuts militated against such an experiment on a voluntary basis. Farmers would also have resisted compulsory crop restrictions on political grounds. The truth was that they, like other pressure groups, preferred a solution that would place the financial sacrifices on other taxpayers.

They found exactly the remedy they wanted in the McNary-Haugen Bill. Credit for devising the new scheme belongs to George Peek and Hugh S. Johnson, executives of the Moline Plow Company, who had become interested farm problems when the market for plows disappeared after the war. The most novel feature of their proposal was to shift the emphasis in farm relief from penalizing hostile pressure groups to creating a stable price for key agricultural commodities. Peek and Johnson believed that this objective could be achieved by empowering a government corporation to deal in such commodities. The latter would presumably maintain the world price plus the protective tariff rate on that portion of a crop sold in the domestic market by buying the remainder at the same total price and dumping it abroad. The losses on exports were to be recouped by an equalization fee assessed against each farmer on the percentage of his crop marketed abroad. In other words, if the world price of wheat was a dollar a bushel, and the tariff forty cents, a farmer who produced 1,000 bushels and exported 200 bushels would be $320 better off under the proposed legislation. He would get $1,400 instead of $1,000 for his crop and would refund as equalization fee the amount of the tariff protection (forty cents) on each of the 200 bushels sent abroad, or a total of eighty dollars. The scheme owed its special charm in agrarian circles to the fact that it proposed to raise prices without restricting production. Utilization of the tariff also strengthened the likelihood that the consumer would pay the bill.

Congress considered four separate versions of the McNary-Haugen bill between 1924 and 1928. The House turned down the initial version on June 3, 1924, because the commodities singled out for special treatment were grown primarily in the Midwest. Its appeal was also too limited to win congressional support two years later. When cotton and tobacco were added to the list of key commodities, the bill cleared both houses in February 1927.

Coolidge promptly vetoed it. His opposition had been announced during the 1924 campaign when he criticized it as a price-fixing measure. As McNary-Haugen advocates picked up supporters in ensuing years, the President had taken a stronger stand in behalf of cooperative marketing. To head off southern support of the legislation, he had appointed a Cotton Committee in October 1926, and authorized $3 million in loans to cotton-marketing organizations. Hence his veto of February 25, 1927, did not come as a surprise. In the accompanying message, he criticized the measure on every conceivable ground. He assailed it as special-interest legislation designed to help the growers of a few staples rather than agriculture in general, he characterized the price-fixing features as a departure from American principles, and he warned Congress that the provision authorizing the Farm Board to collect the equalization fee was an unconstitutional delegation of legislative power. The President also predicted that the plan would lead to further overproduction and retaliatory dumping by foreign powers. Much of the analysis in the veto was sound, but it would have done Coolidge more credit if he had been a consistent opponent of pressure groups and discriminatory trade practices. As the unblushing defender of business interests and of high protective tariffs, he sounded less convincing.

The farm bloc could not muster the two-thirds vote needed to override the veto. Nevertheless it came back the following year with a fourth version of the bill, which cleared both houses by May 1928, only to be killed by another veto. Although the issue bobbed up in the ensuing presidential campaign, the agitation for price fixing had passed its high-water mark. Farmers were forced to settle for legislation already passed until their economic condition took a turn for the worse during the Great Depression.

THE MUSCLE SHOALS CONTROVERSY

On still another front Coolidge waged vigorous defensive warfare, which postponed for several years the entrance of the federal government into the power business. The focal point of the controversy was Muscle Shoals, a thirty-five-mile strip along the Tennessee River where dams had been started during the war to provide power for the manufacture of fertilizers and explosives. The advocates of government intervention, headed by Senator George W. Norris, favored completion of the dams and chemical plants. Their ostensible reason was the enlargement of national defense facilities. What really interested them was the sale of surplus power. They thought that if the government engaged in such activity, it could establish a yardstick of proper rates for the private utility companies.

Neither Harding nor his successor adopted this line of reasoning. The former stopped construction on the facilities and sought to dispose of them. In July 1921, Henry Ford offered to lease them for one hundred years, buy the nitrate plants, and provide forty thousand tons of nitrogen annually if the government would complete the dams under construction.

Before Congress could act on the proposal, Harding died and several utilities companies made competing bids. Coolidge promptly urged the sale of the property to the highest bidder as a sure way to keep the government out of the power business. Norris, who was a resourceful fighter, managed to block this proposal, which the President continued to recommend in every annual message. The balance of strength between the antagonists was so close that Coolidge had to use a pocket veto in 1928 to prevent adoption of the Norris plan.

While the Muscle Shoals facilities slowly depreciated during the controversy, Congress and the President cooperated on the less explosive issue of flood control. The disastrous Mississippi River flood in 1927, which destroyed $400 million worth of property, and rendered 700,000 homeless, led directly to the Jones-Reid Act of 1928. It appropriated $300 million for the erection of levees and spillways at the most dangerous points on the river. Ever mindful of economy, Coolidge unsuccessfully urged Congress to pass a fifth of the cost on to the states.

Although Coolidge had blocked frontal assaults of the public power advocates, the latter were able to work the Boulder Dam Project Act through Congress in December 1928. The measure, which represented an effort to control the turbulent Colorado River, was politically irresistible because it combined flood control, irrigation, and hydroelectric power development. Since 1922 the states of the Colorado basin had been trying to work out a compact for the allocation of river water. Their tentative agreement paved the way for the legislation of 1928. The contribution of the federal government was to be the 750-foot Boulder Dam near Las

Vegas, Nevada, an irrigation canal to the Imperial Valley of California, and plants for generating hydroelectric power. The public power advocates succeeded in wedging the latter provision in the law as a means for the government to recapture its investment of approximately $165 million. The money was to be raised by the sale of both water rights and electric power to states in the Colorado basin. Coolidge disliked the measure but allowed it to become law.

CONGRESS DEFIES COOLIDGE

Because of the President's negative attitude toward farm relief and most other legislative projects, relations between the executive and Congress grew steadily worse during his last two years in office. The G.O.P. had suffered the normal off-year losses in the 1926 election, which reduced their majority in the House and left forty-eight Republicans facing forty-seven Democrats and one Farmer-Laborite. As a result, the Republican leadership had to give the 1924 rebels their old committee assignments to retain even nominal control of the upper house. Inside the party, the insurgents were as rebellious as they had been outside. Strengthened numerically by the election, they harassed Coolidge at every step. Norris teamed up with a freshman North Dakota senator, Gerald Nye, to wage a campaign against excessive election expenditures, which embarrassed several regular Republicans. It eventually ended in a vote by the upper house to deny Frank L. Smith of Illinois and William S. Vare of Pennsylvania their Senate seats. Presidential critics in the Senate also ignored a Coolidge statement declining to run for re-election and adopted a resolution February 10, 1928, expressing opposition to a third term. Thus during the dying months of Coolidge's term, the President and Congress barely remained on speaking terms.

If the negativism of Coolidge is difficult to admire, it is also difficult to condemn without broadening the indictment to include the American public. The widespread apathy toward political problems that characterized the period suggests that the majority of voters preferred inactivity. If such was the case, Coolidge faithfully represented his nationwide constituency.

SUGGESTED READINGS

1. Adams, S. H., *Incredible Era: The Life and Times of Warren G. Harding.*
2. Paxon, F. L., *American Democracy and the World War* (vol. 3).
3. Sullivan, M., *Our Times* (vol. 6).
4. White, W. A., *A Puritan in Babylon.*

CHAPTER EIGHTEEN

THE OUTBREAK OF THE GREAT DEPRESSION

HOOVER BECOMES PRESIDENT

"We'll leave that to the wonder boy." With this tart comment Coolidge passed a number of uninteresting problems on to President-elect Herbert Hoover. The use of the term "wonder boy" was a by-product of the 1928 campaign. Hoover had been presented as an embodiment of all the qualities necessary for putting prosperity on a permanent basis. By successfully organizing Belgian food relief during World War I he had earned the title of humanitarian; as Secretary of Commerce, his untiring effort to promote business cooperation and standardization of production had publicized him as an efficiency engineer. This reputation was combined with such respectable antecedents as birth in a weathered Iowa farmhouse, a heroic fight against poverty to win his bachelor's degree at Stanford University, and a distinguished career as a mining engineer in the Orient.

Business analysts had already prepared the public for the advent of an economic New Jerusalem based on statistical studies and scientific methods of production. Consequently the nomination of a presidential candidate whose name had been identified with the successful application of such techniques was bound to release some florid oratory. Republican campaign managers presented him to the country as an omniscient administrator who would run the United States as if it were General Motors Corporation. Hoover himself also made modest contributions to the growth of the legend. In his speech accepting the nomination, he cheerfully predicted that "we in America are nearer to the final triumph over poverty than ever before in the history of any land."

The build-up continued even after victory had rendered further activity unnecessary. Early in December 1928, Governor Owen Brewster of Maine revealed the existence of a Hoover program for public works that would be held in reserve in case of economic troubles. He went on to assert that fact-finding agencies would recognize the signs of a depression far in advance, thereby enabling the President to prevent it through nationwide construction projects. An economy-minded electorate was also assured that the program would not raise the cost of government; pending projects would simply be deferred until the crucial time. The Republican party succeeded so well in establishing Hoover's reputation as an expert on economic problems that the onslaught of a world-wide depression in the fall of 1929 provoked disillusionment and bitterness.

The Kansas City Convention which nominated Hoover in mid-June of 1928 was the closest the Republicans came to enjoying an unbossed convention during the postwar decade. Coolidge had taken himself out of the race in the summer of 1927. Pushing taciturnity to new lengths, he had issued a one-line statement from his Black Hills vacation retreat on August 2: "I do not choose to run." His political supporters refused to take his withdrawal seriously and organized a Draft Coolidge movement. There is some evidence that the silent man in the White House looked favorably on such activity, but he gave his supporters such scant outward encouragement that the drive quickly lost momentum.

Meanwhile various candidates entered the contest. The farm bloc would have liked to unite behind a senator favorable to the McNary-Haugen plan, but none possessed the necessary stature and political appeal. Borah was willing but he was too much of a lone wolf to accept even the informal discipline of the farm bloc. Blaine of Wisconsin, who had inherited the old La Follette organization, showed excessive zeal for the repeal of prohibition. George W. Norris was the ablest of the group, but eastern Republicans regarded his repeated re-elections to the Senate as a deliberate attempt by Nebraska to insult the party. That left only the aging Frank O. Lowden of Illinois, who had not held public office during the decade and hence had taken no direct part in the parliamentary battles over farm policy. Minnesota instructed its delegation to back Lowden, and he also developed some strength in other midwestern states. Most of the farm bloc's strength, however, was hopelessly scattered among favorite sons. Vice-President Dawes, too, would have liked to inherit the Coolidge mantle. He was able, energetic, and sufficiently conservative for the tastes of the East. On the other hand, he suffered from the obscurity ordinarily attached to his office and had annoyed influential senators by criticizing the rules of the upper house.

Hoover fell into a different category. He had been on the public stage for more than a decade, and he knew how to extract sustained favorable publicity out of any organization over which he presided, whether it was the War Food Administration or the Commerce Department. Eastern businessmen backed him strongly because of his well-advertised efforts in their behalf. Ordinary citizens also favored him because he seemed to be an unselfish public servant aloof from the petty maneuvers of politicians. The fact that he had never held elective office was rated as an asset rather than a liability. A combination of popular support and the silent acquiescence of Coolidge gave him sufficient momentum to win a first-ballot nomination in spite of some dissent.

The convention extended a withered olive branch to the farm bloc by

"Gentlemen, it gives me great pleasure to report we are definitely on the upswing. According to these statistics only 34 people died of starvation in this city this year compared to 41 last year." (O. Soglow, 1934.)

nominating the conservative Senator Charles Curtis of Kansas for Vice-President. Curtis had supported the easterners more than his own section as majority leader in the Senate. He lacked both imagination and initiative. H. L. Mencken dismissed him with the acid comment that he was "half Choctaw and half windmill."

The platform, like other Republican platforms of the decade, was largely devoted to self-congratulation. The failure of the La Follette revolt four years earlier gave the leaders courage to defy the farm bloc on the McNary-

Haugen program; but by promising government aid in establishing a co-operative farm marketing system, they recognized the need to do something for agriculture. The irritation of the "drys" over the flourishing trade in illicit alcohol led to the formulation of a plank pledging vigorous enforcement of the Eighteenth Amendment. The section dealing with foreign affairs contained a denunciation of the League of Nations but proposed further limitations of armaments and the outlawing of war.

When the Democrats met at Houston, Texas, two weeks later, Governor Alfred E. Smith of New York, whose candidacy had been bitterly opposed by the South in 1924, won a first-ballot nomination. The emphasis on party harmony led the convention to select Senator Joseph T. Robinson of Arkansas as his running mate. The platform straddled on practically every issue, including prohibition, the tariff, and farm policy. It denounced Coolidge for his handling of the agricultural problem but presented no practical substitute. It even omitted reference to the League of Nations. Taken as a whole, it suggested that the opposition could not find any Republican action of which it really disapproved.

The nomination of Governor Smith doomed the Democrats to overwhelming defeat because he symbolized in his own person all the forces most obnoxious to members of the dominant Nationalist reaction. Not only was he a representative of the new immigration, but he came from New York City, which rural America regarded as the center of urban vice, opposition to prohibition, the Catholic religion, and alien radical philosophies. His candidacy, therefore, infused a new, if unwholesome, life into the campaign and raised election issues of interest to the entire public for the only time in the decade. As a result, eight million voters who had not participated in the 1924 election were sufficiently aroused to register their opinions at the polls. The drooping nativist forces showed fresh vigor as they girded themselves for a crusade in behalf of the home, morality, and the integrity of Anglo-Saxon institutions.

The campaign featured the worst type of smear tactics and whispered assaults on character. Fundamentalists, who distrusted Smith because he was a Catholic, argued that he would show a religious bias in making political appointments. Others worried about the "dual allegiance" of Roman Catholics to state and church, and were fearful that Smith would accept the guidance of the Pope in secular as well as spiritual matters. His demand for modification of the Eighteenth Amendment encouraged rumor-mongers to spread highly colored tales about his allegedly immoderate use of alcohol; and by way of confirming their charges they cited the fact that he sometimes failed to appear at whistle stops on his transcontinental tour. In retaliation some Democrats stooped to similar tactics: Governor Theodore G. Bilbo of Mississippi claimed that Hoover had danced with a Negro woman during a flood relief tour; others whispered mysteriously about international business connections incompatible with patriotism.

The Democratic nominee deserved fairer treatment from his fellow countrymen. He was the only party leader with proved ability to win votes in Republican years. He had served an unprecedented four terms as Governor of New York and had given the state an honest, efficient administration. His alleged radicalism did not extend beyond a lukewarm advocacy of public power projects and a settled determination to make public service bureaus perform their functions with a minimum of red tape. He refused outright endorsement of a drastic farm relief program like the McNary-Haugen bill, although he would probably have gained some votes by the maneuver.

The months between the nominating conventions and the election saw a steady deterioration in Smith's prospects. Southern Democrats, who had possessed no leader capable of stopping him, deserted in large numbers. Faced by the disagreeable choice of supporting either an urban Catholic who had repudiated the party plank on prohibition or else a Republican, they ceased to function as an organized group. Southern Protestant churchmen, led by Methodist Bishop James E. Cannon, Jr., and the militant Baptist, Arthur J. Barton, were instrumental in convening a meeting of anti-Smith Democrats at Asheville, North Carolina, on July 19, 1928. They raised a trial balloon for Hoover, and the response was favorable enough to encourage bolts by important southern leaders like Senator Furnifold Simmons of North Carolina and Senator Thomas J. Heflin of Alabama.

While the Solid South was crumbling, Smith lost additional ground on his transcontinental tour. Dressed in a pin-striped suit and derby and employing the raspy, nasal accent of New York City's lower East Side, he seemed to many midwestern voters more like a carnival barker than a presidential candidate. His appearance and manner reinforced all the provincial prejudices of the heartland against the urban-immigrant world which he represented. As a campaigner, Hoover was dull and wooden. However, the Midwest recognized him as one of its own sons despite his apostasy on the McNary-Haugen issue. The Ku Klux Klan, the D.A.R., and all the other private organizations enlisted in the Nationalist reaction enthusiastically supported the Republicans.

When the votes were counted, Smith suffered a staggering defeat in the electoral college, receiving 87 votes to 444 for Hoover. Although Smith carried the heavily Catholic states of Massachusetts and Rhode Island, as neither Cox nor Davis had been able to do, he lost the rest of the country including four states of the Solid South. Since no Republican presidential candidate had won a single state in the latter group since Reconstruction, Hoover's victory in Florida, North Carolina, Texas, and Virginia was hailed as a political revolution. Smith made a more respectable showing in the popular vote with 15,016,443 to 21,392,000 for Hoover. Whatever comfort the Democrats could take from the election was based on the fact that the 10,000,000 new voters in 1928 divided approximately 50–50. The Socialist and Communist parties did worse than usual.

HOOVER'S POLITICAL PROSPECTS

The Hoover administration opened on a note of optimism. Farmers were receiving higher prices for their products than earlier in the decade. Industry was operating at full steam and the stock market was making headlines with new highs, which brokers interpreted as evidence of popular faith in continued prosperity. Fewer legislative problems required attention than in the opening year of most new administrations. In fact, beyond a modest program of farm relief and tariff revision, the President had committed himself to practically nothing. The country looked forward to a rule of efficiency experts who would not interfere with private enterprise but would stand prepared to help business help itself.

The anticipated policy could not be detected in Hoover's choice of Cabinet members. As usual, the posts were divided between eminent party leaders, campaign workers who deserved recognition, and personal friends of the President. Hoover continued Mellon and Davis from the Coolidge Cabinet. He selected Henry L. Stimson, who had already served several Republican Presidents with distinction, as Secretary of State. Ray Lyman Wilbur, President of Stanford University and a close personal friend, was named Secretary of the Interior. The Postmaster-Generalship was given to the chairman of the Republican National Committee, Walter F. Brown. Noteworthy appointments outside the Cabinet were Charles G. Dawes as Ambassador to Great Britain and Charles Evans Hughes as Chief Justice of the Supreme Court, the latter replacing the deceased William Howard Taft in 1930.

The deficiencies of the new President as a political leader would probably have stimulated applause rather than criticism had it not been for the onslaught of the depression. At the outset he was willing for the initiative in most legislative matters to rest with Congress as it had done since the war. Like Harding and Coolidge, he conceived of himself primarily as an administrator whose principal duty outside the sphere of routine executive activities would be to resist the unsound proposals of the lawmakers. Since prosperity had obtained for nearly a decade under this conception, his attitude was natural enough. Where he hoped to improve on his immediate predecessors was in the realm of administrative efficiency. He possessed unlimited faith in a committee of experts and was so deficient in political experience that he expected opposition to collapse in the face of factual reports. He believed Congress could be dealt with like a group of business executives, and he showed considerable capacity for resisting enlightenment on this point.

To complicate still further his task as a political leader, Hoover lacked personal warmth and magnetism. Of a naturally shy and retiring disposition, he could not greet strangers enthusiastically or put them at ease with a flow of superficial chatter. Nor was there anything in an engineering education to remedy this defect. At the conference table or the political dinner, he would explode a few pertinent observations and then lapse into silence. His superior intellect would have carried him through a normal presidential term unharmed, but after the stock market crash in October 1929 he was fated to deal almost entirely with unhappy and unreasonable men.

THE FARM BOARD

The President experienced his first difficulties a month after inauguration when he called Congress into special session to act on farm relief and tariff revision. As so often in the 1920's, the Republicans had top-heavy majorities that could not be relied upon. The situation favored the administration more in the House than in the Senate, where a dozen Republican insurgents and farm bloc Democrats, like Dill of Washington, Wheeler of Montana, and Kendrick of Wyoming, held the balance of power. Another barrier to smooth relationships with the upper house was the elevation of Senator James E. Watson of Indiana to the post of majority leader. He was orthodox enough in his viewpoints, but during the preconvention maneuvering he had contemptuously referred to Hoover as a "Britisher" and opposed his nomination. Despite the honest effort of both men to forget, they never really trusted each other.

The first order of business was agricultural legislation. The President's notion of adequate farm relief was the creation of a government agency which would encourage the development of cooperative marketing machinery by means of loans to cooperative organizations. Accordingly he sponsored a bill to create a Federal Farm Board of nine members and placed at its disposal a revolving fund of $500 million for loans to bona fide cooperatives. He sought the good will of McNary-Haugen advocates by including a provision which authorized the Board to establish stabilization corporations. Although he disclaimed any intention of fixing prices, the purpose of the corporations would obviously be to enter the market during deflationary periods and purchase a sufficient part of a particular crop to maintain prices. When market conditions improved, such holdings would be sold.

The farm bloc showed its contempt for a gesture which approached its own position by pushing an amendment for export debentures. The latter would have established a flat government subsidy on agriculture exports equal to one-half the tariff rate. Hoover succeeded in blocking this maneuver, and the original version of the Agricultural Marketing Act received his signature on June 15, 1929.

Cooperatives hastened to qualify for loans from the revolving fund by consolidating local and state marketing units into nationwide organizations like the Farmers' National Grain Corporation, the American Cotton Cooperative Association, and the National Wool Association. The new organizations borrowed substantial amounts of money to modernize and expand facilities and to market the crops of members. As the initial impulse in a long-range effort to reduce farm marketing costs and encourage the growth of cooperatives, the legislation was a success.

Such benefits, however, did not materialize rapidly enough to counterbalance the failure of stabilization operations by the Farm Board. For success in such an enterprise the Board had either to control the acreage planted or to possess sufficient luck to operate in a period of mixed price trends. Unfortunately, neither circumstance prevailed.

Starting in October 1929, the Farm Board, headed by Alexander Legge of International Harvester, authorized marketing organizations to make loans on wheat and cotton at fixed prices. A few months later it ventured into the treacherous waters of price manipulation by forming a Grain Stabilization Corporation and a Cotton Stabilization Corporation. During the ensuing three years these organizations managed to lose $345 million dealing in cotton and wheat. Undoubtedly the earlier operations slowed the price decline in both commodities, but the world-wide surplus of agricultural products grew so steadily that stabilizing operations proved useless in the long run. The only infallible cure for low prices was acreage reduction. The Board reached this conclusion in the spring of 1932 and pleaded with farmers to cut production 30 per cent. They promptly responded by planting a larger crop than ever. During the last year of the administration the Board tried to dispose of some surplus wheat through special large-scale deals with China, Germany, and Brazil. Much of the remainder was turned over to the Red Cross for distribution to victims of the depression. Ultimately, the problems of agricultural surpluses and prices were passed on to the next administration unsolved.

THE SMOOT-HAWLEY TARIFF

Although Congress had allowed Hoover to write his own ticket on farm relief, it exercised its traditional independence in the matter of tariff revision. The tariff message did not call for a general increase but recommended raising the rates on industrial products that were suffering from severe competition. If Hoover expected the schedules to be revised in accordance with such a scientific principle, he was quickly disappointed.

The House increased the rates on over a thousand items and passed the bill on to the Senate where the more leisurely pace gave the lobbyists time for further raids on the consumer. Despite the fact that westerners headed the tariff committees in both houses, the eastern Republicans controlled the proceedings more effectively than they did in 1922. Even so the farm bloc made plenty of trouble. Bitter experience had taught them that high tariffs on farm products did not help their constituents. So a coalition headed by Senator Borah of Idaho revived the debenture plan and added it to the tariff bill in October 1929. This parliamentary maneuver provoked bitter denunciation by easterners. Senator Moses of New Hampshire referred to farm bloc senators as "sons of the wild jackass." Joseph R. Grundy, Chairman of the National Association of Manufacturers and later Senator from Pennsylvania, said that the western states didn't have any "chips in the game." Scornfully he added that if the Constitution had not given them two senators apiece, they would "never be heard from."

It required eight more months of legislative warfare and presidential pressure on the Conference Committee considering the differing tariff bills of the two Houses to knock out the debenture provision. Simultaneously Hoover got the committee to eliminate an amendment requiring congressional approval of all revisions recommended by the Tariff Commission. Shorn of farm bloc riders and restrictions on the Tariff Commission, the Smoot-Hawley bill was signed by the President on June 15, 1930. He did so over the solemn protest of one thousand American economists who had signed a petition urging a veto. They pointed out that the bill increased rates contrary to presidential recommendations, and they predicted that it would raise consumer prices, hamper world trade, complicate the problem of European debt liquidations, and lead to reprisals by other countries. If Hoover agreed with these arguments, he felt unable to heed them because every major pressure group, from industrialists to organized labor, was against them.

The new law raised the protective wall to the highest level in the history of the country, with the average rate exceeding that established under the Fordney-McCumber Act by a full 7 per cent. Although friends and foes alike assumed that the Act would exercise a decisive influence on American prosperity, the protective tariff was soon overshadowed by a whole series of devices designed to manipulate the economy.

PANIC IN THE STOCK MARKET

While senators were heatedly debating the debenture amendment to the Smoot-Hawley bill in the fall of 1929, panic suddenly gripped the stock market. During the opening weeks of October prices had sagged slowly, but nobody anticipated the frenzied liquidation of the 23rd when stocks suffered drops averaging eighteen points. The following day was even more disastrous, and although the hasty but well-publicized organization of a bankers' pool of $240 million for stabilization purposes arrested the decline temporarily, blind hysteria developed on Tuesday, October 29. Stocks fell anywhere from ten to two hundred points, and traders seeking to unload their holdings set an all-time record of 16,410,030 transactions for the day. Even many of those unmoved by panic helped to swell the volume of liquidations because they had been operating on margin and could not raise enough money to save their accounts. Thousands in both categories saw lifetime savings evaporate between sunrise and sunset. After the catastrophe of the 29th, the market settled down to a slow, irregular decline that lasted for more than three years and reduced high-grade railroad and utility stocks to as little as one-seventh of their peak values.

The spectacular collapse of values ended a bull market unprecedented in scope and duration. For the preceding six years prices had risen almost steadily. The average market value of fifty leading stocks increased 228 per cent during the period. In the fifty-seven months between January 1, 1925, and October 1, 1929, the market value of all listed stocks rose from $27,072,552,000 to $87,073,630,000. The momentum for the bull market had been provided by an optimism and speculative enthusiasm which infected all classes of society. The unreflective assumed that everything would eventually pay off, and their naïve confidence came to be shared by businessmen who ought to have known better. Even installment buying did not approach the appeal of the stock market, because goods financed on time had to be paid for eventually while speculation in securities stimulated the dazzling hope of getting something for nothing. Purchase of stocks on margin provided many with a formula to turn the dream into a reality. The buyer simply paid for the bulk of his shares through a loan from his broker, who held the stock as security. Although the interest rate was high, it provoked little criticism since stocks always seemed to go up and thus enabled the buyer to pay off the loan out of profits. He could accumulate so much stock with such a modest down payment that the process of making money became almost automatic. Bellhops, waitresses, fruit peddlers, and countless others, who had never before read the financial page of a newspaper, began to buy stock on margin and talk learnedly about the prospects of Anaconda Copper and Bethlehem Steel. The illusion that the common man had mastered the esoteric science of economics lasted during the four years when stock prices did not drop and force him to put up cash to retain his investment.

Until the summer of 1927 the market had risen at a rate which bore a rough approximation to economic prospects. Thereafter prices shot up rapidly and were fed by an orgy of buying on margin. Broker's loans, which financed these speculative purchases, increased from $3.5 billion in June 1927, to over $8 billion in September 1929. During most of this period the banks served as the ultimate source of funds for brokers' loans. The Coolidge administration showed no alarm over this situation. Indeed, the President encouraged inflationary forces by issuing a public statement in January 1928, that he did not regard brokers' loans as too high. The Federal Reserve Board took a graver view of the speculation. It had lowered rediscount rates during the summer of 1927 to stimulate international trade, but it reversed its policy in 1928, raising the rates several times in the hope of drying up bank credit that moved in speculative channels. These deflationary moves had little visible effect. Coolidge refused to associate himself with a more energetic policy, but two days after Hoover took office, the Federal Reserve Board announced that it would not extend credit to banks financing speculation. This unprecedented step was followed by a cryptic warning from Secretary Mellon, who advised prudent investors to buy bonds.

The boom did not even falter. Interest rates on stock-exchange loans promptly jumped from 15 to 20 per cent. Instead of discouraging speculators from purchasing on margin, the high rates coaxed corporate funds on the loan market to replace the funds of banks that had withdrawn. This development marked the penultimate stage of the boom. Theoretically stock prices were supposed to be based on profit prospects; but when the corporations stepped into the market and spent their own funds to bid up the prices of their own stocks, they did not improve profit prospects. In fact, by investing idle funds in speculation rather than in the expansion of productive facilities, they were tacitly admitting that the era of expanding markets had ended.

These danger signals did not impress the layman, who had always believed in perpetual-motion machines anyhow. Even brokers, business analysts, and college professors talked rapturously about a new economic era and the permanent plateau of prosperity. The speculative fever was so universal that when the bubble broke on October 23, 1929, it caught the entire population unprepared.

During the ensuing three weeks of panic, the lamentations of the victims drowned all other sounds. When, however, an uneasy equilibrium developed between buyers and sellers in mid-November, the business and political leaders found their voices. In general they took the view that the crash, like the Panic of 1907, was primarily a funeral for speculators and would not affect the basic prosperity of the country. Business analyst L. F. Parton assured investors that they had suffered "a unique psychological break rather than a disaster due to a collapse of essential values." Secretary Mellon issued an optimistic statement on New Year's Day, 1930, and Secretary of Commerce Robert P. Lamont predicted that healthy economic conditions would prevail. Since the collapse was not followed by a correspondingly rapid contraction of business activity, most citizens provisionally accepted this analysis.

President Hoover acted with the energy of a man who believed that market trends anticipate economic developments. On November 21, 1929, he called leaders of basic American industries to a White House conference. They agreed to maintain existing levels of production and wages provided labor agreed not to strike or seek pay increases for the duration of the crisis. Later the same day union leaders headed by William Green also met Hoover and gave the required pledge. The new management-labor entente was ratified a few days thereafter at another White House conference. Although a few scoffed at the President's zest for meetings and said that his middle initial "C" must stand for "conference," the majority probably agreed with newspaper correspondent M. S. Rukeyser who hailed the President for his "brilliant effort to link up government and business, and influence, modify, and direct the business cycle."

The same month Hoover sought to counteract deflationary forces with an accelerated public works program. He telegraphed governors and local officials, urging them to increase construction projects. A few weeks later he asked and received from Congress increased appropriations for public works. Up to this point he had already gone further than any of his predecessors in accepting the responsibility of the government to fight depression. He took two additional steps in the fall of 1930. The first was to halt immigration on the ground that newcomers were likely to become public charges; the second was to coordinate the relief activities of private charity groups with those of various state and local agencies.

PANIC BECOMES DEPRESSION

Up to this point the President had believed that he was fighting deflationary tendencies rather than a genuine depression. Events in the winter of 1930–31 deprived him of all grounds for optimism. The management-labor pact, which had on the whole been faithfully observed for a year, began to collapse. Industry started curtailing production, which was promptly reflected in unemployment and wage cuts. Simultaneously, credit contraction expressed itself through a number of bank failures. This in turn encouraged the hoarding of funds and thereby pushed credit-shy farmers to foreclosures. Steadily sagging agricultural prices intensified distress.

The fact that similar developments were taking place all over the world indicated the operation of other forces in addition to the stock market crash in the creation of a depression. Years later experts still disagreed as to the primary cause of the catastrophe, but all found impressive evidence of economic disease lurking behind the façade of American prosperity during the 1920's. One chronic source of economic weakness all over the world was the Great War and its aftermath. In Europe alone, millions had lost their lives, their homes, and their sources of livelihood. Postwar peace treaties added several thousand miles of customs walls, dividing the Continent into separate compartments that pursued aggressive trade policies and thereby put fresh strain on already weakened economies. The United States aggravated the problems by insisting on the payment of war debts and by raising protective tariffs so high that payment had to be made in gold. The worst effects of the policy were concealed for a time by the investment of private American capital abroad, which stimulated recovery and incidentally provided various nations with dollars to repay debts. The withdrawal of funds for speculation, and later for the covering of overextended credit positions in the United States, helped to topple the weakened financial structure of Europe. Most Americans did not realize the seriousness of the collapse in Europe or anticipate the magnitude of the repercussions in a world which had developed close economic interdependence in the preceding years. The most immediate effect on the United States was the rapid contraction of her export trade, which by 1932 had dropped to one-third of the 1929 level. Since she needed to export somewhere between 15 and 20 per cent of her production in order to remain prosperous, this development was very serious indeed.

Another by-product of depression in other parts of the world which also affected the Western Hemisphere was a general reduction of prices for raw materials. Cartels in Europe and monopolies in the United States controlled production tightly enough to cushion the fall of prices for industrial goods. But no such mechanisms existed for arresting the downward trend in coal, rubber, coffee, wheat, and cotton — to mention a few commodities. Hence the purely agricultural states were most adversely affected by the world-wide glut of raw materials.

The United States also suffered a great deal. Agricultural acreage had been rapidly expanded during World War I, and a heavy burden of mortgage indebtedness assumed in the process. Even in the more prosperous years of the 1920's the markets for cotton and wheat did not remain large enough to permit reduction of this indebtedness. Cotton markets disappeared as a result of competition from other fabrics. Wheat faced severe competition, particularly after 1925 when Russia returned to the world market. Surpluses also afflicted the producers of other major crops. Moreover, the relief proposals of the farm bloc never took into account the fact that the problem was based partly on developments outside the United States.

Many economists also emphasized the disparity between personal income and production as a contributory cause of depression, although they gave differing answers as to why the disparity occurred. The majority agreed that by the late 1920's the demand for houses, automobiles, and other durable goods at current prices had been filled except for a smaller replacement market. This left American industry with a greatly expanded capital plant and insufficient purchasing power to absorb the production. In the normal course of events, the reduction of profitable investment opportunities would have produced a depression. The diversion of investment funds into speculative channels probably hastened the collapse.

Once the depression started, its intensity seemed to be a product of the interaction between material causes and human psychology. Like boom, depression depended at least partly on how people felt, and as economic conditions grew worse, citizens behaved with a pessimism that strengthened the operation of deflationary forces. Fear of the future led to curtailment of investment, hoarding of savings, and deferment of the purchase of all but essential goods. These private decisions by countless Americans caused industry to restrict production and to discharge workers. Depression became for a time as much of a perpetual motion machine as the wild upward spiral of the twenties.

In the 1930 elections the Republicans retained nominal control of Congress with forty-eight seats in the Senate against forty-seven Democrats and one Farmer-Laborite, and 219 seats in the House, which gave them a narrow margin of three votes; but before the new Congress met thirteen months later, the death of several Republicans, including Speaker Nicholas Longworth, enabled the Democrats to organize the lower house and elect John N. Garner as presiding officer. The only immediate effect of the election was to strengthen the hand of Hoover's critics. Western Republicans, led by George W. Norris, who had just beaten administration efforts to defeat him in the Nebraska primary, joined the Democrats more openly. During the lame-duck session the coalition actually passed the Norris bill for the government operation of Muscle Shoals but could not secure the necessary two-thirds vote to override Hoover's veto. Shortly after this trial of strength between the legislature and executive, the old Congress adjourned in a storm of recriminations. The partisan temper heralded the return of dead-center government which had prevailed from the end of World War I until the election of 1920.

Meanwhile the depression entered a new and more acute phase that lasted for two years and involved vast numbers of citizens in unprecedented misery. Statistics provide one method of measuring the magnitude of the deflation. We have already noted that from 1929 to 1932 the dollar value of American exports dropped nearly 70 per cent. This curtailment of economic activity was reflected in the unemployment figures, which rose from around one and one-half million on the eve of the stock market crash to nearly fourteen million three years later. This estimate did not include numerous other workers who after 1930 were forced to absorb severe pay cuts or accept work on a part-time basis. At every economic level debts increased and savings disappeared. The banks, which were bitterly resented for calling in loans and foreclosing mortgages, could seldom realize enough cash to withstand the heavy runs of frightened depositors. It had been common during the 1920's for 700 banks to fail each year, the mortality being particularly high among institutions which held farm mortgages. The number of failures nearly doubled in 1930, reached 2,294 the following year, and receded to 1,456 in 1932. The deflationary spiral proved to be impartial in its ravages; salesmen, clerical employees, teachers, and salaried executives shared the fate of industrial workers and farmers.

These statistics fail to provide an adequate picture of the way in which the depression assaulted human dignity, comfort, and morale. Thousands of citizens, brought up to regard charitable institutions as the refuge of the chronically lazy, could not avoid applying for help from such agencies. To make matters worse, the charitable institutions usually made the same assumptions and extended relief on a needlessly humiliating basis. Many of those who recoiled from the inquisitorial methods of social workers, particularly the young unmarried men, became vagabonds. They rode railway boxcars from place to place, picking up meals at soup kitchens and sleeping in little hobo villages built of scrap lumber and tin — bitterly referred to as "Hoovervilles." Men with families struggled pathetically to find some means of self-support. Public-spirited citizens in a number of communities helped them by organizing barter exchanges where various kinds of homemade products could be traded for food or other necessities. By the end of 1932, nearly 150 barter exchanges operated in 29 states. A few communities switched over to wooden money when all the neighboring banks failed.

Generally speaking, the jobless of the cities accepted their adversity quietly. Many of them had experienced the mental anxieties and physical hardships of unemployment at some time in the past. They grumbled with increasing bitterness over the length of their ordeal but showed little inclination for revolutionary violence. Communist agitators, who peddled their ideological remedies for poverty with increasing assurance in the dark days of 1932, were dismayed by the unexpected apathy of the jobless. Large audiences gathered in parks to listen to agitators for want of better entertainment, but sentiment for riots and street fights could not be generated.

AGRARIAN VIOLENCE

The only group that resorted to sporadic violence as a protest against the depression were the farmers, who had no revolutionary objective except to get rid of their burden of debt contracted during the great land boom of 1916–20. Mortgage interest payments had been difficult for most of them to meet even in the most prosperous period, and few had succeeded in reducing the principal. Consequently, when the world-wide surplus of agricultural products led to rapid reductions in prices, their cash income practically evaporated. In fact, the average cash income of the individual farmer dropped to sixty-six dollars in 1932.

The center of rural unrest was Minnesota, Iowa, and the Dakotas, which had also been the center of the postwar land boom. Under the leadership of Milo Reno, the Farm Holiday Association — an offshoot of the radical Farmers Union — called a gigantic strike in nineteen food-producing states during the summer of 1932. Operating on the theory that only a nine-day supply of food was in the hands of retailers, striking farmers sought to withhold commodities from the market until prices rose. From the outset, the strike was doomed by lack of organization in most states and by the unwillingness of all farmers to join it. In the four or five states where enthusiasm ran high, the Holiday Association stationed pickets on the highways outside of market towns. Nail-studded planks were occasionally laid across the paths of trucks that tried to break picket lines. Violence broke out most frequently on the Iowa-Minnesota border. Pickets smashed the windshields of produce trucks or turned them over. Marauders occasionally attacked the property of uncooperative farmers, smashing butter churns and dumping oil into pitchers of cream. The use of state troops against pickets, together with the opposition of farmers who produced perishable products or lacked facilities to store nonperishables, eventually broke the strike. The Holiday Association finally called it off shortly after the 1932 election, although all organized activity had stopped a month or so earlier.

The Holiday Association was more successful in mobilizing farmers to obstruct mortgage sales in the winter and spring of 1932 and 1933. By prearrangement large numbers of them appeared at chattel mortgage sales, intimidated prospective purchasers, and bid a few cents for livestock, agricultural equipment, and household goods, which were promptly returned to the victim of foreclosure proceedings. In cases where the entire property was involved, Holiday members simply congregated outside the sheriff's office and informally held him prisoner until the hour for the sale had passed. As a result, foreclosures had to be advertised all over again. Often state officials who might have enforced legal procedures sympathized with the farmers and refused to act. Occasionally farmers came dangerously close to applying lynch law, and several bankers fled small midwestern towns in fear of their lives.

Agrarian unrest reached a climax just as Hoover was retiring from office in March 1933. Armies of indigent farmers marched on state legislatures to demand laws postponing interest payments on mortgages, and Minnesota actually passed such a law despite its doubtful constitutionality. The repudiation fever ran so high in the North Central states that it threatened to become a nationwide movement. Even the conservative president of the Farm Bureau, Ed O'Neal, predicted revolution in the countryside within twelve months.

THE BONUS MARCHERS

Smaller groups of unemployed workers dramatized their plight by marching on Washington to petition Congress for relief. The most important of these were veterans of World War I who demanded immediate payment of the adjusted service certificates in the spring of 1932. Two years earlier, Congress had passed over Hoover's veto a measure permitting veterans to borrow up to 50 per cent on their certificates before maturity. Most of the lawmakers now felt it would be politically expedient to make additional concessions. Representative Wright Patman of Texas introduced a bill embodying their requests and easily worked it through the House. Hoover, ever fearful of an unbalanced budget, got the Senate to reject the measure. The legislative deadlock touched off the migration to Washington. By late spring of 1932, a substantial number of veterans were camping in hobo villages on the edge of town. Although the April 15 issue of the *Daily Worker* urged a monster demonstration and although Communists engaged in promotional activities, control of the so-called bonus army was not in their hands. Most of the veterans were merely unemployed citizens without anything better to do.

Matters moved to a climax when Congress adjourned July 15, 1932, without granting the marchers anything but travel-pay home. When 5,000 of the 11,000 marchers refused to leave Washington at the expense of the government, the tin village of Anacosta Flats took on an air of permanence distasteful to the administration. Whether by accident or design a scuffle took place between the veterans and the police on July 28. Hoover acted promptly on the request of the district commissioners and called out the Army to restore order. A disproportionately large unit of infantry, cavalry, and tanks under General Douglas MacArthur drove the bonus army from its village. Shortly thereafter, fire broke out and raged unchecked until the shacks were burnt to the ground. The combination of military action and conflagration dispersed the veterans and provided Hoover's critics with an opportunity to denounce him for inhumanity.

THE HOOVER RELIEF PROGRAM

Hoover's response to the deepening economic crisis of 1931–32 was not so energetic as his prompt action after the stock market crash. He resisted demands for a special session of Congress and backed away from proposals for direct government aid to the unemployed. Part of his reluctance was due to his faith in the adequacy of measures already taken, part to his scruples against any marked change in the character of relief. He had always opposed direct government intervention in the economy, especially if it involved subsidies to special-interest groups; he feared that an unbalanced budget would seriously aggravate the depression; and above all he was convinced that enlargement of government activity would destroy democratic institutions.

Hoover's conception of government resembled the old Progressive view that it should be an umpire between pressure groups rather than their agent. However, the President assumed that the welfare of business and of the public were the same thing, and that government could aid industry without forfeiting its status as an umpire. His career as Secretary of Commerce had been identified with this assumption. So it was natural for him to fight the depression by aiding business.

At first the public shared the President's position because it had been taught in the twenties to believe that business was the source of prosperity. But by the summer of 1931 popular demands for additional action mounted. When Hoover stubbornly clung to his original position, he became the victim of unrestrained denunciation. Nevertheless, he was far from idle in 1931. He inspired the organization of various public groups to take care of relief problems at the community level. Building on the structure of coordination committees established a year earlier, he created a new over-all Relief Commission and appointed Walter S. Gifford of American Telephone and Telegraph to head it. The latter launched a monster drive aimed at the twofold purpose of coaxing relief money from new sources and creating an optimistic atmosphere to promote recovery. It expressed itself in everything from postseason charity football games to "Block Aid" volunteer committees, which collected money and provided such jobs as cleaning yards or removing ashes. Vast amounts of energy were poured into these projects but the results were trivial. The problem of unemployment relief had grown to such gigantic proportions that it could not be solved by private means.

DEADLOCK

When the Seventy-second Congress met in December 1931, it exhibited an angry but indecisive mood. A small bipartisan group, headed by the tireless Norris in the Senate and by the excitable La Guardia of New York in the House, favored government intervention of a variety of fronts: large-scale public works, compulsory unemployment insurance, minimum wages, a five-day week, and sundry other measures. They were descendants of the Roosevelt Progressives who had parted company with Taft in 1912, and of the "New Freedom" Democrats. Most of the members, however, agreed with Hoover about the limited role of government in time of distress as well as of prosperity. Since both parties distrusted any novel remedies for the situation, they devoted the session primarily to pre-election maneuvering. In this game the Democrats possessed an advantage which grew with each painful turn of the economic screw. As the popularity of Hoover and the Republicans declined, the Democrats became more boldly obstructive; they had no intention of damaging their election prospects by formulating a positive program which might diminish their chances. So they criticized Hoover indiscriminately and professed to believe that he had caused the depression by unsound administration of orthodox policies.

Thus, despite the rapid deterioration of the economic situation in the spring of 1932, the chief congressional battleground was the budget. Both sides stood for economy and expressed the fear that an unbalanced budget would intensify depression. Democrats from the rural South advocated a manufacturers' sales tax, which would not burden their section as heavily as other levies. The corporal's guard of embryo New Dealers wanted to use the revenue measure to chastise the wealthy, and proposed both increased income taxes and increased inheritance taxes. The Republicans, handicapped by the irresolution of Hoover, spent most of their time waging a defensive battle against the proposals of other groups. In the end a compromise bill was adopted which raised the income tax and instituted a few novel excise taxes. Intended to increase revenues by $1,000,000,000, it fell somewhat short because of declining economic activity.

Almost the same kind of struggle went on over appropriations. Notwithstanding outward enthusiasm for reducing expenditures, the policy never enjoys any real popularity with congressmen because they fear to offend constituents by cutting off pet projects. They usually advocate a great variety of trivial cuts which are quietly restored in conference committee. No sharp variation of this pattern occurred in 1932. After much tedious wrangling, Congress lowered appropriations by $300,000,000, which was $100,000,000 short of what Hoover asked. Since the imposition of new taxes was also less than what the administration wanted, the budget could not be balanced. The deficit finally reached $800,000,000, partly because of unforeseen reductions of tax receipts and partly because of the failure of debtor nations to meet their annual reparations installments.

Advocates of increased government expeditures and debt-ridden business groups combined momentarily in early 1932 behind Hoover's recommendation for increased credit facilities. The new law created a Reconstruction Finance Corporation to make loans on good security to banks, railroads, insurance companies, and various types of manufacturing concerns. An initial capital of $500 million was advanced by the government. The law also authorized the Corporation to borrow an additional $1.5 billion. Pressure from proponents of an enlarged public works program led to several amendments extending the borrowing power of the R.F.C. and increasing the number of purposes for which the money could be loaned. Under the latter provision, funds were made available to state and local governments for a variety of self-liquidating projects. Hoover likewise secured approval of the Glass-Stegall Act in February 1932, which authorized Federal Reserve banks to accept a much wider variety of collateral from borrowers. This measure, like the act creating the R.F.C., fitted the Hoover formula of providing government stimulus to investment and economic activity on a business basis. Critics were later to refer to this program derisively as the "trickle-trickle" theory whereby government gave money to business at the top and hoped it would trickle down to the masses.

The only other constructive measure of the session was the Norris-La Guardia Act which limited in very specific terms the use of the injunction in labor disputes. It also banned the notorious "yellow dog" contract whereby workers agreed not to join a labor union as a condition of employment. The same provision warned employers that henceforth such contracts were not enforceable in any federal court. Elsewhere on the legislative front a stalemate prevailed. Bills to modify the tariff, inflate the currency, provide direct government relief for the unemployed, and relieve the debt burden of farmers were introduced, but they died either in committee or on the floor of Congress. The behavior of the Democratic majority was extremely obstructive and partisan.

THE 1932 CONVENTIONS

The ensuing campaign took place in a curiously artificial atmosphere. Each month the depression grew worse; yet the major parties carried out the canvass as if they believed the voters would not support an administration substantially different from the one the country possessed. Part of their inflexibility was due to their blind respect for traditional political rules and their instinctive fear of introducing new issues. The Republicans felt obliged to stand on the record of Herbert Hoover whatever the consequences, and the Democrats saw no reason to advocate anything positive while the political current was running so strongly against the incumbents. Beyond these routine political considerations, there lurked the possibility that the politicians had accurately sounded the sentiments of the voters and that the latter did not yet favor far-reaching institutional changes.

As usual, the Republicans held their convention first. It opened on June 14, 1932, at Chicago in an atmosphere of gloom. To make a real contest of the election the party would have had to drop Hoover as the Democrats had dropped Cleveland in the depression year of 1896. Custom, the internal structure of the party organization, and the defeatist spirit of the delegates militated against such a bold move. Hoover was nominated on the first ballot without difficulty. Vice-President Curtis aroused more opposition, but he too won on the initial ballot.

The heart of the party platform was a laudatory summary of the measures inaugurated by Hoover to fight the economic crisis, together with a promise of more energetic action along the same general lines. The depression was blamed on world conditions and the unsound schemes of the Democrats, which allegedly prevented a revival of confidence. Although the policies of the Farm Board received an endorsement like all other administration measures, the party made a frantic bid for agricultural votes with a promise to support any economically sound plan "to balance production against demand." The only sour note was sounded by the Republican "wets," who wanted a plank advocating the repeal of the Eighteenth Amendment and had to be content with a straddle.

When the Democrats met two weeks later, the bright prospects of victory led to a spirited fight over the nomination. The 1930 elections had produced a crop of favorite-son candidates, but they were all overshadowed by Franklin D. Roosevelt, the Governor of New York. Recent spectacular victories had made him a logical choice. Selected to replace his close friend, Al Smith, on the New York state ticket when the latter ran for President in 1928, Roosevelt had won the governorship by 25,000 while the rest of the ticket lost by several hundred thousand. Two years later, his availability was again emphasized when he ran his re-election majority up to 700,000. His success seemed all the more impressive because a crippling attack of polio in 1921 had presumably ended his political career at an age when most aspirants are winning their first office. By that time Roosevelt had already served as state senator, Assistant Secretary of the Navy under Wilson, and vice-presidential candidate in 1920. His courageous comeback after nearly seven years of complete invalidism won him considerable popular enthusiasm. Like his distant cousin Theodore, Franklin Roosevelt also possessed a reputation for being a foe of the vested interests, although he had done little to offend any particular interest except possibly the public utilities magnates. Other factors in his political appeal were great reservoirs of surface amiability, a magnificent speaking voice, and a knack for coining colorful phrases like "the New Deal" and "the forgotten man."

Long before the convention actually met, James A. Farley, Roosevelt's campaign manager, had done a first-rate job of selling his candidate to party workers. Tirelessly cultivating them with personal visits and chatty letters signed in green ink, Farley managed to swing a majority of delegates behind Roosevelt before the balloting started. Nevertheless a sharp fight ensued, because a two-thirds majority was necessary to secure the nomination. At the outset all the favorite sons made an informal alliance against Roosevelt. Most of them had little objection to him but they saw that their only prospect of nomination lay in the destruction of the favorite. The confirmed opponents of Roosevelt rallied behind Al Smith, who had developed a definite dislike for his erstwhile protégé, and wanted to make a second try for the Presidency.

The loosely allied members of the "Stop Roosevelt" coalition held together for three ballots although the favorite managed to pick up a few additional votes on each test of strength. Just before the fourth ballot, Speaker Garner decided to throw his big bloc of Texas and California delegates to Roosevelt. When William G. McAdoo, who headed the California delegation, made the announcement of the switch, he touched off a bandwagon movement. The Roosevelt total on the fourth ballot soared to 945 out of 1,148, giving him the nomination with plenty of votes to spare. Garner received his reward immediately as the unanimous convention choice for Vice-President, while McAdoo was repaid with the Democratic senatorial nomination in California.

The platform was both shorter and more concise than usual. It made the same general assumptions about the causes and cures for the depression as did the Republicans, and pledged the party to make the necessary recovery measures more effective. Various planks advocated a balanced budget, a 25 per cent reduction in government expenditures, more productive public works, and the preservation of states' rights. More advanced policies of social security, such as old-age pensions and unemployment insurance, were endorsed. A qualifying clause, which left implementation to the states, reduced the practical significance of these proposals; they boiled down to expressions of sympathy that cost the party nothing. The explosive tariff issue also received cautious treatment in a plank that promised reciprocity agreements rather than flat downward revision. A somewhat firmer line was taken on the agricultural program, promising the farmer both aid and an effective control of the crop surplus. The ultimate in clarity was reached with planks for the repeal of the Eighteenth Amendment and for the establishment of Philippine independence. The cumulative impression was that the Democrats did not differ substantially from the Republicans with regard to solving important economic questions. Both documents pledged their respective parties to operate within the framework of the existing capitalist system.

THE FALL CAMPAIGN

The strategy of the campaign was dominated by the constantly growing unpopularity of Hoover. The public wanted a scapegoat for its misery, and all the resentment accumulated during the three years of depression came to a focus on the hapless President. A more colorful and appealing personality would have managed to divert part of the popular fury. Hoover simply did not know how to dramatize his very considerable efforts against the depression or inspire public confidence. His platform manner was dry and solemn rather than buoyant and operatic. He infuriated voters by what they unjustly regarded as an unsympathetic attitude. Politicians discovered that the unusually sullen crowds would cheer an attack on the President when they would cheer at nothing else. Accordingly, Democratic candidates, from Roosevelt down to the lowliest aspirant for county office, ran against Hoover personally. His record was denounced in local campaigns which did not have the remotest relation to national issues. Whenever possible, Republican congressional candidates for re-election disassociated their campaign from that of the President.

With the tide running irresistibly against the administration, Roosevelt followed the traditional routine of blaming the Republicans for everything that had gone wrong in the twentieth century. He repeatedly assured the electorate of his own flexibility and open-mindedness but seldom promised anything more concrete than a willingness to experiment. The assumption of such a negative role did not give adequate scope to his considerable oratorical talents or his flair for dramatic assertions of leadership. It also misled many citizens who regarded his subsequent New Deal program as something more than an experiment. Whether he deliberately deceived the voters is a moot question which may never be satisfactorily answered. A strong probability exists that he himself did not know what he intended to do in the fall of 1932. While he was trying to crystallize a policy, economic conditions were changing so rapidly that he found numerous excuses for not making up his mind.

In any case, the Democratic campaign did not give the country a very accurate impression of Roosevelt. To both conservatives and radicals he seemed a little bit like a stuffed shirt, a cautious, friendly man incapable of anything but routine tinkering with the economy. Some insurgent Republican senators like Norris, La Follette, Cutting of New Mexico, and Hiram Johnson declared for him, as well as a few retired and politically unimportant Bull Moosers who mistook him for Theodore. The influential Detroit radio priest, Father Coughlin, and the eccentric Senator Huey Long of Louisiana brought another segment of radicals into the Democratic fold, but the more visionary of the left-wingers distrusted Roosevelt and launched a group of splinter parties. Ghosts of Populist days, like "Coin" Harvey and Jacob S. Coxey, came out of hiding. The former accepted a nomination from a convention of currency heretics who met under the shadow of his pyramid at Monte Ne, Arkansas, where information on the reasons for the fall of western civilization was being accumulated. Harvey's Liberty party received competition from Coxey's rejuvenated Farmer-Labor party which advocated a vast public works program financed by bogus currency. Still other groups like the Blue Shirts and the Jobless party went through the motions of naming presidential tickets, although they could not get on the ballot in any state. The splinter parties diverted attention from the Socialists, who nominated Norman Thomas, and the Communists, who ran William Z. Foster.

Hoover had intended to follow the usual campaign practice of an incumbent President, and issue a number of dignified statements from the White House as well as make an occasional speech at a carefully selected eastern site. The September victory of a Democratic gubernatorial candidate in Maine, coupled with alarming reports from the Midwest, forced a hasty revision of plans. The President took the stump and delivered a series of gloomy addresses forecasting the dire consequences of a Democratic victory. In a much-quoted speech at Madison Square Garden, he asserted that if Roosevelt won, "grass would grow in the streets of a hundred cities." The prophecy made little impression on the voters. Most of them found it difficult to imagine how things could possibly get worse.

When the ballots were finally counted, they revealed that the Democrats had won their greatest victory since the Civil War. Roosevelt received 22,821,857 popular votes to 15,761,841 for Hoover and slightly over a million for all the minor candidates. The winner carried forty-two states with 472 electoral votes, while Hoover held only four states in New England plus Pennsylvania and Delaware, with a total of 59 electoral votes. The turnover in Congress was equally drastic. The Democrats won 313 seats in the House to 117 for the Republicans and five for minor candidates. In the Senate, where only a third of the membership had faced the voters, the Democrats emerged with a total of 59, as against 36 for the Republicans and one holdover for the Farmer-Laborites. A dispassionate analysis of the results suggests that the voters had rebuked the Republicans rather than tendered a vote of confidence to the Democrats. Nobody knew whether the defection of the Midwest from a long but sometimes reluctant allegiance to the Republican party was an impulsive gesture of anger or portended a momentous political realignment. Similarly, nobody could be sure for what the new majority party stood. Its membership embraced men of every political complexion, and its leader had committed himself to nothing positive. Never before had the consequences of victory been so difficult to forecast.

THE BANK PANIC

The November election was followed by nearly four months of legislative deadlock. Jubilant Democrats in the lame-duck Congress ignored the proposals of Hoover and dragged their feet while awaiting the installation of the new administration on March 4, 1933. Banking reform was sidetracked and budget balancing postponed. The lawmakers engaged in petty harassments of the President by passing a Bankruptcy Act in unacceptable form and adopting a resolution requiring publicity for loans made by the R.F.C. They rebelled on a broader front when they passed and sent to the state legislatures the Twenty-first Amendment repealing nationwide prohibition, which Hoover had always favored. In the midst of this unproductive session, the necessary states finally ratified the Twentieth Amendment which set January instead of March as the end of the terms for Presidents and congressmen not re-elected the previous November. Unfortunately ratification came too late to affect the situation in 1932–33.

If the new administration had been able to take office in January, it is doubtful that Roosevelt would have enjoyed the unanimous support accorded him in March. What happened during the interval to deepen the economic crisis and create a calamity atmosphere was the collapse of the banking system. Americans had long been familiar with the phenomena of bank panics, which depositors often started by simultaneously withdrawing their funds from a particular institution. Hitherto such panics had not affected the entire banking system, and even the numerous failures of 1931–32 did not disturb the public as a whole. Individual depositors who lost their savings denounced the system as unsound, but most of the failures had involved rural banks which carried large amounts of farm securities in their portfolios. The large urban banks seemed secure, and depositors continued to show faith in them despite occasional bank holidays in 1932 when state governments suspended financial transactions for specified periods. When several governors in succession proclaimed holidays in early February of 1933, the public became alarmed.

The event that turned alarm into outright panic was the declaration of an eight-day state-wide holiday by the Governor of Michigan on February 14. Depositors all over America suddenly reached the conclusion that if the great financial citadels of Detroit were in danger of failure, no bank could be safe. Accordingly they queued up in long lines to withdraw funds, thus increasing the pressure on bank reserves, causing the weaker banks to close their doors, and driving more governors to proclaim holidays. The chain reaction progressed so rapidly that by noon on March 4, when Roosevelt took the oath of office, only a few banks were conducting normal operations. The panic extended the effects of the depression to the articulate, upper-middle class which had hitherto resisted the demands of farmers and unemployed workers for drastic government action. The loss of lifetime savings and securities by prosperous citizens made economic misery a society-wide reality. It undermined the middle-class illusion that adversity struck only the foolish, the lazy, and the improvident. It also momentarily destroyed affection for the *status quo,* in a quarter where such a viewpoint had found politically influential defenders.

The universality of the economic paralysis and the frightening prospect of conducting business without money created a general sentiment in favor of rigorous action. Citizens were psychologically prepared to be grateful for anything the new President did. Virtually all avenues were open to him. In this novel atmosphere of popular acquiescence which verged on resignation, the unprecedented legislative program of the New Deal was formulated.

Developments in the last turbulent weeks preceding the transfer of political power created a deep and lasting antagonism between Hoover and Roosevelt. Rightly or wrongly, the President attributed the panic to the country's alarm over what Roosevelt might do. Shortly after the election, Hoover had sought the support of the President-elect for his own economic program and had been politely rebuffed by the latter's plea of a lack of Constitutional authority to act. On February 17, 1933, Hoover wrote Roosevelt about the banking crisis and asked him to assure the country "that there will be no tampering with or inflation of the currency; that the budget will be unquestionably balanced, even if further taxation is necessary; that the government credit will be maintained by a refusal to exhaust it in the issue of securities." With doubtful judgment, Hoover studded the letter with phrases about the "steadily degenerating confidence in the future" and the need for "a resumption of the march for recovery." Simultaneously he wrote Senator David A. Reed of Pennsylvania that if Roosevelt made such a declaration he would be ratifying "the whole major program of the Republican administration." Whatever the merit of this viewpoint, the provocative tone of the letter drove a further wedge between him and the President-elect, who still refused to commit himself.

SUGGESTED READINGS

1. Beard, C. A. and M., *America in Mid-Passage* (vol. 1).
2. Mitchell, Broadus, *Depression Decade.*
3. Seldes, G. V., *Years of the Locust* [America 1929–1932].

CHAPTER NINETEEN

THE FIRST NEW DEAL

THE NEW PRESIDENT

Nobody knows what kind of presidential debut Franklin D. Roosevelt would have made under normal circumstances. The calamity atmosphere prevailing on March 4, 1933, had created an audience prepared to applaud anything, and as a result the new President drew upon unexpected powers of leadership. His inaugural address heartened a sullen and dispirited people. Quotations from it fail to capture his solemn but reassuring manner, though a flicker of its eloquence is still to be heard in the famous assertion that "the only thing we have to fear is fear itself — nameless, unreasoning, unjustified terror which paralyzes needed efforts to convert retreat into advance." After pleading with his fellow countrymen to renounce pessimism, he went on to promise an immediate special session of Congress. He expressed confidence that the lawmakers would pass the necessary recovery legislation, but he anticipated the possibility of deadlock by adding that if all else failed he would ask Congress for broad executive power "to wage war against an emergency."

The day after the inauguration the promised action began. A proclamation was issued under the authority of World War I legislation ordering a national bank holiday during which no banking transactions could be carried on without the consent of the Secretary of the Treasury. Simultaneously, Roosevelt called Congress to meet on March 9. An Emergency Banking bill was ready for the consideration of the lawmakers before they found time to unpack. During the ensuing 104 days of the special session, the President bombarded Congress repeatedly with special recommendations to aid agriculture, business, labor, homeowners, and the unemployed. His aggressive assertion of leadership served as a tonic to citizens in every walk of life. A new spirit of optimism circulated through the economy. Business activity began to revive before the effect of legislative recovery measures could possibly be felt. This boomlet proved to be disappointingly short, but the President had gauged the popular temper accurately and had pressed forward with unprecedented political support.

The fast pace in Washington during the opening days of the new administration distracted attention from the personal character and political philosophy of Roosevelt. Both of these touched off a long and acrimonious argument as soon as the country regained its appetite for political speculation. From the middle of his first term until after his death, he continued to be a storm center of controversy.

Only his political abilities were so exceptional as to be beyond dispute. He knew how to build up pressure behind recalcitrant legislators, and he was an artist at wrenching sustained favorable publicity from a press that yearly grew more hostile. Time after time he exhibited an uncanny power in gauging just how far public opinion would allow him to go. He also possessed a flair for dramatizing political issues in such a way that he always seemed to be leading the forces of good in a deadly battle with evil. These talents were underwritten by a surface geniality, a knack for putting visitors at ease, and a streak of engaging humor.

Behind the politician was the man, and about the latter few people agreed. Admirers found him a warm-hearted humanitarian who labored consistently for the welfare of the underprivileged. They regarded him as the ideal public servant: courageous, magnanimous, unselfish. Opponents saw the same individual through very different eyes; they considered him a cynical, worldly politician with an insatiable thirst for power, and they condemned him repeatedly for repudiation of pledges, for vindictiveness, and for double-dealing.

The truth doubtless lay somewhere between the extremes. Roosevelt was a highly complex personality in a century when the American electorate usually conferred power on individuals more easily understood. He had courage and magnanimity, as his friends contended, but he was also capable of spitefulness on occasion. His desire to make a favorable impression on subordinates and favor-seekers often led him to stray beyond the boundary of candor into a no-man's land where intonation and phrasing modified the character of a pledge. Whether or not he was guilty of deliberate deception, his manner sometimes opened him to such a charge. The same ambiguity shrouded his ultimate intentions. Evidence exists that his dominant motivation was some vicarious feeling for the sufferings of the underprivileged and a desire to help them. On the other hand, he had an appetite for power that lent plausibility to charges that he pursued it for its own sake. He doubtless suffered from the normal human propensity for setting lofty goals and unconsciously rationalizing the pursuit of power as incidental to the fulfillment of the grand design. If he did seek the welfare of his fellow countrymen and at the same time enjoyed power without admitting the fact to himself, he was not the first President to do so.

Roosevelt's place in the American political tradition is very difficult to assign. His own heterogeneous political following became hopelessly divided on the question; part of it regarded him as the architect of a new social and economic order, while the remainder hailed him as an intelligent conservative who was trying to save capitalism. The opposition took a less sophisticated view and flatly accused him of trying to subvert traditional values and standards.

Not orthodox but at least we're getting somewhere. (Carlisle, The New York Sun, *1933.)*

Such divergent outlooks were possible because the New Deal faced simultaneously in several directions and also went through several distinct phases. It would be more accurate to describe the program as New Deals instead of New Deal and to abandon the quest for a coherent political philosophy behind the reform measures. All this was a direct reflection of Roosevelt's disregard of theory, his preference for a pragmatic approach. If he possessed political principles, he minimized their importance when choosing a method to solve specific problems. Confronted by the necessity of stimulating a stagnant economy, he merely devised successive relief measures for each depressed group without worrying about the consistent applications of principles.

Public opinion was responsive to the pragmatic approach, partly because drastic changes were easier to bear if not formulated in terms of an unfamiliar philosophy. The major pressure groups, habitually engaged in thwarting one another, had been reduced to such abject misery by the spring of 1933 that they momentarily favored cooperation. Rank-and-file citizens blindly followed Roosevelt in the hope that he would end their ordeal. The crusading fervor which had lent a touch of nobility to the prewar Progressive movement was completely lacking in the New Deal army. What passed for crusading actually turned out to be indignation against financiers and bankers who had wasted the savings of the frugal and had deluded the multitude with the promise of riches without cost. Chastisement of the deceivers rather than purification of society was the dominant note. Most of the discontented regarded the redistribution of material resources as a cure for the ills of society. They wanted economic aid from the administration without being reminded that the policy involved a momentous shift in theory from government as an umpire to government as an agent of pressure groups. For such a task the direct, nonideological approach of Roosevelt was ideally suited.

THE ORGANIZATION OF THE ROOSEVELT ADMINISTRATION

The first phase of the New Deal lasted from the spring of 1933 until the 1934 Congressional elections. The only consistent policy that emerged during this period was the indiscriminate extension of relief to all groups. The development of internal contradictions in the program did not deter the President or his advisers from what they regarded as the pursuit of recovery.

The general excitement over the special session of Congress distracted attention from the composition of the Cabinet. This contained about the same proportion of competent public servants and mediocre politicians as the Cabinets of the preceding fifty years. Three appointees survived for twelve years: Cordell Hull of Tennessee, who abandoned a Senate seat to become Secretary of State; Frances Perkins, the professional social worker from New York and the first woman Cabinet member, who served as Secretary of Labor; and the fiercely honest ex-Bull Mooser, Harold Ickes, who battled for conservation as Secretary of the Interior. Farley received the expected reward of the Postmaster-Generalship. Henry A. Wallace, who subsequently served Roosevelt in several capacities, crossed over from the Republican party to become Secretary of Agriculture for eight years. The venerable Claude Swanson of Virginia presided over the Navy Department for a comparable period. The important post of Secretary of the Treasury went to William H. Woodin, a New York corporation executive, who struggled with illness for a year and then yielded to another New Yorker, Henry Morgenthau, Jr. The hero of the Teapot Dome scandal, Senator Thomas J.

Walsh, had been slated to become Attorney General but died en route to the inauguration and was replaced by Homer S. Cummings of Connecticut. The personnel of the remaining Cabinet posts changed several times.

The Cabinet was less influential in the formulation of policy than in most administrations because of Roosevelt's habit of relying on a "brain trust" for advice. The composition of this informal group shifted from time to time. Roosevelt showed an unexpected preference for college professors and for bright young lawyers recruited by Felix Frankfurter of the Harvard Law School. Although the brain-trusters often did not hold government posts, the three most important in the early days of the New Deal — Raymond Moley, Rexford G. Tugwell, and Adolph A. Berle — received important jobs in major departments. Businessmen, ever scornful of policy makers who had never met a payroll, circulated lurid rumors about the recommendations of the professors.

Political scientists and laymen who had long complained about the division of powers as a barrier to rapid governmental action were amazed by the speedy grinding of the legislative mill. Bills introduced one day occasionally became laws the next, while measures of unprecedented complexity cleared both houses of Congress and received presidential approval in a few weeks. Most of the legislation was drafted by Roosevelt's advisers rather than by congressional committees, and the lawmakers accepted this veiled insult without visible protest. Party lines crumbled as Republicans and Democrats, goaded by peremptory orders from constituents, supported the administration's proposals. Nothing like it had been seen since World War I when Congress had also been eclipsed by the executive.

BANKING LEGISLATION

Although Roosevelt had proclaimed a nationwide bank holiday immediately after his assumption of office, such an unnatural situation could not be allowed to prevail for an extended period. The questionable legality of the proclamation reinforced the desirability of hasty action. As a result much of the legislation during the so-called Hundred Days was concerned with banking and kindred financial problems. The emergency legislation of March 9 incorporated many of the suggestions of bankers. Besides validating the presidential proclamation, it conferred emergency power on the government to control gold and currency movements, prosecute hoarders, and prevent the reopening of unsound banks. In addition, it met the urgent need for currency by creating a new circulating medium, Federal Reserve bank notes. These, in contrast to the old Federal Reserve notes which required a 40 per cent gold backing, could be issued by banks against all sound assets. A few critics saw an inflationary threat from the new issues, but the bankers generally were satisfied with the entire Act because it did not diminish the private character of the banking system. They also applauded a companion measure passed two days later which gave the President wide powers to cut the salaries of federal employees 15 per cent and to reduce both the pensions and the allowances of war veterans. As the initial step toward a balanced budget, they believed the law would help restore confidence in the monetary system. In fact, for a few days the business community regarded Roosevelt as a kind of well-intentioned but naïve Democratic embodiment of Hoover. He accepted their coaching with deceptive graciousness. Sound banks were reopened on March 13. For this step Roosevelt had prepared the public on the preceding day with the first of his radio "fireside chats." He assured his listeners that their money would be safer in a reopened bank than "under a mattress." The response was so gratifying that within a week 80 per cent of the banks belonging to the Federal Reserve System had begun to conduct normal business. The state banks reopened more slowly, but about three quarters of them were functioning by mid-April.

The Emergency Banking Law was followed by the Glass-Stegall Act of June 16 which started the disenchantment of the bankers with their rookie protégé. It divorced investment banking from deposit banking in order to prevent speculative activity by institutions in the latter category. It also enlarged the power of the Federal Reserve Banks to curb speculation by member banks. A novel provision was added that guaranteed depositors against losses up to $2,500. Originally adopted on a small scale and for a temporary period, the plan elicited so much enthusiasm that the coverage was eventually raised to $5,000 and the guarantee made permanent. After ten years of operation, nearly 14,000 banks affiliated themselves with the Federal Deposit Insurance Corporation.

THE SECURITIES AND EXCHANGE ACT

The area for discretionary activity by bankers and financiers was further contracted through passage of the Securities Act. The Senate Banking and Currency Committee with the shrewd Ferdinand Pecora as its counsel had been investigating abuses in the flotation and sale of securities since 1932. Armed with an arsenal of evidence about devices used to mulct the public, the Committee drafted and secured adoption of a bill to ensure investors of adequate information about securities offered for sale. The securities law prohibited the public sale of new security issues in interstate commerce or through the mails unless a registration statement concerning the character and scope of the business had been filed with the Federal Trade Commission.

This legislation was amended by the Securities and Exchange Act of 1934. The revised law broadened the coverage to include old securities issues and transferred supervision from the Federal Trade Commission to an independent bipartisan board of five members appointed by the President for five years. The new Securities and Exchange Commission, known popularly as the SEC, was vested with wide supervisory power over stock exchanges and brokers. Officers and directors of companies holding 10 per cent or more of the stock of a corporation were required to file a monthly statement with the Commission of their transactions in that particular security. The provision afforded the small stockholder some protection against manipulation by insiders. The Securities and Exchange Act also enlisted the support of the Federal Reserve Board in curbing speculation by granting it authority to raise or lower within certain limits the percentage of the downpayment for stocks purchased on margin. The same regulation was eventually extended to commodity exchanges as well. Willful violation of the rules carried a penalty of fine or imprisonment or both. For several years the New York Exchange resisted supervision by the SEC, but in 1937 the indictment of Richard Whitney, a former Exchange president, for grand larceny arising out of stock manipulation, broke the opposition. Needless to say, the new legislation did not protect the investor against loss. It did guarantee him a minimum of information about companies that solicited his funds.

INFLATIONARY POLICIES

Long before the completion of this elaborate cycle of regulations, the financial community had become bitterly opposed to Roosevelt. It had believed that the Emergency Banking Law of March 9, 1933, and the accompanying effort to balance the budget committed him to a sound monetary policy. Within a month of his inauguration, his use of emergency powers completely disillusioned them.

The bankers and the political leaders of the preceding administration held the gold standard in awe. Roosevelt did not. He lacked a comprehensive knowledge of economics but saw in a dim instinctive way that a high level of economic activity was usually accompanied by a rising price level. Without troubling himself greatly over the problem of which caused which, he came to the conclusion that an issuance of currency in excess of the amount based on gold reserves would inflate prices and stimulate recovery.

The pressures for inflation during the Hundred Days were formidable. Farmers demanded it as one way of reducing their burden of mortgaged indebtedness. Senators from western states with idle silver mines hoped to tie inflation to the revival of the mining industry. A substantial number of exporters believed that their foreign markets had evaporated partly because many other countries had gone off the gold standard, thereby cheapening their currencies and the prices of their goods abroad. Congress considered a variety of inflationary proposals without any prompting from Roosevelt. The one that the legislators approved was a rider to the Agricultural Adjustment Act of May 12, 1933, known as the Thomas Amendment. It provided the President with three methods of inflating the currency: (1) reduction of the gold content of the dollar; (2) the free coinage of silver at a ratio to gold to be fixed by executive decision; and (3) the issuance of $3 billion in greenbacks to pay off federal obligations or reduce the bonded indebtedness of the United States.

Roosevelt had already started an inflationary policy under his emergency banking powers, and the Thomas Amendment did not change the direction of his policy. What he did was to order all persons to exchange their gold for other coin and currency on April 5, and to prohibit the export of gold on April 19. A supplementary congressional resolution of June 5 freed debtors from meeting their obligations in gold even if a gold payment clause had been written in their contracts.

The effect of these moves was to institute a kind of passive devaluation whereby the dollar, divorced from gold, slowly sank in its relation to the price of other currencies. Roosevelt pursued this policy until October 1933, when he decided to hasten the cheapening of the dollar by authorizing the Reconstruction Finance Corporation to buy gold at a figure substantially above that of the world market. Gold was first purchased at $31.36 per ounce and the price was gradually increased until it stood at $34.45 on January 16, 1934. Since an ounce of gold had been worth $20.67 the day Roosevelt took office, he had devalued the dollar approximately 40 per cent in nine months. Legislation known as the Gold Reserve Act of January 30, 1934, ended the downward drift of the dollar. The President was authorized to fix the gold content of the dollar at some figure between 50 and 60 per cent of its old weight. He promptly fixed a weight of 15 5/21 grains nineteenths fine. In nontechnical language, the decision meant that the new dollar was worth 59.06 cents. The Gold Reserve Act also created a stabilization fund of $2 billion and empowered the Treasury Department to use it for foreign exchange operations. Although Roosevelt retained the authority to change the weight of the dollar within designated limits, he engaged in no further monetary tinkering. Thereafter the stabilization fund was used to maintain a fixed relationship between the dollar and other currencies. However, a chronic inflationary device was introduced into the system by the Silver Purchase Act of June 19, 1934, which in effect forced the Treasury to purchase the entire domestic output of silver at a price far above that of the world market.

RELIEF

Just as the inflationary monetary devices of the New Deal seemed to contradict the orthodox financial policies spelled out in the Emergency Banking Act, so deficit spending for the relief of various depressed groups seemed to contradict the budget balancing measure of March 11. Roosevelt sought to conceal the inconsistency by setting up two budgets: one containing regular expenditures that were being reduced, and the other containing emergency expenditures that were being increased. For the moment, he silenced critics of a rising deficit with his strong insistence on the temporary character of the new policy.

Large-scale spending was carried on through the medium of agencies created by earlier administrations as well as by new organizations. An Emergency Farm Mortgage Act authorized the Federal Land Banks to undertake large-scale refinancing of farm mortgages on terms highly favorable to the debtors. A companion piece of legislation set up a Home Owners' Loan Corporation to extend the same benefits to citizens burdened with residential mortgages. The Reconstruction Finance Corporation, with greatly broadened powers, extended a helping hand to some six thousand banks in distress, to small businessmen threatened with bankruptcy, and to a variety of other groups. The fiction was maintained that the agency loaned money only on good security, but much of its work turned out to be rescue operations carried on irrespective of the prospects of repayment.

The RFC was also converted during the Hundred Days into a vehicle of relief for the unemployed. Congress made a fresh appropriation of $500 million to permit fresh RFC loans to the states. Simultaneously it relaxed restraints so completely that loans actually became grants. A new agency, the Federal Emergency Relief Administration, was created to supervise the distribution of funds. Harry Hopkins, who had directed the New York State Unemployment Relief Administration when Roosevelt was still at Albany, became head of the FERA. For a few months he functioned as a coordinator because actual expenditure of funds remained in the hands of the states. Generally speaking, FERA money went for direct relief — doles that provided only a bare subsistence. As such, it was a stopgap operation slated for liquidation when economic activity revived.

A much more ambitious scheme, which pursued the dual objectives of unemployment relief and the stimulation of economic activity, was the public works program. Congress appropriated an unprecedented $3.33 billion with which Roosevelt created a Public Works Administration under Secretary of Interior Ickes to plan and execute suitable projects. The conscientious and irascible Ickes scrutinized the various proposals for public works so carefully that they did not get out of the blueprint stage quickly enough to relieve unemployment in the summer and fall of 1933. Accordingly, Roosevelt created a temporary Civil Works Administration in November 1933 and put Hopkins in charge. Before the experiment was terminated the following spring, Hopkins managed to employ four million people and spend $33 million. CWA employees did everything from repairing highways to raking leaves.

One other experiment for the relief of distress was the creation of a Civilian Conservation Corps. It provided healthful outdoor work for nearly 300,000 young men — mostly unmarried and between the ages of eighteen and twenty-five — in various national forests. They received room and board in forest camps plus $30 per month, $25 of which was sent to their families.

The cumulative impression created by the policy of 1933 was that Roosevelt intended to tide all depressed groups over the emergency period. At the outset, conservative groups who doubted the reliability of the plans dared not complain about deficit spending for the unemployed because they too were receiving government handouts.

THE AGRICULTURAL ADJUSTMENT ACT

The plight of the farmer also received prompt attention from the President and his obedient Congress. Except for interludes of foreign crop failures and wars, American agriculture had been chronically depressed during most of the preceding hundred years. Both politicians and farmers resisted the conclusion that the system of food production as currently organized did not provide an adequate living for the vast majority of farmers in ordinary years.

A number of midwestern radicals favored production for use, without realizing its implications. Most of them would have been unwilling for the government to sell or give away surplus commodities in direct competition with private producers. They would also have opposed any scheme which sponsored a large-scale consolidation of uneconomic holdings or a transfer of farmers from submarginal land to some other occupation. Actually, the only alternative to permanent subsidy was some plan that would remove both tenants and owners from countless tiny eroded hillside plots.

Neither Roosevelt nor the conference of farm leaders which he convened March 8 in fullfillment of a campaign pledge, cared to consider a drastic solution. The fifty-odd leaders representing every major agricultural organization and shade of opinion disagreed sharply over policy. The majority wanted some variation of the McNary-Haugen plan that would enable farmers to imitate industry by restricting production, stabilizing markets, and raising prices. The bitter experience of Hoover's Farm Board had, however, taught the leaders the futility of pleas for voluntary acreage reduction, and they also recognized the unwillingness of the public to pay subsidies on an ever-growing crop. With these considerations in mind, the conference under the leadership of Henry Wallace, the Secretary of Agriculture, presented a series of recommendations to the President. He in turn passed the report on to a group of advisers, who within a week drafted a bill for congressional consideration. The lawmakers passed the measure after a gentlemanly debate, May 12, 1933.

Known as the Agricultural Adjustment Act, the measure gave the President broad powers to refinance mortgages and gave the Secretary of Agriculture power to control production and to raise farm income by increasing farm prices to the level prevailing between 1909 and 1914, which planners regarded as average years. The target was known as "parity" and it became such a watchword of farmers that wags paraphrased the quotation from St. Paul to read: "Faith, hope, and parity, and the greatest of these is parity." Later legislation switched the emphasis from parity prices to parity income so that the term came to mean "the price for the commodity which will give the commodity a purchasing power with respect to articles that farmers buy equivalent to the purchasing power of such commodity in the base period." But in 1933 parity referred to the more modest goal of re-establishing the 1909 to 1914 price level for agricultural commodities.

The law defined seven commodities — wheat, cotton, corn, hogs, rice, tobacco, and milk products — as basic and authorized the Secretary of Agriculture to pay individual farmers for reducing crop acreage or livestock production. Those who grew other crops clamored for benefit payments, and a year later the umbrella was widened to cover sugar, cattle, rye, barley, grain sorghums, flax, and peanuts. The law also provided that the revenue for payments should be raised by a processing tax or excise levy on the initial processing of basic commodities for the domestic market. Since the millers who ground wheat into flour and their counterparts in other industries had no intention of absorbing the cost of this unique experiment, the processing tax was passed on to consumers in the form of a higher price for the finished product.

Additional power was vested in the Secretary of Agriculture to make marketing agreements with processors and middlemen who might otherwise interfere with the price plans of the program. Such agreements were optional rather than mandatory and were exempted from the operation of the antitrust laws. Congress assumed it would be to the interest of the processors to establish marketing quotas and thereby stabilize prices, and that products besides those defined as basic would also benefit. So that the switches would be open on all tracks at once, the Act conferred on the Secretary sweeping powers to loan money on the security of crops, purchase surplus commodities, and subsidize exports.

THE NATIONAL INDUSTRIAL RECOVERY ACT

The most important unfinished business of the special session was the formulation of a program acceptable to industry and to organized labor. Presidential advisers hoped that expenditures on the unemployed would provide a temporary stimulus to economic activity. But for the moment, Roosevelt accepted the orthodox idea that a genuine revival of prosperity would take place under the auspices of private enterprise. What he wanted specifically was legislation to encourage investment, increase production, and provide jobs. After a considerable amount of infighting between business and labor groups, Congress passed the National Industrial Recovery Act on June 16, 1933.

This elaborate piece of legislation owed most of its provisions to industry's contention that current economic stagnation resulted from cutthroat competition. American business had always disliked competition and had expended tremendous energy trying to get rid of it despite the existence of antitrust laws and other legal barriers. Great progress had been made during the 1920's when Hoover as Secretary of Commerce built a program of standardization and cooperation on the foundations of wartime trade associations. These informal agreements broke down under the stress of depression, and demoralizing price wars ensued. Accordingly, business sought the elimination of the weak legal restraints on collusion and the establishment of industrywide standardization agreements that would be binding. To achieve this objective, businessmen were prepared to take the unprecedented step of inviting government regulation of industry. As P. W. Litchfield of Goodyear Tire put it at a Chamber of Commerce meeting in May 1933: "We have failed to take the necessary steps voluntarily, so the element of government force and compulsion becomes necessary." In the hour of crisis the principle of competition did not receive the support of a major pressure group, although it was presumably a cornerstone of the American system.

The entire business community became reconciled to government regulation as the price for heading off the Black bill, which proposed to establish the thirty-hour work week. The latter had been approved by the Senate in April 1933 and seemed likely to emerge from the House with an amendment providing for a minimum wage as well. At this point business appealed to Roosevelt for a law that would permit industrywide cooperation.

The President agreed to a broader approach, and the government lawyers quickly drafted the NIRA. It provided for codes of "fair competition" by industrial groups or associations. Such codes were to be submitted to the President or his authorized representative and, if approved by the former, were to be binding on all units of the particular industry concerned. In cases where an industry refused to submit a code, the President was empowered to impose one after notice and proper hearings. He also received a vague and sweeping grant of authority to make voluntary agreements with business units and labor unions if such agreements would expedite implementation of the Act. Violators of the codes were subject to fine and imprisonment.

The law made a feeble attempt to establish code standards for the guidance of the President. It enjoined him to see that the codes were drafted by representative associations and were free from provisions that would promote monopoly. On the other hand, since the whole idea of industrywide codes revolved about the desire to eliminate competition, implementation of the law invariably meant the promotion of monopoly. Business expected exactly such a concession as its price for accepting the labor provision of the NIRA known as Section 7A. The latter established a new beachhead for the unions by making it mandatory for every code agreement to contain a collective bargaining clause. The effectiveness of 7A was to depend primarily on the vigilance which the government showed in enforcing it. The language of the clause clearly stated the right of employees to choose their own representatives for bargaining purposes free from coercion or restraint by management.

The NIRA was sold to Congress as an experiment and hence was to be in force for only two years. A specific provision exempted companies cooperating in pursuance of authorized codes from prosecution under the antitrust laws. Moreover, since the NIRA envisaged a substantial price rise, the President was vested with power to suspend the import of commodities that improved their competitive position as a result of code agreements.

THE TENNESSEE VALLEY AUTHORITY

During the Hundred Days, Congress also approved the Muscle Shoals project to which Senator Norris had dedicated ten years of his legislative life. At the insistence of Roosevelt, the law provided for government development of the Tennessee Valley on a scale far larger than Norris had ever anticipated. A public corporation was set up to develop power resources and undertake a wide variety of conservation activities, including flood control, soil erosion, forestation, and withdrawal of marginal lands from cultivation. Congress vested management of the corporation in the hands of three directors appointed by the President. Arthur E. Morgan, President of Antioch College, served as chairman until 1938, when he was ousted as the result of a bitter personal and policy quarrel within the TVA. David E. Lilienthal of Wisconsin, a fellow director, replaced him.

The features of the law which subsequently made the TVA a center of controversy related to the generation and disposal of electricity. The private utility companies were to wage a bitter battle over the constitutionality of government sale of surplus power and over the congressional directive which ordered the TVA to give preference to nonprofit-making state, local, and cooperative organizations in selling power wholesale for distribution. However, in 1933 citizens still smarted from losses incurred because of manipulations in utilities stocks and they refused to heed the warning of the power companies about the socialistic threat of TVA legislation.

CROSSCURRENTS IN EMERGENCY LEGISLATION

Congress adjourned in mid-June after giving the President practically everything he had requested. It was impossible to ascribe a coherent philosophy to the emergency New Deal program. Those who called it socialistic could not satisfactorily explain Roosevelt's zeal for saving banks, railroads, farms, and other institutions of the private property system that were threatened with bankruptcy. Nor was there anything particularly radical about the NIRA, which legalized collusive practices dear to the hearts of business, and the AAA, which sought to organize agriculture for price-fixing activities. None of these measures altered the basic structure of capitalism, although they gave franker expression to the policy of subsidizing pressure groups than ever before.

Those who described the New Deal as an imaginative effort to rejuvenate and preserve the old institutional framework had several embarrassing facts to explain. The currency management policy of the President faced in the direction of totalitarian economic controls by the central government. Similarly, TVA legislation, which set up a public corporation designed to compete with private utilities in the generation and sale of power, did not reflect the convictions of orthodox defenders of free enterprise. Direct government employment to relieve the needy might be justified as an emergency measure, but hardly as a practice consonant with the philosophy of those who made the Constitution.

The only common impulse was the determination to help depressed groups. Roosevelt never translated this outlook into theoretical forms, but his program did have ideological implications. It completed the change launched during the Wilson administration from the concept of government as an umpire to the concept of government as an agent of various pressure groups. Government became, for the moment, the agent of all the articulate groups. As the New Deal unfolded, the emphasis shifted until the economically underprivileged became the primary if not the exclusive beneficiaries of administration policy.

The effect of the emergency New Deal legislation upon economic conditions proved difficult to judge. Business activity revived almost as soon as Roosevelt took office. Between March and July 1933, the index of production rose from 56 to 101, the stock market went up, and farm prices increased substantially. This brief boom was due primarily to the spirit of confidence generated by Roosevelt and developed before the impact of his program could possibly be felt. The feverish activity of the new administration was contagious; for the moment people felt that conditions would improve, they made economic decisions on that basis, and conditions actually did improve.

Unfortunately the boom was a false dawn. It was based on cheap government credit, an anticipation of higher labor and material costs, and a rapid expansion of inventories as a hedge against inflation. Farm prices reached a peak in July, wavered for a few days, and then fell abruptly. Business activity also began to decline sharply in the fall of 1933 because purchasing power had not risen sufficiently to absorb increased production. Indeed, the summer price-inflation left the consumer worse off than he had been in the dismal days of March.

Meanwhile the administration expected its various recovery measures to arrest the break. Heavy reliance was placed on the National Recovery Administration (NRA) established by the President to implement the NIRA. He appointed General Hugh S. Johnson to head the new organization and supervise code-making activities. The selection of Johnson emphasized the importance attached to government planning; he had organized conscription in World War I and had then served as a key subordinate of Bernard Baruch on the War Industries Board. He was picturesque, energetic, temperamental, and a coiner of devastating phrases. He regarded himself as the leader of a crusading army, and his NRA codes as fortifications against depression. He adopted the Blue Eagle as a symbol of righteousness, and allowed all employers to display it who agreed to abide by code regulations. A great Blue Eagle campaign was organized on the pattern of Liberty Loan drives during World War I. Local volunteer committees held pep rallies, parades, and information meetings; while Johnson, like a modern Don Quixote, rode off in all directions, tilting with greedy businessmen, stubborn labor leaders, and uncooperative consumers. And yet, despite his extravagant denunciation of obstructionists as "social Neanderthals," he sought to sell the NRA by voluntary methods rather than invoke the punitive clauses.

The actual process of code making was considerably more prosaic and earthy than the public imagined. An association representing a particular industry presented a draft code to the NRA. An open hearing was held where representatives of industry, labor, and consumer groups maneuvered for advantage in traditional fashion. Thereafter the code underwent exhaustive analysis by NRA officials and was often substantially amended. Further informal conferences sought to narrow down the differences between pressure groups. The concluding step was to secure the approval of the code administrator and the President. The code then went into effect and was binding on all units within an industry whether or not they had participated in the drafting of the code.

Johnson pushed his hastily organized staff at a terrific pace and produced the initial NRA code, which covered the cotton textile industry, on July 9, 1933. It provided for a forty-hour week with a two-shift limit, minimum weekly wages of $12 in the South and $13 in the North, and the abolition of child labor. Roosevelt hailed the child-labor clause as the termination of an "ancient atrocity." The coal code, adopted some two months later, seemed still more favorable to labor. It conceded the right of the United Mine Workers to represent the miners and provided for the setting up of grievance committees and for the stationing of observers where coal was weighed. It also dropped the requirement that miners had to live in company houses and trade at company stores. A few simple code provisions seemed to have won for labor more than the gains of several decades of industrial warfare.

Because associations submitted codes at a much faster rate than NRA officials could process them, all industry was invited on July 27, 1933, to adopt the President's Re-employment Agreement (PRA). This model code pledged employers not to hire children; not to work employees over forty hours a week in stores and banks, nor over thirty-five hours a week in factories; and not to pay a wage of less than thirty cents an hour. PRA was widely accepted pending the adoption of specific codes, which took place at an unbelievably rapid pace. By February 1934, NRA had approved over 550 codes covering most of American industry and including such diverse economic activities as manufacturing, wholesale and retail trade, construction, and a wide category of service industries.

Notwithstanding the great variety in basic codes, certain standard provisions appeared in most of them. Minimum wages and maximum hours were established for labor, although the terms usually differed for each geographic segment of an industry and often the coverage did not extend to every category of employees. All codes banned child labor and proclaimed the right of labor to bargain collectively in accordance with Section 7A. The clauses covering production practices were less uniform. In general, industry sought the maximum in detailed and elaborate rules which covered everything from false advertising to discount regulations. Raw material producers set definite production quotas and established fixed prices. Most codes covering manufacturers prohibited the sale of goods at prices below the cost of production — a provision difficult to apply. A smaller group specified the number of hours that a plant might operate and restricted the installation of new machinery.

The code system enjoyed its greatest popularity before it had begun to function. Once the elaborate machinery was set in motion, disillusionment developed rapidly. The first rumbles of discontent became audible in the spring of 1934, and as the year progressed management, labor, and consumers denounced the experiment with less and less restraint. A review board appointed by Roosevelt to evaluate the functioning of the NRA increased the difficulties of the agency. Under the chairmanship of the famous criminal lawyer and Socialist, Clarence Darrow, it issued a report denouncing the entire system. By autumn, violations of codes began to take place openly. The erratic, high-strung Johnson, who did not react well to criticism, first threatened a crackdown and then resigned in September. Thereafter the direction of the NRA passed to a board with less passion for controversy.

In retrospect it is easy to see why the NRA encountered stormy weather. Industrial codes, like tariff schedules, provided ideal vehicles for experts to trap the unwary. Moreover, citizens representing the largest and most important segments of industry became key figures in code making. As a result, innocent-looking codes often contained features which strengthened big business at the expense of lesser competitors. The small fry complained bitterly and were joined by their oppressors, who really did not like government controls and worked to get rid of them as soon as the maximum benefits of collusion had been realized.

The provisions which guaranteed labor certain minimum working conditions and collective bargaining rights proved illusory. Because of the high level of unemployment, the weakness of labor organizations, and the eagerness of workers to accept jobs on any terms, greater government vigilance was required for the enforcement of code provisions than materialized. Employers obstructed 7A clandestinely at first and later more openly. Seventy per cent of the cases sent to the Labor Board of the NRA during first year of the law involved the flat refusal of employers to bargain collectively. Even where they did so, they interpreted 7A to mean that bargaining could be done with small groups and carried no obligation of recognizing a union which represented a majority of the workers. Roosevelt encouraged the employer interpretation when he intervened to prevent a strike in the automobile industry in the spring of 1934. Company unions continued to flourish as they had done in the 1920's.

Consumers never had any ground for being enthusiastic about the NRA, although the fanfare accompanying its debut may have momentarily confused them. Industrywide price-fixing agreements usually mean higher retail prices. This became quite apparent during the public hearings on codes, and consumers howled indignantly as prices increased without a corresponding rise in their income.

Aside from the conventional conflict between pressure groups, the effectiveness of the NRA was paralyzed by the basic incompatibility of its principal objectives. The regulations designed to raise prices by restricting output and hours of work contradicted the stated purposes, which were to stimulate investment, increase production, and create jobs. For several years industry had lacked confidence to risk fresh capital or step-up output. The code system did not change this attitude. Hence industry counterbalanced concessions with regard to working conditions and wage floors by installing labor-saving devices, replacing skilled with unskilled labor, and enforcing a speed-up on the assembly line. Statistical data indicated that there was little net increase of employment or economic activity under the NRA. Those quarters least charitable to the administration contended that it actually hampered recovery. Probably the judgment was too harsh, inasmuch as the NRA gave a psychological stimulus to the economy during the opening months when it enjoyed general support. In any event the days of the agency were numbered. The Supreme Court declared it unconstitutional about a month before it was slated to expire.

At the outset, the Agricultural Adjustment Act also encountered considerable criticism, but ultimately it won substantial support from the farmers whom it was designed to help. Friction quickly developed between Secretary Wallace and George N. Peek, the perennial McNary-Haugenite who was appointed head of the AAA. True to his earlier principles, Peek favored the subsidy program but disliked curbs on production. He pressed for an aggressive campaign to sell or dump agricultural surpluses abroad before experimenting with crop restriction. On the other hand Wallace favored not only an immediate reduction of acreage but a large-scale destruction of commodities that would normally have matured and reached the market in 1933. He took this extreme position because he feared that the world-wide glut of agricultural products would drive prices down still further. Although he regarded crop destruction as an emergency measure and hoped that reciprocal trade agreements would ultimately open up fresh markets, the gulf between him and Peek grew steadily wider. The latter finally resigned in December 1933 and was replaced by Chester Davis, who willingly carried out the Wallace program.

Meanwhile plans for crop destruction had been carried out. Wallace paid farmers nearly $113 million for plowing under an estimated 4.4 million bales of cotton during the summer of 1933. Both Socialists who believed in an economy of abundance and Republicans who disliked farm subsidies in any form were irritated by the program. Indignation mounted still higher when the AAA purchased and slaughtered thousands of little pigs and pregnant sows to prevent a hog surplus. Opponents of the administration condemned it for destroying food when the poor lacked an adequate diet. Relief agencies actually distributed much of the meat to the needy, but this gesture did not disarm the critics.

The spectacular emergency measure of the AAA to control the surplus distracted attention from long-range plans for the limitation of production. Operating in as decentralized a fashion as possible and through existing agricultural organizations, the AAA established county production control associations which worked out acreage allotments for individual farmers. Curtailment of acreage was entirely voluntary. Nevertheless, the novel opportunity to qualify for benefit payments by performing less work stimulated a high level of compliance.

Between 1932 and 1934 both production and prices of basic commodities showed the effect of the AAA program. Cotton output declined from 13 million bales to 9.6 million bales; wheat, from 548.5 million bushels to 360.1 million bushels; corn, from 587.2 million bushels to 170 million bushels. Prices rose in an irregular pattern: cotton, from $32.60 a bale to $61.80; wheat, from 38 cents a bushel to 84.8 cents; corn, from 31.9 cents a bushel to 81.5 cents. Critics of the AAA attributed these changes to the severe drought of 1934, which reduced production and increased prices more than the planners had intended.

Whether nature or the New Deal was more responsible for the new trend in agriculture, farm income increased spectacularly during the emergency period of the New Deal. Even though the entire price level went up, the farmers' purchasing power rose some 25 per cent. Naturally not all segments of agriculture benefited equally. Producers of basic commodities came out most fortunately, large farmers fared better than small farmers, while the tenant population lost out completely.

Both farmers and self-proclaimed sympathizers who had done little for them during the preceding decade lamented the inroads of the AAA bureaucracy on rural independence and self-reliance. However, irrespective of what they said publicly, farmers welcomed cash payments, as their affirmative vote at AAA referendums indicated.

The effects of other features of the early New Deal were harder to measure. The FERA and CWA programs certainly relieved human misery but did not place enough purchasing power in the hands of the unemployed to stimulate private economic activity on a large scale. After 1934 the distinction between the emergency and the regular budgets was to disappear and deficit spending was to develop as a long-term weapon for fighting depression. Thereafter both its wisdom and its effectiveness would have to be evaluated on a somewhat different basis.

The gold-buying program of the President and the legislation ratifying the devaluation of the dollar were supposed to raise the price level and stimulate investment. Like most short-cut solutions to difficult problems, the policy of controlled inflation did not measure up to expectations. Critics of the New Deal blamed the price inflation of World War II and after on what they regarded as the unsound monetary program of the early 1930's. If gold buying had any immediate effect on the economy, it was not apparent.

The various loan programs of the New Deal, which saved many farmers, homeowners, and business firms from bankruptcy, probably did more to restore confidence and optimism than any other policies of the emergency era. We have already noted that individual features of the New Deal worked at cross-purposes and contradicted each other. Nevertheless the feverish pace of activity had a tonic effect on the economy. Production revived in 1934, employment showed modest increases, and farm prices recovered. Roosevelt stood pat on his emergency program, and when Congress met in January it did little more than pass legislation implementing policies already started and tinker with merchant shipping and airline subsidies. The only noteworthy measure of the session was the Reciprocal Trade Agreements Act which launched a new trend in tariff legislation.

Whether or not a sound basis had been laid for recovery, people felt better and gave Roosevelt credit. Republican congressmen complained that most of the mail from constituents ordered them to be rubber stamps and support the President blindly. The reaction of the redcap in the Washington depot, when asked about the New Deal, was typical: "Well, suh, I don't know nothin' about the New Deal, but if it's that what's gettin' us bigger tips then I'm for it."

Riding such a tidal wave of popular sentiment, the Democrats swept the 1934 congressional elections, increasing their total of Senate seats from 59 to 69 and their total in the House from 313 to 332. For the first time in the twentieth century, the party in power increased its strength in the off-year canvass. Encouraged by this mandate, Roosevelt prepared to open the second phase of the New Deal with another spectacular legislative program.

SUGGESTED READINGS

1. Beard, C. A. and M., *America in Mid-Passage* (vol. 1).
2. Lindley, E. K., *The Roosevelt Revolution: First Phase.*
3. Mitchell, B., *Depression Decade.*
4. Wector, D., *The Age of the Great Depression.*

CHAPTER TWENTY

FROM RECOVERY TO SOCIAL REFORM

PRESSURES FOR RADICAL LEGISLATION

The extraordinary spirit of cooperation displayed during the Hundred Days and the following year evaporated slowly in the last half of 1934. Universal fear of economic ruin had bred a solidarity hitherto unknown except in time of war, and the President had adroitly capitalized this patriotic mood by treating the fight against depression as a military enterprise. The NRA as well as other New Deal agencies had been organized like the industrial mobilization of 1917. Thus, for a time, criticism had been regarded as bordering on treason. Such an unnatural state of affairs could last only as long as the emergency. Even the modest economic revival in 1934 was fatal to political consensus.

Business groups broke ranks first. Instinctively hostile to government regulation, they repented their demands for the NRA before it was slated to expire. Roosevelt's tepid sponsorship of collective bargaining, his abandonment of the gold standard, and his gradual conversion of deficit spending from an emergency policy to a more permanent one, reinforced their determination to break with the New Deal. In a futile effort to influence the elections they organized the Liberty League. Ostensibly nonpartisan, it placed disgruntled Smith Democrats in conspicuous positions and agitated for the restoration of business leadership and principles.

Since industrial groups had completely lost the confidence of the voters during the depression, their defection from the New Deal coalition was important only because it annoyed Roosevelt. Thereafter, he considered businessmen ungrateful for his efforts to save them and listened increasingly to radical advisers who urged vigorous chastisement of the fallen heros of the twenties. As his attitude toward business hardened, conservatives like Ray Moley, Hugh Johnson, and Lew Douglas dropped out of the administration. Harry Hopkins, Rexford G. Tugwell, and two protégés of Professor Frankfurter, Thomas Corcoran and Benjamin Cohen, came forward as architects of the 1935 legislative program.

Perhaps a more important factor in pushing Roosevelt to sponsor a broad program of social and economic reform was the fear that a more radical movement would outbid the New Deal. During the 1932 campaign the more visionary schemes for reconstructing society had been ignored by pessimistic voters, but the extraordinary ease with which the President had thrown together a relief program changed the popular mood. Far wilder plans suddenly seemed attainable, and their proponents — hitherto overshadowed by Roosevelt — began to take a more independent attitude. Father Charles Coughlin, the popular priest-politician, launched an extravagant campaign for currency inflation. A retired physician, Dr. Francis E. Townsend, won the devotion of a large number of the aged with his plan for a government pension of $200 a month for every citizen over sixty years of age; especially attractive was its stipulation for the expenditure of the entire pension within thirty days, which Townsend represented as an infallible short cut to prosperity. In Minnesota a militant state Farmer-Labor party had just re-elected Governor Floyd B. Olson on a platform advocating state ownership of key industries. Most amazing of all was the meteoric rise of Senator Huey P. Long of Louisiana.

As a salesman among the poor whites of Louisiana, Long had developed a talent for persuasion which, when translated to the political field, resulted in his election as Governor in 1928 and Senator two years later. In the process he set up a political machine which established records for corruptness and efficiency. Already dictator of Louisiana before the inauguration of Roosevelt, he made his debut on the national stage as an outspoken supporter of the New Deal. He soon broke with the President and treated the nation to a bizarre brand of defiance, conducting one-man filibusters in the Senate, brawling in eastern night clubs, and receiving diplomats in his pajamas. His loudness, vulgarity, and exhibitionism disgusted large numbers of people, but not the rural voters of Louisiana. They loved the Senator for launching a vast public works program which put roads in rural areas and free textbooks in the hands of school children. The poor whites cared little about the rising debt and the tax burden that fell primarily on other shoulders. By the spring of 1935, Long had widened his following among the rural masses of the South with a "Share the Wealth" program. Proposing confiscatory taxes on the well-to-do, Long promised to make every man a king. Openly boasting that he could carry the entire South, he made noisy preparations for the 1936 presidential election.

Roosevelt recognized the potential menace of Long's activity. If the Senator succeeded in uniting all the radical groups in a new third party, the Democrats might lose enough votes to produce a Republican victory. Accordingly, Roosevelt's 1935 legislative program was formulated with a view to minimizing defections on the left. Part of it had already been planned and was to be sent to Congress as soon as research commissions made their recommendations. But the threatened secession of the radicals probably drove him to take a more uncompromising stand in behalf of underprivileged groups than he might otherwise have done.

Always belittlin'. (Talburt, Scripps-Howard newspapers, *1936.)*

The breakup of the national recovery coalition, foreshadowed by the defection of business groups, thus refashioned the New Deal. Henceforward the movement appealed primarily to the lower middle class and the depressed groups of farms and cities. It appropriated the philosophy of the Wilson wing of the Progressive movement, which had envisaged government as an agent of underprivileged groups. Discredited during the Nationalist reaction of the twenties, this credo now welded together left-wing intellectuals, erstwhile members of the farm bloc, and organized labor. At first Roosevelt led them somewhat reluctantly, but by 1936 election time he was clearly enjoying his job.

DEFICIT SPENDING

Probably the most controversial policy of the New Deal was the employment of public funds to provide a living for the vast army of jobless. This device for fighting depression had been adopted apologetically during the

Hundred Days as a stopgap measure to relieve human misery; at the same time it was expected to stimulate business activity by increasing purchasing power. On this hypothesis Roosevelt had created the Civil Works Administration on a short-term basis, poured substantial amounts of money into its projects, and then discontinued it in the summer of 1934.

Unfortunately, the anticipated stimulus to private enterprise did not materialize. Unemployment figures remained almost as high in the spring of 1935 as when Roosevelt had taken office. Over five million people were being carried on relief rolls, while the total number of jobless approached ten million most of the year and never dropped below eight million until the war boom of 1940. Unwilling to abandon aid to the unemployed or the belief that government aid would ultimately encourage business, Roosevelt groped his way toward a permanent relief policy.

Certain changes which seemed desirable in the light of experience were incorporated into the relief program of 1935. The locally administered FERA program, which had provided relief at subsistence levels, was cheap in terms of money but encouraged idleness and undermined the self-respect of recipients. Roosevelt described the FERA as a "narcotic, a subtle destroyer of the human spirit," and recommended that Congress discontinue it. Shortly thereafter he turned the relief of unemployables back to the states and created a fresh program to take care of the able-bodied who were willing to work. Neither the PWA nor the short-lived CWA provided a suitable model for the new agency because they hired only construction workers and operated in areas which were not always centers of unemployment. To meet these problems Roosevelt shifted emphasis from the employment of people needed on a specific project to the creation of projects which would meet the needs of specific people. It meant the sacrifice of some productive relief schemes in favor of others that would utilize the talents of unemployed white-collar workers. Such a revolutionary approach was open to grave political objections and was certain to alienate businessmen still further. Roosevelt accepted the new program at the behest of Harry Hopkins, who felt that the unemployed should be treated with dignity and allowed, so far as possible, to pursue their customary professions.

Accordingly, a new agency, the Works Progress Administration (WPA), was created May 5, 1935, with Hopkins as administrator. He put the new organization together as rapidly as he had activated the CWA eighteen months earlier. By the end of the year the WPA was providing work for over 2,500,000 citizens. Most of the projects involved the repair of public buildings and roads and the construction of countless parks, sidewalks, bridges, sewers, and dams. Generous amounts of funds were earmarked for the educated unemployed. Dramatists received salaries to write plays which actors presented free of charge at WPA theaters. Musicians were paid to organize orchestras and give concerts. Unemployed artists found satisfaction decorating public buildings. Doctors operated clinics, and historians supervised the repair of American antiquities. A whole group of authors went to work enthusiastically on a series of guidebooks for various states. Even housewives received an opportunity to sew and to can fruit for modest wages. Never before had a relief agency been organized to meet such a variety of needs.

In an effort to neutralize charges about the high cost and extravagance of the program, WPA wage payments were raised above the subsistence level but were kept below the rate prevailing in private industry. This policy did not prevent critics from complaining that WPA reduced the incentive of citizens to take jobs in ordinary business concerns. On a broader basis businessmen condemned the WPA project as wasteful if it produced no tangible economic service; if, on the other hand, it satisfied a community need, it was condemned for competing with private enterprise. Either way, the WPA was destined to run a gauntlet of criticism. During the later 1930's, opponents with some justification added charges that Communistic ideas affected the literary and artistic products of the WPA.

The National Youth Administration (NYA), which sought to help an estimated three million young people whose families were on relief, encountered less criticism. Also organized in 1935, it offered part-time employment to high-school and college students on projects desired by the institutions in which they were enrolled. Although wage payments remained low, NYA served the dual purpose of permitting many young people to complete their education and of keeping them off the labor market. It also made a modest venture in the field of vocational training.

These new relief measures, combined with agricultural subsidies and various other loan programs, kept the budget badly out of balance. The national debt, which had been reduced during the 1920's, increased in the last months of Hoover's administration and much more rapidly thereafter. Standing at $13.2 billion when Roosevelt was inaugurated, it grew at an average of $5 billion per year. This rate created genuine embarrassment for the administration, which had categorically promised to balance the budget. The President tried to wriggle out of his exposed position by continuing to insist that there were two budgets — a regular one which he triumphantly balanced every year, and an emergency one which ran up the debt but which he promised to eliminate as soon as economic conditions permitted. To prove his good faith, he made dramatic fights at regular intervals for small economies. On March 28, 1934, he had vetoed the Independent Offices Appropriation Act, which reduced the pay cuts for government employees. Congress found the votes to override the President but the latter came back in May 1935 with a more daring veto of a Veterans' Bonus Bill providing for immediate payment of the $2.2 million not due until 1945. On this occasion the Senate sustained the President but the measure was repassed over his objections the next year. It is highly doubtful that these efforts to "balance" the regular budget disarmed any critics of deficit financing.

Roosevelt was more worried about the political aspects than about the fiscal dangers of an unbalanced budget. He regarded bankruptcy as a remote threat. Moreover he felt sure that if the government continued the spending policy long enough, confidence would revive and private industry would resume its customary role of providing employment for the great mass of citizens. Unfortunately, his sole attempt to curtail public expenditure in 1937 did not encourage business to take up the slack. Overestimating the sturdiness of the boom in the first half of that year, he had ordered a one-third cut in WPA appropriations for the remaining six months, only to find that unemployment rose as soon as the government withdrew. As a result he quickly revived the old policy, and WPA appropriations increased from $1,019,000,000 in the last half of 1937 to $1,502,000,000 for the same period in 1938. One consolation was the fact that as the debt rose, the cost of servicing it decreased. Monetary operations by the Treasury Department in cooperation with the Federal Reserve Banks kept the interest rates low on government bonds.

If the deficit spending program is judged by its results during the 1930's, it certainly failed to cure the depression. The relief agencies enabled several million people to live comfortably who could not otherwise have done so, but the total number of unemployed remained discouragingly large throughout the decade. Many followers of John Maynard Keynes, the British economist who advocated large-scale government fiscal operations to stabilize capitalistic economies, felt that the President did not spend enough money. Roosevelt's opponents on the other hand, contended that deficit spending prolonged the depression by alarming private investors. Only limited weight can be placed on this argument because Roosevelt cannot be blamed for creating the general pessimism. Doubtless some businessmen were sufficiently disturbed by his fiscal policy to postpone fresh commitments, but experience suggests that a far larger number would have made investments whenever the prospects of profit improved, no matter what they thought of deficit spending as a policy. At any rate both businessmen and banks tacitly discounted the threat of bankruptcy by absorbing large quantities of government bonds. Although in so doing they seemed to be expressing confidence in government solvency, they were under considerable pressure to accept the bonds whether they wanted them or not. So the question of how much government policy discouraged investment cannot be conclusively answered.

The opposition of the business community did not exhaust itself in worry over the threat of national bankruptcy. The spectacle of government directly employing vast numbers of citizens was an open challenge to the private enterprise system. Despite repeated assertions by Roosevelt that the program was a temporary response to emergency, businessmen denounced it as creeping socialism. They did not believe that the government would withdraw if economic conditions improved. In fact, they saw the rapidly growing TVA experiment as the pattern of the future and anticipated ruinous competition from subsidized corporations which did not have to show a profit in order to continue operations. The answer of the New Dealers that the government moved only into areas of the economy where private enterprise saw no prospect of profit merely reinforced the worst fears of businessmen.

Bankers and their sympathizers took particular offense at the inflationary aspect of the debt and the monetary policy which cheapened money and reduced interest rates. Since Federal Reserve rules made it possible to use government bonds as a base for rapid expansion of the currency in circulations, the bankers thought that by continuing to use this weapon the administration could further inflate the currency.

The final reason why businessmen were opposed to a growing debt was the high cost of servicing it — and of all their anxieties, this was the one most immediately justified. The administration had already increased the estate and gift taxes in 1934. The Revenue Act of 1935 increased these levies still further and added some new ones aimed at making the wealthy bear the principal cost of debt management. In an effort to steal the thunder of the radical Senator Long, Congress raised the corporation tax from a flat 13¾ per cent to a graduated rate of from 12 to 15 per cent. An excess profits tax modeled on the levy collected during World War I was also revived. A year later Congress added an undistributed profits tax. This novel measure was intended to tax corporation profits at their source or force distribution of a large percentage of profits in the form of dividends which could in turn be taxed as personal income. The revenue produced by the tax proved to be disappointing, but business regarded it as fresh evidence of the administration's determination to redistribute the wealth. Indeed, the combination of public spending and tax policy drove an ever-deeper wedge between business and the New Deal.

SOCIAL SECURITY

No less a contribution to the welfare of underprivileged groups than the broadened program of relief expenditures, was the Social Security Act of August 1935. Unusually comprehensive for a pioneer measure, it covered old-age pensions, unemployment insurance, the needy aged and blind, dependent children, and a variety of public health services. The only part of the program exclusively under the jurisdiction of the federal government was the old-age pension plan.

Several features of a social security program had been adopted by the autocratic German government of Bismarck in the 1880's and by more democratic European governments in the decade before World War I. The United States had not succumbed to the trend. The traditional opposition to a paternalistic government remained strong, a majority regarded poverty as the penalty for laziness, and a practical economic interest reinforced the attitude of those who did not want to bear the costs. At the time of Hoover's election only eight states had authorized old-age pensions, only two helped to finance them directly, and neither the states nor the federal government had done anything about other aspects of social security. Meanwhile the problem of old age was becoming serious. Medical science had achieved spectacular success in increasing life expectancy. It was estimated that one citizen out of fifteen would be 65 in 1940 and one out of six by 1980. Surveys showed, further, that those who worked beyond 65 were largely members of affluent professional groups rather than unskilled or semiskilled laborers who needed employment. Industry, preoccupied with efficiency, habitually discharged employees in the second category between the ages of 45 and 50.

The depression, which dramatized the problem of unemployment along with that of old age, created considerable sentiment for a social security program sponsored by the federal government. The issue was too complex, however, to be tackled during the Hundred Days — the Constitution raised serious barriers against effective federal action, and there were no actuarial data for informed estimates regarding the probable demands on an unemployment insurance fund. Finally, in June 1934, Roosevelt appointed a Committee on Economic Security under the chairmanship of Frances Perkins to study the entire problem. Several advisory panels of experts were set up to facilitate research. A report issued in January 1935 advocated a comprehensive program based on joint federal-state action. Roosevelt endorsed the recommendations and passed them on to Congress, which used them as the basis for the Social Security Act.

The section of the law governing old-age pensions vested complete management of the program in the hands of the federal government. Except for agricultural laborers, domestic servants, the self-employed, and various professional groups, the measure covered most of the wage earners. All in the latter category, and also the employers, were jointly required to pay a tax equivalent to 1 per cent of the salary of each employee. A schedule of automatic increases fixed a rise in the rates to 3 per cent for 1949. Revenues were to be accumulated in the federal treasury until January 1, 1942. After that date retired workers would be eligible for pensions of from $10 to $15 monthly, computed on the basis of average wages and length of participation in the plan. Another section provided a grant up to $20 a month to states which would match the contribution and set up a program.

The adoption of plans for the second item — unemployment insurance — was left to the states, but the Social Security Act ensured a high level of compliance by the dual device of levying an unemployment tax on all employers and allowing the states to retrieve up to 90 per cent of such revenue provided they passed an enabling law. This federal action overcame the fear of driving industries to other states by payroll taxes, which up to this time had discouraged many states from adopting unemployment insurance plans. All the states now fell into line. There was less speed, however, in approving other provisions of the law which made additional aid available to states adopting health, welfare, and vocational rehabilitation programs.

The Social Security Act, like deficit spending, was denounced by various business groups. They considered it another socialistic scheme to redistribute the wealth and discourage investment, and they also complained about the complicated bookkeeping procedures required for the administration of the funds. As for the first accusation, they did have some justification: the law tended toward socialism in the sense that it extended into new and controversial areas the principle of taxing wealth-producing elements for the benefit of impoverished groups. In the long run, however, the general public rather than the employers paid the costs because the payroll taxes were passed on to the consumer in the form of higher prices.

THE REGULATION OF PUBLIC UTILITIES

On still another front Roosevelt chastised the business groups in 1936 by gaining from Congress an amendment to the Securities Act outlawing certain kinds of public utility holding companies. One of the bitterest battles of the New Deal era was waged against this legislation. The TVA, which had already been forced upon the private power companies as part of the emergency program, was beginning to sell power to state, municipal, and cooperative organizations. The private companies, now fearing that they would be driven out of business, organized a mass bombardment of Congress with letters and telegrams denouncing the proposed amendment as a "death sentence." Twice the House of Representatives rebelled against administration pressure, but Roosevelt with the support of Senator Burton K. Wheeler finally secured adoption of the new legislation intact.

The Public Utility Holding Company Act — as the amendment was called — required all corporations that fell into the holding-company category to file information on their organization with the SEC. The latter was required to examine each company with a view to simplifying its organizational structure and distributing voting power equitably among its stockholders. The so-called "death sentence" followed. It outlawed holding companies beyond the second degree. This provision meant that although an operating company might be controlled by a holding company and the latter by a still larger unit, additional pyramiding was prohibited. It also required holding companies to give up units that were not essential to the conduct of integrated operations. The SEC was directed to complete the process of simplification as soon after January 1, 1938, as practicable. Thenceforward the operations of each holding company were supposed to be confined to a compact economic and geographical area. Whether or not these regulations actually deprived them of the prospect of making a profit, the utilities companies fought the law vigorously in the courts. Some even refused to register until the Supreme Court sustained the validity of the amendment in the Electric Bond and Share case of 1938. The tremendous outcry over the holding company amendment distracted attention from other provisions of the new measure which enlarged SEC supervision over stock issues and corporation accounting procedures.

THE WAGNER ACT

No less controversial than deficit spending and social security was the labor legislation of the New Deal. As has already been noted, the principal vehicle for the organization of labor, the A.F. of L., had gone into eclipse during the 1920's. Membership had dropped from 4,093,000 at the beginning of the decade to 2,769,000 in 1929. Contributing to this decline were the conservative trend of popular opinion, the strikebreaking activity of employers, and reluctance of the A.F. of L. to organize the unskilled workers. The depression had dealt further blows. Unemployment added to the pool of surplus workers and enabled employers to reduce wages and lengthen hours without fear of retaliation. The desperate willingness of the jobless to work on any terms destroyed their bargaining power as well as the usefulness of the strike as a weapon.

The modest economic revival during the early months of the New Deal had shaken the pessimism of the workers. Moreover, Section 7A of the NIRA had forced employers to tolerate the activity of labor organizers in their plants. The A.F. of L. took advantage of the new situation by chartering 584 directly affiliated new unions between July and October of 1933. Some 300,000 members were recruited during this period. Organizers also established precarious beachheads in newer industries like the automotive, the rubber tire, and some branches of the chemical industry. Their efforts resulted in the addition of nearly a million men to the union rolls in 1934.

Employers retaliated by offering concessions to workers who would exercise their collective bargaining rights through a company union. These organizations increased their membership almost as much as the A.F. of L. during the life of the NIRA. Still more discouraging for labor organizers was the fact that when the Court voided the NIRA in May 1935, an estimated 40 per cent of the industrial workers held jobs in plants with no form of labor union.

The failure of labor to realize more benefits from Section 7A of the NIRA was partly due to the attitude of the administration during the emergency period. Initially Roosevelt had shown much more interest in reviving production and employment on any terms than in safeguarding the rights of unions. He regarded work stoppage as detrimental to recovery, and under the conservative influence of Hugh Johnson and Donald Richberg had supported interpretations of 7A that would prevent strikes or end them quickly. This outlook played into the hands of employers who refused to recognize industrial unions and insisted on bargaining with fragmentary groups or with company unions. Although the interpretations of NRA administrators and their advisory labor boards were ambiguous, collective bargaining gradually came to mean that employers could recognize as many worker groups as they chose. Such a position fatally weakened the bargaining power of labor. Unions could not hope to exercise effective economic pressure on employers unless a bargaining unit representing a majority of workers in the plant was allowed to speak for them all.

Disillusioned by the unfavorable interpretations of Section 7A, union leaders dubbed the NRA the "National Run Around" and demanded fresh legislation that would make bargaining rights more explicit. Senator Wagner introduced such a bill in 1934, but lacking Roosevelt's support it was killed. Reintroduced the following January, the measure did not fare much better until the Supreme Court invalidated the NIRA. The elimination of even the weak guarantees of Section 7A caused organized labor to redouble its insistence on the Wagner Bill. Angered by the Court decision and the critical attitude of business toward his administration, Roosevelt gradually took a stronger prolabor line. The result was quick congressional approval of the Wagner-Connery bill, which he signed on July 5, 1935.

The new law, known as the National Labor Relations Act, re-enacted the general collective bargaining provision of NIRA Section 7A in almost identical language. What distinguished it from the earlier measure was the addition of a section which listed five unfair labor practices and explicitly outlawed them. Employers were forbidden (1) to interfere in any way with employees exercising collective bargaining rights, (2) to dominate or grant any support to any labor organization, (3) to use their authority over hiring and firing in a manner which would discourage employees from joining a labor organization of their choice, (4) to discriminate against any employee who complained of violations of the law, (5) to refuse to bargain collectively with the representatives of their employees. The law also met the objections of labor to piecemeal bargaining unions. It provided that the representatives chosen by a majority of the employees should be the exclusive representatives of all employees in the plant. A new National Labor Relations Board (NLRB) of three members appointed by the President with the consent of the Senate was authorized to hear complaints, conduct investigations, and certify the proper employee representatives. The Board also received power to order a secret ballot or use any other method it deemed suitable to determine which bargaining unit spoke for a majority of the workers. Lastly, the Wagner Act authorized the NLRB to issue "cease and desist" orders against employers violating the Act, but such orders were enforceable only through petition to the federal courts.

The unions hailed the new law as Labor's Magna Charta. Their enthusiasm ultimately proved to be justified, but at the outset the new protections for the workingman rested on a shaky legal foundation. The reasoning of the Supreme Court in its decision invalidating the NIRA suggested that the judges would also find the Wagner Act unconstitutional. Consequently many employers refused to bargain collectively or obey the prohibitions against unfair labor practices. This uneasy state of affairs continued until March 1937, when the Supreme Court under threat of reorganization affirmed the constitutionality of every aspect of the law. The new trend in legal reasoning made the NLRB a very powerful agency. Consistently prolabor in outlook, it made rulings which created a formidable body of administrative law protecting the bargaining gains of workers. By the end of the decade it had ordered the dissolution of 340 company unions and had forced drastic reorganization of the remainder. How much of a role the Wagner Act played in the spectacular growth of organized labor to a total of 11 million in 1941 will always be a question. At the very least, it provided labor sufficiently favorable terms to encourage turbulent drives for members in steel, rubber, and other heavy industries during 1936 and 1937.

Employers did not capitulate without a stiff fight. Despite the prohibitions of the Wagner Act, they tried to thwart organizational campaigns with the traditional weapons of spies, stool pigeons, and discriminatory action against union members. Labor retaliated with the sit-down strike, whereby employees without leaving the plant simply refused to work. First utilized successfully in 1933 against the Hormel Packing Company of Austin, Minnesota, this form of strike became a major weapon during the middle 1930's. The Goodyear Rubber plant at Akron, Ohio, was the scene of a five weeks' strike which workers began on February 17, 1936, by remaining in the plant at the end of the day and resisting all efforts to dislodge them. Almost a year later, organizers repeated these tactics against General Motors at Flint, Michigan. In both cases there was some violence, but prolabor governors refused to use state troops against the workers. The attitude of Governor Murphy of Michigan encouraged the employees to continue occupation of the plant at Flint despite a court order directing them to withdraw or face imprisonment as well as a fine equal to the value of the plant.

The Supreme Court decision sustaining the constitutionality of the Wagner Act reduced the attractiveness of violent and illegal tactics. Thereafter, except for a few conspicuous exceptions, employers gave up their overt anti-union activities, and labor gave up the sit-down strike. Nevertheless the National Association of Manufacturers and other groups that spoke for management continued to denounce the Wagner Act as one-sided and urged revision on Congress. The House responded to this pressure in 1940 with a series of amendments which pleased employers, but the Senate took no action. As a result the Wagner Act was not revised until after World War II.

THE RISE OF THE C.I.O.

Although the A.F. of L. had waged a stirring fight for the adoption of the Wagner Act in 1935, the Congress of Industrial Organizations (C.I.O.), a labor movement launched shortly after that legislative victory, was destined to reap the benefits of the law. The C.I.O. conducted most of the successful drives to organize the mass industries between 1936 and 1939, including the controversial sit-down strikes in the rubber and automotive industries. The provision of the Wagner Act which required employers to recognize a bargaining unit speaking for a majority as a representative of all workers in a particular plant favored the C.I.O. program of joining craft, semiskilled, and common laborers in a single union. The new law did not create the industrial union. It simply acted as a catalyst. In fact, the blurring of the distinction between skilled and unskilled workers had been going on since the beginning of the Industrial Revolution. This process was greatly accelerated in the 1920's when manufacturers placed tremendous emphasis on labor-saving devices and the closer coordination of assembly lines. Simultaneously the A.F. of L. had got more and more out of touch with the great mass of workers. Its craft unions had developed a middle-class psychology. Skilled workers did not seek improvement of their status as members of an economic class nor did they organize a labor movement at the political level. Members of each trade union single-mindedly sought wage increases that would permit them to enjoy a middle-class standard of living and pattern of values. Conditions varied from craft to craft. A few unions were run by racketeers in cynical collusion with management; a number of others had to carry on ceaseless warfare against employers for any kind of recognition. A large middle group periodically extracted higher pay from industry, which the latter passed on to the public in the form of higher prices. Such unions functioned as labor monopolies and could maintain their position only by keeping the supply of skilled labor artificially scarce. The vast body of semiskilled and unskilled workers menaced the monopoly and worried the craft unions almost as much as they did the employers. The rank-and-file members of the A.F. of L. feared that organization of the unskilled would end in reduction of wages and living standards for those who had learned a trade. Pockets of technological unemployment in the 1920's gave substance to their suspicions. Consequently the A.F. of L. was not well suited to lead the drive for mass unionization that followed in the wake of the NIRA and the Wagner Act. It tried to guide the movement by organizing federal unions with a membership of skilled and unskilled workers. This gesture did not reflect a change in philosophy but was a makeshift arrangement to ease the absorption of new members into the traditional craft union.

The younger and more zealous advocates of the industrial union within the A.F. of L. fought the use of federal unions. They believed that conditions favored mass organization. At the moment they were particularly bitter toward A.F. of L. leaders who opposed the chartering of a steel union to protect the superannuated Iron, Steel, and Tin Workers Union, which had repeatedly been defeated by management. Controversy broke into the open at the Atlantic City convention of the A.F. of L. in September 1935. A closely divided Resolutions Committee issued majority and minority reports.

Heated debates ended in fisticuffs, with John L. Lewis of the United Mine Workers Union knocking down William L. Hutcheson of the Carpenters Union. The convention did not accept the verdict of single combat which went to the champion of industrial unionism. Hutcheson and his craft-union allies possessed enough votes to reaffirm the A.F. of L. policy of granting only restricted charters for new unions. Eight heads of international A.F. of L. unions who favored mass organization retaliated by holding a meeting at Washington, D. C., November 9, 1935, and forming the Committee for Industrial Organization under the presidency of the bellicose Lewis. The new group announced that its activities would be "educational and advisory" and reaffirmed loyalty to the A.F. of L. President Bill Green and the A.F. of L. executive committee treated the C.I.O. as rebels and schismatics. When the latter ignored an order to dissolve, the executive committee expelled the eight dissident unions in August 1936, and the Tampa Convention of the A.F. of L. ratified this decision.

Strongly favored by the bargaining regulations of the Wagner Act, the C.I.O. spearheaded the drive for the unionization of heavy industry already described. Sit-down strikes and other aggressive tactics enabled the C.I.O. to break the solid antiunion front, but the new organization offended the public in the process. A rising volume of denunciation was heaped on Lewis and the C.I.O. during the summer of 1937, climaxed by widespread applause for Tom Girdler, the president of Republic Steel, who successfully resisted the unionization drive.

Henceforth the C.I.O. had to move more slowly and to employ less controversial methods than the sit-down strike. Important corporations held out for several years. Henry Ford successfully defied the efforts of the United Automobile Workers to organize his plant until the eve of World War II. The smaller steel companies, heartened by the victory of Tom Girdler, held out almost as long, although "Big Steel" had capitulated in 1937. Notwithstanding some strong points of resistance, the C.I.O. effectively withstood all counterattacks and slowly established permanent footholds in the automotive, steel, rubber, electrical, textile, and food-processing industries. It picked up most new members in the late 1930's. However, the A.F. of L. also gained strength, particularly in the more homogeneous of the craft unions, like the Teamsters Brotherhood and the Hotel and Restaurant Employees.

Repeated negotiations between the rival organizations failed to re-establish unity. In 1938 the C.I.O. changed its name from the Committee for Industrial Organization to the Congress of Industrial Organizations. This step was marked by the adoption of both a constitution and permanent administrative machinery. John L. Lewis held the presidency until 1940, when he resigned as a result of his failure to carry the C.I.O. for Wendell Willkie in the presidential election. When he withdrew, he also took his powerful United Mine Workers Union with him and for a time remained independent. He was succeeded in the presidency of the C.I.O. by Phil

Murray, who had earned widespread attention for quietly and effectively organizing "Big Steel."

Employers viewed the schism with mixed feelings. In theory, dissension seemed likely to improve their bargaining position and political prospects. In practice, they suffered considerably from crippling jurisdictional strikes, which seldom had much to do with labor-management relations. Jurisdictional warfare also inconvenienced the public and provided another source of sentiment for amendment of the Wagner Act.

Labor remained on the offensive most of the decade, aided by reviving economic conditions as well as by a sympathetic administration. But the long tide of popular support had run out by 1940, and during the postwar era organized labor was to fight hard to expand the gains of the thirties.

MISCELLANEOUS LEGISLATION

Much of the remaining energy of the Seventy-fourth Congress was devoted to repairing breaches in the New Deal's legislative walls caused by Supreme Court decisions. We have already seen that the invalidation of the NRA led to the relief of labor in the form of the Wagner Act. This piece of general legislation did not replace the code system in the coal and oil industries, which sorely needed effective stabilization measures. Neither coal producers nor miners had shared in the general prosperity of the 1920's, and the depression aggravated all the evils from which the industry suffered. Cutthroat competition and low prices destroyed profits and resulted in repeated wage cuts. An effective code system might have mitigated some of these evils, but operators who made a profit saw no reason to formulate a code that would keep marginal competitors in production. Some would have preferred to sell out to the government rather than adopt quotas and pricing agreements, but public ownership of the mines was such a politically inflammable proposal that the government refused to consider it. The only alternative was a new stabilization measure. Congress cooperated by passing the Guffey-Snyder Bituminous Coal Act, which contained many provisions of the defunct NIRA. It created a National Bituminous Coal Commission composed of representatives of industry, labor, and the public, which was to formulate a coal code and fix minimum wages. A clause, much like Section 7A, defined the rights of miners. Compliance of all segments of the industry was sought by a penalty tax of 15 per cent on all coal mined under noncode conditions. The Supreme Court promptly invalidated the new law in *Carter* v. *Carter Coal Co.* (1936). The administration tried again with the Vinson-Guffey Act in 1937. This met Court standards of constitutionality but only at the price of eliminating most provisions of the older laws for effective regulation of the mines. As a consequence, the industry limped through the 1930's burdened with virtually all the problems that had afflicted it since the turn of the century.

The rapid discovery of oil fields along the Gulf of Mexico, in Oklahoma, and in the Texas panhandle during the 1920's exposed the oil industry to some of the same problems that faced the coal operators. Refining was concentrated in the hands of twenty-odd large corporations and hence was conducted on a reasonably stable basis. But the major refiners had never found it economically worth while to monopolize the production of crude oil. Thousands of wildcat operators drilled wells all over the western half of the United States, producing countless barrels of oil that could not be moved profitably at depression prices. Oklahoma, Texas, and other oil states enacted laws establishing individual quotas. They solicited federal help to prevent one state from profiting by the conservation measures of another and to curb interstate traffic in "hot oil," that is, oil produced in violation of quotas. The federal government welcomed the invitation because it had a strong interest in preventing the waste of an important natural resource. Section 9 of the NIRA made special provision for federal supervision but it was struck down by the Supreme Court like the rest of the Act. Congress sought to preserve the substance of the section by passing the Connally Act in 1935. As an additional safeguard the states worked out a series of compacts governing quotas and the movement of oil.

Smaller independent wholesalers and retailers also regretted the loss of price-fixing agreements formulated under the NIRA. Locked in a deadly battle with various chain store systems, the independents clamored for government protection. They objected to two policies of the chain stores: (1) the practice of cutting prices on key commodities and counting on heavy volume to produce a profit, and (2) the technique of selling a few popular items at cost or a small loss in order to lure customers into the store. Congress obliged in 1936 with the Robinson-Patman Act, which sought to outlaw the latter practice. Still the independents were not satisfied. Like so many other pressure groups, they favored competition only when it operated in a sector of the economy which did not affect their own businesses adversely. What they really wanted was a compulsory price-fixing law, which would protect them from competition and reaffirm the suspension of the Sherman Act. Since many state legislatures had already passed laws legalizing contracts whereby retailers pledged themselves not to sell goods received from the manufacturers below a certain minimum price, the independents now worked for federal authorization of the policy. Roosevelt resisted this development but was defeated when Congress in the Miller-Tydings Act of 1937 blessed price fixing through contracts. Independents also harassed the chain stores with special state taxes but failed to secure passage of a bill for a federal tax on each unit of a chain.

The final area in which the Seventy-fourth Congress legislated to offset a judicial decision was agriculture. The elaborate AAA subsidy and crop-restriction program had received a lethal blow in the Hoosac Mills case (*Butler* v. *the United States*) when the Supreme Court invalidated the processing tax. This decision drying up the source of benefit payments for acreage curtailment was handed down January 6, 1936, but within two months the President approved a substitute Soil Conservation and Domestic Allotment Act. The new measure empowered the Secretary of Agriculture to make payments to farmers practicing soil conservation. To sidestep the Supreme Court's prohibition of earmarking a processing tax for agriculture, the 1936 law authorized conservation payments to be drawn from general revenue. Most of the remaining AAA machinery was left untouched. The substitute law led to marked improvements in farming methods, but the agricultural surpluses, which had disappeared in 1934–35, began to pile up in alarming fashion. As a result the whole farm program was slated for a major overhaul after the 1936 election.

Since neither the AAA program nor its immediate successor dealt with the problem of farm tenancy, Roosevelt created a Resettlement Administration in 1935 to do something for the impoverished farm laborer. Rexford G. Tugwell was appointed director of the new agency. Tenancy had increased from 25 per cent of all farmers in 1880 to 42 per cent in 1935. Moreover, a large number of agriculturalists not covered by this classification worked holdings of an uneconomical size, tilled an eroded hillside or other types of submarginal land, or drifted from place to place as harvest hands. Nobody could be sure just how much cash income these miserable people received, but a census report indicated that 1,700,000 farm families averaged slightly less than $500 per year.

The Resettlement Administration lacked funds and the support of the tenants themselves for a large-scale program of removing them from submarginal lands and training them in a more suitable form of work. Many wanted to continue as farmers and did not have enough flexibility for sudden readjustment in middle age. Industry did not care to employ the older, unskilled men. As for the general public, it looked upon any mass relocation of people as a diabolical Communist program. The unanimity of public opinion on this subject meant that there would continue to be too many farmers on the land. Moreover, mechanization was aggravating the problem.

Under the circumstances the Resettlement Administration could do nothing but tinker with a lot of small and ineffectual experiments. It did establish about 160 resettlement communities and subsistence homesteads in various parts of the country, settling them with families that had been living on submarginal land. It also built three so-called greenbelt towns near Washington, Cincinnati, and Milwaukee as models of scientific town planning. Some projects envisaged full-time farming; others, part-time farming and additional work in local industries. Variable practices also prevailed with regard to the explosive question of group activity. A few operations were carried on cooperatively and the rest individually. The greenbelt towns did not actually cater to farmers at all but attempted to provide a healthful home environment for laborers who worked on the periphery of the big cities.

Subjected to constant criticism, the planners in the Resettlement Administration accomplished very little during the short life of the organization. Conservatives marked it for early extinction and achieved their objective in 1937.

THE 1936 ELECTION

Roosevelt had pushed most of his reform through the acquiescent Seventy-fourth Congress in 1935, so that election year would be free for the coming campaign. The political weather improved considerably for him on the eve of the nominating conventions.

The specter of an effective third-party movement on the Left began to vanish with the assassination of Senator Long in September 1935. Roosevelt quickly made peace with the heirs of Long's state political machine — an agreement that the wags uncharitably dubbed "the second Louisiana Purchase." The abrupt removal of the Senator from public life touched off a disruptive scramble by Coughlin, Townsend, and Gerald K. Smith for control of the loosely knit left-wing movement. The only prominent radical with a talent for leadership comparable to Long's was Floyd B. Olson, the Farmer-Labor Governor of Minnesota. Death ended his career also in August 1936, but not before he had firmly disassociated himself from the national third-party forces and endorsed Roosevelt for re-election. These developments did not prevent the entry of a third-party ticket in the election but doomed it to impotence.

Whatever chances the Republican party might have possessed of beating Roosevelt were destroyed long before the election by the conspicuous activity of businessmen whose political behavior could not be controlled. Although they were the last to learn it, the businessmen had completely lost the confidence of the American people. Since they had taken the credit for the prosperity of the twenties, they received the blame for the crash that followed. Their responsibility had been documented to the satisfaction of the voters by inquisitorial congressional committees which had spent long years unraveling and publicizing dubious financial operations on Wall Street.

The ineffectiveness of the Liberty League in the 1934 elections ought to have convinced businessmen of the political hazards involved in hogging the limelight. Nevertheless, as the 1936 election approached, they showered money on the League in an effort to defeat Roosevelt. Its feeble protestations of nonpartisanship fooled nobody. It did not develop either a farm or a labor division. In fact, it defended the interests of the uncommon man at the top of the economic ladder so vigorously that the Republican candidate finally asked it not to participate in the campaign.

The spectacle of businessmen at Liberty League banquets denouncing the inequities of the New Deal was humorous and repellent by turns. The numerous victims of depression found it amusing to hear the indignant complaints of the wealthy. They also regarded these remote and arrogant supporters of the Republican party as their enemies. No Democrat said anything during the campaign that made as many votes for Roosevelt as the statement of the younger J. P. Morgan to a congressional committee in February 1936 that the destruction of the leisure class meant "the destruction of civilization." Pressed to define the leisure class, Morgan added; "I mean the families who employ one servant, 25 or 30 million families." Others were driven by frustration and anger to make even more foolish statements. Mrs. Walter M. Newkirk, a wealthy Philadelphia society matron, announced a drive to revive a backyard potato patch as a protest against AAA price-fixing. Unfortunately, the Republican party had no way of silencing such friends nor halting their clumsy lunges at Roosevelt.

The Republican professionals did what they could to prevent the campaign from developing as a straight fight between the wealthy and the masses. Their only hope lay in the selection of a candidate not conspicuously identified with the business groups. Consequently they ruled out foes of the New Deal like ex-President Hoover, Senator Arthur H. Vandenberg of Michigan, and Colonel Frank Knox, the wealthy Chicago newspaper publisher and former Bull Mooser. The most obvious choice among the remainder was the aged, erratic Senator Borah. Borah's independent attitude, however, offended many orthodox Republicans, and so, almost by a process of elimination, the party managers agreed upon Governor Alfred M. Landon of Kansas. He received a first-ballot nomination from the dispirited Republican National Convention which met at Cleveland in early June. His political virtues were his competent administration of the state, his reputation for moderate political views, and his success in balancing the budget in Kansas. The latter achievement lost some of its luster when Democrats pointed out that the state constitution prohibited a deficit. Landon's other virtues were offset by his uninspiring personality. He lacked assertiveness, self-assurance, and a sense of the dramatic. His oratorical style was colorless and irresolute. In fact, he gave the impression that he was a sober, hardworking citizen who would be somewhat perplexed by the magnitude of national problems. There was considerably more decisiveness and energy in Landon than he revealed during the campaign, but he offered a painful contrast to the colorful, mercurial Roosevelt. In an effort to balance the ticket, the aggressive Colonel Knox was named for the Vice-Presidency.

The platform opened with the observation that "America is in peril" and proceeded to a denunciation of the entire New Deal experiment. The rhetorical introduction was followed, however, by a series of planks pledging the party to preserve a substantial part of the New Deal program, including the regulation of public utilities, issues of securities, and other aspects of business activity. Collective bargaining, unemployment relief, and emergency payments to farmers were likewise approved. The platform proposed government assistance in disposing of agricultural surpluses abroad instead of continued crop restriction, and promised a balanced budget and repeal of the Reciprocal Trade Acts Agreement. The moderate tone of the document reflected the belief of party managers that survival of the G.O.P. depended upon acceptance of many New Deal policies as permanent additions to the social and economic structure.

Since it was a foregone conclusion that the Democrats would also endorse the New Deal program, the country faced its first election without a major party to defend officially the venerable philosophy of personal initiative and limited government. Those principles still commanded wide support among most Republicans. Still, the conviction of professionals that votes would be lost by committing the party to a program of an older vintage indicated the vast revolution in public opinion during the New Deal years. The philosophy of the abortive Bull Moose movement of 1912 had finally captured both major parties.

The Democrats met at Philadelphia with the idea of creating enough enthusiasm among the local citizens to carry Pennsylvania in November. A handful of conservatives, headed by leaders of an earlier era like Bainbridge Colby and ex-Senator James A. Reed of Missouri, tried to organize a revolt against Roosevelt. They made common cause with Governor Eugene Talmadge of Georgia, a pale reflection of Huey Long who combined a truculent manner with rather conservative ideas. This disjointed coalition accomplished absolutely nothing and the Roosevelt-Garner ticket was renominated by acclaim. The convention also struck down the two-thirds rule which had almost blocked the nomination of Roosevelt in 1932 and had given the South a veto power on Democratic candidates.

The platform wholeheartedly embraced the new philosophy that government has "certain inescapable obligations" to its citizens. These obligations were listed: "(1) the protection of the family and home, (2) establishment of a democracy of opportunity for all people, (3) aid to those overtaken by disaster." The platform went on to recount the progress made under each of these headings and promised more energetic action along the same lines. It endorsed more explicitly than the Republican platform the philosophy of large-scale government intervention in behalf of depressed groups. The real difference between the two parties was that they championed different pressure groups, but this cleavage was not so clearly expressed in the platform.

Following the precedent which he had established in 1932, Roosevelt accepted the renomination in person and delivered one of the most effective speeches of his career. He welcomed the challenge of the businessmen and advertised their identification with the Republican party. Describing them as "economic royalists" he pledged himself to a great crusade that would restore equality of opportunity for the masses. Striking a note of humility, he conceded that the New Deal had made mistakes but he called on Dante to witness that "the Almighty weighs the sins of the warm-blooded and those of the cold-blooded in different scales." Then he concluded on an eloquent note: "We are fighting to save a great and precious form of government for ourselves and for the world. I accept the commission you have tendered me. I join with you. I am enlisted for the duration of the war."

The convention of the rudderless third-party forces, which followed the mammoth Democratic show in Philadelphia, was small and colorless. No one of the "jitney messiahs," as H. L. Mencken dubbed the leaders, would permit the nomination of a rival. Consequently the doubtful honor went to Representative William E. Lemke of North Dakota after a session so secret that newspapermen said he had been nominated in a phone booth.

The third-party forces, which took the name Union party, were handicapped by the support of numerous cranks. Father Coughlin could not deliver a devoted radio audience to the party; Gerald K. Smith received cool treatment from the old Long organization in Louisiana; while most of the old-age pension advocates stuck with Roosevelt. All efforts to dramatize the sober-looking, baldheaded Lemke failed. Even the affectionate nickname "Liberty Bell" Bill had to be withdrawn when somebody remembered that the Liberty Bell was cracked. These numerous handicaps held the Union party to 900,000 votes, which was too little to affect the fortunes of the major party candidates. Lemke did well, however, in comparison with established splinter parties like the Socialists, who polled 190,000 for Norman Thomas, and the Communists, who polled 80,000 for Earl Browder.

As usual, public interest centered on the contest between the Republicans and the Democrats. The *Literary Digest* poll which had successfully forecast several preceding elections enlivened the campaign by publishing results pointing to an overwhelming Landon victory. Roosevelt ignored Landon and ran against Hoover for the second time. He stirred memories of the bleak days of 1932 and expressed fear that depression would return if the Republicans won the election. He also replied to the frenzied assaults of the businessmen with reminders of what he had done for them and expressions of surprise at their ingratitude.

With the desperation of doomed men, the Republicans lashed out in all directions. Senator Lester J. Dickinson of Iowa charged that the destruction of farm products by the AAA had raised prices to a point where large numbers of citizens were forced to live off dogfood. Lesser figures circulated stories about AAA officials driving chickens and turkeys into the water in the presence of starving people. Local workers put signs in vacant store windows blaming the failure of the previous tenant on the New Deal. Such techniques might have been more effective in a preradio age, but the soothing broadcasts of the President dispelled popular fears.

James A. Farley, who again managed the Roosevelt campaign, disputed the *Literary Digest* poll and asserted that the Democrats would carry forty-six states. This daring forecast turned out to be absolutely correct. When the votes were counted, Roosevelt had won every state but Maine and Vermont. In the electoral college he piled up the record total of 523 votes to 8 for Landon. The popular vote was also quite lopsided with Roosevelt polling 27,476,673 and Landon 16,679,583. The defection of Al Smith and the so-called Jeffersonian Democrats was more than counterbalanced by the millions of supporters whom Roosevelt detached from the G.O.P. The magnitude of the Democratic triumph led some political commentators to predict the breakup of the Republican party and the inauguration of an "era of good feeling."

SUGGESTED READINGS

1. Brogan, D. W., *The Era of Franklin D. Roosevelt.*
2. Farley, J. N., *Behind the Ballots.*
3. Lindley, E. K., *Half Way with Roosevelt.*
4. Perkins, F., *The Roosevelt I Knew.*
5. Wector, D., *The Age of the Great Depression.*

CHAPTER TWENTY-ONE

SOCIAL AND INTELLECTUAL CURRENTS IN THE DEPRESSION ERA

The Great Depression took its spiritual as well as its physical toll. Disaster struck so widely and impartially that the fixed points in the universe suddenly seemed to move with the disorderly swiftness of pieces in a kaleidoscope. Traditional beliefs lost their authority, and hallowed institutions toppled under pressure. Even the minority fortunate enough to escape economic distress was engulfed in the long tide of despair that washed through the crumbling foundations of society. The failure of the prewar Progressive movement to preserve old institutions by adjustment to new forces and of the Nationalist reaction to preserve them by the destruction of new forces could no longer be concealed. For better or for worse, a reconstruction of ideas was occurring.

Not all the sufferers were equally prepared to participate in the enterprise. Some lived out the remainder of their days in a state of numb bewilderment. A corporal's guard drew consolation from aggressive affirmations of despair. A few gave vent to inner feelings of emptiness by indulging in pathetic exhibitionism. They climbed flag poles, engaged in dance marathons, or persuaded friends to bury them alive. College students of this persuasion held goldfish-swallowing contests and ate phonograph records. The occult arts provided an escape for others unwilling to look reality in the face. Fortunetellers flourished as never before. Residents of New York City alone paid $25 million in 1931 for the services of palmists and clairvoyants. A harvest of gold was also reaped by astrologers and numerologists.

Most Americans could not satisfy their cravings for inner peace and certitude with such meager fare. Some rethought their religious beliefs. Others ignored the discouraging behavior of the economy and put faith in the New Deal version of the old American dream of success. A small but vocal minority thought the New Deal doctrinally inadequate and too closely associated with outmoded institutions. They embraced the secular religion of Communism which promised to create a paradise on earth by destroying the private property system. These various attempts to impose order and meaning on the demoralized, depression-ridden American society provided the dominant impulse for spiritual, intellectual and artistic expression in the thirties.

THE REVIVAL OF CHRISTIAN FAITH

The search for belief led to a pronounced religious revival. Fictional treatments of Christian themes often hit best-seller lists. The most popular were *Shadows on the Rock* by Willa Cather, *Magnificent Obsession* and *The Robe* by Lloyd Douglas, *The Keys of the Kingdom* by A. J. Cronin, and *The Song of Bernadette* by Franz Werfel. People also read enormous amounts of devotional literature and attended church in larger numbers than during the 1920's.

These surfacc manifestations had their counterpart in the vigorous quest of Protestant theologians for a reinterpretation of the Gospel that stood somewhere between the extremes of Modernism and of Fundamentalism. Neither the Catholic nor the Episcopalian churches participated in this enterprise, partly because they had avoided the controversies of the 1920's and partly because their ecclesiastical structure militated against negotiations on doctrine with other denominations. The Lutherans, who had likewise remained aloof from earlier Protestant disputes, joined in the doctrinal reformulation of the 1930's. Their participation was assured by the new trend of thought in the larger denominations which approached the Lutheran position.

Increasing dissatisfaction with the answers offered by Fundamentalism and Modernism also encouraged Christians to rethink their beliefs. The Fundamentalists defended a prescientific dogmatism repellent to the educated conservatives for whom they professed to speak. The Modernists took an optimistic view of man's nature and destiny, which was severely shaken by human behavior under the stresses of depression and war. Neither problem disappeared as a result of Modernist pleas for reasonable Christian conduct. Indeed, both problems got worse before they got better. The continuation of this unhappy state of affairs led some Modernists to conclude that they could convert bad people like Hitler and Stalin only by setting a better example and providing more education. Others, surveying the events of the 1930's in Germany and Russia, ceased to be Modernists. Either they concluded that man was not a reasonable being or that the human intellect without divine support lacked power to do good.

While the more zealous Modernists parried assaults on their optimistic view of human nature, they were attacked from the rear by John Dewey and the Humanists. Dewey shocked them with the demand that they follow the logic of their position and abandon Christianity completely. In his *Common Faith* (1934), the aging Instrumentalist denounced denominations as a barrier to social cooperation and proposed a religion of humanity. The fierceness of the attack made many Modernists realize how far they had gone in sacrificing the unique elements in Christianity to find a common

"And so we're making this survey to find out how a representative section of the community feels about a government policy of deficit spending." (Anne Cleveland, Everything Correlates, *1946.)*

ground with Naturalism and Humanism. Their vulnerability produced a reaction against further accommodation to secular philosophies and a renewed emphasis on religious faith.

The widespread disenchantment with Modernism culminated in the crystallization of a new Christian conservatism. Known as Neo-orthodoxy, the movement originated in Europe and drew heavily on the teachings of the Swiss theologian, Karl Barth. It crossed the Atlantic during the early years of the depression and received favorable attention in Walter Lowrie's *Our Concern with the Theology of Crisis* (1932) and Edwin Lewis's *Christian Manifesto* (1934). The great American prophet of Neo-orthodoxy was Reinhold Niebuhr of Union Theological Seminary. His *Moral Man and Immoral Society* (1932) and a companion volume of sermonic essays, *Beyond Tragedy* (1937), expounded the key doctrines of the new theology.

Central to the Neo-orthodox position was the restoration of the Bible from the lowly Modernist role of ethical guide to its traditional status as the revealer of Divine Will. The insistence of the Neo-orthodox on the inspired character of the Bible did not carry them to the Fundamentalist position that each verse was true in a literal sense. Their point was that God did not reveal all and that much of revelation transcended human understanding. Hence they concluded that God's will as expressed in the Bible could not be comprehended by rational analysis or by a literal rendition of words. For the truths about God, which required the addition of a spiritual dimension to the rational order of time and space, they relied upon symbol. Even their reliance on biblical symbol was qualified by the admission that only God could resolve the contradictions in the human world. In fact, the Neo-orthodox reaffirmed the old warnings of St. Augustine and of Martin Luther about the inadequacy of reason as a guide to salvation. Faith and reliance on God's mercy was their counsel to the bewildered seeker of light.

The Neo-orthodox rejected the optimistic Modernist belief in man's moral powers and capacity for self-improvement not only because they distrusted human reason but also because they believed in the inevitability of human sin. Their emphasis on sinfulness was so strong that critics sometimes dubbed Reinhold Niebuhr a "sin snooper." The epithet deserves qualification because Niebuhr and the Neo-orthodox did not crusade against drinking, cardplaying, or dancing as the Fundamentalists did. They regarded sin as the chronic manifestation of human pride and appetites in defiance of God's will. Niebuhr agreed with Pascal that humility ended in sin when the humble man took pride in his attitude. He denied that unaided human effort could overcome egocentrism and its blighting effect on personal and institutional relations. As at other points, the Neo-orthodox turned their backs on the scientific-humanistic view of man as an intelligent, self-reliant creature and proclaimed that only God could rescue man from sin. In view of their low estimate of human nature, it was not surprising that they denied the possibility of transforming the social order into the Heavenly Kingdom.

To large numbers of religious-minded people who had been disturbed by the extremes of both Modernism and Fundamentalism, Neo-orthodoxy represented a more accurate rendering of Christian revelation than they had heard for over a generation. Although the Neo-orthodox denounced what they regarded as overemphasis on man's intellectual and moral capacity, they exhibited as much concern for economic justice as did the Modernists. The adherents of the new movement favored measures to help the underprivileged without believing that such aid would cure the fundamental evils in man and society or reduce human dependence on God. Unlike the Modernists, they were convinced that power relationships would continue to prevail in secular affairs at all levels. Hence they shunned the pacifism of their Modernist brethren. This attitude did not make them immune to ideological appeals inconsistent with their basic position, but it kept them from being upset when sermons on Christian ethics did not deter dictators from waging war.

As in the case of most new developments in thought, considerable time was required for Neo-orthodoxy to filter down to the rank and file. During the 1930's it gained a foothold in some Protestant divinity schools, thus assuring wider dissemination a decade hence by newly ordained ministers. Meanwhile the official pronouncements at denominational conventions indicated that Fudamentalism was fading. Many church members, however, continued to believe in the imminence of the Second Coming and the literalist interpretation of the Bible.

OTHER RELIGIONS

The depression era also saw the emergence of new religious sects and the unprecedented growth of older ones that had not formerly commanded a wide following. Some of these were avowedly Christian, others mixed Christianity with oriental philosophies, and a few lacked formal connections with the teaching of Jesus. The only common sentiment was the conviction that religion offered a way of surmounting material adversities.

The New Thought movement blossomed afresh during the depression as it had done in every generation since the Civil War. Heavily indebted to Emersonian Transcendentalism, each variant stressed the spark of divinity in man and claimed for him spiritual powers of a high order. Christian Science, though denying any doctrinal obligations to earlier New Thought movements, made the most converts for this general viewpoint. Founded by Mary Baker Eddy at Boston in 1866, the Christian Science church enjoyed spectacular growth after the turn of the century, especially during the 1920's. It taught that matter, evil, and physical sickness were illusions that men could banish by the employment of their tremendous spiritual powers.

An offshoot of Christian Science, the Unity School of Christianity, offered special facilities for those unable to utilize spiritual power without aid. A department known as Silent Unity was organized at headquarters in Kansas City to answer the letters, phone calls, and telegrams of people in distress. This free service required a staff of a hundred workers during the depression. Unity survived the death of its founders, Charles and Mildred Fillmore, but Psychania, a mail-order version of New Thought, seemed unlikely to duplicate that feat. Launched by Dr. Frank Robinson at Moscow, Idaho, in 1928, Psychania advertised through numerous magazines that the spiritual powers available to Jesus could be appropriated by anyone willing to take a course of fourteen lessons. Subscribers received the lessons in installments. The early ones emphasized faith in spiritual power and the later stressed methods for achieving tranquillity as a prelude to complete communion with God. The public response to Robinson's colorful advertising techniques was extraordinary. During the depression era, nearly 800,000 people enrolled. A separate post office had to be built at Moscow to handle the mail. The founder incorporated Psychania under the laws of Idaho but did not set up an effective nationwide church organization.

On the fringe of the New Thought movement were several quasi-philosophical sects and the spiritualists. Loosely organized and commanding the allegiance of only a few thousand until the 1930's, spiritualism now drew nearly half a million to its services by the hope of communication with the dead or the desire for a preview of life after death. This increased popularity owed something to a vigorous campaign conducted in the 1920's by Arthur Conan Doyle, the author of the Sherlock Holmes stories.

Depression sufferers also responded to the promises of millennial groups. The sect with the greatest appeal was Jehovah's Witnesses, which proclaimed the imminence of the Judgment Day and promised a terrestrial paradise for all who believed in God and did His will. A palatial home at San Diego, California, was even made ready for Jesus to occupy when He returned to earth.

Jehovah's Witnesses stirred up considerable controversy by fierce denunciation of other religious groups and by their refusal to salute the flag in public schools. They subsequently annoyed the patriotic by refusing to participate in World War II on the same terms as other Americans. Their plea for preferential treatment was based on their practice of regarding each Witness as a minister and hence exempt from conscription.

Whatever the merits of their legal position, Jehovah's Witnesses featured individual missionary or ministerial work. They handed out leaflets on street corners or broadcast their message by sound truck. The literary output of the movement was prodigious. Judge Rutherford, who headed the sect in the 1930's, wrote books, essays, and sermons. It is estimated that twenty million copies of his various works were distributed in an average year.

Millennial groups received competition from Father Divine's Peace Mission movement, which set up hotels or "Kingdoms" for its votaries in various cities. The founder, Father Divine, apparently started his career as a wandering Baptist Negro preacher and began calling himself God about 1914. After several vicissitudes, he settled down in Harlem during the early 1920's. His Harlem Kingdom, which provided the model for all later ones, consisted of a church with an attached hotel, featuring separate quarters for men and women, restaurants, stores, and schools. Accommodations and food were offered at remarkably low prices. Critics charged that the system was financed by forced gifts of property to Father Divine as the price of joining a Kingdom. Gifts were and are made, but the available evidence suggests that the sojourners at each Kingdom enjoy cheap food, lodging, and other amenities because the spirit of service dominates. Members are imbued with a cooperative viewpoint and a sense of brotherhood reminiscent of short-lived Utopian experiments on the American frontier. The unselfish devotion to Father Divine leads them to repudiate the profit motive in their daily lives.

The theology of the Peace Mission movement is built out of sermons delivered by Father Divine at evening banquets. These authoritative statements of the faith are regularly printed in *New Day,* the official weekly organ, and are read at banquets or church services of other Kingdoms. Besides claiming control over natural forces and asserting his superiority to such human frailties as death, Father Divine has taken a strong interest in secular problems. He repeatedly endorsed racial amalgamation, but this stand did not create much trouble because the movement committed its members to celibacy.

The appeal of the Peace Mission movement was strongest to people who wanted a haven from the worries and frustrations of a turbulent world. Membership in a Kingdom conferred security, a decent standard of living, and firsthand contact with Father Divine. Success led to the opening up of new Kingdoms. Negro leadership was an effective barrier against penetration of the South, but elsewhere Kingdoms quickly found occupants. Whites as well as Negroes participated in the expansion. After World War II whites actually outnumbered Negroes in some western missions.

Of all the exotic religious cults that competed for the loyalty of the rudderless American, none was more fantastic and sinister than the "I Am" movement. Guy Ballard, the creator of "I Am," represented himself as one of a vast celestial brotherhood embracing great men of all ages who were called "Ascended Masters." As the earthly representative of St. German, the greatest of the Ascended Masters, Ballard claimed vast supernatural powers and the right to transmit messages from the celestial hierarchy to believers. These pretensions would have been harmless enough had not Ballard introduced strong fascistic overtones into the messages from outer space and hoodwinked over a million people in the process.

Disaster overtook the movement December 29, 1939, when Ballard died of cirrhosis of the liver. Mrs. Ballard, who occupied the number two spot in the "I Am" pantheon, tried to retrieve the situation by announcing that her husband had ascended to heaven in a radiant path of light. Nevertheless, the exodus of members was spectacular. A worse catastrophe soon followed when the government indicted "I Am" for using the mails to defraud. Eventually the Supreme Court voided the indictment but not before "I Am" was thoroughly discredited.

THE LITERATURE OF HOPE AND DESPAIR

Many of those who had boldly rejected the religious and moral values of their own society after World War I also felt the need for hopes and beliefs. As long as prosperity lasted, aggressive skepticism had proved a congenial pose to the young. Harboring the traditional instinct to defy the older generation, they had used postwar disillusionment as an excuse for the most outspoken assaults on the faiths of their ancestors. Depression brought such sudden and acute privations that they felt an urgent concern over social and economic problems hitherto left contemptuously to the politicians. Since the intellectuals of the 1920's had always taken themselves seriously, they lavished tremendous energy on the search for truths that would relieve their personal distress as well as the misery of society.

Most of them had burned their bridges too determinedly to take refuge in nonsecular values. The most conspicuous iconoclast to strike his colors was Sinclair Lewis, whose later novels reaffirm faith in traditional Americanism if not in traditional religion. The majority either embraced or sympathized with the secular religion of Marxism, which enabled them to retain their old antipathy toward the middle class as the foes of free expression both in art and in personal living. Acceptance of Marxist theory was not always followed by membership in the Communist party or adherence to its arbitrary formulas for artistic expression. More typical consequences were endorsement of Marxian assumptions about the nature of society, emphasis on environmental conditions as the ultimate cause of poverty and crime, and expressions of faith that spiritual as well as material problems would disappear with the advent of a classless society. The perpetual rebel, Lincoln Steffens, voiced the sentiments of the less doctrinaire when he said of the Russian experiment: "I have seen the future and it works." Even Ernest Hemingway underwent a partial conversion when he praised the Communists among the Spanish Loyalists in *For Whom The Bell Tolls*.

The difference between those who blindly followed the dictation of Moscow and the larger group which accepted Marxian philosophy in a general way is reflected in the literature of the time. The militant party-liners produced a stereotyped plot that dealt with industrial class war. The characters were predatory industrialists, virtuous factory workers, and their families. Labor organizers invariably emerged as heroes and galvanized the masses to overthrow capitalism. By contrast, the undisciplined converts from the "lost generation" permitted themselves much more latitude in plot and characterization. They emphasized the same general theme of exploitation but often terminated action on an inconclusive note.

This arid, Marxist formula had first been tried during the 1920's. From the outset Moscow had encouraged the writing of plays rather than novels, because the masses which were supposed to benefit from literary enlightenment could be more easily coaxed to watch a show than to read a book. These educational efforts failed miserably. Characters who spent all their time on the stage talking about economic problems and the class struggle did not hold the attention of the average audience. Attempts to humanize revolutionary activities by having the heroes make long speeches explaining their behavior only made the plays more dreary. Nobody attended them or remembered that they had been given. The Theater Guild with its subscription audience succeeded, it is true, in producing a couple of less orthodox proletarian plays like Ernst Toller's *Man and the Masses* (1924) and Kirchov and Ouspensky's *Red Rust* (1929). During the twenties, however, the masses stubbornly resisted enlightenment.

The atmosphere of the depression guaranteed more responsive audiences for proletarian plays. After ten years of practice, orthodox Communists began to employ art more skillfully as a weapon of class warfare. Michael Gold, the most zealous of the Moscow-directed Communists in the United States, organized some 375 workers' theaters in the middle thirties. These gave such plays as *Unemployed, Lynch Law,* and *What Price Coal,* dramatizing the Communist version of leading problems. Although such productions often minimized character development, they approached problems more realistically and developed a faster pace of action than their earlier counterparts. The workers' theaters also developed a new medium of communication, the "agitprop" or short revolutionary play, for use at all kinds of gatherings to whip up class consciousness.

The orthodox Communists secured a more respectable and influential outlet for their ideas by infiltrating the WPA Federal Theater. Some nonideological plays like Marlowe's *Dr. Faustus* and a swing version of Gilbert and Sullivan's *Mikado* were produced, but most of the authors were preoccupied with social themes and were militantly left-wing. The most blatantly Communistic play produced by the Federal Theater was *Battle Hymn* (1936) by Blankfort and Gold. The authors used the Abolitionist hero, John Brown, as a spokesman for Marxist ideas. The Communists also gained a foothold in the "Living Newspaper" unit of the WPA Federal Theater. Living Newspaper productions, like the avowedly revolutionary agitprops, did not present plots in the usual sense. They gave a visual report of a controversial problem and forthrightly advocated a solution. Besides annoying Republicans and conservative Democrats with *Injunction Granted* (1936) and *Triple A Plowed Under* (1936), the Living Newspaper unit generated a major storm by advocating rent strikes and public housing in *One Third of a Nation* (1937). Congress became sufficiently irritated in June 1939 to kill the WPA Federal Theater.

Meanwhile some of the younger writers were achieving considerable success with plays which developed social and economic themes on a much broader basis. Often the orthodox Communists criticized these productions because the indebtedness of the authors to Marxian ideas did not prevent doctrinal deviations. Elmer Rice, who experimented with economic themes in his impressionistic play *The Adding Machine* (1923), made heroes of the left-wing foes who allegedly burned the German Reichstag building, in *Judgment Day* (1934). Maxwell Anderson collaborated with Harold Hickerson to condemn what he regarded as class injustice in *Gods of the Lightning* (1928), which was based on the Sacco-Vanzetti case. For those who had missed the point, Anderson repeated his condemnation in *Winterset* (1935). He struck a slightly different note in *High Tor* (1937), which emphasized the futility of efforts by idealists to escape the demoralizing influence of industrialism. Anderson was more interested in exposing old flaws than in advocating Communism; eventually he passed out of his skeptical phase and affirmed faith in spiritual values in *Journey to Jerusalem.* Eugene O'Neill, who showed fitful bursts of social conscience during the twenties and early thirties also abandoned his left-wing interests in *Ah, Wilderness!* (1933) and *Days Without End* (1934).

Clifford Odets idealized the militant labor leader in *Waiting for Lefty* (1935) and demanded a new social order in *Awake and Sing* (1935). John Wexley's *They Shall Not Die* (1934) damned the legalized murder of Negroes in the South, while M. E. Clifford and Hallie Flanagan spoke for bankrupt farmers in *Can You Hear Their Voices?*

Simultaneously, musical comedy began to slip corrosive digs at the *status quo* into the traditional songs and gags written for the tired businessman. Representative of this trend were Kaufman and Ryskind's *Of Thee I Sing* (1931) and *Let 'Em Eat Cake* (1933), Irving Berlin's *Face the Music,* and Kaufman and Hart's, *I'd Rather Be Right* (1937).

As might have been expected, many novelists showed the same preoccupation with economic problems and the same sympathy toward Marxian ideas as the playwrights. A few of them, who were bitterly critical of capitalism, also became disillusioned with Communism and ended as exponents of despair. The most prominent was John Dos Passos. In the last volume of his massive trilogy *U.S.A.,* completed in 1936, he hinted that a proletarian revolution was just around the corner. This note of hopeful expectancy disappeared in *Adventures of a Young Man,* the opening volume of a new trilogy. From disillusionment with Communism he moved on to disillusionment with the New Deal in *The Grand Design.* By the middle of the 1940's he had practically run out of credos in which to disbelieve.

Nathanael West was another author whose novels suggested that the collapse of American society would be an act of mercy. *A Cool Million* (1933) dealt with the plight of contemporary middle class society. The hero, Lemuel Pitkin, is a Horatio Alger-like figure who tries to make his way in the contemporary world by sobriety, frugality, and hard work. Disaster after disaster overtakes him, but his conditioning by patriotic, capitalistic slogans has been so complete that he dies without recognizing their emptiness. The grotesque and tragicomic type of characters that assailed Lemuel Pitkin are reanimated by West in *The Day of the Locust,* (1939) a novel about the nightmare world of Hollywood. Assuming that the film capital accurately reflects America, he savagely condemns his fellow countrymen for their immaturity, their addiction to tawdry values, and their cultural poverty. West feared the irrational, anarchic power of the mob which he saw lurking just below the surface of western civilization. He thought of it as a kind of sociological hydrogen bomb destined to explode when the fascistic agitator fired the right combination of fuses. His *Day of the Locust* ended in a frightening outburst of mob violence which was his pronouncement of the death sentence on capitalist society.

At the other extreme was John Steinbeck. He owed much to the Marxists in his indignant descriptions of human suffering but committed the worst possible heresy in their eyes by advocating a kind of sentimental agrarianism as a solution for human ills. *In Dubious Battle* (1936) dealt with class war in the apple orchards of California. Sympathy with the workers did not prevent him from representing the Communists as more interested in stirring up class consciousness than in improving the situation. His masterpiece, *The Grapes of Wrath* (1939), has justifiably been called the first proletarian novel of which the proletariat was aware. It described the vicissitudes of the Joads, a poverty-stricken family who left the dust bowl of Oklahoma and traveled to California, where the callousness of the orchard owners thwarted the efforts of the migrants to earn a decent living. Although the plot is poor, *The Grapes of Wrath* commanded a wide audience because of the vivid and realistic way in which Steinbeck portrayed the exploitation of unfortunate people. It argued persuasively for the view that the woes of the migrants were due primarily to predatory forces rather than to their own inadequacies. It advertised economic determinism more plausibly than most Marxists. Steinbeck had a sentimental and mystical faith in the overwhelming power of vitality or life forces. His books often ended with an expression of confidence that this dynamic drive would somehow triumph.

Other authors, indebted in varying degrees to the Marxian analysis, wrote about individual groups of sufferers from the depression. In *The Young Manhood of Studs Lonigan* (1934) James Farrell traced the disintegration of a young man trapped in the oppressive lower-middle-class society of Chicago's near south side. Erskine Caldwell described the benumbing misery of southern poor-whites in *Tobacco Road* (1932). Faulkner dealt with the same group in *As I Lay Dying* (1930) and with the degenerate white planter class in *Light in August* (1932). Michael Gold's *Jews Without Money* (1930) focused attention on the plight of the slum-dwelling Jews of an eastern big city, while Richard Wright's *Native Son* proclaimed with disconcerting bitterness the hates and aspirations of the Negro. The case for the industrial workers was ably presented in *The Land of Plenty* (1931) by Robert Cantwell, and *The Disinherited* (1933) by Jack Conroy.

Although Faulkner wrote about the social and economic problems of the South, the doctrinaire aspects of his work were secondary to his preoccupation with subconscious aspects of social behavior. Most of his characters reacted far more vigorously to sexual drives, obscure homicidal wishes, and pathetic desires for recognition than to economic needs. Faulkner's complex and often obscure prose style heightened the impression that his characters lived mainly in a twilight world of the subconscious. These aspects of his work brought him closer to the Symbolists of the 1920's than to the critics of capitalism.

Another important author of the era, who did not fall in any established category was Thomas Wolfe. Blessed with a knack for translating his deep sense of loneliness into moving prose, he recorded the passionate search of a young man for affection and faith in *Look Homeward, Angel* (1929),

Of Time and the River (1935), and *The Web and the Rock* (1939). He frequently interrupted conventional narrative development for long passages of introspection or description. Few authors of the time had his uncanny ability to reproduce on paper the sights, smells, and sounds of the American countryside or city street.

Preoccupation with social and economic problems was not so prominent in the poetry and art of the 1930's as in the prose, although it provided inspiration for some experimentation in these fields. The most noteworthy departure from conventional forms was made by Archibald MacLeish. He tried to introduce an insistent note of realism by employing the techniques which Dos Passos had used in the novel — camera shots, rhythmic patterns suggestive of a movie sound-track, and radio announcers.

Painters functioned with a kindred sense of realism. Thomas Hart Benton, Grant Wood, and John Steuart Curry devoted most of their canvases to austere rural landscapes and gaunt hungry people. Numberless WPA artists emphasized toil and suffering in the bright murals with which they covered the walls of post offices and other public buildings. Some of this work showed strong Marxist tendencies although most of the citizens mailing letters were unaware of the fact.

A MIDDLE WAY

The majority of Americans accepted some Marxist criticism of capitalistic institutions but rejected its formula for rehabilitating social and economic life. As an alternative, they groped their way toward a new philosophy of government that combined older strains of native radicalism with depression-born economic theory. The magnitude of the change was not apparent for a variety of reasons. Neither Franklin Roosevelt nor his immediate followers went beyond vague campaign generalizations toward making an authoritative statement of their position. On the contrary, they tended to use terms which employed nineteenth-century ideals for new and unfamiliar purposes. Political opponents contributed to the confusion almost as much as the friends of the New Deal by indiscriminately labeling all aspects of the reform program Socialistic.

Notwithstanding the absence of an official creed, the sources of the New Deal are easily traced. They lie at the headwaters of the great stream of late-nineteenth-century evolutionary thought. Lester Ward, Oliver Wendell Holmes, and Thorstein Veblen — to mention a few thinkers — expounded the theory that society develops by stages and that institutions should be remodeled to meet the requirements of each successive stage. Pragmatists like Dewey and James enriched the theory with their insistence on the plastic character of the universe and their faith in the ability of man to guide evolutionary processes. Most of these men believed that the fruitful adjustment of institutions to environment required intelligent government planning and they boldly advocated such a policy during the Progressive era.

The position of the evolutionists differed from that of the Marxists with regard both to the direction and the goal of the historical process. Although the evolutionists usually felt that man exercised a decisive role in shaping developments, they did not try to forecast what transitional or final patterns would emerge. The Marxists took the opposing view that man and his beliefs were the product of developments destined to move by stages to a final goal — victory of the working class and the complete socialization of property.

Disagreement of evolutionists and Marxists in theory was overshadowed by the similarity of their approach to practical problems. Both thought that the Industrial Revolution had outmoded the values of nineteenth-century individualism and both looked to government to reconstruct institutions in the interest of underprivileged groups. These areas of agreement were broad enough to provoke conservatives to denounce native evolutionary thinkers as Socialists. Yet their basic approach received a tacit blessing in the Bull Moose platform of 1912 and it also reappeared in the New Freedom program of Woodrow Wilson, who had adopted the evolutionary method of evaluating institutions. Without explicitly acknowledging his philosophical convictions, Wilson committed the Progressive movement to government aid for depressed groups. He favored the intrusion of the state in social and economic life, despite his protestations that he intended to restore the free enterprise system of the nineteenth century. His administration accustomed Americans to the practical application of the hitherto heretical idea that the content of democracy changed as the environment changed. What could not be sold directly as an evolutionary philosophy of institutional development, seeped into the old credo and expressed itself through the venerable terminology of the Founding Fathers.

This trend in the history of political thought was interrupted during the fiercely reactionary period of the 1920's but emerged triumphant again in the New Deal. Like his predecessor Woodrow Wilson, Franklin Roosevelt talked a great deal about the restoration of democracy in a way that seemed to mean a transformation of democracy. Consciously or not, he identified himself with the evolutionary-pragmatic tradition. His appraisal of old institutions was frequently made in a critical vein, as if he assumed that developments had made them obsolete. He also betrayed an evolutionary bias in his conviction that large-scale government activity was essential to create equal opportunity in the current stage of industrial development. He showed too much zeal for nontheoretical experimentation to qualify as a Socialist although persistent effort to extend government services made him suspect. The disorderly tangle of conflicting programs which comprised the New Deal was a monument to his policy of continual improvisation. Nobody interested in the creation of a socialist state would have used subsidies as vigorously as he did to keep the various economic pressure groups alive. The unfolding of the New Deal program suggests that he pursued goals only in a provisional, pragmatic sense. Either he sought an equilibrium capable of providing economic security at all levels, or he sought the less lofty goal of political support from as many groups as possible. In any event, he was prepared to take government action to produce the proper balance of economic forces.

THE NEW ECONOMIC AND SOCIOLOGICAL THOUGHT

A new generation of academicians applied the evolutionary analysis to depression-ridden institutions and came up with conclusions which Roosevelt appropriated in piecemeal fashion. The Keynesian economists were perhaps the most influential thinkers. Despite individual differences in emphasis, the majority of them owed their basic outlook to the British economist John Maynard Keynes, who had searched for the causes of the chronic depression in England during the 1920's. Much oversimplified, the Keynesian thesis was that saving or hoarding of capital by business groups led to unemployment and economic stagnation. Or to put it another way, the wealthy kill prosperity by failing to spend. American professors who accepted this diagnosis sought reasons for the timidity of potential spenders in the 1930's and concluded that our society had reached a stage of development where nearly everybody was afraid to risk capital in new enterprises. Alvin H. Hansen, a distinguished Harvard economist, blamed our plight on the closing of the frontier, the decline in the rate of population growth, and the exhaustion of the inventive genius which had hitherto created new consumer demands for such items as automobiles and radios. This analysis seems unreal in the light of the dynamic performance of the economy after World War II. However, the persistence of stagnation in the 1930's led Hansen to forecast a prolonged depression unless government took over the role of investing and spending which private enterprise had abandoned.

Most Keynesians shared Hansen's conclusion and advocated deficit financing as the only alternative to stagnation. Those who believed that the static stage of the American economy would last for an extended period favored a long-range program of government spending. Others with greater faith in the recuperative powers of private industry envisaged government as a stabilizing instrument which would step up the pace of spending and lower taxes in time of depression, and apply the reverse tactics whenever conditions improved.

Stated either way, the program owed its political appeal to the emphasis on government intervention for the maintenance of the health of the private-enterprise system. Indeed, most New Dealers hailed the technique as a middle-of-the-road solution between capitalism and socialism. They countered thunder on the left by the assertion that public spending would put idle men and machines to work without necessitating the socialization of the economy demanded by Stuart Chase in *The Economy of Abundance* (1934) and by George Soule in *The Coming American Revolution* (1934). Conservative critics who objected to a rising public debt on the threefold ground that it threatened inflation, bankruptcy, and redistribution of the wealth were chided for ingratitude toward their New Deal benefactors. Few businessmen accepted the argument that sacrifices were essential in order to avert revolution and save them from themselves. Nevertheless, the Roosevelt administration informally rested much of its case for the enlarged role of government in society on the contention that America had passed into a new stage where public spending was essential to save democracy. The controversy persisted beyond the New Deal era, but it was settled by Roosevelt in the sense that a large majority came to accept his policy of government intervention to cure economic distress.

The evolutionary hypothesis, which pictured society as developing through a succession of stages and needing new principles for new stages, was applied to the analysis of political and legal institutions as well as economic ones. The arch-individualist of the prewar generation, William Graham Sumner, had gloomily foreshadowed the trend in his *Folkways* (1906) when he conceded that the time would come when his cherished credo would no longer be appropriate. Thurman Arnold, Dean of the Yale Law School and later Assistant Attorney General, sought to confirm the prophecy in *Folklore of Capitalism* (1937). He argued that the American constitutional and legal system exalted a lot of outmoded beliefs to the level of eternal truths. In a chapter entitled "The Folklore of 1937" he ridiculed what he thought to be the current myth of automatically regarding the deeds of private corporations as farsighted and constructive and those of the state as fumbling and inept. He also analyzed the sympathetic terminology applied to the activities of private business and how it obstructed the performance of essential government services. He made no secret of his relativist philosophy and pinned his faith on the emergence of a new public outlook free from the myths of an earlier era.

JOHN DEWEY: DEMOCRACY AND EDUCATION

More influential than Thurman Arnold in conditioning citizens to the repudiation of old values and institutions was John Dewey, the Pragmatist — or Instrumentalist, as he preferred to be called. A contemporary of Ward, James, and Veblen as well as Franklin Roosevelt, Dewey was the most conspicuous link between two generations of thinkers who considered a changing environment the most conspicuous feature of nature. His views about the open, plastic character of the universe and the capacity of man to remake it for the welfare of society were well known before World War I. In the two subsequent decades he amplified them and emphasized the mutually shared experiences of the group as the core of democracy. The depression caused him to stress still more enthusiastically the collectivist implications in his thought, especially the notion that government planning permitted constant revision of group goals in the light of experience. In effect, his definition of democracy as group action was expanded to read: group action directed by the government. The amendment did not modify his basic insistence that democracy lacked a fixed content. He continued to think of it as a process oriented toward realization of the maximum benefits from the environment at any given time.

Embalmed in the awkward sentences of Dewey's books and pamphlets, the theory made no great impression on popular opinion. Dewey, however, was an educator as well as a philosopher and applied his viewpoint to the problems of primary and secondary schools, stirring up so much controversy that his name became a household word. As a result, he received the credit and the blame for an educational theory which he accused disciples of modifying without his consent.

Dewey's basic pedagogical approach was revolutionary enough before it was amended by the Deweyites. In brief, he applied his pragmatic view to the education of children, arguing that they would learn whenever they recognized their interests to be touched. He proposed replacing the traditional curriculum centered on the three R's by one focused on the child. His idea of the optimum learning situation was one where the teachers organized their classroom presentation in terms of the enthusiasms of their pupils. This philosophy of education became important in the early 1920's when it emerged as the official creed of the staff at Columbia University Teachers College, one of the first graduate schools for training teachers. Known as progressive education, the new theory was carried back to public school systems all over the country by superintendents, principals, and teachers who enrolled at Columbia for summer school courses.

The progressive education movement of John Dewey and his leading disciple, Professor William H. Kirkpatrick, was child-centered in theory but group-centered in practice. Despite much talk of stimulating creative expression in individual children, the movement put its central emphasis on the adjustment of the child to the group. This trend was partially concealed by defining individual welfare in a way that really made it the same as group welfare. During the middle 1930's younger professors at Teachers College like George Counts and Harold Rugg, who were more candid about this matter, began to shift the emphasis openly. They thought the curriculum should discourage the development of individualistic traits in pupils and encourage cooperation or group integration. Counts frankly admitted that the new emphasis was more than a pedagogical theory; in a pamphlet entitled *Dare the School Build a New Social Order* (1932) he forecast the collapse of capitalism and the emergence of some type of socialist order. He went on to argue that the public schools should train children for the new society by indoctrinating them in unselfishness, teamwork, and concern for group welfare.

Dewey did not welcome the attempt to convert what he called a method of education into a social and economic viewpoint even though it was his own. He and Kirkpatrick stood by their original formula, "no indoctrination, no orthodoxy, no absolutes," and ostensibly parted company with their disciples. Nevertheless, the group-centered theory became an important ingredient of progressive education during the New Deal era.

The degree to which the progressive education movement affected the outlook of the average American is a highly controversial question. As a philosophy it had more effect on primary and secondary school teachers trained in the postwar generation than on their pupils. They tended to take a more subjective view of standards both in education and in society at large. Many of them showed a sympathetic predisposition toward the experimentation and institutional remodeling undertaken by the New Deal. How much of their attitude rubbed off on pupils either in the form of conscious indoctrination or unconscious arrangement of subject matter is difficult to establish. Any conclusion must be tempered by the recognition that few public schools carried out the principles in a systematic way and that the teachers responsive to progressive doctrines were only one of the influences shaping the views of youngsters in the period. Probably the most that can be safely said is that the younger public school administrators fostered an academic atmosphere favorable to the pragmatic orientation of the New Deal.

Aside from theoretical considerations, Progressive education reduced the emphasis on the three R's. Full development of a child-centered curriculum took place only in private schools where children built Navaho hogans, organized Leagues of Nations, published newspapers, or pursued other projects which interested them. Progressive educators hoped that skillful direction of projects would stimulate interest in the more conventional subjects of the curriculum. Proper layout of floor space in a Navaho hogan was supposed to generate enthusiasm for the study of arithmetic, and parliamentary debates to arouse kindred concern about English grammar.

In the public school system, various practical considerations limited the application of the method. Neither teachers nor facilities could be made available on a scale sufficient to cater to the variety of passing interests shown by individual pupils. Opposition from parents, school boards, and older teachers also curbed the experimental zeal of progressive educators. Consequently, innovations were usually introduced piecemeal. A few school systems either abolished grades or put them on a noncompetitive basis. More frequently they introduced a few compulsory project courses which were called the core curriculum or "social living." Such courses varied considerably in academic content but uniformly featured less of it than the traditional courses which were replaced.

During the depression the inroad of progressive education on the old public school curriculum was sufficiently noticeable to provoke widespread discussion. Critics denounced progressive courses as organized play which lowered academic standards and geared content to the level of the mediocre student. They also blamed the new philosophy for producing high-school graduates unable to cope with the problems of American society. College professors often supported the case of the critics by complaining that the current generation of college students was shockingly ignorant of such basic subjects as arithmetic and English.

Progressive educators lashed back with the contention that they were preparing pupils for the new society and that their critics were the ones who had failed to make the adjustment. Professor Kirkpatrick spoke for the entire movement when he countered charges about student ignorance of arithmetic with the assertion that most people never used mathematics after they left school. Although progressive educators might disagree over whether the curriculum should be child-centered or group-centered, they all felt that method was more important than content. In their view, progressive method provided the student with maximum incentive for self-development in a changing society. They were fully prepared to admit that the continuing quest for a useful education might ultimately require complete abandonment of the traditional public school curriculum. The insistence of progressive philosophy on the open, provisional character of education shocked all citizens who regarded the school as a seedbed for the cultivation of American ideals.

The controversy continued beyond the depression era and failed to produce a clear-cut victory for either side. The proficiency of public school graduates in the three R's dwindled slowly in the 1930's and more rapidly thereafter. The role of progressive education in the process was not so clear. To the limited degree that the so-called "core curriculum" encroached on the time devoted to traditional subjects, progressive theory shared responsibility for the outcome. It also played an unmeasurable role by encouraging some teachers to de-emphasize the three R's or to handle them nonchalantly.

Other factors were at work quite apart from progressive theory. Public school systems did not expand facilities or teaching staffs to keep pace with population growth. As a result teachers had less time to spend working with individual students and correcting their written exercises. Standards inevitably dropped under such conditions. At the same time, recently developed media of entertainment like the cinema and the radio began to compete effectively with homework for the attention of the students. Some people hailed these offerings as possessing great educational value. An occasional movie or radio program justified the praise, but the vast majority of productions in either medium could not be classified as even vaguely educational. Nor was there any evidence that the students chose discriminatingly. The net result of the competition proved to be less attention to academic subjects.

With the educational system, political and economic institutions, religious beliefs, and social standards in a state of flux, it was no wonder that the intellectual history of the depression era was full of crosscurrents. The only dominant mood seemed to be the determination to experiment even if such activity meant abandonment of old ideals and institutions. The depression generation never became sure exactly where it wanted to go, but it was in a great hurry to get there.

SUGGESTED READINGS

1. Arnold, T., *The Folklore of Capitalism.*
2. Beard, C. A. and M., *America in Mid-Passage* (vol. 2).
3. Fainsod, M., and Gordon, L., *Government and the American Economy.*

CHAPTER TWENTY-TWO

THE CONSERVATIVE COUNTERATTACK ON THE NEW DEAL

ROOSEVELT BEGINS HIS SECOND TERM

"Give your mind seriously to the question of the Second Coming," wrote H. L. Mencken to a friend just before Roosevelt's re-election. "The signs and portents are upon us." With these scornful words the aging skeptic predicted a fresh torrent of New Deal social and economic proposals. Nobody had taken him seriously for years, but he came much closer to divining the intentions of the triumphant Roosevelt than did the political analysts who anticipated a period of conciliation and consolidation.

The first authoritative evidence that the Chief Executive intended to amplify and broaden the 1935 New Deal program was provided in his inaugural address of January 20, 1937. Asking whether the nation had reached "the goal of our vision," he answered himself with an indignant negative:

> I see millions of families trying to live on incomes so meager that the pall of family disaster hangs over them day by day.
>
> I see millions whose daily lives in the city and on the farm continue under conditions labeled indecent by so-called polite society half a century ago.
>
> I see millions denied education, recreation, and the opportunity to better their lot and the lot of their children.
>
> I see millions lacking the means to buy the products of farm and factory, and by their poverty denying work and productiveness to many other millions.
>
> I see one third of a nation ill-housed, ill-clad, ill-nourished.

In the ensuing weeks, his program for the improvement of living standards was slowly enunciated through a series of special messages to Congress. He proposed legislation on wages and hours, low-cost public housing, fresh aid to agriculture, reorganization of the executive departments, and the creation of new regional projects modeled on the TVA.

All these recommendations might have been expected in response to campaign pledges. Not so the proposal of February 5, 1937, requesting congressional authorization of a plan to reorganize the Supreme Court.

Beyond a sneer at the judiciary for blocking New Deal legislation in the keynote address of Senator Alben W. Barkley at the Democratic National Convention, the issue had not been raised in the campaign. The chief New Dealer had ignored the Court entirely. Hence his sudden insistence on judicial legislation and its priority over other business took friends as well as foes by surprise.

Elementary political logic should have suggested the hazards involved in pressing the issue. Nevertheless Roosevelt felt confident of early success. The first two New Deal Congresses had done his bidding with alacrity, and the newly elected Congress was more heavily Democratic than its predecessors. In addition he felt that his overwhelming defeat of Landon represented a personal mandate from the voters to proceed as he chose. Such confidence was pardonable for a political leader who had enjoyed an uninterrupted series of triumphs. On the other hand, Roosevelt's unique control over Congress was due more to the economic crisis than to his personal qualities of leadership. Congress had done what he wanted, not because he made obedience more enjoyable than his predecessors had, but because angry voters made it fearful of taking an independent line of action. Ever sensitive to political currents, the lawmakers noticed in 1936 a diminishing demand for blind support of the President. This trend gave them courage to think about reclaiming some of the authority hastily surrendered in 1933. Such a reaction had occurred after every period of executive domination, and it transcended partisan considerations.

A second factor destined to nullify the results of Roosevelt's extraordinary election victory was the instability of his following. As earlier chapters have already indicated, the Democrats habitually suffered from an internecine warfare between a northern urban wing with a prolabor orientation and a southern rural wing hostile to Catholics, labor unions, and radicals. The unanimity of public support for Roosevelt had forced a suspension of this conflict during his first term. Still, the southern congressmen liked very little of the New Deal program for which they had furnished so many votes. The only phase of it that really pleased them was the subsidy for cotton. Deficit spending, social security, and the Wagner Act aroused their antipathy, which was no less intense because it had to be concealed.

Whether the southern congressmen reflected the wishes of their constituents is a moot point. Participation in primaries and general elections seldom exceeded 10 per cent of the adults in the deep South and 25 per cent in the border states. Furthermore, the underprivileged groups most likely to be enthusiastic about the New Deal were disfranchised by state election laws which were originally aimed against the Negroes but had come to affect large numbers of poor whites as well. The situation was further complicated by the ambivalent attitude of the poor whites who did vote. In general they cherished the same economic aspirations as their counterparts in other sections, but their devotion to the Roosevelt program was always qualified by fear that the Negro would also participate in the benefits —

The pitcher still wants a change. (Reg Manning, The Arizona Republic, *1937.)*

perhaps to the point where his social inferiority would disappear. Anxieties on this score drove many to support Negro-baiters like "Cotton Ed" Smith of South Carolina and Eugene Talmadge of Georgia, who had loudly opposed the program from the beginning. The more prosperous southern farmers and businessmen voted regularly and with closer regard for their economic interests. The revival of 1935–36 had already diminished their enthusiasm for the New Deal. Only the age-old habit of supporting the Democratic party as the party of white supremacy kept articulate southerners from grumbling in the 1936 campaign. Once the election was over, they intended to oppose minimum wage laws, deficit spending, and the extension of New Deal power projects.

Heartened by the support of the well-to-do and the mixed sentiments of the poor whites, southern legislators could henceforth fight Roosevelt without seriously jeopardizing their political careers. Their prospects of hamstringing the New Deal were heightened by virtue of the fact that long periods of continuous service in both houses had brought the southerners key committee chairmanships. Most of them had resented the Roosevelt practice of drafting bills and ordering committees to report such bills unamended. Vice-President Garner expressed their annoyance at a private party in 1933 when he complained that the President handed all "the top cards to young lawyers who had never worked a precinct." He went on to say that the "old fellows" would go along for a while but that there would "have to be a showdown soon." What the "old fellows" wanted was a good issue on which to desert Roosevelt. They would have defied him sooner or later. The Court plan gave them opportunity for rebellion on moral and constitutional grounds.

JUDICIAL REVIEW AND THE NEW DEAL

Before we consider the content of the bill and the ensuing legislative battle, we must devote attention to the Supreme Court and the controversies which its activities provoked. The makers of the Constitution had created the Court in accordance with their belief in the separation of powers. They expected it to preserve the original distribution of authority and guard the people as well as the various branches of the government from attempts to violate the Constitution. Opinion at the time differed as to whether the chief threat to the reserved powers of the states and the individual liberties of the people would come from the executive or from the federal Congress. Hamilton made it clear in Article 78 of *The Federalist* that the Court was to pass on the constitutionality of legislation, but the Constitution itself did not contain a clause specifically providing for judicial review. The oversight was deliberate and was intended to undercut one of the objections to ratification. However, it had paved the way for a hundred and fifty years of debate over the proper function of the Court — a debate which produced several acute political crises before 1937.

The original opponents of judicial review argued that each branch of the government was intended to be the judge of the constitutionality of its own acts, with the voters serving as a final court of appeal. Adopted by the Jeffersonians, this view was decisively repudiated in the famous case of *Marbury* v. *Madison* (1803), which affirmed the right of the Supreme Court to pass on the constitutionality of federal legislation. Once the precedent had been established, the opposition shifted its point of attack as circumstances required. Most assaults developed the argument that the Supreme Court functioned as a third and unrepresentative branch of the federal legislature. Judges were repeatedly charged with reading their own social, economic, and legal prejudices into decisions. Critics usually proposed some kind of amendment that would deprive the Court of its independent status and make it more directly responsive to public opinion. Defenders relied on Hamilton's argument in *The Federalist* that the judges in exercising judicial review did not assert the superiority of the Supreme Court over other branches of the government but only the superiority of the Constitution over all three.

During the long and indecisive argument, the character of Supreme Court decisions underwent several distinct changes. From *Marbury* v. *Madison* to the Dred Scott decision in 1857, the Court did not invalidate a single law passed by Congress. Possessing a strong nationalist orientation, it devoted most of its energy to striking down state legislation which poached on areas reserved to the central government.

For fifteen years after the Civil War no pronounced trend in Constitutional interpretation developed. The Court was too busy digesting both the actual and the legal changes that had taken place as a result of the war. After 1880 a clearer pattern emerged with the Court showing marked hostility to the social and economic legislation of the Populist and Progressive eras. This new attitude did not lead to the invalidation of much congressional legislation for the simple reason that the central government had only stated powers. It had not been given a blanket grant of legislative authority over the general welfare, and so it refrained from passing laws in doubtful or disputed areas. Its few ventures in social and economic legislation provoked quick retaliation from the Court. An income tax law was thrown out in 1894, and nearly two decades were required to secure an amendment permitting what a majority favored. The Court also blocked two efforts by Wilson to outlaw child labor. Radicals complained loudly over this situation; but except for the Progressive party in 1924, no organized political group advocated a reform of the judiciary during the prosperous twenties. The old controversy revived when the New Deal embarked on a vast legislative program in areas hitherto considered beyond the jurisdiction of the central government.

While the Supreme Court had been busy erecting barriers against social and economic legislation by the central government, it had also shown aversion to similiar measures enacted by the states in pursuance of their residual powers. Laws establishing minimum wages and maximum hours, regulating the rates charged by railroads and public utilities, and enforcing basic safety or sanitary conditions on industry, frequently suffered judicial death. The judges did not dispute the right of the states to exercise general police powers or to legislate for public health and safety; they merely refused to allow such legislation to stand if it impaired property rights unduly. Their basis for such reasoning was a section of the post-Civil War Fourteenth Amendment, which prohibited states from depriving persons of life, liberty, or property without due process of law. They treated corporations as artificial persons entitled to protection under the Amendment. They also professed to believe that individuals had been deprived of their liberty to contract freely for their services if state laws arbitrarily limited the hours of work. In a series of decisions between 1880 and 1930 the Court made repeated attempts to establish foolproof criteria for judging what constituted undue interference with property rights and individual freedom. Each attempt broke down as economic conditions changed. The Court, however, adhered to the basic rule that if state legislation for public welfare, health, or safety conflicted with the due process clause, the legislation would have to be sacrificed.

The cumulative effect of this doctrine was to place most economic reform programs outside the jurisdiction of both the states and the federal government. It is uncertain whether the Constitution makers had intended to create such a curious situation. In any event the popular demand for government aid to fight depression put the Court under tremendous pressure to modify its outlook. The focal point of concern was destined to be the powers of the central government, because the states lacked both the resources and the similarity of interests to launch a national recovery program.

During the hectic Hundred Days, the President and Congress were more concerned with whether legislation would ease the emergency than whether it was constitutional. With an eye on the Supreme Court, New Deal lawyers usually prefaced emergency legislation with long preambles alluding to the crisis and asserting that it created additional government powers. Administration measures in the category of reform as distinguished from emergency rested their claims to constitutionality on the use of stated powers for new purposes.

Nobody knows what would have happened if Roosevelt had pressed the Supreme Court for decisions in the midst of the crisis. He permitted the tests of New Deal laws to take place initially in the lower courts, as was customary. Before these cases reached the Supreme Court the acute stage of the depression had passed.

As the Constitution had intended, the judges lagged somewhat behind public opinion. All of them had been appointed in the twenty years before the New Deal. Since Democratic and Republican Presidents seldom selected judges primarily because of their views of the Constitution, the proportion of reactionaries to reformers was about the same as in the country before the depression. McReynolds, Van Devanter, Sutherland, and Butler could be counted upon to continue the trend they had inherited. Opposing these four occasionally rather than consistently were Stone, Brandeis, and Cardozo. More flexible in outlook than the reactionaries, they tended to follow the tradition of Oliver Wendell Holmes, the great dissenter, who thought that the Constitution permitted citizens to undertake most of the foolish legislative experiments attractive to them. The remaining two, Owen D. Roberts and Chief Justice Charles Evans Hughes, followed a less predictable course. Hughes had once made the statement at a Bar Association meeting that "the Constitution is what the judges say it is." Such a cynical observation was a little out of character for the Chief Justice. At any rate, during the New Deal period he appeared to be guided more by practical considerations and the desire to preserve the Court's prestige than by a consistent philosophy of law. Roberts offered few clues to his probable behavior. Conservative in temperament, he usually teamed up with Hughes to hold the balance of power. Hence the division in the Court meant that the New Deal administration could not win favorable verdicts by a vote of more than 5 to 4, and was likely to lose the controversial cases 6 to 3, if not 9 to 0.

As a result of two decisions in 1934 concerning the exercise of state legislative powers, the administration was deceived into believing that the Court had undergone a change of heart. A Minnesota law postponing interest payments on mortgages (*Home Building and Loan Association* v. *Blaisdell*) and a New York statute fixing the price of milk (*Nebbia* v. *New York*) were sustained by 5 to 4 votes. Approval of the first involved an infrequently tested provision of the Constitution prohibiting states from impairing the obligation of contract. In the second case, the majority opinion sustaining price-fixing in such an unimpeachably private sector of the economy as the milk business, implied a reversal of a fifty-year trend. It seemed to mean that the exercise of state police powers for social and economic objectives would hereafter be approved, even if the implementing laws conflicted with due process. The reason why Hughes and Roberts deserted the four conservatives on this issue is not altogether clear. Perhaps they had already made up their minds to vote for the invalidation of major New Deal laws and felt the Court would be less vulnerable to criticism if it opened the way for state action in these controversial areas.

The Supreme Court did not begin to hand down opinions on the constitutionality of New Deal legislation until the opening days of 1935. Except for a 5 to 4 decision validating the right of the government to suspend payments in gold even where it had entered into private contracts specifically calling for such payments, opinions went uniformly against the New Deal. On January 7, 1935, the judges struck down Section 9A of the NIRA in the so-called "hot oil" case (*Panama Refining Co.* v. *Ryan*). Four months later they invalidated the Railroad Retirement Act. The big blow was reserved for May 27, 1935, when the Court delivered three verdicts against the New Deal by unanimous decisions. The Frazier-Lemke Farm Moratorium Act and the code-making sections of the NIRA were declared unconstitutional, while the President's removal of William E. Humphry from the Federal Trade Commission was declared illegal (*Rathbun* v. *U.S.*).

These decisions had varying implications. The prohibition on the removal of administration critics from independent commissions before the expiration of their terms was to slow down the process of completing New Deal control over these important agencies. The invalidation of the Railroad Pension Law was more disconcerting because the pending Social Security bill contained several similar features. The majority opinion on the NIRA was the one that provoked genuine consternation in administration circles. It denied that the emergency had created any fresh federal powers, branded code-making as an improper delegation of legislative power, and enunciated the general doctrine that the federal government could not employ the power over interstate commerce as a pretext for regulating industrial and labor conditions within the states. The reasoning seemed to raise an unscalable barrier against all New Deal legislation regulating manufacturing and conditions of work for labor. Corporations gained immunity from supervision by the federal government except with regard to interstate marketing or operations that led to monopolistic practices. In fact, the cumulative impression created by these decisions was that the interstate commerce clause could not be employed as broadly as in the Progressive era.

The triple blow was the last straw as far as the President was concerned. Dropping all restraint at a press conference, he bitterly criticized the NIRA decision and denounced the judges for their "horse-and-buggy definition of interstate commerce."

Roosevelt's annoyance did not interrupt the parade of invalidations. On January 6, 1936, the Court killed the processing tax of the AAA (*U.S.* v. *Butler*) 6 to 3 on the ground that the clause permitting government expenditure for general welfare did not cover payments to special groups like farmers. In mid-March, the Court overturned the Guffey-Snyder Act, which had re-enacted many features of the NIRA for the coal industry. Still later in the year, Roberts broke away from Hughes and joined the four conservatives in outlawing the New York state minimum wage law (*Morehead* v. *Tipaldo*). This decision momentarily canceled the promise of enlarged state powers over economic life held out two years earlier in *Nebbia* v. *New York*). The sole consolation for the New Deal was offered February 17, 1936, when all the judges except McReynolds agreed on the constitutional right of the TVA to sell power generated at Wilson Dam.

When the Supreme Court finally adjourned in May 1936, it was clear that if the judges adhered to the same line of reasoning in the next session they would kill the Wagner Act and the Social Security Act, to say nothing of New Deal measures still in the blueprint stage. Roosevelt did not care to jeopardize re-election prospects by introducing such an explosive issue into the campaign. So he had maintained an unnatural silence until the votes were counted, and then he began a methodical search for a suitable way of disciplining the judges.

THE ROOSEVELT COURT PLAN

The problem proved unusually baffling. Legislation narrowing the appelate jurisdiction of the courts or requiring an extraordinary majority for the invalidation of legislation was likely to meet the fate of the NIRA and AAA. Past experience suggested that a constitutional amendment enlarging the stated powers of the central government would take several years to clear the legislatures of the required thirty-six states, even if promptly approved by Congress. Moreover, the controversial character of an amendment conferring general social and economic powers on Congress increased the likelihood of jealous resistance by the states. In any case an amendment could not be adopted quickly enough to protect New Deal laws from threatened invalidation.

The only alternative was some sort of measure which would enable the President to change the personnel of the Court rapidly. There were no constitutional barriers to an increase in the number of judges. The Court had been enlarged twice before. Attorney General Cummings made this approach seem attractive to Roosevelt by anchoring it in an otherwise nonpartisan measure to speed up court procedure and increase the efficiency of the entire judicial system.

The original draft, transmitted to Congress with a special message, provided that the President should appoint one additional judge for every federal judge who attained the age of seventy and who refused to resign or retire after a six months' interval. Judges who had not served ten years were exempted from the provisions of the bill. A further qualification limited presidential appointments to fifty for the entire federal bench, and banned additions to the Supreme Court that would raise the membership above fifteen. If the bill had passed Congress unaltered, Roosevelt would have been empowered to name six Supreme Court judges immediately. All of them except Roberts and Stone were over seventy.

Matters went badly for the bill from the outset. In the first place, Roosevelt had failed to consult congressional leaders in advance or warn them that some such measure would be presented for consideration. Anger ran high among administration wheelhorses who had interpreted the President's silence as an invitation to state their views and now faced the embarrassment of abrupt retreat. Henry F. Ashurst of Arizona, chairman of the Senate Judiciary Committee that was to consider the bill, had just delivered a speech branding any assaults on the integrity of the Supreme Court as "the prelude to tyranny." Caught flatfooted by the presidential announcement, Ashurst issued a terse statement that he was for the plan, but dragged his feet throughout the legislative battle.

The initial sullenness of congressional leaders was not nearly so ominous as the chorus of voices which denounced the President for trying to deceive the American people. The strategy of burying the crucial proposal for enlargement in a message emphasizing "overcrowded dockets" and "aged or infirm" judges fooled nobody, although it looked like an effort to fool everybody. The maneuver was just clumsy enough to create suspicion regarding Roosevelt's motives and to confirm the dark insinuations about his hunger for power which Republicans had circulated in the 1936 campaign. Radio commentators, ministers, and deans of law schools made angry statements. The anti-New Deal press, which had not completed its postelection demobilization, was glad to launch a new war on the administration. Front-page stories gave prominence to the views of critics, and editorial pages gleefully reminded leaders that they had been warned about Roosevelt's despotic temper. The most telling blow was the repeated charge that he wanted to pack the Court and become a dictator.

Hostile reaction was so explosive and public opinion was so evenly divided that Roosevelt took to the radio within a month. He wisely dropped the pretense that the proposed enlargement was an impartial device to improve the efficiency of the judiciary. Accepting the challenge of the opposition, he reviewed the record of the Court and charged it with passing on the wisdom rather than the constitutionality of legislation. He quoted dissenting opinions to substantiate his thesis and disclaimed any intention of packing the Court or trying to control it on specific issues.

Despite the usual Roosevelt eloquence, the speech produced few converts. The Supreme Court had always enjoyed exceptional veneration. For better or for worse, it was thought to be above politics. Nothing Roosevelt said undermined this conviction. Citizens enthusiastic over other features of the New Deal flatly opposed the plan as a threat to the separation of powers and the integrity of the judiciary.

The attitude of the public was quickly reflected in the Senate, which considered the bill first. Ashurst dragged out the hearings from February until June, giving the opposition plenty of time to organize. The corporal's guard of Republicans remained in the background, while the southern Democrats seized the heaven-sent opportunity to defy the President. The disapproval of chronic anti-New Deal Democrats like Glass and Byrd, the two Virginia senators, and "Cotton Ed" Smith of South Carolina was to be expected. The prospects of the bill really deteriorated when administration stalwarts from the South, like Byrnes of South Carolina and Connally of Texas, joined the opposition. The worst blow of all was the defection of Senator Wheeler of Montana who had identified himself with all radical legislation for over a decade. Since he had sponsored a constitutional amendment which would have permitted Congress to override Supreme Court decisions by a two-thirds vote, his unexpected opposition divided the New Dealers.

Meanwhile developments outside the Senate foreshadowed the defeat of the President. The tacit slur on the efficiency of the Court drove the elderly judges to unite against the legislation. Chief Justice Hughes, as the spokesman for all factions, wrote Senator Wheeler a dignified letter defending the competence of the judges and citing figures to prove that they were abreast of their work.

Shortly thereafter, the Supreme Court began to hand down opinions reversing decisions of the previous year. On May 29, a Washington minimum wage law, similar to the New York law so recently invalidated, was upheld by a 5 to 4 decision (*West Coast Hotel* v. *Parrish*), with Hughes and Roberts deserting the conservatives. This precarious majority sustained the Wagner Act in a series of decisions during April. To do so, the Court had to abandon the narrow interpretation of the commerce clause.

Local labor conditions heretofore regarded as having only an indirect effect on interstate commerce were now conceded to have a direct effect on it. Accordingly the judges concluded that labor legislation fell within the jurisdiction of the central government. The same 5 to 4 majority did the unexpected again, by sustaining the Social Security Act and its taxing provisions which bore a close resemblance to those of the AAA.

THE DEATH OF THE COURT PLAN

Opponents of Roosevelt hailed these decisions as impressive evidence of the Court's ability to reform itself. They asserted that his objectives had been achieved, and called on him to withdraw his bill. This advice proved unacceptable to Roosevelt because he regarded the prevailing Court majority as precarious and unstable. Moreover, his elderly foes showed no signs of retiring to permit him even a single appointment. Behind his stubbornness was the annoyance of a political leader unaccustomed to defeat and unprepared to accept the advice of rebels.

Events moved rapidly toward a climax in early June. Willis Van Devanter, a consistent foe of New Deal legislation, retired and thus further reduced the pressure. On June 14, the Senate Judiciary Committee by a vote of 11 to 8 reported the Roosevelt bill to the floor with an intemperately worded recommendation for its rejection. Faced with certain defeat, the President sought to salvage something by backing a proposal which would have permitted him to appoint two judges instead of six. Majority Leader Joseph T. Robinson of Arkansas, who had been unofficially promised the place of Van Devanter, pressed doggedly for this compromise bill. The prospect for even this modest blow at the Court disappeared when the exhausted Robinson died of a heart attack in mid-July. After his funeral, the rebellious Senate killed the bill by recommitting it to the Judiciary Committee. The only tangible fruit of the long struggle was a law providing for a number of procedural reforms in the lower courts.

Neither side could take much pride in the results of the controversy. The President had tried to undermine the separation of powers after winning re-election on a platform that ignored the issue. Not only had he been decisively defeated but he had unwittingly brought to the surface all the disruptive tendencies in the Democratic party. As we already noted, a revolt of the southerners was in the cards. What Roosevelt's policy now did was to precipitate the split at the moment of his greatest triumph and thereby destroy the prospect for any significant extensions of the New Deal. The enlargement of the group which distrusted presidential intentions and the outbreak of civil war in the Democratic party were a high price to pay for a few favorable decisions on the Wagner Act and the Social Security laws. The steady New Deal trend of Court opinions after 1937 owed far more to the retirement of administration critics and their replacement by

Roosevelt appointees than to the momentary pressure of the Court bill. The New Deal did not win security for its program by frightening the Court into a few favorable 5 to 4 decisions.

Like the administration, the Supreme Court emerged from the controversy with somewhat withered laurels. It had met the challenge to the integrity of the judiciary by a humiliating repudiation of constitutional doctrines consistently followed for fifty years and truculently reaffirmed a year earlier. Its abrupt reversal under pressure lent support to the traditional complaint of critics that constitutional law is nothing more than the opinions and prejudices of the judges. If the members of the Court really believed that in the opinions of 1935 and 1936 they had stated the only legitimate interpretation of the Constitution, they should have stuck to them whatever the cost. As it was, the judges enunciated an interpretation of the commerce clause which they had rejected in outspoken language a few months earlier. Apologists for the Court have said that the laws sustained in 1937 were better phrased than earlier New Deal legislation. Unfortunately, the issue was not one of phraseology but of principle. Perhaps the Court should not be judged by the behavior of Hughes and Roberts, who held the balance of power. However, their sudden about-face made the judges seem more like a body of astute politicians than a nonpartisan group dedicated to the preservation of the Constitution.

The sequel to the political struggle was the emergence of a safe New Deal majority on the Supreme Court. The old judges retired one by one, and Roosevelt appointed more sympathetic replacements. Indeed, before he died in 1945, he named seven judges to the Court. Senator Hugo Black of Alabama, appointed in July 1937 to replace Van Devanter, was an avowed radical and received confirmation from his colleagues primarily because of the tradition of "senatorial courtesy." A subsequent revelation that Black had once belonged to the Ku Klux Klan gave critics a good opportunity to demand his resignation, but he successfully rode out the storm. Subsequent appointment of Solicitor General Stanley Reed, SEC Chairman William O. Douglas, former Attorney Generals Frank W. Murphy and Robert H. Jackson, and Senator James F. Byrnes of South Carolina, aroused less controversy. Only the elevation of Felix Frankfurter in 1941 stirred up opposition comparable to that which had greeted Black. Frankfurter was suspect in conservative eyes because of his militant defense of Sacco and Vanzetti in the 1920's and his well-advertised role as a New Deal brain-truster. After his confirmation, however, he surprised both friend and foe by the orthodox trend of his opinions. In 1942 Roosevelt made his last appointment when Byrnes resigned to accept an important war job. The vacancy went to Wiley B. Rutledge, an Iowa circuit judge. A year earlier Roosevelt had promoted the universally respected Stone to the Chief Justiceship upon the retirement of Charles Evans Hughes.

The cumulative effect of the Roosevelt appointments (1937–42) was reflected in several ways. The new majority withdrew the protection of the due process clause from private corporations, thus widening state regulatory power over economic activity. It also relaxed the procedural limitations on the quasi-judicial activities of New Deal agencies like the NLRB and the SEC. Most important of all was the tolerant attitude toward wider uses of federal powers over interstate commerce, spending, and taxation. In fact, the Court finally tended to assume that all laws were constitutional except those affecting civil liberties. In the latter area, the judges distinguished themselves by extending the protection of the Bill of Rights to individuals during the war years when a contrary trend might have been expected.

REBELLION IN CONGRESS

The epic battle over the Court plan left the lawmakers so irritable and exhausted that they adjourned without acting on the rest of Roosevelt's program. He retaliated by calling a special session in October 1937. In the meantime, the temper of Congress had undergone as drastic a change as if an election had intervened. Topheavy Democratic majorities in both houses had been reduced to unreliable ones. Offended by Roosevelt's insistence on making the Court plan an acid test of party loyalty, some moderates from every section of the country joined the southerners in permanent opposition. As a consequence both the special session and the ensuing regular session, which started in January 1938, took great liberties with his program. His demands were either tabled or else passed in emasculated form. Legislation for the six regional TVA's was stifled in committee. Nevertheless, this opposition did not stop construction of dams and power projects, because congressmen habitually sought to please constituents by securing such projects for their districts. Emphasis shifted to piecemeal activities which did not menace the private utility companies so directly as the TVA. Projects like Bonneville and Grand Coulee on the Columbia, Fort Peck on the Missouri, and Big Thompson on the Colorado, were all destined to generate public power, but the navigation, flood control, and irrigation features made them palatable to Congress.

Advocates of the regional TVA's, who argued that public power projects made electricity available to consumers neglected by private companies, were partially consoled by the creation of the Rural Electrification Administration (REA). Roosevelt had set up the agency in 1936 and had allotted $100 million in relief funds for the extension of electrical service to the 80-odd per cent of the nation's farmers who still did not enjoy it. A year later Congress reluctantly empowered the REA to assist farmer cooperatives formed for the erection of transmission lines in rural areas. The organization of such cooperatives was stimulated by loans at low rates of interest. Fearful of controversy, the agency discouraged the formation of cooperatives and the extension of power lines in areas already served by private companies.

Meanwhile the battle over the TVA continued unabated. Flood control, irrigation, and the manufacture of fertilizer did not produce much controversy, but generating and disposing of power kept tempers ruffled. TVA rates for electricity drove down the rates of private companies 33 per cent during the seven years after 1933 compared to 2 per cent for the preceding seven years. Proponents of the agency argued that TVA rates were a fair yardstick, while the power companies insisted the TVA did not need to operate at a profit. During the last three years of the 1930's, power companies that sold their less profitable subsidiaries received considerable public sympathy. In fact, Wendell Willkie made a reputation which ultimately led to a presidential nomination by his heroic fight to secure the investors of Commonwealth and Southern a fair return when the company sold the government a part of its Tennessee properties. This and similar transactions were also preceded by long court battles which went uniformly against the private companies. During the second New Deal an uneasy deadlock developed. Power companies regained strength to block regional projects like the TVA but could not prevent piecemeal extension of facilities in areas where they offered no service because of poor prospects of profit.

Congress also treated roughly the President's plan for the reorganization of government departments. The measure cleared the Senate in the summer of 1938 practically undamaged. Then various semi-independent bureaus which would have lost their identity or freedom of action under the proposed measure, teamed up with the newspapers in a noisy campaign against reorganization. They frightened the public with assertions that the President wanted to be a dictator, and despite his formal denial of the charge the Rules Committee of the House refused to report the bill. Revived a year later, it passed Congress in greatly amended form. The chief disappointment for the President was the exemption of all the independent bureaus and commissions from the provisions of the law. It authorized him to formulate plans for abolishing, consolidating, or regrouping agencies of the executive department in the interest of efficiency and economy and to transmit the plans to Congress. If the legislators did not pass concurrent resolutions disapproving of them within sixty days, the plans would automatically take effect. Six administrative assistants were also provided to help the President with his work. Roosevelt submitted and secured approval for five plans under the terms of the law but lost his concern over the streamlining of government during the war and created dozens of new agencies without regard to whether they encroached on the functions of those already in existence.

WAGES AND HOURS LEGISLATION

The law regarding wages and hours also had to run the gauntlet of numerous amendments despite the fact that recent Supreme Court decisions made invalidation improbable. Most southern congressmen feared that a statutory minimum wage would arrest the migration of industry southward because low labor cost was the principal attraction offered by the region. Northern manufacturers disliked the idea of regulation and believed that it would strengthen the unions. Farmers generally opposed a measure likely to raise the cost of agricultural labor. The turbulent industrial warfare and sit-down strikes of 1936 and 1937 also reduced popular sympathy for the workers. The upshot was that the measure passed the Senate in the fall of 1937 but failed in the House. The Rules Committee continued to bottle it up until May 1938, when Senator Claude Pepper, an outspoken New Dealer, won renomination. This unexpected indication of public sentiment frightened enough southern representatives to secure 218 signatures for a petition discharging the Rules Committee and bringing the bill to the floor of the House. It quickly cleared Congress and received the President's signature on June 25, 1938. In final form it was burdened with amendments exempting important categories such as agricultural workers and domestic servants from its provisions. Known as the Fair Labor Standards Act, it placed a floor of twenty-five cents per hour under the wages of workers engaged in producing goods for interstate commerce. This minimum wage was scheduled to rise gradually until it should reach forty cents in 1945. The law also applied a sliding scale to hours of work, starting with a minimum of forty-four and reducing to forty hours by 1940. Employees were entitled to time and a half for hours worked in excess of the maximum. Children under sixteen years of age were prohibited from working at most occupations, while those under eighteen were limited to jobs that did not involve special hazards. Finally, the Act vested the enforcement of standards in the Wages and Hours Division of the Department of Labor.

Some 300,000 workers received immediate increases as a result of the minimum wage provision and over 1,300,000 benefited from reduction of hours. For a time some employers managed to evade the requirements but by 1940 a high degree of compliance was achieved.

THE AGRICULTURAL LAW OF 1938

Congress showed more willingness to follow the President's lead in framing a comprehensive agricultural law to supplement the stopgap measures enacted immediately after the invalidation of the AAA. Work on the new measure had been begun during the special session of Congress and was completed February 16, 1938. The provisions owed much to the philosophy of Henry Wallace, who drew his inspiration from the biblical account of the food policy pursued by Joseph in Egypt. Like the Old Testament hero, Wallace proposed to store up surplus crops in good years as an insurance against famine. Farmers would be provided a fair income, and consumers an assured supply of food. A variety of subsidy provisions were written into the law to achieve what Wallace called an ever-normal granary.

The soil conservation payments of the 1936 law were broadened and normalized. All farmers became eligible for such payments by adopting conservation practices, except those who produced commodities in excess of market requirements. The latter proviso was to apply if two-thirds of the farmers voted for national acreage allotments on a particular crop. Once the allotments had been approved, all who grew the commodity had to accept individual marketing quotas or forfeit soil conservation payments. Thus for many farmers the payments became a sort of bonus for cooperating in curtailing surpluses.

Other inducements were offered because Wallace regarded the acceptance of quotas as the key weapon for checking overproduction, maintaining price floors, and establishing the ever-normal granary. For the growers of cotton, wheat, corn, rice, and tobacco — nonperishable crops that could be easily stored and seemed likely to be in surplus supply — price support payments were available. At first farmers received payments only when prices fell below 45 per cent of parity, but they reacted so enthusiastically to the subsidy that Congress later raised the supports to 90 per cent of parity.

Farmers who accepted quotas could also receive a third form of assistance from the Commodity Credit Corporation — an organization with functions somewhat like the old Hoover Farm Board. The 1938 law directed the CCC to make loans on cotton, wheat, and corn whenever the supply of these crops was larger than necessary to meet total market requirements or whenever the price fell a certain percentage below parity. It could also make loans on other crops. Under this procedure the farmer received cash loans ranging anywhere from 52 to 75 per cent of parity on his crop. If prices fell below these levels, he kept the cash; if prices rose, he paid off the loan, reclaimed the crop, and sold it on the open market at a profit. It was difficult to lose under this program, particularly if the CCC made an individual crop eligible for loans and if the Secretary of Agriculture did not insist on a farmer referendum establishing quotas. The abuses under this part of the program did not become important during the war years of chronic food shortages but after the war they reached monumental proportions. Growers of all sorts of commodities secured loans by accepting large quotas or in some cases no quotas at all. Such a liberal policy encouraged them to produce ever-larger quantities of unwanted commodities and dump them in the hands of the CCC. The perishable products were sometimes a total loss to the government. Even some proportion of the nonperishable crops spoiled if the government had inadequate storage space or allowed farmers to store crops on their own premises under poor conditions. Thus the Wallace dream of an orderly planned production collapsed under the fierce postwar pressure of agricultural groups who extracted from the administrators the kind of quota system they wanted. The 1938 law neither controlled the surplus nor established a scientific storage program. It did succeed in putting a floor under commodity prices at the cost of ever-larger subsidies to agriculture. The farmers showed their gratitude by switching back to the Republican party in large numbers after 1938. Thereafter they divided their votes so evenly that both parties were afraid to curtail the subsidy program.

The problem of utilizing the food surplus that accumulated on its hands continued to plague the government during the late 1930's. Large-scale gifts to the unemployed aroused the opposition of those who sold such commodities. Even a substantial segment of the general public disliked government distribution of food surpluses and regarded it as a kind of socialism. On the other hand, many of the same people did not like to see commodities dumped abroad at a heavy loss to the taxpayers. The administration experimented with several types of disposal schemes both at home and abroad. The most successful proved to be the Food Stamp Plan inaugurated at Rochester, New York, in May 1939. Through the cooperation of federal and local agencies, families on relief were permitted to buy a weekly minimum of $1.00 or a maximum of $1.50 worth of orange-colored stamps. Grocers accepted these stamps as payment for any product. Those who bought a dollar's worth of orange stamps were given fifty cents' worth of blue stamps which could be used for the purchase of items designated as surplus by the Secretary of Agriculture. The Rochester Plan was so much more acceptable to both merchants and relief clients that over one hundred and fifty cities adopted it during the next two years until World War II temporarily ended the problem.

While Congress was extending the subsidies to farm owners, it put pressure on the President to discontinue some of the more unorthodox types of aid to farm tenants. The controversial Resettlement Administration was abolished in 1937, terminating various experiments in scientific town planning and subsistence homesteads. In its place Roosevelt created a Farm Security Administration to loan money to impoverished farmers. The FSA made loans contingent upon the acceptance of scientific agricultural practices. The Bankhead-Jones Act of 1937 also authorized it to advance money to selected tenants and agricultural laborers for purchasing farms. Such loans averaged $5,000 and were written for forty years at a modest interest of 3 per cent. An estimated 70 per cent of the applicants for FSA help were tenants.

Both the rehabilitation activities and the financial record of the FSA set an enviable standard for efficiency. Clients were taught better methods of cultivation, stock breeding, and sanitation and they were even offered medical care for a small annual fee. However, its success was probably related to the modest scale of its operations. Many tenants worked land which could not have been rehabilitated at any cost, and the majority of migratory farm laborers continued to live under the shocking conditions made famous by John Steinbeck's novel, *The Grapes of Wrath.*

FEDERAL HOUSING LEGISLATION

The sole New Deal reform measure which cleared the rebellious seventy-fifth Congress in 1937 was the Federal Housing Act. Earlier ventures of the administration in the field of housing had been primarily concerned with the stimulation of the languishing construction industry. The Federal Housing Administration, established in 1934, had been authorized by Congress to insure loans made by private institutions for the renovation of old residential units and the construction of new ones. This program encouraged activity by citizens in the middle income brackets but did nothing for the ill-housed third of the nation which Roosevelt referred to in his second inaugural address. Many of the latter inhabited overcrowded slum dwellings. Private contractors could not construct better ones within the rent scale of relief clients or poorly paid laborers. Moreover, the attempt of the PWA to launch slum clearance projects was frustrated by the courts, which would not allow the government to exercise eminent domain, and by the Comptroller General, who ruled that the Housing Authorities would have to charge rent at prevailing rates.

The law of 1937 removed most of the barriers to a slum clearance program. It established the USHA and empowered it to make long-term, low-interest loans to state or local housing agencies which met certain minimum standards. Provision was also made for a federal subsidy to maintain low rent scales. Congress appropriated $526 million to carry the program for three years. Municipal officials hastened to organize housing authorities and qualify for federal aid. Some notorious slums, like the Bowery on Manhattan's lower east side, were improved beyond recognition. However, less than a million people received better homes under the project. Temporarily, real estate interests proved to be better organized than citizens who sought better living quarters, and blocked proposals for broadening the program in 1940.

THE NEW DEAL WAR ON BUSINESS

Despite the various setbacks administered to the New Deal legislative program, Roosevelt carried the war to the enemy on the administrative front. As presidential appointments changed the outlook of quasi-judicial agencies like the Federal Trade Commission and the Interstate Commerce Commission, these agencies treated business with increasing severity. Roosevelt also reversed the NIRA policy of encouraging cooperation between different units of an industry by launching a trust-busting program in 1938. Thurman Arnold, a leading critic of business, was brought from the Yale Law School to head the antitrust division of the Department of Justice. Larger appropriations enabled him to investigate monopolistic practices on a broad front. Since the abortive crusade of Theodore Roosevelt against the trusts, economic developments had strengthened the trend toward business concentration. Moreover, none of the forces that had provided the initial impulse for industrial combinations had ceased to operate. As a result, the fruits of this latest trust-busting drive were to be meager indeed.

Arnold won a few pyrrhic victories against the "block booking" practices of the motion picture industry and the collusive operation of automobile finance companies. He also received some helpful publicity from the Temporary National Economic Committee (TNEC), a sort of 1938 version of the Pujo Committee, which released new data on business concentration. Notwithstanding these disclosures, the voters remained apathetic and the bulk of business unreformed. A half century of agitation had done nothing to restore competition between small private units. By World War II only two types of economic structure seemed possible: a group of privately owned industrial giants engaging in some economic competition but closely regulated by the government, or a group of publicly owned giants operated directly by the government. The ideological predilections of Americans suggested that they would acquiesce in the first without officially accepting it. By the late thirties, trust-busting had degenerated into a New Deal political weapon for harassing opponents. It could no longer be considered seriously as a device for restoring competition. Indeed, in the basic industries competition could not be restored except at the cost of tremendous havoc.

THE 1938 ELECTIONS

The revolt of the southern Democrats against Roosevelt's leadership provoked the President to retaliatory measures in the 1938 elections. He undertook a campaign against party conservatives generally and intervened in several primaries where his foes faced strong opposition. On June 24, 1938, he fired the opening shot in a radio address urging Democratic voters to nominate liberal or New Deal candidates. Two months later, he embarked on a transcontinental political tour. He endorsed some wheelhorses like majority leader Alben W. Barkley of Kentucky and Senator Elmer Thomas of Oklahoma, ignored lukewarm supporters, and specifically called for the defeat of Senators Walter George of Georgia, Millard Tydings of Maryland, and "Cotton Ed" Smith of South Carolina.

Precedents for presidential intervention in midterm party primaries were not very encouraging. Voters treasured their independence in the selection of candidates and usually regarded outside advice as unwarranted interference with states' rights. Southern senators were particularly difficult to dislodge because of the small electorate and the consequent ease with which a political machine could be built up. Moreover, the floodtide of New Deal sentiment had ebbed and voters felt less inclined to do exactly what the President wanted. Most vexing of all, the opposition press described the campaign against disloyal Democrats as a purge — a term which in 1938 terminology suggested a dictatorial effort to crush legitimate opposition. This comparison of Roosevelt's tactics to those of Hitler and Stalin was wildly extravagant, but it improved the prospects of his foes.

The results of the primaries were unfavorable to the President. Some of the incumbents whom he had endorsed won renomination, but so did the senators whom he had tried to defeat. The only scalp he could hang on his belt was that of John J. O'Connor, chairman of the Rules Committee of the House, who had been instrumental in bottling up the Executive Reorganization bill. The general election brought even worse news. Democratic membership in the Senate dropped from 75 to 69, and in the House from 333 to 262. The party still retained a comfortable paper majority. However, the combination of victorious southern Democrats and an enlarged Republican minority was enough to produce a legislative deadlock for the remainder of Roosevelt's second term.

The anti-New Deal coalition declared an unofficial moratorium on social and economic legislation. The only noteworthy laws to clear Congress in the next two years were the Hatch Acts, which sought to prevent the participation of the WPA and other government organizations in political campaigns. Passed at the behest of presidential foes who charged that WPA agents had worked to defeat them in the 1938 elections, the first Hatch Act outlawed the active participation of all but policy-making federal officials in political campaigns. A year later, a second Hatch Act extended the same restrictions to state officials paid partly out of federal funds.

The increasing preoccupation of Roosevelt with foreign relations after 1937 enabled him to accept the new balance of political forces on the domestic front more cheerfully than would otherwise have been the case. In fact, the world crisis helped him re-establish political contact with the southern conservatives and unite the party for the 1940 elections.

Nevertheless, none of these developments killed the New Deal. It had completely lost momentum before outside events rushed in to fill the vacuum. Like earlier reform movements, it had quickly taxed the limited appetite of the voters for institutional change. The tremendous Roosevelt victory of 1936 was an expression of popular gratitude for the economic revival rather than a mandate for fresh experiments. A vast majority had accepted Social Security, government responsibility for direct measures against depression, and comprehensive regulation of business activity as permanent additions to the American system. Rightly or wrongly, these reforms had achieved a status beyond the power of the opposition party to undo if and when it won a presidential election. Notwithstanding the crystallization of this new political consensus which involved a drastic reinterpretation of the Constitution of 1787, the voters did not favor outright competition of government with private enterprise. Nor did they endorse all the Rooseveltian proposals to extend the welfare state. Democratic victories after 1936 owed more to the exploitation of foreign policy issues and the fears of voters that Republican victory would start a new depression. Years were needed for the public to digest the fundamental changes launched in the first and second New Deals.

SUGGESTED READINGS

1. Alsop, J., and Cattledge, T., *The 168 Days.*
2. Corwin, E. S., *The Twilight of the Supreme Court: A History of Our Constitutional Theory.*
3. Pritchett, C. H., *The Roosevelt Court.*

CHAPTER TWENTY-THREE

AMERICAN RESPONSES TO THE BREAKDOWN OF THE POSTWAR STATUS QUO

THREE PHASES OF FOREIGN POLICY

During the depression decade, when Americans were preoccupied with domestic problems, international developments had taken an alarming turn. From 1929 until Pearl Harbor in 1941, the European *status quo* established by the Treaty of Versailles and the Asian *status quo* established by the Washington treaties deteriorated steadily. Only the Western Hemisphere escaped the instability that developed elsewhere.

American policy went through three distinct phases during this period. In the first, which lasted frim 1929 to 1932, the effort of the Hoover administration to preserve the *status quo* through economic cooperation on an international basis, was hampered by an incipient isolationist movement. The second phase started in 1933 with the isolationists gaining the upper hand and continued until mid-1937. Occasional expressions of concern in Washington over world developments sharpened the tone of foreign policy but did not modify its basic orientation toward aloofness from the quarrels of Europe and Asia. In effect, America was gambling that successful aggression anywhere on those continents would not affect her own world position. The third phase of American policy began in 1937 when the expansion of Japan and Germany had proceeded far enough to make Washington aware of the threat to security. At first the country discounted expressions of alarm from the administration and resisted its cautious efforts to take a diplomatic position on the side of the *status quo* powers. Although the minority that supported the President grew larger each time the revisionist states expanded, the isolationists were at first strong enough to prevent Roosevelt from making commitments outside the Hemisphere.

THE MANCHURIAN CRISIS

The Far Eastern *status quo* was the first to break down. A series of brushes between Chinese Nationalists and Japanese troops guarding the South Manchurian Railway reached a climax on September 18–19, 1931, when the Japanese seized Mukden, Changchun, and other cities along the line. The so-called Mukden incident which inaugurated a fourteen-year effort by Japan to conquer China provided an excuse for the reactivation of Tokyo's expansionist program but was not the cause of it. The resort to military action reflected Japanese concern over the rapid comeback of the hitherto weak and disorganized Chinese state.

Its revival had begun in 1924, when the revolutionary leader Dr. Sun Yat-sen entered into close collaboration with the Soviet Union. The latter renounced all extraterritorial privileges and concessions granted to the Tsarist regime, including special political and economic rights in the Chinese Eastern Railway. The treaty implementing these voluntary disavowals was followed by large-scale Bolshevist aid to China — military advisers, army equipment, and financial assistance. The announced reason for this generosity was to help the republican government in Canton reunify China and expel all foreign influence; the ultimate objective was to create a Communist regime. As such, it represented one aspect of an over-all plan to prepare the way for a proletarian revolution in Asia by encouraging agitation against the colonial powers.

The first part of the program worked well enough. The rejuvenated army of the Republic swept triumphantly northward and by 1928 had established a loose control over the whole area south of the Great Wall. War lords in the semiautonomous border provinces pledged their allegiance to the Chinese government, which moved its capital from Canton to Nanking. This operation was accompanied by a revival of antiforeign sentiment reminiscent of the Boxer agitation. Clashes between natives and foreigners took place at Shanghai and Canton in 1925, at Wanhsien in 1926, and at Nanking in 1927.

Meanwhile, General Chiang Kai-shek, the successor of Dr. Sun Yat-sen and leader of the nationalistic Kuomintang party, had discovered the true intentions of the Bolsheviks. So in 1927 he expelled his Russian advisers from the country and the native Communists from positions of influence in the government, the army, and the party. Subsequent withdrawal of Russian aid did not check the energy of the Nationalist movement nor the popular determination to abolish all foreign privileges.

The point of pressure on nonresident powers at the end of the 1920's was in Manchuria, where the Japanese had railroad concessions, harbor leases, and other economic privileges. In December 1929, Nanking prevailed upon Chang Hsueh-liang, the local Manchurian war lord, to acknowledge the suzerainty of China. This move was paralleled by the organization of boy-

"If we don't hang together, will we all hang separately?" (The Daily Express, *London, 1933.*)

cotts against Japanese goods and a variety of measures designed to destroy the value of Japanese treaty rights in South Manchuria. Simultaneously the government sought to deprive Russia of her last remaining foothold in North Manchuria. Matters came to a head in March 1930, when Nationalist forces seized the Chinese Eastern Railway and arrested Russian employees of the road. Moscow reacted so sharply that Nanking backed down in order to avert a war for which it was not ready.

All these developments were deeply disturbing to Japan. She relied on Manchuria for an increasing supply of raw materials to feed her industrial machine and as an outlet for surpluses both of population and of manufactured goods. Apart from immediate interests she had certain long-range objectives which depended upon domination of China. Accordingly, after pursuing an unadventuresome policy during the 1920's while consolidating the gains of World War I, she decided to upset the *status quo* in the fall of 1931.

This resolve was based on a coincidence of factors. The increasingly aggressive behavior of the Chinese put a premium on preventive action before they became stronger, and at the same time the disunity of the nonresident powers minimized the prospect of effective retaliatory action. Great Britain had recently gone off the gold standard and was preoccupied with her domestic crisis. France was devoting her attention to the maintenance of the *status quo* in Central Europe. Like Great Britain, the United States was wrestling with the depression, and the American public could be counted upon to oppose a policy that might lead either to war or to the imposition of economic sanctions on Japan.

THE STIMSON DOCTRINE

Accordingly, when Japan followed the occupation of strong points along the South Manchurian railroad on September 19 and 20 with a conquest of the entire province, the nonresident powers reacted indecisively. Each was determined to avoid involvement in military operations in behalf of China and to place the blame for inaction on the shoulders of others if possible. The complicated and overlapping character of the arrangements for maintaining the *status quo* encouraged reliance on this kind of strategy. The United States was certain to balk at collective action under the auspices of the League of Nations. Therefore the European states could cover up their own reluctance by invoking the Covenant and by rejecting as inadequate any American counterproposals for action under the Nine-Power Treaty. A similar deadlock could be expected over the question of League enforcement of the Kellogg-Briand Pact.

China set the ponderous League machinery in motion on September 21 by appealing to the Council, which promptly commenced hearings. As expected, the United States took a somewhat independent line. On September 22, Secretary of State Stimson informed the Japanese ambassador that America was gravely concerned over the threat to the Kellogg-Briand Pact and the Nine-Power Treaty. In response to an invitation from the Council he appointed Prentiss Gilbert of the American consulate in Geneva to attend sessions on the dispute. He reduced the value of this gesture, however, by making it clear that America would not be bound by any collective decisions and that she would not even discuss any subject except the Kellogg-Briand Pact. Eventually the Council, despite unofficial American opposition, adopted a resolution on December 10, 1931, establishing a neutral commission under the chairmanship of Lord Lytton to make an investigation. The commission was authorized to visit Manchuria and report its recommendations back to the Council.

Opinion differs as to whether the negative attitude of Washington toward the League activity offered Japan comfort and encouragement. Apparently the policy was predicated partly on the belief that the Japanese military clique had launched the invasion in defiance of the Cabinet and that restraint would facilitate restoration of civilian control over foreign affairs in Tokyo. In December the opposite development occurred and the moderate government was replaced by one more responsive to the army. The methodical mopping up of isolated pockets of Chinese resistance in Manchuria continued. When Chinchow, the last Chinese stronghold in the southern part of the province, fell on January 2, 1932, Washington was confronted with the painful necessity of formulating a new policy.

Events of the preceding three months had not appreciably changed popular opinion in America. The habit of reacting indignantly to adverse developments in the Far East was so deep-seated that denunciations of Japan were widespread. Nevertheless, the most vocal segments of the press, the pulpit, and the major political parties coupled their condemnation with assertions that the United States ought to mind its own business. Senator Borah of Idaho spoke for a growing isolationist group when he urged complete withdrawal of American forces from China. President Hoover did not belong to this school, but he was a pacifist by conviction and unwilling to take any steps that carried risk of war. Only Secretary Stimson favored an energetic response. The President vetoed his proposal for the imposition of economic sanctions against Japan on the dual grounds that they might provoke armed retaliation and might contract still further America's dwindling foreign trade. The only remaining alternative was a verbal chastisement of Tokyo. Such a maneuver seemed likely to fail since Japan was aware of the strong isolationist sentiment in America.

Stimson, seeing the desirability of joint action, asked Great Britain and France to associate themselves with a policy of refusing to recognize political changes in the Far Eastern *status quo* that were accomplished by force. He proposed to base this stand on the Japanese violation of the Nine-Power Treaty rather than on violation of the League Covenant. This policy was precisely what the British and French did not want. They feared that Washington would be unwilling to follow up strong diplomatic representations with action, and furthermore they had already reconciled themselves to remaining in the Orient on Japanese terms and were in a position to keep the League from offending Tokyo. When they declined to cooperate, Stimson addressed a joint note to China and Japan on January 7, 1932. It announced the refusal of the United States to recognize any impairment of its treaty rights or any assaults on the territorial and administrative integrity of China. The Stimson Doctrine of nonrecognition was to be a cornerstone of America's Far Eastern policy throughout the 1930's. It had no immediate effect, however, except to demonstrate the disunity of the nonresident powers and hence to encourage fresh assaults on China.

After establishing a puppet state called Manchukuo in mid-January 1932, Japan dispatched an invasion armada to Shanghai in retaliation for a Chinese boycott. The initial bombardment of the city took place on January 28 and was followed by a month of sporadic fighting, disorder, and terror. The Japanese quickly got the upper hand and wantonly destroyed human life and property. This renewal of aggression prodded Stimson into restating the American position on February 23, 1932, in a long public letter to Senator Borah, the chairman of the Senate Foreign Relations Committee. The League Assembly passed a resolution along similar lines on March 11,

1932. In effect it committed League members to withholding recognition of the puppet state of Manchukuo if the Lytton Commission subsequently found Japan to be the aggressor. The Commission did not report until October 2, 1932, when it issued an exhaustive analysis of the controversy. It denied Japanese claims that they had invaded Manchuria in self-defense and recommended the creation of an autonomous Manchuria within the Chinese Republic. Several weeks were spent by a committee of nineteen from the League Assembly in a futile attempt to secure Japanese acceptance of the report. When finally the Assembly passed a resolution declaring that Japan had violated the League Covenant, Nipponese representatives walked out of the session. Tokyo followed this gesture of defiance by giving notice of its withdrawal from the League on March 27, 1933. The great powers were reluctant to support the legal judgment, which was promoted by the small powers in the Assembly, and balked at the use of sanctions or other collective measures of discipline.

By allowing Tokyo to depart unscathed, the League demonstrated the inability of an organization of sovereign states to override the wishes of individual members. More important, the whole incident served notice that Great Britain and France, the dominant League powers, had no intention of checking the revisionist program of Japan either as members of a world organization or as sovereign states. Henceforward they could no longer be counted upon as effective participants in the Far Eastern balance.

AMERICAN FAR EASTERN POLICY (1933–37)

The revolutionary modification of power relationships in the Orient necessitated a reappraisal of American policy. The Stimson Doctrine had been formulated to preserve the *status quo* of the 1920's, with the United States balancing off the other nonresident states against Japan. By 1933, however, the European powers that had signed the Washington treaties were out of the picture, Russia was a doubtful quantity, and China, on the other hand, had graduated from the status of a prize of the great powers to a weak but contending factor in the balance.

The new alignment opened two major alternatives for the United States. Either it could try to preserve the *status quo* enunciated in the Stimson Doctrine by committing more American power in behalf of China or it could accept a new and less favorable Japanese version of the *status quo*. If it intended to head off further Nipponese expansion at the expense of China, prompt economic retaliation against Tokyo was essential. In view of Japan's sensitivity to economic pressure from Washington in 1940 and 1941, it seems likely that such a policy would have served as a brake on expansion in the mid-1930's before Tokyo became heavily involved on the mainland.

The incoming Roosevelt administration behaved as if it were prepared to acquiesce in additional Japanese modifications. From 1933 to 1937 it failed to contest the piecemeal encroachments in China, ignored the Stimson Doctrine, and declined to build up American naval strength to the level authorized under the London Treaty of 1930. Even the occasional protests against Japanese treaty violations, which had accompanied the recession of American influence between 1913 and 1918, were avoided.

The intensification of isolationist sentiment is usually relied upon to justify the trend of American policy during Roosevelt's first term. Undoubtedly a number of forces outside the control of the President helped to generate pressure for a wholesale reduction of commitments overseas. These factors will be evaluated in connection with American-European relations in the thirties (pages 552–555) because they arose mostly out of popular fear of involvement in a European war. Still, the President's contribution cannot be ignored. His preoccupation with domestic problems suggests that he shared the outlook of his fellow countrymen. Undoubtedly his example promoted indifference to Far Eastern affairs.

Tokyo drew the expected conclusions from American apathy. The most obvious springboard for fresh assaults was Manchukuo from which Japanese troops moved south and west to the Great Wall. They occupied all the intervening territory as well as the Chinese province of Jehol. Completely deserted by the nonresident powers, Nanking confirmed Japanese control of this area in the Truce of T'ang-ku, May 31, 1933. Japan devoted eighteen months to the consolidation of her gains. By the spring of 1935 she had resumed her southward push, overrunning the next tier of five provinces in northen China under the guise of an autonomy movement. Washington and London took cognizance of this maneuver on December 5, 1935, by dispatching a joint note of reminder to Tokyo that both governments were "closely observing" developments and would protect their treaty rights. Japan ignored this vague warning, and the observers lapsed into their customary silence. Penetration of these new areas was always followed by the imposition of discriminatory tariffs, taxes, railroad rates, harbor fees, and other imposts which made a mockery of the Open Door and the Washington treaties. Tokyo justified the exclusion of other states from normal economic intercourse with China by announcing a "Japanese Monroe Doctrine" for East Asia. This policy was stated semiofficially on April 17, 1934, but evoked only a mild protest from Washington twelve days later. The State Department's reaction was equally restrained when Tokyo evicted American, British, and Dutch oil firms from Manchukuo the same year.

While Japan advanced on the mainland, she took measures to upset the *status quo* in naval power in the Pacific and thereby minimize the risk of retaliation. On December 29, 1934, she gave the required two-year notice that she would no longer accept the 5:5:3 ratio in capital ships which had been reaffirmed in the London Treaty of 1930. Reiteration of her demand for naval parity at a second London conference in the fall of 1935 produced a deadlock. After she bolted the conference, American, British,

French, and Italian delegates agreed to a new formula for limitation of naval armaments. This new London Treaty of 1936 was meaningless, of course, without the adherence of the Japanese, and the self-imposed restrictions soon became a dead letter.

Washington responded to the Japanese notice canceling the London Treaty with naval maneuvers in oriental waters. The effectiveness of this gesture was impaired by the persistent American refusal to increase the size of the fleet even to the authorized levels. Congress passed legislation for the construction of capital ships but appropriated no funds for construction, with the result that the naval position of the United States in the Pacific deteriorated steadily from 1931 to 1938. The impression that she intended to reduce her Far Eastern commitments was confirmed by passage of the Tydings-McDuffie Act of March 1934, which established timetables for Philippine independence and scheduled complete American withdrawal for 1946.

The only move that held out hope of bolstering America's position was recognition of the Soviet Union on November 16, 1933. Since the Russian revolution of 1917, successive administrations had resisted the establishment of diplomatic relations with the Bolshevik regime. Washington had felt justified in withholding recognition because the Communists refused to recognize debts incurred by former governments and to refrain from plotting the overthrow of capitalist states. Roosevelt took the initiative in reopening official contact, mostly to encourage the revival of trade between the two countries. On invitation from the White House, Maxim Litvinoff, the Soviet Commissar of Foreign Affairs, came to Washington for negotiations which were to end in an exchange of ambassadors. Litvinoff assured a favorable outcome by agreeing to negotiate settlements of American claims and debts and by giving formal assurances that Russia would stop Communist propaganda in the United States. Since the Soviets did not subsequently honor these pledges, the revival of trade did not materialize. On the other hand, the determination of the Soviet Union to protect its interest in northern Manchuria prevented Japan from concentrating complete attention on China and Southeast Asia.

Meanwhile, four years of feeble protests from the United States and other nonresident powers against encroachments on China's northern provinces encouraged Tokyo to resume full-scale warfare. A brush between Nationalist and Japanese troops in the outskirts of Peking on July 7, 1937, provided an excuse for the invasion of China. Neglecting the formality of a war declaration, Tokyo carried out the assault simultaneously by land and by air. Heavy bombardment of Shanghai, Nanking, Canton, and Hankow inflicted severe damage on property and resulted in the death of numerous noncombatants. The Chinese resisted doggedly, but they were no match for the well-equipped Japanese armies. The major cities on the mainland fell one by one and the Nationalist forces retreated slowly into the interior. Japan continued to display great striking power, but by the end of 1938 she was bogged down in sparsely settled western China where guerrilla units harassed her overextended supply lines.

The undeclared war in China forced the nonresident powers to reappraise their Far Eastern positions. The massive Japanese aerial assaults on overcrowded Chinese cities provoked world-wide denunciations. Pressure mounted on occidental governments to make specific protests against the destruction of the lives and property of their nationals in the foreign section of Shanghai and other cities.

The slowness of the reactions of policy makers in Washington confirmed both the weakness of the American military establishment and the official reluctance to consider Far Eastern developments seriously. At the outset Roosevelt refused to recognize the existence of the war, because recent neutrality legislation would have required him to apply an arms embargo against both belligerents. He was technically within his rights because neither side had declared war. Most commentators, however, interpreted his decision as a gesture to aid the Chinese, on the theory that the Nationalist government would be helped more by arms shipments than Japan would be hurt by being denied them. This reasoning was probably justified since the embargo did not cover such crucial items for the Japanese war machine as gasoline, fuel oil, and scrap iron.

On July 16, 1937, Secretary of State Hull made a general announcement that the United States would apply the principles of the Good Neighbor policy to the Far East. He did not mention China specifically but reiterated American determination to avoid entangling alliances and to cooperate in modifying treaties as the need arose "by orderly process." This statement implied that the United States would accept some modification of the Far Eastern *status quo* provided the Japanese were willing to use negotiation rather than war. However, a supplementary assertion on August 16 took a different tack and came close to a reaffirmation of the Stimson Doctrine of nonrecognition.

RETREAT IN EUROPE PARALLELS RETREAT IN ASIA

While struggling irresolutely in the summer of 1937 against the consequences of a four-year withdrawal from the Far East, Washington also discovered that a similar policy in Europe had begun to yield the same results. The eight-year cycle of American-European relations had opened in 1929 with an effort on the part of the Hoover administration to find some basis for cooperation on the general problems of depression and disarmament. This approach was abandoned by Roosevelt in 1933. Preoccupied with his domestic recovery program, the President virtually ignored Europe during his first term. Notwithstanding his disposition to retreat from an active role in both theaters, American withdrawal was more complete in Europe than in Asia. Several factors help to explain this development. For one thing, nothing authoritative like Washington's warning against entanglements in Europe existed to discourage American involvement in the Orient. Secondly, the history of the preceding thirty years had accustomed Americans to regard European stability as self-sustaining and Far Eastern stability as dependent upon their intervention. Except during World War I, the Old World had curbed revisionist powers without the help of the United States, whereas Asia had needed the sustained vigilance of Washington to keep colonial powers from getting out of hand.

The tendency to participate systematically in the Far Eastern balance was also encouraged by the tacit assumption that war would be less likely to result from such activity in Asia than in Europe. This belief, in turn, owed something to feelings about the superiority of whites over Orientals which developed at the turn of the century. A final factor which affected the American outlook was a deeply rooted disposition to defend existing treaty obligations. Americans had made no commitments to uphold the Versailles settlement, but they had associated themselves with naval disarmament and Four-Power and Nine-Power treaties to preserve the Far Eastern *status quo*. Whatever the relative importance of each consideration, the cumulative effect was to make the United States more fearful of involvement in Europe than in the Orient.

BREAKDOWN OF THE VERSAILLES SETTLEMENT

The history of American-European relations between 1929 and 1937 begins with the Great Depression, which affected both the power structure of Europe and the attitude of the Continental states toward Uncle Sam. During the first phase of the economic crisis (1929–33) its impact on Europe was twofold: (1) it gradually destroyed the will and the ability of the French to impose the crippling economic clauses of the Versailles Treaty on Germany; (2) it killed the disposition of the great powers to cooperate on economic problems. Restrictions on the movement of commodities and gold slowly multiplied. Democracies and dictatorships alike brought trade with foreign countries under state control, limited imports, and took precautions against retaliatory measures by their neighbors.

The United States was involved in the intensification of European economic warfare because of her efforts as a creditor to collect war debts. In an earlier chapter we noted that the United States had repeatedly insisted that there was no connection between the debts owed her by her wartime allies and the reparations paid to them by the Germans. We also observed at the same time that the international banking fraternity had destroyed the practical value of this distinction by drawing American capital into the intricate network of intergovernmental loans. Between 1924 and 1930, American businessmen had invested nearly $2.5 billion in a variety of German enterprises. In addition, the Young Plan of 1929 had recognized the interlocking character of the debt structure by making the semiannual reparations installments of the Germans approximately equivalent to the semiannual debt installments of their European creditors to the United States. Washington might say anything it pleased about the separation of reparations and war debts; the fact remained that the United States kept the system going by loaning money to the Germans. Their government siphoned off these funds for reparations payments to the Allies, who in turn used them for debt payments to the United States.

Trouble was bound to develop when the depression stopped what looked like a perpetual-motion machine. The ink had scarcely dried on the Young Plan before heavily industrialized states like Germany and Great Britain began to experience distress and to look for ways to avoid its provisions. Austria and other Central European countries with flimsy postwar financial structures also felt the immediate impact of the depression. Meanwhile, the stock market crash of October 1929 and the deterioration of prospects of profit frightened American investors. They shut off the flow of long-term investment capital to Germany and Austria, but not of short-term notes which presumably carried less risk. In the spring of 1931 Chancellor Brüning of Germany sought to avert an economic crisis by proposing a customs union to a willing Austria. France, interpreting this bid as a preliminary feeler for a merger of the two countries, acted promptly to block it. After some prodding from their government, French bankers, who held a substantial fraction of the outstanding German and Austrian short-term notes, demanded immediate payment. Unable to withstand the pressure, Brüning withdrew the projected union but not in time to stop a disastrous run on German and Austrian banks. On May 11, 1931, the oldest financial institution in Central Europe, the Kredit-Anstalt of Vienna, failed. The news of the disaster created a panic in German money markets and led to heavy withdrawals of gold.

THE HOOVER MORATORIUM

Germany hovered on the edge of bankruptcy. She could not meet the payments on her short-term notes, to say nothing of her impending $1 billion reparations installment. France had done most to create this dangerous situation. She regarded financial chaos in the Reich as the best guarantee against the revival of German power. Unlike the other Western European states, France had thus far escaped the worst effects of the depression and expected her favorable position to continue. Consequently she intended to take retaliatory financial action against any powers that attempted to rescue Germany. Like France, the United States with its mixed agricultural and industrial system was to experience a relatively delayed reaction to the world-wide slump. Nevertheless the Hoover administration took a graver view of the German crisis than did Paris. It had refused to join the British in granting the Brüning government stopgap financial aid prior to the failure of the Kredit-Anstalt. The subsequent business panic alerted Hoover to the possibility that Germany would suspend payments on a wide range of bonds and short-term notes held by American investors. Fearful of a German default on all obligations if the European states tried to collect the reparations installment due on July 1, 1931, the President proposed a one-year moratorium on all intergovernmental payments.

This unexpected American gesture of international cooperation was made on June 21. It came too late to give much of a psychological boost to the sagging economies of Europe. The President did not delay his offer because he doubted its wisdom but because he feared an adverse political reaction at home. Great Britain, Germany, and a number of smaller states accepted the moratorium immediately. France temporarily withheld consent because she resented any interference with her policy of reducing Germany to financial impotence. It required only two weeks to convince the French that the Weimar Republic would escape bankruptcy, whereupon they accepted the moratorium and availed themselves of its benefits. Simultaneously they tried to discourage London and Washington from further financial operations in behalf of Germany by promoting fresh withdrawals of gold from both countries. Acting through the official Bank of France, they managed to drive England off the gold standard on September 21, 1931. This eliminated John Bull as a source of credit for the states of Central Europe and left them at the mercy of France. A similar government-inspired liquidation of French assets on Wall Street fed deflationary forces in the United States but fell short of its immediate objective. Having failed to break American financial power in a test of strength, France promptly switched to the alternate method of persuasion. Prime Minister Laval paid a special visit to Washington on October 22 for three days of conversation with Hoover. His twofold purpose was to extract from America a pledge of noninterference in the financial affairs of Germany and a reduction of the French war debt.

Hoover readily agreed not to renew the moratorium but refused to commit himself on the debt issue. In professing his willingness to have the French take the initiative after the expiration of the moratorium, the President made a virtue of necessity. His experiment in international cooperation had encountered a critical reception at home. Most Americans feared that the moratorium was the preliminary step to a general debt cancellation and stoutly opposed any relaxation of European obligations. Hoover had accurately assessed the popular mood because when Congress reconvened, in December 1931, it ratified the one-year moratorium but rejected a presidential request for the creation of a commission to re-examine the entire debt structure.

France and most of the remaining European states continued to hope that the United States would relax its position if they scaled down German obligations. Sentiment for such a step grew rapidly during the spring of 1932 as economic conditions deteriorated. In mid-June, on the eve of the expiration of the moratorium, the states of Western and Central Europe met at Lausanne, Switzerland. By this time it had become apparent that the Weimar Republic could no longer make reparations payments and that her creditors would not load the burden of debts owed to America on their own people. Even the French had begun to feel the repercussions of the depression and recognized the risk of further demands on Germany. The common misery created a spirit of liberality and they lowered German reparations to $714 million. Their action came close to being an outright cancellation, since they had originally billed the Weimar Republic for $33 billion. On the other hand, they made their new arrangement with Germany contingent upon American willingness to accept a similar cancellation of war debts.

Popular reaction in the United States proved to be uniformly hostile. With economic paralysis spreading, taxpayers were in no mood to assume the fresh burden of the European war debt. Parallel discussions of disarmament at the Geneva conference, which had opened in February 1932, fanned American resentment because a group of powers headed by the French resisted reductions in armaments and military expenditure while stoutly insisting that they were too poor to pay the war debt. This stand smacked of hypocrisy to most Americans, particularly after the French bloc had given an indifferent reception to a dramatic Hoover proposal of June 22, 1932, for a flat one-third reduction of all land and naval forces. The position of France and her allies continued to be that they would not sacrifice their military superiority over Germany without pledges of automatic help from Great Britain and the United States. Since both states steadfastly refused to give the necessary guarantees, the bloc persisted in its policy of heavy expenditures for armaments. The Geneva Disarmament Conference held intermittent sessions until February 1934, by which time German rearmament had proceeded far enough to make further discussions useless.

The protracted deadlock between the United States and Europe over the interrelated questions of war debts and disarmament stimulated the rapid revival of American isolationist sentiment in the summer of 1932. Hoover bowed to these pressures during his last months in the White House. On July 14, 1932, he denounced the Lausanne agreement and reaffirmed the traditional American insistence that reparations and war debts were separate questions. However, intergovernmental payments gradually came to a halt. Germany discontinued reparations installments after the Lausanne conference; France and most of the Continental states defaulted when debt payments to the United States fell due on December 15, 1932. Great Britain, Czechoslovakia, Italy, Finland, Latvia, and Lithuania met their obligations as usual, partly because Hoover had held out some hope of relief by agreeing to American participation in a conference on economic questions. The next installments fell due on June 15, 1933, during the London Economic Conference, and this group of states made token payments. When the conference broke up without any offers of relief from the new American President, Franklin Roosevelt, they suspended payments altogether. Only Finland, which enjoyed a favorable balance of trade with the United States, continued to meet its semiannual installments in full.

THE LONDON ECONOMIC CONFERENCE

To the end of his term as President, Hoover stoutly maintained that the depression had been caused by world conditions and could be cured only by international cooperation. One of his last acts before retiring from the White House was to commit the United States to discussions at London on world economic problems. By the time the delegates convened on June 12, 1933, control over American foreign policy had passed to Franklin Roosevelt. The new President refused to allow the problem of war debts to be placed on the agenda despite the insistence of several European governments that settlement of the issue was a prerequisite for the revival of international trade.

With the discussion of intergovernmental payments excluded, the delegates struggled to find a basis for agreement on tariff reduction and currency stabilization. It soon became apparent that the United States was not disposed to compromise on those issues either. Low-tarriff countries like Great Britain held out for a rate-cutting plan that would bring neighboring tariff walls down to their level. The United States countered with a proposal for a flat percentage cut, which meant a trifling reduction of the high schedules established by the Smoot-Hawley law of 1930. Although Secretary of State Cordell Hull, who headed the American delegation, was a firm defender of low tariffs, he could not commit Roosevelt to a policy of wholesale reductions.

While the delegates searched for a compromise formula on tariff cuts, the United States refused to agree to currency stabilization. The question had become important in 1931 when a number of states had gone off the gold standard and cheapened the value of their monetary units to stimulate exports. During the ensuing two years devaluation reached epidemic proportions. Roosevelt had taken the United States off the gold standard in March 1933, and had let the dollar sink to 59 cents by mid-April. However, he had given informal assurances on the eve of the London conference that the United States would consent to currency stabilization. What made him change his mind was a mild price rise and business revival in America during May and June. Fearful that international stabilization would jeopardize his domestic recovery program, he radioed a message which was read to the conference on July 4, 1933, rebuking the delegates for concentrating on monetary questions. Known alternately as "the bombshell" message and the "Second Declaration of Independence," it destroyed the incentive of other states to compromise and, although the conference dragged on for three additional weeks, economic recovery on an international basis was dead. Thus, Roosevelt made his debut on the world stage as an isolationist.

America did not bear sole responsibility for the situation. Other states clung just as stubbornly to their positions. Germany appeared briefly in the role of obstructor, while the Soviet Union did not receive an invitation to the conference or show any desire to cooperate with capitalist countries. Nevertheless it is difficult to avoid the conclusion that the negative attitude of America hastened the drift of European states toward economic nationalism.

INTENSIFICATION OF ISOLATIONIST SENTIMENT

The decision to spurn world leadership on this occasion rested primarily with President Roosevelt. His behavior has often been explained as a capitulation to irresistible isolationist pressure against his better judgment. This view is difficult to accept because he enjoyed unique freedom of action in 1933. It is true that he did not have unlimited choice of alternatives in foreign affairs, but he was certainly secure enough politically to soften a policy that he opposed. Hence his uncompromising statement to the London conference ought to be taken at face value. It indicates that he began his Presidency as a leader of the isolationists rather than as their captive. His brand of isolationism tended to be pragmatic. It was reflected in his determination to sacrifice international cooperation in the interest of domestic economic recovery. Unlike the theorists who wanted to build a Chinese Wall between the United States and Europe, he merely wanted to ignore Europe altogether. The casual attitude of the debtor nations toward their obligations increased his temptation to do so. Moreover, he shared the view of most Americans that the security of the United States would not be affected by any developments in Europe. On this assumption he virtually ignored European affairs from 1933 to 1936. Like Harding, he deviated from his position long enough in 1934 to recommend American membership on the World Court. He also urged selective tariff cuts. The Senate rejected the first proposal, but both houses passed a bill in June 1934, authorizing him to negotiate trade agreements and put them into effect without legislative approval. He was empowered to cut rates by as much as 50 per cent in return for reciprocal concessions from other countries. In effect, the Democrats took the reciprocity principle from the G.O.P. and substituted it for their traditional policy of wholesale tariff reductions. On this basis Roosevelt negotiated fourteen separate agreements during the next three years. Congress renewed the Act in 1937 and again in 1940. Inasmuch as the Smoot-Hawley tariff had established the highest rates in American history, the limited reductions under these agreements did not result in the abandonment of the protectionist principle. Aside from these two modest gestures of international cooperation, the President concentrated on his domestic recovery program. His prevailing emphasis on economic nationalism created an atmosphere favorable to the growth of more extreme isolationist theories, which were translated into legislative restrictions on American foreign policy.

Probably the most important idea to catch the popular fancy was the familiar doctrine that the pursuit of foreign economic interests produces wars. This belief had begun to gain respectability in 1932 when the Senate Banking and Currency Committe investigated the business in foreign securities. In addition to the discovery that Wall Street manipulators had tricked the public into buying many unsound issues, the committee had also uncovered evidence of a close connection between overseas investment and foreign policy. Following this clue, isolationists began to search for data on steel manufacturers and munitions makers which would prove that they had promoted World War I. A widely quoted article "Arms and the Man" in *Fortune* magazine (March 1934) dwelt on the international character of the armament business. Sensational books like George Seldes' *Iron, Blood, and Profits* and H. C. Engelbrecht and F. C. Henighen's *Merchants of Death* took up the same theme. Gerald P. Nye, with the support of Robert M. La Follette, Jr., Burton K. Wheeler, George W. Norris, and other Senate isolationists therefore worked a resolution through the upper house, in April 1934, establishing a special committee to investigate the munitions industry. Under the chairmanship of Nye the committee made several discoveries: (1) that native bankers who had loaned money to the British and French favored American participation in World War I on the Allied side, (2) that the warring coalitions of Europe had bombarded the United States with propaganda designed to promote sympathy and active support, (3) that American industrial firms were prone to accept orders for war materials from hostile as well as from friendly powers, and (4) that the War Department in Washington kept on file military plans for use against potential enemies. To a contemporary reader, the pursuit of such activities would seem like a normal feature of international politics. To the average American of the middle 1930's, however, the revelation that private economic groups within states possessed interests was repulsive; that these groups would promote such interests by a variety of methods, including war, was startling beyond belief. Nye skillfully activated dormant isolationist sentiments. His investigation popularized the simple thesis that self-interested parties at home and abroad had tricked Uncle Sam into an unnecessary war against Germany. Citizens who accepted Nye's conclusions also shared his faith in preventive legislation. They felt that the United States could avoid involvement in another European war if Americans were protected against their temptation to get a stake in the outcome. The crystallization of this sentiment in 1934–35 paved the way for the short-lived experiment of legislating neutrality.

NEUTRALITY LEGISLATION

The first step was taken on April 14, 1934, when Congress passed the Johnson Act. It prohibited American citizens and corporations from loaning money to any country which had defaulted on its debt payments to the United States. More comprehensive legislation followed in August 1935 making it unlawful for American vessels to carry munitions or implements of war if the ultimate destination of the shipment was a belligerent port. A companion provision authorized the President to disavow government responsibility for American citizens who ignored an official warning and traveled on the ships of belligerent powers. Roosevelt disliked the restraints imposed on his executive authority by the mandatory arms embargo and prevailed upon Congress to limit the life of the measure to six months. Matters soon passed out of his control, however, and the legislators extended the arms embargo to May 1, 1937. On the eve of its expiration, in February 1936, they also added several amendments. The first required the President to ban loans and credits to belligerents, but permitted him to decide whether a state of war existed; the second compelled him to invoke the neutrality legislation against states that entered a war after the outbreak of hostilities; and the third exempted any American republic at war with a nonhemispheric state from the provisions of the Act.

If Roosevelt disliked the second neutrality law, which deprived him of discretionary authority to aid the victims of aggression, he gave no indication of it during the 1936 campaign. In fact on January 6, 1937, he accepted without complaint a congressional resolution applying the familiar bans against American involvement in the Spanish Civil War.

Permanent neutrality legislation superseded the patchwork of laws and resolutions on May 1, 1937. The new measure re-enacted all the earlier restrictions on the export of loans and war materials to belligerents. The provision of the 1935 law disclaiming responsibility for American citizens traveling on belligerent vessels was turned into an outright prohibition of such travel. Dissension among isolationists over whether shipments of raw materials would constitute a violation of neutrality resulted in a compromise amendment. It empowered the President to insist that belligerents who purchased nonmilitary commodities pay cash for them and transport them away from the United States. This so-called "cash and carry" clause was to expire after two years unless Congress renewed it.

The neutrality law of 1937 climaxed the effort of isolationists to eliminate all sources of friction between the United States and Europe. It was a monument to the faith that economic interests and travel on belligerent ships were responsible for American involvement in 1917 and that the prohibition of such activities would guarantee peace. This estimate of the motivation of foreign policy contained an element of truth and attracted many people who were not isolationists. But it failed to take account of American security requirements which had also created pressure for intervention on the side of the Allies. The problem of protecting America's world position continued to exist in the 1920's and 1930's and would ultimately draw the United States into a second world war. The isolationists left the question out of their calculations because they wanted to believe that developments in Europe were irrelevant to the welfare of America.

Words fail to convey the intensity of the popular commitment to the isolationist viewpoint between 1934 and 1938. The lonely Cassandras who professed alarm over German and Italian aggression were either dismissed as unwitting mouthpieces of British propaganda or denounced as agents of munitions makers and international bankers. College students agitated for the abolition of military training at land-grant colleges and solemnly swore that they would not fight except in defense of American soil. Pacifist organizations rapidly gained recruits and vied with one another in extravagant pleas for disbanding the armed forces. A Gallup Poll in April 1937 demonstrated the effectiveness of the isolationist-pacifist agitation when it reported that 70 per cent of those queried considered American participation in World War I to have been a mistake. A kindred distrust of executive discretion in foreign policy provided inspiration for proposals to make American participation in armed conflict contingent upon majority approval. A resolution introduced by Representative Louis Ludlow called for a national war referendum except in cases of an armed invasion of America or her possessions. The Ludlow resolution reached the floor of the House over the opposition of the administration and was narrowly defeated on January 10, 1938, by a vote of 209 to 188. The extraordinary grass-roots support for this visionary proposal reinforced the verdict of the Gallup Poll.

HITLER AND MUSSOLINI ON THE MARCH

The growth of isolationist sentiment during the middle thirties coincided with the rise of a genuine threat to the stability of Europe. Earlier chapters on the Versailles settlement have already called attention to the inherent instability of the postwar balance. Enforcement rested upon a weak but willing France and a reluctant, irresolute Great Britain whose principal interests were overseas rather than on the Continent. These two powers faced the herculean responsibility of policing Germany, Italy, and Russia and maintaining order in the huge vacuum area from the Baltic to the Mediterranean. Despite the partial reversion of Great Britain to a policy of aloofness, France proved adequate to the task of enforcing the *status quo* during the 1920's. Her temporary success was due to the exhaustion of Germany, the reduced nuisance value of an Italy without strong allies, and the diplomatic isolation of Russia. Furthermore, though the depression eventually destroyed her ability to preserve this artificial superiority, she was among the last of the industrial countries to feel its effects. We have already noted that she had sufficient financial power between 1929 and 1932 to preserve economic ascendancy over depression-ridden Germany and to retaliate successfully against Germany's would-be rescuers. This policy thwarted Hoover's efforts to make a contribution to European stability and weakened the economic position of the British. Both emerged from the episode with less incentive to intervene on the Continent.

No sooner had the French established sole dominance over Germany in 1932 than the full force of the depression hit them and forced them to relax their grip. This development occurred just at the time that Hitler came to power and the Reich began to recover from its economic distress. Some revision of the Versailles Treaty would have been inevitable in any event, but the interaction of four factors enabled the Germans to get completely out of hand and to make a bid for control of Europe. They were as follows: (1) the maniacal fury of Hitler, who pushed the economic resurgence of Germany at breakneck speed and who concealed his wild revisionist objectives behind a deluge of promises that deceived the unwary; (2) the economic collapse of France, which sapped her will to check Hitler at a time when he might have been stopped cheaply; (3) the fatal disagreement of the French and British about Hitler's intentions, with the latter assuming that his objectives were limited and restraining Paris on critical occasions; (4) the aloofness of the United States and its tendency to withdraw further from Europe as the risks of participation grew.

It took Hitler about four years from the time he became Chancellor of Germany on January 30, 1933, to destroy the restraints of the Versailles settlement. He withdrew Germany from the League of Nations and the World Disarmament Conference on October 14, 1933. He commenced rearmament in 1934 by integrating his private Nazi Storm Troop units into the army and increasing the military budget. On March 16, 1935, he felt secure enough to throw off the mask. He denounced the disarmament clauses of the Versailles Treaty and reinstituted conscription. As on later occasions, he averted retaliatory action by detaching Great Britain from France. With a great show of moderation, he proposed an Anglo-German naval agreement. London swallowed the bait on June 18 and signed a treaty conceding to the Reich equality in submarines and a surface fleet 35 per cent as large as the British Navy.

Meanwhile, Hitler's success had loosened the entire French alliance network on the Continent. Fearful that Paris would abandon them if Germany expanded eastward, several Central European powers opened negotiations with Hitler. Poland signed a ten-year nonaggression pact in January 1934, and Yugoslavia accepted a trade treaty a few months later. France tried to counter these developments by coaxing the Soviet Union and Italy into a new anti-German front. Of the two powers, Russia gave the more encouraging response. She joined the League of Nations in 1934, repeatedly endorsed collective security at Geneva, and sought a full-dress military alliance with the French. Nevertheless, neither Great Britain nor the small states trusted her intentions, and they protested against the projected alliance. This created misgivings in Paris, with the result that the French settled for a watered-down version of the original terms in May 1935.

As the French backed away from a binding commitment with Russia out of deference to Great Britain and their Balkan allies, they redoubled their bids for Italian support. Unfortunately the Fascist dictator, Benito Mussolini, was in an adventurous mood. In the 1920's, the strong position of the British and French had prevented him from pursuing the Italian dream of a Mediterranean empire, and so he now welcomed their preoccupation with Hitler. He did not object to cooperating temporarily with the western powers if they were willing to pay a generous price, but he knew that his long-range objectives could be secured only at the expense of the British and French. His response to feelers from the French Prime Minister Laval in the summer of 1935 was to demand a free hand in Ethiopia in exchange for support against Germany. Although Ethiopia did not belong to France, Laval struck a bargain at her expense. Apparently he assured Mussolini that France would look in the other direction while the Italians conquered the last independent state in Africa. Laval may have gone further and undertaken to keep the League of Nations from intervening in behalf of Ethiopia.

The whole scheme foundered on the unexpected intransigence of London. Mussolini invaded Ethiopia on October 3, 1935, and despite French efforts to silence the British, the latter pushed a resolution through the League Council four days later condemning Italy as an aggressor. After some debate the League voted economic sanctions against the Italians and put them into effect on November 18. Although the French failed to block the imposition of an embargo on Italy, they prevented the League ban from extending to critical materials like coal and oil. In this backstage maneuver they received the cooperation of the British, who were reluctant to press for sanctions that might have stopped Mussolini altogether. The wavering policy of London reflected concern over public feeling at home and an unwarranted fear of Italian naval power in the Mediterranean.

The upshot of League action was to irritate Mussolini without effectively crippling his war machine. He denounced the British for their interference and proceeded with the conquest of Ethiopia, which was completed on May 9, 1936. The friction between the Italians and the British encouraged Hitler to remilitarize the Rhineland. Confident that only an isolated France would protest, he occupied the zone on March 7, 1936. His calculations proved correct. Paris was indignant but backed away from a military test when Italy and Great Britain refused to support her.

The occupation of the Rhineland was the decisive event in the breakdown of the European balance. It provided protective covering for the hitherto vulnerable German armament industry of the Ruhr and by the same token it sealed France off from access to possible allies in Eastern

Europe. The net effect of the power realignment in the winter of 1935–36 was to wreck the French postwar system for containing Germany. The Ethiopian episode had seriously undermined the prospect for a western bloc composed of Great Britain, Italy, and France and had exposed the uselessness of the League as an instrument of preserving the *status quo*. Simultaneously the dramatic resurgence of German power had created almost prohibitive risks for Balkan states that wanted to maintain their connection with the French. In short, France was confronted with an isolation almost as complete as she had imposed on Berlin for fifteen years.

FOREIGN POLICY UNDER NEUTRALITY LEGISLATION

The American response to the European crisis was apathetic because the average citizen neither understood the significance of Old World developments nor cared to be enlightened. A few showed sympathy for the underdog Ethiopians, but the majority interpreted the outbreak of war and the great-power disputes at Geneva as fresh confirmation of Europe's incurable devotion to violence. This inaction strengthened popular determination to remain aloof and prodded Congress into passing the first neutrality law (August 31, 1935).

When Italy attacked Ethiopia on October 3, 1935, Roosevelt had to proclaim the mandatory arms embargo against both belligerents. He disliked this because it applied only to munitions and not to raw materials, which were more accessible to the Italians than to the Ethiopians. He therefore sought an amendment which would have extended the ban to all commodities suitable for use by a war machine. Congressional isolationists denounced his proposal as an attempt to identify the United States with the League policy of sanctions against Italy, and they succeeded in tabling it. Secretary Hull countered on November 15, 1935, with the proclamation of a moral embargo against the shipment of critical materials to Italy in excess of normal requirements. Thereafter American diplomatic activity subsided and the ban on arms shipments was lifted at the end of the Ethiopian war.

Neither the President nor Congress took any official notice of the remilitarization of the Rhineland. According to the memoirs of Democrats close to Roosevelt, he began to comment with increasing frequency on the gravity of the European situation during the spring of 1936. But if he felt the need for a reappraisal of foreign policy, he managed to conceal it from both his advisers and the American public.

The outbreak of the Spanish Civil War on July 18, 1936, gave Hitler and Mussolini a fresh opportunity to tilt the European balance further against the *status quo* powers at an inconsiderable cost. At the outset the conflict was a purely Spanish affair arising out of a rebellion by General Francisco Franco against the Madrid government. The big landholders, the Catholic

Church, and conservative mercantile interests backed Franco, while a Popular Front representing workers, peasants, and various radical groups with conflicting objectives rallied behind the government. At the initiative of the British and French, twenty-seven European nations met in London and established a nonintervention committee on September 9, 1936, to localize the war and to prevent outside aid from reaching either side. Roosevelt promptly adopted a parallel policy and secured congressional approval for a special neutrality law covering civil wars.

Most powers faithfully observed the rule of nonintervention. The Germans and Italians, who had established an informal Rome-Berlin Axis in the fall of 1936, sent Franco volunteers and military equipment, while the Russians with less success tried to give the Madrid government similiar help. These violations took place on an expanding scale in 1937 and 1938 with the result that Franco eventually emerged victorious and aligned Spain diplomatically with Germany and Italy. Since Spain was weak in manpower and industrial resources, her adherence to the revisionist camp was important primarily from a geographical standpoint. It complicated British problems in the Mediterranean and gave the French another hostile frontier to watch.

The United States erred in minimizing the stakes involved in the war, but popular sentiment overwhelmingly supported nonintervention. Roosevelt found it easier to endorse strict neutrality in this crisis than in the Ethiopian one, because any display of partisanship would have annoyed either the American Catholics, who favored Franco, or the liberals, who favored the Spanish government. As evidence of German and Italian intervention increased, Roosevelt grew apprehensive. In the summer of 1937 he began to cast about for a new policy toward both Europe and Asia.

SUGGESTED READINGS

1. Bailey, T. A., *A Diplomatic History of the American People.*
2. Beard, C. A., *American Foreign Policy in the Making,* (1932–40).
3. Bemis, S. F., *A Diplomatic History of the United States.*
4. Nevins, A., *The New Deal and World Affairs.*
5. Wolfers, A., *Great Britain and France Between Two Wars.*

CHAPTER TWENTY-FOUR

AMERICA GOES TO WAR AGAIN (1937-1941)

ROOSEVELT ABANDONS ISOLATION

Diplomatic circles all over the world began to buzz on October 6, 1937, as the result of a foreign policy speech delivered twenty-four hours earlier by President Roosevelt in Chicago. The novelty of Roosevelt's expression of concern over international problems would have ensured him of an interested audience in any case. What made his pronouncement a sensation was its contents. He denounced the revisionist powers of Europe and Asia as a threat to peace; predicted worse behavior on their part; and called upon other states for concerted action to quarantine the offenders as health officers quarantine the carriers of communicable disease.

Although Roosevelt did not spell out exactly what the United States was prepared to do, his proposal for a quarantine suggested the intriguing possibility of American participation in an alliance to preserve the *status quo*. Secretary of State Hull seemed to confirm this interpretation the following day when he endorsed the action of a League committee which had found Japan guilty of violating the Kellogg-Briand Pact and the Nine-Power guarantee of the Open Door in the Washington treaties. Hull also approved the committee proposal for a conference of the signatories of the Nine-Power agreement to negotiate a settlement of the Sino-Japanese dispute.

The desire of Roosevelt to change American foreign policy is beyond question, but his motives for wanting to do so have been a matter of controversy. Circumstantial evidence points strongly to a relationship between the growing resistance to the New Deal program at home and the revival of the President's interest in world problems. The "quarantine" speech was made against a background of business recession and the rebellion of southern Democrats against the Court plan. Consequently, Roosevelt's critics accused him of trying to distract public attention from domestic problems by launching an adventuresome foreign policy. Conversely, the defenders of the President contended that he had long been sensitive to the world crisis but had held his peace because of the futility of challenging the dominant isolationist sentiment.

The truth doubtless lies somewhere between the extremes. It is difficult to accept the view that Roosevelt had been an unwilling hostage of the isolationists until 1937. For four years he had shown a strong preoccupation with domestic recovery, accepted neutrality legislation without complaint, and betrayed little anxiety over the deterioration of the *status quo* in Europe and Asia. The timing of his conversion to an interventionist policy was probably geared to the simultaneous deterioration of the international situation and of popular support for his recovery program. The behavior of Germany and Japan became more menacing just as Roosevelt lost his incentive to push forward on the domestic front. Nobody knows which factor weighed more in his reappraisal, but the American public and the world were startled by the abruptness of his policy shift.

Notwithstanding his eloquence and persuasiveness, Roosevelt could not hope to discredit overnight a viewpoint which he had helped to cultivate by his outward indifference to world developments. Aside from the difficulty of securing public support, he was proposing to launch an adventuresome foreign policy from the least favorable power position that America had occupied in the Far East during the twentieth century. Between 1932 and 1937 only China had disputed Japanese expansion. Great Britain and France had been preoccupied successively with the depression and with the resurgence of Germany. Neither could be expected to concentrate more than a fraction of its waning strength on the Orient, nor could China be expected to roll the Japanese back from their advanced position on the mainland. Russia was reviving, but the threat of German expansion in Central Europe made her a doubtful factor in Far Eastern politics. The virtual disappearance of all the counterweights in the oriental balance meant that Roosevelt was undertaking sole responsibility for checking Japanese expansion. Worse still, he was embarking on this momentous policy with his country virtually unarmed.

The consequences would ultimately depend upon the kind of settlement Washington was prepared to make. Japan had become too deeply involved in China to withdraw voluntarily from all her recently acquired holdings. On the other hand, she did not want war with America. Several times in the next few years she offered the United States a settlement on the basis of current possessions or something less. Since peace on these terms would have purchased America a breathing spell for rearmament, considerations of power politics argued for acceptance. But Roosevelt's Far Eastern diplomacy from 1938 to 1941 was dominated by an uncompromising attitude and pointed irresistibly to war.

The Roosevelt-Hull endorsement of collective action against Japan got off to a conspicuously bad start. Before the conference of the signatories of the Nine-Power Treaty could meet, the uproar of isolationist groups forced the President to repudiate the implications of his "quarantine" speech. In a "fireside chat" on October 12, 1937, he reassured his countrymen that the conference would confine itself to the exploration of peaceful methods

"The nation is not all taking your warward step, Mr. President." *(McCutcheon,* The Chicago Tribune, *1941.)*

for settling the Sino-Japanese dispute and that the United States delegation would not tie its hands with any prior commitments. These disclaimers doomed the Brussels Conference from the outset. The delegates met on November 3, heard Japan declare that she would tolerate no outside interference in the settlement of her dispute with China, and broke up on November 24 after a routine reaffirmation of the principles of the Washington treaties.

The mild stand of the administration did not silence the isolationists, who still constituted the majority of the people. For five years they had followed the President's lead in ignoring the Far East and now refused to believe his unexpected assertion that Japan was menacing the American position. Their sustained agitation for a complete withdrawal from China forced Roosevelt to take a second step backward and pull the small detachments of troops out of the international settlements in Shanghai and Peiping. American civilians were also urged to leave, and the government evacuated those who took its advice.

GROWING TENSION IN THE FAR EAST

Emboldened by the apparent dissension in the United States, Japanese aviators climaxed a series of disagreeable incidents in Chinese waters by repeatedly bombing the American gunboat *Panay* on December 12, 1937. Two were killed and thirty wounded in the sinking. Tokyo had no excuse for mistaking the identity of the ship because it was displaying the American colors conspicuously at the time of the attack. The average citizen did not take nearly so grave a view of the affront to national honor as an earlier generation had taken of the *Lusitania* incident. Public opinion overwhelmingly preferred a complete withdrawal to a stubborn defense of American rights that might end in war. According to a Gallup Poll taken a month after the incident, 70 per cent favored noninvolvement.

The administration took a much stiffer line than the public. On December 14, 1937, it sent a sharp note to Japan demanding reparation for damages and additional safeguards against repetition of the incident. An apology crossed the note en route, indicating that irresponsible military officials rather than the government had precipitated the incident. Eventually Tokyo paid damages of $2,214,007.36, which Secretary Hull accepted along with expressions of regret on December 24, 1937.

The sequel to the settlement of the *Panay* incident was a deterioration rather than an improvement in American-Japanese relations. Throughout 1938 Tokyo blandly multiplied her violations of the Open Door, and Washington matched each with a protest. An exchange of notes in the autumn clarified the positions of the two powers. On November 18 Japan asserted in guarded fashion that the Open Door was dead and invited the United States to participate in the trade of East Asia under what amounted to Nipponese supervision. The State Department rejoinder of December 31, 1938, flatly rejected both the assertion and the invitation. It again affirmed America's determination to uphold treaty obligations and informed Tokyo that the only proper remedy for unsatisfactory treaties was negotiation of disputed points. The polite language of diplomacy partially concealed the width of the gap separating the two powers. The Japanese refused to negotiate except on the basis of a new *status quo,* and the Americans refused to discuss anything until Tokyo pulled back within the boundaries established by the Washington treaties. The apparent willingness of each party to hold conversations was dependent upon the other's making the key concession.

Developments in 1939 increased the chances that the deadlock would lead to war. The United States had begun to rearm in May 1938, with the passage of the Vinson Naval Expansion Act which authorized the expenditure of approximately a billion dollars over a ten-year period. The avowed purpose of this legislation was to create a two-ocean navy capable of dealing simultaneously with Japan, Germany, and Italy. Hence, with each passing year, the United States would be in a better position to enforce its hitherto academic insistence on the restoration of the Far Eastern *status quo* of the 1920's. The temptation of Japan to fight before America grew stronger was increased by the latter's policy of stepping up the flow of credits, supplies, and military equipment to China. As the Japanese armies became increasingly bogged down in the western provinces in 1939, Japan also became increasingly vulnerable to the threat of an American embargo on strategic raw materials. An added goad was the revival of instinctive American reflexes for energetic measures. During 1939 isolationist sentiment remained strong, but it began to focus more exclusively on the problem of keeping out of the impending war in Europe. Prominent isolationists objected less vigorously to unneutral policies of the administration in the Far East. Tokyo still preferred to avoid war but she was fully prepared to take risks by expanding into new areas that would reduce her economic dependence on America.

After the spring of 1939 the timing of her blows was to depend upon (1) the degree of coordination that Japan could achieve with the revisionist powers of Europe, and (2) the opportunities that would develop in the Far East as a result of developments elsewhere.

HITLER ON THE MARCH

Meanwhile, in the European theater the *status quo* deteriorated more rapidly between 1937 and 1939. Only by rigid enforcement of the disarmament, economic, and territorial clauses of the Versailles Treaty could France have maintained her artificial advantage over Germany in the balance. Once Hitler had smashed the initial pair of restrictions in a series of actions climaxed by the remilitarization of the Rhineland (March 7, 1936), nothing short of war would stop him. The French recognized the hopelessness of their isolated position and tried to assure themselves of British support for the impending showdown by allowing London to take the initiative in all dealings with Hitler. The Chamberlain government cheerfully accepted the responsibility. It continued to operate on the assumption that Hitler was a sort of poor man's Bismarck who would show his gratitude for reasonable concessions by acting as a stabilizing force in Central Europe. In an effort to secure his cooperation, London was willing to abandon the wavering allies of France in the Balkans and to ignore the Soviet Union.

International relations unfolded within this context during the next three years. The tempo of developments was geared to Hitler's timetable — a flexible schedule of aggression affected by his intuitive estimates of what his divided opponents would tolerate and by the progress of German rearmament. Aside from broadening the scope of intervention in Spain and stepping up the propaganda campaign aimed at Germans outside the Reich, Hitler was relatively quiet in 1937. The deceptive calm ended abruptly on March 12, 1938, when he invaded and annexed Austria. This bloodless victory put Czechoslovakia in the claws of a German pincer. Shortly thereafter, Hitler demanded that Prague give up its sovereignty over the border provinces containing the Sudeten Germans. The Czechs appealed for help to the French and Russians with whom they had defensive alliances. France made her support conditional on the approval of Great Britain, and the latter regarded intervention as hopeless. A four-power conference of Germany, Italy, France, and Great Britain met at Munich, September 29–30, 1938, and turned the Sudetenland over to Germany after receiving explicit pledges from Hitler that he would make no further territorial demands. Prime Minister Chamberlain hailed the agreement as assuring "peace for our time" and envisaged an era of cooperation between the western powers and a contented Germany.

Hitler's repeated threats to fight, during the weeks before the Munich conference, encouraged Roosevelt to make his first open venture in European diplomacy since the ill-fated "quarantine" speech. On September 26, 1938, when it appeared that Hitler would break off negotiations with Great Britain over a procedural squabble, the President cabled the German Chancellor and urged him to settle the dispute peaceably. A noncommittal response and an aggravation of the tension on the 27th resulted in a second appeal which was addressed simultaneously to Hitler and to Mussolini. Inasmuch as the Italian dictator telephoned his German counterpart the next day and won the latter's consent to a Munich conference, the intervention of Roosevelt may have helped to avert war.

By this time most Americans regarded Hitler as a bully and sympathized with the Czechs. They had, however, no more intention than the British of fighting to prevent the dismemberment of the little republic. They still enjoyed the twin illusions that the revisionist program of Hitler could not affect the security of the United States and that Germany could be stopped without any American commitment. The developments of 1939 and 1940 were needed to convince the average citizen that America did not live in a world by herself.

The hope of permanent peace lasted only long enough for Prime Minister

Chamberlain to send out Christmas cards bearing a photograph of the plane that had carried him to Munich. On March 15, 1939, Hitler tore up the Munich treaty and occupied the remains of truncated Czechoslovakia. Three weeks later Mussolini occupied Albania without serious resistance. Meanwhile, Hitler had set the stage for a fresh crisis by demanding that Poland permit the Reich to build an extraterritorial motor road across the corridor separating East Prussia from Germany.

Reactions to these developments demonstrated the disunity of Hitler's foes. Two days after the Germans had entered Czechoslovakia, Acting Secretary of State Sumner Welles condemned the action in unrestrained terms. Mussolini also received a verbal chastisement after his bloodless conquest of Albania. Roosevelt followed with an extraordinary appeal to the two dictators on April 21, 1939. He asked them to pledge not to attack any one of the thirty enumerated states for a ten-year period. He also offered to honor such a pledge by promoting a conference on disarmament and equal access to the raw materials of the world. Hitler and Mussolini avoided a direct reply until they had wrenched from several small states an admission that they did not fear an attack. Thereupon they blandly announced that the pledge was unnecessary.

The President had acted without consulting the European *status quo* powers. Whether he saw the desirability of joint action is uncertain. In any event, the American public would not have tolerated participation in a collective security program to stop Hitler. The only contribution that Roosevelt felt able to make was to press for revisions of the neutrality law which would favor the western powers. Mindful of America's key role as a source of supply for the Allies in World War I, he concentrated his efforts on repeal of the mandatory arms embargo, which provided for a ban on the shipment of all military commodities upon the outbreak of war. Roosevelt regarded this clause as an invitation to Hitler to attack the western powers at the earliest possible moment so that their access to American arsenals would be cut off and their control of the seas would be neutralized. In effect, he took the position that the embargo favored Germany and would promote war.

Congress was unmoved by these arguments. Both houses rejected bills to repeal the embargo as well as a compromise proposal to extend the coverage of the cash-and-carry provision to weapons, ammunition, and other war materials. When Roosevelt saw that Congress intended to adjourn without taking action, he called a White House conference of legislative leaders on May 19, 1939. He reiterated his earlier argument and predicted that a European war would break out by fall unless Congress repealed the embargo. Senator Borah openly disputed the forecast, and Vice-President Garner asserted that the necessary votes for repeal could not be rounded up. Confronted with such a discouraging response, the Chief Executive gave up the fight temporarily but threatened to renew it in the fall if Europe went to war.

A curious air of unreality hung over the debate between Roosevelt and the isolationists in the spring of 1939, because neither side was prepared to take the steps necessary to stop Hitler. Doubtless the Chancellor appreciated the fresh demonstration of isolationist sentiment, but his choice of war or peace was to turn on whether his potential victims in Europe could unite against him rather than on whether an uncommitted America repealed the arms embargo.

After the German occupation of Czechoslovakia, Great Britain and France made it clear that they would fight if Hitler attempted further expansion. Unfortunately, such a combination was not sufficient to intimidate him. Sensing the need for a stronger coalition, they opened negotiations with Soviet Russia in April 1939. The prospects for an alliance were clouded at the outset by suspicions on both sides. The British and French distrusted Communism and were almost as willing to let Hitler take Eastern Europe as to let Russia "liberate" the area. Hence they sought an agreement with the Soviet Union that would limit the conditions under which it provided aid to neighboring countries. Conversely, the Russians feared that the western powers would negotiate another Munich agreement after embroiling them in a quarrel with Hitler. So Moscow demanded an ironclad defensive alliance and discretionary authority to send troops across the borders of neighboring countries to forestall Hitler.

Negotiations proceeded at leisurely pace throughout the spring and summer of 1939 with neither side showing any disposition to make concessions. Meanwhile Hitler had made up his mind to attack Poland even though this meant that he would face war with Great Britain and France. In an effort to assure a victory, he opened secret negotiations with Russia in early August. The two powers struck a bargain on the basis of a partition of Poland and an informal division of the remainder of Central Europe into German and Soviet spheres of influence. The only terms that were published were a trade agreement (August 19, 1939) and a nonagression pact (August 23, 1939).

The world was stunned by the news of this alliance, partly because ideological differences had hitherto been regarded as a barrier to friendly relations between the two states and partly because the Soviet Union had continued its parallel negotiations with the western powers until the day it accepted Hitler's proposals. Both Berlin and Moscow were to reap substantial dividends from their partnership. Hitler received the most immediate benefits because the assurance of Russia's benevolent neutrality cleared the way for him to attack Poland without risking a two-front war. In return, the Soviet Union obtained an opportunity to retake most of the territory it had lost as a result of World War I.

Twenty-four hours after the announcement of the nonaggression pact, Roosevelt addressed an urgent appeal for a peaceful settlement to Chancellor Hitler, the President of Poland, and the King of Italy. Neither of the principals would yield. Confident of victory over a coalition that did not include Russia or the United States, Hitler now couched in the form of an ultimatum his demands for Danzig and a motor road across the Corridor. Reassured by national pride and promise of help from the western powers, Poland flatly rejected the German terms and completed her mobilization. She did not have long to wait. On September 1, 1939, Nazi legions poured across the border, and two days later Great Britain and France declared war.

Roosevelt immediately issued the necessary proclamations to invoke the neutrality legislation. He also called a special session of Congress to repeal the arms embargo as he had threatened to do if war was declared. With considerable fanfare he advertised his recommendation as a proposal to restore the traditional policy of basing American neutrality on international law. If he had the Wilsonian version of neutral rights in mind, he needed to urge far more than the repeal of the arms embargo. By this time sympathy for the foes of Hitler had replaced popular indifference to developments in Europe. Nevertheless, such sentiment could be mobilized behind legislation only if Americans were assured that armament sales to the British and French carried no risk of war. Roosevelt undertook to give the necessary assurances by coupling the repeal bill with a request for authority to prohibit American ships from sailing into danger zones. On this occasion, he first employed the argument that aid to the foes of aggression would strengthen their ability to resist and thus keep the war away from American shores. Some pure isolationists took a contrary view. They asserted that the repeal of the arms embargo would be equivalent to changing the rules after the start of the war and would invite retaliation. The willingness of the President to retain other features of the neutrality legislation and to add a ban on American shipping in war zones carried the day for his proposal. It convinced a decisive number of waverers that the sale of munitions on a cash-and-carry basis would not involve the United States in war. On November 3, 1939, Congress approved both of Roosevelt's requests, with minor changes, by a vote of 55 to 24 in the Senate and 243 to 172 in the House.

THE FIRST PHASE OF WORLD WAR II

Claims that America had abandoned isolationism were premature. The majority still clung to the view that the position of the United States would not be affected at all. This assumption seemed to be confirmed by events during the opening stages of the war. The Germans took up a defensive position on the western front and quickly overran Poland. Warsaw fell in less than a month, and organized resistance ended two weeks later. The British and French had made only token attacks and received an invitation from the victorious Chancellor to a peace conference in mid-October. The Allies flatly rejected his offer, but neither side launched an offensive. Fighting came to a virtual standstill in the fall and winter of 1939–1940. Referred to by the wags as a *Sitzkrieg,* the lull in operations encouraged the belief that France's Maginot Line and Germany's Siegfried Line were impregnable. Most observers expected a repetition of the pattern of World War I, with the belligerents settling down to a protracted siege of each other's economies. This impression had been strengthened at the outset by an Allied announcement (September 8, 1939) of a long-range blockade against Germany, and by a retaliatory Nazi proclamation of a counter-blockade three days later. During the ensuing months Great Britain and France multiplied the restrictions on neutral shipping without regard for the rules of international law, while the Germans sowed mines and preyed indiscriminately on merchant vessels headed for the British Isles. Washington informed the belligerents that it reserved all the rights to which Americans were entitled under international law, but the neutrality law reduced the practical effect of this lofty announcement by prohibiting citizens from doing most of the things that had created incidents between 1914 and 1917. The State Department made a series of halfhearted protests to London over interference with transatlantic mail and merchant shipping. These representations were politely brushed aside.

Once popular wrath over the German conquest of Poland had subsided, Americans turned the full force of their moral indignation on Russia as she moved to secure her share of the spoils. Her association in the partition of Poland shattered the lingering illusions of all but fanatical Communists that the Soviet Union was an unselfish, peace-loving state. Whatever restraint Americans had exercised during this cynical exhibition of power politics, vanished completely when Russia attacked Finland in December 1939. Finland's gallant resistance evoked unprecedented displays of sympathy, for the little Baltic republic had been the sole European country to continue its war debt payments throughout the 1930's. Roosevelt denounced "the dreadful rape of Finland" and instituted a moral embargo against the export of military supplies to the Soviet Union. Although neutrality legislation was an obstacle to positive American aid to Finland, the administration explored the possibility of a loan through the Import-Export Bank. Before a decision could be made, the Soviet armies pierced the Mannerheim Line which protected Helsinki, and forced Finland to accept a dictated peace on March 8, 1940.

The contrast between the inactivity of Germany and the aggressive behavior of the Soviet Union during the winter of 1939 and 1940 convinced most Americans that Russia was the chief menace to peace. This opinion survived for barely six weeks. On April 9, 1940, Hitler abruptly ended the *Sitzkrieg* phase of the war by launching a *Blitzkrieg.* In a matter of days, land armies overran Denmark, while combined naval and air operations across the Kattegat quickly gave the Nazis control of the principal Norwegian cities. Scarcely pausing to regroup his forces, Hitler struck again on May 10, this time to the west. German armored units supported by bomber and fighter planes swept through Holland, Belgium; and northern

France. Territory which the British and French had contested inch by inch in 1914 fell in less than three weeks. An English expeditionary army, cut off from the main Allied forces retreating southward, was pinned against the sea at Dunkirk and was evacuated across the Channel with difficulty. Mussolini added to the problems of the beleaguered French government by declaring war against the Allies on June 10. Two days later Paris fell, and onrushing German armies fanned in all directions to stamp out the last isolated centers of resistance. The aged Marshal Pétain replaced Paul Reynaud as Prime Minister on June 16 and surrendered to the Germans on June 22. Hitler had performed the incredible feat of knocking France out of the war in forty-three days.

Washington was completely unprepared for the sensational German victory. Roosevelt had sent Sumner Welles to the major capitals of Europe in February to explore the possibilities of a negotiated peace and had received a discouraging report. Anticipating a long war, the President had made preparations for a gradual build-up of military power that would not alarm the isolationists unduly. He began to doubt the adequacy of existing armament plans when Hitler conquered Denmark. Fearful that the Chancellor would also try to occupy the Danish islands of Iceland and Greenland, Roosevelt took preventive measures which made increased military commitments probable. On April 18 he brought Greenland under the protection of the Monroe Doctrine and authorized the Coast Guard to patrol the island. Great Britain rescued him from responsibility for Iceland by occupying it on May 10. Prompt action kept these two island stepping-stones, which dominated Anglo-American shipping lines, out of German hands.

Any lingering doubt that the United States needed to speed up rearmament was dispelled when the Nazis began their triumphant sweep across northern France. On May 16, 1940, Roosevelt made a special request to Congress for increased military appropriations. After warning that national security would be imperiled if a hostile power seized any territory on the periphery of North America, he demanded rapid enlargement of ground forces and the production of fifty thousand war planes per year.

The same day the British Prime Minister, Winston Churchill, who had replaced Neville Chamberlain a week earlier, sent an urgent appeal for ammunition, aircraft, and a loan of over-age destroyers. Premier Reynaud of France addressed a more desperate appeal as the Germans surged toward Paris. Even if the neutrality law had not been a barrier to large-scale emergency aid, Roosevelt felt reluctant to give the limited armaments that America could spare to governments which might capitulate and be obliged to turn their supplies over to the Germans. Hence he offered nothing more tangible than sympathy until after France had surrendered. When it became clear in late June that the British would continue the war, he secretly ordered the War and Navy Departments to scrape "the bottom of the barrel" for John Bull. In pursuance of his directive, considerable quantities of small weapons and ammunition were turned over to private firms for resale to the British. War Department officials also promised Churchill some fourteen thousand war planes in the next year and a half. By midsummer of 1940, Roosevelt had reached the conclusion that the survival of Great Britain was essential to American security. He also recognized the urgency of British needs, but the imminence of the 1940 election caused him to postpone the formulation of a systematic program of aid.

ROOSEVELT INCREASES THE PRESSURE ON JAPAN

During the year and a half after Munich, Japan tried to take advantage of America's increasing preoccupation with Europe. A crisis threatened to develop in the summer of 1939 as Japan opened negotiations for a German alliance and simultaneously intensified pressure on Great Britain. With the latter facing almost certain war with Hitler, the hard-pressed Chamberlain government capitulated and on July 24 recognized the authority of Tokyo in all territory occupied by the imperial armies. Fearful that these concessions would embolden Japan, Washington stepped into the picture two days later by denouncing the American-Japanese commercial treaty of 1911. This action cleared the way for placing an embargo on shipments of munitions and critical raw materials at the end of six months. The effectiveness of the threat was increased on August 23 when Germany signed an alliance with the Soviet Union instead of with Japan in order to avoid a two-front war in Europe. This double blow not only jeopardized the major source of supplies for Tokyo's war machine but enabled Russia to take a more active role in the Far East. Moscow promptly stepped up the undeclared border warfare in North Manchuria and rejected repeated bids during the next eighteen months for a general settlement that would have freed Tokyo to push southward. The initial phase of the European war also disappointed the Japanese. Since Hitler failed to follow up his rapid conquest of Poland with an all-out attack on Great Britain and France, it was difficult for Tokyo to apply pressure effectively on the European powers in the Far East. Expansionist projects were temporarily shelved and the Japanese Foreign Office adopted a conciliatory tone with Washington to avert the threatened embargo. Secretary Hull hoped he could gain concessions in return for a new treaty, but deadlock quickly developed over familiar issues. Shortly before January 26, 1940, when the old treaty was to expire, the United States announced that it would continue exporting critical material to Japan on a provisional basis. This statement served notice that America intended to use trade as a weapon for enforcing good behavior in the Far East.

The incentive for Japan to meet American standards of deportment decreased sharply in May 1940 when Hitler overran the Netherlands and France, thus orphaning the Dutch East Indies and French Indo-China and reviving expansionist dreams in Tokyo. As a consequence, the moderate

Yonai government fell on July 16, 1940, and was succeeded by a coalition under the nominal control of Prince Fumimaro Konoye. The new Prime Minister had a reputation for caution, but his appointment of the anti-American Matsuoka as Foreign Secretary and the rash General Hideki Tojo as Minister of War foreshadowed a renewal of expansion southward.

The threefold objective of the new cabinet was to finish the war in China which had dragged on for four years, to negotiate an alliance with Germany, and to seize suitable springboards for the conquest of the Dutch East Indies. On July 12 the retiring Yonai government had begun cutting the supply lines to China by extracting from the British a promise to suspend traffic on the Burma Road for three months. Konoye applied similar pressure on the feeble Vichy French government of Indo-China and it acquiesced in the closing of the Haiphong-Kuming railroad — the other major artery to Chungking, the temporary Chinese capital. After some resistance, Vichy also signed on September 24 an agreement authorizing Japan to build air-strips and to station troops in northern Indo-China. Three days later Germany, Italy, and Japan signed a tripartite agreement which pledged each of the contracting parties to cooperate militarily, politically, or economically if any one of them were attacked by a power not currently at war. Since the treaty contained a specific disclaimer of hostility toward Soviet Russia, the obvious intent was to threaten the United States. Instead of being frightened by these developments, the Roosevelt administration retaliated energetically.

It had tried to forestall the midsummer Nipponese push southward by partial implementation of the long-threatened embargo; on July 26 it banned the export of aviation gasoline, lubricants, and scrap metal to Japan. When this attempt at preventive action failed, Washington countered Nipponese occupation of northern Indo-China with loans to Chiang Kai-shek and additions to the embargo list. Between September 1940 and the end of the year, Nationalist China received $100 million from the United States, and Japan's opportunities to purchase American metals, chemicals, and machine tools were further curtailed. Meanwhile Roosevelt had prodded the British into reopening the Burma Road on October 8 and had promoted exploratory talks with them and the Dutch about the joint defense of the West Pacific. Three-power staff discussions followed in the spring of 1941, but plans for concrete action foundered on the inability of Washington to state under what circumstances it would fight.

The willingness of the administration to trade punches probably discouraged Tokyo from taking further advantage of the colonial powers, which had been badly beaten in Europe. But Washington seemed certain to run considerable risk if it continued such a policy in 1941. Further curtailment of trade seemed likely to hasten the Nipponese drive for control of the raw materials of the Dutch East Indies, while continued aid to China carried with it the danger of provoking Tokyo into a direct attack on America.

THE 1940 ELECTION

The steady deterioration of American-Japanese relations in 1940 helped improve Roosevelt's prospects of re-election, and the German conquest of France gave a still more dramatic boost to his ebbing political fortunes. No single event in American history had come so close to creating widespread panic among the voters as the sudden appearance of Nazi legions on the Atlantic coast opposite North America. Overnight it revived the popular instinct to avoid changing leaders in a crisis. If another candidate with Roosevelt's experience in foreign affairs had been available, the President would have faced stiff competition; as it was, he enjoyed a clear field. The political climate of the thirties had discouraged able men from attempting to make their reputations as experts in international relations. The only Republican of the requisite stature was Herbert Hoover, a holdover from an earlier era whose identification with unpopular domestic policies disqualified him as a candidate. The Democrats were even poorer in talent because Roosevelt had systematically eliminated all potential rivals.

As usual the Republican convention met first. The principal candidates were two senators with isolationist records — Robert A. Taft of Ohio and Arthur H. Vandenburg of Michigan — and Thomas E. Dewey, a youthful New York prosecuting attorney. When the delegates assembled at Philadelphia on June 24, the front runners received an unexpected challenge from Wendell L. Willkie of Indiana. By all rules of politics, his candidacy ought to have failed. A former Indiana Democrat and president of the Commonwealth and Southern Corporation, he suffered the double handicap of being a recent convert to the G.O.P. and a utilities magnate. Worse still from the standpoint of party managers, he was virtually unknown. Nevertheless, in a phenomenal upset, he was nominated as the Republican standard bearer on June 28. The convention chose Senator Charles L. McNary of Oregon as his running mate and adopted a platform noteworthy for its cautious tone on both foreign and domestic affairs.

It is difficult to separate the emotional from the practical reasons for the choice of Willkie. He had great personal magnetism, a straightforward manner, and a Lincolnlike face which made him an appealing contrast to the solemn, unimaginative Republican candidates of the depression era. His mild internationalism and qualified endorsement of New Deal social reforms also seemed like assets to the Republican strategists, who took the support of isolationists and conservatives for granted and counted on the liberal views of their candidate to detach waverers from the Roosevelt camp.

The Democrats convened at Chicago on July 15. Roosevelt had coyly parried all efforts to make him declare whether he would be a candidate for a third term. His persistent silence, however, was interpreted as a tacit expression of availability and resulted in the withdrawal of all aspirants who hoped to have a political future. On July 16 he sent a message to the convention indicating his preference for retirement but proclaiming his willingness to abide by its decision. After the formalities were out of the way, he received a first-ballot nomination over the opposition of a few conservatives headed by James A. Farley and Senator Harry F. Byrd of Virginia. At the request of the President, his former running mate, John N. Garner, who had given covert encouragement to anti-New Deal Democrats in Congress, was dropped from the ticket and Secretary of Agriculture Henry Wallace was substituted.

Roosevelt intended to model his re-election bid on the 1916 campaign of Woodrow Wilson, striking a lofty nonpartisan tone and pleading preoccupation with the European crisis as an excuse for limiting his political activity. To make his aloofness convincing, he had appointed Henry L. Stimson as Secretary of War and Frank Knox as Secretary of the Navy on June 20, 1940; both men were prominent Republicans and exponents of national unity.

Roosevelt's debut as an elder statesman created serious campaign problems for Willkie because he agreed with the President on the issue of aid to Great Britain and would not stoop to purely political criticism. His initial move was to attack New Deal social and economic policies and to support administration foreign policy. For the first month he concentrated his fire on his silent opponent for seeking a third term and on the Democratic party for dishonest and inefficient administration of reform legislation. He balanced his condemnation with an endorsement of the Burke-Wadsworth Selective Service law which Roosevelt worked through Congress in early September. He also gave qualified approval to an unprecedented executive agreement of September 2, whereby the United States granted Great Britain fifty over-age destroyers in return for ninety-nine-year leases on air and naval bases in Newfoundland and the Caribbean. The President had resorted to an executive agreement instead of a treaty in the hope of giving Great Britain stopgap aid without opening up an election debate on foreign policy. Willkie missed a golden opportunity to put new life in his lagging campaign by exploiting popular fears that Roosevelt might precipitate a war through further action of this sort.

Isolationist groups were not so reluctant to take up the cudgels against the President on foreign policy. In early September they organized a bipartisan America First Committee under the chairmanship of Robert E. Wood, a top executive of Sears, Roebuck and Company, and hammered away on the theme that Roosevelt was a warmonger. Internationalist groups also set up a bipartisan organization to propagandize their viewpoint. It was called The Committee to Defend America by Aiding the Allies and was headed by William Allen White, Kansas editor. As the campaign entered its final stages, it became clear that the outcome would hinge on whether Roosevelt successfully combated the charges of the isolationists.

The President responded to the challenge with a vigorous eleventh-hour campaign. In a three weeks' speechmaking tour through the big doubtful states of the East and the Midwest, he insisted that vigorous support of Axis foes was not incompatible with peace. Repeatedly he defended the policy of aid to Great Britain as the best method for keeping the war away from American shores. Fearful of last-minute damage from isolationist charges of warmongering, he tried to reassure mothers with a specific pledge: "Your sons will never have to fight in any foreign war." Opinions differ as to the honesty of the motives which prompted him to make such a categorical statement. However, there can be little doubt that he told a majority of Americans what they wanted to hear: that the expansion of the revisionist powers could be stopped without involvement in war.

To the disgust of the isolationists, who had no major party candidate of their own, Willkie refrained from extravagant attacks on Roosevelt's foreign policy. His assaults on the New Deal failed to attract the voters. As a result, the President was re-elected on November 5, 1940, but by a considerably smaller margin than four years earlier. The final count gave Roosevelt 27,243,000 popular votes and 449 electoral votes, and Willkie 22,304,400 popular and 82 electoral votes. The Chief Executive also carried the Democratic party to comfortable majorities in both the Senate and the House. Minor party candidates polled less than 500,000 votes.

AID SHORT OF WAR

History repeated itself in that the winner of the election duplicated the performance of Woodrow Wilson twenty-four years earlier: he took America into war after running for re-election on a peace platform. To a large extent the conduct of both men was based on national illusions regarding foreign affairs. Both had asserted that the paramount object of American policy was the preservation of peace. Since the isolationists had adopted the same position, the "great debate" before the 1940 election took place in an unrealistic context. Neither the supporters nor the foes of the President were prepared to sacrifice American interests in the cause of peace. However, both sides took the line of least resistance politically and gave contrary assurances to the voters. In effect they gambled that the military enterprises of the revisionist powers would not be successful enough after 1940 to force America to choose between peace and defense of her world position. Had the isolationists won the 1940 election, they might have been able to keep their pledge for a longer period than the internationalists did. Nevertheless, at some point even the bitter-end advocates of hemispheric insulation would have met the growing challenge to American interests with a military response. The victorious Roosevelt was destined to renounce his pledge within a year because he advocated a policy of deliberately provoking the revisionist powers. Whether he understood the contradictions that lurked in his program and concealed them from the electorate or whether he remained unaware of their implications is a question. Probably he shared the traditional propensity of his countrymen for disregarding the rules of the Western State System in the formulation of American policy. In any event, he interpreted his re-election as a mandate for vigorous aid to the nations resisting Germany and Japan.

The principal obstacle to the implementation of a large-scale aid program was the legislative ban on loans to belligerents and nations that had defaulted on war-debt payments. By the end of 1940 Great Britain had mobilized and spent more than two-thirds of her dollar resources. Unless Roosevelt found some way to waive the cash-and-carry provisions of the neutrality law, he would soon be compelled to suspend delivery on the huge British orders for warplanes, tanks, and cargo ships. Urgent messages from Churchill stimulated his fear that Great Britain might collapse if American aid were withheld.

Reluctant to reopen another frenzied debate on foreign policy by a frontal attack on neutrality legislation, Roosevelt sought to circumvent it through a "Lend-Lease" program. In essence, he proposed that the United States manufacture and loan a wide variety of armaments to states at war with the Axis and accept repayment in goods and services after the end of hostilities. He issued a trial balloon at a press conference on December 16, 1940, explaining that the plan would operate on the same principle as the individual who without first demanding payment lent his neighbor a garden hose to put out a fire. Two weeks later he amplified his proposal in a "fireside chat," telling a large radio audience that Great Britain and the British fleet stood between the New World and Nazi aggression. He went on to add that Churchill asked for supplies rather than men and urged Americans to make their country "the great arsenal of democracy." Heartened by a favorable public response, he asked Congress for the necessary authority to undertake the program.

It was possible to disagree with Roosevelt's Lend-Lease proposal and his entire policy of creeping intervention without being an isolationist. However, the extreme isolationists stole the spotlight and led the opposition. Senator Burton K. Wheeler of Montana indignantly called it a program to "plow under every fourth American boy," and the *Chicago Tribune* echoed his charges. The extreme isolationists had, however, ceased to command the support of the country. The House passed the bill on February 8 and the Senate followed suit on March 8. Roosevelt signed it three days later and managed to wrench a $7 billion appropriation out of Congress to finance the program.

No sooner had he secured tacit legislative approval for the suspension of the "cash" provision of the Neutrality Act than he took the next logical step and undermined the companion "carry" provision. Growing German submarine activity in the North Atlantic reduced the probability that Lend-Lease shipments would reach the British Isles in volume unless the

United States helped with the patrol of supply lines. Nazi U-boats destroyed 537,493 tons of merchant shipping in March 1941, and 653,960 the following month. To stop these staggering losses Roosevelt embarked on a series of piecemeal measures that culminated in an undeclared naval war with Germany. The next step was taken on March 25, 1941, when he authorized American navy yards to repair British vessels. Three days later he loaned Great Britain ten Coast Guard cutters for antisubmarine operations. He also authorized the seizure of thirty Axis merchant ships in American ports before the end of the week. A larger number of Danish merchantmen were impounded to prevent them from returning home, where they would have fallen into Nazi hands.

Since these gestures fell far short of terminating German harassment of British supply lines, Roosevelt edged his way toward the establishment of a convoy service. The device he used to disguise this momentous step was a proclamation on April 10 extending the American neutrality patrol from coastal waters to the mid-Atlantic. In this arbitrary amendment to international law, he announced that between the American coast and 25° west longitude, American naval vessels would search for submarines and warn British vessels of their presence. He tried to soften the impact of this unneutral action on Berlin and on native isolationists by promising that patrol units would not attack German U-boats.

Hitherto the Nazi government had refrained from torpedoing American vessels, but it reversed this policy after Roosevelt's proclamation. On May 21 a submarine sank an American freighter, the *Robin Moor,* in the South Atlantic. Popular reaction was restrained, but the President delivered a radio address six days later announcing the determination of the administration to continue the patrol. He also hinted that more drastic measures would be taken if necessary to keep supplies flowing to Great Britain. This warning was the prelude to the occupation of Iceland by American marines on July 7, and the institution of regular convoy service between the United States and Iceland on July 26. Thus in three months the President had moved from a policy of patrolling the West Atlantic to a policy of sinking hostile naval units that threatened American and British shipping in the area. On September 11 he took the additional step of extending convoy coverage to British and neutral vessels after a German U-boat had sunk the United States destroyer *Greer.*

The proclamation of April 10 enlarging the American patrol zone had provided the pretext for the gradual shift in the status of the United States from a neutral to an unofficial belligerent. The interpretation of the neutrality law ignored its intent and sabotaged its safeguards against encounters between American and belligerent vessels on the high seas. Isolationists were powerless to interfere because the President set policy in the patrol zone by virtue of his power as commander-in-chief of the armed forces. Their experience demonstrated afresh the futility of legislative restrictions on executive control of foreign policy. It would have required explosive public opposition to deter the President, and such an outburst was not forthcoming. A decade of isolationist propaganda had made the average citizen ashamed of his emotional outbursts over incidents on the high seas prior to World War I and hence indifferent to these matters in 1941. A clear majority accepted the standard explanation for expanding American naval activity in the West Atlantic. Roosevelt defended each successive step on the twofold ground that Hitler threatened the security of the Western Hemisphere and that German power could be kept at arm's length only if the United States safeguarded the flow of Lend-Lease goods to Great Britain. Roosevelt's alarm over the Nazi challenge to America's world position and his insistence on energetic countermeasures were undoubtedly justified. At the same time, it must be remembered that his isolationist policy from 1933 to 1937 had helped to create the challenge and to deprive America of other sensible alternatives. Roosevelt's supplementary assurances that active aid to Axis foes would preserve peace were contradicted by the spread of the undeclared shooting war with the Germans. He had some excuse for believing that he could give aid on the limited basis of 1940 and escape involvement, but he must have been aware of the probable consequences of Lend-Lease.

By October of 1941 Roosevelt had exhausted all the indirect methods for countering Germany except by an extension of American convoy service beyond the West Atlantic to British ports. He could not take this final step without the repeal of the restrictive clauses in the Neutrality Act of 1939. On October 9 he made the necessary recommendations to Congress. Isolationists made a futile stand, but on November 13 the House ratified Senate action of the preceding week authorizing the President to arm merchant ships and send them through the war zone to British ports. German submarines were active during the congressional debate, sinking the destroyer *Kearny* on October 17 with a loss of eleven lives and the *Reuben James* on October 31 with a loss of 115 lives.

After this the only major provisions of the neutrality law still intact were the prohibitions on passenger travel and on private loans to belligerents. The United States had not reverted to the Wilsonian stand on neutral rights. Neither the President nor the American public showed any concern about freedom of the seas or kindred issues which had excited an earlier generation. Those matters as well as the neutrality law which tried to deal with them had become irrelevant to the question whether America would participate in World War II.

While Roosevelt stepped up the tempo of the undeclared naval war with Germany in the summer and fall of 1941, he also took measures on the diplomatic front which pushed the United States closer to full-scale involvement. The most promising opportunity for enlarging the anti-Hitler coalition occurred on June 22, 1941, when Germany invaded the Soviet Union. The outbreak of this unexpected war climaxed a year of increasing friction between Hitler and Stalin over the division of Central Europe and the

Middle East. Roosevelt did not make any immediate move to aid Russia under the Lend-Lease Act because relations between Washington and Moscow had deteriorated steadily since the Nazi-Soviet pact of 1939. The Russo-Finnish war and the ensuing absorption of Latvia, Estonia, and Lithuania by the Kremlin had revived all the latent American antagonism toward Communism. Moscow's accompanying propaganda barrage against "Yankee imperialism" made matters worse, to say nothing of the activity of local Communists in fomenting strikes in war industries and in establishing valuable connections in the government. Under the circumstances it is not surprising that Americans shed few tears when Hitler turned his efficient armies against the Russians. Roosevelt probably shared the immediate reaction. His reluctance to aid the Russians was reinforced by the estimates of his military advisers that the Communist empire would collapse in three months.

Notwithstanding initial American indifference to the fate of Russia, Great Britain promoted collaboration between Washington and Moscow within two months. In accordance with the amoral precepts of power politics, Churchill promptly welcomed Russia as an ally and prepared to help her against the common enemy without harboring any illusions about the character of Communist aims. He also made an effort to convert Roosevelt to his viewpoint when Harry Hopkins, Lend-Lease administrator and personal envoy of the President, arrived in London on July 14, 1941. The main purpose of the mission was to arrange a conference between Roosevelt and Churchill. The latter eagerly accepted the invitation to a rendevous "in some lonely bay" on August 9. He also persuaded Hopkins to visit Moscow for conversations with Stalin. When Hopkins reached the Kremlin, he received an optimistic report about Russia's prospects of withstanding the Nazi invasion. He also discovered that Stalin was not disposed to let his ideological principles stand in the way of American aid and would graciously consent to receive Lend-Lease equipment and to cooperate in expediting its delivery. Stalin also showed enthusiasm for American participation in the war and volunteered to allow American soldiers under their own commander to fight anywhere on the Russian front.

THE ATLANTIC CHARTER

While Washington pondered this sudden display of magnanimity, preparations were concluded for the first face-to-face conference between Roosevelt and Churchill. The two leaders and their military staffs secretly met on the American cruiser *Augusta* just off the coast of Newfoundland. The President had in mind a joint declaration of what he regarded as moral principles to strengthen the spirit of the states resisting Hitler. Churchill was obviously more interested in extracting some sort of statement about the conditions under which the United States would fight. Extended conversations failed to budge Roosevelt from his original determination to avoid a specific diplomatic or military commitment. As a result, Churchill had to settle for additional convoy help and a pledge of Lend-Lease aid for Russia. In return he agreed to a statement subsequently known as the Atlantic Charter. In phrases reminiscent of the Fourteen Points, both governments pledged themselves to organize the postwar world in accordance with general principles. Among these were: (1) the four freedoms — freedom from fear, want, aggression, and war; (2) the right of people to choose their own form of government; (3) the prohibition of territorial aggrandizement and territorial changes contrary to the wishes of the people involved. The text of the Atlantic Charter, with other news of the Roosevelt-Churchill meeting, was published on August 15 after the two leaders had returned safely to their own countries.

Shortly thereafter, Roosevelt opened negotiations with Russia that culminated in an Anglo-American-Soviet conference at Moscow in late September 1941. The principal result of the discussions was an Anglo-American commitment to furnish Russia a billion dollars' worth of aid by June 30, 1942. Congress endorsed the agreement indirectly by tabling a motion to bar the Russians from the benefits of the Lend-Lease program, whereupon the President on November 7, 1941, declared them eligible for aid. It was unfortunate that Churchill did not accompany his diplomatic matchmaking between the United States and Russia with a word of caution about marriages of convenience. Within a few months opinion in Washington would veer to the view that the Communists wanted the same kind of postwar world as Uncle Sam.

By the fall of 1941 the average American citizen had developed a split personality. He approved the undeclared shooting war on the high seas and closer Anglo-American-Soviet cooperation, while resolutely opposing participation in the world conflict. So pronounced was the antiwar sentiment that Congress rebelled against an administration bill to renew the draft law. By limiting the proposed extension to six months, the resolution cleared the Senate by a safe majority, but it encountered rough sledding in the House and just squeaked through by a margin of 203 to 202 on August 12.

With an irresolute public willing to have America act as arsenal and paymaster for an anti-Hitler coalition but unwilling to authorize a conscript army for more than six months, the initiative passed to Berlin. And while Washington concentrated its attention on Europe, the war clouds gathered in Asia.

THE FAR EASTERN CRISIS

First premonitions of disaster came on January 26, 1941, when Foreign Minister Matsuoka warned America that she would have to change her attitude toward Japan or face the consequences. His bellicosity reflected the growing impatience of Tokyo. The military groups favored simultaneous resumption of the southward push and of the drive against Nationalist China irrespective of how the United States acted. A moderate element, composed primarily of exporters and manufacturers, feared the outcome of a war with America and wanted to avert it if possible. This group was willing to sacrifice some recent gains in Asia, provided the United States would end the embargo, discontinue aid to China, and recognize the improved Japanese position on the mainland. There was no sentiment for peace on the old American terms of complete withdrawal from China.

The moderates enjoyed a temporary ascendancy in Tokyo partly because of the hope that Washington would relax its doctrine of nonrecognition and partly because the expansionists were reluctant to move south with a hostile Russia in the rear. Therefore the Foreign Office pursued the double-barreled policy of trying to neutralize the Russian threat and to effect a general settlement with the United States. This approach revealed that Japan was exposed in two areas and could not make up her mind which way to move. What looked to the outside world like a flexible policy was a grim contest between factions of the cabinet that worked at cross-purposes. Foreign Minister Matsuoka regarded the noncommittal attitude of Russia as the chief obstacle to the resumption of expansion and worked tirelessly to remove it. In March 1941 he visited Berlin and was assured by Hitler that German-Russian relations had cooled. The Nazi dictator did not divulge his plan for a summer attack on the Soviet Union but did hint at the possibility of war between the two states. The most he would promise Matsuoka was to fight the Russians if they interfered with the proposed Japanese assault on British and Dutch possessions in South Asia. Fearful that Germany might make another last-minute settlement with the Soviet Union as she had done in 1939, Matsuoka added Moscow to his itinerary. After several sessions of hard bargaining, he secured a five-year nonaggression pact from Stalin on April 13, 1941. The value of this agreement was qualified by the refusal of Russia to settle outstanding differences between the two countries or to shut off aid to Chinese Communists fighting Japan.

Meanwhile the more cautious Konoye had opened secret negotiations with Washington behind his Foreign Minister's back. Using Catholic missionaries in Tokyo as intermediaries, the Prime Minister proposed a three-point program as a basis for agreement with the United States: (1) virtual Japanese nullification of the Tripartite Pact, (2) withdrawal of troops from China, (3) revival of economic cooperation between the United States and Japan. After Secretary Hull had responded favorably, Konoye informed the army leaders. They recoiled at his generosity but eventually agreed to a formula for withdrawal from China after direct negotiations with Chungking and after a merger of the Chiang Kai-shek government with the Japanese puppet regime. In return they demanded from the United States both a loan and a resumption of normal economic relations. This overture was embodied in a note to Washington on April 9, 1941. It probably represented the maximum that Japan would be willing to concede. The proposed arrangements for China did not represent a belated capitulation to American insistence on restoration of the 1931 *status quo;* they offered the United States diplomatic and military concessions in return for recognition of Japan's political and economic gains on the Asian mainland.

Secretary Hull, in a noncommittal response to the Japanese note on April 16, reiterated the traditional American position. Apparently Washington intended to concede nothing, to intensify the pressure on Japan, and to keep negotiating until it could confront Tokyo with overwhelming military and economic power. The Japanese cabinet deferred a counterproposal until the return of Matsuoka, who was infuriated when he found out that negotiations had been carried on behind his back. The next Nipponese note of May 7 bore the stamp of the Foreign Minister and was less conciliatory in tone. It proposed that the two countries pledge themselves not to go to war with each other — a transparent device for tying Washington's hands while Tokyo attacked British and Dutch possessions in South Asia. Hull rejected the proposition flatly, as well as a second bid of May 12 which offered less than Konoye had offered on April 9. Talks continued in leisurely fashion through May and early June with the United States refusing to budge from its stand that a complete Japanese withdrawal from China was a prerequisite to any settlement.

The persistent inflexibility of Washington and the decision of Hitler to attack Russia on June 22 seriously weakened the position of the moderates in Tokyo. Matsuoka fell from power on July 16, but the involvement of Russia in the European war generated irresistible pressure on the Konoye cabinet for a resumption of expansion southward. One of the last acts of the deposed Foreign Minister had been to send Vichy France an ultimatum on July 14 demanding the cession of specified areas in southern Indo-China for Japanese air, land, or naval bases. His replacement, Admiral Toyoda, kept up the pressure on the helpless French and they capitulated on July 23, 1941.

The same day Secretary Hull told the new Japanese ambassador to the United States, Admiral Kichisaburo Nomura, that the conduct of Tokyo was making further negotiations futile. The following day Roosevelt warned Nomura that he might embargo the export of oil to Japan unless the Imperial government pulled out of Indo-China. On July 26 he applied the threatened embargo on oil and other vital materials not covered by earlier bans, froze all Japanese funds in the United States, and closed the Panama Canal to Nipponese shipping. He also announced the mobilization of the Philippine militia. In a demonstration of diplomatic solidarity with the United States, the British and Dutch announced a similar embargo on oil shipments to Japan.

These retaliatory measures pushed the Far Eastern crisis into its penultimate stage and forced Tokyo to choose between retreat or continued expansion at the risk of war. The stiffened attitude of the administration commanded widespread support at home but only because the public knew nothing about the preceding negotiations or the growing desperation of Japan.

As matters turned out, the Japanese hesitated once more. Under heavy pressure from the military clique for an immediate attack on Singapore and the Dutch East Indies, the desperate Konoye appealed on August 7 to Roosevelt for a personal conference to discuss methods of reducing tension. The President was encouraged by Hull to reject the proposal unless Japan agreed to the American terms on China in advance. Konoye renewed his plea for direct talks on August 18 and on September 6, 22, and 25. The contents of all these offers suggest that Japan was prepared to sacrifice both the Tripartite Alliance and part of her gains in China for a settlement with the United States. No reciprocal disposition to bargain existed in Washington. The administration slammed the door shut on successive proposals by making an agreement conditional on Japanese withdrawal from China and termination of all other encroachments on the Open Door. This policy rested ultimately on the assumption that the relative strength of powers remains static for an indefinite period. This belief in turn interacted with an older American insistence on the sanctity of treaty obligations. As a result, the administration felt obliged to enforce the *status quo* established by the Washington treaties long after the conditions underwriting it had disappeared. It was to fight a four-year war for a dispensation that could not be restored and to wind up with a new *status quo* less satisfactory than the one proposed by Konoye in the fall of 1941.

After Roosevelt had rejected a final private appeal by Konoye on October 13 for some sort of compromise, developments pointed irresistibly to a military solution of the Far Eastern crisis. The Prime Minister resigned on October 17 and was succeeded by General Tojo, who headed the war party. Two weeks of irresolution ensued while the Emperor, the Navy, and business groups struggled to avert war. The deadlock was broken on November 5 when Tojo agreed to a final round of negotiations with the understanding that he could order an attack on the United States if no agreement had been reached by November 25. The same day he issued orders to the Japanese armed forces to be ready for military operations in early December.

Meanwhile another futile series of conversations between Hull and Nomura was launched on November 7. Ten days later Tokyo dispatched a special envoy, Saburo Kurusu, to Washington with what the Imperial government regarded as an ultimatum. He delivered his message on November 20. Twenty-four hours later the State Department intercepted a dispatch to Nomura and Kurusu. It ordered them to continue the conversations until November 29 but warned them of rapid developments after that date. Word also reached Washington on November 25 that Japanese troopships had been sighted off Formosa — a rumor promptly confirmed by British and Dutch protests.

In the face of these threats, Washington took an uncompromising position. On November 26, Hull rejected the Japanese note of November 20 and suggested a "mutual declaration of policy." The counterproposal contained nothing new. It simply invited the adherence of the Imperial government to the terms upon which the United States had been insisting as the basis for Far Eastern peace since 1937. On November 24 and again on the 27th Washington anticipated the possible consequences of its action by alerting military commanders in the Pacific to a Japanese surprise attack. The President and his advisers believed that if such a blow materialized it would be aimed at exposed American outposts like Guam and the Philippines, though they considered an assault on British and Dutch colonies in Southeast Asia more probable. Roosevelt credited the Japanese with an awareness of the internal cleavage over American foreign policy and assumed that they would avoid acts of direct provocation likely to restore national unity. What he foresaw was a rapid envelopment of Singapore and the Dutch East Indies while isolationists immobilized America with debates about the impropriety of intervention. Reports of Japanese troop concentrations in Indo-China during the last week of November seemed to confirm the forecast. American military commanders in the Pacific accepted this view. It gave them no excuse for a relaxation of elementary vigilance. Nevertheless they were lulled into a false sense of security which left them unprepared for the tragic sequel at Pearl Harbor.

The miscalculation was ironic in the extreme because America paid a severe penalty for one of her few efforts to base Far Eastern diplomacy on rational considerations. Roosevelt had every right to expect that Japan would attack the British and Dutch immediately and conciliate the United States until the European powers were defeated. American possessions did not bar the path to the East Indies, while American opinion was far from unanimous about the desirability of aiding the British and Dutch. The situation invited Japan to continue her reliance on the Tokyo version of "divide and conquer," which was "occupy and apologize." However, the policy of piecemeal conquest was the sole alternative that the contending factions within the Imperial government had refused to consider. The advisers of the Emperor had left themselves only a choice between a humiliating retreat and a war with the United States. Hence the final breakdown of negotiations in late November set the stage for a direct attack on America.

PEARL HARBOR

On November 25 a Japanese carrier task force left the Kuriles for an assault on Pearl Harbor, the great American bastion in the mid-Pacific. The receipt of Hull's uncompromising "mutual declaration of policy" in Tokyo the next day convinced the wavering Emperor that there was no alternative to war. With the Germans at the gates of Moscow and Hitler committed to fight the

United States as soon as Japan struck, Hirohito approved the plan of the High Command on November 29.

An uneasy week ensued while the Japanese aircraft carriers crept closer to Pearl Harbor and the Japanese army made preparations for the attack on Singapore and the Dutch East Indies. In Washington, Kurusu and Nomura tried to maintain the pretense that Tokyo was still seeking a settlement. However, the large-scale movement of Japanese troops toward Malaya could not be concealed and became the subject of repeated conferences between Roosevelt and his military advisers during the first week of December. The consensus was that Japan would soon start a war in the South Pacific and that the United States ought to enter the conflict on the side of the British and the Dutch. Still, the President dared not make a solid commitment to these potential allies because he despaired of getting a war resolution through Congress. Instead he dispatched an urgent appeal to the Emperor Hirohito on December 6 for some action that would dispel the threat of war. The same afternoon the belated reply to the Hull proposal arrived at the Japanese embassy in Washington. Since the United States had cracked the Nipponese code a year before Pearl Harbor, notice that Tokyo was breaking off negotiations reached Roosevelt before the ambassador delivered it on the fateful morning of December 7.

By the previous evening the carrier task force under Admiral Nagumo had slipped undetected within range of Pearl Harbor. The Japanese were stalking big game, because Admiral Husband E. Kimmel had concentrated the American Pacific fleet at that great base. Responsibility for the protection of the Navy rested with the Admiral and with General Walter C. Short, who commanded the ground and air units at Pearl Harbor. Neither of them expected an attack nor bothered to deploy their forces in an appropriate defensive posture. Hence when the Japanese planes flew over Pearl Harbor in two waves at 7:55 A.M. and 8:50 A.M. on the morning of December 7, they dropped their bombs unmolested. Within two hours the entire base had been reduced to twisted metal and smoking fragments of wood. All eight of the battleships and most of the smaller units were either destroyed or disabled. The same fate overtook the Air Force, which failed to get a single plane off the ground.

When news of the disaster reached the mainland in midafternoon, the initial reaction of the public was compounded equally of disbelief and of wild indignation. These emotions dominated because citizens knew next to nothing of the diplomatic negotiations preceding the rupture. Ignorant of the magnitude of the crisis, they were unprepared for a Far Eastern war and furious over a treacherous attack. Incredulity vanished in late afternoon on the heels of reports about Japanese landings on Malaya, Siam, the Philippines, and American islands in the Pacific, leaving only an uncomplicated desire for revenge. The next day, Monday, December 8, Congress gave a striking demonstration of national unity. In less than an hour it approved the President's request for a declaration of war against Japan. Only the negative vote of Representative Jeanette Rankin of Montana prevented the joint resolution from carrying unanimously. On December 11 Hitler and Mussolini honored their pledge to Japan by formally declaring war on the United States. Congress returned the compliment the same day and America entered the European conflict.

Notwithstanding the fact that the isolationists experienced the greater immediate embarrassment from Pearl Harbor, neither side emerged from the four-year debate with much cause for satisfaction. The internationalists were probably right in advocating vigorous countermeasures against the revisionist powers in 1940–41, but only because Roosevelt's previous neglect of world problems had deprived the country of realistic alternatives. They were either naive or dishonest in giving categorical assurances that their policy would keep America out of war. At the very least, the internationalists ought to have told the country that their program carried strong risks of involvement.

The isolationists were certainly wrong in their assessment of America's world position, but behaved more candidly and consistently than their foes. Had their advice been followed, it is probable that American involvement would have been postponed several years, although it would probably have occurred under less favorable circumstances than in 1941. The real difficulty stems from the fact that no responsible leader advocated the application of American power to world problems during the middle thirties when such action had some prospect of forcing adjustments on a peaceful basis. Roosevelt switched suddenly in 1937 from a policy of ignoring all changes in power relationships to a policy of trying to undo changes completely. This kind of reversal could only lead to war. Nobody knows how many Americans disapproved of both the internationalists and interventionists, but lacked the leadership to rally behind a different policy. Whatever their numbers, they were drowned out by the intellectuals who promoted a militant isolationism until 1937 and divided into a pair of warring groups thereafter.

SUGGESTED READINGS

1. Bailey, T. A., *A Diplomatic History of the American People.*
2. Beard, C. A., *President Roosevelt and the Coming of the War.*
3. Bemis, S. F., *A Diplomatic History of the United States.*
4. Langer, W. L., and Gleason, S. E., *The Challenge to Isolation, 1937–40.*
5. Rauch, B., *Roosevelt: Munich to Pearl Harbor.*

CHAPTER TWENTY-FIVE

MOBILIZATION FOR TOTAL WAR

FREE EXPRESSION IN WORLD WAR II

On the morrow of Pearl Harbor, America turned to the formidable task of mobilizing for victory. The sneak attack by the Japanese created a solidarity which would have been impossible a week earlier. Momentarily, the designations of *isolationist* and *internationalist* ceased to have any meaning. Senator Burton K. Wheeler and Colonel Charles A. Lindbergh tendered the administration pledges of cooperation. The *Chicago Tribune*, the Hearst papers, and other journalistic critics of Roosevelt's foreign policy reversed themselves and urged the nation to support the Commander-in-Chief. The hitherto influential America First Committee quietly disintegrated. The reorientation of isolationist thinking was hastened by the German and Italian declarations of war which came less than twenty-four hours later. This development left the erstwhile foes of intervention so exposed that reaffirmation of their position would have invited charges of treason. No prominent isolationists cared to run such a risk, but most of them recanted with mental reservations. Their pledges of support for the war effort were genuine enough, but they still blamed Roosevelt for provoking the Axis Powers to attack America and they silently cursed the crisis which prevented an immediate post-mortem on his foreign policy.

Probably the most wholesome by-product of solidarity was a respect for civil liberties wholly lacking in World War I. Toleration flourishes most readily when dissent shrinks to a minimum as it did during the conflict. The minority groups which had denounced the Wilsonian crusade either no longer existed or else took a different view of American obligations. Hence there was no mass sentiment for setting in motion Public Safety Committees and volunteer patriotic organizations.

Citizens of German and Italian ancestry supported the war against the Axis as unreservedly as the rest of the population. The lukewarm among them were hard to find, and the public showed no interest in the handful of

German spies and saboteurs rounded up by the Department of Justice. Even the trial and imprisonment of domestic Fascists like William Dudley Pelley, George Christians, and Ralph Townsend for violation of the espionage laws aroused little excitement. A more ambitious attempt to convict twenty-eight pro-Nazis of sedition ended in a mistrial which nobody seemed to regret. Left-wing groups, once critical of participation in what they called imperialistic wars, abandoned their old position. Communists, who took their cue from Moscow, vied with administration spokesmen in extravagant denunciations of Fascist states. Socialists were caught in the midst of a quest for new ideological bearings, and the war compounded their confusion; in the end most of them rallied to the support of their own country. No Socialists courted martyrdom after Pearl Harbor as Eugene V. Debs and Victor Berger had done twenty-five years earlier. Nor did firebrands from splinter left-wing groups, like the defunct I.W.W. and the Nonpartisan League of World War I, outrage patriots with wild diatribes against the war. In fact, the cohesiveness of Americans was so great that they tolerated occasional pacifistic sermons and sneers at the Red Cross.

Administration policy reflected the popular attitude toward civil liberties so faithfully that it violated them at the one point where the majority lacked a sense of justice. This capitulation to ugly prejudices took the form of a forced uprooting of 112,000 loyal Japanese-Americans from their homes on the West Coast. Victims of hysteria, they were removed by General John L. DeWitt, who declared the western sections of the Pacific Coast states and Arizona to be a war zone. Interned first in temporary stockades and later transferred to ten relocation centers in western deserts, the Nisei suffered untold hardships. Eventually 18,000 who were suspected of disloyalty were imprisoned in a camp at Tule Lake, California, and the remainder freed. Barred from returning to the West Coast by local opinion, most of them resettled in the East and Midwest. The Supreme Court declined to challenge the evacuation and detention although these people were American citizens and guilty only of an indiscreet choice of ancestors.

Although the restraints on free expression were not as great in World War II as in World War I, propaganda and censorship practices turned out to be considerably worse. Woodrow Wilson had organized his wartime propaganda around the idea that enemy peoples were not congenitally wicked, but were misled by irresponsible autocratic rulers. During World War II, Washington encouraged the impression that the Germans and Japanese were evil to a man and deserved no mercy. This viewpoint created much unnecessary mischief and nerved enemy peoples to fight longer and more desperately. It also involved the United States in the futile and costly policy of destroying states and subsequently rebuilding them to withstand the Russians.

The War Department managed to establish an effective censorship of war news by insisting that it alone should decide what information about military operations was suitable for release. These tactics annoyed the champions of

The battle against inflation: The "topkick" greets the rookies. (Jerry Doyle cartoon reprinted from The Philadelphia Daily News, *1942.)*

freedom of the press. They argued that the military lowered a security curtain to conceal evidence of their own blunders and to enjoy immunity from criticism. The administration tried to steer a middle course, really pleasing nobody. On December 19, 1941, Roosevelt established an Office of Censorship with Byron Price, an experienced journalist, as its director. This unit was made responsible for the screening of information in letters passing between the United States and other countries. Since the censors were expected to delete everything from data on troop movements to weather reports, the job required nearly 10,000 employees. Trouble did not develop so much over the censorship of mail as over the voluntary code binding newspapers and radios not to release military news unless cleared by appropriate officials. This arrangement meant in effect that the War and Navy Departments decided what information would be released.

Repeated criticisms of military censorship by writers, newscasters, and publishers drove the President to create a mediating agency — the Office of War Information (OWI) in June 1942. Vested with extensive powers to coordinate and disseminate information on all aspects of the war, it aroused great expectations. Its director, Elmer Davis, a popular radio commentator, quickly organized foreign and domestic branches, both of which ground out voluminous material on war policies and postwar objectives. Moving pictures, radios, newspapers, and magazines carried the administration viewpoint so persuasively that Congress all but killed the domestic branch of OWI on the eve of the 1944 election. Unfortunately, dissemination of effective propaganda was not quite the same thing as serving up uncensored news on the progress of the war. The appointment of Davis did not appreciably change the basic situation.

OBSTACLES TO RAPID MOBILIZATION

The problem of preserving cohesiveness and uniformity of thought under wartime conditions was mild compared with that of inspiring cooperation in economic mobilization. For one thing, patriotic sentiment did not produce a uniform spirit of self-sacrifice on the home front. Some citizens gave unstintingly of their time and energy, serving on draft or ration boards, acting as air-raid wardens, volunteering to entertain servicemen on leave in unfamiliar communities, and working as harvest hands in labor-scarce communities. Others felt that their obligations were discharged by strict obedience to government regulations for the conservation of critical materials. Disconcertingly large numbers rationalized their patriotism to the point where it became synonymous with their own economic interests. Such people made sacrifices only after rational calculation and only after assuring themselves that others made proportional sacrifices. This psychology fed on the attitude of major business, agricultural, and labor pressure groups, which were better organized than in 1917 and were disposed to quarrel about the terms of their participation in mobilization. Reservations about patriotic obligations also grew as the initial fright caused by the attack at Pearl Harbor receded. Recollection of the fact that America had never lost a war provided them with an additional incentive to carry on business as usual.

The example set by the administration encouraged a leisurely approach to problems of mobilization. Official expressions of alarm over deficiencies in the war machine were not always matched by decisive action. Despite repeated references to the gravity of the fuel and manpower shortages, motorists were not denied the rationed gasoline for Sunday drives, nor sports fans the athletes for major league baseball games. Mobilization officials justified such concessions to the public as productive of higher morale. In some cases, relaxation of controls undoubtedly paid dividends but it often produced the opposite result, encouraging people to regard wartime controls as unimportant or unnecessary. Roosevelt unintentionally reïnforced the deep-seated popular contempt for the bureaucracy by his reluctance to discharge ineffective subordinates. Instead of making a clear-cut decision in such instances, he usually transferred their powers to new agencies. This method of dealing with incompetence frequently blurred the lines of responsibility, created a no-man's land between competing agencies, and added to the general confusion.

The final product was difficult to evaluate. Conscientious junior administrators and war workers, afflicted by blundering superiors as well as by endless red tape, found it hard to believe that the total enterprise could succeed. Yet, in the end, mobilization did succeed beyond their fondest expectations. Troops were equipped and transported to remote theaters in the Pacific, new deadly weapons like the bazooka and the atomic bomb were developed, and allies all over the world were generously supplied with critical war goods. America accomplished this astounding feat with a minimum of inconvenience. The manufacture of automobiles and most electrical appliances for civilian use was discontinued. Items like cigarettes, chocolates, and nylon stockings disappeared periodically from shop windows. Meat, shoes, rubber tires, and many other items were rationed. Even so, most Americans enjoyed a higher standard of living during the war than in the depression decade.

What people hailed as the miracle of production was not a miracle in the sense that the United States set herself impossible goals and fulfilled them. The mobilization partook of the miraculous because she reached readily attainable goals despite inconsiderable sacrifices on the home front and an unhurried approach to the problems of building a war machine. It is difficult to avoid the conclusion that the fortunate circumstances of geography, near economic self-sufficiency, and considerable unused plant capacity played a key role in the success of the war effort. Security from bombing attacks, abundant resources, and an economy capable of expanding production substantially on the basis of existent facilities more than counter-balanced the irresolution and halfheartedness of mobilization.

THE MOBILIZATION OF MILITARY MANPOWER

The most immediate and pressing job of the planners in December of 1941 was mobilization of manpower. As in 1917, they faced the double problem of meeting the production requirements of the military and the home fronts while adjusting the economy to the withdrawal of ten to twelve million young men from the labor force. At the outset more attention was paid to the build-up of the armed services because the Axis took the offensive on three continents and their adjoining seas. The members of the Allied coalition did not expect immediate help from American troops in Europe and Africa, but none of them thought the war could be won in either sector without them. Meanwhile the brunt of the battle to prevent the Japanese from overrunning East Asia, the South Pacific, and Australia fell on the United States. The pre-Pearl Harbor army available for meeting these staggering commitments was a conscript force of 1.6 million recruited under the Burke-Wadsworth Act. The nucleus of career men comprised only a small part of the total. Since public opinion would have rebelled against a training program that prepared the rookies for overseas combat, and since no responsible strategist anticipated an invasion of the United States, the conscript army had not been taught to do anything in particular. Worse still, the well-advertised reluctance of Congress to renew the draft law in the fall of 1941 made soldiers restless and uncooperative. Morale also suffered because much-needed training weapons were diverted from army camps to overseas foes of the Axis. Occasionally, draftees suffered the indignity of being forced to drill with broomsticks on their shoulders.

Despite the pyramiding of such frustrations during the months before the outbreak of the war, no controversy over the principle of conscription developed after Pearl Harbor as it did after American entrance into World War I. Citizens did not challenge the constitutionality of involuntary military service nor dispute the superiority of conscription over the hit-and-miss volunteer system. Congressional opposition to the draft likewise melted away when the conflict started. Inasmuch as the machinery already existed, all that Congress needed to do was to amend the Burke-Wadsworth Act. On December 13 it removed the ban on the use of draftees overseas, and a few days later extended the term of service to the duration and six months. Subsequent amendments made additional age groups eligible for conscription. All hitherto unregistered males between the ages of 20 and 44 became subject to call, while those over 44 but under 65 were placed in a special manpower pool which could be tapped for essential industries. Resistance to a lowering of the draft age lasted until June 1942, but in the end the Army had its way. The reduction of the draft age to 18 lowered the pressure for the conscription of older men, and before the end of 1942 the Army stopped calling up men between the ages of 38 and 44. Congress wrote into the draft laws provisions for relieving conscientious objectors, citizens with numerous dependents, and medical and divinity students. It also authorized deferments for skilled industrial personnel, otherwise subject to the draft, until replacements could be trained. These broad statements of policy guided the Selective Service Director, General Lewis B. Hershey, and his organization, which consisted of 54 state and territorial agencies, 515 boards of appeal, and 6,443 local boards. Administration of the law lacked uniformity, because local boards were forced to draw their monthly quotas out of manpower pools which varied in composition. Some drafted husbands and fathers early in the war. Others with an abundant supply of young unmarried men avoided that unpopular step for nearly two years. Boards in the latter category often applied a liberal deferment policy to skilled industrial workers and farm laborers. Appeals from the decisions of local boards usually involved dependency cases, conscientious objectors, and certain religious sects.

As the impersonal machinery of conscription drew into the armed forces ever-larger numbers of men with families, pressure mounted for more generous pay and dependency allotments. Congress responded in mid-1942 by raising Army privates and their counterparts in other services from $21 to $50 per month. Proportionate increases were granted to the upper ranks, making the American enlisted men and officers the most highly paid in the world. Later the same year Congress approved the Service Men's Allotment Act, granting $50 to the wives of those in the armed forces. Soldier gratitude for this legislation was tempered by a provision deducting $22 from their pay. However, the same law added to the basic dependency allotment $12 for the first child and $10 for each additional child. Later the rates were raised to $30 and $20 respectively.

In June 1944 Congress passed a rehabilitation law, popularly known as the G.I. bill, which authorized compensation to unemployed veterans at the rate of $20 a week for 52 weeks. Similar compensation provisions were made for self-employed veterans. The bill also obligated the government to guarantee 50 per cent of loans up to $2,000 sought by veterans buying homes or setting up in business. Other sections appropriated money to enlarge the Veterans Hospital System and to increase the placement facilities for ex-servicemen in the United States Employment Service. The most novel feature of the rehabilitation law was a provision commiting the government to finance veterans who desired a college education. Under this arrangement veterans were eligible to receive up to $500 a year for books and tuition plus $50 a month for subsistence. The program covered the full four-year college course and encouraged the enrollment of married men through enlarged subsistence payments. Funds were also made available for vocational training in every profession from welding to bartending.

Although most conscription and rehabilitation legislation revolved about the problems of creating and demobilizing a mass army, the personnel of other branches were entitled to the same pay scales and benefits. Draft boards eventually registered 31 million men and called up over 9 million for service. At the same time the threat of induction in the Army — and most especially into the infantry — indirectly stimulated volunteering for other branches of the armed forces. At peak strength, the Navy boasted 3,883,250, the Marine Corps 599,693, and the Coast Guard 241,902. The grand total that served in all four branches some time during the war was 15,145,115. To free a substantial number of military personnel from routine clerical, inspectional, and instructional jobs that could be performed by women, the government took the unprecedented step of organizing the Women's Army Corps (the WAC) and the Women Accepted for Volunteer Emergency Service (the WAVES). The former unit was incorporated into the regular Army and headed by Colonel Oveta Culp Hobby; the latter was organized as a branch of the Navy under the direction of Lieutenant Commander Mildred McAfee. More than 100,000 young women volunteered for service in the WAC and approximately 86,000 in the WAVES. Pay scales were the same as for men of similar rank in the Army and Navy. A small percentage of both units saw service overseas, but the greater number performed their duties in the United States.

The relatively rapid mobilization of the armed forces made it necessary for the government to show comparable haste in constructing camps, producing weapons, and training military personnel in the operation of them. The same problem had existed at the outset of World War I on a smaller scale and, as in that instance, was ultimately solved because of the tremendous productivity and technological know-how of Americans. These two assets more than counterbalanced the waste motion, red tape, and inept planning characteristic of the early stages of such projects. Aside from the magnitude of the enterprise, mobilization for World War II was more difficult in that it involved training men to fight under a variety of conditions and to operate unbelievably complicated equipment. The planners responded to this challenge by reproducing the North African environment in the California desert, the Apennines in Colorado, and the New Guinea jungles in Louisiana. They also established numerous airfields in the southwestern United States where weather permitted flight training over 250 days a year. At first, the Army Air Force suffered from a serious shortage of instructors, but eventually this arm of the service grew from a modest 292,000 on the eve of Pearl Harbor to a total ten times as great in 1945. Instruction in the operation of fighters and bombers proved to be just one phase of a program which taught military personnel to operate everything from submarines to radar equipment.

The four-year mobilization of military manpower enabled the United States to field a fighting force capable of meeting her global commitments. The product seems impressive when measured against pre-Pearl Harbor standards. Nevertheless, the number of able-bodied youths inducted into the armed services represented a smaller percentage of the total population than did the military establishment of any other major belligerent.

THE DRIVE FOR FULL PRODUCTION

The policy of conscription which the government relied upon to develop a strong military arm was not employed on the home front. All through the war, civilian workers, farmers, and businessmen escaped direct regimentation. Their activities were channeled into essential production by a hit-and-miss system which featured patriotic appeals, economic pressures, and subsidies concealed in varying degress. Subtle bribery in the form of price, wage, or profit guarantees often assured cooperation that would not otherwise have been forthcoming. Some recalcitrants fell in line when government rationing of critical materials prevented them from manufacturing nonessential products.

Like all semivoluntary systems for achieving precise results, the combination of inducements to secure full production from civilians was unsatisfactory from a number of standpoints. The farmers proved to be most easily handled, because they geared production to prices. Accordingly, all the planners needed to do was to offer generous price guarantees for commodities in short supply. With the enthusiastic support of the powerful farm bloc, Congress assured farmers a minimum price of 110 per cent of parity for basic crops. The prolonged disruption of agricultural production in devastated areas abroad assured higher crop prices and converted rural enthusiasm for price floors into complaints against price ceilings. Farmers also grumbled about the scarcity and high cost of livestock feed, the shortage of harvest hands, and the curtailed production of farm machinery. Nonetheless, they made every effort to increase production. Nature gave a generous assist in the form of good weather. As a result, the three years after Pearl Harbor saw record crop yields. The wheat harvest topped all previous records in 1944, while equally impressive gains were registered in corn, meat, and fats. Net cash income from farming increased more than 400 per cent between 1940 and 1945. Prosperity not only enabled farmers to extinguish debts which in some cases had hung over their heads since the 1920's, but to build up savings accounts. Simultaneously, farm tenancy declined from 38.7 per cent in 1940 to 31.7 per cent in 1945, reflecting the dual effect of improved agricultural income and the growth of job opportunities in war industry.

The mobilizers found no single formula for coaxing higher production out of industry quite so effective as the price guarantees that stimulated farm output. Businessmen did not always jump to accept cost-plus contracts from government despite the assurance of generous profits. Some were reluctant to engage in the production of unfamiliar items. Others hesitated to lose carefully developed consumer markets by switching to the manufacture of war goods. The more cautious did not want to retool even with government financial aid, on the theory that the war might end before worth-while profits could be reaped. Even in cases where the cost-plus contracts offered sufficient inducements, they encouraged wasteful production policies. Many firms padded their payrolls with scarce labor and otherwise increased their overhead, secure in the knowledge that government would absorb the costs.

Workers also proved restless, quarrelsome, and assertive where their rights were concerned. The labor force grew from 48 million to nearly 60 million during the war, but the increase in size was at the expense of efficiency. Over 15 million in the age brackets of greatest productivity were withdrawn by the armed services and were replaced by 7.5 million unemployed, 2 million housewives over the age of thirty-five, a like number of older citizens who came out of retirement, and an indeterminate number of children between the ages of fourteen and eighteen. Productivity increased sharply. Part of the gain was the result of technological improvements, and the rest was due to the fact that labor worked longer hours. The average work week increased from 40.6 hours in 1941 to 45.2 hours in 1944.

In lieu of a labor conscription program, the government established a War Manpower Commission in April 1942 to channel workers from nonessential into defense industries. Headed by Paul V. McNutt, a former Governor of Indiana, the WMC gradually developed rules that discouraged job-hopping. Workers in defense plants were forbidden to quit without the approval of the United States Employment Service. Such regulations reduced turnover but failed to serve the positive function of forcing bartenders, bookies, and other nonproductive workers into industry. Roosevelt long resisted worker conscription because of the opposition of organized labor. In his annual message in January 1944, he cautiously endorsed the idea but made no real effort to push it during the presidential campaign. With the election out of the way and the Germans on the offensive in December 1944, he renewed his plea for a labor draft law. The House acted promptly but the Senate stalled until the collapse of Germany destroyed popular interest in the measure.

Just as critical as the need for recruiting ever-larger supplies of labor to cope with the demands of a war economy was the problem of cutting production losses due to absenteeism. The loss of man-hours through strikes had been a negligible problem during World War I because organized labor lacked a secure foothold in most basic industries. Although a hastily convened labor-management conference promised to settle all disputes affecting essential industry by negotiation, over 3,000 strikes erupted in 1942, 3,752 in 1943, and 4,956 in 1944. During the 44 months of war, some 14,700 strikes idled 6.7 million workers for periods varying from a few days to several weeks. Man-days lost were estimated at 36 million, the worst year being 1943 which accounted for more than one-third of the total. Actually, the record of organized labor seemed worse than it was. Small wildcat strikes and jurisdictional squabbles rather than crippling shutdowns of essential industry accounted for most of the work stoppage. The vast majority of workers honored their no-strike pledge. What made organized labor so vocal and militant was its fear that it would make a larger sacrifice for the war effort than other pressure groups.

The administration proved more willing than the public to make concessions that would allay union fears. The National War Labor Board, established on January 12, 1942, maintained a consistent prolabor attitude despite the fact that equal representation was given to management, labor, and the public. Composed of twelve men under the Chairmanship of William H. Davis, it handled all disputes that could not be settled through the conventional channels of collective bargaining or conciliation. The most open manifestation of its partiality to organized labor was in its vigilant protection of union rights based on the Wagner Act. Awards even ordered employers to grant the closed shop whenever a majority of workers favored it. Generous protection for unions was afforded by the maintenance-of-membership clause which permitted them to recruit newly hired employees during the life of a contract. It gave labor organizers a period of grace during which they could use the ample privileges granted under the Wagner Act to win new members.

The indulgent attitude of the NWLB toward organized labor did not make it immune to criticism from that source. Far from being grateful, the unions accepted the guarantees of the Wagner Act as their birthright and badgered the Board for wage increases. Like the farm organizations which believed that almost any agricultural problem could be solved by higher crop prices, the unions endorsed upward revision of pay scales as the magic means of improving productivity and industrial relations. Employers showed an unprecedented sympathy toward demands for higher wages because of war-contract rules permitting them to pass all costs of production on to the government. Nevertheless, the NWLB, which was authorized to freeze wages by executive order under the War Powers Act, could not permit indiscriminate pay increases without jeopardizing the entire stabilization program. Resistance to wage demands provoked a flurry of strikes in 1942. In July 1942, the Board established a general pattern for pay increases by granting a 15 per cent raise to employees of several small steel companies. Known as the Little Steel formula, the new yardstick offered labor a compensatory raise to cover the increase in living costs after 1939.

Once the original wage freeze had been cracked in mid-1942, union leaders regrouped their forces for an attack on the formula. Work stoppages reached serious proportions in the spring of 1943. A nationwide transportation strike was narrowly averted, but John L. Lewis called the miners out of the pits three times in two months. Neither the President's appeal to the miners over the head of Lewis nor government seizure of the mines did more than postpone the breaching of the Little Steel formula. The victory of the defiant Lewis was denied by the government and partly concealed in pay increases to compensate miners for a shorter lunch period and for travel to and from the pits. Public wrath at the behavior of the miners goaded Congress to pass the Smith-Connally War Disputes Act over the President's veto in June 1943. The new legislation sanctioned government seizure of strike-ridden war plants, provided criminal penalties for those who tried to promote strikes in government-operated plants, and forced unions to give a thirty-day notice before taking a strike vote of its members. This restrictive law also annoyed labor leaders by prohibiting union contributions to political campaign funds. Simultaneously, several states in the South and West passed laws curbing union activities.

Whether the concerted effort of organized labor to secure pay increases was any more detrimental to the mobilization effort than the self-interested maneuvers of other pressure groups cannot be easily determined. Living costs rose more than 30 per cent during the war, but the earnings of union workers increased 70 per cent. Two factors qualified the impressiveness of this pay raise. Part of the gain was due to overtime work which would presumably end after the war. Furthermore, most of the increases went to the 15 million organized workers, while the remainder of the labor force either barely kept up with the rise in cost of living or fell far behind it. Even if labor as a whole did not make disproportionate gains, the public thought it did, and regarded the strikes as unwarranted.

ALLOCATING STRATEGIC MATERIALS

In theory, the mobilization of material resources ought to have proceeded more smoothly than the mobilization of human beings. However, the construction of an industrial war machine was characterized by the same initial slowness, frustrating confusion, and political maneuvering that hampered the organization of producers and fighters. In the long run the uniformity of delays and waste motion on both sectors of the mobilization front was an advantage because it meant that the training of soldiers and the fabrication of their weapons would be synchronized. Still, the ultimate effectiveness of the industrial economy could hardly have been anticipated in 1941 and 1942 except by people with the blindest faith in their destiny. As in the mobilization of human resources, American success owed less to intelligent planning than to inbred technological skills, abundant time for repairing blunders, and freedom from enemy air attack.

World War I experience provided the government with a record of mistakes to be avoided in converting industry for the struggle against the Axis. Several prewar studies of industrial mobilization also helped the planners to become aware of the relation between technical production problems and quasi-political matters like labor, price, and taxation policy. Additional stimulus for anticipating the stresses of conversion was provided by the hard-pressed British and French, who ordered vast quantities of American goods long before the attack on Pearl Harbor.

These advantages did not immediately translate themselves into farsighted prewar mobilization plans. The administration tended to let matters drift, because it saw the political unwisdom of preparing energetically for war while promising to preserve peace. Roosevelt took the first step in August 1939 by appointing Edward R. Stettinius, Jr., of the United States Steel Corporation to head a War Resources Board. Staffed mostly by representatives of heavy industry, the WRB fell under a murderous cross fire from New Dealers and isolationists. Before Roosevelt dissolved it two months later, the Board submitted a plan for gradual mobilization. The President made no attempt to act on it or on a more drastic plan presented by Bernard Baruch, the chairman of the War Industries Board during World War I. Nothing further was done until the fall of France in May 1940, when Roosevelt revived the Advisory Commission to the old Council of National Defense. He drew the membership from all the major economic groups, including consumers, and entrusted the chairmanship to William S. Knudsen, the president of General Motors Corporation. The Advisory Commission, like its predecessor, was doomed because Congress did not regard industrial mobilization as an urgent enough matter to warrant a statutory concentration of power in the hands of a single agency. Wary of risking an open political fight on the issue, Roosevelt resorted to his favorite escape mechanism — creation of another agency to supersede the Advisory Commission. Established on January 7, 1941, and known as the Office of Production Mobilization, the new organization was expected to coordinate civilian and military production. Knudsen, who served as a symbol of American technological wizardry, survived the shakeup but was forced to share his authority with Sidney Hillman of the C.I.O. The OPM commenced operations just in time to reap the harvest of criticisms precipitated by the inconveniences of partial mobilization. Shortages of steel, rubber, aluminum, electric power, and railroad rolling stock plagued manufacturers of consumer goods as well as the automotive and other industries attempting to convert to war production. Rising prices intensified the scramble for scarce raw materials, while the struggle between the OPM and other government agencies led to the virtual breakdown of the priorities system.

On August 28, 1941, Roosevelt repeated his administrative sleight of hand, abolishing part of the OPM, reorganizing the remainder, and creating a Supply Priorities and Allocation Board under the chairmanship of Donald M. Nelson, a senior executive of Sears, Roebuck. Since nothing had really changed but the names of the boards and the faces of the powerless men who staffed them, confusion continued on the production front. Chaos did not end until the attack on Pearl Harbor freed the administration from the necessity of soft-pedaling industrial mobilization to placate isolationists. Once America entered the conflict, Roosevelt demanded and Congress quickly passed the first War Powers Act on December 18, 1941. Modeled on the Overman Act of World War I, it authorized the President to reorganize and redistribute the powers of mobilization agencies. Congress also amended existing laws to expedite the procurement of essential supplies and to pave the way for government use of property confiscated from the enemy.

Roosevelt moved promptly, merging the remnants of older mobilization agencies into a brand-new organization, the War Production Board, created with the War Industries Board of World War I in mind. Donald M. Nelson was made chairman in January 1942 and was given virtually the same dictatorial powers over industry that Wilson had conferred on Bernard Baruch twenty-five years earlier. The work was broken down into six major divisions: purchases, production, materials, industry operations, labor, and civilian supply. The new organization relied on the Industry Advisory Committees that had been so helpful to Baruch in 1918. It also reached down to the individual war plants through some five thousand labor-management committees. These intermediary groups served as a two-way transmission belt for all suggestions aimed at improving efficiency.

Nelson started out energetically enough. During the early months of 1942 he gradually shut down the production of automobiles, electrical appliances, and a whole range of metal goods used by civilian consumers. Residential construction except for the housing of defense workers was also discontinued. This policy freed fresh plant capacity for the manufacture of war equipment and helped to check the drain on scarce raw materials. Unfortunately it worked severe hardship on small industries that could not convert easily to war production. Some of them received relief from the Small War Plants Corporation (SWPC), an agency organized to secure war contracts for small business. Informal suspension of the antitrust laws and the pooling of industrial patents afforded some additional help. While WPB regulations drove some companies to the verge of bankruptcy, they brought others unheard-of prosperity. Many took advantage of changes in the 1940 tax law to expand their capital facilities and write off construction costs over a five-year period. Further expansion was stimulated by congressional appropriations, parts of which entered the economy through the planned expenditures of the WPB.

Notwithstanding a hopeful beginning, Nelson's career as industrial dictator proved to be short-lived. Convivial and easygoing, he lacked the aggressiveness to dominate all the agencies competing for power. The defense secretaries prevented him from controlling the all-important allocation of priorities on critical materials. Leon Henderson, who had presided over the Office of Price Administration and Civilian Supply since its inception in April 1941, jealously guarded his limited powers, thereby blocking overall coordination of price policy. Nelson succeeded in stimulating the industrial build-up but failed to stop the wild scramble for scarce raw materials and to break the numerous bottlenecks.

The rising volume of criticism in the fall of 1942, coupled with the passage of an anti-inflation act in October, gave Roosevelt the opportunity to make a reorganization uniting the administration of industrial production, rationing, and price control. He retained the harassed Nelson as chairman of the WPB, but transferred most of its authority to a super-agency — the Office of Economic Stabilization. The tough but able James F. Byrnes was enticed from the Supreme Court to head the new organization and ride herd on all groups in the war economy. He quickly established such firm control of steel, copper, and other scarce metals that the production bottlenecks disappeared. He also managed to coordinate allocation, rationing, and price policies, minimizing frictions between the civilian and military sectors. He purchased these successes at the price of excessive attention to detail. As a result, Roosevelt made the last of his numerous reorganizations in May 1943, creating an Office of War Mobilization for Byrnes, who was thereafter known as "Assistant President." Another southerner and former congressman, Fred M. Vinson of Kentucky, was prevailed upon to leave the bench and take over the job of Economic Stabilizer vacated by Byrnes. Thereafter except for an occasional obstacle the mobilization of the war machine proceeded smoothly and efficiently.

Some aspects of industry that had provided serious problems for planners in 1917 caused less trouble during World War II. For a time mobilization was hampered by a shortage of boxcars, but no crisis developed comparable to the one that had forced government operation of the railroads in Wilson's time. The carriers moved more men and material than ever before and with a minimum of confusion. Depression had forced railroads to improve efficiency and inaugurate drastic economies as a price of survival. These harsh lessons were learned so well that the Office of Defense Transportation (ODT), directed by Joseph B. Eastman, had less to do than its World War I counterpart.

Technological improvements resulting in the more rapid construction of ships enabled America to weather an initial shortage without serious distress, despite the crippling blows struck by Axis U-boats. Shipbuilder Henry J. Kaiser developed an assembly line technique which produced ten-thousand-ton cargo boats in a month and a half — or roughly one-third of the time required during World War I. General supervision of the shipbuilding program was entrusted to a War Shipping Administration (WSA) headed by Vice-Admiral Emory S. Land. Simultaneously, the government pressed forward energetically with a program to create a fleet more than twice as large as the one partially destroyed at Pearl Harbor.

The complexity of modern industry made it inevitable that deficiencies of key raw materials normally imported from countries overrun by the Axis would create special problems. Rubber was a case in point. No real effort had been made to build a rubber stock pile before the outbreak of war. Consequently when the Japanese overran Malaya and the Dutch East Indies in the spring of 1942, the United States lost 90 per cent of its normal supply and had little prospect of opening up additional sources of rubber abroad. The President met the crisis by appointing a special committee under the chairmanship of Bernard Baruch to investigate the situation and make recommendations. The committee proposed a drastic program for conserving rubber tires by rationing gasoline and limiting automobile speed to 35 miles per hour. It also urged immediate development of a vast synthetic rubber industry. Roosevelt promptly accepted both recommendations. William M. Jeffers, president of the Union Pacific Railroad, was placed in charge of the Rubber Division of WPB on September 15, 1942. He turned out to be a very fortunate choice. A hard-driving administrator, he cut through a jungle of obstacles and created a synthetic rubber industry that was producing 760,000 tons by 1944 — or 20 per cent more than the normal annual prewar imports from East Asia. At the same time, small but important supplementary supplies were found in Ceylon, Latin America, and Liberia.

Efforts to keep key raw materials produced abroad from reaching the Axis were often as important as opening up new sources for the use of the United States. The manifold ramifications of this double-barreled policy transformed it from a purely domestic mobilization problem to a diplomatic and strategic one involving a multitude of government departments. The Board of Economic Warfare (BEW) headed by Vice-President Henry Wallace, and the Reconstruction Finance Corporation under the supervision of Jesse Jones, Secretary of Commerce, competed with each other in coaxing additional supplies of critical materials from Latin-American countries. Repeated quarrels between Wallace and Jones over everything from price policy to purchasing methods eventually drove Roosevelt to another reorganization in July 1943. Both were stripped of authority over strategic materials and their responsibilities were transferred to a new Office of Economic Warfare headed by Leo Crowley. Later consolidations pulled the Lend-Lease Administration and other agencies into a catchall Foreign Economic Administration.

The global battle for the control of key commodities also involved the State Department, which alternately cajoled and threatened neutrals selling goods to the Axis. The effectiveness of the pressure varied directly with the fortunes of war. During the early stages, Sweden sold iron ore, Turkey chrome, and Spain wolfram to the Germans, despite State Department protests. For a time the United States engaged in preclusive buying of these and other commodities to take them off the market. When American military victories improved the diplomatic weather in 1944, all three neutrals discontinued sales of strategic materials to the Axis. Spain was the most stubborn and reversed herself only when the American government suspended oil shipments to Franco.

PRICE CONTROL

Closely intertwined with the problems of mobilizing manpower and the industrial machine was that of stabilizing prices. As the disposable income of an ever-growing labor force increased more rapidly than the supply of goods and services for civilians, severe inflationary pressures developed. If allowed to flourish uncontrolled, they seemed certain to touch off a crippling round of strikes and to unsettle the price structure for producers and consumers alike. Continuous inflation also posed the threat of sharply increasing the total cost of the war.

One way the administration proposed to meet the situation was by instituting wholesale and retail price controls and by sponging up surplus purchasing power with heavy taxes. Roosevelt had made a beginning by setting up an Office of Price Control and Civilian Supply in April 1941, but the first chairman, Leon Henderson, lacked the necessary power to control rents or prices. Even after Pearl Harbor, Congress was reluctant to grant statutory authorization for what many members regarded as socialistic regimentation. Various pressure groups abetted the procrastination of the legislators by wrangling about the terms of a price freeze in the same way that they disputed over the schedules in a tariff bill. Discussion lasted nearly nine weeks and might have continued longer if prices had not begun to rise at the unprecedented rate of 2 per cent a month. Congress finally acted on January 30, 1942, establishing an Office of Price Administration (OPA) and empowering its administrator to set reasonable ceilings on the prices of commodities which had risen rapidly or threatened to do so. The law also authorized the administrator to ration goods for personal consumption and to propose rent control in defense areas.

Within three months Henderson had completed a hasty survey of the price structure, and on April 28, 1942, he issued the General Maximum Price Regulation establishing ceilings for most commodities sold at either wholesale or retail. He used the highest price level of March 1942 as a yardstick and refused to authorize ceilings above it. During the same period OPA instituted rationing. The list of rationed goods was gradually extended until it included shoes, gasoline, fuel oil, sugar, meat, butter, and canned goods. The law contained one fatal loophole because the farm bloc had succeeded in amending it to prevent the imposition of ceilings on agricultural commodities below 110 per cent of parity. As food prices soared in the summer and fall of 1942, labor unions threatened to strike for higher wages to offset increases in the cost of living. Since any general rise in the wage level would mean higher prices for manufactured goods and generate fresh agitation for compensatory adjustment of ceilings on all commodities, Roosevelt moved abruptly to stop the vicious inflationary cycle. On September 7, 1942, he sent Congress a special message demanding comprehensive powers over economic life and threatened to act without statutory authority unless the legislators responded by October 1.

Congress complied reluctantly the day after the deadline, thus enabling Roosevelt to set up the Office of Economic Stabilization under Byrnes. He was also authorized to stabilize salaries, wages, and prices — including agricultural prices — at the levels prevailing September 15, 1942. In addition, the application of rent control was permitted throughout the country. Byrnes promptly proclaimed a general wage and price freeze. Unfortunately, the inflationary door had been slammed shut too late to please organized labor. Leaders complained that living costs had risen nearly 25 per cent between the beginning of the boom in 1941 and the spring of 1943. They demanded termination of the wage freeze and called for pay increases in excess of the 15 per cent allowed under the Little Steel formula. Roosevelt countered on April 8, 1943, by ordering his stabilization agencies to "hold the line" against what he referred to as unwarranted increases. When John L. Lewis defied him by ordering the first of his coal strikes on May 1, OPA launched a campaign to roll back food prices, which was climaxed a week later with a 10 per cent reduction in the retail prices of meat, coffee, and butter. This counterattack headed off most of the impending strikes but irritated the farmers, whose representatives tried a variety of methods to remove the ceilings from agricultural prices. In the end, none of the attempts to breach the price-wage structure after May 1943 achieved more than nominal success. The cost-of-living index, which had spiraled so rapidly before the rollback in food prices, increased only 1.5 per cent during the remaining twenty-seven months to VJ Day. OPA purchased this achievement at the cost of considerable popular discontent. Leon Henderson resigned in December 1942. His successor, the lame-duck senator from Michigan — Prentice M. Brown — survived only nine months, giving way to Chester Bowles, a New York advertising executive, in October 1943.

By comparison with World War I, when price fixing at the retail level was not attempted and living costs rose 63 per cent, the record of the stabilization authorities in checking inflation after mid-1943 deserves considerable praise. Altogether, living costs increased slightly less than 3 per cent from 1939 to 1945. On the other hand, satisfaction over the official figures should be tempered with the recollection that a considerable quantity of scarce commodities found their way into black markets and sold at prices far above OPA ceilings.

WAR FINANCE

Besides instituting a wage and price freeze to curb inflation, the administration formulated its wartime financial program partly with a view to drying up excess supplies of money. Keynesian theory provided the inspiration for the new approach to taxation and borrowing operations. It envisaged government as a balance wheel in the economy which would increase expenditures and lower taxes in periods of depression and reverse the procedure when prosperity returned. Applied specifically in the context of a war boom, it required steep tax rates to check inflation.

The administration was more interested than Congress was in a Keynesian program adjusted to fit political realities. The legislators cared nothing for theories and especially resented lectures on fiscal policy from Treasury Department tax experts. As a result, the war Congresses approached the problem of finance with a preference for borrowing and an aversion to high taxes. Of the total expenditures during the fiscal years from 1941 to 1945, only $131 billion or barely 41 per cent came from tax receipts. This ratio of taxation to borrowing represented a modest improvement over the 33 per cent raised by the revenue acts of World War I. The law passed in October 1942 and hailed by Roosevelt as "the greatest tax bill in history" was intended to raise an additional $7 billion. When the President proposed a fresh increase of $16 billion in his budget message of January 6, 1943, Congress balked. Even when the request was scaled down to $10.5 billion, it did not win many friends. Congress stalled until February 1944 and then passed a measure granting only $2.2 billion in additional revenue. The chagrined President took the unusual step of vetoing a revenue bill, provoking a similarly unprecedented resignation by Alben W. Barkley from his post as Senate majority leader. The Democratic caucus in the upper house turned the incident into a large-scale rebellion by unanimously re-electing Barkley. Thereupon both the Senate and House overrode the veto by wide margins. This election year rebuke was the most crushing defeat administered to the President since the rejection of his Supreme Court plan, and it ended all prospects of tax revision.

The failure of Congress to arrest inflation by adopting higher taxes is usually concealed behind a flurry of statistics about the magnitude of the rates actually authorized. The law of October 1942 did produce more revenue than would have been needed to meet the cost of a typical $8 billion prewar budget. Citizens shocked by the extravagance of the New Deal found the high taxes during the war years almost beyond belief, but the scale of other comparable economic activities increased as much if not more. What made wartime taxation especially noteworthy was the full exploitation of the income tax as a device for raising revenue. In 1939 only 4 million citizens were touched by the federal income tax. The coverage increased to 17 million in 1941, and to over 50 million under the Revenue Act of 1942, which broadened the tax base by lowering the exemptions to $500 for single persons and $1,200 for married couples. The law also increased the normal tax rate from 4 per cent to 6 per cent, and imposed a schedule of surtaxes ranging from 13 per cent on the first $2,000 of taxable income to 82 per cent on income in excess of $200,000. Pyramided on all these levies was a "Victory Tax" of 5 per cent withheld from salaries by employers. Later legislation discontinued it, or, more properly, incorporated it into the surtax structure.

The addition of so many millions of citizens to the income tax rolls complicated the problems of both the Bureau of Internal Revenue and the new taxpayer. The former possessed neither the personnel nor the procedures to detect tax evaders quickly, while the latter had no experience in systematically saving money for annual payments. Each stood to gain by some method of withholding tax payments in installments at the source. Beardsley Ruml, a New York financier, proposed a plan whereby employers would deduct the federal income tax from wages and salaries. To make withholding payments current, Ruml contended that the government should forgive the tax of the preceding year.

Described as the "skip a year" plan, it picked up considerable support from citizens who labored under the happy illusion that they would be relieved of income tax payments for a year. Although the administration feared a loss of revenue, it eventually accepted a compromise plan whereby the taxpayer filed returns for both 1942 and 1943 income, but received a 75 per cent reduction of the tax for the year in which he owed the smaller amount. The new system went into effect July 1, 1943. A year later Congress relieved citizens whose entire income was from wages or salaries and totaled less than $5,000 from filing complicated income tax forms. Those receiving income from other sources were required to estimate it and make quarterly payments to the Treasury.

Mindful of the political risks involved in increasing the tax bills of individuals without laying comparable burdens on business, Congress raised the tax on corporate profits to 40 per cent. It also levied an excess-profits tax of 90 per cent which quieted popular fears that industrialists would grow rich off the sacrifice of others. This tax was difficult to administer, produced less revenue than anticipated, and encouraged corporate extravagance and waste. A more satisfactory source of additional revenue was excise taxes on liquor, luggage, jewelry, telephone calls, railroad tickets, and a wide range of amusements.

Since the revenue fell far short of meeting war costs, the annual deficit could be made up only by borrowing from individuals, corporations, and banks. In the process the national debt increased from $49 billion on June 30, 1941, to $259 billion on June 30, 1945. The administration sought to minimize the inflationary pressures generated by such a rapid rise. Taking its cue from the economists who knew that bonds sold to private citizens or nonbanking institutions did not provide a base for the expansion of currency and credit, the Treasury Department aimed a four-year sales campaign at those groups. The response was phenomenal. Individuals bought approximately $40 billion worth of bonds, either outright or through a payroll deduction plan. The most popular type was Series E which could be purchased in denominations as low as $18.75 and carried a maturity value of $25 if held for a full ten years. Other types designed for institutional investment sold at higher prices, paid interest semiannually, and brought the Treasury an additional $60 billion. The remaining $87 billion was absorbed by the Federal Reserve System and commercial banks. Under existing laws, the banks used it as a reserve against which they issued loans, thus indirectly feeding the threefold increase in the money supply during World War II. As we have already seen, the resulting inflationary pressure put the whole stabilization program under severe strain, intensified resistance to price controls, and encouraged the multiplication of black markets.

BY-PRODUCTS OF MOBILIZATION

The unplanned by-product of mobilization on the domestic front was the fulfillment of the New Deal program — or at least that part of it which envisaged extension of government services and redistribution of wealth. Before the end of the depression decade, support for both policies had waned. The New Deal spending program had relieved human misery but fallen short of providing the momentum for economic recovery, while its tax program had frightened the already wary investors without changing the basic pattern of income distribution.

Developments after Pearl Harbor reversed economic trends as well as trends in public opinion. Not only did war mobilization stimulate government planning on a larger scale than ever before, but it did so in a patriotic context that silenced critics and compelled popular acquiescence. Sweeping extensions of government power and sharp increases in tax rates, that would hitherto have been labeled socialistic, commanded widespread support as war measures. Price control, rationing, and trade regulations characteristic of totalitarian regimes were also accepted without serious complaint.

After demobilization it became apparent that the impact of World War II on the internal structure of all societies, including America's, was revolutionary and had stimulated a lasting socialization of institutions. Two developments on the domestic front stood out as permanent legacies of the war: the enlarged role of the central government in economic life, and the marked reduction of the gap between the incomes of the wealthy and the poor.

The first can be illustrated by the rise in the proportion of public expenditures to the gross national product. In 1939 the federal government contributed $7.9 billion out of a total of $88.6 billion — or less than 10 per cent; in 1944, $89.5 billion out of $199.22 billion — or 45 per cent; and in 1953, $59.5 billion out of $364.5 billion — or 17 per cent. Although the ratio of government spending to the gross national product had receded from the wartime high in 1953, it was nearly twice as large as in 1939. Besides an enlarged role in expenditure and investment, the government retained substantial powers over the disposal of a wide variety of exports.

The effect of war expenditures was to raise the economic status of depressed groups, while the effect of inflation and high taxes was to reduce the fortunes of the middle class. A few business groups in a position to initiate inflationary price movements actually gained. Others, who could secure prompt adjustments of wages and prices to compensate them for depreciation in the value of the dollar, either gained or lost relatively little.

As a rule, the organized pressure groups such as manufacturers, farmers, and unionized workers came out best. The chief sufferers were unorganized workers, citizens who lived on fixed income, and numerous white-collar and professional people. To the degree that inflation impaired the economic position of individuals in the two latter categories, it functioned as a leveling influence and redistributor of wealth.

High taxation supplemented inflation in changing the distribution of income. Although wartime revenue laws broadened the tax base, the steeply graduated surtax rates resulted in very heavy burdens for individuals with annual incomes in excess of $10,000. The aggregate effect of expenditures, inflation, and taxation was to reduce the extremes of poverty and wealth.

The postwar years brought little modification of the basic wartime pattern. Government continued to be a big factor in the national economy, while spending and taxation policies tended to favor the lower and middle income groups. Thus, although President Roosevelt after Pearl Harbor had officially abandoned the role of "Dr. New Deal" for that of "Dr. Win-the-War," the New Deal as a social and economic reform movement won its greatest victories in the process of economic mobilization. Americans persisted in denouncing the slogans and objectives of the welfare state, but their so-called "mixed" postwar economy resembled the welfare state more than the old free-enterprise state of the twenties.

SUGGESTED READINGS

1. Goodman, J. (ed.), *While You Were Gone: A Report on Wartime Life in The United States.*
2. Harris, S. E., *Economics of America at War.*

CHAPTER TWENTY-SIX

AMERICA WINS A GLOBAL CONFLICT

THE FIRST MONTHS OF THE WAR

In Johann Strauss's *Gypsy Baron,* Sandov Barinkay boasted that he "would breakfast on tomorrow's question marks." The Americans were not in a boastful mood, but they subsisted on question marks for several months after Pearl Harbor because the initiative lay with the Axis. In the Pacific theater, the Japanese followed the bombing of Pearl Harbor with a massive offensive, enveloping most of southeast Asia and occupying the archipelagoes that converged on Australia. American, British, and Dutch possessions were quickly overrun in a series of seaborne invasions. Guam fell December 11, 1941, Wake Island two weeks later, and Hong Kong on Christmas Day. Simultaneously, Japanese units landed on the Malay peninsula and the Philippines, while other units stationed in Indo-China successfully invaded Thailand. January of 1942 was a month of uninterrupted disasters. Outnumbered American and Filipino troops abandoned Manila on January 2, retreating for a final desperate stand on Bataan peninsula. Three weeks later a joint American-British-Dutch fleet in the Strait of Macassar momentarily turned back a Japanese armada headed for the East Indies, but subsequent battles in the Java Sea destroyed the Allied fleet. This disaster, coupled with the fall of Singapore on February 15, cleared the way for Japanese conquest of the Indies, which was completed March 9. Other Nipponese units operating farther west pushed southward from the Carolines to the Solomon Islands, where they constructed bases and made methodical preparations for the attack on Australia. By mid-May, Port Moresby, the last Allied base in southern New Guinea, was in jeopardy, while Darwin, the northernmost city in Australia, was suffering from heavy air raids.

Meanwhile the American forces on Bataan peninsula fought a grim delaying action. General Douglas MacArthur, who had directed the retreat from Manila, was transferred to Australia on March 17, 1942. His successor, Jonathan Wainwright, abandoned Bataan for a final stand on Corregidor and other island forts off the tip of the peninsula. Nearly 40,000 troops who covered this retreat were taken prisoner April 9. The remaining 11,574 held out an additional month, but tropical heat, malaria, and malnutrition took such a heavy toll that Wainwright finally surrendered on May 6.

Just as the Japanese were wiping out the last pockets of resistance in the Philippines, they completed the occupation of Burma, cut off the flow of American supplies to China, and cast greedy eyes at India and Ceylon. As it turned out, they had reached the limit of their expansion, except for the subsequent occupation of Kiska and Attu in the Aleutian Islands. A temporary halt would have been necessary in any event to relieve the strain on overextended lines of communication and to consolidate the vast gains already made. The unsuccessful efforts of the Japanese to resume their drive proved that their "pause" was really a loss of initiative. American naval power, knocked out at Pearl Harbor, had been rebuilt sufficiently during the ensuing six months of uninterrupted setbacks to contain the Nipponese thrust on Australia. The turning point was the battle of the Coral Sea from May 4 to 8. Coupled with the restoration of British naval superiority in the Indian Ocean, it ended the threat of Japanese domination of the South Pacific.

Despite the loss of the Philippines, Malaya, and the rich oil, tin, and rubber producing islands of the East Indies, the situation in Asia was less grave for the Allied coalition by mid-1942 than in Europe and Africa. The German advance on the Russian front, stalled just outside of Moscow in December 1941, was resumed after the spring thaw. Confined to the region south of Kursk, it aimed at the complete conquest of the Ukraine and the capture of the Grozny oil fields on the northern slopes of the Caucasus. One spearhead pointed due east toward Stalingrad, the great industrial city on the Volga, and the other southward along the Black Sea coast. Here the Germans rolled forward on a continuous front during the summer and fall of 1942. Although the northern front stabilized on an irregular line running from the southern end of Lake Ladoga to Vyazma, the rapidity of the advance elsewhere seemed likely to knock Russia out of the war.

In North Africa, where German troops had reinforced the faltering Italians, their combined armies under the masterful leadership of Marshal Erwin Rommel pierced the British defenses along the Gazola-Bir Hacheim line in a continuous battle from May 26 to June 17, 1942. The remnants of the British army fled from Libya to Egypt, where they set up a fresh defense line at El Alamein approximately seventy miles from Alexandria. By the end of August, Rommel was ready to renew the attack. If he succeeded in breaching the fortifications at El Alamein, then Cairo, Suez, and the entire Middle East would fall to the Germans.

The situation in the North Atlantic was almost as critical. Great Britain had regained control of the skies over the home islands and banished the threat of a cross-channel invasion. However, German U-boats roamed the shipping lanes and came perilously close to choking off the flow of the

The three fates. (Fred O. Seibel, The Richmond Times-Dispatch, *1945.)*

Lend-Lease supplies so desperately needed on the Russian and North African fronts. Allied convoys headed for the Russians ports of Archangel and Murmansk were vulnerable to land-based German bombers as well as U-boats. Approximately one-fourth of the ships that plied the dangerous Arctic route failed to reach their destinations in 1942. The overall losses of neutral and allied shipping for that year approached 8 million tons.

THE UNITED NATIONS COALITION

While the scattered foes of the Axis held on grimly, waiting for the balance to turn, unified plans for counterblows were being perfected. The first effort to coordinate Allied military strategy came during the darkest days of the war. Winston Churchill arrived in Washington on December 22, 1941, and the ensuing conferences with Roosevelt led to agreement on all key issues: the pooling and distribution of munitions, the creation of a combined chiefs of staff in Washington and of a joint British-Dutch-American command in the Pacific, and the formulation of military strategy. On the latter question, the conferees wisely concluded that Germany with her tremendous technical knowledge and industrial potential was the more dangerous enemy. Accordingly, they decided to aim the first major offensive blows against the Nazis while standing on the defensive in the Pacific. Tentative plans were laid for a joint British-American invasion of North Africa in March 1942, but the problems of logistics proved too formidable at such an early stage in the war and forced postponement of this diversionary attack.

While Roosevelt and Churchill were formulating their over-all military strategy, they also stepped up the tempo of Anglo-American diplomacy. All states currently at war with the Axis, as well as those already conquered and represented by governments in exile, were drawn into a grand alliance. Known henceforth as the United Nations, this coalition formally came into existence on New Year's Day, 1942. The representatives of twenty-six governments signed a declaration, affirming their loyalty to the principles embodied in the Atlantic Charter and pledging themselves not to make a separate peace with the Axis. The adherence of the South American states and the European governments in exile to the Declaration of the United Nations had less immediate material effect on the course of the war than the abstention of such strategically located neutrals as Sweden, Spain, and Turkey.

The participation of Soviet Russia in the Allied coalition was another matter. It enhanced the prospects of ultimate victory for the United Nations because the Russians were fighting the Germans on a two-thousand-mile front in Europe and worrying the Japanese with a hostile neutrality in East Asia. Desperation rather than agreement with the objectives of the Atlantic Charter motivated Soviet policy. Its leaders would have preferred to sit on the side lines while the bourgeois states fought a war of mutual destruction. Prevented by Hitler from enjoying a spectator's role, Stalin sought the maximum help from his new allies and offered the minimum of cooperation in return. Many historians have ascribed his suspicious attitude to resentment over the attempted isolation of Soviet Russia by several great powers during the 1920's. Doubtless the previous hostility of capitalist states strengthened a mistrustfulness which also fed on ideological convictions. However, the prewar policies of the West served as an excuse rather than the cause of Stalin's unwillingness to establish a partnership with the British and Americans. Beneath the surface manifestations of friction was the divergence between the aims of a revisionist Russia and a *status quo* Anglo-American bloc. Whether considered in the context of world revolution or of the material interests of the Russian state, Stalinist policy continued the aggressive expansionist tradition of the Tsars. As early as December 1941, when the British Foreign Secretary, Sir Anthony Eden, visited Moscow to negotiate an Anglo-Russian alliance, Stalin presented postwar demands for Soviet annexation of the Baltic states plus specific slices of Finland, Poland, and Rumania. In effect, he was proposing restoration of Russia's 1914 frontiers which would push her European boundaries considerably west of those enjoyed in 1939. Six months later Churchill extracted a twenty-year treaty of alliance from Stalin without making any commitments regarding the disposal of territory. What made the negotiations significant was the fact that Stalin revealed his huge annexationist appetite when the enemy stood outside the gates of Moscow. His sweeping demands at a moment of dire extremity foreshadowed still larger demands when his prospects improved. Even Allied agreement to restore the 1914 frontiers would have obligated the United Nations coalition to acquiesce in Russian annexation of small states in violation of the Atlantic Charter.

DISAGREEMENT WITH RUSSIA

The early indications of incompatibility between Russian and Anglo-American war aims ought to have suggested caution in dealing with Stalin, especially since the annexationist demands of December 1941 represented his minimum program. However, Roosevelt ignored the warnings of Churchill and took the view that Russia wanted the same kind of postwar world as the other great powers in the United Nations. He assumed that the manifestation of self-interest by the Russian leaders was due to misguided fear and suspicion of the West, and this assumption involved him in a policy of ever-broader concessions. This formula suited the Russians. They found it distasteful to be pleasant and were happy when their complaints softened resistance to their demands. In calculated fits of graciousness, they subscribed to various idealistic war aims and even officially dissolved the Comintern — the international Communist organization — in 1943. However, they resisted close coordination of the Allied war effort and often acted unilaterally in matters of diplomacy and military strategy. Official Russian newspapers insinuated that delays in the establishment of a second front were due to sinister capitalistic influences in Great Britain and America. Less official sources kept the Allies on tenterhooks by repeatedly spreading rumors about the possibility of a separate peace between Russia and

Germany. Notwithstanding the accumulating evidence of divergence between Russian and American aims, Roosevelt persisted in hoping that kind treatment would eventually soften Russian obstruction. Instead, it permitted the expansion of Russian power to a point where the Kremlin did not need to pay even lip service to the objectives of the United Nations unless such expressions of sentiment served broader propaganda purposes. Such a stage in Allied relationships did not materialize until Russian soil was cleared of German troops in 1944. However, even in the opening months of the war Stalin defended Russian interests with a vigor not characteristic of states that had everything to lose by parting company with their allies.

The most pressing issue over which Russia and her British and American allies contended in 1942 was the opening up of a second front in Europe. Molotov arrived in Washington on May 29 and urged an Anglo-American invasion of the Continent strong enough to force the diversion of forty German divisions from the eastern front. He also hinted darkly that delay might knock Russia out of the war, leaving the Atlantic powers to face Hitler alone. He left the United States without a definite promise, although the President was sufficiently alarmed by the threat of a complete Russian collapse to consider a limited cross-channel attack on northern France. Subsequent conversations between Roosevelt and Churchill and their military staffs, starting in Washington on June 21, revealed strong British objections to any kind of limited diversionary operations on the Continent. The simultaneous arrival of news that the Rommel offensive in North Africa was threatening Egypt gave added weight to the British position. Momentarily, the United States bent all its military energies toward bolstering the position of the British Eighth Army under General Bernard Montgomery at El Alamein. When the immediate crisis passed in mid-July, Roosevelt sent his unofficial adviser, Harry Hopkins, as well as General George C. Marshall and Admiral Ernest J. King, to London in the hope of reactivating the proposal for a cross-channel invasion. Churchill stubbornly resisted the project, suggesting as an alternative measure a joint Anglo-American invasion of North Africa. His plan possessed two attractions: it offered a real opportunity to drive the Germans and Italians out of Africa, and it envisaged an offensive on a scale better suited to current Anglo-American military resources than a cross-channel operation. The principal drawback of the plan was its unacceptability to the Russians. They understandably doubted that the attack on North Africa was a large enough enterprise to force the transfer of many Germans from the eastern front. Moreover, they objected to the concentration of Anglo-American resources on the reconquest of what in Marxist terminology was a colonial area. Notwithstanding these objections, Roosevelt accepted the Churchill plan of starting the reconquest of Europe through the back door. General Dwight D. Eisenhower, the Commander of the European Theater of Operations, was entrusted with the organization of a joint Anglo-American task force and ordered to make landings on the North African coast not later than October 30, 1942.

THE ALLIED COUNTEROFFENSIVE

The diplomatic and military planning undertaken by Roosevelt and Churchill during the dark half-year that followed Pearl Harbor began to bear fruit in the closing months of 1942. A steady stream of favorable developments outside the intended theater of operations augured well for the success of the North African campaign. The hitherto irresistible advance of the Japanese was halted in the west on the borders of India, and in the South Pacific along a line that stretched from the tip of New Guinea westward. Simultaneously, the offensive of the German Sixth Army on the lower Volga lost momentum before Stalingrad. By mid-November, General Paulus had given up hope of taking the city during the 1942 campaign and had established hedgehog defenses for the winter on its outskirts. Farther north the Germans had spent another fruitless year trying to capture Leningrad. The most helpful development of all was the successful offensive of General Montgomery. On October 23 he launched a surprise attack against Marshal Rommel, which after ten days destroyed the armored divisions of the Italo-German forces and sent the remaining units in flight across western Egypt and Libya.

While the battle for Egypt was in progress, an Allied expedition hit the Atlantic and Mediterranean coasts of French Morocco on November 8, 1942, and occupied the ports of Casablanca, Algiers, and Oran. The surprise was so complete that the forces of the Vichy French government offered only token resistance. Marshal Pétain, who headed the puppet regime in Vichy France, promptly severed diplomatic relations with the United States and called on his forces in North Africa to fight the invaders. Matters might have gone less well for Anglo-American troops if Hitler had not retaliated by invading the rest of Unoccupied France on November 11, 1942. As it turned out, Admiral Jean Darlan, who commanded the Vichy French forces, was a thoroughgoing nationalist. He defied Pétain, negotiated an armistice agreement with General Eisenhower, and thereby assured the Allies of the support of some fifty thousand French troops in North Africa.

The arrangement of a "cease-fire" with the "fascist" Darlan outraged large segments of American opinion, ranging all the way from militant left-wingers to restrained internationalists like Wendell Willkie. The rumpus in America subsided on December 24 when a fanatic assassinated Darlan. This development, however, further clouded the political situation in North Africa. General Charles de Gaulle, who headed the Free French group in London, and General Henri Giraud, a military hero and escapee from a German prison camp, contended for the mantle of Darlan. Roosevelt had sponsored Giraud and was reluctant to drop him even though he commanded little support either in North Africa or in France. Churchill showed more regard for political reality in pressing the claims of de Gaulle although the latter was haughty, opinionated, and egotistic. In January 1943, Roosevelt and Churchill brought the rival French leaders together for handshakes and photographs at Casablanca. It was hoped that the meeting would produce a kind of *de facto* cooperation until Frenchmen received an opportunity to decide between the claims of the two. Such expectations proved unjustified and the French leaders remained on bad terms until the Americans finally allowed Giraud to sink into obscurity.

Important military decisions could not be postponed while Allied diplomats struggled to resolve these political issues. The capitulation of French Morocco provoked large-scale German intervention in Tunisia to provide a haven for Rommel's retreating army and to deny the Anglo-American forces the most suitable jumping-off-spot for an invasion of Sicily. Hitler poured troops, armored units, and air power across the Mediterranean before the British Eighth Army under Montgomery could converge with Eisenhower's combined American-British-French forces. A full-scale campaign followed, opening with a surprise German offensive in the vicinity of Faid Pass on February 11, 1943, and closing with the encirclement and surrender of all Axis forces in Tunisia on May 12. Hitler paid dearly for his effort to retain a toehold in North Africa. Altogether the Axis lost fifteen divisions, nearly 2,500 planes, 250 tanks, and a like number of ships. The combined total of casualties and prisoners was 349,206 for the German-Italian armies compared to 70,000 for the Allies.

Pausing only long enough to collect a new invasion armada and soften up the enemy with an intensive aerial bombardment, Eisenhower landed an army of 160,000 on the beaches of Sicily on July 10, 1943. The British Eighth Army, still ably commanded by Montgomery, and the American First Army, under General George S. Patton, quickly overran the island. Patton had already established a reputation for daring utilization of armored units in North Africa. His brilliant performance in Sicily hastened the rout of Axis forces, which were cleared from the island by August 18.

The rapid advance of the Allied armies was destined to end when they crossed the Strait of Messina and invaded Italy. Encouraged by the collapse of Mussolini's government on July 25, Roosevelt and Churchill had opened negotiations with the new regime of Marshal Pietro Badoglio. An armistice agreement for the surrender of Italy was signed on September 3, but German units forestalled the Allied plan to seize Rome and other key points. Hitler re-established a Mussolini government at Lake Como and made methodical preparations to contest every inch of the Italian boot. The terrain favored this enterprise because, except for the Po Valley in the extreme north, Apennine ridges crisscrossed the entire peninsula. Neither armored divisions nor air power could assure prompt Allied penetration of such rough, mountainous country. Natural obstacles coupled with German resourcefulness counterbalanced the growing superiority of American military equipment.

The Allied landings at Reggio Calabria and Taranto, which began the same day that the Badoglio government signed the armistice, were secondary attacks and encountered little opposition. The main invasion at Salerno Bay a week later (September 9) provoked such fierce German counterattacks that the American Fifth Army of General Mark Clark was nearly split and driven into the sea. Eventually Clark managed to consolidate the beachhead and occupy Naples on October 1. The British advance up the central and eastern sectors of the boot was more rapid, but by mid-November the Germans managed to stabilize the entire front along the Gustav Line just north of Naples. Thereafter Allied progress was slow and painful. Each time British and American forces breached German fortifications, Hitler's armies made an orderly retreat and established a new line along the next series of Apennine ridges. The slow timetable up the peninsula vindicated the German policy of fighting long delaying actions. The Gustav Line was not broken until May 1944 despite a diversionary American landing at Anzio just south of Rome on January 22. The Germans abandoned Rome on June 4 and retreated to prepared positions 150 miles north of the capital. Entrenched behind the so-called Gothic Line, they successfully withstood all attacks from September 1944 until the collapse of their military fortunes elsewhere in the final months of the war.

The great Allied victories of 1943 in North Africa, Sicily, and southern Italy broke Axis power in the western Mediterranean and finally destroyed the German threat to Suez. Thereafter both sides recognized that the outcome of the world conflict would be decided in other theaters, but fierce bloody battles for the control of the Tuscan hills continued until VE Day.

While British and American troops were establishing their first foothold on the Continent in 1943, their naval units gained the upper hand in the all-important battle of the Atlantic. The monthly toll of merchant ships taken by German U-boats dropped below 200,000 tons for the first time in May 1943. Methods for protecting convoys and detecting U-boats improved so rapidly that when the Allies attempted the cross-channel invasion thirteen months later they did not lose a single ship to submarine torpedos. German losses of U-boats mounted from approximately 100 per month in 1942 to 237 in 1943 and 241 in 1944. This spectacular reversal of Allied fortunes in the North Atlantic paved the way for the final defeat of Germany.

WARFARE IN THE PACIFIC

Despite the preoccupation of America with the European theater in 1943, her military build-up proceeded so rapidly that she also undertook limited offensive operations in the South Pacific. Lengthening supply lines and a deficiency of advance bases had forced the Japanese to pause north of Australia in midsummer of 1942. They were hurriedly building airstrips on the Solomon Islands and completing the conquest of southern New Guinea when the Americans launched their counteroffensive. On August 7, 1942, marines under General Vandergrift landed on Florida, Tulagi, Gavutu, and Guadalcanal islands in the Solomon group. Tulagi fell after three days, but Guadalcanal became the scene of a prolonged and bloody battle. At the outset the Americans managed to capture the nearly completed Japanese airstrip which they renamed Henderson Field. They withstood numerous counterattacks, but the outcome remained in doubt for nearly six months because the Japanese flew reinforcements nightly from their huge base at Rabaul, New Britain. Wryly referred to as the "Tokyo Express," this operation repeatedly snatched the fruits of victory from the gallant marines. Only after a series of American naval victories had made the surrounding seas untenable did the Japanese withdraw from Guadalcanal on the night of February 7–8, 1943.

Shortly after the American landings in the southern Solomons, General Douglas MacArthur launched a counteroffensive against the Japanese who had moved within thirty-two miles of Port Moresby, the last Allied base in New Guinea. Advancing on September 28, 1942, he drove the enemy back to the Buna-Sananada area. After a four months' campaign, he cleared the Japanese out of Papua. Organized resistance ended January 22, 1943.

The success of the two-pronged offensive in New Guinea and the Solomons destroyed the Japanese threat to Australia and to Allied supply lines in the South Pacific. It also cleared the way for a gigantic pincer movement to isolate Rabaul, the chief Japanese base to the north of Papua. The remaining months of 1943 were consumed in this enterprise, with Admiral William F. Halsey directing an island-hopping campaign in the north Solomons and General MacArthur directing a similar operation from New Guinea. Both commanders employed the strategy of bypassing strong pockets of Japanese resistance and seizing points suitable for airfields and harbors. With a mixed force of Americans, Australians, and New Zealanders, MacArthur captured the northern New Guinea base of Finschhafen in September 1943 and invaded New Britain in December. Simultaneously Halsey was moving northward from Guadalcanal to Bougainville, which he occupied in November. Meanwhile the rapidly growing American Air Force had begun to bomb Rabaul from the new bases. The campaign for the neutralization of Rabaul was completed shortly after the end of the year, the pincer being closed with successful landings on Negros island in February 1944 and St. Mathias island in March 1944.

On the all-important Russian front, developments also favored the Allies during 1943. As in the Mediterranean and South Pacific theaters, the foundations for later victories were laid in the final months of 1942. The German defenses on the outskirts of Stalingrad were broken by a vigorous Russian counterattack which began on November 20, 1942, and cut off 330,000 Nazi troops. Efforts by General von Mannstein to relieve the isolated Sixth Army failed, and General Paulus surrendered February 2, 1943. The disastrous defeat at Stalingrad was the prelude to a Russian offensive along the entire eastern front which steadily gained momentum. By October the

Russians had recaptured most of their homeland lying east of the Dnieper River and south of Lake Ladoga. The ensuing winter offensive carried them within sight of their old 1939 frontiers.

WARTIME DIPLOMACY: CASABLANCA TO TEHERAN

As the final defeat of Germany and Japan became more probable in 1943, the members of the Allied coalition stepped up the tempo of diplomatic activity. A succession of conferences was held to hammer out agreements about impending military campaigns, terms of surrender, disposition of enemy territory, and the organization of the postwar world. During this crucial year, America began to make the military and political decisions which subsequently deprived her of some fruits of victory. Seeds of future trouble were sown at the Casablanca conference, where Roosevelt and Churchill, flanked by their respective diplomatic and military advisers, held full-dress conversations from January 14 to 24, 1943. The principals spent considerable time debating the merits of a cross-channel invasion of France the following summer and agreed to postpone it a year in favor of the Sicilian campaign. They lavished additional hours on a fruitless attempt to resolve the quarrel between Giraud and de Gaulle. The most momentous decision was announced on the last day by Roosevelt after an insufficient discussion of its implications. Speaking with the consent of Churchill and presumably other members of the United Nations, the President proclaimed that the Allies would carry on the war until the Axis Powers agreed to unconditional surrender. The enunciation of such a policy reflected all the idealistic American presuppositions about the war: that it was being waged against the forces of evil embodied in Germany, Italy, and Japan; that the destruction of these states, coupled with a vague but universal application of the Atlantic Charter, would restore a more radiant version of the post-Versailles *status quo;* and that other members of the Allied coalition — including Soviet Russia — favored a revival of the pre-1931 balance of power or something approximating it.

None of these assumptions underlying the unconditional surrender policy seems justified in the light of historical experience. The destruction of great powers had hitherto led to the creation of vacuums which in turn invited intervention by states nearest the vacuums. Although the United States expected the war to restore a stable *status quo,* the policy bade fair to produce the opposite result. In fact it threatened a worse instability than before the war by destroying the last states capable of supporting a multiple balance. Complete victory over Germany and Japan would leave only the Soviet Union and the United States, surrounded by vacuums where allies had been exhausted and enemies shattered in the process of attempting to reconstitute the *status quo.* Aside from the instability inherent in a simple balance, the prospect of sharing world power with Russia ought to have frightened America. Until Hitler made war on both states and thereby drove them into alliance, the United States and the Soviet Union had disagreed for twenty years about everything from domestic institutions to foreign policy. Moreover, the expansionist appetite of Russia between 1939 and 1941 while she was collaborating with Germany indicated that she was a dynamic rather than a *status quo* power like the United States. Such a record hardly justified the American assumption that the temporary wartime cooperation of the two states would assure a common attitude toward postwar objectives. On the contrary, it underlined the risks of a military policy which was destined to produce vacuums on both sides of Russia. These risks stood out with particular clarity in the case of central Europe, where the complete destruction of German power would hand the Soviet Union the dominant position on the Continent to which Hitler had aspired.

The Casablanca declaration of the unconditional surrender policy simplified matters for the expansionist-minded Russians. They could subscribe wholeheartedly to it and occupy most of the areas they wanted as collaborators in the crusade against the evil Fascist powers. When the war ended or when America woke to what they were doing — whichever came first — the Russians could use all the disarming slogans of the Atlantic Charter to justify their subjugation of enemy territory. Meanwhile they intended to maintain a cooperative demeanor at conferences, avoid territorial demands, and compete with the Americans in enunciating lofty peace proposals. If all went as planned, the Russians were likely to have the vacuum in Eastern Europe so completely under control by the end of the crusade against Fascism that only a fresh war could oust them.

Although Russia did not participate in the Casablanca conference or in further Roosevelt-Churchill conversations at Quebec from August 14 to 24, 1943, she served as host to the Conference of Foreign Ministers which opened in Moscow on October 18. Almost two years had elapsed since the inconclusive Anglo-Russian talks about postwar objectives in December 1941, and during this interval the Allies had gone their respective ways. Furthermore, the Soviet Union was openly critical of her western allies for failure to carry out the cross-channel invasion and open a second front in 1943. Unofficial Communist sources insinuated that Great Britain and the United States plotted the exclusion of the Soviet Union from peace discussions about areas where she was not directly concerned. Both Secretary of State Cordell Hull, who represented America, and Foreign Secretary Anthony Eden, who represented Great Britain, arrived at Moscow braced for a stormy session. To their amazement, agreements were quickly reached on most points, including the treatment of a conquered Germany. Molotov and Stalin accepted the tentative draft of an American plan calling for the establishment of an Inter-Allied Control Commission to supervise the surrender, occupation, de-Nazification, and disarmament of Germany. The so-called Hull plan also incorporated the principle that the Reich would be required to pay reparations for damages inflicted on other countries in manpower and goods but not in money. Its vagueness about German boundaries suited the Russian preference for postponing demands until the military situation clarified.

The world received no intimation of Allied decisions about Germany at the Moscow conference except a three-Power declaration over the signatures of Roosevelt, Churchill, and Stalin. Issued November 1, 1943, it promised prompt punishment of German war leaders, including both Nazi leaders and lesser figures guilty of atrocities. More impressive still was a four-power declaration, with which China associated herself, pledging the signatories to establish a new international organization along the lines of the defunct League of Nations.

The phenomenal degree of consensus achieved by the Foreign Ministers on the German question overshadowed the sharp disagreement over Poland. The Soviet Union had severed diplomatic relations with the Polish government-in-exile in London and had begun to deal with a group of Polish Communists in matters affecting both states. Hull urged Molotov to restore relations with the London group but was rebuffed in a way that revealed the Kremlin's intention of recognizing only a satellite Polish government. Molotov's promises to acquiesce in the reconstitution of Austria as an independent state, and to join in the war against Japan after the defeat of Germany, softened the shock of Russian intransigence on the Poland question.

In retrospect it is easy to see that the Soviet Union made no concessions at the Foreign Ministers' conference fatal to her plan of dominating Eastern Europe. In fact the major agreement, which envisaged the surrender and occupation of Germany, suited the long-range interests of Russia better than those of the United States. However, the conciliatory attitude of the Soviet leaders caused Americans of various political persuasions to hail the Moscow conference as a great success. The ailing seventy-two-year-old Hull was accorded a hero's welcome on his return and invited to give Congress a personal report. His optimistic account of negotiations encouraged the assumption that Russia cherished the same ideals and postwar objectives as America.

Since plans had been laid at the conference for a personal meeting of the Big Three, Roosevelt welcomed the new opportunity to strengthen Allied unity. He optimistically hoped that his personal powers of persuasion would remove the last suspicions from Stalin's mind regarding the motives and aims of the United States.

The Big Three finally agreed to meet at Teheran, the capital of Iran, after Stalin had rejected several proposed sites farther from the Soviet Union on the plea that he had to maintain personal supervision of the Russian military effort. Roosevelt paused en route at Cairo for conversations with Churchill, Chiang Kai-shek, Lord Louis Mountbatten, Allied Commander in southeast Asia, and General Joseph Stilwell, the American commander in the Burma-China theater. The Cairo discussions from November 23 to 27 were concerned with the problem of reconquering Burma and reopening supply lines to the beleaguered Chinese. Final plans called for dual offensives in Burma by Stilwell's American-Chinese army attacking from the north and by British troops attacking from India. Both drives got stalled in the opening months of 1944. The British spent most of the year parrying Japanese counterattacks on Chittagong and Imphal in India. As a consequence, the reconquest of southern Burma was delayed until Japanese power collapsed on all fronts near the end of the war. Stilwell cleared enough of north Burma after a year of fierce fighting in jungle-covered mountains to open the Ledo road in January 1945. Thereafter a steady stream of supplies reached Chungking, the Chinese capital.

After reaching decisions on what continued to be a minor theater of the war, Roosevelt and his advisers flew from Cairo to Teheran on November 27, 1943, for four days of conferences with Churchill and Stalin. The President made ostentatious efforts to convince Stalin that the Americans and British had not agreed on a common strategy in advance. Indeed, he hammered home the point by holding at least one secret conversation with Stalin. Aside from his effort to establish personal rapport with the Russian dictator, Roosevelt sought the closest possible coordination of military operations. Stalin was most concerned about the cross-channel invasion of France, and although Roosevelt categorically promised such an attack would take place in the summer of 1944, he refused to name the exact time and place or choose a commander. His reticence on the last point reflected his desire that General George C. Marshall, Chief of Staff, be accorded the honor and responsibility of liberating Europe, which was balanced off against his fear that Marshall could not be spared for the task. Conversations at Teheran strengthened Roosevelt's conviction that Marshall was indispensable in his role as coordinator of America's far-flung military enterprises. In the end, the President decided to appoint Eisenhower Supreme Commander of the European invasion forces and communicated the decision to him on the return journey from Teheran.

Stalin and Roosevelt were much more enthusiastic about the establishment of a second front in the west than Churchill was. The latter suggested an Anglo-American invasion of the Istrian peninsula and of southeastern Europe. Stalin opposed the project on the ground that it would not divert a sizable number of German divisions from the eastern front, but a weightier reason was his unstated objection to the intervention of the western powers in the Balkans. Roosevelt did not share the British mistrust of Russian intentions in Eastern Europe and agreed with Stalin that Germany should be attacked directly in force from the west. On other matters greater cordiality prevailed. The Big Three edged toward the idea of partitioning Germany and adopting a severer policy of chastisement than originally contemplated under the Hull plan. They also approved the principles of a Roosevelt plan for a United Nations Organization to prevent future wars. Another demonstration of solidarity occurred when Stalin repeated his promise that Russia would enter the Pacific war after the defeat of Germany.

The Teheran conference marked the zenith of great-power unity. Roosevelt felt that the twenty-five-year-old barriers of ideological suspicion separating Russia and the western powers had fallen forever. Unwilling and unable to anticipate the collapse of Allied solidarity when the military crisis passed, the President expected the advent of a new era. Akin to the Wilsonian vision of 1919, his hopes flowered in a faith that Russia and other states would henceforward pursue ideals instead of conventional self-interests. Before the Big Three convened again at Yalta in February 1945, Russian policy in Eastern Europe had spoiled the hopes of those who were willing to examine the evidence. Solidarity varied inversely with military success and the creation of vacuums on the borders of Russia. Thus, when the Allied military machine ground forward during 1944 and 1945 into territory formerly held by the enemy, American-Russian relations worsened — slowly at first and rapidly after complete victory was assured.

THE ALLIED INVASION OF EUROPE

In 1944 the capacity of the Allied coalition to inflict damaging blows on the Axis powers was greatly enhanced by the rapid build-up of American and British air power. As early as 1942 in the European theater, the RAF had switched from aerial bombardment of specific targets to the more devastating system of mass raids on industrial areas. At first the new pattern of attack did not disrupt German production or transportation very seriously, because the British needed to conserve their air power and hence conducted raids only at night. The bomb tonnage dropped on Germany rose from 50,000 tons in 1942 to over 200,000 tons in 1943, reflecting large-scale use of American-made Liberators and Flying Fortresses. These heavily armored bombers delivered mass attacks in broad daylight, supplementing the nightly raids of the RAF. However, severe losses in October 1943 forced suspension of daylight raids pending the development of a long-range fighter escort for the bombers. The P-51, which first appeared over Germany in February 1944, solved the problem of protection. Coupled with the introduction of radar bombsights and other miscellaneous improvements, it enabled the British and Americans to dominate the skies. Round-the-clock bombing of German aircraft factories and industrial plants was inaugurated after the invasion of France in midsummer. Altogether 1.2 million tons of bombs fell on the hapless Reich in 1944, turning cities into living hells. Just before the final collapse of Germany, waves of eight thousand to nine thousand bombers pulverized the transportation system. When the Allied armies converged on Berlin in April 1945, they found production at a standstill and people reduced to abject misery.

The build-up of air power occurred more slowly on the Pacific front, partly because the main Allied effort was concentrated on Germany and partly because the center of the Japanese empire remained outside bomber range until the summer of 1944. General James Doolittle and a heroic band of aviators had taken off from the deck of the aircraft carrier *Hornet* and bombed Tokyo on April 14, 1942. Despite this daring gesture, American planes during the next two years were used primarily to provide tactical support for naval operations and troop landings on the various island chains. Only after the capture of the Marianas did the United States acquire land bases from which the new B-29 Superfortresses could blast the home islands. Between November 1944 and the end of the war in August 1945, the Air Force dropped 160,000 tons of bombs on Japan — or approximately 12 per cent of the amount dropped on Germany during a comparable period. The total damage was almost as great because of the tremendous concentration of industry and population in a small area. Especially after March 9, 1945, when the Air Force started dropping fire bombs on Tokyo, Osake, Kobe, and other Japanese bamboo cities, the destruction was fearful. One such raid on Tokyo devastated sixteen square smiles and caused 185,000 casualties. Long before the Americans dropped the still more terrifying atom bombs on Hiroshima and Nagasaki, air raids had made the lot of the Japanese almost unendurable.

As the aerial arm of the Allied war machine softened up the resistance of the Germans in the spring of 1944, General Eisenhower, the Supreme Commander of the Allied Expeditionary Forces, made careful preparations for the decisive gamble of the war — the invasion of Europe. Assigned the code name OVERLORD, the cross-channel attack was originally scheduled for May 1, 1944. However, a shortage of landing craft forced the postponement of OVERLORD until the first week of June, when less favorable weather conditions prevailed. A sudden storm prevented the departure of the invasion armada on the 5th, and it was not able to put to sea until the morning of the 6th. Several grim hours later the first sea-borne troops hit the beaches along a sixty-mile strip of the Cotentin peninsula in Normandy and moved inland to join their air-borne divisions which had been landed behind the German lines the preceding night. Initially light resistance was encountered except at Omaha beach, where a furious German counterattack almost drove the Americans back into the sea. Otherwise fortune favored the invaders, who packed their beachheads full of supplies and equipment. Within two weeks they had landed 1.1 million men and then they fanned out along the Normandy coast, capturing the important port of Cherbourg as well as Caen and Saint-Lô. Consolidation of the beachheads was facilitated by the confusion of the German High Command. Field Marshals Erwin Rommel and Karl von Rundstedt had discounted the landings on the Cotentin peninsula as diversionary maneuvers and persisted in believing that the main invasion would be aimed at the Calais area. Eisenhower successfully deceived them by the unprecedented feat of unloading heavy mechanized equipment without the use of port facilities and by concealing troop movements with furious air or naval bombardments both before and after the landings.

The German Seventh Army tried to contain the invaders within the Normandy beachhead. It was enveloped and cut to pieces between Falaise and Argentan during a fierce battle from August 19 to 23. Other German armies, confronted with a similar threat, fled precipitously to prepared positions in the Siegfried Line. Paris fell after only token resistance on August 25 and the American Seventh Army, which had landed in southern France just outside the port of Toulon ten days earlier, joined the mop-up of isolated German units. The triumphant sweep of the Allied forces continued to the Siegfried Line or Westwall. Antwerp and Brussels fell in early September, and Luxemburg was liberated simultaneously. Thereafter the Allies encountered tougher going but kept up unremitting pressure on the discouraged Germans. An effort of the British Third Army to outflank the northern end of the Westwall failed when paratroopers were unable to hold a bridgehead across the Rhine at Arnhem. The First, Second, and Ninth American Armies tried to pierce the middle of the line with Cologne and the industrial areas of the Ruhr Valley as their ultimate objective. Aachen fell October 21, 1944, and the advance carried as far as the Roer River where heavy German resistance forced a halt on December 14. Farther south, Metz fell to the American Third Army and Strasbourg to the Seventh Army. However, the broken character of the terrain aided the defenders, who stabilized their position above and below Strasbourg.

Meanwhile the Russians had synchronized their attack with the Anglo-American invasion and launched a tremendous offensive on June 23, 1944, along the entire front. The Finns collapsed first and signed an armistice on August 25. Elsewhere on the north front the Russians advanced rapidly, recapturing all the southeastern shore of the Baltic by the end of 1944 except the city of Memel and the Courland peninsula. In the central theater, the Russians reached the Vistula River in late July but were held up the rest of the year by the stubborn German defense of Warsaw, and by their unwillingness to aid non-Communist Poles fighting the Germans inside the city. After the latter had smashed the resistance movement, the Russians took Warsaw on January 17, 1945. Farther south the demoralized Rumanians capitulated on August 23, 1944. Bulgaria tried to maintain her neutrality but was occupied on September 8. The Russians then swung northwest up the Danube Valley, taking Belgrade on October 20 and laying siege to Budapest, which surrendered in February 1945.

MacARTHUR RETURNS TO THE PHILIPPINES

While the Allied offensives in Europe were driving the Germans back within the frontiers of the Fatherland, the scattered forces of the United Nations on the opposite side of the globe began to converge on the Philippines. Immediately after the isolation of Rabaul in March 1944, MacArthur routed the Japanese from the northern coast of New Guinea. A series of amphibious operations, culminating in the capture of Morotai in September 1944, brought the islands to the south of the Philippines under American control. Simultaneously the greatly enlarged fleet in the Central Pacific was approaching the Philippines from the east. In mid-1943 it had recaptured Attu and Kiska and had swung far south at the end of the year to seize Makin and Tarawa in the Gilbert Islands. Saipan, Tinian, and Guam, the most strongly fortified of the Marianas, fell in June and July of 1944. In the process American naval units and carrier-based planes under Admiral Raymond A. Spruance inflicted a severe defeat on the Japanese fleet. September and early October were consumed in occupying key islands in the western Carolines. These victories freed the fleet to cooperate with the units accompanying MacArthur in the invasion of Leyte, the largest of the southern Philippine islands. As a result the Americans concentrated overwhelming naval power against the last major Japanese fleet, which made a desperate effort to turn back the invasion armada in the Gulf of Leyte. In three major engagements on October 24 and 25, the Japanese were completely defeated, losing three battleships, four carriers, nine cruisers, and eight destroyers. Thereafter the seas around the Philippines passed into the control of the Americans, and MacArthur could proceed with the invasion of Mindanao and Luzon. He landed at Lingayen Gulf on the northeast coast of Luzon on January 9, 1945, and after fierce fighting captured Manila on March 3rd. The reconquest of the Philippines cost the worn-out Japanese military machine and navy nearly 10,000 planes and some 400,000 troops. In addition it blocked the communications between Japan and its crumbling empire in the East Indies, Malaya, and Indo-China. As 1944 ended, America was systematically occupying the jumping-off-spots for the invasion of Japan itself.

THE RE-ELECTION OF ROOSEVELT

Notwithstanding the fact that an uninterrupted succession of Allied military victories all over the world created formidable problems, diplomatic exchanges between members of the coalition were carried on through regular channels and kept at a minimum in 1944. Representatives of the Big Four (the United States, Britain, Russia, and China) met at Dumbarton Oaks from August 21 to October 7, 1944, and made a tentative draft of a charter for the postwar world organization in pursuance of the Moscow Declaration. Farther north at Bretton Woods, New Hampshire, delegates from forty-four states met for three weeks, starting July 1, 1944, to work out an agreement that would reduce the incidence of economic warfare and provide reconstruction loans. Both conferences made a beginning but did not draft plans in final form.

Developments took place at such a slow pace partly because America, the kingpin of the coalition, was convulsed by a presidential election.

Mindful of the thorny path trod by President Wilson, Roosevelt refused to identify himself with any particular plan of international organization or territorial settlement that might alienate substantial blocs of voters. His reluctance to press for another international conference in 1944 was reciprocated by Churchill and Stalin. Both recognized the possibility that Roosevelt might lose the election and preferred to postpone making commitments until after the voters reached a decision. Delay suited Stalin especially well because he wanted Russian troops to be in effective control of Poland and as many Balkan states as possible before returning to the conference table.

Although the Republicans had gained sharply in the 1942 elections, increasing their seats in the House from 162 to 209 and in the Senate from 28 to 38, their presidential prospects had not improved materially since 1940. Nothing had occurred during the war years to change the allegiance of numerous citizens who voted Democratic out of habit or conviction. Those apprehensive about a postwar depression still blamed the Republicans for the economic crisis of the 1930's and credited the New Deal for the full employment accompanying mobilization. Other voters who were prepared to desert the administration because of annoyance over conscription, price control, or other forms of regimentation, were canceled out by erstwhile critics of the Democrats reluctant to change leaders in the middle of war. Conservative southerners denounced the New Deal's concessions to labor unions and Negro workers in war industry, but tradition restrained them from voting for the G.O.P. Isolationists hated the administration to a man, but leading Republicans spurned their support. Wendell Willkie, the titular head of the party, had become an outspoken internationalist, and in 1943 most Republicans in Congress had supported resolutions committing the United States in general language to a future world organization. The vote of 360 to 29 in the House, and 85 to 5 in the Senate, indicated that isolationism had lost much of its appeal. Hence the Republicans faced the formidable task of winning an election without criticizing internationalism, New Deal social and economic reforms, or patriotic wartime legislation.

In the spring of 1944 it appeared as if the party would produce several candidates for the presidential nomination, but when the convention assembled in Chicago on June 26, only one serious contender remained. Wendell Willkie had withdrawn after suffering a severe defeat in the Wisconsin primary. The youthful Commander Harold Stassen, who had won three terms as Governor of Minnesota before enlisting in the Navy, aroused little enthusiasm outside his native state. The white hope of the old-line conservatives, Governor John W. Bricker of Ohio, faded rapidly despite an energetic preconvention campaign. William Allen White's characterization of Bricker as "an honest Harding" put in words a widespread fear that the Ohio governor lacked the requisite energy and imagination to make a good wartime chief executive.

The deflation of these balloons led to a first-ballot nomination of Governor Thomas E. Dewey of New York by a vote of 1056 to 1. The youngest

Republican standard bearer since Theodore Roosevelt, Dewey had a reputation for honesty, administrative efficiency, and moderate views on controversial issues. More important still, he was the first Republican to be elected Governor of New York in two decades and hence stood a better chance than recent G.O.P. presidential nominees of carrying the crucial northeastern states. The convention balanced the ticket geographically by giving Bricker second place on the ticket. It also adopted a platform that committed the party to the preservation of basic New Deal reforms and to American participation in postwar international organization. Voters were spared the inconvenience of confusing the document with the Democratic platform by the inclusion of the usual denunciations of New Deal centralization, waste, and inefficiency.

The Democratic convention, which did not meet until July 19, 1944, went through the routine procedure of renominating Franklin D. Roosevelt. Although he waited until July 11 to announce his availability in an open letter to National Chairman Robert E. Hannegan, it had been a foregone conclusion for months that he would accept an unprecedented fourth nomination. The usual coterie of southern conservatives tried to block the selection of Roosevelt, but they could muster only 89 first ballot votes for Senator Harry F. Byrd of Virginia out of 1066.

More than the usual excitement was attached to the selection of the vice-presidential nominee because many delegates shared the unspoken conviction that Roosevelt would not live long enough to complete another term. During the winter of 1944 he had suffered from a bronchial ailment that he could not shake until after a month of vacation in South Carolina. As an aftermath of his illness, White House physicians had advised him to reduce his weight between ten and fifteen pounds, and the President had complied. He claimed that he felt better at the lower weight, but he looked considerably worse because part of the loss came out of his face and neck, causing his cheeks to sag. His stubborn refusal to purchase shirts with smaller necks heightened the visual impression that he was failing physically in the summer of 1944. Rumors that the had suffered a stroke encouraged the wrangle over the vice-presidential nomination.

Most of the southerners as well as many moderate Democrats above Mason and Dixon's line were determined to block the renomination of Wallace. The former disliked him for his militant championship of underprivileged Negroes and poor whites. The others were frightened by the boundless quality of his enthusiasm for all sorts of eccentric projects. Roosevelt might have insisted on his renomination if he had not also harbored reservations about the emotional stability and political judgment of Wallace. The desire to avoid a fuss rather than anxieties about his own health caused Roosevelt to drop the Vice-President. He gave Wallace a public endorsement but pointedly refrained from insisting on his nomination. Simultaneously he encouraged James F. Byrnes to run for the office. This strategy was upset by Sidney Hillman, a C.I.O. official who had organized a Political Action Committee after the 1942 elections to get out the labor vote in the forthcoming presidential contest. He told Roosevelt that the conservative Byrnes was unacceptable to the unions and to the northern Negro voters. Since the Political Action Committee had already demonstrated its power by blocking the renomination of several antilabor congressmen in the 1944 primaries, Roosevelt bowed to Hillman and deserted Byrnes for a compromise candidate. He indicated that either Justice William O. Douglas or Senator Harry S. Truman would be acceptable. While both men fitted the specifications of Hillman, Douglas aroused the same resentment among southern conservatives as Wallace did. On the other hand, Truman was a sufficiently obscure and noncontroversial figure to run the gauntlet of party factions unscathed. He had supported all New Deal labor legislation without being a disagreeable, doctrinaire advocate of it. Moderates could swallow his voting record because he had a reassuringly practical manner. Even southern conservatives were encouraged by the fact that he hailed from the border state of Missouri, and they assumed that he would share their dismay over wartime reductions of the barriers between Negroes and whites. One other virtue enhanced his attractiveness — a reputation for honesty and efficiency as chairman of a special committee that investigated mismangement in war industry. The negotiations culminating in the decision to nominate Truman as Vice-President consumed several days before the opening of the Democratic convention. Had Roosevelt possessed any intimation of his impending death, he might have considered a longer list of running mates. As it turned out, campaign considerations rather than the question of qualification for executive office dictated the choice.

At the convention matters were arranged to give an air of spontaneity to the nomination of Truman. Party managers allowed Wallace to lead on the first ballot, and spokesmen for the C.I.O.'s Political Action Committee organized extravagant demonstrations in his behalf. He faltered on the second ballot, and Truman received the nomination on the third ballot. Shortly thereafter the convention adopted a platform pledging the party to preserve New Deal reforms and provide vigorous leadership in international affairs.

The ensuing campaign was a frustrating experience for Dewey. Military victories kept piling up during the summer and fall of 1944. He could not criticize the conduct of the war without risking retaliatory slurs on his patriotism. Nor could he denounce the New Deal legislation of the 1930's without providing ammunition for the PAC drive to register workers who had migrated since the 1940 election. Foreign policy offered no attractive issues because isolationism was dead and internationalism was being successfully marketed by the Democrats as the original discovery of Franklin Roosevelt. The dearth of suitable controversies left Dewey with no alternative except to exploit popular doubts about the President's health. He wisely avoided a direct statement on the subject but pounded repeatedly on the theme that the Democratic administration was staffed by tired old men. His tactics alarmed Roosevelt sufficiently to force him to the hustings. He made speeches in Washington, Chicago, Wilmington, Boston, and New York, allowing himself to be driven through the latter city with the automobile top down in a pouring rain. His last-minute display of physical robustness was the prelude to another victory on November 7. The distribution of votes in 1944 did not vary markedly from the pattern set in 1940, although both the total popular vote and the President's share of it declined. Roosevelt received 25,602,505 ballots, and Dewey 22,006,278. The margin in the electoral college was more one-sided. Roosevelt carried 36 states with 432 votes, and Dewey 12 states with 99 votes. The PAC campaign to get transplanted war workers to the polls may have been decisive, because outside the Solid South and the border the President built up his pluralities in the large industrial cities. The congressional elections strengthened the control of the Democrats. They picked up 22 House seats and emerged with a standoff in the Senate, thereby retaining their majority of 20.

THE YALTA CONFERENCE

As soon as his mandate had been renewed, Roosevelt pressed for a fresh conference of the Big Three to deal with accumulated problems. Some of them arose out of disputes at Dumbarton Oaks over the charter for the proposed world organization. Others concerned the treatment and disposition of enemy territory already conquered by members of the Allied coalition. Still others revolved about the coordination of military strategy for the final drive against the Axis powers and the allocation of responsibility among the various occupation armies after the foes had surrendered.

As usual Stalin objected to leaving Russia, and so Roosevelt and Churchill agreed to meet him at Yalta in the Crimea, which had been the winter resort of the Tsars. Preliminary Anglo-American conversations were held en route at Marrakech in French Morocco between Edward R. Stettinius, Jr., who had replaced Cordell Hull as Secretary of State, and Anthony Eden. They reviewed frictions between the two western powers and presented their findings to Roosevelt and Churchill, who paused for conversations at Malta on January 31 and February 1. Disagreements over the composition of the new Italian government and the character of British intervention in Greece were resolved. Stettinius confided to his memoirs that Roosevelt looked physically fit and alert after his long voyage on the cruiser *Quincy*.

From Malta the Big Two proceeded by air to the Crimea, where they conferred with Stalin from February 4 to February 11, 1945, about Europe, Asia, and the embryo world organization. The Yalta conference has frequently been described as marking the high tide of Allied unity. The metaphor is justified in the sense that the Big Three reached agreement on an imposing number of questions. It is misleading in the sense that the principals purchased agreement by ignoring or concealing differences of intention and interpretation. What happened was that Roosevelt continued to assume an identity of postwar objectives on the part of the western powers and the Soviet Union. Hence he dismissed the possibility that Russia would interpret the agreements to suit herself as soon as the defeat of the Axis powers removed the incentive for cooperation with the West. He did not live long enough to see the full effect of his miscalculation regarding the objectives of Russia. However, even at Yalta Stalin's intransigence on the Polish question foreshadowed things to come.

Reconstitution of a free Poland was a topic high on the agenda at Yalta as it had been at the Moscow conference fifteen months earlier. Aside from the fact that she had suffered unspeakable indignities at the hands of the Nazis, Poland was a symbol. Churchill felt a moral obligation to restore her independence, since England had entered the war to preserve that independence. Roosevelt also regarded the decision of the great powers on Poland as a crucial test of the Atlantic Charter which would be closely watched all over the world. He felt an additional obligation to make a firm stand because Polish-Americans showed lively concern over the fate of their distant relatives in Europe. Stalin, on the contrary, was determined to make Poland a satellite of Russia and proposed that the western powers recognize the Communist-dominated Lublin government. When Churchill and Roosevelt refused, Stalin offered to include a few leaders of the Polish government-in-exile. Again they balked. Thereupon the Russian dictator promised to reorganize the Lublin government so that it would include representatives of all Polish groups at home and abroad and also undertook to hold free elections at the earliest practicable date. The western leaders accepted this illusory concession, and within two weeks the Kremlin expelled western observers from Poland as a prelude to the liquidation of anti-Communist leaders.

Aside from his determination to dominate Poland, Stalin displayed a conciliatory attitude at Yalta. He feared Germany as his only rival on the Continent and enthusiastically assented to the demands of his colleagues for harsh surrender terms. If anything, he was inclined to outbid them in urging the destruction of German power, on the theory that both the United States and Great Britain would soon withdraw from Europe. This impression was strengthened by Roosevelt's incautious remark that American occupation troops would remain on the Continent only a year after the surrender of Germany. Stalin also felt disposed to go along with the proposed world organization which would give Russia a veto on collective military action against her encroachments in the vacuum area of Eastern Europe.

Against this background negotiations for the dismemberment of Germany and the creation of the United Nations Organization proceeded smoothly. It was agreed that East Prussia would be partitioned, with the northern half going to the Soviet Union and the southern half going to Poland. In return for territorial compensation in the west, Poland was expected to cede to the Soviet Union her eastern provinces containing Ukranians and White Russians. The Big Three refused a Russian request for a specific reparations bill of $20 billion but accepted the figure as a basis for future negotiations and agreed to establish a Reparations Commission with headquarters in Moscow. Composition of the Inter-Allied Control Commission provoked a mild dispute because the western powers wanted to include France and the Russians objected. In the end Stalin yielded after receiving assurances that the French occupation zone in Germany would be carved out of an area already allotted to the western powers. Determination of the exact boundaries of Germany was left for future conferences, although the Big Three reaffirmed their intention of dismembering the Nazi state.

The earlier deadlock at Dumbarton Oaks over representation in the projected United Nations Organization was resolved at Yalta in favor of America. Stalin had originally demanded representatives for each of the sixteen Soviet Republics, but agreed to settle for representatives from Russia, Ukrania, and White Russia. Fearful that the Senate would object to the Soviet Union having more members in the General Assembly than the United States, Roosevelt also got Stalin's consent to three American representatives. The concession, however, proved unnecessary to win Senate approval, and Roosevelt accepted a single representative. More important was Stalin's assent to the President's proposal that all states at war with Germany on March 1, 1945, be admitted to the United Nations. This concession paved the way for the entrance of the Latin-American states, which were expected to vote with the United States. In view of the limited powers envisaged for the General Assembly, the preponderance of the western bloc in that body did not mean much. Neither the United States nor Russia proposed to tamper with the veto power of the permanent members in the more important Security Council.

The best-kept secret of the Yalta conference was the Russian pledge to enter the war against Japan within three months after the surrender of Germany. In return, Roosevelt promised to restore all Russian territory and all special privileges lost to the Japanese in the war of 1904–1905. These included (1) the southern half of Sakhalin Island, (2) the lease of the naval base at Port Arthur on the southern tip of the Liaotung peninsula, (3) the privilege of jointly operating the Chinese Eastern and the Southern Manchurian railroads with the government of Chiang Kai-shek. The President also agreed to a transfer of sovereignty over the Kurile Islands from Japan to Russia and recognized Soviet control over Outer Mongolia. Although the renewal of Russian railroad concessions was certain to impair Chinese control over Manchuria, Stalin eased Roosevelt's anxieties by offering to recognize Chinese sovereignty over the area and to sign a treaty of alliance with the Nationalist government at Chungking.

The Far Eastern accord, like the agreement on Poland, was subsequently denounced by critics of Roosevelt as a sellout to the Russians. The more charitable inferred from his early death that the President erred at Yalta because of declining physical and mental capacities. The rest charged him with either an inexcusable error of judgment or a willful desire to strengthen Russia at the expense of his native country. Neither assertion will survive objective examination. His judgment reflected the view of his military advisers, all of whom overestimated the Japanese capacity for continuing the war. Foreseeing a fanatical defense of the home islands, they thought that resistance would last until mid-1946 and cost America a million casualties unless Russia intervened. Whether Roosevelt and his advisers had the data for a better guess is a moot point. The issue of Russian participation in the Japanese war would never have arisen at Yalta had it not been for the unconditional surrender policy which the supporters of the President uncritically accepted. The subsequent deterioration of the American position in the Far East stemmed from the determination to destroy Japan rather than to cut it down to reasonable size.

THE FINAL OFFENSIVE AGAINST GERMANY

The Big Three were not to meet again until July 1945 at Potsdam. By that time death had claimed Franklin Roosevelt (April 12) and a political reversal had forced Winston Churchill to relinquish power in the middle of the conferences. However, the decisions made at Yalta guided the military operations of the United Nations during the final months of the war. The desperate Germans opened 1945 with a strenuous effort to sustain a counterattack launched by General von Rundstedt on December 16, 1944. Striking through the Ardennes forest at the southern end of the Siegfried Line, he had advanced nearly fifty miles in the last two weeks of the year. His objective was the Allied port of Antwerp. The offensive lost momentum at the Moselle River in early January, and the Allied armies smashed the salient to bits at the end of the month. Known as the "Battle of the Bulge," this proved to be the last gasp of the collapsing German armies. The Anglo-American forces quickly regained the initiative, piercing the Westwall on a broad front in February and overrunning the Rhineland in March. Cologne surrendered on the 6th and other cities on the left bank quickly followed. The Allies crossed the Rhine on the 24th and completed the encirclement of 250,000 Germans in the Ruhr a week later. Nonetheless organized resistance continued on all fronts until the armistice on May 8, 1945, with a world audience watching breathlessly to see whether the Anglo-American or the Russian army would reach Berlin first. Most of the spectators were not aware until later that the outcome of the race had been fixed. Although the Big Three had not agreed at Yalta to stop their armies along any particular line, they had allocated occupation zones on the basis of an earlier plan. The zones assigned to the Americans and the British were west of the Elbe River. Roosevelt did not consider it desirable to continue the offensive beyond the Elbe and to take Berlin, which would be in the Russian zone. His attitude reflected the views of Eisenhower and Marshall who, anticipating a final Nazi stand in the so-called "National Redoubt" of the Bavarian Alps, gave priority to a rapid conquest of that area.

The speed of the Anglo-American advance in February and March, which was synchronized with Stalin's cynical installation of Communist governments in Poland and Rumania, created pressure for a new policy. His worst fears of Soviet intentions confirmed, Churchill urged a rapid advance of the Anglo-American forces on Berlin and Prague. Repeatedly he asked Roosevelt to authorize the occupation of both cities, arguing that they should be held until Stalin reversed his policy in Poland. The Churchill plan was militarily feasible because on April 1 the Allied victory in the Ruhr had removed the last army barring the route to the German and Czech capitals. Roosevelt turned a deaf ear to Churchill's entreaties. When the President died on April 12, the Russian armies were still stalled on the Oder River, whereas the vanguard of western armies had reached the Elbe at a point only fifty-three miles from Berlin. Churchill hastily addressed a fresh plea to the inexperienced Harry Truman. The new President, on the advice of General Marshall, stood firm behind the original plan of conquering the National Redoubt instead of advancing on Berlin and Prague. As a result, Eisenhower sent Patton to Bavaria on April 21 for the mop-up of what proved to be a nonexistent Nazi army. Other Allied units turned slowly southward along the Elbe where they established contact with the Russians on April 27. Even at that late date, Prague might still have been liberated by American troops. Eisenhower, however, respected the wishes of Stalin and remained west of the river, allowing the Russians to enter Prague on May 8. The irresolute leadership in Washington, reinforced by the indifference of the American High Command to political considerations, destroyed the last opportunity of the western powers to retrieve with military operations what they had lost by diplomacy. Their occupation of Prague and Berlin might well have forced Stalin to respect his pledges of free elections in Poland and Rumania.

Meanwhile, Marshal Gregory K. Zhukov, who had paused on the Oder River while Russian troops fanned out to liberate Danzig, Königsberg, and Vienna, burst into West Prussia on April 15. A week later his troops reached the outskirts of Berlin and fought their way slowly to the heart of the city. Hitler had lingered in his capital until the last, hoping that his foes would turn on each other. By April 29 the burning city resembled Valhalla at the End of the World, and the Fuehrer planned an exit worthy of his Wagnerian heroes. He appointed Admiral Karl Doenitz his successor and married his mistress, Eva Braun. After a twenty-four-hour interval, the pair committed suicide. Their bodies were burned in the chancellery garden in accordance with careful instructions. Two days earlier, Italian partisans had captured and shot Mussolini.

The death of the two dictators symbolized the end of an era, although remnants of the German military machine fought on for an additional week. The units in northern Italy and Austria laid down their arms on May 2. Scattered divisions in Holland, Denmark, and northwest Germany followed suit two days later. The final surrender document was signed by Colonel General Alfred Jodl at 2:41 A.M., May 7, in Eisenhower's presence. Within twenty-four hours all organized fighting on the Continent had ceased for the first time in six years. The news of victory touched off spontaneous demonstrations in Allied capitals, but Churchill gloomily confided to his memoirs that his mind was "oppressed by forebodings."

THE DESTRUCTION OF JAPAN

No sooner had hostilities been ended in Europe than the United States launched a vast transfer of military units to the Pacific. Japan gave up before most of them could be shifted. We have already noted that the American occupation of the principal Mariana islands in the summer of 1944 had provided bases for the bombardment of Japan's home islands and that the naval engagement in Leyte Gulf had destroyed her fleet. After October of 1944 the United States dominated the skies and seas of the West Pacific. It was only a question of time until Japan quit. Iwo Jima, 750 miles south of Tokyo, fell to American marines on March 16, 1945, after some of the bloodiest fighting of the Pacific war. Okinawa, a larger island in the Ryukyu group and 400 miles closer to Japan, was invaded by Army and Marine Corps units on April 1. The defenders put up the same fanatical resistance on Okinawa as they had at Iwo Jima. Japanese aviators made suicide attacks on American warships and landing craft. Heedless of their losses, the ground troops contested each inch. When they were finally routed out of all the caves and jungles on the island, the Japanese had sacrificed 111,000 soldiers and nearly 4,000 planes.

The ability of a crumbling military establishment to contest Okinawa from April 1 until June 21 convinced MacArthur that the Japanese would defend the home islands with comparable fury. Neither he nor Admiral Nimitz expected the Pacific war to end until mid-1946. Both had underestimated the effectiveness of air attacks. By May of 1945, the Emperor and a sizable peace party had recognized the necessity of ending the war. Accordingly Premier Baron Kantaro Suzuki, who had replaced General Kuniaki Koiso on April 18, opened secret conversations with the Soviet ambassador, Jacob Malik, in the hope of securing Russian mediation. These efforts proved fruitless because Stalin had no intention of forfeiting concessions promised at Yalta. The unwillingness of the United States to accept less than unconditional surrender also strengthened the hand of the military extremists who successfully resisted implementation of the peace program for two months.

The Potsdam Declaration of July 26, calling upon Japan to surrender or face "utter devastation," reopened the debate in Tokyo. Issued over the signatures of Truman, Attlee, and Stalin, it served notice on the Japanese that Russian intervention was imminent and their position hopeless. Suzuki, backed by the Emperor, decided to accept the Potsdam Declaration but could not compel the cooperation of the army leaders. Seeking to avert a military coup by rejecting the Declaration, the Japanese Prime Minister provided the United States with an excuse for unveiling the atomic bomb. On August 6 a lone B-29 dropped this new and frightful explosive on Hiroshima. The ensuing blast leveled 4.4 square miles of the city and killed nearly 80,000 residents. Three days later the Russians declared war on Japan, and the American air force dropped a second bomb on Nagasaki. The battered Empire of the Rising Sun had reached the limit of endurance. On August 10 the Suzuki cabinet informed Washington that it was prepared to accept the Potsdam terms provided the Allies safeguarded the status of the Emperor. Washington countered by insisting on the subordination of the Emperor to the Supreme Commander. The military and naval officials in Tokyo urged further resistance, but the Emperor forced acceptance of Allied terms on August 14. An insurrection of army leaders threatened to prolong the agony of Japan. In the end, the cabinet prevailed and sent envoys to General MacArthur who worked out the specific details of the surrender. The formal ceremony took place September 2 in Tokyo Bay on board the battleship *Missouri* where Foreign Minister Mamoru Shigemitsu signed the surrender documents in the presence of General MacArthur and other representatives of the Allied Powers.

As far as the Americans were concerned, the defeat of Germany and Japan had irrevocably smashed the forces of evil. They looked forward to a new era of world-wide brotherhood and prosperity, confident that even the Russians would relax in the utopian atmosphere of the *Pax Americana.*

SUGGESTED READINGS

1. Churchill, W., *The Grand Alliance.*
   The Hinge of Fate.
   Closing the Ring.
2. Hall, W. P., *Iron Out of Calvary: An Interpretive History of the Second World War.*
3. Sherwood, R., *Roosevelt and Hopkins.*
4. Wilmot, C., *The Struggle for Europe.*

CHAPTER TWENTY-SEVEN

THE QUEST FOR PROSPERITY AT HOME AND PEACE ABROAD

On April 12, 1945, less than six months after he had been elected to an unprecedented fourth term, President Roosevelt was stricken by a cerebral hemorrhage and passed away within an hour. Although alarming rumors about his health had circulated during the campaign and had been supported by visible evidence of his declining weight and vitality, his abrupt death came as a shock.

Mourning for the deceased was mingled with anxiety about national leadership. Roosevelt had enjoyed widespread prestige because of his unique feat in surviving as Chief Executive during the twelve turbulent years of depression and war. Many youngsters could not remember living under any other President. The older generation had come to accept his indestructibility as a fact — the New Dealers cheerfully, and the Republicans with resignation.

Both parties had adjustments to make. The Republicans had grown so accustomed to regarding Roosevelt as a permanent incarnation of evil that the transfer of their ferocious hatred to lesser Democrats required quite an effort. They were also confronted with the political consequences of his death. With reasonable luck their foes could cultivate public veneration of the deceased war leader as another Lincoln, and exploit patriotic gratitude for his services to keep the party in power. Even his most rabid critics were sobered by the realization that their adversary might be more formidable dead than alive.

The Democrats were likely to suffer the most immediate damage. As the majority party entrusted with the conduct of the war, they were responsible for furnishing a new leader. Roosevelt had made this task more difficult by refusing to tolerate either rivals or understudies. His sin of omission, coupled with the curious Constitutional procedure governing the presidential succession, prevented the party from grooming a replacement. In a legal sense the Democrats had chosen a successor when they nominated Harry S. Truman as Roosevelt's running mate. Unfortunately, tradition had outlawed the practice of using the Vice-Presidency as a stepping stone to the Presidency. Except when the Chief Executive died in office, the Vice-Presidency led to a political graveyard. This rule worked so consistently that convention delegates usually selected a candidate who would balance the ticket geographically or appease a disgruntled faction. The nominee rarely stood high in the party councils or had a wide popular following. The system did no particular harm as long as a President lived to complete his term, but it committed both the nation and the majority party to untried leaders whenever a President died prematurely. Occasional crises had occurred prior to 1945 but never during a great war when confidence in American leadership was so essential both at home and abroad.

TRUMAN BECOMES PRESIDENT

The first reaction bordered on dismay. When Truman took the oath of office at 7:09 P.M. on April 12, he was a shadowy, unfamiliar figure to the average citizen. The politically illiterate either did not know his name or remembered it only as the second word in a campaign slogan. Republicans who read their newspapers carefully were most apt to recall that he had been identified with a political machine in Missouri. Democrats knew that he had received his nomination because of distinguished service as head of a special Senate committee which investigated waste in war industries. Otherwise, memories of his career as a prewar New Deal senator were vague. He had shunned the limelight in a decade made to order for the champions of social causes. Neither the controversies of the New Deal nor the debate over foreign policy in the 1930's had tempted him to bid for a national following. No important piece of legislation bore his name, and none of the metropolitan newspapers had bothered to report his speeches. Even during the 1944 election, he had been overshadowed by the retiring Vice-President, Henry Wallace.

An inquisitive public quickly learned the facts about the early life of the new President. Born in 1884 at Grandview, Missouri, he divided his youthful years between a farm and neighboring Kansas City. Deficient eyesight kept him out of sports and blocked his ambition to attend West Point. The outbreak of World War I temporarily rescued him from an uninteresting job as a bank clerk. He found soldiering a congenial profession and rose to the rank of Major in the Missouri National Guard. After being demobilized in 1919, he married a childhood sweetheart and opened a clothing store in Kansas City. When this fledgling business was wiped out in the postwar depression, he drifted into politics as a protégé of the Pendergast machine. From 1922 to 1924 he held the elective post of District Judge for eastern Jackson County, the Missouri equivalent to the County Commissionership in other states. After being defeated in 1924, he made a political comeback two years later and was elected Presiding

Bringing up baby. (Burt Thomas, The Detroit News, *1945.)*

Judge for all of Jackson County. He ran this office honestly and efficiently, took the graft out of highway construction, and gave the county a fine network of roads and a new courthouse.

When the operations of the Pendergast machine branched out into state politics, Truman was promoted to the United States Senate in 1934. Before his first term ended, Pendergast went to prison for income tax evasion, and the machine was broken up. The reform wing of the Democrats worked hard to defeat Truman in 1940 but he scored an upset victory. Although he would have preferred to complete his public career in the Senate, he accepted the vice-presidential nomination primarily because it was thrust upon him.

Nothing in his political career prepared him for the staggering burdens of the Presidency. His initial reaction was very much like that of his fellow countrymen. To close friends he expressed doubt as to his adequacy for the tasks ahead. Photographers caught the mood of insecurity in their first pictures; he looked bewildered, solemn, and ill at ease.

The President benefited almost immediately from a great wave of popular support. Paradoxically the very qualities that frightened people at the outset, endeared him to them after his first days in office. His self-confessed inadequacy and humility, united with a simple promise to do his best, provoked unusual demonstrations of cooperation. He fitted perfectly the role of underdog. Even the Republicans were temporarily moved to genuine pledges of support.

Truman's first acts as President capitalized on both the expressions of popular good will and the older habit of wartime solidarity. He promised to carry out the policies of his predecessor and assured administrative continuity by asking the members of the Roosevelt Cabinet to remain at their posts. He made a dramatic bid for the cooperation of Congress by visiting the Senate unannounced to lunch with his old colleagues and by asking Senator Kenneth D. McKellar, the president *pro tem* of the upper house, to attend Cabinet meetings. He also made a gracious plea for bipartisan support, to which Senator Taft responded by calling at the White House with a delegation of Republican legislators. Ex-President Hoover followed his example a few weeks later, thus ending a twelve-year boycott. The Republican press adopted a restrained bipartisan tone. Editors predicted an end to chronic party warfare and executive-legislative antagonism. They hailed the President as a moderate who would inaugurate a new era of good feeling. After expecting too little of him, they fell into the opposite error of expecting too much.

PROBLEMS OF RECONVERSION

The harmony of the opening months of Truman's administration did not survive the war. The first indication of a new mood appeared in Congress, which rebelled long before public opposition crystallized. Economic issues connected with reconversion turned out to be the chief bone of contention, but behind them were the crosscurrents of a constitutional struggle between executive and legislature. The constitutional struggle seemed to be entering the second phase of a familiar cycle: Congress, which had been overshadowed by the President throughout the war, began to fight back. It sought early termination of executive war powers irrespective of whether the President had usurped them as commander-in-chief or had received them through specific grants. It was also concerned over the steady growth of executive authority since the beginning of the New Deal. The legislators strove for an equilibrium like the one that had prevailed in the 1920's and regarded Truman as likely to acquiesce in the role of a weak President.

The minority in both houses wanted to use the same constitutional struggle as a means of reviving the political fortunes of their party. They could not hope to win elections by reaffirming the principles of the 1920's. Their sole chance seemed to lie in exploiting a major social and economic crisis.

Reconversion, which was bound to be painful for some groups, fitted the need perfectly. It offered the administration unusual opportunities to make mistakes. On the other hand, the Republicans would run few risks by exploiting irritation over shortages, high prices, industrial unrest, and other by-products of demobilization. Consequently, Republican congressmen gradually shifted from patriotic cooperation, to regretful criticism, and finally to indignant obstruction. They did not have long to wait for the problems they had anticipated. Within a month of VJ Day, the last vestiges of patriotic restraint were discarded by various groups in the American economy. These began to bid against each other for a wide range of capital goods and raw materials that had been in short supply throughout the war and could not be produced in volume for some months. Consumers also showed a strong desire for scarce commodities like automobiles, electrical appliances, nylon hosiery, and chocolate bars. A large money supply interacted with pent-up demand to create tremendous pressure for price inflation. Total dollars in circulation jumped from 43.6 billion in 1940 to 106.4 billion at the end of 1945. The rising volume of money was fed both by savings and by the growth of the public debt. That portion of the debt held by banks in the form of bonds was particularly inflationary, because under the rules of the Federal Reserve system it could be monetized. Each dollar of bonds functioned as a reserve deposit against which a bank could loan six dollars. Currency circulation also increased as citizens began to turn in war bonds and convert other types of savings into cash. Altogether savings of $140 billion were available for spending, and few Americans cared to defer their purchases. The resulting disparity between the supply of money and the supply of goods foreshadowed a race between manufacturers to raise prices and laborers to raise wages.

Other ominous clouds hung on the horizon. Since the boom of the 1920's the construction of new houses, as well as the repair of existing ones, had lagged behind the needs of the nation. The shortage was aggravated between 1942 and 1945 when 6.5 million marriages took place and only 1.5 million household units were built. The end of the war moved the problem closer to a crisis as demobilized soldiers and their families were forced to double up with in-laws.

Behind this problem was one that many people feared would be the greatest of all — whether veterans would find jobs to finance construction of the homes they needed. Economists forecast a repetition of the demobilization pattern of World War I, estimating that unemployed veterans and war workers would number from 10 million to 15 million during the period of reconversion. Many of them advocated a large-scale public works program and a government guarantee of full employment as the only safeguard against a catastrophic depression.

TRUMAN REORGANIZES HIS CABINET

While reconversion problems were piling up, President Truman completed the reorganization of his administration. Only three holdovers from the Roosevelt Cabinet — Harold Ickes, Secretary of the Interior; Henry Wallace, Secretary of Commerce; and James V. Forrestal, Secretary of the Navy — survived VJ Day. Edward R. Stettinius was appointed United States delegate to the United Nations to make room for James F. Byrnes as Secretary of State. Henry Morgenthau gave way to Fred M. Vinson as Secretary of the Treasury, and Frances Perkins to Lewis Schwellenbach as Secretary of Labor. Clinton Anderson of New Mexico left a safe seat in the House of Representatives to replace Claude Wickard in the top job of the sprawling Department of Agriculture. Robert P. Patterson was promoted to Secretary of War when the aged Henry L. Stimson retired. Robert Hannegan took over the Postmaster Generalship from Frank Walker, and Tom Clark became the new Attorney General. Turnover in the Cabinet was to be rapid. Thirty-four members served Truman for varying intervals during a seven-year period compared with the twenty-five for Roosevelt during a twelve-year period. Generally speaking, Truman delegated power more generously to members of his official family than his predecessor had done. By the same token he showed less tendency to protect them when they produced controversies within the administration. As a result, several of his original appointees left with ill-concealed hostility for their chief. No official or unofficial adviser ever occupied the unique position of Harry Hopkins under Roosevelt. The President, however, came to lean heavily on the counsel of Fred M. Vinson even after the latter had been promoted from Secretary of the Treasury to Chief Justice of the Supreme Court in 1946. Other important advisers were John F. Snyder, head of the Office of War Mobilization and Reconversion (later Secretary of the Treasury), John R. Steelman, who held various jobs, and Clark Clifford, a presidential assistant and speech writer.

During the four months between the death of Roosevelt and VJ Day, Truman gained in self-confidence and zest for his job. The extraordinary public support during the last months of the war heartened him, and the gradual departure of holdovers from the Cabinet gave him the satisfaction of being master in his own house. He shed the self-deprecatory manner and harassed look so characteristic of his first weeks in office. As the months lengthened into years, critics complained that he grew cocky and overconfident. He certainly seemed so to political opponents, who repeatedly expressed doubt about his capacity for performing the duties of President. His friends talked of his fighting spirit, determination, and willingness to take responsibility for decisions.

The controversy regarding his ability and personality lasted beyond his administration. Whatever the ultimate verdict of history, his skill as political leader cannot be disputed. He lacked Roosevelt's oratorical ability and flair for generating the crusading spirit. His formal speeches were flat and toneless, but no one excelled him in the knack of making effective extemporaneous talks. He was folksy, earnest, and persuasive. He possessed the psychology of Main Street, but he also saw it objectively enough to diagnose the political temper of the average small-town or rural American. Even his commonplace appearance was an advantage in politics, where distinction breeds suspicion more often than trust. Above all he was a scrapper who earned affection because of his persistent combativeness. His friends cared little whether he won or lost but felt reassured to know that he was fighting special privilege, a "do-nothing" Congress, or an insubordinate Army general. Foes found little to admire in Truman's insatiable thirst for controversy. They deplored his name-calling and his occasional resort to pool-hall phrases as unworthy of a President. They also feared that his absorption in political maneuvering cloaked a careless attitude toward urgent domestic and world problems. These fears were verbalized in charges of incompetence, which grew louder during Truman's second term.

THE RELAXATION OF WAR CONTROLS

Like his Republican opponents, Truman approached the problems of reconversion with an eye cocked on the 1946 elections. His basic task was to frame a policy broad enough to satisfy both the northeastern and the southern wings of his party. These populous units had been at odds on domestic issues since 1937 and had achieved a semblance of wartime solidarity only by observing an informal truce for the duration. With the restoration of peace, old cleavages seemed destined to re-emerge. The urban Democrats of the North wanted high wages, more comprehensive unemployment insurance, and bigger pensions for the aged. But below Mason and Dixon's line, the rural Democrats disliked the idea of being taxed to support welfare programs that would be of more benefit to another section. Inasmuch as at the moment the prices of cotton, tobacco, and peanuts remained above the floor guaranteed by government, southerners were in a fine tactical position to denounce all subsidies as violations of American political principles. At the same time, they had reasons for disliking the prolabor attitude of northern Democrats. Strong unions meant organizational drives in the South and an end to the cheap labor supply which gave textile manufacturers of that area a competitive advantage. In addition, unionization seemed certain to threaten the social structure which kept the Negro in a subordinate position. Aside from eastern labor and southern agriculture, the prewar Democratic coalition had drawn support from small business and white-collar groups, western mining interests and cattlemen; but these elements were neither so populous nor so important in election calculations as the workers and farmers. Still, if reconversion slowed down production for an extended period, all groups might embarrass the administration by voting as indignant consumers.

Two general reconversion policies were open to Truman. Either he could use his war powers until their expiration to regulate all phases of the economy or he could withdraw government controls as quickly as possible. The first course appealed to the New Deal element as a way of easing the transitional economic stresses from war to peace. It suffered from two obvious defects: the possibility that interim controls might not work, and the political hazard of extending regimentation beyond the end of the war. The alternative program of indiscriminate relaxation of controls suited business but seemed certain to release strong inflationary forces and squeeze consumers badly.

Truman chose to steer between the two, combining the relaxation of controls over most scarce materials and wages with the retention of price ceilings on consumer goods. This formula was intended to offer something to all groups and to forestall dissension in the Democratic party.

Relaxation of controls took place with great fanfare. Immediately after VJ Day, the WPB terminated the wartime priority system and swept away 210 regulations within a week. Among the conspicuous casualties was order M126 which had prohibited the use of iron and steel in 1,200 items ranging from jukeboxes to golf clubs. The government still retained import-export controls and the right to distribute scarce materials like copper, tin, rubber, timber, and textiles. Simultaneously it cancelled war contracts totaling billions of dollars, instituted a sale of surplus properties at bargain prices, suspended Lend-Lease operations, and secured quick congressional approval of reductions in both individual and corporate taxes. The excess-profits tax, so annoying to business, was repealed altogether.

The public also demanded quick demobilization of the armed forces. Truman responded by setting up a schedule calling for the discharge of 50,000 soldiers in September 1945, and an acceleration of the pace each month until December, when the rate would increase to 650,000. A comparable schedule was fixed for other branches of the armed forces and a point system devised to assure prior discharge of men with overseas service. However, the pressure of parents for immediate release of sons in uniform proved to be so formidable that the schedule was scrapped and a wholesale exodus was sponsored by the government. Nearly 1,112,000 soldiers and 500,000 sailors received their discharge in December 1945. The military authorities sustained this pace until the armed forces had dropped to the 2.2 million prescribed by Congress. The job was completed in July 1946, disbanding a military establishment which had reached a wartime peak of 15 million. Neither the prospect of deteriorating relations with Russia nor the enlargement of American commitments outside the Western Hemisphere dampened popular determination to hasten the release of impatient military personnel.

THE REAFFIRMATION OF NEW DEAL OBJECTIVES

The prompt demobilization measures were well received in all quarters and encouraged conservatives to believe that Truman would pursue policies somewhat to the right of the New Deal. These hopes received a rude setback on September 6, 1945, when he sent a message to Congress containing twenty-one specific recommendations. Ostensibly a program to forestall postwar recession, he reaffirmed all the orthodox New Deal doctrines and proposed that some of them be extended to new areas. He called for a statutory boost in minimum wages from 40 cents to 65 cents per hour, an increase in social security benefits, and an extension of social security coverage to provide health insurance, low-cost housing, and slum clearance. He also recommended long-range planning to develop national resources, construction of useful public works, and provision for technical assistance to businessmen and farmers. He gave Negroes special consideration in a proposal that the wartime Fair Employment Practices Act be put on a permanent basis. Banking on the good will already gained by the relaxation of controls, he asked Congress to extend his war powers over prices and wages until reconversion stresses disappeared.

Cynics dismissed the message with the wisecrack that Truman was trying to take advantage of the rules for the release of military personnel and had made enough points to be discharged as commander-in-chief. Conservatives were stunned, and erstwhile New Dealers elated. The old prewar coalition of southern Democrats and Republicans promptly reconstituted itself in Congress and pigeonholed all the recommendations except the one for the extension of war powers.

The only other New Deal proposal to be reported out of committee was the full-employment bill. Introduced in the Senate by an administration spokesman, James E. Murray of Montana, the measure sought to make government responsibility for the relief of unemployment an official policy. It directed the President and his staff to prepare an annual national production and employment budget which would estimate the total expenditure of funds necessary to maintain full employment. It also required a Congressional Joint Committee on the National Budget to use the report as a basis for appropriations that would sustain "a full volume of employment and production."

As originally drafted, the measure went beyond the official New Deal economic policy of the 1930's. The fiscal theory of the depression had envisaged government spending as a temporary device to encourage private investment. But the limited gains in employment and productivity during the depression decade, compared to the phenomenal gains of the war years when spending had also risen steeply, brought a revision of theory. The New Dealers came to feel that planned government expenditures would assure full employment, high productivity, and a rising standard of living. Roosevelt had endorsed the policy during the 1944 campaign, and Henry Wallace had popularized it in a pamphlet entitled *60,000,000 Jobs*.

Because of the public clamor over full employment, Congress felt obliged to demonstrate its enthusiasm for prosperity. So in March 1946 it passed an emasculated version of the Murray bill. It knocked out all provisions for the implementation of mandatory planning but retained the clause establishing the official board of economic soothsayers. Composed of three members and known as the Council of Economic Advisers, the board was authorized to advise Congress and the President about fiscal problems and to issue an annual report on the economic health of the nation. Congress removed all temptation for the advisers to become planners by redefining the goals of the legislation as "maximum" employment rather than "full" employment. From a major feature of postwar reconversion policy, the full-employment law had been whittled down to the point where it did nothing more than create a new statistical bureau in Washington.

INFLATION AND STRIKES

Meanwhile troubles developed for the administration on other fronts. The reduction of taxes and controls over materials without a corresponding relaxation of wage and price controls quickly produced inflationary pressure. Deprived of overtime on war contracts, organized workers all over the country sought to recoup wage losses by demanding forty-eight hours of pay for a forty-hour work week — or a 30 per cent raise. Union spokesmen contended that such an increase was necessary to counterbalance the rise in living costs between 1941 and 1945. Businessmen were prepared to make some adjustments provided the administration permitted proportionate price increases. Irrespective of administration policy, however, they regarded an across-the-board raise of 30 per cent as excessive and likely to force many companies into the red. Furthermore, many small firms feared that sharp price increases would result in the loss of business to competitors, while large integrated industries felt that abrupt changes might annoy consumers and stir up antitrust suits. Still others foresaw mass unemployment and believed the time ripe for the resumption of warfare against organized labor, which now boasted an all-time high of 14 million members.

As we have already noted, the administration was bound to be directly involved in the impending disputes because the President had important emergency powers over prices and wages. Obviously he faced less political risk from a policy of preserving price ceilings and permitting wage increases than from any other program. Workers and consumers would be grateful, whereas the businessmen who stood to lose most from a price freeze would probably vote Republican in any event. Officials in charge of the reconversion program encouraged Truman to believe that the policy of political expediency was also the policy of statesmanship. They argued that reduction of corporate taxes would permit business to grant wage increase of approximately 25 per cent and still maintain earnings without price relief.

Truman convened a Labor-Management conference in late November of 1945, partly to sell his stabilization formula and partly to discuss methods for preventing industrial disputes. Unfortunately, the success of all mediation procedures depends upon the existence of a basis for agreement, and in this case the principals did not have one. Organized labor stood inflexibly behind the 30 per cent increase, and management was unwilling to grant more than 5 per cent or 6 per cent unless there were a price increase. The conference adjourned on an inconclusive note, and an epidemic of strikes spread to every major industry after the end of the year. The worst month was January 1946, but before the epidemic subsided in June nearly 2 million men had lost a total of 113 million man-hours on strike. Neither side resorted to the violent methods which had characterizated the industrial disputes of the 1930's, nor was there any of the hysterical fear of Communism that had been so pronounced during the reconversion strikes of 1919. The warfare was so gentlemanly that the average citizen would hardly have been aware of it except for continued shortages of consumer goods and the near paralysis of the economy on several occasions.

Whether Truman could have prevented the situation by a different policy is uncertain. Once the strikes began, he tried to force a settlement that would cause as little damage to his formula as possible. Emergency reconversion powers provided him with more leverage for dealing with disputes in industries defined as essential than in those outside that category. Whenever essential industries became strikebound, he could invoke the Smith-Connally War Disputes Act and reopen them under government operation. In such cases the transfer of control was purely formal. Its purpose was to open the way for a new contract between the government and the workers, granting the latter the points in dispute. During the war the owners usually ratified government concessions as soon as the plant was turned back to them. After the patriotic compulsions bred by the crisis had disapppeared they could not be counted upon to acquiesce in labor's demands so readily. There was the further hazard that workers might not accept even the more generous contract proposals of the government. Notwithstanding these dangers latent in frequent use of the Smith-Connally Act, Truman seized the oil refineries in order to avert a work stoppage in October 1945 and the meat-packing industry a few weeks later.

Truman customarily prepared the public for government operation by appointing a board to investigate and publish the essential facts regarding the dispute. He relied still more heavily on this technique to forestall or settle disputes in consumer goods industries not subject to seizure under the Smith-Connally Act. The Railway Mediation Act of 1926, for instance, had given legal status to the fact-finding board in that industry and it also made a cooling-off period mandatory while the investigation was taking place. Board recommendations did not bind either party, but public opinion was expected to endorse the findings and force acceptance of its terms.

In December 1945 the President asked Congress for a law that would extend the principles of the Railway Mediation Act to all major industrial disputes. Before he made the request he had repeatedly asked industries threatened by strikes to accept presidential fact-finding boards voluntarily. This method was especially appealing to him because he could exercise discretion in the selection of members and thereby secure decisions in harmony with his stabilization program. Such manipulation jeopardized the impartial character of the board but not sufficiently to impair the judicial atmosphere surrounding the transaction or to disillusion the public.

Businessmen distrusted the boards for precisely the reasons that commended them to Truman. As a group, they were convinced that all panels he appointed would find facts to warrant a wage increase. They also contested the assumption that government was entitled to know all the facts about a private enterprise — a doctrine that had not been seriously advanced even by the New Deal.

An early showdown was certain when 180,000 members of the United Automobile Workers called a strike in General Motors plants in twelve states on November 21, 1945. The vice-president of the UAW, Walter Reuther, threw down the gauntlet immediately by publishing a financial statement purporting to show that General Motors could grant workers a 30 per cent pay increase and still earn double the annual profits from 1935 to 1939 at existing car prices. The corporation stoutly contradicted Reuther's contention and refused his request to examine their books, ignored the recommendation of a presidential Fact-Finding Board for a wage increase of 19½ cents per hour, and insisted on the private character of its operation. Since the issue was more doctrinal than financial from the standpoint of the corporation, it held out until the fact-finding formula had been repudiated as a basis for negotiations. After 113 days, it settled for a pay boost of 18½ cents per hour — only a penny less than the one recommended by the board several weeks earlier. Chrysler and Ford settled on identical terms without a strike.

The General Motors dispute was but one of a series that slowed reconversion. In almost every case the administration was reluctant to permit price increases. The event that forced the formulation of a new program was the steel strike. After weeks of fruitless negotiation, 750,000 steel workers walked out on January 24, 1946. Production shrank alarmingly. Inasmuch as the workers demanded the conventional 30 per cent pay increase while the United States Steel Corporation, acting as spokesman for the industry, refused to discuss a raise without a price boost of seven dollars per ton, some relaxation in price ceilings was inevitable. Truman announced the new formula on February 14, 1946, after lengthy conferences with stabilization officials. It called for a general markup sufficient to permit labor a pay raise that would offset the 33 per cent increase in the cost of living since 1941. According to administration arithmetic, the workers had already received a 15 per cent raise under the wartime Little Steel formula and were entitled to an additional 18 to 20 cents per hour. A settlement was quickly worked out on the new basis. The administration permitted an increase of five dollars per ton in the price of steel, and the industry in turn granted an 18½-cent pay increase. The price-wage pattern established for steel was widely imitated, ending some strikes and forestalling others.

Unfortunately the respite lasted only two months. By mid-May, work stoppage in rail transportation and in the coal mines threatened to strangle all economic activity. The unions rejected the formula of February 14 as a basis of settlement. In the resulting crisis, the administration reverted to the earlier policy of taking over strikebound industries under the Smith-Connally Act.

The railroad dispute had been smoldering longest and flared up in the most sudden and paralyzing work stoppage in American history. The explosion was all the more humiliating to the administration because it followed a period of fruitless negotiations prescribed by the Railroad Mediation Law which Truman regarded as a model formula for producing industrial peace. The deadlock had started in July 1945 when all twenty Brotherhoods — as the railroad unions were called — demanded wage increases averaging 30 cents per hour and changes in working rules. When the carriers rejected these terms, eighteen of the Brotherhoods agreed to arbitration and accepted a compromise. The engineers and trainmen, however, stuck to their demands and called a strike for March 11, 1946. Truman postponed the showdown for two months by invoking the cooling-off provisions of the Mediation Act. After both Brotherhoods rejected the award, the President ordered government seizure of the railroads on May 17. To his surprise, the recalcitrant engineers and trainmen struck against the government itself on May 23. Within a matter of hours, the shutdown of the entire rail transportation system was complete. The Brotherhoods declined to move either passenger or freight trains except a few which carried milk, troops, or hospitalized military personnel.

Accustomed only to management's defiance of wage awards, Truman was suddenly confronted with the rebellion of labor and the necessity of doing something about it. He took to the radio on the evening of May 24 and demanded that the two Brotherhoods give up their strike by the next afternoon. He promised the nation that all the emergency power at his disposal would be used to move trains if necessary. As the deadline approached without word from A. F. Whitney and Alvaney Johnson, the heads of the defiant Brotherhoods, Truman went before Congress to demand legislation assessing drastic penalties against workers who struck industries operated by the government. He recommended criminal penalties against recalcitrant union leaders and employers. He also proposed that strikers be deprived of seniority rights and drafted into the armed services.

Just as the President was beginning to deliver his message, his aides received word that the trainmen and engineers had capitulated. An angry House of Representatives passed the bill 306 to 13, but the Senate allowed it to die when it became clear that full service would be restored.

The short but dramatic tie-up of transportation distracted public attention from a coal strike that had lasted longer and delivered more crippling blows to production. It also removed temporarily from the spotlight John L. Lewis, the president of the United Mine Workers and the most unpopular labor leader in America. Lewis had earned his reputation after three decades of hard fighting for the rights of the miners in a manner that antagonized both the governmental authorities and the average citizen. Between 1940 and 1949 he compiled a record of seventeen major strikes, an average of two a year. He had defied every President from Wilson to Truman and still possessed sufficient energy for quarrels with industrialists, coal operators, and other labor leaders. Because of his knack for recruiting opponents, people found it difficult to weigh the claims of the miners objectively or to understand why Lewis spurned the increase of 18½ cents permitted under the February 14 formula. When he called the miners out on strike on March 31, 1946, without specifically stating his demands, his many critics attributed the move to the desire for publicity, power, and leadership of the labor movement.

During the period of bargaining before the strike Lewis concealed his wage demands in order to concentrate on better safety rules and a huge health and welfare fund from the coal operators. Their fierce objection to fringe benefits, particularly a welfare fund controlled solely by the union, made the strike inevitable. After six weeks the nation's coal pile dwindled to the vanishing point. Steel mills banked their furnaces, automobile plants shut down, and the Office of Defense Transportation declared an embargo on rail shipment of all but the most vital commodities.

Having demonstrated his tremendous power, Lewis proclaimed a twelve-day truce on May 13 and sent the miners back to work. The imminence of the rail strike made a settlement imperative. Since the formula of February 14 could not be stretched to justify an increase in prices that would cover all the fringe benefits demanded by Lewis, the government seized the mines on May 22, two days before the railroad strike. Popular indignation against the trainmen and engineers now deflected attention from the coal crisis, making it politically easier for the administration to give Lewis what he demanded. A week later a new contract was signed. The terms provided for a wage increase of 18½ cents per hour, a longer vacation with pay, and more comprehensive safety rules. The principle of the health and welfare fund was accepted with the proviso that it would be fed by a five-cent royalty on each ton of bituminous coal mined. A compromise agreement settled the controversy over control of the fund. It was divided into two parts: a welfare and retirement fund to be administered by the union and the operators jointly, and a medical fund to be administered by the union alone.

The eight months' bout of strikes just about exhausted the political credit of the administration. The attempt to hold the line on prices and to utilize fact-finding boards as vehicles for justifying wage increases alienated businessmen. The formula of February 14 for selected price increases irritated manufacturers, retailers, landlords, and farmers, who had not received similar adjustments. Consumers became increasingly vexed as industrial disputes persisted. Even organized labor, for whom the Truman administration had made such sacrifices, resented the emergency strike bill recommended by the President during the railroad tie-up. Hardly a group in the old Democratic coalition supported the administration wholeheartedly on the eve of the 1946 campaign.

THE CONTROVERSY OVER PRICE CONTROL

With the approach of June 30, 1946, the spotlight shifted from labor legislation to the controversy over extension of the law authorizing the President to fix rental ceilings and retail prices. Congress had not granted Wilson such sweeping economic powers during World War I, and many economists blamed the inflation of 1919–1920 and the panic of 1921 on the failure to enforce price controls. This explanation of the postwar depression became official doctrine before World War II. Roosevelt created an Office of Price Administration (OPA) by executive order in April 1941, and Congress provided a statutory basis for presidential price fixing ten months later. Prices and rents crept slowly upward during the first year of the war but after Roosevelt issued his "hold the line" order in 1943 the rise was negligible.

Congress renewed price-fixing authority on a yearly basis during the war. As long as patriotic considerations dominated popular thinking, there was little open opposition. But the refusal of the administration to abandon price fixing when it terminated other controls shortly after VJ Day made OPA a controversial symbol of Truman's reconversion policy. Critics blamed industrial disputes, black markets, and the continuing shortages of critical goods on price controls and demanded immediate termination of regulations. The administration countered with a plea for congressional renewal of OPA powers as the sole guarantee against runaway inflation.

Public reaction to the impending legislative battle was indecisive. Nearly every citizen in his role as consumer opposed a rise in prices, but this sentiment could not readily be converted into support for the administration. For many citizens were also producers, processors, landlords, salesmen, or workers struggling to balance their professional economic interests against their interests as purchasers. The majority of the pressure groups wanted the retention of price controls on items they consumed and the elimination of price controls on items they produced. They were thus in a mood to do some of the log-rolling traditionally associated with tariff bills.

The group that provided widest support for a compromise bill was agriculture. Of the 435 members in the House of Representatives, 256 came from farm districts, and on price control were the backbone of the Democratic-Republican coalition that wrote the bill. Their constituents were reluctant to remove ceilings on durable goods like farm machinery and automobiles or soft goods like clothing, but they were equally determined to write some formula into the law which would permit a rise in the prices of agricultural commodities. A world-wide shortage of grains and fats assured higher agricultural income once controls were relaxed. Besides justifying such a policy on the ground of belief in a free market for agricultural goods, farm spokesmen also pointed to increased costs of feed, labor, and overhead. They sought converts among consumers with the assertion that relaxation of ceilings on food prices would coax currently scarce supplies of meat and butter into the market on a larger scale.

Congressmen responsive to business or to organized labor took more extreme positions. The former advocated outright repeal of OPA and echoed the argument of the National Association of Manufacturers that suspension of controls would encourage production and bring lower prices after a brief inflationary period. Organized labor reflected its own interests and the viewpoint of the administration by reiterating the familiar insistence on the retention of rigid controls until production increased sufficiently to obviate the threat of a price rise. The N.A.M. conducted a nationwide advertising campaign against OPA, while Chester Bowles, a former advertising executive and the director of the Office of Economic Stabilization, headed the administration counterattack. None of the arguments altered the fact that America had fought a long, exhausting war and was destined to suffer reconversion shortages irrespective of the policy adopted. The real question was what pressure groups would bear the brunt of transitional inconvenience.

Three days before the deadline of June 30, Congress extended the Price Control Act for a year, with a series of provisions permitting certain increases, which Bowles denounced as "booby trap" amendments. Congressional leaders told Truman that the bill represented maximum concessions to his viewpoint and urged him to sign it. The President, however, took the advice of the stabilization officials, who regarded the bill as unworkable. Bowles resigned and Truman vetoed the bill as a "bonanza formula for inflation."

Many Republicans were delighted by his decision. Their elation was short-lived. The first week of a free market brought a price rise of 4.5 index points on 982 representative commodities, or nearly one-third as much as had occurred during the entire war. Both Republicans and southern Democrats were convinced that a substitute bill was necessary. Before it could be passed and sent to the President on July 23, further price rises occurred. The Bureau of Labor Statistics estimated that during the 26 days when controls were inoperative, the prices of 28 key consumer items increased 24.8 per cent.

Truman also feared the possibility of severe political repercussions and permitted himself to be stampeded into signing the new measure although it was less satisfactory from his standpoint than the previous one. The only concession to the administration assured industry a price level that would guarantee profits equivalent to those made in 1940 — a leaner year than 1941, which had been designated as the base year in the original bill. Even under the less generous formula, a substantial price rise seemed inevitable because wholesalers and retailers as well as manufacturers were authorized to pass increased production costs on to the consumer. This dubious advantage was more than counterbalanced by an amendment exempting meat, poultry, grain, dairy products, and a few other commodities from control until August 20. To assure confusion and deadlock in the administration of ceilings for agricultural products, the antiadministration coalition inserted a provision dividing authority among OPA, the Department of Agriculture, and a new decontrol board which was supposed to be a final court of appeal. With the important modifications noted, the new law extended price controls and rent ceilings until June 30, 1947.

When the smoke cleared away, it became evident that the Republicans and their southern Democratic allies had outmaneuvered Truman. The new law contained about as many exceptions as a typical low-tariff bill. During the weeks before the reimposition of agricultural price ceilings on August 20, farmers marketed their commodities at a furious pace. Meat, which had been in short supply, flooded the market and brought premium prices, but the rush of livestock to the slaughterhouses ended abruptly when the decontrol board again fixed prices for meat. Truman resisted the pressure for decontrol until frantic pleas of officeholders seeking re-election forced a retreat. On October 14 he made a radio speech announcing the immediate removal of price ceilings on meat and the gradual abandonment of other ceilings except on rents.

Truman's capitulation reflected the bleak prospects for the Democrats in the off-year elections. A strong current of dissatisfaction had set in during the summer. Irritated voters were looking for a scapegoat, and as the months slipped by without relief from shortages, strikes, and rising prices, discontent came to a focus on the hapless Truman.

The Republican campaign pitch was simple and obvious, summed up in the slogan: "Had enough?" The G.O.P. exploited every facet of annoyance and blamed all postwar troubles on administration planners. The minority leader in the House, Joe Martin, promised the electorate that a Republican Congress would "take the meddling hands of the political despots out of the farmhouses, out of the grocery stores . . . and rescind some of those 76,541 directives." The result was a crushing defeat for the Democrats, who lost control of both houses for the first time since 1928. Republicans in the Senate increased from 39 to 51, while in the lower house they picked up 58 seats, raising their total from 188 to 246.

THE WORLD BALANCE IN 1945

Meanwhile the Truman administration was experiencing similar difficulties in international affairs. By VJ Day a multiple balance had been converted to a simple balance composed of two states — the United States and Russia — and their subordinate allies. Between the pair lay huge vacuum areas where erstwhile enemy peoples, nervous neutrals, rebellious colonials, and newly liberated but ineffectual states uneasily eyed each other and the giants. The ingredients for recurrent quarrels were present in the vacuums because economic, nationalistic, and religious animosities divided the resident powers. A breathing spell of several decades might have led to the consolidation of several strong units in these weak and currently defenseless areas. Such a period did not materialize because the giants quickly began to intervene. The United States would have preferred to stay out of the vacuum altogether because, as a *status quo* power, she felt that there was little to be gained in these areas that she did not already enjoy. Least of all did she seek territorial acquisition there. However, Soviet Russia reacted differently to the opportunity. A dynamic power with an ideology for softening up the resistance of potential victims and a geographical location favorable for intervention in the vacuum, she swallowed Poland and Rumania before the war ended. These thinly concealed conquests were not the last manifestation of anticapitalist suspicions but the prelude to fresh adventures. Continuance of the offensive eventually drove the United States to countermeasures. As a result, the history of American foreign policy during most of the decade from 1945 to 1955 revolved about a feverish quest for a way to arrest Russian expansion short of war.

AMERICAN RELIANCE ON THE UNITED NATIONS

The first phase of postwar policy, which was characterized by faith in world organization, emerged against a backdrop of increasing enthusiasm for the export of American ideals. As such it featured a familiar repetitive pattern. In fact, popular thought about foreign policy had reached the same point in the cycle on VJ Day that it had reached a generation earlier on Armistice Day, 1918. This revival of Wilsonian internationalism attracted bipartisan support on a scale that would have astounded the father of the League. Except for a few isolationists who resisted the embarrassment of a public recantation, elimination of dissent was complete. Moderate counsel was shouted down by giving it the current odious designation of "isolationist." The middle position was eroded away in foreign affairs in the 1940's as it had been in domestic affairs in the 1920's. Some people continued to belong to the middle, but poor leadership and the tactics of the extremes rendered them ineffectual. Ignoring the fate of the League, most Americans hailed the proposed United Nations Organization as the hope of a war-weary world. They expected it to end alliances and balance-of-power politics, forestall action by potential aggressors, and provide a forum for the peaceful settlement of disputes. Presumably the UN would achieve these objectives without receiving much more authority than its predecessor, the League of Nations.

The majority relied on two further considerations to justify their confidence in world organization. One was the belief that the refusal of the United States to join the League had caused its failure, and hence that her adherence to the new organization would assure its success. The other was a blind conviction that the victor powers — especially the United States and the Soviet Union — agreed completely about postwar objectives and would work together within the UN.

These assumptions provided the foundation for America's confidence in the UN as the custodian of peace and the *status quo.* All of them were rooted in the belief that other states shared America's estimate of her motives and aims. Those best disposed toward her felt that her peace objectives were an inextricable mixture of altruism and unconsciously rationalized power interests. Critical states suspected America of trying to establish a *Pax Americana* and regarded the UN as a device for sweetening compliance with her program. A large middle group did not know what to believe. Whatever their analysis, all showed a predictable reluctance to override their own interests at the behest of the UN. This attitude precluded universal indignation against what America might term aggression and thereby reduced the likelihood that the UN would effectively intimidate disturbers of the *status quo.*

STRUCTURE AND POWERS OF THE UNITED NATIONS

As already indicated, the main outlines of the United Nations Organization had been agreed upon by the Big Three at the Yalta conference. On that occasion they made provision for the convocation of an international conference at San Francisco to draft a charter. The delegates of forty-six states that had declared war against the Axis met on April 25, 1945, and devoted two months to their difficult assignment. On June 26 they produced a document that representatives of all the states were willing to sign, though in some cases with great reluctance. American newspapers gave the Russians credit for most of the disputes that slowed the work of the conference, although the small states led by Australia exhibited unexpected ability to obstruct at crucial points. The principal source of disagreement developed over the distribution of authority. Russia favored a structure that would concentrate power in the hands of the major wartime allies, whereas the small states wanted to democratize the organization as much as possible. The United States occupied an ambiguous position in this quarrel because her practical objectives and her ideological loyalties diverged.

The charter that finally emerged represented a solid victory for the great-power viewpoint. The familiar device of a bicameral system of representation was employed to conceal the antidemocratic character of those arrangements. The charter provided for a General Assembly which possessed little power but featured equal representation of states, and a Security Council which possessed substantial power but featured a restricted membership.

Member nations were each allowed one vote in the General Assembly, although they could have as many as five delegates. Russia constituted the only exception because of a compromise provision in the charter granting her three votes. The Security Council was a more exclusive body composed of five permanent members (the United States, Great Britain, Russia, France, and China) and six rotating members selected by the General Assembly. The charter authorized the General Assembly to consider any question and make recommendations to the Security Council on all matters within the jurisdiction of the United Nations Organization. It had no power to compel action by the Security Council beyond formal discussion of recommendations. In essence, the General Assembly was nothing more than an international forum for the ventilation of grievances by the small powers. Authorities differed about the value of such discussions; in 1945 the majority seemed to believe that they would lead to greater harmony.

Theoretically, debates in the General Assembly on issues affecting the peace and welfare of member states were supposd to lead to action by the Security Council. The charter vested in the latter the power to commit the resources of the United Nations against aggressors — resources which would presumably include an international army. This remarkable grant of authority was qualified by restrictions fatal to energetic action. Questions of procedure might be settled by a minimum of seven members, but a unanimous vote was required to authorize action on any substantive question. Opposition by a single permanent member of the Security Council could prevent the use of UN machinery against an aggressor. The charter also slammed the door on constitutional relief from obstruction with a provision giving permanent members the right to veto proposed amendments. The drastic limitation imposed on the Security Council by the veto power was one of the few matters about which the Russians and Americans — to say nothing of other major powers — agreed both at Yalta and at San Francisco. It served notice on the world that the UN would be a league of sovereign states and that the great powers would obey international authority only when it suited their interests.

There was nothing remarkable about the unwillingness of states to surrender any portion of their sovereignty. What defied belief was the American expectation that permanent members of the Security Council would refrain from using the veto to protect their own interests. This expectation owed its vitality to American assumptions already examined: that all wartime allics cherished the same postwar objectives and that all thrcats to the United States-sponsored *status quo* would provoke their unanimous indignation. Events soon demonstrated the readiness of the great powers to use the veto. As it turned out, the Russians employed it most often, because states belonging to the American power bloc constituted a majority and controlled the UN machinery. Had the situation been reversed, the United States would undoubtedly have wielded the veto to thwart the designs of Russia and her satellites.

Besides the two-chamber system of representation reminiscent of the League of Nations, the UN featured an International Court of Justice like the old World Court. The new judicial body was subject to the same limitations as the old. It possessed only the jurisdiction that sovereign states chose to grant. The charter also provided for a Secretariat headed by a Secretary General to perform routine administrative tasks.

Since the UN, like its predecessor, was a league of sovereign states, it could not look forward to much success in dealing with political or substantive questions. On the other hand, the new organization sponsored many more allied and subsidiary agencies for dealing with nonpolitical international problems than the League of Nations did. Among these were the UN Economic and Social Council to advise about health and welfare problems, the International Monetary Fund for currency stabilization and the expansion of world trade; the International Bank with a total capital of $9.1 billion for long-term loans to build up the productivity of economically backward or war-ravaged countries; and the UN Relief and Rehabilitation Administration for short-term operations on a gift basis in the same areas. The last named organization spent approximately $4 billion from 1945 to 1947 on the relief of displaced persons and other war victims. In a slightly different category was the Trusteeship Council, created to supervise former League mandates and former Axis territory. The effectiveness of these organizations varied directly with their ability to avoid entanglement in political issues. Agencies that sought to disseminate scientific and medical information enjoyed a large measure of success. Other units might have functioned more successfully if completely divorced from the political structure of the UN.

With the current of war-bred illusion running strong in America, the charter and other measures gained quick congressional approval. The Senate received the charter July 2, 1945. The Foreign Relations Committee, headed by Senator Tom Connally of Texas, reported it to the floor unamended after only five days of hearings. A perfunctory week of debate ended in ratification on July 28 by the overwhelming margin of 87 to 2. This enthusiastic reception contrasted sharply with the rough treatment accorded the League Covenant twenty-six years earlier; in fact, the United States earned the distinction of being the first to join the new world organization. A larger number of Republicans opposed the ratification of the Bretton Woods agreement establishing the International Monetary Fund and the World Bank, as well as the passage of a reciprocal trade agreement broadening presidential tariff-cutting powers, but both measures were approved by comfortable margins in the summer of 1945. A proposed loan of $3.75 billion to Great Britain encountered rougher going. Intended as a substitute for Lend-Lease that would tide the faltering English economy over a difficult transitional period, it aroused the wrath of nationalists who remembered Britain's default on debts in the 1930's. Seven months elapsed before Congress finally approved the loan in July 1946, by a close vote. The stubbornness of the opposition foreshadowed the end of the honeymoon period between the administration and Congress on foreign affairs. Thereafter the lawmakers scrutinized more critically all measures providing for loans or other forms of overseas aid.

Americans gave other indications of their concern over postwar international problems. Through UNRRA, they contributed $2.7 billion for the relief of war-devastated China and Central Europe. The American Red Cross, churches, and private charity groups gave additional millions in food and clothing. At the same time the armed forces assumed responsibility for emergency aid to the homeless and starving thousands in Japan and in the American zone of Germany. Elsewhere the United States offered surplus military property and Lead-Lease supplies to her nearly bankrupt allies in Western Europe at cut-rate prices. She also financed purchases through relief and rehabilitation loans from the Export-Import Bank or other agencies. Close to $5 billion worth of additional goods was distributed as a result of such arrangements.

RUSSIAN-AMERICAN CONFLICT

Notwithstanding the evident desire of America to make amends for her aloofness after World War I and to assume leadership in establishing the foundations for a lasting peace, she encountered frustrations at every point. The deterioration in Soviet-American relations, which had begun after the Yalta conference, continued unchecked save for a brief interlude of ceremonial politeness at the Potsdam conference. Called to deliver Japan an ultimatum of surrender and to complete plans for the treatment of conquered Germany, the Potsdam conference completed both tasks in seven days (July 25 to August 2, 1945). Of the original triumvirate of Allied war leaders that had first met at Teheran, only Stalin survived as chief of state. Truman had already replaced Roosevelt, and half way through the Potsdam conversations Churchill stepped aside for Clement Attlee as a result of the British election. The Big Three reaffirmed the Yalta agreement to demilitarize Germany, root out Nazism, and prosecute war criminals. The deadlock of long standing on reparations was resolved. The Russians accepted a proposal of James F. Byrnes, who had recently replaced Stettinius as Secretary of State, that each Allied power take reparations from its own zone. They also agreed to exchange specified amounts of food and raw materials from their zone for 15 per cent of the capital equipment in the western zone. They postponed the thorny problem of a German peace treaty, and by evading a final decision on the western boundary of Poland they left the Communist-dominated Lublin government in occupation of German territory east of the Oder-Neisse line. However, they established a Council of Foreign Ministers and directed it to draw up peace treaties for Italy and the erstwhile allies of the Axis in the Balkans.

Despite the atmosphere of cordiality prevailing at Potsdam, the Big Three were not destined to meet again for ten years. As long as the war continued, Russia avoided open defiance of the United States. Once Japan surrendered, she began a systematic campaign to exploit opportunities in the newly created vacuum areas. During the closing months of 1945 Communist parties in Hungary, Rumania, and Bulgaria joined coalition governments as the prelude to subversion. Usually the Communists sought cabinet portfolios that would give them control of the police. The arrest of prominent political opponents followed, and effective retaliatory action was blocked by the presence of Red Army units. Eventually a coup would take place, resulting in the expulsion of all non-Communist ministers from the government and paving the way for a conventional purge. The timetable differed from state to state, but by the end of 1946 all three had been reduced to the status of Soviet satellites like Poland. Only Finland and Greece still remained outside the Russian orbit. What Winston Churchill referred to as an "Iron Curtain" descended on most of the vacuum areas in Central Europe. Besides suppressing free expression, confiscating property, and persecuting religious leaders, the Sovietized states began to follow a foreign policy identical in every particular to that of Russia.

The United States made repeated protests against the open violation of the Yalta agreement governing the treatment of people in the liberated areas. She also sent stiff notes to the satellite states as they stepped up the tempo of their purges and multiplied the harassments of neutral observers. Depending on the circumstances, the Soviet Union and her clients ignored protests, made evasive replies, or blandly announced that they were eliminating Fascist elements. At the outset American reaction to Russian policy was mixed. Many erstwhile Roosevelt supporters who had staked so much on their hopes of postwar Russo-American collaboration were reluctant to admit defeat. They interpreted Soviet moves as the product of fear and accepted the comforting view that Russia would settle down once she had constructed a layer of friendly states to insulate her from German attack. Others exhibited varying degrees of surprise and dismay but were uncertain what the United States ought to do.

THE PEACE CONFERENCE OF 1946

By employing a little more finesse and politeness, the Russians might have exploited the American attitude for some months longer without a basic modification of policy. But the Kremlin relied increasingly on bluster, abuse, and obstruction, even when such tactics promised very little prospect of gain. The long wrangles over the treaties with Italy and the Balkan states formerly allied with Germany were a case in point. The Council of Foreign Ministers met first at London in September 1945 but could not agree on the treaties until four conferences and eighteen months later. Even after enough progress had been made to call a twenty-one-nation peace conference at

Paris on July 29, 1946, the wrangling was so heated that another meeting of the Council became necessary. In fact, the contracting parties did not sign the treaties for Italy, Hungary, Bulgaria, and Rumania until February 10, 1947. Molotov, the Soviet Foreign Minister, showed unexpected resourcefulness in obstructing business. He argued about everything from conference procedure and the agenda to minute substantive matters. In instances where he intended ultimately to yield, he held out as long as possible and destroyed whatever good will he might have extracted from the concession. Worse still, he made long and bitter speeches that reflected on the motives and integrity of other states. For the first few months Soviet invective was concentrated on Great Britain as the prime example of cynical imperialist state, but the United States was soon elevated to the number one spot in the hierarchy of capitalistic war-mongering devils. Goaded by these tactics, James F. Byrnes, the American Secretary of State, fought back with increasing stubbornness.

The Russians lost far more through the alienation of the American public than they gained in concessions, because the interest of the United States in transfers of territory among the Balkan states behind the Iron Curtain was tepid. Byrnes pressed hard and unsuccessfully for Soviet agreement to an Austrian treaty. The Kremlin balked at the termination of the occupation of Austria because it would have ended the Russian excuse for keeping troops in Hungary and Rumania to protect supply lines to Vienna. Byrnes made more headway in resisting the truculent claims of the satellite Yugoslavia for the Austrian province of Carinthia and the Italian city of Trieste. In the end the Russians agreed to an arrangement whereby Trieste became a free city under the UN. A deadlock subsequently developed on the choice of a governor for the area, and as a result the troops of the western powers continued to occupy it. Aside from these disputes, the Russians and Americans argued long and bitterly over reparations, with the Kremlin finally accepting a smaller amount from Italy than it had originally demanded. The net result of the long diplomatic battle was that Russia called the tune in areas occupied by her troops, and the western powers did the same. In Austria, where a joint occupation prevailed, the great powers failed to reach an agreement.

The eighteen months' quest for peace with former German allies by the American President and his much-traveled Secretary of State produced a bitter pun in Washington: "Truman fiddles while Byrnes roams." However, popular apathy over the terms of the treaties became clear when the Senate promptly ratified them by the overwhelming margin of 79 to 10.

FRICTION OVER GERMANY

The acrimonious tone that poisoned the deliberations of the Council of Foreign Ministers characterized Russo-American relations across the board. Matters went from bad to worse in Germany, where the four powers had agreed to try war leaders, eradicate Nazi influence, treat the Reich as a single economic unit, cooperate on reparations policy, and establish democratic institutions. Only the first pledge was kept by the various occupying states. After long preliminary examinations, twenty-two high Nazi officials were brought to trial before an International Military Tribunal at Nuremberg. The court sat with brief interruptions from November 21, 1945, to October 1, 1946, and brought in nineteen convictions and three acquittals. Twelve of those convicted were sentenced to death, and the others drew long prison terms. Hermann Göring cheated the executioner by swallowing poison. Although the tribunal maintained the view that the accused had committed crimes against humanity forbidden by international law, much of the world preferred to believe that the victors had tried the vanquished. Opinion outside the countries involved was especially shocked by the conviction of generals for obeying military orders. While the prosecutors did their work at Nuremberg, occupation officials in all four zones were making a vigorous effort to remove Nazis from positions of influence and power. This policy was supposed to create both democratic institutions in Germany and popular enthusiasm for them. By 1949 the powers in the three western zones had managed to establish a democratic structure on paper, but whether German compliance with parliamentary procedures would outlive the occupation era was uncertain. The Russians also chastised the Nazis eagerly in their zone, but the product was a totalitarian regime like the ones being established elsewhere in Eastern Europe. They used their animus against Nazism and Allied approval of "labor" as "reparations" to justify the retention of thousands of German prisoners in slave-labor camps.

Divergent interpretations of the economic provisions in the Potsdam agreement hastened the drift toward permanent division of Germany. Reparations proved to be a fruitful source of controversy. At first the United States cooperated with the Russian program of dismantling factories and shipping them eastward as reparations. This policy ignored the crucial role of German industry in the economic recovery of Western Europe. Moreover, it aggravated unemployment within the western zones, which were already paralyzed by war destruction, food shortages, and the burden of a large refugee population. By the fall of 1946 the United States had begun to reverse the policy of destroying German industry which had caused economic chaos. It was also becoming apparent that Russian reparations systematically bled the western zones, transferring the ultimate cost of occupation and relief to the American taxpayer.

The Russians provided the excuse for the termination of this program by refusing to ship food westward from their predominantly agricultural zone and by resisting the establishment of a uniform German currency. These tactics were designed to blackmail the western powers into giving Russia a voice in the management of Ruhr industries. They drove the British and Americans into a bizonal merger at the end of the year, and the French joined it later. The new Trizonia foreshadowed the complete breakdown of four-power administration in the Reich and the establishment of two Germanies. The western powers justified their action on the ground that the Russians had violated the clause of the Potsdam agreement calling for the administration of Germany as a single economic unit. The Soviet Union retaliated with charges that their erstwhile allies had repudiated the Potsdam provisions governing reparations. While the recriminations continued, the Americans took the lead in rebuilding the West German industry that they had recently tried to destroy. The equally stubborn Russians proceeded with their plans for completing the Sovietization of East Germany. Only in divided Berlin, which was a four-power island surrounded by the Soviet zone, did the pretense of joint administration continue. The physical isolation of the German capital from the western zones left the other occupying powers at the mercy of the Russians, who were to provoke a crisis in 1948 by trying to oust them.

RUSSIA OBSTRUCTS THE UNITED NATIONS

Soviet aggressiveness in Eastern Europe during the year and a half following VJ Day did a great deal to dispel the American belief that Russia would cooperate in the creation of a brave new world. But the most disillusioning development of the period was Soviet obstruction in the UN. Quite unwisely, America had expected the Russians to acquiesce in a *status quo* otherwise unacceptable to them, if it were backed by the majesty and weight of the world organization. Behind this optimism were the assumptions already mentioned so many times: that each state, including Soviet Russia, preferred peace above all; that each state accepted the United States version of peace as intrinsically desirable; and that in order to avert war each state would unhesitatingly accept a UN command contrary to its interests.

As might have been anticipated, the Russians behaved in exactly the same way toward the United States in the UN as in direct diplomatic negotiations. This fact became apparent when the new organization met for the first time at London early in 1946. Although the United States possessed a large working majority and was initially gratified by the passage of a resolution establishing the permanent home of the organization in America, quarrels dominated the session. The Soviet Union steadfastly refused to participate in the International Monetary Fund, the International Bank, and several other agencies. She also obstructed the organization of the international police force authorized by the charter to enforce peace. More disturbing was her determination to invoke the veto if necessary to choke off investigation of her aggressive activities in various parts of the world. During 1946 it was used to sidetrack a resolution for the investigation of Communist-backed guerrilla warfare in Greece and to prevent the admission of new states to the UN. When the Security Council permitted Iran to present a complaint against the continued presence of a Soviet army in its northern provinces beyond the period specified by treaty, the Russian delegate walked out of the deliberations. Moreover, he continued to absent himself whenever the matter was discussed. Eventually the army was withdrawn in response to a variety of pressures. These episodes made it clear that Russia would employ the veto indiscriminately as well as other obstructive procedures if her interests were touched.

DEADLOCK ON DISARMAMENT

Worst of all, the Russians refused to accept American disarmament proposals under the auspices of the UN. Immediately after VJ Day, the United States had begun to demobilize, cutting the military forces to one-tenth of the wartime peak within six months. This drastic reduction was undertaken partly in response to public demand for the release of conscripts and partly because of the unwarranted assumption that the creation of the UN would inaugurate an era in which large armies would be unnecessary. Such a notion reflected America's interest in economy and her hope that the *status quo* would be self-sustaining without the maintenance of substantial military forces. This view was all the more appealing to Americans because their unilateral disarmament had not interrupted the manufacture of atomic bombs or broken the American monopoly on atomic secrets.

Nevertheless, the United States recognized the futility of any disarmament scheme which failed to provide for the control of this new and frightful weapon. Aside from the probability that others would soon develop such weapons and end her immunity against sudden devastation, America felt a genuine desire to relieve world anxiety about the A-bomb and free atomic energy for peaceful purposes. Accordingly Bernard M. Baruch, acting on behalf of the American government, presented a bold and generous disarmament proposal to the UN Atomic Energy Commission on June 14, 1946. The Baruch Plan called for the establishment of an International Atomic Development Authority, which would by stages take over ownership and control of all mines, factories, laboratories, or other facilities connected with the production of atomic energy. The Plan also vested complete power in the International Authority to conduct inspections anywhere in the world and punish violators.

The Baruch Plan asked the Russians to make sacrifices that they regarded as unwarranted. The provision of such an Authority with unlimited rights of inspection would have caused any sovereign state to hesitate. It was especially unpalatable from the standpoint of the Russians, who suspected that the Authority would be under the control of the pro-American majority. They made a counterproposal to outlaw the manufacture and use of the atomic bomb, vesting enforcement in the Security Council, where the veto could be invoked. Further discussion produced Russian acquiescence in the principle of unlimited international inspection, but the Kremlin stubbornly refused to give up the power to veto the punishment of violators which the United States regarded as necessary for effective international control. With neither side willing to compromise on this crucial issue, the American dream of a comprehensive disarmament program was rudely shattered.

The deadlock on the Baruch Plan foreshadowed a new atomic armament race. In fact the UN gave up work on an arms reduction formula in 1948. Meanwhile the United States continued to build up her stockpile of A-bombs, and the Soviet Union toiled feverishly to break the American monopoly. The world learned that the Russians were in the race on September 23, 1949, when President Truman issued a statement crediting them with the detonation of an A-bomb. Four months later, he again recognized Russian progress by issuing orders for the construction of a superhydrogen bomb. Little was heard about the project until eyewitnesses reported a new and terrifying blast in the Pacific in November 1952. Shortly thereafter the American government conceded that a hydrogen bomb had been exploded. Unofficial estimates indicated that this bomb was seven hundred times more powerful than the type dropped on Hiroshima. The United States did not enjoy a monopoly in the new category so long as in the case of the A-bomb, for Russia announced in August 1953 that she too had set off a successful hydrogen blast. If the claim was valid, the Soviet Union seemed likely to gain ground on America in the atomic armament race.

The rapid improvement of nuclear weapons created a great controversy in the United States and elsewhere regarding their significance. The optimists considered the increasing destructiveness of the bombs a development that would preclude their use. Relying on the reasonableness of leaders in Russia and America, they foresaw an era of uneasy peace interrupted by occasional petty wars with conventional weapons. An equilibrium based on mutual fears of the giants had little to recommend it, but only people completely out of touch with the situation made a more hopeful estimate. Those who looked to history rather than to human reason for comfort found none. Frightfulness of weapons had not hitherto been a deterrent to their use. Worse still, the ideological overtones of Russian-American antagonisms, which were stated in terms of principles and ideals rather than of self-interest, increased the incentive for both powers to unleash their destructive might regardless of the physical consequences.

Such lugubrious speculations did not discourage Americans from pressing the armament race but made them uncertain of the degree to which nuclear weapons outmoded traditional methods of fighting. As a consequence, discussions of military strategy were never completely dormant during the decade from 1945 to 1955. Popular aversion to conscription and universal military training created many partisans for the view that the next war would be decided by nuclear bombs rather than by armies and navies. Congress extended Selective Service for only eleven months on July 1, 1946, and reluctantly approved a stronger version a year later. It repeatedly rejected the pleas of the Truman administration for a universal military training program. The trend toward over-all cuts in military spending was arrested temporarily in 1948 when the Communists seized power in Czechoslovakia and also blockaded Berlin. After his re-election, however, Truman took over leadership of the congressional movement for further reduction of the defense establishment. The Army bore the brunt of the ensuing cutback, dropping to a low of 600,000 men on the eve of the Korean War in mid-1950. Thereafter a substantial military build-up took place in all branches of the service. Nonetheless, a substantial congressional minority led by Senator Taft continued to oppose the commitment of United States troops overseas whenever the issue came up, urging instead a reliance on the atomic bomb and the Navy to protect American interests.

If the advent of nuclear weapons produced divided councils on military strategy, it underscored the danger of an "atomic" Pearl Harbor and thereby stimulated the movement for unification of the armed forces. Intraservice rivalry prevented agreement on a precise plan of unification until July 1947, when Congress finally passed the National Security Act. The law established a single department which was to be presided over by a Secretary of Defense with Cabinet rank and supervisory powers over the Secretaries of the Army, Navy, and Air Force. It also provided for the creation of several planning agencies: a Joint Chiefs of Staff National Security Council, a Securities Resources Board, and a Central Intelligence Agency. This impressive legislative integration did not immediately lead to complete unification at the operating level, but the first Secretary of Defense, James V. Forrestal, proved adept at minimizing the frictions between admirals and generals.

While the controversy on unification of the armed forces was raging, Congress passed an Atomic Energy Act on August 1, 1946. It vested the President with sole power to order the use of the atomic bomb in warfare. It also created a government monopoly on fissionable materials and a five-man Atomic Energy Commission to direct research and production. Despite a determined fight by Senator Vandenberg to give military leaders a major voice in determining atomic energy policies, the final version of the measure established the principle for full civilian control. A supplementary provision authorized a Military Liaison Committee to advise the Atomic Energy Commission.

Doubtless some of the American strategic and legislative decisions taken to cope with problems created by the A-bomb would have been necessary even in the event of nuclear disarmament. Still, the failure of the UN to secure Russian compliance with the Baruch Plan came as a severe shock in the United States. One final blow completed the American disenchantment with world organization as a method of keeping peace — the growing tendency of Russia to use UN as a sounding board for Communist propaganda. By the end of 1946, the Soviet delegate on the Security Council had launched open criticism of United States policies. He soon followed it with denunciations of America as a "war-mongering," "imperialistic," state, and these epithets were paid back with interest. Such exchanges exposed the impracticality of settling disputes between states by public debate. When put to the test, the old Wilsonian principle of "open covenants, openly arrived at" degenerated into "open insults, openly arrived at." For better or for worse, the Russians and the Americans conducted their feuds through the UN but reverted to the conventional practice of private diplomacy on the rare occasions when they sought agreement. This development ushered in a new phase of the "cold war."

POLITICS AS USUAL

On the domestic front deadlock prevailed in 1947–48. Truman repeatedly urged enactment of his old twenty-one-point program which opponents denounced as a prelude to a welfare state. He also recommended federal aid to education, a national system of health insurance, and the admission of displaced persons from behind the Iron Curtain. He prodded Congress on several occasions to restore his wartime powers for controlling inflation.

Besides rejecting most of the program for extension of government subsidies and services, the Eightieth Congress carried on the conventional party warfare with investigations of the executive department, appointments, taxation, and the budget. Thirty-six major investigations covered every conceivable topic from Communist infiltration of the government to the boxcar shortage. The public reacted apathetically. The Republicans did not have much more luck when they fought appointments. Their most notable effort in 1947 was directed toward blocking the transfer of David E. Lilienthal from the chairmanship of TVA to the chairmanship of the Atomic Energy Commission. Some objected to him as a blundering New Deal bureaucrat; others took the more extreme view that he was a Communist. In the end a number of Republican senators, headed by Vandenberg of Michigan, joined the Democrats, and Lilienthal was easily confirmed. By May 5, 1948, the Republicans scented victory in the presidential elections and stopped confirming appointments except to the Cabinet and military posts.

Taxation was another area where the parties could maneuver for position without much political risk. The G.O.P. made the orthodox assumption that the voters would show gratitude to the party in the presidential election for a reduction in personal income taxes. Accordingly, congressional leaders piloted a $4 billion tax-relief bill through both houses in June 1947. By so doing, the Republicans temporarily abandoned their repeatedly expressed concern over the size of the public debt. The President was equal to the occasion and reversed the position of his own party. In a message vetoing the bill he made his debut in the unaccustomed role of an advocate of conservative fiscal policy. He warned that the legislation would be inflationary and denounced it as "the wrong kind of tax reduction at the wrong time."

Enough Democrats supported his position to sustain the veto. However, the political appeal of tax relief was so irresistible in the election year 1948 that a lopsided bipartisan majority passed a new bill calling for $4.8 reduction and easily repassed it over a second veto.

The Republicans sought to rehabilitate the party reputation for concern over the public debt by cutting the Truman budget so deeply that the debt could be reduced despite tax relief. During the opening weeks of the first session, Republican leaders predicted spending cuts as deep as 20 per cent. Such promises could not be fullfilled, of course, without jeopardizing national security or irritating important pressure groups. Military appropriations defied the budget cutters, and foreign aid escaped substantial reduction. Responsible politicians dared not tamper with the billions earmarked for the veterans, the farmers, the traditional pork-barrel expenditures, and the interest on the national debt. The process of elimination left only the executive departments as a happy hunting ground for the pruners. Even there reductions could be hazardous, as the Republicans were to discover when they lost votes in the Rocky Mountain area because of cutting the funds of the Department of the Interior. After much oratory and backstage maneuvering, the G.O.P. cut the budget approximately 8 per cent and inaugurated an unusual two-year period of balanced budgets.

THE TAFT-HARTLEY ACT

The sole area where the Republicans defied a major pressure group was that of labor legislation. When John L. Lewis again reduced the coal pile in December 1946, the walkout of the miners produced a worse impression than usual because they struck against the government. They even defied an injunction until Judge Alan Goldsborough fined Lewis $10,000 and the United Mine Workers $3.5 million. Although Lewis's determination to appeal ultimately led to a reduction of the fine, the issue was aired in the papers for several weeks and provided an excellent backdrop for corrective legislation.

The Taft-Hartley bill incorporated many features of the Case bill which Truman had killed with a veto in 1946. The most controversial feature of the proposed law was a provision authorizing the government to obtain injunctions that would force an eighty-day ban on strikes threatening national health or safety. A supplementary clause required employers or unions desirous of terminating a contract to give sixty days' notice. Workers who struck during this cooling-off period lost rights otherwise safeguarded by the law. Another provision weakening union control over workers was the outlawing of the closed shop and of coercive tactics against nonunion laborers. Since the bill permitted the union shop, the prohibition of the closed shop did not raise a formidable barrier to the organization of workers; it simply relieved employers of contractual provisions making the employment of union men mandatory.

More troublesome for the unions were the restraints on what management called "unfair practices." Some took a negative form such as the prohibition of jurisdictional strikes, secondary boycotts, and contributions for political purposes. Others required labor unions to perform certain positive acts — collective bargaining, fullfillment of contract terms, and publication of financial statements. In addition, union officers were required to sign affidavits that they did not belong to the Communist party or support any organization advocating the overthrow of the United States Government. To administer the complicated provisions of the bill, Congress proposed enlargement of the National Labor Relations Board from three to five members, establishment of a special counsel, and organization of a new conciliation service outside the Department of Labor.

The Republican party was by no means united behind all the labor curbs of the Taft-Hartley bill, but the congressional leaders received enough support from southern Democrats to secure a heavy majority in both houses. Like the union leaders, Truman would have preferred no bill at all. At most he was willing to accept extension of the Smith-Connally War Disputes Act which permitted him to take on strikebound industries and arrange his own terms of settlement. Consequently on June 20, 1947, he vetoed the bill with the unexpected observation that it would "inject the government into private economic affairs on an unprecedented scale." The House promptly voted to override the veto 331 to 83, and the Senate followed suit, after a short filibuster, by a margin of 68 to 25. Union leaders promptly denounced the Taft-Hartley Act as "a slave-labor law." As it turned out, curbs on labor were as ineffective as the older laws designed to curtail industrial monopolies. Unions continued to conduct economic warfare against both management and consumer as their interests required. Part of their immunity was due to the intrinsic limitations of legislation as a weapon for modifying basic economic trends; part was due to the timidity of politicians, who feared their power to retaliate. The only immediate beneficiaries of the Act seemed to be the lawyers, who henceforth earned handsome fees from labor as well as from business for advice on how to circumvent restrictions. The long-range effect was impossible to forecast in 1947 because, like the Wagner Act before it, it faced a substantial period of interpretation by the NLRB and the federal courts. Whether or not such a process would ultimately justify the fears of organized labor, the short-term results indicated that it was no "slave labor" law as the unions contended. Nevertheless, they continued to denounce the Act and to threaten the Republicans with retaliation.

THE PRESIDENTIAL SUCCESSION

Partisan spirit affected the consideration of legislation and constitutional amendments governing the presidential succession. The line prescribed by the Act of 1884 descended from the Vice-President to the Secretary of State and then to other Cabinet members. Truman wanted it changed so that elective officials would precede appointed officials. Specifically, he sought an amendment placing the Speaker of the House and the President *pro tempore* of the Senate ahead of Cabinet members. The Republicans did not see much merit in the proposal or pass it until they had gained control of Congress and elected the presiding officers of both houses.

The same year the Eightieth Congress also passed and sent to the state legislatures for ratification a proposed amendment prohibiting more than two elective terms for any President or more than one if he served more than two years of a predecessor's term. Eventually approved by the necessary thirty-six states on February 26, 1951, the Twenty-second Amendment specifically exempted Truman from its provisions, but probably was one of the factors that discouraged him from seeking re-election in 1952.

THE 1948 ELECTION

The Republicans approached the election of 1948 with heartfelt optimism for the first time in twenty years. Precedents favored victory. Since the turn of the century, no party in power had lost both houses in off-year elections without losing the next presidential election. History also appeared to bless the policy of obstruction, because the Republicans had won in 1920 and the Democrats in 1932 after their legislative majorities had indiscriminately opposed the policy of a President whose party controlled only a minority in each house. Repeated Gallup polls as well as other samples of public opinion confirmed the existence of a Republican trend. Best of all, the hitherto invincible coalition of sectional groups forged by Roosevelt threatened to crack wide open. The Solid South, profoundly irritated by Truman's insistence on a civil rights program for Negroes, repeal of the poll tax, and passage of an antilynch law, made preparations to launch its own presidential ticket. Simultaneously the disgruntled Henry Wallace was busy lining up supporters for a third party that might detach a large slice of the labor vote from the Democrats. The reality of this menace became apparent in February 1948 when a Wallace-endorsed candidate of the American Labor party won a by-election to fill a congressional vacancy in a New York City district that had gone Democratic for years.

The improving prospects of the G.O.P. guaranteed a lively preconvention fight for the nomination. The personal aspects of the contest were to some degree concealed behind the recurring quarrel over election strategy between the party wing that favored a straight anti-New Deal platform and their critics who regarded a qualified endorsement of Roosevelt legislation as essential for victory. In general, the more bellicose and rigid Republicans on domestic issues came from the Mississippi Valley, and the compromisers from the eastern seaboard states.

The record of the Eightieth Congress showed a midwestern orientation and produced a strong contender for the presidential nomination in Senator Robert A. Taft of Ohio. Both the speaker of the House, Joseph Martin of Massachusetts, and the majority leader, Charles Halleck, deserved as much credit for the performance of Republican legislators as Taft. The latter, however, had captured the affection of the more bitter foes of the administration by his persistent denunciations of Truman and all his works. Taft was so uninhibited that he made a special appeal to those who disliked the hedging typical of politicians. He gave a good example of this characteristic in the fall of 1947 when reporters asked for his solution to the meat shortage and received the answer, "Eat less." He was not nearly so conservative as he sounded. His outspoken criticism of the Democrats fed partly on a fierce and honest indignation over the growth of government at the expense of the individual. It also drew nourishment from his long tenure as spokesman of a minority which did not have any responsibility for translating words into policy. He had opposed everything from the Nuremberg "war crimes" tribunal to the OPA and had been the chief advocate of the labor law so obnoxious to union leaders. Personal magnetism might have softened the sting of his opinions, but he was solemn-faced and humorless and lacked popular appeal.

The candidates reflecting the views of the more moderate eastern wing of the party were Governor Thomas E. Dewey of New York and former Governor Harold Stassen of Minnesota. Although tradition frowned on the renomination of defeated presidential candidates, Dewey had considerable political appeal. He had run a close race against Roosevelt in 1944, had won re-election as Governor of New York in 1946 by an overwhelming margin, and was not handicapped by a long list of controversial congressional votes on national issues as Taft was. Stassen appealed to the same elements as Dewey did, but he lacked organizational backing. After the war he had assumed the role of the earnest internationalist and had visited Moscow and other European capitals to qualify himself as an expert on world affairs. His claim to the title was tacitly contested by Senator Arthur H. Vandenberg who supported administration foreign policy. Although Vandenberg did not openly avow his candidacy for fear of jeopardizing his self-appointed position as elder statesmen of the party, supporters advertised his availability as a compromise candidate. General Douglas MacArthur was less coy about his willingness to accept the nomination. The hero of the Pacific war was, however, virtually eliminated by a defeat in the Wisconsin primary, which had been the graveyard for Wendell Willkie's hopes four years earlier.

When the Republican convention met at Philadelphia in June, Dewey held a substantial lead. His major opponents and the lesser favorite sons could not form a solid opposition. He received 434 votes on the first ballot to 224 for Taft and 157 for Stassen. The second ballot brought him so close to a majority that the convention made his nomination unanimous on the third and final roll call. The platform was considerably more moderate in tone than the pronouncements of most leading congressional spokesmen. The party promised to uphold the UN and the European aid program. It renewed previous pledges for the reduction of government expenses and taxes and advocated special legislation to root out Communism. In general it also endorsed many of the schemes that the party had refused to support during the Eightieth Congress: broadened civil rights, a higher minimum wage, inflation controls, public housing, and aid to displaced persons.

The Democrats, who met in the same hall at Philadelphia nearly two weeks later, were gloomy and demoralized. Many southern politicians had threatened to bolt the convention altogether if Truman sought renomination. Wallace gave every indication of willingness to court defeat as a third-party candidate if the sacrifice would also ruin the chances of Truman. Urban bosses nominally pledged to the President, like Jake Arvey of Chicago and Frank Hague of Jersey City, were convinced that Truman could not win and searched frantically for a substitute. The popular General Dwight D. Eisenhower, with the infectious grin and the unknown political views, loomed up as the ideal compromise. He had, however, already rejected feelers from the Republican party and broke the incipient Democratic boom with a categorical refusal to run. The would-be President-makers quickly switched their attention to William O. Douglas, Associate Justice of the Supreme Court, who likewise rejected the proffered nomination. In the end they made a dispirited re-entry into Truman's camp. The return of the rebels enabled the President to win a first-ballot nomination over Senator Richard B. Russell of Georgia, the candidate of the anti-Truman South, by a vote of 947½ to 263. As *Time* magazine put it: "No one strong enough to take the nomination from Harry Truman wanted it. And no group which wanted it was strong enough to take it away." Few candidates expressed interest in the vice-presidential nomination. When the venerable Senator Alben W. Barkley of Kentucky was sounded out, he demanded that the convention act quickly: "I don't want it [the nomination] passed around so long it is like a cold biscuit."

The civil rights plank of the Democratic platform completed the estrangement of the southerners. The committee had drafted a typically vague pronouncement on this controversial issue only to have the convention overturn it. The substitute plank categorically endorsed legislation for the enforcement of Negro rights and was the work of the youthful, militant northern Democrats headed by Hubert H. Humphrey of Minnesota. Many of his associates belonged to a new organization, the Americans for Democratic Action (ADA), who opposed Communism but favored a leftward orientation. Otherwise the platform was an uninteresting document which enumerated the achievements of the administration. It pledged the party to continue the policy of preventing Soviet expansion and to enact the Truman program of domestic legislation known as the "Fair Deal."

The threatened defections quickly materialized. A convention of States'

Rights Democrats — or Dixiecrats as they came to be called — met at Birmingham, Alabama, on July 17. After adopting resolutions for continued segregation of Negroes, they nominated Governor J. Strom Thurmond of South Carolina for President and Governor Fielding Wright of Mississippi for Vice-President. A few days later a call was issued for the formation of a new Progressive party. Delegates convened at Philadelphia to nominate Henry A. Wallace for President and Democratic Senator Glen H. Taylor of Idaho for Vice-President. On domestic issues their platform closely followed that of the Democrats. The foreign affairs plank proposed a kind of diplomatic revolution in which the United States would seek a settlement with Russia and destroy her stock of atom bombs.

The ensuing campaign ended in one of America's greatest political upsets. Counted out by everybody but himself, Truman led the Democrats to their fifth successive victory in a presidential election. Several factors conspired to deceive professional politicians as well as laymen regarding the outcome.

The most damaging miscalculation was made by the Republicans. Misled by their victory in the 1946 congressional elections as well as by the forecasts of pollsters, they assumed that the G.O.P. had become the majority party and waged the campaign accordingly. There was little basis for their optimism. Off-year elections had always been a notoriously unreliable gauge of party strength because far fewer people participated than in presidential contests. Moreover, the major political rhythm in American history featured parties in succession rather than parties in alternation. Long periods of one-party supremacy were the rule, indicating that voters did not change their allegiance casually. After the presidential vote had stablized at approximately 50 million in 1940, the Republican share had never exceeded 23 million. What the Republicans had to do was win the support of citizens who habitually voted against them or did not vote at all.

Unfortunately for the party, the leaders believed they could win the election solely on irritation over conversion. The record of the Eightieth Congress was negative enough to arouse misgivings among voters tired of the Democrats but fearful that the Republicans would repeal basic New Deal reforms if given full control. The vague, platitudinous speeches of Dewey served to reinforce such suspicions. The return of an agricultural surplus in the summer of 1948, coupled with G.O.P. legislation to reduce parity supports, nettled farmers. Organized labor had been irretrievably alienated by the Taft-Hartley Act. In fact, the only group entirely pleased with the Republican record was business. For twenty years business support had been an election handicap, and the Republican campaign did nothing to dispel popular mistrust of such long standing.

The obverse side of the Republican obtuseness was Truman's skill in advertising it. He performed the minor feat of convincing Democrats that they ought to vote Democratic. One aspect of his campaign was a clever two-year drive to pin the label of negativism on the Republican-dominated

Eightieth Congress. When it refused to pass his legislative program or revive inflation controls in the regular session of 1947, he had expressed concern over high prices and called a special session in November. He repeated the performance again in 1948, recalling Congress on July 26 after the adjournment of the national conventions with the sneer that the Republicans could show their sincerity by enacting the major planks of their platform. Their failure to cooperate set the stage for his campaign attacks on the "do-nothing Congress" and his forecasts of depression in the event of a Republican victory.

The President also courted and won key pressure groups. Unlike Henry Wallace and other erstwhile New Dealers who harbored an ideological humanitarianism, Truman was a professional "liberal." His mind worked like an adding machine when it came to totaling pressure-group votes. In key northern states he nailed down the bulk of the urban Negro population which had increased approximately 80 per cent since 1940, by all-out advocacy of civil rights. He held most of the labor vote with repeated recommendations for broadened social security, public housing, and inflation controls. Lastly, he made fatal inroads on Republican midwest farm support by forecasting a break in agricultural commodity prices comparable to 1929–1933 if the G.O.P. came to power. His success in the Mississippi Valley was aided by a devastating campaign technique — the intimate, folksy, rear-platform or "whistle stop" attack. In a section traditionally mistrustful of the urban East, the impression left by him contrasted favorably with the one left by the smooth, fluent Dewey who looked and sounded like the New York lawyer he was.

The outcome of the election was uncertain for some hours after the polls closed on November 2. By the following morning small but unchallengeable pluralities in the farm states of Ohio, Illinois, Iowa, and Wisconsin assured the re-election of the President. He carried 28 states and 304 electoral votes; Dewey, 16 states and 115 electoral votes; Thurmond, 4 states and 38 electoral votes. The division of the popular vote was not greatly different from 1940 and 1944, except for the inroads of the third parties on the Democratic total. Truman received 24,105,812; Dewey 21,970,065; Thurmond 1,169,021; and Wallace 1,157,172. The outcome vindicated the President's strategy. The electoral vote which he picked up in doubtful northern states by advocating civil rights more than counterbalanced his losses on that issue in the South. He also succeeded in outbidding Wallace for the support of northern labor while the former Vice-President was seriously damaging himself by his complacency toward Communism at home and abroad. An analysis of the vote distribution indicates that Truman held together the old New Deal coalition. Labor supported him less warmly than it had Roosevelt, but he recaptured a part of the farm vote lost by his predecessor in 1940 and 1944.

SUGGESTED READINGS

1. Churchill, W., *Triumph and Tragedy.*
2. Dallin, D. J., *The Big Three.*
3. Daniels, J., *Frontier on the Potomac.*
4. Lippmann, W., *United States Foreign Policy: The Shield of the Republic.*
5. Reeves, E., *The Anatomy of Peace.*
6. Wilmot, C., *The Struggle for Europe.*

CHAPTER TWENTY-EIGHT

THE FAIR DEAL GIVES WAY TO MODERN REPUBLICANISM

THE FAIR DEAL ERA

When President Truman took the oath of office for his second term on January 20, 1949, optimism ran high among Democrats committed to a program of extending government services. Exuberant members of the ADA as well as hard-headed party professionals interpreted the election to mean that the majority of voters had shed their postwar irresolution and resumed their New Deal orientation. Especially among the intellectuals and the administrators of the depression era, hopes for a new reform crusade burned brightly. The amazing productivity of the war economy had elevated their confidence in public planning from a faith to a dogma. They believed that they possessed a unique formula for the abolition of poverty — a middle way between capitalism and Communism. What the new-style liberals proposed was an enlarged, systematic version of the New Deal which would feature indirect government planning. They envisaged such intervention in the form of public expenditures to stimulate production, manipulation of tax schedules to increase the purchasing power of depressed groups, and control of credit to prevent deflation. Only a few bureaucrats thought that the Truman administration could apply the formula with scrupulous regard for the requirements of the economy at any given time. Most liberals were prepared to settle for a rule-of-thumb approach with government promoting new forms of social security as rapidly as political conditions warranted. The whole idea of extended social and economic services came to be identified with the phrase "welfare state."

Proponents called this program the Fair Deal, and foes dubbed it creeping socialism or a blueprint for a welfare state. Truman had repeatedly recommended measures to extend government services between 1945 and 1948; but before his re-election, prospects for their enactment were remote and Fair Deal congressmen made only token fights in their behalf. An epic legislative battle loomed ahead when the President, encouraged by his vote of confidence, again demanded a higher floor under minimum wages, a medical insurance program, federal aid to education, subsidies to permit construction of low-cost dwellings, and authorization for government enforcement of civil rights.

The administration offensive of 1949 failed to develop momentum. The most controversial proposals were sidetracked without ever being brought to a vote, while the remainder received legislative approval only after undergoing substantial amendment. In fact before the Eighty-first Congress adjourned, the sixteen-year reform tide had ebbed and liberals of all shades were exposed to a powerful undertow that swept them off their feet. The first phase of the tidal movement saw the collapse of their legislative program; the second phase saw them fighting desperately to clear themselves of disloyalty charges.

Several factors were responsible for the reversal of political fortunes. In the first place, the liberals misread the results of the election. The Democratic majority of ninety-one in the House and ten in the Senate was nominal, like all congressional majorities after 1938. The prompt re-emergence of the coalition between Republicans and southern Democrats indicated that the majority had voted for the preservation of existing reforms rather than the inauguration of a new program. It soon became clear that the deep-seated popular fear of Republicans as reactionaries and architects of depression was balanced by a popular aversion to the ambitious schemes of Fair Deal Democrats. The dominant pressure groups expected Truman to increase the size of the subsidies provided by New Deal legislation. They were quite willing to support higher Social Security payments and higher minimum wage floors. But they did not share the liberals' vision of a prosperous new society based on government intervention in new areas. Postwar prosperity also dulled the appetite for experimentation. Pressure groups were less disposed to cooperate on a program than during the depression when their desperate condition cleared the way for mutual concessions. As the boom continued into the mid-1950's with only mild setbacks, more and more citizens lost interest in reform legislation of any type. The major parties reacted to popular sentiment by gradually converging on policies and principles until by 1956 they met in dead center and were as indistinguishable as the Democrats and Republicans in 1924. Simultaneously the postwar constitutional trend of transferring the initiative in domestic policy from the executive to Congress continued.

The final factor that turned deadlock into a headlong retreat for the liberals was the exposure of the Communist affiliations of a few erstwhile New Dealers in 1948 and 1949. Within a few months the inquisitorial machinery of congressional committees, which had been trained on conservatives and businessmen since 1933, was redirected against liberals. Moreover, public sympathy gravitated quickly toward the former, thereby

"My program calls for a mammoth federal dam and a vast irrigation system that will convert this barren dust bowl into a veritable Eden of lush and prosperous farms, after which I shall press upon the Production and Marketing Administration the need for an adequate subsidy to purchase all the surplus farm produce of the entire area." (Robert Day, The New Yorker, *1950.)*

strengthening the opposition to all legislative measures tinged with socialist implications. In the end this combination of factors destroyed the political credit of Truman's second administration.

CIVIL RIGHTS

The controversy that most seriously impaired the effectiveness of the Democratic majority in the Eightieth Congress was Truman's attempt to secure legislation providing for federal enforcement of Negro rights. An earlier effort during the Reconstruction period after the Civil War had been given up as a bad job in 1876 when federal troops were withdrawn from the South. For nearly sixty years thereafter, the status and destinies of the Negroes had been left to southerners who reassumed their dominant pre-Civil War position. At first, coercive organizations of whites, like the Ku Klux Klan, frightened the Negro into submission, but after 1890 the emphasis shifted from violence to legal methods. With the connivance of the Supreme Court, whose decisions cut the heart out of the civil rights guarantees of the Fourteenth and Fifteenth Amendments, most southern states rewrote their constitutions. The amended documents exploited the Supreme Court doctrine that the Negro could be discriminated against as long as he was not singled out as a race. They permitted poll taxes and other devices which excluded him from participation in government but were broad enough in wording to exclude poor whites as well.

Southerners also took advantage of a second Supreme Court doctrine which held that the legal requirement of the "equal protection" clause of the Eighteenth Amendment was fulfilled provided the Negroes enjoyed equal but separate facilities. Under this legal umbrella they segregated the two races in hotels, railroads, schools, restaurants, and all other public or semi-public places. It was not customary for either the Supreme Court or the state authorities to worry about whether the Negro really obtained equal facilities. In fact, most public buildings and conveyances put at his disposal were far inferior to those enjoyed by whites. This kind of discrimination showed up most flagrantly in the field of education. Negro schools were either inadequate or nonexistent, as the illiteracy rate of 30 per cent in 1910 indicated. Even those who somehow got through college found southern graduate schools in law and medicine closed to them. Besides his legal disabilities, the Negro also suffered from grinding poverty and lack of opportunity. Part of this handicap was due to discrimination against hiring him for a job even though he had the qualifications. As a result, low living standards prevailed in most areas of the South, though there is, to be sure, little indication that white skin would have improved the situation.

The social ferment of the 1930's, coupled with the wartime migration of Negroes northward to work in war jobs, brought the issue of racial discrimination to a head. Many northern congressmen and senators from urban states suddenly found their constituencies jammed with Negroes interested in the plight of their southern brethren. Between 1940 and 1948 the Negro population in New York City jumped from 460,000 to 810,000; in Chicago from 260,000 to 420,000; in Philadelphia from 250,000 to 410,000; and in Detroit from 190,000 to 380,000. These increases reflected a minor political revolution because in these populous states where the electorate was almost evenly divided between Republicans and Democrats, the Negroes came to hold the balance of power. Truman recognized the political potency of the northern Negroes by seeking to perpetuate a wartime Fair Employment Practices Committee (FEPC), but it was filibustered to death by Senator Bilbo of Mississippi. As the 1948 election approached, Truman repeatedly recommended revival of the FEPC, repeal of the poll tax, and passage of an antilynching law. He also sought to identify the Democratic party with the cause of the Negro by appointing a Civil Rights Committee which made an exhaustive survey of the problem. Besides endorsing all the earlier proposals, the Committee urged legislation to prohibit discrimination or segregation on all types of interstate transportation. It also proposed that all federal grants to states for housing, education, and similar purposes be made contingent on acceptance by the appropriate officials of the nonsegregation principle. Congress refused to act on the report of the Committee in an election year. Truman promptly forwarded it to the new Congress in the winter of 1949 and demanded that it be used as the basis for legislation. Republican endorsement of a Civil Rights program in the 1948 party platform and the aggressive lobbying of the National Association for the Advancement of Colored People seemed to assure a top-heavy congressional majority on this issue.

The bitterness of the southerners against antidiscrimination legislation reappeared as soon as the President renewed the fight. Thoughtful citizens from below Mason and Dixon's line had also been touched by the New Deal reform currents of the 1930's and recognized the need for improving the status of the Negro. They denied, however, that the government could legislate improvements in race relations and pleaded for time to work out the problem at the local level. A more articulate group opposed all concessions and denounced the northerners for trying to interfere. Since no southern politician who wanted to remain politically active dared advocate a government-imposed pattern of race relations, the sectional bloc in Congress unanimously opposed the President. No parliamentary devices for holding up the will of the majority existed in the House, but southern senators announced their intention to filibuster the legislation to death as they had done with antilynching bills in the past. Hence the major test in the Senate revolved about the effort of pro-Civil Rights forces to strengthen the ineffectual rules governing the limitation of debate. Several Republican senators joined the southerners, and the administration fell short of rounding up the necessary two-thirds majority to amend the rules. This setback cleared the way for a southern filibuster and the ensuing defeat of the legislation.

SUPREME COURT DECISIONS AND SEGREGATION

Meanwhile, the trend of Supreme Court decisions had begun to run strongly in favor of the Negro. During the late 1930's and early 1940's, the Court invalidated a series of efforts by the Texas Democrats to bar Negroes from voting in its primaries, which habitually settled elections in the one-party South. After the war, judicial decisions reinterpreted the "equal protection" clause of the Fourteenth Amendment by declaring that Negroes were entitled to enjoy facilities of the same quality as whites. Decisions invalidating the conviction of Negroes in trials where they were barred from juries, and requiring railroads to provide the same service for whites and blacks, did not create much of a stir. But the application of this doctrine to southern education carried revolutionary potentialities. The Court first outlawed segregation in state graduate schools by ordering admission of a Negro to the Texas Law School. The decision made it clear that a color line would be unlawful even if a state provided a separate school or made arrangements to pay for the tuition of Negroes in an out-of-state school. The second stage was launched by a unanimous Supreme Court opinion in May 1954 which declared segregation in the public school system unconstitutional. The Court sought to soften the impact of this decision by postponing enforcement for a year, during which period it proposed to hear the petitions of interested parties. Thirteen months later it vested the supervision of desegregation in the judges of the federal district courts. The Supreme Court set no time limit for the completion of public school desegregation, insisting only that the responsible judicial authorities enforce a reasonable pace in their respective districts.

The reaction in the affected areas varied. The border states, Delaware, and the District of Columbia, which had smaller Negro populations than the states of the Solid South, engaged in some grumbling but made preparations to comply. Delaware and the District of Columbia did not even wait for the year of grace allowed by the original decision. Both carried out integration during the school year 1954–55 without serious disturbances. Tennessee and Kentucky also made a cautious beginning. Racial mixing at the primary level did not create formidable social problems, but in the higher grades dances and some other school functions were discontinued to forestall incidents. The academic background of whites was usually better than that of Negroes in the comparable grade, thus complicating the teacher's task of maintaining current standards. The protests of white parents against integration were often indirect and took the form of moving their residence from school districts that absorbed large numbers of Negro pupils.

Elsewhere, in the South, the decision provoked expressions of open defiance, whispered pledges of passive resistance, and guarded assurances that the law would be obeyed. The most violent reaction occurred in Georgia, Mississippi, and South Carolina. The legislatures of these states passed standby laws permitting abolition of the public school system, which their governors promised to invoke if the Supreme Court attempted to enforce desegregation. Other states adopted a wait-and-see attitude. Whether the effort to end segregration by judicial decision would be more successful than the abortive Truman attempt to end it by legislation remained to be seen. In any event, the softening of southern opposition to segregation would require a long time. Even if such legal disabilities were ultimately removed, the southern Negro would face a further transition period characterized by formal equality but private discrimination — such as prevailed in the North at mid-century.

Notwithstanding the many barriers to full racial equality in 1955, the Negro had enjoyed a half-century of real progress. His economic and educational opportunities had improved markedly in the North, and the postwar industrialization of the South stimulated similar hopes in those states. Outside of Dixie he had also managed to break down white resistance to joint participation in sports, the theater, and other types of entertainment. In 1945 the versatile singer and actor Paul Robeson performed in the title role of Shakespeare's *Othello,* supported by a predominantly white cast. About the same time the Brooklyn Dodgers took the courageous step of playing the Negro baseball star, Jackie Robinson, against other major league teams. A decade later, Negroes studded the line-ups of clubs in most leagues. Some states, notably New York, aided the trend with laws prohibiting job discrimination. For the North, the big problem was not whether the status of the Negro would be improved but whether progress would take place at a fast enough rate to satisfy most of the colored people.

CONGRESS BLOCKS OTHER MEASURES

The determination of Truman to push civil rights legislation over the protests of the southern Democrats provoked retaliation. Their traditional dislike of the administration program was now reinforced by vindictiveness, and they obstructed enactment of other Fair Deal measures with unusual vigor. They turned down all versions of federal aid to education for fear it would encourage the establishment of government standards of eligibility. The measure also got tangled up in a sectarian controversy over whether aid should be confined to public schools or extended to those operated by various religious denominations.

Opponents of enlarged government intervention in American life had to work harder to defeat the National Health Insurance bill. This bill proposed the financing of medical, dental, and hospital services by a compulsory 3 per cent payroll tax on employees making less than $3,600 and on their employers. The American Medical Association fought the principle ferociously. It denounced medical insurance as socialized medicine, forecast a depersonalized, mechanical type of service under such a system, and pictured physicians as tireless, selfless servants of the sick and wounded. Many people who did not favor the Truman bill also disliked the *status quo* to which the A.M.A. was attached. The Association maintained control over the profession and used its influence to control the expansion of medical schools. Despite some ideological differences, the A.M.A. functioned very much like the A.F. of L. and in effect operated to prevent doctors from becoming too numerous and competing with one another. In the end, Congress weakened the administration bill and contented itself with voting enlarged appropriations for medical research, education, and hospitals. Other proposals to repeal the Taft-Hartley Act, to increase taxes by $4 billion, and to re-establish inflation controls also died.

THE EXTENSION OF THE NEW DEAL

The principal accomplishment of the first session of the rebellious Eighty-first Congress, which sat continuously from January through October of 1949, was to increase the benefits from legislation passed in the New Deal era. It raised the minimum wage floor from 40 cents to 75 cents, but balanced the increase by reducing the categories of workers covered under the law. This modification was adopted at the behest of southern congressmen who wanted to retain the sectional advantage over northern industry resulting from low wage costs.

Another law revived public housing on such a broad basis that every major pressure group stood to benefit from its terms except the private real estate interests. Under the New Deal program 192,000 units had been built. The National Housing Act of July 1949 authorized construction of 810,000 additional units during the next six years. It also permitted loans of one billion dollars to supplement local slum-clearance projects, and subsidies to cover the difference between the rents that low-income tenants could afford and the actual costs of operation. Builders were coaxed into erecting rental units by guarantees of loans for construction. Farmers were enabled to construct new buildings and repair old ones on terms as favorable as those covering urban dwellings. Home owners not covered by these provisions were offered low-cost loans for maintenance or enlargement of existing residences.

Although surpluses of many agricultural commodities had begun to pile up in government warehouses, both parties feared the political consequences of depriving farmers of the high wartime price supports. The Republicans blamed the loss of crucial midwestern states in the preceding election on their 1948 law which sought to replace rigid supports of 90 per cent of parity with a sliding scale. The Democrats accepted their diagnosis and as a result the 1949 law postponed the day of reckoning with the farmer. It authorized for an additional year 90 per cent supports on crops defined as basic, called for a gradual drop to 75 per cent by 1952, and authorized the Secretary of Agriculture to suspend the reduction of price supports in either year if he chose. It also permitted the Secretary to support crops not defined as basic. It allowed substitution of 1945–50 for 1909–14 as the base period in calculating the parity formula which in turn governed the level of supports. Since the parity program had originally been devised to assure farmers a normal income, the authorization of an alternate and abnormally prosperous base period for use in setting up price guarantees contradicted the purpose of the legislation. The only sour note from the standpoint of the farmer was that after 1950 the Secretary of Agriculture could decline to support commodities in excess supply at 90 per cent of parity. Under such circumstances, farmers had the choice of voting production quotas on themselves by a two-thirds vote to save 90 per cent support prices or accepting the token reductions in 1951 and 1952 scheduled by the law.

The success of the farmers in hanging on to wartime price supports dispelled any lingering notions that their motives and objectives were different from those of other pressure groups. The new legislation did nothing to discourage the continued production of commodities that the market could not absorb. Each year after 1949 Congress was compelled to increase the appropriations for price support and crop loans. Truman's new Secretary of Agriculture, Charles F. Brannan, tried to sell farm organizations on an alternate program which he believed would stabilize rural income. Known as the Brannan Plan, it proposed to continue a revised formula for non-perishables but to let the prices of perishables be determined in a free market. Producers in the latter category would be reimbursed through a direct cash subsidy whenever prices fell below a stated minimum. Although the Plan seemed likely to discourage the continual enlargement of perishable surplus, most farm organizations disliked it. Under the current arrangement, government subsidies to agriculture were concealed in the form of crop loans. Theoretically farmers could always pay off their loans and reclaim their commodities from the government warehouse. But they had no intention of doing so except in the unlikely event of a price rise that carried above the 90 per cent support level. The Brannan Plan would have dispelled the vague business atmosphere from this kind of transaction and substituted an exposed subsidy for a concealed one. The indelicacy of the plan affronted the well-to-do farmers who thought of themselves as defenders of private enterprise against government handouts. Their spokesmen in Congress blocked all amendments that would have modified price supports and thereby postponed the day of reckoning until after the next presidential election.

There was considerable sentiment for the broadening of Social Security benefits. By 1950, one out of twelve citizens was over sixty-five. Postwar inflation had drastically reduced the purchasing power of New Deal pensions. Moreover, the war had expanded the working force in various professions not covered by the pension system. The new law, signed by Truman on August 28, 1950, made self-employed workers, domestic servants, and some professional groups eligible for pensions. Still excluded from the program were medical practitioners of all sorts, lawyers, architects, and farm owners. In all, about 10 million people were added to the pension rolls — raising the total coverage to 45 million. Payments also rose sharply. Married men with three years of service could receive as much as $120 per month, and single men $80 per month.

OTHER FAIR DEAL LEGISLATION

The enlargement of the pension system was the last victory for Truman's Fair Deal. The outbreak of the Korean War in July 1950 and the exposure of Communist activities in the United States reinforced the trend against social experimentation. The remaining legislative achievements were limited to areas where political considerations did not operate so strongly. The most spectacular progress occurred in the reorganization of the federal government. Congress had reorganized itself in 1946, raising salaries to $12,500 with a $2,500 tax-free expense account, starting a pension system, and eliminating committees with overlapping jurisdiction. It had also conferred modest authority on Truman to reshuffle executive agencies and created a Commission to make further recommendations on the subject in 1947. Composed of six Republicans and six Democrats and with former President Hoover as chairman and future Secretary of State Dean Acheson as vice-chairman, the Commission issued twenty-one reports in two years. It proposed consolidation of departments, introduction of uniform accounting procedures, and a variety of other measures to promote efficiency. It estimated that implementation of its recommendations would save the government approximately $3 billion a year.

Because of the nonpartisan character of the reports, Congress passed a General Reorganization Act in June 1949. It ratified the Commission's recommendations in principle and authorized the President to draw up specific reorganization plans. However, the legislators reserved to themselves the right to veto any plan by adverse vote of either house within sixty days of its submission. As it turned out, they used the veto sparingly. The principal casualty was a Truman proposal for a Department of Public Welfare with a secretary of Cabinet rank, which annoyed opponents of national health insurance. Despite several changes in personnel, the Commission continued to study the administration of government departments and make recommendations until Hoover retired in 1955. The persistence of vested interests within various executive agencies, as well as the inability of government to change its character and operate like a business, impaired the effectiveness of the reorganization plans.

DISPLACED PERSONS

Partisanship encroached to a somewhat larger degree in the formulation of laws governing the admission of displaced persons. Both parties felt obliged to make some gesture in behalf of homeless eastern Europeans uprooted by Nazis or Communists; after all, the relatives of these peoples cast a good many votes in Cleveland, New York, and Detroit. Various Nativist groups, however, resisted any liberalization of immigration quotas. Submerged controversy also developed over the relative merits of admitting Jews, Catholics, and political victims on the one hand, and victims of oppression on the other. The Eightieth Congress passed a bill in June 1948 admitting 205,000 persons, and its successor increased the number to 415,000. Both acts were loaded with restrictions that made it difficult for displaced persons to take advantage of the enlarged quota. Unsympathetic administration by the State Department after 1952 held admissions below the level permitted by the law.

THE CONTROVERSY OVER COMMUNIST INFILTRATION

Throughout the 1930's and early 1940's successive Democratic administrations had either ignored or been indifferent to Communist infiltration of the national government. They did not regard Communism as a conspiratorial movement which jeopardized national interests. Popular opinion began to change after World War II, when it became apparent that Communists holding key government posts in Czechoslovakia and Hungary had helped to promote bloodless Soviet revolutions in those states. In 1949 a more dramatic example of subversion occurred in China, which fell under Communist control only four years after being liberated from Japan. The replacement of the Chinese Nationalist government by a Communist one constituted such a serious diplomatic reverse for the United States that increasing numbers of Americans began to blame the Truman administration for neglecting national interests. In view of what had happened elsewhere, they also suspected that the administration was indifferent to the fate of China because it harbored Communist policy-makers. The only development needed to turn popular suspicions into urgent demands for a "witch hunt" was the discovery of a known Communist official in the government.

A series of investigations miscarried before foes of the administration found an appropriate case. The individual accused was Alger Hiss — the perfect example of the young New Deal intellectual. He had graduated from Johns Hopkins and the Harvard Law School, acted for one year as secretary to Oliver Wendell Holmes, and moved to the State Department in 1936, where a decade of service was climaxed by participation in the Yalta conference and the UN Charter conference at San Francisco. On the latter occasion he had held the post of Secretary General, but shortly thereafter he left the government service and became president of the Carnegie Foundation for International Peace.

Superiors of Hiss in the State Department had heard whispers that he was a Communist but had accepted his denials at face value. In the spring of 1948 Thomas Donegan, a special assistant to the Attorney General, gave a federal grand jury in New York a damaging FBI report on Hiss. Before the grand jury could act, the Un-American Activities Committee entered the case. In testimony before it Whittaker Chambers, a former avowed Communist, who had left the party in 1938 and later became an editor of *Time* magazine, identified Hiss as a prewar card-carrying member. The charge had no effect on the election because of low public esteem for the Committee, the doubtful reputation of Chambers, and the convincing denials of Hiss. Nevertheless, Richard M. Nixon and other Committee members who were dissatisfied with Hiss's testimony, refused to drop the case.

Eventually Chambers substantiated his charges with copies of secret State Department documents allegedly delivered to him by Hiss in 1937 and 1938. A cloak-and-dagger atmosphere hung about the latest revelation, because Chambers produced the damning documents in the dead of night from a disemboweled pumpkin hidden on his farm. Hiss repeated his denials that he was a Communist, had given State Department documents to Chambers, or even seen his accuser after January 1, 1937. The Committee turned back to the grand jury what had grown into a formidable mass of circumstantial evidence linking Hiss with the Communist party. Since the statute of limitations protected him from indictment for espionage, the grand jury indicted him for perjury.

The first trial terminated July 8, 1949, with the jury hopelessly deadlocked, but a retrial ended in his conviction and sentencing to five years of imprisonment. The evidence left no reasonable doubt about the justice of the verdict. Particularly damning was the similarity between the handwriting of Hiss and that appearing on some of the stolen documents. His personal refusal to admit his guilt and the chorus of New Deal intellectuals — some in high office — that denounced the verdict, produced a very disagreeable impression on the average citizen. Such behavior seemed to confirm the theory that Communists bored from within and that they could not be identified by their behavior or views. Even men of moderate views regarded the case as an object lesson.

The case against Hiss had not been documented convincingly enough by the fall of 1948 to influence the presidential elections, but it began to damage the Democrats in 1949. The response of the administration failed to reassure the growing body of critics. To accusations that they had tolerated Communist infiltration of the government and thereby betrayed America's interests, the intellectuals and Fair Dealers rejoined that their intentions had been pure and that they ought to be judged in terms of their motives rather than of the results. When this argument failed to silence the opposition, they shifted their ground, insisting that toleration of Communists had not affected American policy or damaged American interests. In effect, the administration argued simultaneously that ignorance excused its action and that the results did not impair America's position. Its effort to present a moving target shattered public confidence. Thus, as soon as citizens concluded that the government was trying to cover up and explain away its behavior, they made an explosive demand for corrective action. By late 1949 the question whether there had been one Communist or fifty in the government no longer seemed important to them; the rank and file had simply ceased to believe that the administration was a safe custodian of national interests. Although Truman in March of 1947 had set up a Loyalty Board to detect Communist spies in the government, and although his Justice Department had secured a grand jury indictment of twelve leading Communists in the summer of 1949, the public was not impressed. Against this background of growing mistrust of the administration, the new "witch hunt" developed.

THE RISE OF McCARTHY

Public anxieties about the Communist menace, growing out of the Hiss case and the exposure of the twelve, were promptly exploited by Senator McCarthy of Wisconsin. In a speech to the Women's Republican Club of Wheeling, West Virginia, on February 9, 1950, he asserted that there were 205 Communists in the State Department. Equally extravagant statements had been made by fanatical opponents of Communism throughout the 1930's and 1940's without visible effect on the voters. In the changed atmosphere of 1950 the accusations created a sensation. Overnight the Senator became the leader of the anti-Communist crusade. As the self-proclaimed defender of American institutions, he launched a four-year cycle of investigations that made him the most controversial figure in national politics and a household word all over the world.

Citizens who watched McCarthy perform in the role of investigator learned to expect certain standard techniques: irresponsible accusations, incessant juggling of statistics, disconcerting shifts from one point to another, vilification of his non-Communist critics as tools of Communism, and the editing of documents presented as evidence. The opening gambit against the State Department was typical. Having stated that 205 members of the Communist party worked and made policy in that agency, McCarthy repeatedly revised his total until it ranged from "over 200" to 57. Eventually, he proclaimed his intention of resting the entire case against the State Department on an investigation of Owen Lattimore, Far Eastern expert and Johns Hopkins professor, whom he called "the top Soviet espionage agent in the United States." Even this reduction of the target did not materially improve McCarthy's prospects of proving that Communists worked in the State Department because Lattimore was not an employee of the Department. Nevertheless the Senator did force an investigation of Lattimore by a subcommittee of the Senate Foreign Relations Committee. Undaunted by a verdict granting Lattimore a clean bill of health, McCarthy trained his guns on Senator Millard Tydings, of Maryland, the chairman of the subcommittee. With the help of a doctored photograph that purported to show an intimate conversation between Tydings and Earl Browder, McCarthy encompassed the defeat of the Maryland senator in the 1950 election.

Political success encouraged McCarthy to redouble his efforts. The volume of investigations increased during the Eighty-second Congress as Democrats sought to steal the issue. The climax came in 1953–54 when the Republicans regained control of Congress and extended the search to institutions of higher learning, philanthropic foundations, and all sorts of private organizations. State legislative and local committees applied the McCarthy technique at the grass-roots level. As chairman of the Committee on Government Operations, McCarthy roamed over the whole field. In his frantic search for facts on Communists, he even demanded that government employees violate security regulations and furnish him with information classified as secret or confidential. Until he finally overreached himself in 1954, his political following increased with each successive investigation regardless of whether he discovered any Communists.

The liberals and the New Deal intellectuals quickly raised their voices against the threat to civil liberties. They complained about the persecution of individuals for views held a decade earlier, the arbitrary and truculent questioning of witnesses by congressional committees, the refusal of the FBI to confront the accused with informers, and the harassment of college professors by means of loyalty oaths and investigations of textbooks and courses. The use of such tactics coupled with the explosive reaction of citizens toward suspected Communists increased the hazards of forthright advocacy of left-wing doctrines. The penalty for defiant radicalism was not formal suppression but frequently loss of jobs and social ostracism. The prospects of such a sentence scared some liberals out of exercising free speech, but many others never became too frightened to attack McCarthy.

As long as the liberals spearheaded the opposition, the Senator was politically invulnerable. Their contention that individuals with Communist sympathies had never influenced foreign policy was as oversimplified as the McCarthy thesis. The testimony of Owen Lattimore, extracted over a five-year period by congressional committees and a federal grand jury, belied the contention of innocence and purity. Before a circuit court of appeals threw out the perjury charges against Lattimore in June 1955, he established both his innocence of espionage and his guilt of uncritical sympathy for Soviet policy in Asia. Such guilt raised questions about his role as an occasional adviser to the Department. People were entitled to ask whether liberals like him exercised a decisive influence on foreign policy at critical junctures and whether their left-wing orientation clouded their judgment regarding American interests. The fact that most liberals refused to admit the relevancy of such questions in a discussion of the loyalty issue did not justify the McCarthy position. On the other hand, their attitude drove into his camp waverers who at least professed to take the matter of loyalty seriously.

The beginning of the end for McCarthy came in 1952 with the election of a Republican President pledged to root the Communists out of the government. During 1953 the Senator defied and investigated the administration of his own party as stubbornly as he had harassed the Truman administration. The showdown approached in the spring of 1954 when he launched an investigation of the Army for giving a routine promotion and an honorable discharge to Irving Peress, a dentist strongly suspected of Communist leanings. Evidence indicated that the ponderous Army bureaucracy was guilty of negligence, but military officials gave out as little information as possible. The Senator retaliated with exaggerated charges about the existence of a vast Communist conspiracy in the Army and a violent tongue-lashing of General Zwicker, the officer technically responsible for the promotion of Peress. Secretary of the Army Stevens made the countercharge that McCarthy had blackmailed the Army into granting special favors to Private David Schine, a former associate of the Senator and an employee on his Government Operations Committee.

During a long investigation of both charges which followed, McCarthy yielded the committee chairmanship to Senator Karl Mundt of South Dakota but prevented a judicial presentation of evidence by raising points of order, introducing irrelevant material, and browbeating witnesses. Although the Army officials did not emerge from the encounter with credit, the investigation hurt McCarthy most because it was televised and gave many admirers a disconcerting sample of his inquisitorial tactics.

The administration preferred to back away from a fight with McCarthy that might split the G.O.P. on the eve of the off-year elections. Still, the Senator remained unrepentant and goaded his foes within the party unmercifully. As a result old charges were revived about his personal finances, his connections with the real estate lobby, his insulting characterizations of colleagues, and his abuse of General Zwicker. In early August of 1954, a Republican senator, Ralph Flanders of Vermont, introduced a resolution to censure McCarthy. The Senate appointed a special committee of three Republicans and three Democrats to consider the charges. All members, with the possible exception of Senator Ervin of North Carolina, were avowed conservatives and had hitherto avoided intimate involvement in the controversy. The choice of members lent a mildly judicial tone to the hearings which was sustained by the conduct of the chairman, Senator Arthur V. Watkins of Utah. He refused to tolerate the introduction of irrelevant material and gaveled McCarthy into silence whenever the latter went off on obstructive maneuvers. The committee sifted the evidence on forty-six separate charges and after a month of deliberation recommended that McCarthy be censured on two counts: obstructing the work of the Senate by refusing to give the subcommittee information about his personal finances, and impairing the dignity of the Senate by contemptuous references to other senators.

Although the committee recommendations were made well in advance of the November election, leaders of both parties saw the wisdom of ducking the issue until the voters had spoken. The lame-duck Senate reassembled on November 15, and after a session of nearly a month — prolonged by the temporary incapacity of McCarthy with an elbow injury — it voted censure by a margin of 67 to 22. With some justice McCarthy claimed that he had been condemned for behavior frequently practiced by other senators, but neither he nor his foes bothered to point out that the Senate had avoided the basic issue of his position on civil liberties.

Cynics ridiculed the censure as a slap on the wrist. A year earlier they might have been right. As matters turned out, the action was the final blow to the ebbing fortunes of McCarthy. It climaxed a growing popular boredom with the issue. Ordinary citizens continued to believe that Communists should be rooted out of the government, educational institutions, labor unions, and other positions of trust in American society; but they believed that the Eisenhower administration would complete the job, and they were tired of McCarthy as well as a little ashamed of their earlier enthusiasm for his methods.

THE McCARRAN ACT

In the meantime the investigations had produced little legislation, partly because of constitutional barriers against deprivation of free expression and partly because of reluctance to drive the Communists underground. The outbreak of the Korean War in 1950 had strengthened the hand of legislators favoring drastic measures and in September Congress had passed the McCarran Internal Security bill. Key provisions of the measure required registration with the Attorney General of members carrying a Communist party card and of all Communist and Communist-front organizations, withdrawal of passport privileges and of employment opportunities in defense plants from citizens belonging to such organizations, and the barring of all would-be immigrants who had ever belonged to Communist or other totalitarian parties. The bill also authorized the government to detain Communists and other saboteurs in detention camps upon the outbreak of war. Truman had promptly exercised his veto on the ground that the proposed invasion of civil rights was too sweeping. Congress ignored his objections and repassed the bill by the necessary two-thirds vote. The new restrictions proved very difficult to administer and became the object of numerous court tests. After this no further legislation of consequence was passed until the summer of 1954 when pre-election maneuvers by Fair Deal Democrats resulted in the amendment of a Republican bill outlawing the Communist party altogether.

CROSSCURRENTS IN THOUGHT

A major by-product of the Communist scare had been that it deprived the already discredited intellectuals of the creative impulses provided by left-wing ideology since the 1930's. The majority either recanted by making a stereotyped repudiation of Communist ideology or reactivated the safer formulas of postwar disillusionment. The former group contained Whittaker Chambers, Richard Wright, and a host of others who wrote movingly of their spiritual ordeal but ended making the same strictures against Communism as old-line conservatives.

The bruised, sensitive spirits of the late 1940's and early 1950's made far less original contribution to literature than youth in the 1920's. Hemingway continued to imitate himself with *The Old Man and the Sea* and to provide inspiration for a new group headed by Chandler Brossard, whose *Who Walk in Darkness* features the adolescent outlook of *Farewell to Arms.* The only variant of the older repudiation of values was James Jones's war novel *From Here to Eternity.* A kind of sublimated homosexual creed emerges in the statements and behavior of the army bugler Prew who is Jones's spokesman. He condemns marriage, religion, and all other institutions that interfere with the sacred male comradeship manifested in gambling, drinking, and the pursuit of prostitutes. Prew also serves as the vehicle for expressing the old Naturalistic philosophy that realistic filth is art.

The Symbolists did not seem to be at quite the dead end of the Naturalists. William Faulkner continued to be the dominant influence in the field. His novel, *A Fable,* won wide acclaim although like earlier works it was written in a style so involved as to obscure the message for all but the elect. Faulkner's technique of using the rural South as the setting of his novels and peopling it with a variety of grotesque characters attracted able imitators. Truman Capote in *Other Voices, Other Rooms* and Carson McCullers in *The Heart Is a Lonely Hunter* demonstrated the vitality of the tradition. A few authors like Saul Bellow and Paul Bowles cautiously tried to use it for discussion of political and economic themes in a non-Marxist context.

For the intellectuals unwilling to work in the older traditions and unable to find a new cause capable of releasing creative instincts, only the pursuit of fads remained. They successively developed enthusiasm for yoghurt, charades, madrigal singing, block-printed Christmas cards, tropical fish, and high-fidelity musical reproduction — safe and tame substitutes for the stirrings and rebellions of the twenties and thirties.

The average American remained untouched by the dilemmas and frustrations of the intellectuals. He worried vaguely about the hydrogen bomb and more urgently about his religious beliefs. The insecurity of life led him to attend church more often and to seek some practical resolution of doctrinal differences between the Neo-orthodox and the Modernist theologians. As before, he was most responsive to a religious emphasis that left the initiative in the drama of existence primarily with man. The phenomenal popularity of Norman Vincent Peale's *The Power of Positive Thinking* (1952), which held out the possibility of compelling divine help through prayer, attested to the durability of Modernist optimism among Protestants.

Despite the established appeal of the novel, the newspaper, the moving picture, and the radio, television tended to become the most influential medium for entertainment as well as for the dissemination of ideas. By 1950 nearly ten million homes boasted TV sets. During the ensuing four years the rapid construction of coaxial cables made reception feasible in rural areas and smaller cities, quadrupling the number of spectators. Only the very poor and the very hostile remained without sets. The staple of the programs was variety shows, sports contests, serialized horse operas and mystery thrillers, full-length movies, and newscasts. High-class plays and scientific, political, and educational programs appeared less regularly. Commercial TV stations, like radio before them, geared their offerings to people who were susceptible to the incessant hammering of advertisers. The government set aside a substantial number of wave lengths for educational stations, but high production costs slowed down state universities and other groups interested in providing such services.

The postwar rise of juvenile delinquency and the simultaneous drop of scholastic achievement in the public schools led to considerable criticism of television programs. The agitation ultimately produced a congressional investigation of the industry but no perceptible change in the content or tone of its productions. The complacency of station owners is reflected in the statement of Charles Connell: "We are living in the age of the jerk. Most people have been tasteless slobs since their antediluvian beginnings. They don't mind it. They don't even know it. They think other people are jerks. I see very little to get excited about regarding the quality of our enthusiasms."

TRUMAN'S TROUBLES

Meanwhile time was running out on the harassed Truman administration. The Republicans registered sharp gains in the 1950 congressional elections, increasing their membership in the Senate from 42 to 47, and in the House from 171 to 199. Thereafter, the administration's control of Congress was purely nominal. Southern Democrats courted a national party disaster by collaborating with Republicans to conduct 130-odd investigations. Most of them proved abortive but a few struck pay dirt. Disclosures fell into three categories: the first concerned individuals close to the President who had accepted valuable gifts from lobbyists in return for favors; the second involved key officials in various government departments encouraged by long tenure to line their pockets at the expense of the public interest; and the third exposed connections between Democratic municipal administrations and underworld figures.

Presidential cronies under fire included John Maragon, who was convicted of accepting fees for favors to businessmen, and Major General Harry Vaughn, the inept, blustery military aide of Truman, who violated the spirit if not the letter of the law. Departmental grafting centered in the Bureau of Internal Revenue and the Reconstruction Finance Corporation. Investigating committees discovered that prosecutions for income tax evasions had been sidetracked through gifts to Bureau officials. Seven out of sixty-four District Collectors of Internal Revenue and over one hundred lesser figures in the Bureau were forced to resign. Scandal even touched T. Lamar Caudle, Assistant Attorney General, who quit under fire for accepting favors from tax delinquents. RFC officials were charged with making unwise loans because of the intervention of fixers who possessed White House connections. The names of Donald Dawson, presidential assistant, and E. Merle Young, husband of a White House stenographer, bobbed up repeatedly in these accusations. Neither was ever prosecuted, although the administration received much unfavorable publicity because Mrs. Young had allegedly accepted a fur coat worth $1,540. Republicans described Truman as being surrounded by officials who passed out favors for 5 per cent fees, Deepfreeze units, and mink stoles. The President reacted to criticism by reorganizing both the RFC and the Bureau of Internal Revenue. District tax collectorships, traditionally regarded as patronage plums, were converted into civil service jobs. Truman also appointed Newbold Morris, an independent Republican, to investigate the tax division of the Justice Department, but Congress hamstrung Morris by refusing him power to subpoena tax information, and Attorney General J. Howard McGrath artfully obstructed the accumulation of important data. In the end, Truman admitted failure by simultaneously firing both Morris and McGrath.

The special Senate crime investigating committee probably would not have damaged the prestige of the party if its transactions had not been televised. As it turned out, the committee chairman, Estes Kefauver, a Democratic senator from Tennessee, teamed up with the Bible-quoting Republican senator, Charles Tobey of New Hampshire, to put on a spectacular show. The former acted like a fearless young Galahad, and Tobey got so worked up that he wept over his own denunciations of vice. Leading figures of the underworld were hailed before the committee and cross-examined. Careful questioning revealed close cooperation between criminal elements and Democratic officials in New York City, Chicago, New Orleans, and Miami. Several Democrats lost local elections in 1950 and 1951 because of scandals uncovered by the Kefauver committee.

THE TAFT-EISENHOWER CONTEST

As the 1952 election approached, the accumulation of troubles threatened the Democrats with overwhelming defeat. To the alliterative Republican chant of "corruption and Communism" was added Korea as the months slipped by without successful negotiation of a truce. The prolongation of the so-called Korean police action, which had started in June of 1950 and dragged on indecisively for two years, galled the public on several counts. It produced a high casualty rate and resulted in the drafting of 47,000 young men per month. It absorbed vast amounts of money and kept taxes high. Worst of all, the war had seemingly reached a dead end where neither victory nor defeat was possible. Public impatience began to assume a menacing tone by the spring of 1952.

Notwithstanding the hostile trend of voter sentiment, the Democrats might still have won the impending election if the Republican party had nominated Taft, as it almost did. The Ohio senator had important qualifications. He had won re-election in pivotal Ohio in 1950 by a wide margin despite the outspoken opposition of labor unions and other Fair Deal pressure groups.

He had also been largely responsible for making party domestic policy in successive postwar Congresses. Both politicians and detached observers agreed that he overshadowed other Republican legislators from the standpoint of ability and capacity for work. Moreover, he enjoyed the enthusiastic support of isolationist Republicans. The objections to Taft had not changed materially since his initial try for the Presidency in 1940. Critics regarded him as outspoken, solemn, and reactionary. He seemed to combine all the personality traits which made the electorate distrust the G.O.P. Various public-opinion polls confirmed fears about his poor prospects as a vote getter. Nevertheless, he announced his candidacy in October 1951 and methodically began to round up delegates. His preconvention campaign demonstrated his handicaps afresh. In general he won his delegates from states that habitually went Republican or never went Republican. The doubtful eastern states, so essential to victory, were controlled by Republicans who stood between the party conservatives and Truman. In the judgment of the moderates the twenty-year supremacy of the Democrats could not be ended if Taft became the party candidate.

The eastern Republicans found it easier to agree upon the necessity of stopping Taft than of presenting a candidate of their own. Dewey could not be rammed down the throats of the convention for a third time, and neither Stassen nor Warren possessed much political appeal. The ideal candidate from the standpoint of the easterners was General Dwight D. Eisenhower. He had a phenomenal popularity that refused to die even after enthusiasm over his military achievements had receded. He looked more like a good-humored bachelor uncle than a stony-faced general, and he wore the laurels of European victory modestly. Best of all, he had taken no stand on controversial political issues. As a candidate he could be all things to all men. This asset had made him attractive to Democrats trying to ditch Truman and his civil rights program in 1948; it loomed large four years later in the minds of Republicans who thought victory depended on the wooing of the independent voters.

The problem for the eastern Republicans was not whether Eisenhower would be a good candidate but whether they could persuade him to make a fight for the nomination. His promotion, success, and recognition had all been achieved in close cooperation with Democratic politicians. His current assignment as organizer of the European army identified him with the administration's foreign policy. Moreover, it was no secret that Truman wanted Eisenhower to run for President as a Democrat and could have delivered the nomination to him without a fight.

Despite the more certain rewards of continuing his associations with the Democrats, Eisenhower regarded himself as a Republican and intended to accept a nomination only under that banner. Unfortunately from the standpoint of his backers, he was just as determined not to campaign for the honor. Like many military men he found politicians and their method of reaching decisions distasteful. If the country wished to draft him, he would accept; otherwise he would finish out his army career. This attitude, coupled with his refusal to do anything while in uniform that could possibly be construed as political, complicated the task of his supporters.

The Taft managers, who controlled the Republican National Committee and the convention machinery, faced the double threat of Eisenhower as a rival aspirant for the Republican nomination and as a possible Democratic standard bearer. Their first task was to taunt the General into such a categorical pledge of his Republicanism that the Democrats would lose interest in him. Properly executed, this maneuver would also bring to the Taft camp some wavering delegates who feared that the rejection of Eisenhower might make him a Democrat.

The General was too much an amateur and too sincere to continue the concealment of his political affiliation. Instead he listened to Senator Henry Cabot Lodge, Jr., and permitted the fact of his membership in the Republican party to be announced in early January. Victories for the General in the New Hampshire primary and an unprecedented write-in vote in the Minnesota primary failed to arrest the accumulation of delegates by Taft. So Eisenhower was driven to do what he had said he would not do — resign his command and make an active campaign for the nomination. He returned a few weeks before the Republican convention, shook hands with delegates, conferred with party leaders, and stumbled through a series of platitudinous speeches.

When the 1,206 delegates and alternates assembled at Chicago in early July, Eisenhower occupied roughly the same position with relation to Senator Taft as Theodore Roosevelt had occupied with relation to the elder Taft in 1912. Like Roosevelt forty years before him, Eisenhower was the choice of rank-and-file Republicans but could count only 392 sure votes. Similarly, Taft enjoyed the enviable position his father had once held. Not only did he control 469 delegates, but the convention machinery as well. This advantage, reinforced by precedent, seemed to assure the seating of 68 contested Taft delegates from three southern states. The parallel between the two conventions failed at one crucial point. The bloc of delegates nominally pledged to favorite sons or uncommitted was much larger in 1952 than in 1912. At the 1952 convention it exceeded 300 and included mostly delegates from large states like California, Michigan, and Pennsylvania. Strong Eisenhower sentiment existed in several of these delegations. However, if the convention seated the contested Taft men from Texas, Louisiana, and Georgia, the Senator would be close enough to a majority to exert a strong pull on the doubtful delegations.

History repeated itself when Eisenhower adopted the Roosevelt tactics of 1912 and appealed to public opinion in the hope of forestalling a convention decision to seat the Taft delegations from the three southern states. The General and his supporters took the line that the Taft delegates had been fraudulently selected and should be banned by the convention. Appropriating the custodianship of party honesty and morality, they forecast the collapse of the great crusade against the corruption-riddled Democrats if the Republican nominee owed his selection to such delegates.

The argument sounded better than it actually was. The traditional Republican practice of permitting southern states with a negligible party following to send almost as many delegates as northern states of comparable population, invited manipulation. The skeletal organizations south of Mason and Dixon's line existed only to enjoy patronage when the party controlled the White House. In fact southern leaders actually discouraged potential members from joining the party because a flourishing organization would threaten the patronage monopoly. The loose state regulations governing parties in the South also encouraged snap conventions and other practices that conserved their unrepresentative character. Inasmuch as Taft had spent many years building up his organization, it was not unnatural for his lieutenants in southern states to exclude renegade Eisenhower Democrats from delegate conventions. The ensuing wrangle in Texas and elsewhere led to rump conventions and the selection of Eisenhower delegates who claimed that they represented the popular will. Twenty-three Republican governors issued a statement taking the same position and warning the convention that it must go to the country with clean hands. Their ascription of virtue to the Eisenhower forces was not so much a moral judgment as a reflection of their belief that the General would be more likely to carry their states in November than Taft.

The issue of honesty meant as little to the Republican National Committee which placed the contested Taft delegates on the temporary roll of the convention as it did to the Credentials Committee which ratified the verdict. The only hope left to the Eisenhower forces was an appeal to the convention itself. This desperate expedient had failed Theodore Roosevelt in 1912 because of a rule permitting delegates seated temporarily by the National Committee to vote in all contests but their own. It worked for Eisenhower because the convention by the close margin of 100 votes out of 1,206 adopted the so-called Langlie rule prohibiting delegates challenged by one-sixth of the National Committee from voting on contests. On this critical issue most favorite-son and unpledged delegates supported Eisenhower. The unexpected amendment of the rules from the floor marked the turning point of the convention. Its immediate effect was to disqualify any disputed Taft delegates from voting on the fate of their brethren from other states, but its long-range effect was to assure the nomination of Eisenhower.

A test vote followed on the Georgia delegation. Deprived of support from the contested Texas and Louisiana delegations, the Taft forces lost by a larger margin than on the Langlie rule. Further resistance was useless and the convention unseated the 68 disputed Taft delegates and gave their places to Eisenhower men. The General owed much of his success in the preliminary skirmishes to Governor Dewey, who provided professional leadership as well as 92 votes from his state delegation.

By the time the convention was ready to ballot on the nominees, a number of unpledged delegates had climbed on the Eisenhower band wagon. The initial roll call gave Taft 500 and Eisenhower 595. The General was so close to a majority that members of the Minnesota delegation requested that their votes be changed from Stassen to Eisenhower, thus making a second ballot unnecessary. The convention nominated Senator Richard M. Nixon of California for Vice-President. Nixon was still under forty years of age but had gained widespread recognition as a member of the House Un-American Activities Committee which had exposed the Communist affiliations of Alger Hiss.

The platform was critical of the Democratic administration at home and abroad. It pledged the party to eliminate corruption from government and to restore a sound fiscal policy but was prudently vague about what expenses and subsidies would be eliminated. In a bid for southern votes, the Republicans added a plank advocating the transfer to the states of the tidelands oil.

Although Taft congratulated Eisenhower at the convention, both the Ohio senator and his supporters were bitter over the outcome. They felt that the strategy of drawing presidential candidates from the moderate eastern wing of the party had backfired three times in a row. Besides believing it was their turn to select a nominee, they considered Eisenhower an outsider and resented his bid to take over the party. For a time Taft threatened to sit out the campaign, but after a long vacation at Murray Bay he gave several speeches for the ticket. Most of his supporters followed his example.

THE EMERGENCE OF STEVENSON

The Democrats, mindful of their upset victory in 1948, were more optimistic than they ought to have been. They assembled in Chicago a week after the Republican convention had ended. Truman had surprised friends and foes alike by withdrawing his name from consideration in early spring. Various indications made it clear that he favored Governor Adlai Stevenson of Illinois despite an official proclamation of neutrality. Stevenson attracted the professional politicians for several reasons. He came from a distinguished family and was the namesake of a grandfather who had served as Vice-President under Grover Cleveland. A more practical consideration was his demonstrated vote-getting ability in a large doubtful state. From an inconspicuous law practice and wartime service in the State Department, he had vaulted into the governorship of Illinois in 1948 by a margin of 572,000 while Truman squeaked through with 33,000. Fluent, hardworking, and popular, Stevenson showed strength in an area where the party was weak. Like all governors, he had the advantage of being uncommitted on controversial national issues.

The nomination did not look so attractive to Stevenson as he did to the professionals. He nipped an incipient January boom by announcing on

February 4, 1952, that he would run for a second term as Governor of Illinois. Pressure was redoubled when Truman withdrew from the race. In late April, Stevenson issued a second statement taking himself out of the presidential contest, but he stopped short of categorical rejection of a draft. Colonel Jake Arvey, inheritor of the Chicago Kelly-Nash machine, interpreted the omission correctly in his artful southside prose: "I think I understand the Governor. He is not a candidate . . . If however . . . the nomination [were] given him . . . then no man could say no."

While supporters were organizing the draft, a number of candidates threw their hats in the ring. Senator Kefauver, the crime investigator, entered several of the presidential primaries and rolled up impressive votes. He had, however, earlier angered Truman for exposing the questionable activities of urban Democratic machines and by entering the New Hampshire primary and beating the President. Other Democrats not sympathetic to the Fair Deal also distrusted him as a brash newcomer who would not wait his turn for party preferment. Senator Richard B. Russell again sought the nomination as the candidate of conservative southerners. Vice-President Barkley and the Mutual Security administrator, W. Averell Harriman, ran as avowed Fair Dealers, while Senator Kerr of Oklahoma entered the lists in the dual role of liberal and oilman.

Even after the balloting started, Stevenson clung to his role, but the C.I.O. veto of the elderly Barkley eliminated his only rival with a national reputation. The administration did not intervene in the first two ballots and as a result the convention momentarily took on a spontaneous unmanaged air. On the third ballot Truman and the urban bosses started the stampede for Stevenson. Kefauver, who had led on the first ballot, tried vainly to get the floor and join the Stevenson parade. When the roll call was completed and showed Stevenson only two and a half votes short of a majority, the permanent chairman, Sam Rayburn, allowed Kefauver to move that the nomination be made unanimous. Both Truman and the new standard bearer delivered fighting speeches to the delegates the same night. The following morning the convention threw a sop to the lukewarm southerners by nominating Senator John J. Sparkman of Alabama for Vice-President. The platform was noteworthy primarily because it contained a much subdued version of the civil rights plank adopted in 1948. Although a clash between northern and southern delegates was barely averted by voting down a motion for a loyalty pledge to the candidates, there were serious southern defections. A few weeks after adjournment Governor James F. Byrnes of South Carolina issued a statement declaring the Stevenson position on civil rights unsatisfactory and announced his support for Eisenhower. Governor Allan F. Shivers of Texas also bolted to the Republicans because Stevenson would not come out for state ownership of tidelands oil. Elsewhere below Mason and Dixon's line, state tickets were organized which made it possible for orthodox Democrats to vote for Eisenhower without voting the Republican ticket.

THE ELECTION OF 1952

The campaign proved uneventful. Eisenhower drew huge crowds everywhere he went. His speeches were uninspiring, but his jerky delivery, punctuated by frequent gropings for words, left hearers impressed with his earnestness and sincerity. The combination of a record of solid competence and a faltering platform manner was politically irresistible.

Stevenson labored under special handicaps. Whether he intended it or not, he was a perfect symbol of the Fair Deal intellectual. His fluent speech, subtle wit, bland manner, and bow ties made him seem for all the world like one of the bright career bureaucrats whom McCarthy had taught many citizens to suspect. Professors of literature were wild about Stevenson, but party hacks who worked the precincts frequently could not understand what he was saying. He also suffered because he was not well known by the voters. A systematic build-up might have overcome this disadvantage, but all efforts foundered on Truman's determination to share the limelight and repeat his colorful rear-platform campaign of 1948.

Midway through the campaign, fireworks developed over the discovery by the Democrats that a group of California businessmen had made funds available to Nixon to help cover his expenses as senator. Partisan demands for his resignation echoed and re-echoed. Eisenhower remained tight-lipped for several days to see which way the wind was blowing. Exposure of the fact that Stevenson had used a similar fund to supplement the salaries of his aides at Springfield, plus an impassioned Nixon defense of his integrity on TV, caused Eisenhower to acclaim his running mate.

When the votes were counted, they revealed a smashing personal victory for Eisenhower. He received 33,936,252 popular votes to 27,314,992 for Stevenson. The electoral college margin was just as lopsided, with the Republicans carrying 39 states with 442 votes and the Democrats 9 states with 82. By winning Texas, Florida, and Virginia, Eisenhower almost duplicated Hoover's feat of capturing four states in the Solid South in 1928. He proved to be much more popular than his party. Republican congressional candidates got slightly more than 50 per cent of the vote, giving them slight majorities of 49 to 47 in the Senate and 221 to 214 in the House.

THE EISENHOWER ADMINISTRATION

The new administration got off to a slow start on January 20, 1953. Eisenhower was a novice in the art of government. Nothing in his previous career prepared him for a post where responsibility was shared with other agencies and where persons beyond his control could obstruct the implementation of his policies. Nor did he have adequate experience or insight into domestic problems. Over the years he had evolved a vague laissez-faire philosophy, but he could hardly assess its practical potentialities or limitations until he learned some of the economic facts about agriculture, manufacturing, and labor. From the outset he applied himself diligently to repair the gaps in his knowledge. But even in the White House, where the opportunities for learning were unparalleled, his education took time. Accordingly, he felt his way carefully during his first year in office. There was nothing aggressive or operatic about the quality of his leadership. He avoided head-on collisions with Congress and contended himself with legislative recommendations which were exceedingly modest by New Deal or Fair Deal standards.

It is clear in retrospect that a more ambitious program would have suffered the fate of Truman's Fair Deal. The election had confirmed popular addiction to dead-center government. Voters hoped that Eisenhower would terminate the Korean War, introduce a more upright and efficient tone in the national administration, and root out Communists suspected of holding key government jobs. They felt little enthusiasm for Eisenhower's campaign strictures against government paternalism and could be counted upon to resist any serious interference with the intricate structure of federal subsidies established during the New Deal era.

This sentiment received expression in legislative defiance of executive leadership. Voters saw a guarantee of stability in the postwar congressional drive to recapture powers conferred on the President during depression and war. They perpetuated an executive-legislative deadlock into the middle 1950's by continuing to elect Congresses closely divided between Republicans and Democrats.

The Eighty-third Congress, which took office with Eisenhower, was typical, but special factors made it unusually indifferent to presidential requests even during the so-called "honeymoon period." The over-all Republican majority in both houses was smaller than any given to a newly elected President since 1916. To make matters still worse, the G.O.P. had languished in a minority status so long that its representatives in Congress assumed a negative attitude almost instinctively. A few adjusted to responsibility quickly, but others needed months to overcome the habit of automatically changing their position whenever they found themselves in agreement with a President.

Such disruptive tendencies aggravated the consequences of the normal split in the majority party. Voters accustomed to the almost chronic feuding of the Democrats had forgotten that the G.O.P. was also a combination of sectional groups and would suffer inner stresses when it became responsible for the formulation of policy. The split, which re-emerged in 1953, followed the same geographical lines as in the 1920's, but the issues were somewhat different. The old antagonism between the agricultural Midwest and the industrial East still existed but received less direct expression than formerly. Sectional economic overtones could often be detected in Republican quarrels about foreign policy. Even so, the most obvious cause of cleavage was disagreement over the proper method of protecting America from expanding Communist power. The Midwest had strong sympathy for the McCarthy technique of dealing with native Communists, and favored a provocative policy against Communism in Asia and a reduction of commitments against Communism in Europe. For the most part, sectional antipathy to foreign economic aid was pronounced although many midwestern farmers showed enthusiasm for subsidy programs which stimulated absorption of agricultural surpluses abroad. Most eastern Republicans took an opposite position on these questions. They opposed Communism but regarded the McCarthy "Red hunt" as undignified, unfair, and destructive of civil liberties. They considered Europe more vital to the defense of America than Asia and saw virtue in economic aid for non-Communist states.

Eisenhower unquestionably belonged to the eastern wing of the party but found that the midwesterners were strategically located in the chairmanships of important committees. Especially in the Senate, where the dominant cabal selected Taft as majority leader, the President lacked an outstanding spokesman. The sudden illness and death of Taft in August 1953 led to his replacement as majority leader by Senator William F. Knowland of California, who was outspokenly critical of the administration's foreign policy.

Despite the poor prospects of cooperation with Congress, Eisenhower launched his administration with high hopes of reversing the fiscal policy of the Fair Deal and creating an economic environment congenial to private enterprise. He selected a Cabinet which reflected his sympathy with business. Recognizing his heavy obligation to Governor Dewey, he appointed John Foster Dulles as Secretary of State, and Herbert Brownell as Attorney General. Dulles was a New York lawyer with a broad background in foreign affairs. Truman, in pursuit of a bipartisan foreign policy, had utilized his services as a State Department adviser. Dulles had also enjoyed a short term in the Senate by appointment. Brownell, like Dulles, was a Dewey protégé and had served the Governor in various capacities for over a decade. Three other Cabinet posts went to prominent business leaders: the Treasury portfolio to George M. Humphrey of the M. A. Hanna Company; the Department of Defense to Charles E. Wilson of General Motors; and the Department of Commerce to Sinclair Weeks, a Massachusetts industrialist. A successful farmer, Ezra Taft Benson of Utah, was appointed Secretary of Agriculture, and a western governor, Douglas McKay of Oregon, became Secretary of the Interior. Arthur Summerfield was rewarded for his campaign services by selection as Postmaster General. Friends and foes were surprised by the appointment of Martin Durkin, a Democrat and an A.F. of L. official, as Secretary of Labor. Disagreement with Eisenhower over amendment of the Taft-Hartley Act led to Durkin's resignation in the fall of 1953, and he was replaced by James P. Mitchell of New Jersey. The Cabinet was rounded out by Oveta Culp Hobby, wartime director of the WAC, as Secretary of Health, Education, and Welfare, after Congress confirmed an executive reorganization plan creating the new department.

The appointment of a Republican Cabinet did not lead to abrupt or spectacular changes in the executive departments. Most key subordinate officials had been granted civil service status during the preceding twenty years and could not be replaced despite their Democratic leanings. Eisenhower's problem of securing sympathetic administration of his policies was illustrated by the fact that he had managed to appoint only 1,500 executive-level officials after a year in office.

The tone of constitutional decisions handed down by the federal courts and of orders issued by the independent commissions and other quasi-judicial agencies also changed slowly. The President could appoint Republicans to such posts only as the terms of Democrats expired. In the case of multimember commissions with staggered terms, several years were required to produce a Republican majority.

MILD DEFLATION

The area in which the transfer of controls could be most readily detected was monetary policy. Under the direction of Secretary Humphrey the administration launched a modest deflationary program. The Federal Reserve Board stopped buying government bonds to peg prices at par. As a result bond prices declined quickly. Most banks were unwilling to sell bonds at a loss and began borrowing from Federal Reserve to meet the loan requirements of customers. The Federal Reserve Board in turn raised interest rates. Throughout the summer and fall of 1953 money grew more scarce and loans more expensive.

The administration also tried to reduce government spending. Eisenhower appointed Joseph M. Dodge, a Detroit banker, as Director of the Budget and ordered him to go over estimated expenditures with a fine-tooth comb. Simultaneously, the President requested all executive departments to eliminate waste. The number of government employees was quickly cut from 2,550,000 to 2,450,000 merely by omitting replacement of those who quit. The administration effected other token savings, but neither Dodge nor the President dared recommend cuts in defense expenditures, veterans' appropriations, and foreign aid. Efforts by the Secretary of Agriculture to save money through reduction of nonmandatory price supports touched off wild cries from farm congressmen.

What started out in January as an attempt to balance the budget ended in August with Eisenhower fighting to prevent the deficit from getting larger. He asked Congress for a postponement of the promised tax cut until 1954 and for a six months' extension of the excess-profits tax. The Senate complied, but Dan Reed, the chairman of the Ways and Means Committee in the House, bottled up the extension bill because of irritation over the postponement of tax relief. Eventually, Speaker Martin of Massachusetts employed an unusual parliamentary device to discharge the Ways and Means Committee of the bill and to secure passage by the House. Despite the grudging cooperation of Congress, Eisenhower wound up with an estimated $3.8 billion deficit. He did not immediately give up his hope of a balanced budget, but after 1954 he spoke, like Franklin Roosevelt before him, of this particular campaign pledge as an ultimate objective. Whatever the politicians might say, deficit financing ceased to be an issue on which the attitude of the major parties differed.

Economists disagree as to whether the deflationary policies of the administration contributed to the economic recession which began in the late summer of 1953. The role of such policies was certainly modest compared with the repercussions from the suspension of the Korean War and from the steady accumulation of surpluses. In any event, the economy went through a transitional period of over a year marked by considerable contraction of business activity and deflation of prices. The sharp break in the market for raw materials during the spring of 1953 heralded the slump. The prices of key farm commodities dropped from 10 to 15 per cent in the eighteen months from December 1951 to June 1953. Wheat fell from $2.57 per bushel to $1.96, corn from $2.00 to $1.51, and beef steers from $378.25 to $220. Boxcar loadings fell off sharply and the steel mills seldom operated at more than 65 per cent of capacity from January to October 1954. Unemployment, though not severe by prewar standards, was acute in a few localities with depressed industries.

While the economy suffered from post-Korean War economic pains, the dissension-ridden Eighty-third Congress stumbled toward adjournment. It allowed wartime controls over wages, prices, and rents to lapse. It killed the controversial Reconstruction Finance Corporation. Positive accomplishments were even more meager. Beyond the extension of the excess-profits tax for six months and the reciprocal trade law for a year, Congress passed only two major administration proposals: a bill authorizing the entry of 214,000 European refugees in addition to the quota, and another giving the states title to offshore oil lands. Bills authorizing the St. Lawrence Seaway, statehood for Hawaii, and extension of Social Security coverage were tabled, as well as a series of amendments to the Taft-Hartley Law.

INTRAPARTY WARFARE

The coolness of Congress toward administration proposals was emphasized by the evaporation of the nominal Republican majority on critical occasions. Led by Senator McCarthy, the right wing criticized and harassed Eisenhower as unremittingly as it had his Democratic predecessor. From his vantage point as chairman of the Committee on Government Operations, McCarthy investigated everything from the overseas libraries of the State Department to the Army, and announced that his path was beset by Communists at every turn. He organized the unsuccessful Senate fight against confirmation of Charles Bohlen as Ambassador to Russia and interfered with what he regarded as inadequate State Department efforts to block trade with Red China.

Eisenhower absorbed this punishment without audible protest and contented himself with mildly worded statements outlining his own program for safeguarding the government against Communist infiltration. He also used various nonpolitical settings to make temperate affirmations of his belief in free expression. This passive resistance disillusioned many of his supporters and seemed to confirm Democratic sneers that he was an amiable straw man like General Grant. Ultimately his technique of allowing McCarthy unlimited opportunity to overreach himself paid off (see page 690), but in the fall of 1953 it pushed the administration to the verge of demoralization.

The simultaneous convergence of so many troubles led the voters to rebuke the Republicans at the polls. Two by-elections for House seats in normally Republican districts of New Jersey and Wisconsin resulted in smashing Democratic victories. New Jersey also chose a Democratic governor for the first time in a decade. These setbacks frightened Republicans into closing their ranks and convinced Eisenhower of the necessity for more energetic executive leadership. His year as an apprentice in an unfamiliar job had ended and with it his ignorance and illusions. He still had a doctrinaire enthusiasm for the private enterprise system of the 1920's as well as a reverent attitude toward businessmen. He was still determined to do what he could to create a favorable climate for private investment and to withdraw the government from economic activities which individuals or corporations could perform. On the other hand, he saw the political necessity of scrapping budget-balancing plans and deflationary monetary plans. He and his advisers recognized that a full-scale depression would permanently alienate the voters from the Republican party. Hence, without making a public recantation, he adopted the New Deal-Fair Deal theory of utilizing government spending to check recession. His annual message to Congress, in January 1954, proposed large-scale public works, broadened Social Security, and tax reduction. Simultaneously, the administration's fiscal operations were reoriented to make money abundant and cheap.

LEGISLATION IN 1954

Notwithstanding further grumbling from the Republican right wing over proposed increases in government spending and the impending showdown with McCarthy, the Eighty-third Congress passed a large part of the presidential program. It appropriated $1.93 billion in grants-in-aid to the states for highway building. It extended Social Security benefits to cover various categories of self-employed people and part-time workers. Even cleaning women who split their services among several employers became subject to payroll taxes and eligible for pensions. Henceforth housewives as well as businessmen were expected to make Social Security deductions and keep careful records; this requirement created formidable administrative problems. A kindred welfare law authorized construction of 35,000 new public-housing units. Even the controversial St. Lawrence Seaway bill cleared Congress, because it had become apparent that Canada would proceed alone if necessary.

Three major pieces of legislation bore a distinctly Republican stamp: tax reduction, substitution of a sliding scale for fixed farm price supports, and the authorization of participation by private enterprise in atomic power development. The provisions of the tax revision bill reflected Eisenhower's avowed intention of granting the greatest relief to businessmen and large-income groups who had borne the brunt of successive tax increases. A Democratic move for an across-the-board raise in the personal exemption was beaten, and relief of low-income groups was granted only to retired workers. The latter received a tax credit of 20 per cent on income up to $1,200. Tax reduction for individuals in middle-income brackets took the form of a cancellation of payments on the first seventy dollars received from dividends. Businessmen rejoiced over a provision cutting wartime excise taxes on jewelry, furs, luggage, and transportation. The law also provided for the overhauling and streamlining of the internal revenue code.

Overhauling of the agricultural law of 1949 was the latest in a series of efforts to establish a permanent farm policy. Leaders of both parties accepted the principle that government should establish floors under farm prices to avert an agricultural depression on the scale of the 1930's. Controversy revolved around the question of what price level should be supported. The first law to implement this policy had been passed in 1938 and guaranteed a calamity floor at 45 per cent of parity (see page 532). Wartime legislation to stimulate the output raised the support level to 90 per cent of parity and committed the government to maintain it for two years after the war. As we have already seen, the operation of the 1948 law which envisaged a sliding scale of 60 per cent to 90 per cent parity was postponed. Its 1949 successor re-established 90 per cent parity until 1952 and in the latter year Congress again extended wartime floors until 1955. The reluctance of the politicians to tamper with high-price props was based on their belief that the Republican-sponsored law of 1948 providing for the sliding scale had caused the G.O.P. to lose the election.

Inasmuch as farmers held the political balance of power in several key midwestern states, Congress avoided a showdown until the surplus became unmanageable in 1954. By the summer of that year mandatory price propping of basic crops at 90 per cent parity had forced the government to take off the market and store $5.4 billion worth of wheat, cotton, corn, peanuts, and tobacco. Even the decision of the wheat and cotton farmers to accept acreage allotments in 1953 had been more than counterbalanced by increased acreage yields. The government held enough wheat to provide the average family with a thousand loaves of bread and enough cotton to provide it with eighty-eight shirts. Besides encouraging the production of surpluses, the 90 per cent floor on basic crops kept grain prices high for cattle, hog, and chicken producers who were not eligible for mandatory supports. Such a system was flagrantly discriminatory, since the producers of basic crops took in only one-quarter of the total farm cash receipts but received the three-fourths of the government dollars loaned for price props. So the administration introduced a bill to lower the mandatory price supports on the so-called basic crops. It encountered rough going from the politically powerful congressmen from wheat and cotton states. A compromise version finally cleared both houses in August of 1954 and was signed by the President. It provided that supports could be lowered to 82½ per cent in 1955 and 75 per cent in 1956. It also authorized the Secretary of Agriculture to dispose of surpluses through sales or gifts. During the fiscal year 1954–55, wheat valued at $1.3 billion was sold at a cut rate to foreign countries outside the Iron Curtain. The government donated an additional $200 million worth of flour, milk, and butter to charity and relief organizations, drought victims, veterans' hospitals, and school lunch programs.

The law authorizing participation of private industry in the development of peaceful atomic energy projects led to a mild scuffle between friends and foes of public power. The latter, mistrustful of the Eisenhower preference for projects directed by private enterprise, found what they thought to be a better issue in the Dixon-Yates contract. The controversy was precipitated by the growing demand at the Atomic Energy Commission for electric power. The TVA, which had hitherto furnished most of the power for atomic projects in the Tennessee Valley, proposed to meet the requirements of the AEC by constructing a steam-generating plant at Fulton, Tennessee. A group of southern utility magnates headed by Edgar H. Dixon and Eugene A. Yates offered to organize a new corporation, the Mississippi Valley Generating Company, for the purpose of building a 650,000 kilowatt plant at West Memphis, Arkansas. Eisenhower endorsed the proposal in his budget message of January 1954. Six months ensued during which it was examined by the Federal Power Commission, the Bureau of the Budget, the Tennessee Valley Authority, and the Joint Committee on Atomic Energy. In mid-June, the President sought to terminate the delay by ordering the agencies involved to sign a contract with Messrs. Dixon and Yates.

This gesture brought the quarrel into the open. Advocates of public power professed to believe that the administration veto on the Fulton plant was the first step in a campaign aimed at the destruction of the TVA. They denounced the financial terms of the Dixon-Yates contract as excessively generous to the utility group and proclaimed that a TVA plant would cost the taxpayer less in the long run. The administration denied both contentions, but proponents of public power thought they had found a campaign issue and would not let the controversy die. Senator Langer of North Dakota, an independent Republican and bitter foe of the utilities, conducted hearings throughout the campaign as a one-man subcommittee on monopoly.

Even after the elections, which demonstrated public apathy to the issue, congressional opponents of the administration employed a number of parliamentary devices to block implementation of the contract. Eventually their agitation anchored it so firmly in politics that it became hazardous as a business proposition. Eisenhower canceled the project in July 1955, after assurances from the mayor of Memphis that the municipal administration would build a plant capable of correcting local power deficiencies.

THE OFF-YEAR ELECTIONS

The midterm congressional campaign was conducted in a most unorthodox manner. Statistics showed that since the turn of the century, except in 1934, every administration had lost some seats in such elections. Since the Republicans barely controlled the Congress and faced some retaliation because of the economic recession, Democratic prospects seemed unusually bright. The foes of the administration found it difficult, however, to develop issues and were afraid to attack Eisenhower. For the most part they took the cautious line that a Democratic Congress would give the President more support than one controlled by his own party.

Initially Eisenhower dismayed hard-pressed Republican candidates by declining to participate actively in the campaign. In mid-September, when Maine chose its first Democratic governor in twenty years and re-elected its Republican congressional delegation by sharply reduced majorities, the President consented to a series of campaign speeches. He again gave a devastating demonstration of his technique of making partisan pleas which sounded nonpartisan. With the Democrats defying tradition to promise support of the President, and Eisenhower ignoring unfavorable precedents to demand election of a Republican Congress, nobody knew what to expect. The result was the closest off-year election since 1930. The Democrats picked up 21 House seats for a margin of 232 to 203, and one Senate seat for a margin of 48 to 47. Subsequently Senator Wayne Morse of Oregon, who had been classified as an Independent in the Eighty-third Congress, voted with the Democrats to organize the upper chamber.

Nobody could draw comfort from the election except the proponents of dead-center government. The Democrats gained enough support to control both houses, but the Republicans lost far less than was normal in an off-year election, thus demonstrating the continued popularity of Eisenhower. The Democrats indirectly acknowledged the hollowness of their victory by refraining from the expected cry that the President had been repudiated. On the contrary, they gave him formal pledges of cooperation.

ECONOMICAL REVIVAL

Just as the political misfortunes of the Republicans in 1953–54 had been to some degree dominated by recession, so their reviving credit with the voters in 1955 depended on the re-emergence of boom conditions. During the last quarter of 1954, steel production enjoyed a sharp upturn, boxcar loadings increased, automobile sales — sparked by the early introduction of new models — skyrocketed, and the chronically sluggish coal and textile industries picked up noticeably. Not only did these trends continue into 1955 but elated businessmen resumed the expansion of capital facilities. Investors evaluated the future so optimistically that they bid up the value of all listed stocks from $137.9 billion on May 30, 1954, to $182 billion on May 31, 1955.

The spectacular rise in employment, production, and profits during the first half of 1955 tended to obscure an equally spectacular long-term rise in the standard of living. This development can be measured in various ways. During the boom year of 1929 there were 695 cars per thousand families, while in 1955 the total had jumped to 890 per thousand families. In the same period the disposable income of the population increased over 400 per cent. Much of the gain took place in the decade following World War II. Factory wages, which averaged $1.046 per hour in January 1945, went up to $1.87 per hour in May 1955, representing an increase in real income of approximately 19 per cent. Farmers, businessmen, and individuals living on fixed income did not fare quite so well as industrial workers, but they too enjoyed greater purchasing power.

Citizens whose memories of the crash in 1929 were still fresh found several disturbing parallels between the two boom eras. Both periods witnessed an orgy of corporation mergers. The spectacular integrations of the 1920's (see page 401) were matched in the decade after 1945. Federal Trade Commission statistics showed 200 consolidations in 1950, 713 in 1951, and 822 in 1952. Especially noteworthy were the merger of Nash with Hudson, and Studebaker with Packard, in the automobile industry; Olin with Mathieson in the chemical industry; Sunray with Midcontinental in the petroleum industry. Two huge New York banking systems, Chase and Manhattan, pooled their resources in 1954, and only the direct threat of antitrust action postponed the proposed integration of Bethlehem Steel and Youngstown Sheet and Tube. Other corporate giants like American Machine and Foundry, Pullman Company, and American Cyanamid diversified by swallowing up smaller firms. Critics lamented the mergers as a deadly threat to competition, while the architects of consolidation insisted that the pooling of resources would create more effective competitive units. Evidence pointed both ways. Moreover, the Justice Department found difficulty in applying the antitrust law which called for prosecution of mergers tending to diminish competition.

The clarity of the monopoly issue was further clouded by the McGuire Fair Trade Act of 1948. It made retail price-fixing agreements between a manufacturer and a single vendor binding on all vendors of the commodity involved. The McGuire Act applied to businesses in the thirty-eight states with Fair Trade laws. Enforcement of such retail price-fixing began to break down in 1954, often with the connivance of manufacturers who diverted surplus production to discount houses. Simultaneously, scattered decisions in state courts cast doubt on the constitutionality of the Fair Trade laws. Indeed, America seemed no closer to the formulation of a consistent policy on monopoly in 1955 than in the days of Theodore Roosevelt.

The prosperity of the 1950's also brought about an incautious boom psychology reminiscent of the 1920's. Stock prices rose with unprecedented speed between January 1954 and July 1955. The industrial stocks making up the Dow-Jones average penetrated the peak level of the 1929 bull market on June 26, 1954, and continued their steep ascent to a record 460 on July 6, 1955. Railroads took longer to regain the 1929 level, and utilities lagged farther behind, but all three averages skyrocketed far above their postwar lows. Financial analysts disagreed about the danger of such a rise. Some expected a catastrophic break comparable to the one from 1929 to 1933. Others argued that stocks had been undervalued for years and were simply catching up with the rest of the economy. The optimists pointed to the Federal Reserve Board rules requiring large down payments of cash for stock purchases — 75 per cent after January 1955 — and to the investment of pension and insurance funds in high-grade common stocks as important market stabilizers not operating in 1929. An investigation of the stock market by the Senate Banking and Currency Committee in February 1955 neither cast much additional light on the causes of the rise nor scared the investors who were bidding up prices.

If the bull market of 1955 differed from its predecessor at some points, installment buying looked monotonously the same. Citizens of the atomic age lubricated their buying spree by purchasing vast quantities of automobiles, television sets, and household appliances "on time." During the decade after VJ Day, the installment debt increased more than 1200 per cent (i.e., from $2.5 billion to $31.6 billion).

The rosy appraisal of the future, which encouraged consumers to assume staggering debts, stimulated industry to plan for ever-larger markets. General Motors, American Telephone and Telegraph, and a host of other corporations took advantage of investor eagerness to increase working capital and expand productive facilities. Promoters launched new projects with a fanfare worthy of the twenties. Automobile manufacturers talked airily of two- and three-car families and of an annual market for ten million cars by 1960. William Zeckendorf, who headed the real estate firm of Webb and Knapp, announced in early June 1955 an agreement with the Pennsylvania Railroad to develop its New York City passenger station. The irrepressible Zeckendorf told reporters that he would build the most costly commercial structure in the world — a $100 million Palace of Progress twice the size of the Pentagon and half again as large as the Great Pyramid of Gizeh. Faith in the prospects of the economy was contagious; Americans were again selling themselves on the old dream of permanent prosperity.

PREPARATIONS FOR THE 1956 ELECTION

With the economy healthy except for agriculture and with reform sentiment all but dead, both parties began to concentrate on the 1956 election a year in advance. Eisenhower formulated most of his recommendations to the first session of the Eighty-fourth Congress with a view to making further inroads into groups that normally voted Democratic. This strategy led to requests for an increase in the statutory wage minimum from 75 cents to 90 cents per hour, a three-year program of federal aid to education, a ten-year highway-building plan, and voluntary health insurance. Less politically oriented proposals included a three-year renewal of executive authority to negotiate reciprocal trade treaties, an extension of the draft law, a pay increase for the armed services, and a large foreign-aid appropriation.

The Democratic congressional majority, led by Sam Rayburn in the House and by Lyndon Johnson in the Senate, acted favorably on the tariff, military,[1] and foreign-aid bills. The legislators killed Eisenhower's social and economic program except for the minimum wage increase, in which instance they outbid the President by raising the floor to one dollar on July 20, 1955. In the House, where the Democratic majority was more manageable, Rayburn secured passage of a bill authorizing a flat twenty-dollar tax cut, and another restoring mandatory 90 per cent price supports on basic agricultural crops. The administration, with the help of southern Democrats, succeeded in blocking this bid of Fair Dealers for support of low-income groups. As usual, Eisenhower declined to put serious pressure on Congress in behalf of his program. Hence little had been accomplished when the legislators adjourned in mid-August.

Republican strategists, who had pinned their hopes of victory in 1956 on Eisenhower, received a severe jolt when the President suffered a heart attack on September 24, 1955, while vacationing in Colorado. He was confined to the hospital for seven weeks and worked on a restricted schedule for several months thereafter. Party leaders nevertheless subjected him to unremitting pressure to run for re-election and at last he assented on February 29, 1956. Republican campaign plans were again thrown into confusion when he underwent an operation for ileitus on June 9, 1956, but he recovered well in advance of the national convention.

When Congress met for its second session in January 1956, the ailing Eisenhower resubmitted his social and economic recommendations of the preceding year which the lawmakers had tabled. In an attempt to head off a fresh assault on flexible price supports, he proposed a supplementary

[1] The draft extension law (July 26, 1955) aimed at an increase in military reserves from 800 thousand to 2.9 million by 1960. It offered youngsters in the 17 to 18½ age group the opportunity to avoid the draft by volunteering for six months of active service and seven and a half years in the active reserves or in the National Guard units until the age of 28.

system of farm subsidy payments. Known as the Soil Bank Plan, the new measure was tied to an appropriation of $1.2 billion which would be distributed among farmers who took a specified portion of their acreage out of crops in surplus supply and planted it in soil-building grasses. With an eye to the urban Negro as well as the farmer, he also urged the establishment of a commission to investigate racial discrimination.

The Democrats responded to the presidential recommendations by employing a flexible strategy. They dragged their feet on some measures, loaded others down with crippling amendments, and passed a few with voter-appeal in a more generous form than requested. Southerners managed to kill the proposed commission on discrimination as well as a new version of federal aid to education. Democrats from both wings of the party collaborated to add a provision for 90 per cent price supports to the Soil Bank bill, but Eisenhower vetoed it on April 15. Fear of voter retaliation in the farm belt forced them to submit a separate soil bank bill, which the President signed on May 28.

In hope of sharing the credit with the administration, the Democrats cleared and sent to the White House a variety of measures which increased long-range spending commitments. These included (1) a sixteen-year highway-building program to provide a forty-one-thousand-mile road network between state capitals and major population centers, (2) an amended Social Security law which qualified totally disabled workers for pensions at fifty and women workers at sixty-two, (3) a housing law authorizing the government to subsidize construction of thirty-five thousand new low-rent dwelling units over a two-year period. Congress showed less willingness to vote great sums for foreign aid. A bipartisan revolt finally ended in a compromise which authorized the expenditure of $4.04 billion — slightly less than what the President had requested.

EISENHOWER AND STEVENSON AGAIN

With the national conventions moved to mid-August, Congress adjourned in time for legislative leaders to give undivided attention to preliminary political maneuvers. Activity was especially evident in the Democratic camp, where Adlai Stevenson was climaxing a vigorous campaign for renomination which he had started in November 1955. In the process he had tried to shed his reputation as a wise-cracking intellectual and to cultivate the manner of the homespun, healthy, outdoor man. He was not very convincing in his new role, but he did not receive serious competition because of the widespread conviction within the party that the nomination would be worthless in 1956. Only Senator Estes Kefauver had provided opposition in the primaries, and Stevenson had won every trial run except in Minnesota. A last-minute roadblock was thrown up against him by Harry Truman, who had worked for some months behind the scenes to line up delegates for Governor Averell Harriman of New York. The belated Harriman boom collapsed almost before it started when Kefauver withdrew from the race on July 31 and endorsed Stevenson. This brought Truman out in the open. He tried to revive the Harriman candidacy with a public endorsement on August 11, two days before the convention opened. The delegates however, gave Stevenson a first-ballot nomination with 905½ out of a possible 1,372 votes. Kefauver edged out Senator John F. Kennedy of Massachusetts for second place on the ticket. In an effort to avert a party split over civil rights, the convention took an ambiguous stand on the issue. Other planks in the platform reiterated the familiar promises to promote peace and prosperity.

Inasmuch as the renomination of Eisenhower was a foregone conclusion, the only preconvention excitement on the Republican side arose out of an abortive campaign by Harold Stassen in late July to substitute Governor Christian Herter of Massachusetts for Richard M. Nixon as the vice-presidential nominee. Apparently Stassen was the spokesman for highly placed Republicans who disliked Nixon but hesitated to oppose him openly.

The Republican delegates assembled at San Francisco for the opening session on August 20. Forty-eight hours later the Eisenhower-Nixon ticket was renominated by acclamation. Like the Democrats, the Republicans adopted a civil rights plank that avoided a clear-cut stand on the enforcement of desegregation decisions handed down by the Supreme Court. Other planks paralleled those of their opponents closely enough to preclude any kind of campaign except a popularity contest.

Long before election day it became evident that the Democrats were in the majority but that many of them would vote for Eisenhower. Well-bred hints by the Democratic National Committee that the President would not live out his term made little impression on the electorate. Efforts to picture Eisenhower as an amiable, well-meaning stuffed shirt were equally unproductive. Stevenson indirectly acknowledged the hopelessness of his position by a desperate bid for votes with proposals to end the draft and to suspend H-bomb tests. The injection of these issues into the campaign provoked countercharges that Stevenson was irresponsible. As usual, Eisenhower de-emphasized partisanship in his appeal to the country. He substituted television appearances and a series of airplane trips to doubtful states for the traditional swing around the country.

The voting on November 6 confirmed the predictions of the pollsters and professional politicians. Eisenhower won 41 states and 451 electoral votes, while Stevenson carried only 7 states and 74 electoral votes. The President duplicated his feat of 1952 by capturing four states in the Solid South and increased his portion of the popular vote from 55 per cent to 58 per cent. But he could not carry his party to victory in Congress. Approximately four out of ten voters split their tickets, returning the Democrats with a 49 to 47 majority in the Senate and a 234 to 201 majority in the House. For the first time since 1848 the voters had simultaneously returned to power a President of one party and a Congress of the opposing party. Their action was a fresh endorsement of dead-center government.

As Eisenhower started his second term in January 1957, it was apparent that party battles over domestic issues would be fought on a very narrow front. His recommendations for a new study of the monetary system, a relaxation of immigration barriers, a civil rights commission, and a $71.8 billion budget foreshadowed a continuation of the petty partisan warfare that had characterized his first term.

SUGGESTED READINGS

1. Cooke, A., *A Generation on Trial.*
2. Chandler, L. V., *Inflation in the United States, 1940–48.*
3. Lubell, S., *The Future of American Politics.*
4. Myrdal, G., *An American Dilemma.*

CHAPTER TWENTY-NINE

A DECADE OF CONTAINMENT

DISILLUSIONMENT WITH ORGANIZATION DIPLOMACY

The ability of the Soviet Union to expand her power in 1945–46, and to prevent retaliatory UN action by invoking the veto, gradually impaired American confidence in organization diplomacy. When Russia gave unmistakable signs of embarking on fresh expansion in the opening months of 1947, Washington resorted to countermeasures outside the framework of the United Nations. By this time, the United States had tacitly written off the countries already behind the Iron Curtain and was prepared to settle for a new and less favorable *status quo* that confined Russia within her current boundaries. The new policy came to be known as "containment" and involved America in frustrations from the outset, because it left the initiative with the Soviet Union, the dynamic state. From her central position the Soviet Union could simultaneously probe the weak spots in surrounding vacuum areas with a minimum of effort. By contrast, the United States had to remain on the defensive, waiting for the foe to act and hopping all over the globe to parry each new thrust. Thus, containment confronted Washington with the dismal prospect of dissipating strength on little enterprises all over the periphery of the vacuum. It would never seem a very heroic policy to Americans; hence they were not likely to apply it except in a haphazard, piecemeal way.

The only escape — aside from a frontal attack on the Soviet Union, which America refused to consider — was to act as the holder of the balance by restoring two regional equilibriums. This condition might have been created in Europe by balancing off the western states against Russia and in Asia by balancing off China against Russia. The United States was dimly aware of the desirability of such a policy but unwilling to encourage the revival of genuinely independent states for regional balancing operations. The necessity of promoting the self-interest of such states and of ignoring both their ingratitude and their defiance collided with America's determination to export her own ideals. The upshot was that Washington fell back on containment and tried to sell it as the method for preserving the democratic American way of life. Most of the people in vacuum areas, however, did not want to become Americans. They were more willing to accept economic aid, but it too produced discord. For tactical and ideological reasons, America wanted her expenditures to promote capitalistic institutions, while most recipients of aid — particularly the newly independent states of Asia — associated capitalism with their former colonial status. Accordingly, misunderstandings and irritations dogged American efforts to promote containment through economic aid.

The individual most responsible for a theoretical formulation of containment policy was George F. Kennan, the counselor of the embassy at Moscow and long-time State Department adviser on Russian problems. What Kennan had in mind was a large-scale build-up of American strength in Europe and an extension of military and economic aid to countries in the vacuum west of the Iron Curtain that would resist Russian subversion. In an unsigned article in the July 1947 issue of *Foreign Affairs,* he asserted that a long-term, vigilant containment of Soviet power offered the only prospect of achieving peace and security.

AID TO GREECE AND TURKEY

Five months before Kennan tried to sell his views to the public, America had formally commenced her policy of containment. The incident responsible was a momentous note delivered by the British ambassador to the Washington government on February 24, 1947. It stated that Great Britain could no longer assume the responsibility for blocking Communist expansion in the eastern Mediterranean area and that she would pull out of Greece altogether. Inasmuch as British support of a rightist Greek government from 1944 to 1947 had forestalled the effort of the Communist-dominated EAM party to gain control of the state, the threatened withdrawal alarmed America. The gravity of the situation was emphasized by the fact that the EAM controlled much of northern Greece and received a constant flow of military supplies from the Communist satellite states of Yugoslavia and Bulgaria. EAM guerrillas even operated in the hills around Athens, robbing, killing, and blowing up bridges. It was doubtful that the non-Communist government could survive the chaos once the British withdrew. If the Russians succeeded in gaining control of Greece, Turkey would be outflanked and threatened with subversion. In fact, the Turks had already been subjected to repeated Russian demands for naval bases on the Bosporus. Soviet ambitions in this area were based on an age-old Russian dream of gaining warm-water ports in the Mediterranean, which Britain had successfully checked for a century and a half. In retrospect Britain's decision to abandon responsibility for Greece seems momentous because it foreshadowed the liquidation of her commitments in vacuum areas all the way from the Middle East to Central Asia.

"Well, boys, Monroe wanted to prevent Europeans from interfering with American affairs. We've got to prevent them from interfering with European affairs." (Verdens Gang, *Oslo, 1947.*)

President Truman responded to the crisis by appearing before Congress on March 12, 1947, and requesting $400 million for aid to Greece and Turkey. He might have saved much subsequent confusion by announcing that the United States proposed to extend economic and military aid to sovereign states endangered by Russian expansion; such a statement would have prepared the public for later aid to the totalitarian states of Spain and Yugoslavia. Instead, he gave a statement which by its mingling of ideology and power objectives confused Americans more than Europeans. After pointing out that a primary goal of American policy was to create conditions for the emergence of democratic institutions all over the world, he branded the imposition of totalitarian regimes on free people as a threat to peace and to American security. He concluded with the assertion that the United States should "support free peoples who are resisting attempted subjugation by armed minorities or by outside pressures." This statement of policy came to be known as the Truman Doctrine.

Although the opposition made a noise out of proportion to its numbers, Senator Arthur H. Vandenberg, who headed the Foreign Relations Committee of the upper house, declined to take a narrow political view. He rallied a substantial bloc of Republicans behind the President and contributed a face-saving amendment which authorized America to lay down the foreign aid burden whenever the UN was prepared to take it over. After a debate that lasted two months, Congress approved the initial appropriation of $400 million on May 15, 1947. The affirmative vote was 67 to 23 in the Senate, and 287 to 107 in the House. Vandenberg's bipartisan approach to foreign policy continued uninterrupted for the next five years despite occasional grumbling by the minority that it was not adequately informed by the administration. Senator Vandenberg put this complaint aptly when he said that the G.O.P. always received invitations to participate in the crash landings but not in the take-offs.

Aid to Greece and Turkey proved to be the most successful application of the containment policy, although it required three years and additional appropriations of $259 million to complete the job of reorganizing the economies and armies of both countries. Progress was slower in Greece than in Turkey because of guerrilla warfare and government resistance to much-needed reforms. Matters took a sharp turn for the better when Marshal Tito of Yugoslavia broke away from the Russian orbit in 1948 and shut off the flow of supplies from his country to the EAM. The program went well in Turkey from the outset because the Turks nursed a long tradition of hostility toward Russians whether in the guise of Slavs or of Communists.

THE MARSHALL PLAN

While the public was still digesting the novelties of the Truman Doctrine as applied to Greece and Turkey, the administration proposed another variation of containment policy. The new plan was unveiled by General George C. Marshall, who had replaced James F. Byrnes as Secretary of State, in an address at Harvard University on June 5, 1947. In brief, he offered American financial help to European states if they would get together, formulate comprehensive plans for economic recovery, work out arrangements for mutual assistance, and send Washington a specific statement of their needs. The wording of the invitation was so general that it did not exclude Britain, Russia, or the states behind the Iron Curtain.

This generous proposal was made against a background of deepening political and economic chaos in Western Europe. The $10 billion already sent across the Atlantic under a variety of stopgap programs did not seem to have done much more than avert starvation. In 1947 Europe was still suffering from numerous ailments including devastation, inflation, unemployment, and evaporation of foreign markets. Unless productive facilities could be restored on a large scale, both England and the Continental states threatened to become chronic charity cases. Worse still, the persistence of low living standards provided a fertile field for Communist agitators who enthusiastically fomented strikes, riots, and sabotage. Flourishing Communist parties in France, Italy, and several of the smaller European countries were looking for a crisis that would catapult them to power. Only a bold, coordinated program of reconstruction offered Europe much prospect of again becoming self-supporting. Whether reviving productivity and prosperity would also reduce the Red menace was uncertain, but the Marshall Plan rested on the assumption that Communist sentiment falls as living standards rise.

Elated by the sudden turn of events, the British and French Foreign Ministers met with Molotov at Paris on June 27, 1947, to consider the American offer. Molotov exhibited fierce hostility and withdrew from the conference after a few days, thereby passing up a golden opportunity to obstruct containment from the inside. Great Britain and France then invited representatives of twenty-four states to meet in Paris on July 12 for a discussion of specific needs. Six states behind the Iron Curtain and two just in front of it declined the invitation after advice from Moscow. The remainder worked until mid-September drawing up lists of needs that would fit into an integrated program. Altogether they requested $22.4 billion in the form of grants and loans. Before transmitting the proposal to Congress on December 17, 1947, Truman cut the total down to $17 billion and recommended that appropriations be spread out over a four-year period. Congress debated for nearly three months. A sizable bloc of Republicans led by Senator Taft tried to make deep cuts in the appropriation, while the isolationist *Chicago Tribune* denounced the entire scheme as a "global WPA" and an "Operation Rathole." Conservatives were handicapped by the unsolicited help of American Communists. Senator Vandenberg, who led the bipartisan coalition for the administration, improved the prospects of the bill by making adroit concessions to the waverers. He reduced the initial appropriation from $6.8 billion for fifteen months to $5.3 billion for twelve months and eliminated altogether a clause committing Congress to the total amount. The Communists removed all doubt that the Plan would be approved by seizing control of Czechoslovakia in February 1948. Final passage was held up until March 31, but Congress acted in time to help the Christian Democrats win the Italian election of April 18. Together with personal letters written by Italian-Americans to relatives in the homeland, the Plan apparently kept the former Fascist state out of the Communist orbit. Under the Economic Cooperation Administration (ECA), which administered the Plan in conjunction with the Committee of European Economic Cooperation, $12 billion was spent on reconstruction programs between April 1948 and December 1951. By the latter date, most of the countries receiving assistance had managed to restore or exceed their 1938 production levels without a substantial revival of east-west trade. American restrictions on the shipment of key industrial equipment behind the Iron Curtain and Soviet trade practices sharply curtailed the exchange of goods between the Marshall Plan countries and Eastern Europe.

If the Marshall Plan was a success as an economic recovery program, it was of questionable value as a device for counteracting the appeal of Communism in Western Europe. Local Communist parties in France and Italy continued to hold their popular following intact, to dominate labor unions, and to retain their grip on many municipal governments. Contrary to American beliefs, fat people were not happy people. Instead of making Europeans more contented, improved living standards taught them that progress was really possible and made them impatient for more. Furthermore, economic aid failed to function as ideological competition for Communism. Its inadequacy was inevitable because subsidies do not constitute an idea-system or a way of life. The meaning of democracy could not be reduced to a formula of technological progress and exported, because it involved voluntary belief in a set of values. In so far as Americans imagined that they were selling democracy through the Marshall Plan, they were bound to be disappointed over the results.

SPAIN AND YUGOSLAVIA

Another reason for America's distrust of her own ideological assertions was provided when she edged toward the restoration of cordial relations with Fascist Spain. The House of Representatives had not included Spain on the original list of countries eligible for Marshall Plan aid, and only strong administration pressure caused the legislators to reverse themselves. Out of deference to world opinion, the United States continued the ban on Spanish participation in the Plan and in the NATO. Later the hardening of her determination to contain Soviet expansion was accompanied by a corresponding relaxation of her hostility toward the government of Franco. Diplomatic relations were restored in 1950, and shortly thereafter the Import-Export Bank loaned Franco $62.5 million. The logic of power politics dictated closer cooperation between the two states. Spain had a large but poorly equipped army and an antiquated economic system. With adequate help she would be willing to put both at the service of the anti-Communist coalition. Despite her manifest weaknesses, she was potentially a more reliable ally for the United States than France and Italy, which contained large Communist minorities. Her rugged terrain and geographic isolation made her an ideal redoubt for a final stand in the event that Soviet armies overran the rest of Western Europe. These considerations eventually outweighed the objections of American liberals to a Spanish alliance. As a result the Eisenhower administration signed an executive agreement with Franco on September 26, 1953, which granted Spain $226 million for military and economic aid. In return, the United States received the right to use specified naval and air bases on the Iberian peninsula.

The American public experienced difficulty in rationalizing aid to Yugoslavia. It distrusted Tito even though he had succeeded in taking his satellite out of Russia's orbit in 1948, and in defying the Communist dictator at Moscow. Between 1949 and 1953 nearly $120 million was spent to help him maintain this hard-won independence. Nevertheless he showed only perfunctory gratitude, continued to advertise his Communist philosophy loudly while waging a violent propaganda war with Moscow, and rejected offers of direct military alliance with the West. After Khrushchev came to power in Russia in 1954, Tito edged toward closer relations with the Kremlin.

He did, however, accept a modified version of a defensive pact in June 1954, linking Yugoslavia, Turkey, and Greece. At the same time his independent policy in the Adriatic almost led to an open rupture with Italy over Trieste, which was supposed to be a free territory but which had been occupied by British, American, and Yugoslav troops since 1947. After repeated mediation efforts by the United States, Yugoslavia and Italy finally agreed in October 1954 to partition Trieste.

THE NORTH ATLANTIC TREATY ORGANIZATION

Meanwhile, Russian countermoves added to American frustrations over containment at the economic level. One reaction was to revive the Cominform — or Fourth International — as a substitute for the Comintern, which had been dissolved as a gesture of wartime solidarity in 1943. No realist believed that Russia had really broken up her international network of subversive Communist parties. Therefore when the Soviet Union announced the meeting of a nine-nation Cominform on October 5, 1947, the United States knew that revolutionary agitation was entering a more militant phase. Besides serving notice of an all-out fight on the Marshall Plan, Moscow also introduced the Molotov Plan which was aimed at greater economic integration of countries behind the Iron Curtain.

While Americans pondered the implications of economic warfare in Western Europe, the Russians gradually tightened the noose around the little four-power island of Berlin. In protest against unification of the American, British, and French zones, they began to restrict the inbound movement of people and freight from western Germany on April 1, 1948. A crisis was precipitated on June 24 when they shut off non-Russian traffic to Berlin except by air, with the obvious intent of forcing either the withdrawal of the western powers or the suspension of their program for zonal integration. The Kremlin reckoned without the stubbornness of the aroused British and Americans, who promptly established an airlift for supplying their beleaguered zones. Although the siege continued until mid-May of 1949, the western powers succeeded in supplying both their garrisons and the civilian population. The combined British and American air forces had made 277,264 flights before the Russians called off the siege in return for another conference on the German question. The airlift was costly and inconvenient, but it proved to be a morale builder in the non-Communist world and increased the respect if not the affection of the Germans for the western powers.

The siege of Berlin, which followed so closely on the heels of the Communist coup in Czechoslovakia, alarmed Western Europe sufficiently to set in motion plans for coalescence. On March 17, 1948, Great Britain, France, Belgium, the Netherlands, and Luxemburg had taken the first step to restore a regional balance of power by signing a fifty-year alliance. Known as the Brussels Pact, the agreement committed the signatories to aid each other in the event that any one of them was attacked. Elated by this turn of events, the United States opened negotiations to broaden the coverage of the Pact. She not only sought membership in this alliance but pressed for the inclusion of other states receiving Marshall Plan aid. Since this would involve participation in a regional power bloc outside the framework of the UN, the administration sent up a trial balloon in the form of a resolution affirming support of such regional defense agreements. Vandenberg pushed this through the Senate on June 11, 1948, by a vote of 64 to 4.

Shortly thereafter representatives of the Brussels powers plus Norway, Denmark, Iceland, Portugal, Italy, Canada, and the United States met in Washington to draw up the North Atlantic Treaty. The new agreement was signed April 4, 1949. The preliminary clauses paid lip service to the UN and stressed the defensive character of the treaty. The key provision was a stipulation binding the signatories individually or collectively to aid each other in case of attack. Since the wording precluded an automatic commitment by the United States to fight in behalf of her allies, Congress was assured that its power to declare war was unimpaired. The Senate ratified the treaty on July 21, 1949, by a vote of 82 to 13, and two months later both houses voted an appropriation of $1.45 billion with which to arm the allies. The alliance was enlarged to include Greece and Turkey in 1951. Although no explicit admission was made, American adherence reversed the old policy of aloofness from foreign entanglements and completed the repudiation of organization diplomacy through the UN.

The United States quickly discovered that it was easier to appropriate funds than to create a force capable of withstanding the Russians. Early in 1950 General Eisenhower accepted the task of building the NATO army. No sooner had he established headquarters in Paris than troubles began. The eight European states who were to receive American arms dragged their feet about such basic matters as conscripting soldiers and raising funds. They also showed little enthusiasm for participating in an international army under the command of an American, even though each national unit was to retain its identity. On the other side of the Atlantic, public opinion bridled at the prospect of sending large numbers of American troops overseas. Taft and Hoover teamed up in a campaign to prevent the President from detaching more than four divisions for the defense of Europe. At the same time, the outbreak of the Korean War in June increased American preoccupation with the Asian theater. The cumulative effect of these developments was that the NATO army remained largely a paper force despite the rapid build-up of American military aid appropriations from $200 million in 1950 to $4.4 billion in 1953.

BARRIERS TO THE PROJECTED EDC

Inevitably, the United States and her European allies began to toy with the idea of recruiting additional manpower for NATO by rearming West Germany. Such a solution had been foreshadowed in 1949 when the western powers created the German Federal Republic with its capital at the ancient city of Bonn on the Rhine. Although the sovereignty of the new Reich had been restricted in several important particulars, the United States and her associates reversed the policy of dismantling German industry. In fact, the same year the Bonn Republic was created, the United States made it eligible for participation in the European aid program. A remarkable economic recovery followed.

The French first suggested that the Bonn Republic be allowed to participate in the defense of Western Europe. Ever-mindful of the fact that German soldiers had burst over the northeastern frontiers of France three times in eighty years, the Paris government wanted special restrictions on the rearming of their former enemies. Specifically it proposed a new organization, the European Defense Community (EDC), to supersede NATO. Under this plan West Germany would not be permitted to rebuild her own army but would contribute a quota of men to a six-nation EDC force. German troops would lose their identity in an integrated military establishment to which France, Italy, Belgium, the Netherlands, and Luxemburg would also contribute.

Great Britain, seeing a further dilution of sovereignty in the scheme for an international army, flatly refused to join in EDC, but the United States, which would presumably arm and command the new force, enthusiastically seconded the French proposal. Coming on the heels of the Schuman Plan for a coal-steel pool by the same six nations, it seemed to foreshadow a federation of Western Europe. Better still, it offered promise of recreating on a small scale, outside the framework of the UN, the international police force which the Russians had blocked in the world organization. Finally, it fanned the dying embers of American faith in organization diplomacy under United States leadership.

The dangers latent in EDC ought to have been more apparent in America. If the members of NATO showed a disinclination to contribute soldiers to an organization that would preserve the identity of national units, they were likely to move still more slowly in building an international army. Furthermore, the only reliable way of strengthening the incentive of Western European states to defend themselves against Russia was by holding out to them that their sovereignty would be preserved. The long-range prospect of membership in a federation hostile to the national interests of individual states was hardly more appealing than the Russian brand of internationalism. Rightly or wrongly, most Europeans outside the Iron Curtain did not consider the choice between Washington and Moscow as obvious or as inevitable as it appeared to Americans. They would have preferred to make no choice at all, but to pursue the goal of separate existence and national interests — hence their lack of enthusiasm for EDC or any scheme which promised to be merely a prelude to the extinction of sovereignty.

The initial enthusiasm of the Americans for EDC was echoed in West Germany. Konrad Adenauer, the Chancellor of the Bonn government, like Stresemann a quarter of a century earlier, would have agreed to almost anything to end occupation of the Reich and restrictions on German sovereignty. Consequently the United States, Great Britain, and France signed a peace "contract" with West Germany at Bonn on May 26, 1952. It could hardly be called a settlement, since Germany was still divided, Russia was as averse as ever to an all-German treaty on western terms, and the Allies were pledged not to negotiate a separate peace. The agreement, however, had the effect of a treaty. Contingent upon ratification, West Germany regained virtual sovereignty. The next day at Paris, a representative of the Adenauer government signed the EDC agreement along with representatives of the other five participating members.

Shortly thereafter West Germany ratified the peace contract and the EDC agreement. On July 1, 1952, the United States Senate also approved both treaties. The French, who had initiated the EDC plan, promptly developed misgivings. Fear of an armed Germany revived on such a scale that it threatened to overshadow preoccupation with Moscow. Even those reconciled to German rearmament disliked the proposed internationalization of the armed forces. This mood of irresolution was strengthened by the outspoken opposition of de Gaullists and of Communists who hated EDC for different reasons. Both the war in Indo-China and the anticolonial movement in North Africa added to the divisive influences in the country. As a result, successive French governments professed loyalty to EDC but refused to risk a ratification vote on it in the Chamber of Deputies. This stalling continued for two years.

Meanwhile opposition also revived in West Germany, where the Parliament had already approved EDC. The unpleasant experience of the Germans during World War II was sufficient to account for much of their revulsion against militarism. Furthermore, they had even less incentive than the French to fight for Western Europe. Their primary objective was reunification of Germany, and a close tie-up with the western powers seemed likely to postpone rather than hasten achievement of that goal. Confronted with the alternatives of a shotgun wedding to the American or the Russian bloc, they would doubtless have preferred the former. But they were heartily sick of both and in no case cared to be the battleground of the rival coalitions. As the agitation against EDC mounted in France, the four-party alliance that kept the pro-Western government of Dr. Adenauer in power grew more unstable.

EISENHOWER CONTINUES CONTAINMENT

Amidst evidence that the deadlock would grow worse, the chief antagonists changed leaders. General Eisenhower replaced Truman as President of the United States on January 20, 1953. Two months later Joseph Stalin died and a quadrumvirate headed by Georgi Malenkov took his place. Neither change foreshadowed any drastic reorientation of policy in Europe. The new regime in Russia spoke less vituperatively about the non-Communist world, partly because the habitual rudeness of Soviet diplomats during the Stalin era had needlessly alienated neutral states and partly because it sought a relaxation of containment pressures that would permit internal consolidation of power. There was no relaxation of the drive to prevent rearmament of West Germany or integration of the North Atlantic alliance system.

At the outset the Eisenhower administration appeared to be more aggressive than its predecessor. Both the new President and his Secretary of State, John Foster Dulles, indicated that America would resume the diplomatic offensive and make a concerted effort to free the satellite peoples behind the Iron Curtain. What the so-called "new look" in foreign policy turned out to be was an intensification of American ideological activity. It fell short of provocative appeals for revolt by the satellites. In fact, when the East Germans rioted momentarily against their oppressors in June 1953, the United States offered no tangible gestures of support. Her aloofness during this abortive uprising underscored the impossibility of effective intervention behind the Curtain short of war, and Eisenhower was no more willing than Truman to take such risks. In the end, American policy settled down in the well-worn grooves of containment.

The more vigorous tone of the administration frightened and annoyed the lukewarm allies of America in Western Europe. A substantial cutback of appropriations for conventional military weapons was accompanied by a veiled threat that aggression would be met by "instant" and "massive retaliation" — presumably with nuclear weapons. The language was clear enough to disturb the North Atlantic states. It seemed to imply that America would oblige them with a "radioactive" rescue in the event of a Russian invasion.

Secretary of State Dulles also struck a vaguely coercive note in his effort to prod the dilatory French into ratifying EDC. He warned them that further delay would necessitate an "agonizing reappraisal" of American foreign policy. Pressure eventually caused the government of Pierre Mendès-France to bring EDC up for ratification on August 30, 1954 — nearly twenty-seven months after it had first been proposed. The Chamber of Deputies promptly jettisoned it by a vote of 319 to 264, with ninety-five Communists casting the decisive ballot. Mendès-France, who was no friend of EDC, indicated that he would support a multilateral alliance including West Germany, provided Great Britain agreed to maintain troops in Europe. Under heavy pressure from the United States, Britain made the necessary commitment. Accordingly a fifteen-power conference, which included fourteen NATO states plus West Germany, negotiated a new series of agreements on October 23, 1954. The principle of a Western European defense structure based on national contingents was re-established. The Bonn Republic was admitted to the new organization and authorized to contribute twelve divisions, although the French forced the inclusion of certain restrictions on German military power. Ratification followed promptly in all countries, including France. Nevertheless the creation of the new army proceeded at a snail's pace. The German Parliament showed marked reluctance to authorize the necessary conscription legislation and favorable action was not taken until the fall of 1955. At that date a Western European army capable of stopping Russia seemed as far away as it had in 1950.

THE SUMMIT MEETING

As the years of cold-war tension in Western Europe continued, Winston Churchill, who had returned to power after a Conservative victory in 1951, repeatedly advocated a meeting of the Big Four. Neither the United States nor Russia responded to the idea with particular warmth until 1955, when Soviet leaders perceptibly toned down their denunciations of American policy. Their new line was characterized by more objective treatment of world news in Russian newspapers, professed willingness to lower the barriers against tourist travel in the Soviet Union, and expressions of interest in exchanging agricultural and cultural representatives with America. The tentative extension of olive branches culminated in a sudden statement of desire to resume negotiations on the long-deadlocked Austrian treaty. Prompt concessions verified Soviet good faith and led to termination of the four-power occupation and to the restoration of Austrian sovereignty in the spring of 1955. Despite subsequent negotiation of military alliances with her Eastern European satellites in retaliation for French ratification of the new NATO treaty, Russia had convinced the United States that negotiations on other questions would be worth while.

Accordingly preparations were made for a Big Four meeting at Geneva on July 18, 1955, with the understanding that the agenda would not be limited in any way. The mutual desire of the United States and Russia to sustain a conciliatory atmosphere precluded the former from bringing up the question of the satellite countries, and the latter the question of admitting Red China to UN. Not a single chief of state who had attended the Potsdam meeting in 1946 was on hand for the summit meeting at Geneva. Except for President Eisenhower, the conferees were new stars in the diplomatic firmament. Anthony Eden represented Great Britain; Edgar Fauré sat for France; and Nikolai Bulganin was the official spokesman of the Soviet Union, although Nikita Khrushchev, the First Secretary of the Communist party, masterminded Russian strategy from behind the scenes.

The unexpected amiability of the Russians made more news than the transactions of the conference. They drove to their headquarters in an open car, gave generous interviews to the press, posed patiently for innumerable photographs, and exuded good will from every pore. The discussions lasted five days and canvassed such subjects as German reunification, European security, and disarmament. Disagreements were frequent but both sides expressed themselves with restraint. Eisenhower created the most excitement when he offered to permit aerial inspection of the United States by Russian planes if the Soviet Union would reciprocate. Conceding that his proposal would not solve the problem of disarmament, the President represented it as a desirable first step in the relaxation of tension and suspicion. Bulganin did not reply immediately but allowed the plan to die a slow death by raising polite objections in a subsequent exchange of letters. Many observers attributed Russian apathy to the belief that the Soviet Union would yield more vital information than she would gain by such an exchange. Although no outstanding problems were solved at Geneva, the Big Four established a favorable atmosphere for further negotiations. Before the conference adjourned, they agreed to hold another meeting of Foreign Ministers at Geneva in November. During the interval Chancellor Adenauer, who had rejected an invitation to Moscow before the Big Four Conference, visited the Russian capital. He reluctantly agreed to the establishment of formal diplomatic relations in return for a promise that German prisoners still held by the Soviet Union would be released.

When the Foreign Ministers assembled in October 1955, the spirit of Geneva had begun to wear a little thin. It quickly became apparent that the United States and Russia were as far from agreement on the German question as ever. Both advocated reunification of the Reich but neither would permit it on a basis favorable to the other. The United States proposed popular elections to choose an all-German government; the Russians rejected this because of inability to control the outcome. Their counterproposal for the creation of a provisional government representing all elements was equally unacceptable to an America mindful of the way Stalin had manipulated the provisional government in Poland. Deadlock on Germany inevitably led to deadlock on the related question of European security. Disarmament was scarcely discussed, and Molotov summarily dismissed the proposals of Dulles for a raising of the Iron Curtain. The latter squared accounts by ignoring the Russian plea for the revival of east-west trade in strategic materials. When the conference adjourned on November 16, 1955, it was clear that the cold war would continue unabated despite the novel and refreshing politeness of the antagonists.

RUSSIAN REVERSALS IN 1956

Matters took an unfavorable turn for Russia during the summer and fall of 1956 when serious unrest developed in the satellite states of Eastern Europe. On February 14, 1956, Khrushchev unintentionally stirred up dissatisfaction by denouncing the ruthless methods of his predecessor, Stalin, and by showing favor to hitherto discredited Communist nationalists in Iron Curtain countries. This policy was encouraged by Marshal Tito, who persuaded the Kremlin to approve in principle the autonomy of local Communist parties. A week later Polish workers greeted the news of relaxed control by rioting against depressed living conditions and the presence of Soviet troops. This uprising was the prelude to mass disturbances which lasted from October 19 to October 23 and ended in the installation of a new Polish Politburo headed by an avowed Titoist, Wladyslaw Gomulka. The emergence of Gomulka seemed to foreshadow a greater measure of Polish independence from Moscow, but Soviet leaders coupled their concessions with prompt measures to prevent Poland from regaining her sovereignty. They poured Russian troops into East Germany to cut Poland off from outside help and strengthened occupation armies already stationed inside the country.

Simultaneously Hungary rebelled aganist Soviet rule with greater violence. Student riots in Budapest on October 20 and 21 caused Moscow to replace the unpopular Erno Gerö with the more nationalistic Imre Nagy. Far from quieting the restless Hungarians, this concession led to demands for the withdrawal of Soviet troops and the establishment of a neutralist foreign policy. Encouraged by the defection of Russian-trained Hungarian army units, a mass uprising of workers and peasants took place. Bewildered occupation forces withdrew from Budapest on October 30 and for a moment it looked as if Hungary might actually recover her independence. Indecision ended in the Kremlin on November 4, and Russian troops attacked Budapest. It took nearly three months to stamp out the last embers of revolt. In mid-November, Imre Nagy, who had joined forces with the revolutionaries, sought sanctuary in the Yugoslav embassy and was abducted when he tried to leave it. A new Soviet puppet, Janos Kadar, replaced him. As the hopes of independence faded, thousands of Hungarians fled across the western border to Austria. They were housed temporarily in refugee camps while the states of the free world wrestled with the problem of finding them new homes.

By using force to crush the Hungarians, Khrushchev and Bulganin virtually nullified the effect of their two-year drive to convince the world that they were a couple of harmless Santa Clauses. All over the world neutralists expressed dismay over Russia's behavior, while in Western Europe many disillusioned intellectuals gave up their membership in Communist parties. Although the sequel to the Hungarian episode indicated that the new generation of outraged neutralists would also have short memories, the spectacular outbursts of discontent behind the Iron Curtain in 1956 exposed the shaky foundations of Soviet Russia's empire in Europe. Whether this demonstration of weakness would cause the masters of the Kremlin to pursue a less adventuresome foreign policy remained to be seen.

CONTAINMENT IN THE MIDDLE EAST

Although American aid to Greece and Turkey in 1947 and the subsequent inclusion of both countries in NATO blocked direct Russian penetration of the Mediterranean, the expanding Soviet state threatened to reach its goal by an end run through the Middle East. Stretching from Iran to Egypt across the seat of some of the world's oldest civilizations, the Middle East was an unusually chaotic vacuum area. Formerly under the domination of Great Britain and France, it had been virtually cut loose to fend for itself as a result of the reverses suffered by those states in other areas during World War II. After VJ Day the British still clung to isolated strong points such as the Suez Canal, and struggled to preserve their commercial interests in oil-rich Iran and Arabia. Their weakness stimulated a nationalistic fever that was to infect the entire Arab world. Compounded of resentment against marginal living standards and interference by outside powers, nationalism assured a responsiveness in the Middle East to the kind of agitation at which Russia specialized.

Despite the fact that the British seemed to suffer the greatest immediate loss from Russian intervention, the United States had an important stake in the area. Aside from her considerable oil concessions in the Arabian peninsula and the Persian gulf, she dared not allow the Russians either the strategic or the economic fruits of domination in the Middle East. Immediately after World War II she had considerable prestige among the Arab peoples as a friend of independence, and she also enjoyed the good will of rulers who had become prosperous from the royalties on American oil concessions. She threw away these advantages, however, and at the same time seriously weakened the position of the British when she identified herself with the aspirations of the Jews for a national home in Palestine.

Jewish agitation for the fulfillment of this ancient dream had the enthusiastic support of a well-organized Zionist movement in the United States. The Jews undoubtedly deserved well of the world, for they had suffered frightfully at the hands of the Nazis and had been cruelly uprooted from homes elsewhere in Europe. Several states offered to absorb substantial numbers of them after the war. This solution would have pleased the Arabs, who currently outnumbered the Jews approximately two to one in Palestine and had resided there for over a thousand years.

The British emerged from the war with primary responsibility for Palestine based on an old League of Nations mandate. On the other hand, they knew that it would be fatal to their waning influence to offend the Arabs. This calculation led them to resist Zionist pressure and to turn back several boatloads of refugees in 1945 and 1946. Repercussions were evident at once in America. Governer Dewey of New York, who was seeking re-election, urged the British to admit 100,000 Jews. Truman, promptly echoing this plea, made the issue a matter of United States policy.

The irritated and weakened British sought to sidestep the impending crisis by transferring their responsibility to the UN in April 1947. Under pressure from the United States, the Security Council recommended the partition of Palestine. Russia promptly supported the scheme, recognizing the limitless opportunities that it provided for spreading dissension in the Middle East. The Arab states refused to be cowed by the unexpected agreement of Russia and the United States. They rejected the partition but reluctantly accepted a temporary UN trusteeship which permitted refugee Jews and armaments to trickle into Palestine. The trusteeship policy was pursued with the connivance of the United States, which sought to create favorable conditions for the emergence of a Jewish state without provoking the wrath of the Arabs. This tortuous diplomacy looked like a retreat from the policy of partition and subjected Truman to ungracious charges at home that he had capitulated to sinister oil interests. Such impatience proved premature. By the spring of 1948 the Jews had received enough financial contributions and manpower from abroad to risk the formation of an independent Israel. They announced their intention to the world on May 14, 1948, and the United States recognized the new state the same day.

The poorly equipped armies of the Arab states promptly converged on Israel but were thrown back by the small but better trained Jewish forces. A stream of Arab refugees who had left businesses and homes in Palestine accompanied the retreating armies. Eventually UN mediation slowed down the fighting and established the *de facto* partition of Palestine which the United States had sought in the first place.

THE SUEZ CRISIS

The debut of the new nation aggravated the instability of the Middle East. Egypt, Jordan, and Syria especially remained unreconciled to the existence of Israel. For a time the attention of the Egyptians was concentrated on forcing the British to withdraw from the Suez Canal zone. The Churchill government capitulated in 1954 after considerable prodding from the United States. Meanwhile a group of army officers headed by General Mohammed Naguib had ousted the incompetent King Farouk and had begun to reorganize the Egyptian military establishment. Naguib was in turn overthrown in the spring of 1954 by Colonel Abdul Gamel Nasser, who quickly stepped up the undeclared war with the Jews along a section of the border known as the Gaza Strip. He was unsuccessful in his request for arms from Great Britain and the United States but found Russia willing to furnish them through her satellite, Czechoslovakia. Shipments began in the fall of 1955, much to the dismay of the western powers, who accused Russia of violating "the spirit of Geneva."

Whether this aid foreshadowed closer ties between Russia and Egypt was not clear until nine months later when the whole situation deteriorated very rapidly. The incident that touched off the explosion was an Anglo-American announcement on July 19 that both powers had withdrawn an earlier offer to help Egypt finance a huge dam at Aswan on the Nile. This decision reflected their annoyance at the pro-Soviet trend of Nasser's policy and his eagerness to mortgage the economic future of Egypt in order to pay for Communist arms. Nasser retaliated a week later by nationalizing the Suez Canal which would otherwise have remained in the hands of the internationally owned Suez Company until its charter expired in 1968.

The reaction to the seizure of the canal was more violent in London and Paris than in Washington. Already resentful of Nasser for his ill-concealed efforts to foment rebellion in their African colonies, the British and French recoiled at the prospect of a hostile Egypt astride the vital artery upon which they depended for shipments of oil. They immediately demanded some form of internationalization of the waterway that would modify Egyptian control. America associated herself with these proposals but balked at the use of force on the ground that it might push Egypt and perhaps the entire Arab world into the Russian camp. Her restraining influence resulted in a series of conversations between the western powers and Egypt which dragged on from mid-August until the end of October. After it had become apparent that Nasser would concede nothing, the British and French resorted to arms. Israel provided an excuse for military operations on October 29 when she crossed the frontier and made a thrust toward Suez. The next day the western powers issued an ultimatum to Tel Aviv and Cairo, proclaiming their intention of reoccupying the canal zone unless hostilities ceased within twelve hours. As expected, neither Israel nor Egypt complied and thereupon the British launched from Cyprus a series of air raids on military installations around Cairo. Allied troop landings followed on November 5 and 6. Port Said, at the northern end of Suez, capitulated without a struggle and the invasion army began to move slowly along the waterway. Meanwhile, during the same week the Israelis successfully occupied the Gaza Strip and overran the Sinai peninsula to the Gulf of Aqaba. Soviet military equipment was of little use to the untrained Egyptians.

The outcome of the war was not decided by the participants. The United States, which had not been consulted by her allies in advance of the invasion, tried vainly to discourage them from continuing operations. Emboldened by the aloofness of America, the Soviet Union threatened to use guided missiles and at the same time stepped up deliveries of military equipment to the pro-Soviet government of Syria and offered to send volunteers to help Nasser.

In the face of these menacing gestures, Great Britain and France announced that a cease-fire was in effect on November 7, and Israel followed suit two days later. Simultaneously the United States sponsored a proposal for the dispatch of a UN emergency force to Egypt with the dual objective of forestalling Russian intervention and paving the way for the withdrawal of the British and the French. The first units landed on November 15. Russia dropped her campaign for volunteers the same day after a sharp warning from Eisenhower. Sustained American diplomatic pressure on the British and French led them to accept a face-saving formula whereby UN units would replace their troops in the canal zone pending a permanent settlement. The withdrawal started on December 16 and was completed on December 22.

The United States experienced more trouble in persuading Israel to end its occupation of Egyptian territory in the Sinai peninsula, the Gaza Strip, and the Gulf of Aqaba. What Tell Aviv hoped to exact as the price of withdrawal was an Egyptian pledge to permit the passage of Israeli ships through the Suez Canal and the Gulf of Aqaba. Nasser not only resisted concessions but made the reopening of the canal contingent on the evacuation of Egypt by Israeli troops. Inasmuch as the primitive economy of the Nile Valley had suffered less from the loss of canal tolls than had Western Europe from the loss of oil shipments, America redoubled her efforts to pry the stubborn Israeli out of Gaza and the Gulf of Aqaba in February 1957. Fearful of UN economic sanctions and the suspension of various American aid projects, Israel withdrew completely in mid-March. In return Nasser permitted UN salvage crews to speed up their removal of wreckage from the canal so that it was reopened on April 7, 1957.

Throughout the crisis the United States had acted as an honest broker, refusing to take sides despite the defiant behavior of Nasser, the Anglo-French assumption of automatic American support, the saber-rattling of Russia, and the agitation of Zionist groups in America. Unfortunately, Washington could not restore the situation which had existed before the attack on Egypt. Russia had penetrated the Middle East and found willing collaborators in the Egyptians and Syrians despite Anglo-American efforts to build a barrier against her.

IRAN

The Middle East containment policy had been undertaken in 1953 to free Iran from the threat of Russian domination. Tension in that country had become acute two years earlier when Prime Minister Mossadegh confiscated the property of the Anglo-Iranian Oil Company. Lacking technicians to operate the refinery at Abadan and the tankers to haul the oil, Mossadegh nonetheless refused all compromise formulas for partial reimbursement of the British. American attempts, prompted by the fear that loss of oil revenue would bankrupt the Iranian government and lead to Communist control, only irritated both parties. The sudden ouster of Mossadegh by General Zahadi in 1953 brought prompt offers of American financial aid to Iran and paved the way for an Anglo-Iranian agreement that opened the refineries a year later.

American containment diplomacy, which had produced a mutual defense pact with Pakistan in May, 1954, aimed at a regional agreement including Iran and Iraq. Egypt, Syria, and Saudi Arabia were as bitterly opposed to the scheme as Russia. They feared that such a program would protect Israel from Arab retaliation and perpetuate domination of the Middle East by the western powers. However, the prospect of an adverse reaction from Israel's immediate neighbors did not modify America's determination to build a Middle Eastern Treaty Organization (METO). For tactical reasons she stayed in the background while Great Britain organized the northern tier of Middle Eastern states. Encouraged by fresh grants of American aid, Iraq and Iran signed a treaty with Great Britain, Turkey, and Pakistan in mid-1955. Known as the Bagdad Pact, the new multilateral treaty envisaged a regional METO like NATO in Europe. As has already been noted, Russia circumvented the barrier by making an arms agreement with Egypt. Shortly thereafter, Syria, Saudi Arabia, and Egypt formed a new Middle Eastern bloc.

During the ensuing Suez crisis, America moved gradually to a policy of outright participation in the Bagdad Pact. Eisenhower warned Russia that the United States would not tolerate an attack on Iran, Iraq, or Turkey. He followed up this statement on January 5, 1957 by asking Congress to authorize a Middle Eastern program of "military assistance and cooperation with any nation or group of nations which desires such aid." He also requested an appropriation of $200 million for immediate use in the Middle East. Congress granted the necessary authorization on March 9 and a few day later the United States formally entered METO. Thus by the spring of 1957 she was committed to a full-fledged containment policy in the Middle East. With Syria and Egypt linked diplomatically to Russia, and all the Arab states hostile to Israel, the settlement of the Suez crises seemed like an interlude before a new storm.

CONTAINMENT IN THE FAR EAST

Nerve-racking and frustrating though it was, the policy of the United States prevented a major break-through by Russia in Europe and the Middle East from 1947 to 1956. In the Orient, containment did not work nearly so well because after 1949 the two resident powers, Russia and China, functioned as allies, systematically probing soft spots all the way from Tibet to Korea. Whether the United States could have devised a policy to forestall such cooperation is a matter of varied opinion. Preoccupied by the menace of Japan, America had failed to recognize the spectacular revival of Chinese power which enabled the Nationalist regime to resist the Japanese almost single-handed from 1931 to 1941 despite the distraction of civil war with Communists. The contrast between the performance of China during the Boxer Rebellion and that in the decade of the thirties was impressive. The continuous fighting and concomitant economic disorganization had put her under a severe strain which World War II intensified. Nevertheless she managed to hang on until VJ Day, when not only Japanese but British and French power in the Far East had crumbled. As a result, she emerged from the fifteen-year ordeal with the fires of nationalism blazing, notwithstanding her internal weakness.

Under the circumstances China could not be expected to accept her old role as a junior partner of the United States. Irrespective of what regime wielded power in Peiping, the articulate groups, humiliated by two decades of appalling reverses, lonely resistance, and frustrating coalition warfare, were determined to revive the strength of China. With all the old enemies except the Russians humbled, they sought nothing less than the restoration of the peripheral areas of the empire detached by the colonial powers in the century after 1840. In this enterprise they could count on the enthusiastic moral support of the millions of Chinese scattered throughout southeastern Asia in Indonesia, Singapore, Indo-China, and Burma. It seems safe to assume that had Chiang Kai-shek been able to survive, his regime would have terminated its dependence on the United States at the earliest practicable moment, as his sporadic defiance of American advisers indicated. He never got firmly enough in the saddle after the war to disillusion the Americans as the Russians had done. Instead his mass following melted away, transferring its support to a regime that was stronger, more efficient, militantly nationalistic, and not identified with the agonies of the preceding twenty years.

When the Americans held their post-mortems on China policy during the crucial years from 1945 to 1950, they blamed the deterioration of their position exclusively on the Communist regime. The rise of the Communists to power undoubtedly hastened the process, but the United States was headed for trouble in the Far East in any event. Her wartime policy had assured the emergence of a China with far greater potential strength than Japan could ever have hoped to muster. Once America had made this decision, the balancing of China against Russia was the only method capable of producing stability. The device seemed all the more feasible since a centuries-old clash of Chinese and Russian interests had characterized Far Eastern power politics. However, such a policy would have involved treating China as an independent state and making it worth her while to avoid a Russian alliance. Instead, America recognized neither the desirability of creating a balance nor the changed power position of China; she drifted into a policy which encouraged the Sino-Russian alliance. This disastrous decision was followed by the most disheartening experience in containment anywhere on the globe. With the only two major powers in eastern Asia united in probing the vacuum areas from which the Japanese, British, French, and Dutch were withdrawing, America was destined to experience a series of reversals. Short of a major war which she refused to risk or the establishment of a balance of power which she refused to consider, there was no method for terminating the frustrations of containment.

AMERICA WITHDRAWS SUPPORT FROM CHIANG KAI-SHEK

The drama of postwar developments in China unfolded against a backdrop of increasing uncertainty in Washington as to whether it should support the Nationalist government of Chiang Kai-shek or keep hands off the internal situation. Even before VJ Day, reports from General Albert C. Wedemeyer, who had replaced Joseph W. Stilwell as commander of the American forces in China, and other reports from Ambassador Patrick Hurley, indicated the probability that withdrawal of American support would pave the way for a Chinese Communist government. This prospect dismayed the General and the Ambassador far more than it did the State Department. It is unlikely that there were any Far Eastern experts in the State Departments who were card-carrying Communists, but as a group they sympathized with the Chinese Reds. The latter had established themselves at Yenan in the northwest corner of China in 1935 and had beaten off repeated efforts of Chiang Kai-shek to dislodge them. Part of the State Department enthusiasm for the Communists reflected its New Deal orientation and took the form of assertions that Mao Tse-tung, the head of the Yenan regime, was an agrarian reformer rather than a Communist. This impression had been strengthened by the reports of newspapermen who accompanied Henry Wallace to Yenan in 1944, when he unsuccessfully urged on Chiang and Mao a common front against the Japanese. Even the American military mission was impressed by the orderly, efficient way the Communists governed their villages. Contrasted with the monstrous disorder and corruption of the Nationalist regime, the miniature Communist state of the northwest looked good.

Aside from these quasi-ideological considerations, the Far Eastern experts were annoyed with Chiang because he tried to act like the head of a sovereign state. He frequently ignored American advice, seemed insufficiently grateful for aid, and actually complained privately about Roosevelt's restoration of Russian concessions in Manchuria. Unfortunately such matters as agrarian reform and the stubbornness of Chiang affected the discussion of China policy more than the crucial demands of international politics and the issue of which regime the Chinese people were likely to support. If the United States ignored the former and made a bad guess on the latter question, she faced serious consequences.

A month before his death, Roosevelt attempted to clarify American policy in China with a compromise formula. The United States would continue to support Chiang Kai-shek but also would apply simultaneous pressure on both the Nationalists and the Communists to suspend their civil war and form a coalition government. When Truman became President in April 1945, he followed this general policy. Immediately after VJ Day, American Army Air Force units moved three Chinese Nationalist armies from the interior to the coastal cities. Part of the Pacific fleet transported an additional 400,000 troops under Chiang Kai-shek's command to various Manchurian ports. In such key cities as Tientsin and Peiping, American marines served as armies of occupation until National units could take over. The prompt action of the Truman administration forestalled the possibility of Communist troops taking control in areas where the Japanese were surrendering. As early as November 1945, General Wedemeyer reported to Washington that the government of Chiang was not firmly seated, and proposed an energetic effort to prop it up.

Presidential advisers recoiled from a choice between large-scale intervention in behalf of the corrupt Nationalist regime and a complete withdrawal which would probably assure a Communist victory. Runaway inflation, unemployment, food shortages, and the widespread apathy of the Chinese masses to Chiang reduced the incentive to save him. General Wedemeyer's prediction that generous aid to the Generalissimo would improve the morale of his government and release a burst of reforming zeal was generally discounted. Even those who believed Wedemeyer, disliked the prospect of undertaking such an expensive long-range program. They reinforced their doubts by forecasting fierce political repercussions if the administration committed the American people to fresh economic and military intervention so soon after a victorious war.

Unwilling to help Chiang Kai-shek effectively and lacking the frankness to recognize Mao openly, the administration drifted. It sent General Marshall to China in December 1945 with instructions to press for a truce and some sort of coalition government representing both the Kuomintang and the Communist parties. Since General Wedemeyer and other observers agreed that procrastination would favor the Communists, truce negotiations seemed certain to strengthen the position of Mao whether he joined a coalition or not. Thus the dispatch of the Marshall mediation mission was Washington's way of saying that it would accept a Communist regime in China but would not take responsibility for bringing Mao to power. The adoption of this policy assured the triumph of the Chinese Reds without giving them any reason to be grateful to the United States. Worse still, it encouraged the intervention of the Russians, who had hitherto done little for Mao because of their conviction that the United States would keep Chiang in power. Once Truman adopted the mediation policy, the Soviet Union stepped up its aid to the hitherto ignored comrades south of the Amur River. Red army units occupying Manchuria turned over vast quantities of captured Japanese weapons to local Communists, who promptly smuggled them to party members farther south. Before they withdrew in the spring of 1946, the Russians had stripped Manchuria of nearly $2 billion worth of industrial equipment and had left flourishing Communist organizations behind. The arming of Chinese Reds was also simplified by the corrupt officials of Chiang's government who sold them American weapons. This procedure was so thoroughly systematized in the later years of the civil war that United States might as well have armed Mao directly.

Meanwhile, General Marshall spent a futile year trying to bring the Communists and the Kuomintang together. Both sides grudgingly agreed to a temporary cease-fire, but neither would grant the concessions necessary for a joint administration. During the negotiations the economy continued to deteriorate, and the Communists capitalized on the rising tide of popular dissatisfaction. Marshall returned to Washington in January 1947 after condemning both groups and declaring that the salvation of China lay with a liberal group within the Kuomintang. Unfortunately, this element possessed neither organized support nor the prospect of getting any.

The United States withdrew all her military forces from China, except a small marine contingent, as Chiang and Mao prepared to resume the civil war. On paper the Nationalists possessed an overwhelming superiority in manpower and equipment, including surplus weapons and Lend-Lease supplies made available by the United States in 1945–46. However, their strength literally melted away in the summer and fall of 1947. Corruption, defeatism, and banditry turned the countryside against them, while inflation and poor distribution of food alienated the urban population. Communist guerrillas sprang up everywhere, spreading confusion behind the lines. General Wedemeyer, sent back to China in July 1947 for an estimate of the military situation, again urged a policy of all-out aid to Chiang Kai-shek. The President did nothing except secure a $400 million appropriation for the Nationalists from Congress in April 1948. This gesture prolonged the agony of Chiang and annoyed the Communists. Mukden fell to the Red armies in October of 1948. The Nationalists vowed that they would make a determined stand south of the Yangstze River, but their armies fell apart before they could be defeated. Chiang was forced out of office in January 1949 by the desperate Kuomintang politicians, who sought to open negotiations with Mao. The Communists pushed relentlessly southward, overrunning Hankow, Shanghai, and Canton in late spring. The remnants of the Nationalist government followed Chiang to Chungking, from where they were flown to Formosa in December 1949.

RED CHINA

The victorious Reds established a People's Republic of China at Peiping, proclaimed their solidarity with Soviet Russia, launched a ruthless purge of their foes, and made preparations for driving out foreigners and confiscating their property. As the campaign broadened, it blossomed into a frenzied nationalistic crusade against western influences. The avowedly anti-American tone of the new regime gave Washington something to think about. The transfer of 475 million Chinese from the status of lukewarm and occasionally resentful allies to defiant foes could hardly be hailed as a victory for American diplomacy. The best that could be done was to try to represent it as a matter of indifference. A State Department White Paper issued on August 5, 1949, undertook this dialectical exercise. It absolved the United States of all responsibility for the collapse of Nationalist China, implied that a farsighted diplomatic service had anticipated this denouement, and even undertook to congratulate the administration for refusing to waste money on a lost cause. According to a Gallup Poll in May 1949, a substantial majority of Americans had favored the curtailment of aid to China and hence presumably approved of the sentiments expressed in the White Paper.

Public complacency ran thus high because the American public naively overlooked the unpleasant fact that drastic shifts in the balance of power have far-reaching consequences. In this particular case, the result was going to be a series of Russian-Chinese excursions into the vacuum areas of eastern Asia. The new allies formalized their partnership in a thirty-year mutual aid pact signed in Moscow on February 14, 1950. Each signatory pledged itself to aid the other in the event of attack by Japan and her allies. This alliance was the prelude to the Korean War which exploded on June 25, 1950, and shattered the American illusion that the loss of China had changed nothing in the Orient.

While the Chinese and Russians plotted fresh moves in the fall of 1949, the United States groped her way toward a new policy. If she had considered recognizing the Communist regime in Peiping, the rough treatment meted out to missionaries and American citizens dissuaded her. Peiping's consistently bellicose behavior stiffened United States resistance to the admission of Red China to the UN. Except for occasional verbal chastisements of the Peiping government, the Truman administration took a defensive position in eastern Asia. On January 5, 1950, the President, reiterating his hands-off policy in the Formosa Strait, indicated that the United States would not interfere with any attempt by Red China to take Nationalist-held Formosa. A week later Secretary of State Dean Acheson was still more specific. He announced that the United States would defend a perimeter that ran through the Aleutians, Japan, the Ryukyus, and the Philippines. Incautiously he went on to deny the responsibility of America for protecting Korea, Formosa, and southeastern Asia from military attack. This repudiation of obligations in the vacuum area would have been dangerous enough if China and Russia functioned as counterweights in a simple balance; it was an invitation to aggression after the formation of the Sino-Russian alliance.

Administration policy came under increasing Republican criticism in the fall of 1949. A senatorial bloc headed by Taft of Ohio, Wherry of Nebraska, McCarthy of Wisconsin, and Knowland of California repeatedly assailed Truman for selling out China to the Communists. After Acheson declared Korea and Formosa to be outside the American defense perimeter, their indignation boiled over in charges that a clique of Communists dominated the State Department. This attack would have been of more practical value two years earlier when Chiang Kai-shek still held a strong position on the mainland. As it was, the Republicans waited until the prospects of the

Generalissimo had deteriorated hopelessly and then demanded that the United States provide aid for the Formosa government. Under the circumstances nothing short of a full-scale war would have sufficed to oust the Communist regime, and the Republican leaders were no more prepared than Truman was to commit American armies. Taft talked wildly about freeing Chiang's army on Formosa for an invasion of the mainland, but it was hard to resist the conclusion that it would not have fled to Formosa in the first place if it had been capable of successful operations in China.

All that the Republicans accomplished by their belated agitation was to create public pressure for driblets of aid to the Formosa regime under the foreign-relief program. This step irritated the Chinese Communists without materially improving the prospects of Chiang. It drove Mao closer to the Russians and thereby made the American position in the Orient less tenable than at any time since 1900.

THE KOREAN WAR

The congressional post-mortems on China policy were interrupted unexpectedly by the outbreak of hostilities in Korea. Since the turn of the century, Korea had been a victim of great-power rivalries. Granted nominal independence after the Sino-Japanese War in 1895, she was brought under the control of the Nipponese as a result of their victory over Russia a decade later. Incorporation in the Empire of the Rising Sun stimulated rather than subdued Korean nationalism. Roosevelt took cognizance of this sentiment at the Cairo conference in November 1943, and made a vague promise to establish an independent Korea after the war. When the Japanese armies on the mainland surrendered in August 1945, the Russians occupied North Korea and the Americans South Korea, with the 38th parallel as the dividing line between the zones. At the outset it was assumed that the arrangement would be a temporary one. Both the United States and Soviet Russia paid lip service to the principle of a unified, independent Korean state. Moreover, "38th parallel" had no significance except as an administrative device of the occupation authorities. It was neither an economic nor a geographical nor an ethnic boundary.

Unfortunately, as the Americans and Russians moved down divergent paths, the line separating the occupation zones gradually hardened into a permanent boundary. North of the 38th parallel, the Russians established the conventional puppet regime, sovietized Korean institutions, and trained an army. South of the 38th parallel, the Americans imposed democratic institutions on the native population and invested considerable funds in economic reconstruction. They paid less attention to the creation of an effective military force than the Russians did. As a consequence, the South Koreans were virtually defenseless when the American troops withdrew in 1949, although nominally they passed under the protection of the UN.

Despite the deadlock between the United States and the Soviet Union, nobody regarded partition as a permanent solution, least of all the Koreans. The division of the country restricted the normal exchange of goods between the industrial north and the agricultural south and thwarted the nationalist drive for unification. Although the presence of the occupying powers aggravated the differences between Koreans and nourished factionalism, these problems would doubtless have been solved on a nonideological basis if both the United States and Russia had withdrawn. Unfortunately, the removal of United States troops, followed by disclaimers of responsibility for continental East Asia, tipped the balance within the divided state strongly in favor of the heavily armed regime backed by Russia. The North Koreans needed little encouragement to send their armies across the 38th parallel, and the Russians ran few risks by egging them on. If the United States declined to intervene, Korea would be reunified on a Communist basis and pass into the orbit of Moscow. If the United States decided to rescue the South Koreans, she would be fighting far from home and on terrain which would neutralize her superiority in mechanized equipment. To the Kremlin the prospect of pinning down American strength in an unimportant area under such disadvantageous conditions must have seemed almost as attractive as the subversion of all Korea. The probable rearmament of a *status quo* America, which was not likely to start a general war, seemed unlikely to counterbalance these benefits. Obviously, each alternative involved some drawbacks, but the fruitful possibilities open to the Soviet Union far exceeded those available to the United States. Only in the remote event that Washington abandoned the frustrations of containment for a global war would a Korean adventure backfire on Russia. Such a reversal in American policy seemed so remote that the Kremlin was willing to take a calculated risk. If worst came to worst, the cynical Stalin could always disclaim responsibility for the North Koreans and abandon them to their fate.

The North Korean army surged across the 38th parallel on June 25, 1950. The same day an indignant United States rammed through the Security Council of the UN a resolution branding the invaders as aggressors, urging an immediate cease-fire, and calling upon members of the world organization to assist in the restoration of peace. This remarkable maneuver was made possible by the absence of the Soviet delegate. The latter had boycotted the Security Council since its refusal to replace the representative of Chiang with the representative of Mao and hence was not present to wield the expected veto. Friends of the UN regarded his absence as an act of Providence. Critics considered Russian indifference to UN intervention was a more probable explanation.

On no other postwar issue did such a discrepancy exist between what the policy makers said they were trying to do and what they did. From the outset, the administration proclaimed and perhaps believed that its conduct was vindicating the UN. Nevertheless its insistence on the identification of

UN with American objectives suggested the opposite conclusion. Like any league of sovereign states, it lacked the power to compel the obedience of members on issues contrary to their interests and hence it was doomed to be an instrument of power politics. This fact became painfully apparent on June 27, 1950, when the Security Council called upon UN members to provide military assistance to South Korea and only sixteen out of sixty responded favorably. The insubordination of Russia, her satellites, and a number of neutrals demolished the assumption that aggressive action would excite universal indignation and create a unanimity that would be fatal to alliance obligations. Still, the Americans ignored the obvious.

Truman commanded American air and naval forces to resist the North Koreans on the same day that the Security Council authorized military action. Three days later, the President ordered to Korea most of the unseasoned occupation army in Japan. Shortly thereafter the UN empowered Truman to appoint General Douglas MacArthur commander of the international army in Korea. Notwithstanding the President's insistence that American intervention was a United Nations police action rather than a war and did not need explicit congressional approval, the enterprise exhibited all the conventional characteristics of war. It also remained primarily an American affair. Except for South Korea, the United States furnished the largest number of soldiers. The contingents contributed by Great Britain, Turkey, Australia, and the Philippines gave an international flavor but were too small to affect the outcome. The United States likewise provided most of the air power, military equipment, and supplies. The dominant role of America in what was supposed to be a United Nations police action became more apparent as her objectives in Korea changed and as she imposed her new objectives on the world organization.

The initial goal of intervention was the expulsion of the North Koreans from territory south of the 38th parallel. Inasmuch as South Korea had become a responsibility of the UN after the withdrawal of American troops in 1949, this obligation seemed clear and legitimate. It required three months for the armies under the command of General MacArthur to repel the invaders. Initially, the North Koreans possessed an overwhelming advantage and by September 12, 1950, had pushed the ill-prepared American–South Korean divisions into the southeastern corner of the peninsula. Only the superiority of American air power kept the defenders from being driven out of Pusan, their last major port. Despite their inability to stem the offensive, the forces under MacArthur bought valuable time for a build-up of American strength. The entire complexion of the war changed on September 15 when he made an amphibious landing at Inchon behind the enemy lines. The North Koreans fled in panic to avoid complete encirclement and within two weeks had retreated behind the 38th parallel.

With the original objective achieved, most of the states that had supported collective action were anxious to call it quits. The United States took a different view. She assumed that the North Koreans would, if given a breathing spell, simply regroup and attack again. Both the State Department and the Joint Chiefs of Staff regarded the military situation as favorable enough to permit a rapid conquest of North Korea. The prospect of complete success encouraged Truman to draw the UN beyond its original objective of repelling aggression to sponsorship of Korean unification. Accordingly the United States wrenched from a reluctant Assembly an ambiguously worded authorization for MacArthur to cross the 38th parallel. Even if the United States refused to recognize what she was doing, the rest of the world knew that she had shifted her objective.

The ensuing invasion was undertaken on the assumption that neither Russia nor China would intervene. This proved costly. The Peiping regime had already been annoyed by Truman's order of June 27, 1950, instructing the American Navy to neutralize Formosa and to prevent either attacks on the island by Mao or attacks on the mainland by Chiang. Moreover, the Chinese Communists needed no encouragement from Russia other than the offer of armaments to interfere with the establishment of a hostile Korean state on their border. As early as September 30, 1950, the Chinese Premier Chou En-lai had issued a public warning that China would not tolerate the invasion of North Korea. Nevertheless MacArthur advanced rapidly, heedless of the potential threat on his flank. In late October, as the victorious American troops approached the Yalu River, which served as the boundary between China and North Korea, a swarm of Chinese "volunteers" drove a wedge into his overextended divisions. Within a month his panic-stricken armies were driven out of North Korea. Bitter cold and guerrilla activity behind the American lines complicated the task of regrouping the demoralized UN units. In January 1951, the lines were stabilized approximately on the 38th parallel.

The intervention of the Chinese caught both MacArthur and the administration flat-footed. Prominent Republicans who had supported the President in June, and had voted to authorize the use of American troops in the police action, became bitterly critical. One faction reacted by demanding that the United States withdraw from what they called "Mr. Truman's War." Another group, encouraged by MacArthur, took the opposite tack and demanded that America bomb the Chinese bases in Manchuria and unleash Chiang Kai-shek for attacks on the mainland. The Democrats were almost as badly divided as the Republicans and looked about for some exit which would do them the least political damage.

The administration followed a vacillating middle course. It was unwilling to pull out of Korea and admit defeat. It was equally unwilling to risk the possibility of war with Russia which might conceivably follow air raids on the industrial targets and supply lines of her Chinese ally. Almost by a process of elimination, Truman settled on the policy of continuing the limited undeclared warfare against the North Koreans and the Chinese. The ultimate objective now shifted from the unification of Korea to the chastisement of the Chinese for unwarranted aggression. The new policy was heralded in February 1951 by an American-sponsored resolution branding Red China as aggressor, which cleared the UN Assembly by a vote of 44 to 7.

General MacArthur reacted adversely to the new program for Korea. He saw no possibility of proving to the Chinese or anybody else that "aggression does not pay" as long as the Peiping regime could supply the North Koreans without fear of retaliation. His opinions became so outspoken that Truman summarily removed him from all his commands on April 11, 1951. The dismissal of a popular military hero revived the slumbering controversy on Korean policy. The General received a rapturous welcome from his countrymen after his return to the United States. In a series of public pronouncements capped by a speech to a joint session of Congress, he assailed the policy of the administration and emphasized his opposition to the plan for limited warfare in Korea. The Armed Services Committee of the Senate provided him with an additional opportunity to elaborate his views. It also heard an administration rebuttal from General Bradley of the Joint Chiefs of Staff. Eventually the public lost interest in MacArthur, but not before he had invigorated the opposition to the war.

THE KOREAN CEASE-FIRE

It looked as if the administration would have an opportunity to liquidate the unpopular police action when a Russian delegate in the UN urged a cease-fire and armistice on June 23, 1951. A Chinese spokesman endorsed the proposal, and negotiations opened two weeks later. The exploratory talks began at Kaesong but were later shifted to Panmunjom, a neutralized zone near the 38th parallel. They continued for over two years despite sporadic outbreaks of heavy fighting. Chinese and North Korean negotiators proved to be adept imitators of the Russians in the art of stalling. For a time they deadlocked the discussions by stipulating that all foreign troops be withdrawn from Korea — a proviso calculated to leave South Koreans as defenseless as before the initial invasion. They also insisted that the armistice terms provide for the compulsory repatriation of some 83,000 North Korean and Chinese prisoners who had indicated an unwillingness to return to their homes. The United States flatly rejected both demands.

Meanwhile the American voters had expressed their frustration over the deadlock as well as over domestic irritations by returning the Republicans to power in the 1952 election. Before he took office, President-elect Eisenhower fulfilled a campaign pledge by making a three-day visit to Korea in December 1952. Truce negotiations were reopened in April 1953, amidst mounting evidence that this time the Communists really intended to reach an agreement. They removed the chief stumbling block by dropping their demand for compulsory repatriation and agreeing to the establishment of a neutral commission which would be empowered to supervise the release of prisoners. Further progress was made when both sides accepted a cease-fire line corresponding to the current military line, a demilitarized zone between North and South Korea, and a separate neutral commission for the enforcement of armistice terms. Disturbed by the prospect of an agreement which would leave Korea divided, Syngman Rhee, the fierce old President of South Korea, made an eleventh-hour effort to disrupt the negotiations. Besides threatening to take independent action if the peace conference provided for by the armistice terms did not produce a unified Korea in ninety days, he suddenly freed 27,000 anti-Communist North Korean prisoners of war in June 1953. These defiant gestures were ignored by the delegates at Panmunjom, who put the finishing touches on the armistice agreement and signed it on July 27, 1953.

The armistice ended the fighting in Korea but did not bring peace. The Repatriation Commission did its work in an atmosphere of mutual recrimination, with each side accusing the other of coercing prisoners and of falsifying the lists of captives. The ensuing peace conference ended in deadlock, indicating that the *de facto* partition of Korea would be continued for the foreseeable future. To placate Syngman Rhee, the United States substituted a bilateral defense pact with South Korea for the nebulous protection of the United Nations. The new treaty committed the signatories to consultation in case of a threatened attack rather than automatic military action. It was ratified by a Senate vote of 81 to 6 on January 26, 1954. Supplementary agreements assured a steady flow of American economic and military assistance to South Korea.

COMMUNIST PRESSURE IN INDO-CHINA

The negotiation of a truce in Korea did not terminate Sino-Russian penetration of the Asia vacuum but simply deflected it to other areas. The new point of pressure was Indo-China where the Communist Viet Minh rebels had been fighting the French and their native Viet Nam allies since 1946. Until the Korean armistice, the fighting in north Indo-China had been indecisive. Thereafter Red China sharply increased her aid to the Viet Minh rebels with the result that Ho Chi Minh and his Communist guerrillas inflicted a series of crippling defeats on the French in the winter of 1953–54.

Mindful of the threat to Singapore, Indonesia, Thailand, and Burma which would follow a Communist victory in Indo-China, the United States contributed nearly $3 billion worth of military aid to the French. This generous help was unavailing. In March and April of 1954, the Viet Minh overran the lush rice fields of north Indo-China and destroyed a French army which had tried to save the fortress of Dien Bien Phu. At this critical juncture the Eisenhower administration toyed with the idea of direct American intervention. Popular hostility to what might become another Korea, as well as the prospect of warfare in difficult jungle terrain, forced the President to shelve this idea.

With the French exhausted, the British reluctant to annoy China, and the Americans in an unheroic mood, the sole alternative was a truce on Communist terms. The great powers had already agreed to hold a conference at Geneva in April 1954 to discuss Korea and Indo-China. So sixteen states that had participated in the UN police action plus Russia, China, and North Korea took part in the discussions. The Communist negotiators evaded an agreement on Korea and were encouraged by the rapid deterioration of the French position to postpone a settlement. At length, when the summer monsoon had closed the campaign season in south Asia, Molotov and Chou En-lai consented to a French proposal for the partition of Indo-China. The agreement of July 21, 1954, awarded the area north of the 17th parallel to the Communist government of Ho Chi Minh, and left the south temporarily in the control of the French.

The United States opposed the partition proposal and refused to associate herself with the Geneva settlement. Aloofness was not, however, enough to save the administration from criticism. Secretary of State Dulles got caught in a savage cross fire from pro-Chiang members of both parties. They denounced American participation in the same conference with Communist China and predicted that it would lead to recognition of the Peiping regime. When the terms of the agreement were made public, their anger knew no bounds. Senator Knowland, the Republican majority leader, labeled it a "Far Eastern Munich" and upbraided his own administration for selling out Asia to the Communists. Even presidential spokesmen conceded that the Sino-Russian bloc had won another significant victory.

CRISIS IN THE FORMOSA STRAIT

No sooner was the Indo-China crisis out of the way than Peiping announced its intention of conquering Formosa. Although Eisenhower had terminated the neutralization of Formosa on February 3, 1953, the withdrawal of the American Seventh Fleet from patrol duty did not immediately change the status of the island. Chiang continued to make hit-and-run raids on coastal installations and merchant shipping as he had formerly done. The Communist regime retaliated by assembling an invasion army opposite Formosa and warning the United States that interference would precipitate a war. The war of nerves reached a crescendo in February and March of 1955. Despite their threats and bluster, the Chinese Communists knew that the American fleet could break up any invasion armada with ridiculous ease. What they counted on was the disinclination of Washington to get involved in a war over Formosa. The Eisenhower administration confirmed their diagnosis to the extent of evacuating Nationalist troops from small islands off the coast. The spotlight immediately switched to Quemoy and Matsu, two larger and heavily fortified islands in the Formosa Strait. While Americans debated the merits of resisting a Chinese attack on the islands, Peiping suddenly choked off the agitation in midsummer of 1955. The near certainty of defeat and the unwillingness of the U.S.S.R. to provide military and economic aid for such a hazardous project probably accounted for the retreat of the Chinese Reds. Evidence of increasing rivalry between Moscow and Peiping over the right to exercise the dominant role in southeast Asia also indicated that the period of fruitful collaboration between the two states might be drawing to a close. China made a bid for leadership at the African-Asian conference held at Bandung, Indonesia, in April 1955. Russia countered with a state visit by Khrushchev and Bulganin to India, Burma, and Afghanistan the following November.

ATTEMPTS TO BUILD AN ANTICOMMUNIST BLOC

If America paved the way for the defection of China to the Russian camp, she struggled feverishly against the consequences of her blunder after 1949. As in Europe, she sought to build a containment policy on the basis of friendship with the lesser states of Asia. The outbreak of the Korean War emphasized the desirability of friendship with the erstwhile Japanese foe. The benevolent MacArthur dictatorship in Japan, which had executed the war criminals and democratized the structure of Nipponese society, came to an end in the spring of 1951. Over the protests of Soviet Russia and other members of the Communist bloc, the United States piloted a Japanese peace treaty through a conference of fifty-two nations convened for that purpose at San Francisco. The formal signing took place September 8, 1951. Japan received the restoration of her sovereignty on paper but not in actuality. As a matter of fact she was forced in subsequent treaties to confirm American rights to maintain troops and naval bases on her home islands. The Senate ratified the entire package of agreements by heavy majorities on March 20, 1952. The establishment of closer relations with Japan did not create the incentive for the Nipponese to rearm and support the diplomatic position of the United States. What Americans expected from their former enemies was gratitude instead of apathy. But only the pursuit of self-interest through an independent policy would spur the Japanese to defend themselves, and the operation of that motive awaited the full restoration of sovereignty.

The Philippines fell into a different category. Liberated in 1945 and granted independence on July 4, 1946, the new state willingly gave the United States ninety-nine-year leases on some twenty-three military and naval bases. These infringements on Philippine sovereignty were sweetened by generous American economic concessions which included a $620 million grant for war damages, tariff preference, and a favorable exchange rate for the peso. As a result, the mutual security pact signed on August 30, 1951, brought the United States a more enthusiastic ally than the similar treaty with Japan. She extended her Far Eastern network of pacts two days later by signing defensive agreements with New Zealand and Australia.

American bids to the newly independent states of southeastern Asia were poorly received. Suspicion of the white man, apprehension about the revival of Western imperialism, and burgeoning nationalism fed neutralist sentiment in Indonesia, Ceylon, Burma, and India. Local Communists also stimulated anti-American sentiment by artfully insinuating that Uncle Sam gave economic aid from sinister motives. Even the dramatic Eisenhower proposal of December 8, 1953, calling on states to pool their atomic resources for peaceful purposes, elicited little enthusiasm in power-hungry neutralist countries. Populous India took an especially hostile view of American activity in southeastern Asia. Her Prime Minister, Jawaharlal Nehru, aspired to leadership of a neutralist bloc and considered American containment policy as more menacing than the threat of Communist subversion. He became especially incensed when his repeated protests failed to block consummation of a mutual security treaty between the United States and Pakistan in May 1954. What Nehru disliked most about the pact was a provision for arming Pakistan, with whom he had an unresolved quarrel over the province of Kashmir.

While Nehru's untiring denunciations of American policy echoed and re-echoed in Indian bazaars, the United States was working furiously to set up a regional South East Asia Treaty Organization comparable to NATO. Eight states already tied to the United States by agreements of various kinds met at Manila on September 5, 1954. Except for Thailand and Pakistan, the neutralist powers of southeastern Asia boycotted the conference. After only three days of deliberation, Great Britain, France, Australia, New Zealand, Thailand, Pakistan, and the Philippines joined the United States in a defense pact. Known as SEATO, the new agreement did not contemplate the creation of an allied army for the defense of Asia. It simply bound the signatories to consult one another and concert defense measures in the event of aggression or subversion. Whether a regional military alliance like NATO would emerge from this modest foundation remained to be seen. In an obvious bid for the support of their absent neutralist brethren, the delegates to the conference also signed a Pacific Charter, pledging their states to promote self-government.

The intricate network of Asian pacts sponsored by the United States to check Communist expansion in the vacuum area suffered from the aloofness of India and the hostility of China. With Nehru stubbornly neutral and Mao tied to the Soviet Union, there was little prospect that the United States could establish a regional balance of power in Asia even if she saw the desirability of doing so. The continuation of containment policy, based on alliances with the smaller states, gave promise of more anxieties and setbacks.

AMERICA AND THE WESTERN HEMISPHERE

In the Western Hemisphere, where the United States exercised preponderant power, her postwar foreign policy did not get bogged down in discouragements and frustrations. Resentment developed in Latin America as elsewhere in the world. Part of it was due to the fact that the huge American wartime purchases of raw materials ended abruptly, jolting the perennially shaky economies of many states below the Rio Grande. They hungered for aid programs on the scale of the Marshall Plan and were resentful to discover that the United States regarded the problems of ex-enemy countries like Italy as more urgent than those of loyal hemispheric allies. As elsewhere, Latin-American Communists fulminated against the United States, tailoring the local formula to fit the ancient fears of "Yanqui imperialism." Notwithstanding a rising tide of anti-American sentiment, most of Latin America continued to dance to Uncle Sam's tune.

The Latin-American state least susceptible to this leadership was Argentina. She had shown consistent prewar sympathy with the Nazis and had reluctantly declared war against Germany just before VE Day. Ill-advisedly, Washington attempted to interfere with the effort of Colonel Juan Perón to consolidate his dictatorship, which had begun in 1945. Protests by American Ambassador Spruille Braden and publication of a State Department Blue Book implicating Perón in Nazi conspiracies to overthrow the governments of neighboring republics, increased the popularity of the Argentine dictator at home. Running against Braden rather than his domestic opponents, Perón was elected president by a heavy majority in 1946 and proceeded to strengthen Fascist institutions at home. Chastened by the bitter fruits of intervention, the United States switched to a policy of conciliation. American-Argentine relations did not become genuinely friendly, but Washington took a more indulgent view of the totalitarian antics of the anti-Communists as the Red menace increased elsewhere in the world. When hostile elements finally overthrew Perón in the fall of 1955, America showed little enthusiasm over the change.

Much more grave than the defiant attitude of Perón was the establishment of a Communist-infiltrated government in Guatemala. The closeness of the tiny "banana republic" to the Panama Canal bothered Washington more than the radical economic program sponsored by the government. In 1953 the State Department used Guatemala's expropriation of properties belonging to the United Fruit Company as an excuse for issuing a stiff protest. It also pushed a resolution condemning Communist infiltration of the Hemisphere, through the tenth Inter-American Conference at Caracas in March 1954.

A crisis developed two months later when Communist Poland shipped a large cargo of arms to the Guatemalan army. This was too much for the United States. She denounced the Communist menace as a violation of the Monroe Doctrine and promptly airlifted armaments to Guatemala's neighbors. More important, she encouraged the Guatemalan exiles who invaded their native land in June 1954 and overthrew the Communist-tainted regime within a matter of days. America hastened to bolster the new regime with economic aid and moral support. The ostensibly native flavor of the Guatemalan revolution did not save the United States from bitter criticism for intervention in the internal affairs of other hemispheric countries. However, the criticism was a small price to pay for the elimination of a pro-Communist government so near the Panamanian life line.

The hostility characterizing the relations of Argentina and Guatemala with the United States during much of the postwar period was the exception rather than the rule in Latin America. For the most part, the states south of the Rio Grande subscribed with monotonous and unenthusiastic regularity to American-sponsored resolutions demonstrating hemispheric solidarity. A special conference held at Rio de Janeiro in August 1947 approved a treaty binding all the American states to armed support of each other in the event of an attack from any quarter. The only barrier to the automatic application of the guarantee was a provision requiring that the dispute be referred initially to the Security Council of the United Nations. Eight months later the Ninth International Conference of American Republics met at Bogotá, Columbia. Latin-American delegates hoped that the United States would offer them a little Marshall Plan and were visibly disappointed by a proposal for a half-billion-dollar loan from the Import-Export Bank. Washington showed more interest in measures to unite the Americas against the Red peril. Preoccupation with this issue was intensified by a local revolt of Communists and other dissidents which rocked Bogotá and forced suspension of the conference for several days. At length, in April 1948, the delegates adopted an anti-Communist resolution, established a defense council, and formed a closer union of American states. Pledges of solidarity were reaffirmed at a Washington conference in the spring of 1951. As already noted, the Tenth International Conference held during the Guatemalan crisis branded Communist infiltration as a threat to the Americas. It also approved an Argentine resolution demanding the elimination of European colonies in the Western Hemisphere. Out of consideration for her British and Dutch allies the United States abstained from voting. The resolution passed 19 to 0.

By the middle 1950's America had begun to loosen the purse strings and grant Latin-American economic aid under Point Four and other programs for the development of backward areas. None of these measures gave the states below the Rio Grande as much help as they wanted. Nevertheless the overwhelming strength of the United States gave them no alternative but to go along with her foreign policy.

AMERICA: QUO VADIS?

By 1957 Americans had all but given up hope of a lasting peace. Outside of the Western Hemisphere the power position of the United States had deteriorated steadily since the end of World War II, whereas Russia had expanded her influence aggressively during the same period. All that Washington had to show for ten years of reliance on a containment policy was a number of grumbling allies, most of whom were unreliable. Other recipients of American aid outside the Iron Curtain had repaid Uncle Sam with surly neutrality or outright flirtations with the Soviet Union.

The results of the containment policy might have been still worse but for American superiority in atomic weapons. Even this advantage disappeared in October 1957, when the Russians accomplished the scientific and technological feat of launching a satellite that began to circle the earth in a predictable orbit. Within a month they repeated their triumph with a second orbiting satellite. Many American scientists inferred from these achievements that Russia could also launch intercontinental missiles with atomic warheads capable of destroying American cities.

Just how much the sudden emergence of the Soviet Union as the leader in the field of missile development affected the over-all power position of the United States was not immediately clear. However, the development dramatized America's need for a policy more effective than containment. Aside from an all-out war, which most Americans did not want, the only realistic alternative policy was the reconstitution of a balance of power in Europe and Asia. Whether Washington could shake the habits and illusions of the past resolutely enough to achieve this objective was uncertain in the fall of 1957. In any event, the cold war seemed likely to continue.

SUGGESTED READINGS

1. Harris, S. E., *The European Recovery Program.*
2. Middleton, D., *Defense of Western Europe.*
3. North, R. C., *Moscow and the Chinese Communists.*
4. Thomas, L. V. and Frye, R. N., *The United States and Turkey and Iran.*

INDEX